# dbt Analytics Engineer Exam Prep

A six-week study plan

Laurence Lee

Edition 1 – 2026
Snowleaf Press

Published by Snowleaf Press · First edition, 2026.
ISBN: 978-1-918744-02-6



Aligned with the current study guide (dbt Core 1.11).

Companion repository: `github.com/snowleafbooks/dbt-analytics-engineer-certification`
Code samples, errata, and exam-update notes are published there.

# Contents

# Cheat Sheet — dbt Analytics Engineer Certification

Quick recall only. One glance, one fact. Organised by the 7 blueprint domains, then commands, then selectors, then gotchas.

---

## Exam logistics

- **Version:** dbt Core 1.11 study guide
- **Questions:** 65 (a few unscored, unmarked)
- **Duration:** 2 hours · ≈ 1.8 min / question
- **Passing score:** 65% · all questions equally weighted
- **Result:** shown immediately on submission
- **Delivery:** online proctored · Caveon Web browser · Talview scheduling · 24-hour cancellation
- **Language:** English and Japanese
- **Validity:** 2 years
- **Prerequisites:** SQL · Git — the guide's own Checkpoint 0 list; 6+ months of dbt experience is *recommended*, not required, and is no longer qualified as Core
- **Formats:** 6 official buckets — MCQ (single + multi grouped as one), FITB, Matching, Hotspot, Build-list, DOMC; treat MCQ-single and MCQ-multi as separate tactics (see Ch 1 §1.3 for first-principles, Ch 15 §15.1 for the seven-tactic split)
- **Out of scope:** Mesh · Semantic Layer · dbt Fusion / Core 2.0 · 1.12-only behaviour · deep Python models
- **Domain weights:** NOT disclosed

---

## Topic 1 — Developing and optimizing models

### Core references

- `ref('model_name')` — registers DAG edge, for dbt-managed models
- `ref('model_name', v=2)` — versioned model
- `source('source_name', 'table_name')` — raw tables under a `sources:` key in any properties YAML (no required filename)

### Five materializations

- `view` (default)
- `table`

- `incremental`
- `ephemeral` (inlined CTE)
- `materialized_view` (adapter-specific — Snowflake uses `dynamic_table`)

## Incremental model essentials

- `unique_key`
- `is_incremental()` guard around the delta filter
- `on_schema_change` — one of: `ignore` (default), `fail`, `append_new_columns`, `sync_all_columns`
- `incremental_strategy` — one of: `append`, `merge`, `delete+insert`, `insert_overwrite`, `microbatch`
- `merge_update_columns` / `merge_exclude_columns` — restrict which columns `merge` overwrites on a matched row; merge-strategy options only
- `full_refresh: false` on the model beats `--full-refresh` on the CLI
- `--full-refresh` to rebuild from scratch

### event_time

- event_time: <column> — config on models, seeds, snapshots **and** sources
- The column name is yours (`ordered_at`, `session_began_at`, `last_loaded_ts`); dbt enforces none. The **type** is not: date or timestamp filters correctly, numeric errors loudly, and text is the trap — it compares as a string, so most rows land right and a row stamped exactly on a batch boundary silently slips into the previous batch
- Prefer a real event timestamp; an ingestion/load column is allowed only where the table carries nothing better, and mis-bins late arrivals
- Three surfaces: `+event_time:` in `dbt_project.yml` · properties `config:` · inline `{{ config() }}`
- **Required** for microbatch auto-filtering and `--sample`; **recommended** for Advanced CI compare-changes

## Microbatch

- `incremental_strategy: microbatch` — a strategy value, not a materialization
- Always required: `event_time`, `begin`, `batch_size`
- `batch_size` — `hour` · `day` · `month` · `year` (there is no `week`)
- Model body is an unguarded `select` — no `is_incremental()`, no date predicate
- `lookback` — default `1`; reprocesses that many batches back from the current time. No bookmark, no catch-up: if the job stops longer than `lookback` the gap is never replanned
- `concurrent_batches` — unset auto-detects; `{{ this }}` in the SQL forces sequential
- Backfill: `dbt run --event-time-start X --event-time-end Y` — both required, UTC; start inclusive, end exclusive
- Batch plan: a first build or `--full-refresh` spans `begin` → now; an incremental run spans `lookback` batches back from now. Never derived from the data
- `dbt retry` reprocesses only the failed batches
- Custom `get_incremental_microbatch_sql` gets batches only under `require_batched_execution_for_custom_microbatch_strategy` (`false` at 1.11) — off, it is called once for the whole range and warns `D020`
- Upstream `ref()`/`source()` with no `event_time` → full scan every batch, silently — unless *no* input declares one, which warns at parse
- Parallel batch **execution**: Snowflake and BigQuery only; first and last batch never parallel

- `.render()` on a `ref()` opts that one reference out of auto-filtering

| Adapter | Batch replacement | `unique_key` |
|---|---|---|
| Postgres | `merge` | **required** — batch 1 passes without it, batch 2 fails |
| Redshift, Snowflake | `delete+insert` | not required |
| BigQuery, Spark | `insert_overwrite` | not required |
| Databricks | `replace_where` | not required |

### `--empty` and `--sample`

- `--empty` — on `run`, `build`, `compile`, `snapshot`; limits every `ref()`/`source()` to zero rows
- The SQL really executes and relations are really created — full column list; the zero rows are guaranteed on the INPUTS, and the output follows from them
- Data tests pass **vacuously** over zero rows: `--empty` is a compile/schema gate, never a data gate
- Limits input **rows**, not input **dependencies** — a missing upstream relation still fails
- `--sample` — on `run` and `build` only
- Relative: `--sample="3 days"` · static: `--sample='{"start": ..., "end": ...}'`
- Grains: `hour` · `day` · `month` · `year` (plurals accepted); `3 weeks` exits 2 on `Invalid grain size`
- **Fails open**: no `event_time` on the sampled relation → the run succeeds and processes every row
- `event_time` must sit on the relation being **sampled** (usually the source), not the reading model
- `.render()` opts one reference out of either flag; both are silently ignored for Python models

## Snapshots

```
snapshots:
  - name: orders_snap
    relation: source('raw', 'orders')
    config:
      unique_key: id
      strategy: timestamp
      updated_at: updated_at
```

- YAML `snapshots:` takes a `relation:`, not a query — the body is a fixed `select *`, so it cannot filter, alias, or project a column subset
- `schema:` routes through `generate_schema_name`; legacy `target_schema:` hard-codes one location, and switching between them relocates the relation
- `snapshot_meta_column_names` — renames the `dbt_*` metadata columns
- `dbt_valid_to_current` — non-NULL sentinel for the currently-valid row (default NULL)

Legacy form, still valid — and the only form that can snapshot a query:

```
{% snapshot orders_snap %}
{{ config(
    schema='snapshots',
```

```
    unique_key='id',
    strategy='timestamp',
    updated_at='updated_at'
) }}
select * from {{ source('raw','orders') }}
{% endsnapshot %}
```

- File: `snapshots/*.sql` wrapped in `{% snapshot %}` ... `{% endsnapshot %}`
- Command: `dbt snapshot`

| Strategy | Trigger | Required |
|---|---|---|
| `timestamp` | `updated_at` column advances | `updated_at:` |
| `check` | Values in watched columns change | `check_cols: ['c1','c2']` or `'all'` |

- Added columns: `dbt_valid_from`, `dbt_valid_to`, `dbt_scd_id`, `dbt_updated_at`
- `hard_deletes` — rows no longer in source: `ignore` (default), `invalidate` (close them out), `new_record` (tombstone row)
- `new_record` adds a `dbt_is_deleted` column; `ignore` and `invalidate` do not
- Legacy boolean `invalidate_hard_deletes: true` equals `hard_deletes: invalidate`; setting both keys on one snapshot is an error
- Retrofitting `hard_deletes` onto a POPULATED snapshot is not a migration — `new_record` stops with `Snapshot target is missing configured columns`; add them by hand
- `--full-refresh` never resets snapshot history — `dbt build --full-refresh` runs the snapshot normally. To rebuild, drop the table by hand and re-run `dbt snapshot`

## Seeds

- CSVs in `seeds/` become tables of the same name
- `dbt seed` — truncate-and-insert by default
- `--full-refresh` — drops + recreates (required after a table schema change)

| Seed config | Purpose |
|---|---|
| `column_types: {col: varchar(10)}` | Override inferred column types |
| `quote_columns: true` | Wrap every column name in quotes |
| `delimiter: ';'` (or any single character) | Use a non-comma separator |

## Config precedence (more-specific wins)

1. `{{ config() }}` in model SQL
2. YAML `config:` in `.yml`
3. `dbt_project.yml +config`
4. dbt's built-in default — `view` for `materialized`; a few, `incremental_strategy` among them, are dispatched per adapter

**One exception:** `pre-hook` / `post-hook` are **cumulative, not overridden** — a project-level hook and a resource-level hook both run (Ch 5 §5.4).

## Jinja context

- Data: `ref`, `source`, `var`, `env_var`
- Model: `this`, `target`, `run_started_at`, `adapter`, `builtins`
- Declarative: `config`
- Graph: `graph.nodes`, `graph.sources`, `graph.exposures` (populated after parse)

**`this` vs `target`**

| Variable | What it is | Reach for it to |
|---|---|---|
| `this` | the current model's relation — `database.schema.identifier` | read the model's own table in a hook |
| `target` | the active connection profile — `target.name`, `.schema`, `.database` | branch behaviour by environment (dev vs prod) |

## Jinja primitives / helpers

| Jinja call | Purpose |
|---|---|
| `log(msg, info=true)` | Print to stdout (use `info=false` for debug log only) |
| `return(value)` | Early exit from a macro with a value |
| `{% if execute %}` | Guard blocks that must run in the **execute pass** only, not parse |
| `run_query(sql)` | Execute SQL at runtime; returns `agate.Table`. Must be inside `{% if execute %}` |
| `{% call statement('n', fetch_result=true) %}…{% endcall %}` | Run SQL in a macro; pull results with `load_result('n')` |
| `fromjson(s)` / `tojson(obj)` | JSON string ↔ dict |
| `as_text`, `as_number`, `as_bool`, `as_native` | Cast a `var`/`env_var` string to the intended type |
| `debug()` | Drops into `ipdb` at that point in the compiled Jinja. Registered only when `DBT_MACRO_DEBUGGING` is set — `--debug` does not enable it |
| `var('key', default)` | Read a project-level variable (from `vars:` in `dbt_project.yml` or `--vars` CLI flag). Usable anywhere Jinja runs |

## Macros

- `dispatch:` in `dbt_project.yml` — entries of `macro_namespace:` + `search_order:`; consulted IN ORDER, so the overriding project comes first
- File lives in `macros/`
- Invoke from SQL: `{{ my_macro(col) }}`
- Invoke from CLI: `dbt run-operation my_macro --args '{arg: 3}'`

```
{% macro my_macro(arg) %}
  {% do return(arg * 2) %}
{% endmacro %}
```

**Adapter dispatch** (cross-warehouse macros):

```
{% macro my_macro() %}
  {% do return(adapter.dispatch('my_macro')()) %}
{% endmacro %}

{% macro default__my_macro() …%}{% endmacro %}
{% macro snowflake__my_macro() …%}{% endmacro %}
```

- Naming: `<adapter>__<macro>` — adapter prefix first; `default__` is the fallback
- `search_order` in `dbt_project.yml` under `dispatch:` controls package-level lookup

**Override macros** (dbt calls these if present in `macros/`):

| Override macro | Purpose |
|---|---|
| `generate_schema_name(custom, node)` | Customize target schema per model |
| `generate_database_name(custom, node)` | Customize target database per model |
| `generate_alias_name(custom, node)` | Customize table/view name per model |

## Python models

- `.py` file in `models/`
- `def model(dbt, session):` returns a DataFrame
- Use `dbt.ref(...)`, `dbt.source(...)`, `dbt.config(...)`
- Materializations: `table` or `incremental` only
- Supported adapters:
  - Snowflake — Snowpark
  - Databricks — PySpark; `submission_method: all_purpose_cluster` (default) · `job_cluster` · `serverless_cluster` · `workflow_job`
  - BigQuery — `submission_method: serverless` (default) · `cluster` · `bigframes`

## Grants

- `grants: {select: ['role_a', 'role_b']}`
- Applied post-materialization
- dbt reconciles exactly on every build (adds listed, revokes unlisted)
- `+` on the privilege name (`+select:`) merges with parent-scope grantees instead of replacing them; works at any config layer

## Hooks — project-level (`dbt_project.yml`)

- `on-run-start` — before any resource
- `on-run-end` — after last resource

**Triggered by:**

- `build`

- `run`
- `seed`
- `snapshot`
- `source freshness`
- `test`

**Not triggered by:**

- `parse`
- `clean`
- `deps`
- `debug`
- `run-operation` — it opens a connection, but hooks are bound to the node graph
- `compile` and `docs generate` — the reference page lists both; at 1.11 neither fires

## Hooks — model-level (individual model sql file)

- `pre_hook:` — before materialization
- `post_hook:` — after materialization
- `{{ this }}` resolves to the model's relation inside a hook — use it when you need to read from the underlying DB (e.g. `delete from {{ this }} where ...` in a pre-hook)

### `dbt_project.yml` top-level keys

- `name`, `version`, `profile`
- `model-paths`, `seed-paths`, `test-paths`, `snapshot-paths`, `macro-paths`, `analysis-paths`
- `clean-targets`; `target-path` DEPRECATED here (`D011`) — use `--target-path` / `DBT_TARGET_PATH`
- `vars`, `models`, `seeds`, `snapshots`, `sources`, `data_tests`, `unit_tests` — the two test keys are UNDERSCORED, every path key is dashed. `tests` = legacy alias
- `on-run-start`, `on-run-end`
- `dispatch`, `require-dbt-version`

### `profiles.yml` structure

```
my_project:
  target: dev
  outputs:
    dev:
      type: snowflake
      account: xy12345.us-east-1
      user: dbt_user
      password: "{{ env_var('DBT_PWD') }}"
      role: TRANSFORMER
      warehouse: TRANSFORM_WH
      database: ANALYTICS
      schema: dbt_dev
      threads: 4
```

- Lives at `~/.dbt/profiles.yml`; override with `--profiles-dir`
- `profile:` in `dbt_project.yml` selects the top-level key
- `target:` picks the output block; override with `--target`

- Common keys: `type`, `account`/`host`, `user`, `password`, `database`/`dbname`, `schema`, `threads`, `role`, `warehouse`, `keepalives_idle`

### `dbt docs`

- `dbt docs generate` — writes `target/catalog.json` + `target/manifest.json`, and a `run_results.json` that overwrites the prior run's, killing a pending `dbt retry`
- `--no-compile` writes `catalog.json` only — the `manifest.json` and `run_results.json` rewrites are compile-gated, so both survive and so does a pending `dbt retry`
- `dbt docs serve [--port 8080]` — renders locally

## Descriptions in YAML

```
models:
  - name: dim_users
    description: "User dimension."
    columns:
      - name: user_id
        description: "Surrogate key."
```

## Doc blocks

Define in **any `.md` file** under any resource path — `macros/` as much as `models/` (filename is free; the `.md` extension is the requirement):

```
{% docs pii_email %}
Hashed email column (SHA-256).
{% enddocs %}
```

Reference from a `description:` in a properties YAML, via the `{{ doc() }}` Jinja function:

```
models:
  - name: dim_users
    columns:
      - name: email
        description: "{{ doc('pii_email') }}"
```

- One `.md` may hold many `{% docs %}` blocks
- A `{% docs __overview__ %}` block overrides the docs site landing page — the block name is what matters, not the file name

### `persist_docs`

- `persist_docs: {relation: true, columns: true}` — pushes descriptions into warehouse object comments
- Supported: Postgres, Redshift, Snowflake, BigQuery, Databricks, Apache Spark

### `meta` vs `description`

- `description` — human documentation
- `meta` — free-form key-value metadata (e.g. `owner: '@team'`), lives in `manifest.json`

## Packages

`packages.yml` + `dbt deps` → installs to `dbt_packages/`

## Five package source shapes

- **Hub** — `package: dbt-labs/dbt_utils` (underscore slug, not hyphen)
- **Git** — `git: "https://github.com/..."` with `revision:`
- **Tarball** — `tarball: "<url>"` with `name:` (required)
- **Local** — `local: "../relative/path"`
- **Private** — `private: "org/repo"`; `provider: github|gitlab|ado` is a 1.12 requirement, not a 1.11 one (docs use `ado` for Azure DevOps)

## Pin styles (Hub)

- Exact: `version: "1.2.1"`
- Range: `version: [">=1.0.0", "<2.0.0"]` — a LIST of comparators, never a comma-joined string (`">=1.0.0,<2.0.0"` raises `SemverError`)
- Single comparator: `version: ">=1.0.0"` is a legal range with no ceiling — it takes the newest release the registry offers, so it pins nothing
- Omitted `version:` is NOT legal on a Hub entry — validation raises before `dbt deps` downloads anything (an omitted Git `revision:` merely warns, which is the opposite way round)

### `package-lock.yml`

- Records resolved versions + SHA
- Commit for reproducibility; `.gitignore` for auto-update

---

# Topic 2 — Model governance

## Contract

```
config:
  contract:
    enforced: true
columns:
  - name: user_id
    data_type: int
    constraints:
      - type: not_null
```

- `data_type` is required on every column when `enforced: true`, on the materializations that enforce a contract — `table`, `view`, `incremental` (`ephemeral` and `materialized_view` accept the config and build green with it missing). A missing one fails inside the materialization at `dbt run`, not at parse
- `alias_types` — default `true`; maps generic type names to the adapter's own
- Preflight check runs before DDL

### Constraints (6 types)

- `not_null`
- `unique`
- `check`
- `primary_key`
- `foreign_key`
- `custom` — free-form `expression` emitted verbatim into the DDL; the escape hatch for platform-specific clauses
- Inert without `contract.enforced: true` — declared without one, they are silently dropped
- Only `foreign_key` takes `to` / `to_columns`; `check` and `custom` take `expression`
- `foreign_key.to` takes `ref()` / `source()` only — a raw table name stops the parse
- `warn_unenforced` (definable but not enforced) and `warn_unsupported` (not definable) both default `true`
- Definable ≠ enforced

| Adapter | `not_null` | `primary_key` / `foreign_key` | `unique` | `check` |
|---|---|---|---|---|
| Postgres | enforced | enforced | enforced | enforced |
| Redshift | enforced | definable | definable | — |
| Snowflake | enforced | definable | definable | — |
| BigQuery | enforced | definable | — | — |
| Databricks | enforced | definable | — | enforced, post-build `ALTER TABLE` |
| Spark | definable | definable | definable | definable |
| Athena | — | — | — | — |

- Postgres is the only adapter enforcing all five standard types; `custom` is emitted verbatim and never validated by dbt

### Versions

- `versions:` list under the model in `.yml`
- `latest_version:` — the default when `ref()` omits `v=`
- `deprecation_date:` — emits warning before, `DeprecatedReference` after
- File naming: `model_name_v1.sql`, `model_name_v2.sql` (override with `defined_in:`)
- Reference specific: `{{ ref('model', v=2) }}` (alias `version=2`)
- `latest_version_pointer` — NOT a 1.11 feature; accepted and creates nothing

### Access levels

- `private` — only same-`group` models can `ref` it
- `protected` (default) — any model in the project
- `public` — cross-project (Mesh — out of scope)

### Groups

- Defined in `.yml` under `groups:`
- Required: `owner:` (with `name:` or `email:`)

- Bind a model to a group with `group:` config

---

# Topic 3 — Debugging

## Error families

- Parsing — YAML does not load; nothing reaches SQL. Banner: `Parsing Error`
- Compilation — Jinja, macro, unresolvable `ref()`. Banner: `Compilation Error`
- Dependency — graph validation; at 1.11 cycles only. Guide category name, not a printed banner
- Database (warehouse SQL errors)
- Runtime (dbt execution failures)

## `ref()` error cases

- Missing model — typo or file absent
- Cyclic — two models ref each other
- Disabled — `enabled: false`
- Wrong version — `ref('model', v=9)` when only v=1,v=2 exist

## YAML errors

- Tabs vs spaces
- Indentation off by one
- Misplaced key (config under properties or vice versa)
- Wrong scalar type (`true` vs `'true'`)
- Unknown property name (flagged only on BigQuery, Databricks, Redshift, Snowflake)

## Triage path

1. `dbt run` → read the error banner
2. Open `target/compiled/<project>/<path>/<model>.sql`
3. Paste into warehouse → fix SQL
4. `dbt test` → confirm
5. Commit

## Debug commands

- `dbt debug` — validates profile + warehouse connection
- `dbt debug --connection` — connection only
- `dbt compile --inline "<sql>"` — compile ad-hoc snippet (writes to `target/`)
- `dbt --log-level debug run` — verbose logs

## Configs vs properties

- **Properties** (structural YAML): `description`, `columns`, `constraints`, `versions`, `data_tests`
- **Configs** (runtime flags): `enabled`, `materialized`, `grants`, `persist_docs`, `freshness`

## Flags commonly tested — and which side of the subcommand they take

Global configs, accepted **left** of the subcommand (`dbt --target dev ls`):

- `--target <name>`
- `--profile <name>`
- `--fail-fast`
- `--no-partial-parse`
- `--warn-error` — promote warnings to errors (CI gate)

Accepted only **right** of it (`dbt ls --vars ...`); `dbt --vars ... ls` is `No such option`:

- `--profiles-dir <path>`
- `--project-dir <path>`
- `--threads <n>`
- `--vars '{key: value}'`
- `--full-refresh`

**Every boolean flag has a `--no-` twin** (`--no-full-refresh`, `--no-version-check`, `--no-populate-cache`, `--no-partial-parse`, `--no-write-json`, `--no-introspect`): the pattern is `--flag` / `--no-flag`.

Logging:

- `--log-level` / `--log-level-file` — console `info`, file `debug`
- `--log-format` / `--log-format-file` — `text` · `debug` · `json` · `default`; neither defaults to `text` and neither to `json`
- `--quiet` — suppresses non-error console output, file log untouched
- `--log-path` — CLI or `DBT_ENGINE_LOG_PATH`; also a top-level project key

Others worth knowing:

- `--no-write-json` — skips `run_results.json` / `manifest.json`, so a later step's artifacts survive
- `--no-introspect` — `compile` still hits the warehouse without it
- `--no-version-check` — bypasses `require-dbt-version`
- `--defer-state` — deferral state only, separate from `--state`
- `--max-depth <n>` — bounds `+` on `dbt ls`
- `--lock` / `--add-package` / `--upgrade` — `dbt deps`
- `--output-dir` — `dbt docs generate`
- `--show` — `dbt seed` flag, takes no value (NOT a selector)

## Flags — four meanings, four surfaces

- Four unrelated things are called "flags": global config · behaviour-change · `warn_error` / `warn_error_options` · the read-only Jinja `flags` object
- Precedence: CLI > env var > `dbt_project.yml flags:` > `~/.dbt/user_settings.yml` > default — rung 4 is documented but Core 1.11 does not read it
- Behaviour-change flags: `dbt_project.yml flags:` **only** — never CLI, never env var
- `--state`: CLI or env var **only** — never `dbt_project.yml`
- `log-path`: IS an accepted top-level project key; `log_path:` under `flags:` is ignored
- Env var prefix `DBT_ENGINE_<CONFIG_NAME>`; booleans take any ordinary spelling — `1`/`True`/`true`/`yes` set, `0`/`False`/`false`/`no` clear
- Lifecycle: Introduced (gated, old default) → Mature (default flips, old path warns) → Removed

- Already mature at 1.11 (some since earlier), default `true` there: `require_explicit_package_overrides_for_builtin_materializations` · `require_resource_names_without_spaces` · `source_freshness_run_project_hooks` · `require_generic_test_arguments_property`
- `enable_truthy_nulls_equals_macro` — off by default; on, `equals()` treats `NULL = NULL` as a match instead of `UNKNOWN`
- `require_unique_project_resource_names` — `false` at 1.11: a cross-type logical name duplicate WARNS; on, it is a `Compilation Error` at parse
- 14 core behaviour flags at 1.11 — the 4 above are `true`, the other 10 are `false`; seven of the ten flip at 1.12, and the three of those seven worth carrying are `skip_nodes_if_on_run_start_fails` · `state_modified_compare_more_unrendered_values` · `validate_macro_args`
- `--warn-error` takes no warning name; `--warn-error-options` is the granular surface — `error` takes `"all"` / `"*"` or an array, `warn` and `silence` take an array only

---

## Topic 4 — Troubleshooting pipelines

### `dbt build`

- Runs `run` + `test` + `seed` + `snapshot` + functions in DAG order — FIVE types
- Short-circuits: upstream test failure or model error → downstream nodes `skipped`

### `--fail-fast (-x)`

- Stops on the first `error` / `fail` / `partial success` and cancels the in-flight queries
- Every unbuilt node is recorded `skipped` — CANCEL is a log line, never a node status
- The exit code is `1` with or without it; only the run summary differs

---

## Topic 5 — Tests

### Four taxa

- **Generic** (built-in) — `unique`, `not_null`, `accepted_values`, `relationships`
- **Singular** — any `.sql` file in `tests/` returning failing rows
- **Custom generic** — `{% test %}...{% endtest %}` in `tests/generic/` or `macros/` (either is discovered)
- **Unit tests** — `unit_tests:` YAML; mock `given:` rows in, `expect:` rows out; assert logic, not data. Optional keys include `description`, `versions`, `config`, `overrides`, `static_analysis`

### Unit tests

```
unit_tests:
  - name: test_discount_applied
    model: fct_orders
    given:
      - input: ref('stg_orders')
        rows:
```

```
      - {order_id: 1, amount: 100}
expect:
  rows:
    - {order_id: 1, amount: 90}
```

- Declared under `unit_tests:` in a properties YAML under `models/` — the documented home; the parser accepts `tests/` too
- Keys: `name`, `model`, `given`, `expect`, plus optional `versions`, `config`, `overrides`
- Assert model **logic** against mocked inputs; data tests assert warehouse **data**
- `overrides.macros` / `.vars` / `.env_vars` replace entries in the render context, so they reach **nested macro calls**, not just the model's own text; the docs promise only direct references — design to the narrower rule
- Unit-testing an incremental model requires an `is_incremental` override, or parsing fails; with `is_incremental: true` it also needs an `- input: this` entry
- `dbt test` runs them by default; under `dbt build` the per-model order is unit test → materialize → data test
- Skip in prod with `dbt build --exclude-resource-type unit_test`
- `unit_test:` is a selector **method** (takes a name); `test_type:unit` is a selector **value**

## Test configs

- `severity: error` (default) or `warn`
- `warn_if: '> 10'`
- `error_if: '> 100'`
- `store_failures: true` → writes to `<schema>_dbt_test__audit.<test_name>` (suffix on the active schema); unset defers to `--store-failures`
- `store_failures_as: table | view | ephemeral` — wins over `store_failures` in both directions; `ephemeral` means *do not store*
- `fail_calc` — the expression counted, default `count(*)`; a bare `sum()` errors on zero rows
- `where: "order_date >= current_date - 7"` — narrows the scan
- `limit: 100` — cap returned failing rows (doesn't reduce scan)

## Severity evaluation order

### With `severity: error` (default):

1. `error_if` checked first — if met, errors
2. Otherwise `warn_if` — if met, warns

An explicit threshold **replaces** the `'!= 0'` default — but only for the key you set: `warn_if: '> 10'` with `error_if: '> 100'` lets 1–10 failing rows pass, 11–100 warn and >100 error, while `warn_if: '> 10'` alone still errors on the first failing row against the default `error_if`.

### With `severity: warn`:

- Only `warn_if` is checked; `error_if` is skipped.

## Indirect selection modes

- `eager` (default) — runs a test if any referenced node is selected
- `cautious` — runs only if ALL referenced nodes are selected
- `buildable` — cautious, widened: every referenced node must be selected **or** an ancestor of a selected node
- `empty` — runs no tests indirectly

### Test selectors

- `--select test_type:generic` (also `singular`, `unit`, and `data` — the parent of `generic` + `singular`; `unit` is disjoint from all three)
- `--select test_name:unique`
- `--select tag:daily`

### Pass/fail

- Test passes when the query returns **zero rows**
- Failing rows = assertion violations

---

## Topic 6 — External dependencies

### Exposures

```
exposures:
  - name: weekly_kpis
    type: dashboard
    owner: {name: Finance Analytics}
```

- Required: `name`, `type`, `owner`
- Types: `dashboard`, `notebook`, `analysis`, `ml`, `application`
- Optional (conventional): `depends_on`, `maturity`, `url`, `description` — `depends_on` takes `ref()` / `source()` calls; a bare name parses and creates no edge
- Maturity values: `high`, `medium`, `low`
- `loaded_at_query` — full alternative to `loaded_at_field`; `filter` does NOT apply to it

### Source properties

- `quoting` (database / schema / identifier) — defaults `true`, except **Snowflake** where it defaults `false`

```
sources:
  - name: raw
    database: raw_db            # override default
    schema: public              # override default
    tables:
      - name: orders            # logical name used in source()
        identifier: ORDERS_RAW  # physical warehouse name (when different)
        loaded_at_field: _etl_loaded_at
        freshness:
          warn_after: {count: 12, period: hour}
          error_after: {count: 24, period: hour}
          filter: "_partition_date >= current_date - 3"
```

- `filter:` — applied to the freshness query only, not to `source()` refs

### Source freshness

- period: one of minute, hour, day
- Opt out per-table: freshness: null
- Command: dbt source freshness → writes target/sources.json
- Selector: source_status:fresher+

---

## Topic 7 — State & defer

### State artifacts in target/

- manifest.json — graph + all node metadata
- run_results.json — last run's execution results
- sources.json — last freshness check
- catalog.json — docs metadata

### State sub-methods

Used with --select (plus --state <dir>) in dbt run, dbt build, dbt test, dbt ls — the classic Slim CI pattern.

- state:modified / state:modified+
- state:modified.body — SQL changed
- state:modified.configs — config changed; meta counts, tags and group do not (no state selector compares those two)
- state:modified.relation — database, schema or alias changed
- state:modified.persisted_descriptions — description changed
- state:modified.macros — a macro the node uses changed, directly or indirectly
- state:modified.contract — contract changed
- state:new — resource not in prior manifest; catches new sources and exposures, which state:modified does not
- state:old — resource in both manifests
- state:unmodified — the exact inverse of state:modified; for a node, in both and unchanged

Sample: dbt build --select state:modified+ --defer --state ./prior-artifacts

### Result selectors

Used with --select after a prior run — reads run_results.json in --state <dir>. Typical in dbt run, dbt build, dbt test.

- result:error+ — anything that errored, tests included
- result:fail — tests that returned failing rows
- result:pass — tests that returned none
- result:skipped+ · result:warn+ · result:success+

Sample: dbt build --select result:error+ --state ./prior-artifacts (rerun what errored last time)

### Defer

- `--defer` — **unselected** nodes resolve to the prior state's relations
- Requires `--state <dir>`
- Both flags read the same `manifest.json`
- `--favor-state` — prefer state-artifact relations even when a local one exists (more aggressive than plain `--defer`)

### Slim CI recipe

```
dbt build --select state:modified+ --defer --state ./prior-artifacts
```

#### `dbt retry`

- Re-runs from prior failure point using `run_results.json`
- Does NOT accept `--select`
- Re-parses on invocation; the failed-node list is frozen from the prior run
- To replay a saved state: `dbt retry --state <dir>`, not a copy of `run_results.json` back into `target/`

#### `dbt clone`

- Zero-copy on Snowflake / Databricks / BigQuery — and only if the source relation is a `table`
- Pointer view fallback otherwise — other adapters, and any non-table relation
- Requires `--state <dir>`

---

## Commands grid

| Command | Purpose | Key flags |
|---|---|---|
| `run` | Compile + execute model SQL | `--select`, `--exclude`, `--full-refresh`, `--empty` |
| `build` | `run` + `test` + `seed` + `snapshot`; short-circuits | `--select`, `--resource-type` |
| `test` | Execute data and unit tests | `--store-failures`, `--indirect-selection` |
| `seed` | Load CSVs from `seeds/` | `--full-refresh` |
| `snapshot` | Execute SCD2 snapshots | `--select`, `--exclude` |
| `compile` | Render SQL to `target/compiled/` | `--select`, `--inline` |
| `docs generate` | Write `catalog.json`, `manifest.json`, `run_results.json` (`--no-compile`: catalog only) | `--no-compile`, `--empty-catalog`, `--static` |
| `docs serve` | Serve docs locally | `--port` |
| `ls / list` | List resources | `--output`, `--resource-type` |
| `deps` | Install packages | `--add-package`, `--upgrade` |

| Command | Purpose | Key flags |
|---|---|---|
| `run-operation` | Invoke a macro | `<macro>`, `--args '{...}'` |
| `source freshness` | Check `loaded_at_field` against thresholds | `--select source:...` |
| `debug` | Validate connection | `--connection`, `--config-dir` |
| `parse` | Emit `manifest.json` only | (global) |
| `clean` | Delete `clean-targets` paths | — |
| `retry` | Re-run from failure point | — (no `--select`) |
| `clone` | Zero-copy clone from prior state | `--state`, `--select`, `--full-refresh` |
| `init` | Scaffold new project | `<name>` |
| `show` | Preview query results | `--select`, `--limit`, `--inline` |

---

## Node-selection grid

### Graph operators

- `model+` — model + descendants
- `+model` — model + ancestors
- `+model+` — both
- `model+N` — model + N levels of descendants
- `N+model` — N levels of ancestors + model
- `@model` — model + descendants + ancestors needed to build those descendants

### Set operators

- Space between args → **union** (`a b`)
- Comma in one arg → **intersection** (`tag:a,tag:b`)
- `--exclude <selector>` → subtract

### Selector methods (21 total)

- `fqn:` · `tag:` · `path:` · `file:` · `package:` · `config:`
- `resource_type:` · `source:` · `exposure:`
- `metric:` · `semantic_model:` · `saved_query:` *(Semantic Layer — out of scope)*
- `test_name:` · `test_type:` · `unit_test:` · `state:` · `result:` · `source_status:`
- `version:` · `group:` · `access:`

### Named selectors

- `indirect_selection:` inside a `selectors.yml` definition beats the `--indirect-selection` CLI flag; `parents` / `children` inheritance cannot be modified

- Defined in `selectors.yml`

- Invoke with `--selector <name>`

- Typically not combined with `--select` / `--exclude`

## Indirect-selection modes (for tests)

- eager (default) · cautious · buildable · empty

### .dbtignore

- Gitignore-style syntax; matching files are treated as if absent

---

## Gotchas — the traps the exam loves

- **source ≈ (database + schema).** A source is identified by its YAML name, but by convention teams declare one source per (database, schema) and group all its tables under it. The exam tests this convention.
- **@ operator** is descendants-first, not ancestors-first.
- **+model upstream, model+ downstream** — the prefix/suffix distinction matters. **The model itself is always included** in +model, model+, and +model+.
- **, vs space** in selectors — comma = intersection, space = union.
- **| is NOT a dbt selector operator.** Not listed in the docs.
- **result:fail is tests only** and result:failed is not a value. + after it matches nothing — a test is a leaf — so reach for 1+result:fail to rebuild the model behind a failure.
- **merge without unique_key** silently degrades to append-only — no error, just wrong semantics (duplicates).
- **on_schema_change: ignore** drops added columns silently; removing a column causes the run to **fail**.
- **dbt_project.yml key for data tests is data_tests:**; tests: remains valid as a backwards-compatible alias, and one resource cannot carry both keys.
- **dbt show** previews seeds and snapshots as well as models, tests, analyses and inline SQL — and showing a seed runs the loader.
- **dbt snapshot --full-refresh** exits on Error: No such option — **run**, **build**, **seed**, **compile**, **clone**, **retry** and **show** all register the flag; **snapshot** and **test** are the two node-SQL commands that never do.
- **dispatch naming:** <adapter>__<macro> — adapter prefix FIRST (e.g. snowflake__my_macro, default__my_macro).
- **run_query yields Jinja Undefined during parse, not None.** Always wrap in {% if execute %} — dbt does two passes, and **run_query/statement** only produce results on the execute pass.
- **doc() is a Jinja function, not a macro.** It lives in YAML strings (descriptions); .md files only *define* the blocks.
- **Exposures required fields:** name, type, and owner — the reference page does not mark owner required; the parser rejects an exposure without it.
- **target/compiled/** vs **target/run/** — compiled is pre-execute; run has the executed statement incl. create/insert wrappers.

# Chapter 1

# Introduction to the exam

> **Scope.** Give you a clear map of the dbt Analytics Engineer Certification before you touch any dbt content. By the end you will know what the exam is made of, what it deliberately leaves out, and where this book fits in the official learning path.

---

## 1.1 What this exam is, and who it's for

The **dbt Analytics Engineer Certification** validates that you can build, test, document, and maintain dbt models in a real project. It is not a dbt platform UI test and not a Snowflake/BigQuery/Databricks SQL test. It is a dbt Core 1.11 test, scoped to what an analytics engineer does in a working project week-to-week. The dbt Mesh line is finer than it looks: contracts, versions, groups and `access:` are in scope as single-project mechanics; multi-project deployment, cross-project `ref()` and project dependencies are not. §1.5 carries the full boundary. The official exam landing page is `getdbt.com/certifications/analytics-engineer-certification-exam`.

**Who the exam is for (per the current study guide):**

- SQL-fluent practitioners — comfortable with joins, aggregations, CTEs, and window functions without reaching for a reference.
- Git-literate — you've pushed a feature branch, opened a PR, handled a merge conflict.
- **6+ months hands-on dbt experience.** The guide recommends it rather than requiring it — it says "We recommend at least SQL proficiency and 6+ months of dbt experience", and its own *Prerequisites* checkpoint names only SQL and Git. The certification page counts "experience working with dbt or dbt Core", so terminal and platform reps both count.

**Who it is not for:**

- Absolute beginners. If you haven't yet run `dbt build` on your own project, take the **dbt Fundamentals (dbt Studio)** course first. The exam assumes you've already internalized the `ref`/DAG/materialization loop.
- Architects who design dbt projects but don't author models. The exam tests authoring mechanics — config precedence, selector syntax, test configuration — more than it tests design philosophy.

**Why take it.** Three practical reasons: (1) it is a vendor-backed dbt credential — the analytics-engineering one, alongside dbt Labs' Architect certification — so it signals baseline competence to hiring managers; (2) studying for it is the fastest way to notice the dbt features you have never reached for in production (almost certainly including `--empty`, `--sample`, microbatch, and `dbt clone`); (3) it forces a read-through of the official docs.

---

## 1.2 The seven domains of the current blueprint

The current study guide lists **seven topic domains**. They are the complete topic scope of the exam. The sub-bullets below are paraphrased from the guide's own outline; read them for shape and emphasis, not for wording. Memorise the shape of the list — it tells you where dbt Labs thinks the weight sits, and that is the only weighting signal you get. The guide carries no revision number of its own: it is versioned against the dbt Core release it supports, so cite it as the dbt Core 1.11 study guide.

### Topic 1 — Developing and optimizing dbt models

*Fourteen bullets — nearly half the outline. Treat it as the core model-building domain.*

- Identifying and verifying raw object dependencies
- Understanding the core dbt materializations
- Modularity, and how to apply DRY principles
- Using the commands `build`, `run`, `test`, `docs`, `show`, `snapshot`, and `seed`
- Designing a logical model flow and clean DAGs
- Defining configuration in `dbt_project.yml`
- Using dbt packages
- Creating Python models
- Granting access to models with the `grants` config
- Defining snapshots in YAML
- Choosing the incremental strategy that fits a dataset's characteristics
- Validating model logic and schema definitions in a dry run with `--empty`
- Running models in sample mode with `--sample`
- Advanced materializations, microbatch in particular

### Topic 2 — Managing dbt models governance

*Three bullets. The verb is "managing", not "understanding" — expect scenarios, not definitions.*

- Adding contracts to fix the shape of a model
- Versioning models, and deprecating old versions
- Defining constraints in YAML to enforce data integrity at the platform level

### Topic 3 — Debugging data modeling errors

*Five bullets — the second-largest domain by bullet count, and the one whose questions most often arrive dressed as something else.*

- Reading logged error messages
- Debugging through compiled code
- Debugging `.yml` compilation errors
- Building and testing a fix before merging it
- Managing dbt behaviour with flags

### Topic 4 — Troubleshooting and optimizing dbt pipelines

*Two bullets — tied with Topics 6 and 7 for the smallest domain on the outline.*

- Troubleshooting and managing failure points in the DAG
- Using `dbt clone`

### Topic 5 — Implementing dbt tests

*Three bullets. The first explicitly covers both data tests and unit tests; expect both in scenarios.*

- Applying generic, singular, custom, custom-generic and **unit** tests across models and sources
- Testing assumptions about models and sources
- Placing testing steps in the workflow

### Topic 6 — Implementing and maintaining external dependencies

*Two bullets.*

- Implementing exposures
- Implementing source freshness

### Topic 7 — Leveraging the dbt state

*Two bullets.*

- Understanding state and state selection
- Using `dbt retry`

Three current-scope points matter before you read on. **There is no documentation domain** — `dbt docs` appears inside Topic 1's command list and exposures sit in Topic 6, so no question maps to a documentation domain. **Topic 1's last five bullets name high-yield skills**, which §1.5 maps to the chapters that teach them. **The topic outline is not exhaustive**: model access, distinguishing a pure-SQL issue from a dbt one, and combining state with result selectors remain real dbt behaviour a stem can rest on — two of the ten official sample questions turn on source resolution, and one is a git-branching item.

### The inferred-weighting caveat

dbt Labs **does not publish domain weights** — not in the study guide, not on the certification landing page, not inside the dbt Learn course. Nothing is gated; do not go looking. Two signals are all you get: thirty-one sub-bullets spread across the seven domains, and ten released sample questions. The table below is my inference from those two. **It is a study-time allocation and nothing more** — no column in it is a claim about how the exam is weighted, and no percentage in it comes from dbt Labs.

| Topic | Sub-bullets (of 31) | In the 10 official samples | Suggested share of study time |
|---|---|---|---|
| 1. Developing and optimizing models | 14 | 6 | Dominant (est. **40–50%**) |
| 3. Debugging | 5 | 1 | Mid (**10–15%**) |

| Topic | Sub-bullets (of 31) | In the 10 official samples | Suggested share of study time |
|---|---|---|---|
| 5. Tests | 3 | 1 | Mid (**10–14%**) |
| 2. Governance | 3 | 1 | Small-to-mid (**8–12%**) |
| 6. External dependencies | 2 | 0 primary, 1 secondary | Small (**4–8%**) |
| 4. Troubleshooting pipelines | 2 | 0 primary, 1 secondary | Small (**3–7%**) |
| 7. State | 2 | 0 | Small (**3–7%**) |

Rows are ordered by inferred weight, not by topic number. One of the ten samples is a git-branching item that maps to no current domain — git is a Checkpoint 0 prerequisite now — so the sample column is read against the nine in-scope samples. The band midpoints sum to roughly 95 rather than 100, because they are ranges and not a partition; do not try to make them add up.

Topic 1 holds 14 of the 31 outline bullets and six of the nine in-scope samples — the largest share of the outline by a wide margin, which is why it gets the largest share of the study plan. What that converts to in scored questions is not published. When study time runs short, Chapters 4, 5 and 11 pay back fastest.

---

## 1.3 Question formats — six official buckets, seven tactics

The current study guide lists six question-format buckets. dbt Labs groups single-answer and multi-answer multiple-choice under one "multiple-choice" heading; this book splits them, because they fail in different ways — hence seven headings below rather than six. The guide states plainly that its sample questions do not represent all question formats, so do not infer from the ten samples that hotspot, matching and DOMC are rare.

### 1. Multiple-choice — single answer

Classic. One correct answer among 4–5 options. The majority of questions on the exam.
*Worked example:*

> Which materialization is the default when `materialized:` is not configured?
> A. `table`
> B. `view`
> C. `ephemeral`
> D. `incremental`
> **Answer:** B. `view`.

### 2. Multiple-choice — multi-answer ("select N")

Same layout, but the stem asks for "two answers" or "all that apply." Partial credit is **not** awarded — you must pick exactly the right set, no more and no fewer.
*Worked example:*

> `dbt build` errored on `stg_orders` and skipped the one model downstream of it. Nothing else in the run failed. You want to re-run the errored model and the model its failure blocked. Which **two** invocations do that? (Choose two.)
> A. `dbt build --select result:skipped+ --state ./prior`
> B. `dbt build --select state:modified --state ./prior`
> C. `dbt retry`
> D. `dbt build --select result:error+ --state ./prior`
> E. `dbt build --select result:failed+ --state ./prior`
> **Answer:** C and D. `dbt retry` resumes the last invocation from where it failed; `result:error+` selects the errored node plus its descendants. On 1.11.14 both land on the same two nodes. A is a real token, but it matches the skipped child and not the model that errored; B tracks code changes rather than run status; E is a typo dbt accepts in silence, matching nothing at exit 0. Ch 12 §12.5 has the status tokens.

The format is what to take from this one, not the selectors. Pick C alone — correct, as far as it goes — and you score exactly what you would have scored for picking E. A multi-answer item is a set-equality question wearing five options.

### 3. Fill-in-the-blank (FITB)

A sentence or YAML snippet with one or more blanks. You type the missing token exactly — no tolerance for typos or synonyms. Keep your spelling on `is_incremental()`, `on_schema_change`, `--full-refresh`, `packages.yml`, and `profiles.yml` letter-perfect.

*Worked example:*

> To indicate that a model should be built in chunks on subsequent runs, configure its `materialized:` to ______.
> **Answer:** `incremental`.

### 4. Matching

Two columns; drag items from the right onto items on the left. Typical exam use: match a command to its purpose, or a selector syntax to its graph semantics. A single wrong pair marks the whole item incorrect.

*Worked example:*

> Match each command to its primary effect.
>
> 1. `dbt compile`
> 2. `dbt docs generate`
> 3. `dbt deps`
> 4. `dbt debug`
>
> a. Render SQL to `target/compiled/` without executing it
>
> b. Produce `catalog.json` and `manifest.json`
>
> c. Install packages from `packages.yml`
>
> d. Validate profile resolution + warehouse connectivity
>
> **Answers:** 1-a, 2-b, 3-c, 4-d.

### 5. Hotspot

A screenshot (usually of code, a YAML file, or a DAG) with clickable regions. You click the single region that answers the stem. Be ruthless about *reading the stem* — hotspots often give you a crowded image and a narrow question.

*Worked example:* (described; the real exam shows a clickable image)

> (Screenshot of a `dbt_project.yml`.) Click the key whose value decides which directories `dbt clean` is allowed to delete.
>
> **Answer:** the `clean-targets:` key.

### 6. Build-list

Click items from an unordered pool to build an ordered list — typical use is "order these build steps" or "order these commands for a slim CI run." The study guide names *Build list* as one of its six formats and says nothing about how the pool behaves, so read the stem: it, and not a convention, tells you whether every pool item belongs in your answer.

*Worked example:*

> Put these slim-CI commands in the order they would run in a typical CI pipeline that only builds what changed.
>
> Pool: `dbt deps`, `dbt compile`, `dbt build --select state:modified+ --defer --state ./prior`.
>
> **Answer:** `dbt deps` → `dbt compile` → `dbt build --select state:modified+ --defer --state ./prior`. (Note: a separate `dbt test` is *not* in the pool because `dbt build` already runs tests interleaved with the run.)

### 7. Discrete Option Multiple Choice (DOMC)

The format most candidates have never seen. **DOMC shows you one option at a time.** You click Yes (this is correct) or No (this is not correct), and another option appears. You can't review all options simultaneously, and you can't go back. The engine draws from a large option pool; the set of options you see is not identical to what another candidate sees.

*Worked example:* (simulated — the real DOMC item sequences one option per screen)

> Stem: "Which statement about `dbt deps` is true?"
>
> - Option 1 appears: *"`dbt deps` installs packages listed in `dbt_project.yml`."* → click No (packages live in `packages.yml`).
> - Option 2 appears: *"`dbt deps` writes a `package-lock.yml` on first successful install."* → click Yes.
> - (DOMC ends and scores based on your Yes/No decisions; you are not told how many options will appear.)

**DOMC strategy:** treat every option as an independent true/false, answer it on its own merits, and **resist the urge to assume there's "one right answer"** — there may be several true statements in the pool. Answer each as-is.

---

## 1.4 Scoring, time budget, and logistics

- **65 questions, 120 minutes.** That works out to ~**1.8 minutes per question.** Internalize this.

- **65% to pass.** Scored questions are equally weighted (1 point correct, 0 incorrect). No penalty for wrong answers; always answer everything.
- **Some questions are unscored.** Every sitting embeds an undisclosed number of "research" items that do not count toward your score, indistinguishable from the scored ones. Answer every question as if it counted.
- **Score is visible immediately** on submit. No waiting.
- **Proctoring:** online proctored, and it runs in a Caveon Web browser rather than your everyday one. You'll need a stable webcam, a cleared desk, and a government ID.
- **Price: $200 USD**, printed in the guide as `$200*` without an associated note. Confirm what you actually owe at registration, and distrust any specific voucher figure you find elsewhere. Retakes cost the fee again.
- **Scheduling and cancellation:** free reschedule or cancellation through Talview up to 24 hours before your slot; no-show = no refund.
- **Language:** English and Japanese, per the guide's logistics table. Read the current list on the registration page before you book.
- **Validity:** 2 years from the date the certification is awarded.
- **Accommodations:** `accessibility@dbtlabs.com`. **Certification questions:** `certification@dbtlabs.com`.

### Why the 1.8 min/Q budget matters

1.8 minutes is an average, not a per-question ceiling — it sounds generous until you meet a build-list with 8 items or a code-scenario MCQ with a 20-line SQL snippet. Expect the mix to be uneven: a good few that resolve in seconds, most in a minute or two, and a handful that take real thought. The recommended way to absorb that unevenness is to **move on from anything over 2 minutes on the first pass** and leave time at the end for what you left. Whether you can flag an item and return to it depends on the exam interface — check what it offers in the tutorial before the timer starts, and if it does not let you revisit, answer every question when you first see it rather than planning a second pass.

**Concrete strategy:**

- First pass: answer everything quick. Set aside anything that requires reading SQL or checking your memory of a config key — flagging it if the interface allows, answering your best guess if it does not. Target $\leq 90$ seconds average.
- Second pass, where the interface permits one: return to what you set aside. Be willing to guess on hotspots and DOMC — they're hard to brute-force late.
- Never leave a question blank — a blank is a guaranteed zero.

---

## 1.5 What this exam does NOT test

The study guide targets **dbt Core 1.11** — stated on its cover, again in its logistics table, and confirmed on the certification landing page. Answer from current 1.11 behaviour; behaviour that changed after 1.11 is not what you are being asked about. The following are either explicitly out of scope or so far out of scope that dbt Labs does not mention them:

| Feature | Status | Why it's here |
|---|---|---|
| **dbt Mesh as a multi-project pattern** (project dependencies, cross-project `ref()`, public models as products) | Out of scope | The topic outline lists no cross-project workflow, and Topic 2's governance bullets — contracts, versions, constraints — are all local to a single project. Worth naming, because it confuses people: the official path *does* carry a dbt Mesh model-governance course, and it is there for contracts, versions and access, not for cross-project deployment. |
| **dbt Semantic Layer** (MetricFlow, semantic models, metrics YAML, saved queries) | Out of scope | Absent from the topic outline, and absent from every checkpoint's reading list. |
| **dbt Fusion / dbt Core 2.0** | Out of scope | Fusion is a separate engine with its own adapter list — Postgres, which this book's companion project runs on, is not on it. The outline names no Fusion-only behaviour. A docs page gated to "dbt v2.0 and later" is telling you the feature is not examinable. |
| **dbt Core 1.12 behaviour** | Out of scope | 1.12 ships after the version the exam pins. The trap is a behaviour flag that exists at 1.11 but defaults `false` and flips at 1.12 — `state_modified_compare_more_unrendered_values` is the one you're most likely to meet. Answer from the 1.11 default. |

| Feature | Status | Why it's here |
|---|---|---|
| **dbt Canvas, dbt Insights, and the platform's Catalog UI** | Out of scope | Paid platform surfaces — the docs gate Canvas and Insights to an Enterprise plan, and Catalog to a Starter, Enterprise or Enterprise+ plan — and none of them appears in the topic outline or in any checkpoint's reading list. One naming trap sits here: Catalog "builds upon dbt Docs", the site `dbt docs generate` produces, and *that* site is in scope through Topic 1's `docs` command even though the paid product built on it is not. |
| **Advanced dbt Studio features** | Not prominent | The exam tests dbt Core mechanics that work the same in dbt Studio and the terminal. Studio-specific UI is not drilled. |

### What IS in scope that you might be tempted to skip

- **Python models.** Listed explicitly in Topic 1 (`Creating Python models`). How often they appear is not published, so treat the emphasis here as a recommendation rather than a forecast. The two things worth knowing cold are (a) the platforms the Python-models page lists — Snowflake (Snowpark), Databricks (PySpark) and BigQuery (BigQuery DataFrames or Dataproc) — and (b) the difference between Jinja `{{ ref() }}` and `dbt.ref(...)`. Read `/docs/build/python-models` once.
- **Git.** Not a named topic bullet — it sits in the Checkpoint 0 prerequisites alongside SQL, as "Familiarity with branching strategies, basic commands, and pull requests" — and yet one of the ten official sample questions is a git-branching item. Know the basics: branching, merging, PR hygiene, and the trap that recurs — `git fetch` = download only, `git pull` = fetch plus an integration step, which in this merge-based workflow is a merge. Appendix A is the refresher.
- **Grants.** Listed as a Topic 1 sub-bullet. Know `grants: {select: ['role_a']}`, that grants are applied post-materialization, and that `grants` is distinct from governance `access:`.
- **Exposures.** A Topic 6 sub-bullet. Know the shape, per `/reference/exposure-properties`: `exposures:` in a `.yml`, `type:` one of `dashboard|notebook|analysis|ml|application`. The parser requires `name`, `type`, and `owner`; `depends_on:` is conventional and `description:` / `url:` / `maturity:` are optional.

**These eight current-outline skills** are high-yield reading because each is explicitly named in the topic scope.

| Current-outline skill | Topic | Where it is taught |
|---|---|---|
| Snapshots defined in YAML | 1 | Ch 5 |
| Choosing an incremental strategy to fit a dataset | 1 | Ch 4 |
| `--empty` dry runs | 1 | Ch 11 |
| `--sample` mode, and the `event_time` config it depends on | 1 | Ch 11, Ch 4 |
| Microbatch | 1 | Ch 4 |
| Constraints declared in YAML | 2 | Ch 13 |
| Behaviour management through flags | 3 | Ch 10 |
| Unit tests, folded into Topic 5's first bullet | 5 | Ch 7 |

---

## 1.6 Setting up — use the companion repo

The fastest way to prepare for this exam is to keep a real, green-building dbt project open while you read. Rather than install from scratch, clone this book's companion repo:

```
git clone https://github.com/snowleafbooks/dbt-analytics-engineer-certification.git
cd dbt-analytics-engineer-certification
```

The repo is a lab designed for this book: it opens in a VS Code Dev Container, runs on Postgres 15, and green-builds end to end. Its `requirements.txt` is the one place the dbt Core and adapter versions are pinned — read it after cloning, and check out the release tagged for this edition of the book if `main` has moved on. It exercises the concepts this book drills that a local warehouse can run:

- Sources and freshness; materializations; all four Postgres incremental strategies, microbatch included; `event_time`
- Snapshots defined in YAML with `hard_deletes`; seeds
- Tests, native unit tests and custom generic tests included
- Macros with dispatch; packages; documentation with `persist_docs`
- Governance: groups, `access:`, contracts, constraints, grants
- Behaviour flags; `--empty` and `--sample`; state and defer; slim CI

Warehouse-specific features — Python models, zero-copy clones, Delta Lake properties, Unity Catalog column masks — stay in the book's source-backed examples because they do not translate to Postgres; Chapter 14's Credora walkthrough is where those live instead.

### First end-to-end sanity check

From inside the companion repo:

```
dbt debug           # validates your profile + warehouse connection
dbt deps            # installs packages
dbt build           # run + test + seed + snapshot in DAG order
dbt docs generate   # writes catalog.json + manifest.json
dbt docs serve      # opens the lineage site on localhost:8080
```

If any of the first four commands fail, fix it before reading further — the rest of this book assumes the companion's dbt loop runs clean.

---

## 1.7 The official learning path — how to use it alongside this book

The study guide recommends a **four-checkpoint** path, and says explicitly that you can reorder it. Here it is at a glance, with the book chapters each checkpoint pairs with. Appendix B carries the full course, reading and documentation lists per checkpoint.

| Checkpoint | What it covers | Book chapters |
|---|---|---|
| **0 — Prerequisites** | SQL (joins, aggregations, CTEs, window functions) and git (branching strategies, basic commands, pull requests). | **Appendix A** (the prereq refresher). |
| **1 — Build a Foundation** | The largest checkpoint by a wide margin: dbt Fundamentals plus materializations, refactoring, analyses and seeds, snapshots, incremental models, and Jinja/macros/packages. Seven courses, and a documentation list long enough to be a study plan on its own — incremental strategy, microbatch, `--empty` and `--sample` are all on it. | **Ch 2** (first project, `ref`, the DAG), **Ch 3** (sources), **Ch 4** (materializations, incremental, microbatch), **Ch 5** (snapshots, seeds), **Ch 6** (Jinja, macros, `dbt_project.yml`), **Ch 8** (packages), **Ch 11** (CLI, `--empty`, `--sample`). |
| **2 — Govern and Debug Your Models** | Contracts, model versions, constraints, model access, debugging errors, `dbt compile`, behaviour changes and global-config flags. One course — the dbt Mesh model-governance module. | **Ch 13** (contracts, constraints, versions, access), **Ch 10** (debugging, `dbt compile` as a triage step, behaviour flags). |
| **3 — Build Resilient Pipelines at Scale** | Advanced testing, unit testing and exposures as three separate courses, plus `dbt clone`, cloning incremental models, source freshness, state, the `state` method, and `dbt retry`. | **Ch 7** (tests, unit tests), **Ch 9** (exposures), **Ch 3** (source freshness), **Ch 12** (state, defer, `dbt clone`, `dbt retry`), **Ch 14** (real project). |

Three features of the path matter. There is **no deployment checkpoint**: the four are Prerequisites, Build a Foundation, Govern and Debug Your Models, and Build Resilient Pipelines at Scale, and every testing course sits in the last of them. **Unit Testing** and **Exposures** are courses in their own right there, listed beside *Advanced Testing.* Model governance is a named course — the *dbt Mesh — Model Governance module* in Checkpoint 2 — which signals that contracts, versions and access are expected knowledge rather than advanced reading.

One caution, because the path is easy to misread. It does not list every document a question may turn on: node-selection syntax, general resource properties, `env_var`, `target`, `schema`, `database`, tags, hooks and operations, custom schema, threads, and `dbt run-operation` remain assessable. One official sample question is a pure graph-operator item and another turns on the `schema` property in `sources.yml`. The learning path is a reading suggestion; the topic outline in §1.2 is the assessment scope.

My recommendation: if you have worked on dbt extensively in the past, start with this book and the companion repo, and consult the official courses only on the topics Mock 1 shows you're weak in. If you have fewer than 6 months of dbt experience, use the companion repo alongside this book to build the hands-on reps the official courses would otherwise provide. §1.8 sets out the week-by-week tracks; Appendix B carries the per-checkpoint lists. Neither is repeated here.

---

## 1.8 How to use this book

Pick the track that matches your calendar and your hands-on dbt comfort. The technical chapters have a consistent study loop: scope and learning goals, sub-topics with doc refs, a real-project tie-in (skippable), and end-of-chapter practice questions with answers and explanations. Ch 1 is orientation; Ch 15 is exam strategy. Formal chapter drilling runs from Ch 2 through Ch 14.

**6-week aggressive track.** Best for working analytics engineers who already use SQL and Git daily.

| Week | Chapters | Weekend drill | Cumulative Qs |
|---|---|---|---|
| 1 | Ch 1, Ch 2, Ch 3 | 58 Qs (Ch 2–3) | 58 |
| 2 | Ch 4, Ch 5 | 69 Qs | 127 |
| 3 | Ch 6, Ch 7, Ch 8 | 78 Qs | 205 |
| 4 | Ch 10, Ch 11 | 62 Qs + Mock Test 1 timed | 332 |
| 5 | Ch 9, Ch 12, Ch 13 | 87 Qs + Mock 1 weak-domain re-drill | 419 |
| 6 | Ch 14, Ch 15, cheat-sheet review | 20 Qs + Mock Test 2 timed, then rest | 504 |

The ordering is deliberate in three places. **Ch 4 and Ch 5 own week 2 outright**, because between them they carry microbatch, `event_time`, incremental-strategy selection, snapshots in YAML and `hard_deletes` — the densest Topic 1 material in the book, and Topic 1 is the largest share of the outline. **Ch 6, Ch 7 and Ch 8 share week 3** so their Jinja, testing and package work can reinforce each other. And **Ch 9 sits in week 5, after Ch 11**: §9.5.5 leans on the selector methods and graph operators Ch 11 teaches, so reading it any earlier means reading it out of order.

*Weekend-drill counts are per-week loads; the last column is the running total, and it counts each mock in the week you sit it. Both are taken from this printing — 374 chapter drills, plus 65 questions in each of the two mocks. Count the paper in front of you rather than trusting the last column.*

**8-week relaxed track.** Better if dbt is not your day job yet, or if you are studying around production work.

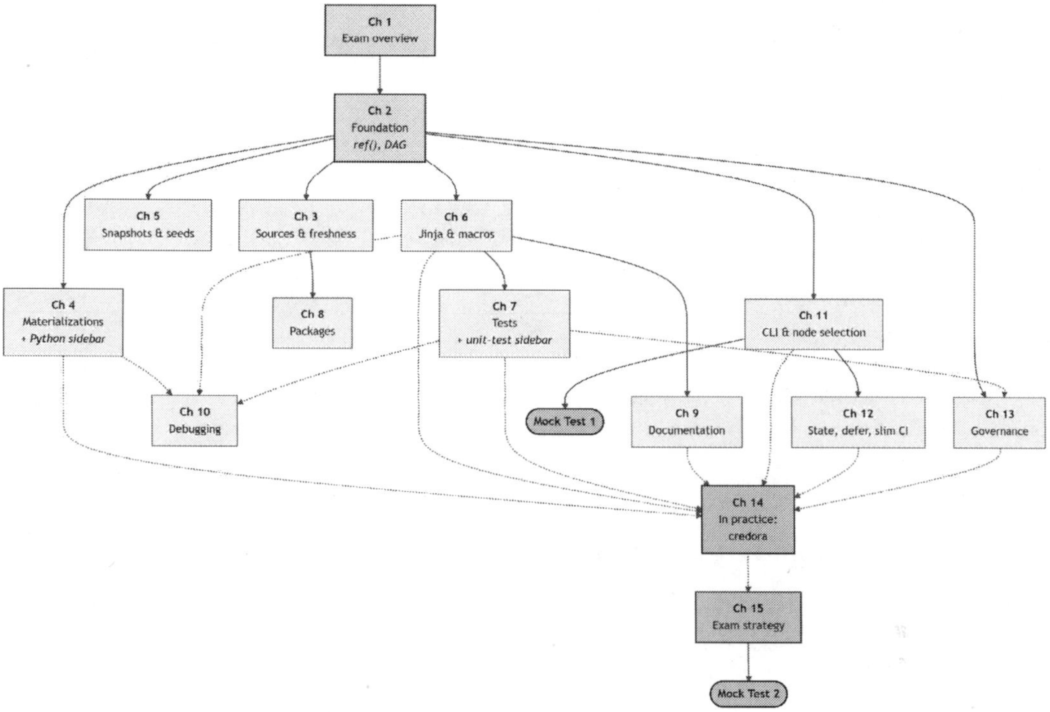


Figure 1.1: Chapter dependency map. Solid arrows are required prerequisites; dotted arrows are softer "useful before" links. Mock Tests sit at the natural checkpoints in the study tracks below.

| Week | Focus |
|---|---|
| 1 | Ch 1, Ch 2 |
| 2 | Ch 3, start Ch 4 |
| 3 | Finish Ch 4, Ch 5 |
| 4 | Ch 6, Ch 7 |
| 5 | Ch 8, Ch 10 |
| 6 | Ch 11 + Mock Test 1 |
| 7 | Ch 9, Ch 12, Ch 13 |
| 8 | Ch 14, Ch 15, cheat sheet, Mock Test 2, exam |

**2-week cram track (not recommended).** Cheat sheet → skim Ch 1, Ch 2, Ch 4, Ch 6, Ch 7, Ch 10, Ch 11 → Mock 1 → re-drill weak areas → Mock 2. This path cuts the analyze-level depth needed for debugging and state questions, and it skips snapshots in YAML (Ch 5) and constraints (Ch 13) entirely, both of which are named bullets on the current outline. Use it only when the exam date is already fixed.

### The three artefacts to return to

- **Cheat sheet (front of book).** Use it twice: once now, for orientation, then once more the morning of the exam. It mirrors the 7 blueprint domains one-to-one.
- **Mock Test 1** (end of book, after Ch 11 in the 6-week plan). Baseline difficulty — calibrated against the ten official sample questions, including analyze-level items. Aim for the 65% bar these mocks use, which is 43 of 65.

- **Mock Test 2** (end of book, after Ch 15 and 1–3 days before the exam). **Written one notch harder than these mocks' baseline**, so a comfortable score here is a good sign. Neither mock is the exam, and neither score predicts one: use both to find the concepts you missed or guessed, and re-drill those.

### The hands-on companion repo

Every chapter from 4 onward teaches a concept that the exam expects you to have actually *done*, not just read about. Every concept in Chapters 4–13 that works on a local warehouse is wired up in the companion repo from §1.6 — `https://github.com/snowleafbooks/dbt-analytics-engineer-certification` — as a concrete example you can run, break in a targeted way, and diff. A dedicated `exercises/` folder has 22 deliberately-broken cases for triage practice against the debugging chapter.

You never need to open the companion to pass the exam — this book is self-contained. But using it collapses the gap between "I read about incremental models" and "I've built one, broken it, and fixed it," which is where exam readiness actually lives. The repo's README has a quickstart; the coverage map at `https://github.com/snowleafbooks/dbt-analytics-engineer-certification/blob/main/REPO-COVERAGE.md` maps every exam concept to the specific file in the repo that demonstrates it.

# Chapter 2

# A first dbt project: structure, `ref`, and the DAG

> **Scope.** Every other chapter in the book assumes you can build a dbt project from empty directories, wire its models together with `ref()`, read `dbt_project.yml` without flinching, and trace a model from a `.sql` file to a row in the warehouse. If you have been shipping dbt for six months, skim §2.1 and read §2.3–§2.6 carefully — that is where the cert's Topic-1 questions actually live.

---

## 2.1 The minimum viable dbt project

A dbt project is a directory. Exactly one file is required — `dbt_project.yml` — and a project that builds anything also has at least one `.sql` file under `models/`. Everything else is optional. It is genuinely worth doing once from scratch, because the cert asks several questions that are only answerable if you have built the skeleton without a wizard's help.

### The required pieces

At minimum, a working project contains:

```
my_first_project/
├── dbt_project.yml
└── models/
    └── my_first_model.sql
```

And a `profiles.yml` somewhere dbt can find it. dbt takes the first hit of four: the `--profiles-dir` flag, the `DBT_ENGINE_PROFILES_DIR` environment variable (legacy spelling `DBT_PROFILES_DIR`), the working directory, then `~/.dbt/profiles.yml` — so a copy sitting in the project root is read *before* the home-directory one. **`profiles.yml` is still not part of your project**: the project is the code you commit, the profile is the secrets you don't.

The two are read in a fixed order, and that is what makes a startup failure diagnosable. dbt loads the project first. Run any project-loading command in a directory that has no `dbt_project.yml` and it stops at `Runtime Error: No dbt_project.yml found at expected path <cwd>/dbt_project.yml` — before it has looked for a profile at all. Delete both and you still get that error, not a profile one. Only once the project has loaded does dbt resolve the connection, and a `profile:` naming something `profiles.yml` does not define fails separately, with `Could not find profile named '...'`. So the error text tells you which of the two you are missing, and no model is listed either way.

### `dbt_project.yml` — the five-line starter

`name` and `profile` are strictly required — a file with nothing else parses clean. The conventional starter looks like this:

```
name: 'my_first_project'
version: '1.0.0'
profile: 'my_first_project'

model-paths: ["models"]
```

That is enough for dbt to parse the project. `name` is a required identifier using letters, digits, and underscores only; it must not start with a digit. `profile` tells dbt which block to look up in `profiles.yml` for warehouse credentials. `model-paths` defaults to `["models"]`, so you can drop it — it is printed here because the exam asks which directory keys exist.

See `/reference/project-configs/name` and `/reference/project-configs/profile` for the reference definitions for each of those keys.

### `profiles.yml` — and why it isn't in the project

`profiles.yml` lives at `~/.dbt/profiles.yml` by default. A minimal Postgres profile (the shape used by this book's companion repo):

```
my_first_project:
  target: dev
  outputs:
    dev:
      type: postgres
      host: localhost
      user: dbt_user
      password: "{{ env_var('DBT_PWD') }}"
      port: 5432
      dbname: analytics
      schema: dbt_dev
      threads: 4
```

Three things to notice.

1. **The top-level key `my_first_project` matches `profile:` in `dbt_project.yml`.** That is the only link between the two files. If you rename one and forget the other, dbt raises a "Could not find profile" error at load time.
2. **`target: dev` selects which `outputs:` block is active by default.** The outputs block can contain any number of targets (`dev`, `ci`, `prd`, etc.). `dbt run --target prd` switches which block dbt reads. The values under each target — `schema`, `dbname`/`database`, `host`, etc. — are defined here in `profiles.yml` and surfaced inside a model as `{{ target.name }}`, `{{ target.schema }}`, `{{ target.database }}`.
3. **Profiles are *machine-local secrets*, not project artifacts.** Your teammate's `profiles.yml` points at their scratch schema; yours points at yours; CI's points at its service account. `dbt_project.yml` is the same on every machine. This split is why dbt projects can be committed to Git with credentials nowhere in sight. See `/docs/local/profiles.yml` for the full shape.

### The first model

Create `models/my_first_model.sql` with a single line of SQL that doesn't depend on any tables (the same snippet runs cleanly on any warehouse the companion repo supports):

```
select 1 as id, 'hello' as message
```

From the project directory, run:

```
dbt run --select my_first_model
```

dbt parses the project, compiles the model, executes the compiled SQL against your warehouse, and materialises it as a view (the default). Query the resulting object — `select * from dbt_dev.my_first_model` on Postgres — and you should see one row. **If that round-trip doesn't work, stop and fix it now.** Every chapter hereafter assumes it does. See `/reference/commands/run`.

If you want to see the SQL dbt will actually send without executing it, run `dbt compile --select my_first_model` — the rendered file lands under `target/compiled/<project>/models/my_first_model.sql`. `dbt show --select my_first_model` goes one step further: it runs the compiled SQL and prints a preview of the result rows. Point it at an incremental model and the compiled SQL still carries its `is_incremental()` watermark filter, so what you preview is the incremental delta — empty immediately after a build.

### What just happened

Parsing → compile → execute. dbt discovered the `.sql` file under `models/`, rendered any Jinja (there was none), wrote the rendered SQL to `target/compiled/my_first_project/models/my_first_model.sql`, then wrapped it in `create view` DDL and ran that against the warehouse. We'll unpack the full lifecycle in §2.5.

---

## 2.2 `ref()` and the DAG

A dbt project with one model is not yet a dbt project in any interesting sense. The moment you have two models where one depends on the other, you meet the function the cert tests hardest: `ref()`.

### What `ref()` does

`ref()` is a Jinja function that returns a schema-qualified reference to another dbt model. Inside a model's SQL, instead of writing `select * from my_first_model`, you write:

```
select * from {{ ref('my_first_model') }}
```

At compile time, dbt resolves `{{ ref('my_first_model') }}` to the fully-qualified relation — `"analytics"."dbt_dev"."my_first_model"` — with database and schema resolved through the active target, never from a literal in your SQL. In dev, that schema is your personal scratch schema; in CI, it's the CI schema; in prod, it's the prod schema. **You never hard-code the schema. `ref()` knows what target you're on and fills it in.**

The reference page is `/reference/dbt-jinja-functions/ref`. Three things the page is explicit about:

1. `ref()` takes the model name. A two-argument form names the package or project first — `ref('dbt_utils', 'model_name')` — which is how you disambiguate two models that share a name across your project and an installed package (Ch 8). For versioned models, a `v=` (or its long form `version=`) kwarg selects a specific version (Ch 13 material).
2. `ref()` registers a **dependency** — dbt records a directed edge from the current model to the referenced model in the internal graph.

3. The referenced model must exist in the project. If it doesn't (typo, missing file, `enabled: false`), dbt raises a compilation error at parse time, before any SQL touches the warehouse.

### The DAG falls out of `ref()`

You don't write the DAG. You write `ref()` calls, and dbt infers the DAG from them. Every `{{ ref('x') }}` in a model's SQL becomes an edge "this model depends on `x`" in the graph. When you `dbt run` (or `dbt build`), dbt topologically sorts the graph and executes models in dependency order.

Here's the simplest two-model example:

```
-- models/stg_orders.sql
select 1 as order_id, 100 as amount
```

```
-- models/orders_summary.sql
select sum(amount) as total_amount
from {{ ref('stg_orders') }}
```

Running `dbt run`:

```
1 of 2 OK created sql view model dev.stg_orders ......... [CREATE VIEW in 0.12s]
2 of 2 OK created sql view model dev.orders_summary ..... [CREATE VIEW in 0.09s]
```

dbt ran `stg_orders` first because `orders_summary` refs it. Add `{{ ref('orders_summary') }}` to `stg_orders` while `orders_summary` still refs it and you get a **circular dependency** — dbt detects the cycle at compile time and refuses to run either model. See `/docs/build/sql-models` for the ref/DAG discussion.

### Running subsets: `dbt ls --select`

`dbt ls` (alias of `dbt list`) prints the resources dbt would act on, without running anything. It's the safest way to preview what a selector resolves to — pair it with `--select` to slice the DAG:

```
dbt ls --select orders_summary          # just the model itself
dbt ls --select +orders_summary         # orders_summary and all its upstreams
dbt ls --select orders_summary+         # orders_summary and all its downstreams
dbt ls --select +orders_summary+        # orders_summary plus upstreams and downstreams
```

The `+` prefix/suffix is the graph operator. We'll cover the full selector language in Ch 11; for now, `+model` is the one pattern that keeps coming up because it lets you answer the question "what would I need to rebuild to rebuild X?" without drawing anything. See `/reference/commands/list` (the `dbt ls` alias) and `/reference/node-selection/graph-operators`.

### Why never hard-code the schema

A frequent exam pattern asks you to spot the bug in a model that does something like `from dev.my_schema.stg_orders` instead of `from {{ ref('stg_orders') }}`. Three things go wrong the moment you hard-code:

1. **CI and prod break.** Your hard-coded `dev.my_schema` does not exist in CI or prod. The model fails on merge.

2. **The DAG is wrong.** dbt has no way to know that `stg_orders` is upstream of this model. It might try to run them in the wrong order, or let you delete `stg_orders` without warning.
3. **Refactoring is unsafe.** Renaming `stg_orders` to `stg_raw_orders` doesn't flag any downstream usage. With `ref()`, dbt tells you at compile time.

The rule, repeated everywhere in the cert: **if a table was produced by a dbt model, use `ref()`. If it was not, use `source()` (Ch 3). There is no third option.**

---

## 2.3 Project structure at scale

A project with two models doesn't need a folder convention. A project with 200 does. dbt Labs' published guidance — `/best-practices/how-we-structure/1-guide-overview` — codifies the structure every cert question assumes.

If you have come from a data-lakehouse background, this is the **Medallion architecture** — bronze / silver / gold in Delta or Iceberg — under dbt's names, **staging / intermediate / marts**, with one offset: medallion *bronze* is the raw landed layer, which maps to a dbt **source** rather than to staging. Staging is bronze with light cleanup, intermediate is silver-shaped joins and re-graining, marts are business-facing gold tables. The dbt names are the ones the exam uses.

### The three layers

```
models/
├── staging/      # stg_*.sql      - one-to-one with source tables
├── intermediate/ # int_*.sql      - transformations used by multiple marts
└── marts/        # fct_*, dim_*   - business-facing entities
```

Each layer has a narrow job.

**Staging (`stg_`).** One model per source table, renaming columns, casting types, and doing light cleanup. Staging models should have a **one-to-one** relationship with source tables and avoid joins. A staging model is the only place in the project where `{{ source(...) }}` appears — everything downstream refs the staging model instead. See `/best-practices/how-we-structure/2-staging`.

**Intermediate (`int_`).** Purpose-built transformation steps that bridge staging and marts. Typical uses are joining multiple staging models to produce a reusable building block, re-graining (aggregating from event-level to session-level, for example), or pivoting. Intermediates are usually materialised as views or ephemeral — they are not meant to be consumed directly. See `/best-practices/how-we-structure/3-intermediate`.

**Marts (`fct_`, `dim_`).** The end of the line: business-defined entities, usually materialised as tables because they are read by BI tools and downstream consumers many times per day — or as **incremental** once a full rebuild costs more than the added complexity is worth. `fct_` for facts (events, transactions, measurements), `dim_` for dimensions (entities like customer, product, account) — a dimensional-modelling overlay on the structure guide's own plain-entity naming (`orders`, `customers`). A mart may `ref()` another mart, and the guide expects it to; the only prohibition is the one the DAG enforces anyway, which is that the references must not close a loop. Materialization, though, is a workload decision rather than a naming rule, and the guide states it as a progression: start with a view, build it into a table once the view is too slow to *query*, and go incremental only once the table is too slow to *build*. So a mart that is still small or still changing shape may legitimately sit as a view. Read a stem for cost and query pattern; the layer name does not settle the materialization on its own. See /

`best-practices/how-we-structure/4-marts` for the layer and `/best-practices/best-practice-workflows` for the prefixes.

## Why the naming matters

The `stg_`, `int_`, `fct_`, `dim_` prefixes are not arbitrary style — they are scannable signals of *where in the DAG a model sits* and *how stable its contract is.* An exam question that shows you a model named `int_order_pivoted` is telling you, without saying so, that it is a reusable intermediate, probably unmaterialized as a table, and not meant to be consumed by a BI tool. Recognize the prefix, know the expected role.

The staging layer's convention goes one level finer than the prefix. A staging file is named `stg_[source]__[entity]s`, and the two underscore runs do different jobs: the single underscore after `stg` separates the layer prefix from the source system, and the **double** underscore separates the source system from the entity. `stg_shopify__orders.sql` is the Shopify system's `orders` table, one staging model to one source table. Multi-word entities keep single underscores inside the entity half — `stg_shopify__order_items` — so the double underscore stays unambiguous, which is what lets you read `stg_stripe__customers` and `stg_shopify__customers` side by side without guessing which system each came from.

A concrete medium-sized folder layout:

```
models/
├── staging/
│   ├── stripe/
│   │   ├── stg_stripe__customers.sql
│   │   ├── stg_stripe__charges.sql
│   │   └── _stripe__sources.yml
│   └── shopify/
│       ├── stg_shopify__orders.sql
│       └── _shopify__sources.yml
├── intermediate/
│   └── finance/
│       └── int_payments_joined_to_orders.sql
└── marts/
    └── finance/
        ├── fct_orders.sql
        └── dim_customers.sql
```

Two sub-conventions from the dbt Labs guide worth memorising:

- **Sub-folder per source system under `staging/`.** One folder per upstream system (Stripe, Shopify, Salesforce) keeps ownership obvious.
- **Sub-folder per business domain under `marts/`.** `finance/`, `marketing/`, `product/` — not by grain, not by materialization.

## The shape of a healthy DAG

Draw the graph left to right and a well-structured project looks like an arrowhead pointing right: widest on the left, where one staging model stands per source table, narrowing as models combine. The guidance behind that shape is **narrow the DAG, widen the tables**. Several inputs converging on one post-staging model is expected and healthy — that is what a model is *for*. Several outputs fanning out of one model is the warning sign, because it usually means a widening that should have happened once was deferred to every consumer instead.

Read a fan-out the way you read a repeated join. If nine marts each `ref()` the same intermediate model and each bolts one column onto it, those columns belong in the intermediate model and the marts should be reading a wider table. The mart-side form of the same heuristic counts **concepts**, not joins: once a mart brings together more than four or five of them, that is the point to stop and ask whether the reusable part belongs in an intermediate model. Read it as a warning sign rather than a limit — the guidance says so itself, and supplies its own counter-example both ways: eight staging models brought together with nothing but simple joins might be fine, while four concepts woven with heavy window functions could already be too much. What actually decides it is complexity, whether the grain changes, and whether the same join is being repeated somewhere else.

Intermediate models carry their own naming grammar. They are named `int_[entity]s_[verb]s` — `int_payments_pivoted`, `int_orders_joined_to_customers` — because what distinguishes one intermediate from another is the operation, not the source. The double underscore drops away at this layer and reappears only when a model is deliberately source-scoped (`int_shopify__orders_summed`). Their subdirectories are cut by **area of business concern** — `finance/`, `marketing/` — not by source system. That is the point at which the project stops being source-conformed and starts being business-conformed.

Intermediate models are also the layer you do not expose. Ephemeral is the guide's default recommendation at this layer, because an ephemeral model leaves no relation for anyone to find. The alternative, when a broken build is hard to debug from inlined CTEs alone, is a view in a custom schema that consumers are not granted on. Either way the contract holds: nothing outside the project reads an `int_` model.

The convention pays off a third time at selection time: **folders are the primary selection and grouping mechanism, and tags are for the exceptions.** `dbt build --select marts.marketing` costs nothing to maintain, because the folder already exists and every new model lands in it. `dbt build --select tag:marketing` costs a tag on every model and a review comment every time somebody forgets one. Reach for a tag when the set you need genuinely cuts across folders — a nightly subset, a PII group — not when it *is* a folder.

See `/best-practices/how-we-structure/3-intermediate` and `/best-practices/how-we-structure/5-the-rest-of-the-project`.

## Folder-level configs via `dbt_project.yml`

The payoff of the convention is that you can set configs at the folder level in `dbt_project.yml` and have them cascade to every model inside:

```
models:
  my_first_project:
    staging:
      +materialized: view
      +schema: staging
    intermediate:
      +materialized: ephemeral
    marts:
      +materialized: table
      +schema: analytics
```

That block says "every model under `models/staging/` is a view, every model under `models/intermediate/` is inlined as a CTE, every model under `models/marts/` is a table." The `+` prefix is the signal that this is a *config* (not a property).

> **What +schema: actually does.** Setting +schema: staging does **not** override the target's schema; by default, dbt *concatenates* it onto the active target's schema as <target.schema>_<custom> — so a developer with target.schema = dbt_dev lands models in dbt_dev_staging, while CI's target.schema = analytics_ci lands them in analytics_ci_staging. The concat is implemented by a built-in macro called generate_schema_name, which a project can override (typically in macros/) to swap the rule — for example, to use <custom> directly without the target prefix in production. The cert occasionally tests recognition of the default concat shape.

### The other dbt directories

models/ is not the only place dbt looks. The project structure supports a standard set of directories, each with a corresponding top-level path key in dbt_project.yml (see /docs/build/projects):

| Directory | Path key | What it holds |
|---|---|---|
| models/ | model-paths | .sql (and .py) model files — and the .yml files that declare sources and unit tests |
| seeds/ | seed-paths | CSV files loaded by dbt seed; may be co-located with models/, because the file types do not collide |
| tests/ | test-paths | Singular .sql tests; generic test *definitions* go in a generic/ subdirectory beneath it |
| macros/ | macro-paths | Reusable Jinja macros — the one path that cannot be co-located with models |
| snapshots/ | snapshot-paths | SCD2 snapshot definitions |
| analyses/ | analysis-paths | Ad-hoc .sql that compiles but doesn't execute |

Memorise the names of these keys; the cert asks about them directly. You can change the paths in dbt_project.yml — e.g., model-paths: ["transforms"] — but the defaults are near-universal, and every one of the six resolves to the directory name above when the key is absent. See /reference/project-configs/model-paths for the pattern.

Two file-level rules travel with these directories. A properties file may carry either extension — dbt reads .yml and .yaml alike — but a model entry's name: inside one must match the model name exactly, **including case**. Write Dim_Customers against a dim_customers.sql and dbt attaches nothing, says so at warning level (Did not find matching node for patch with name 'Dim_Customers'), and builds the model on its defaults. A green run is not evidence that the properties file was applied.

---

## 2.4 dbt_project.yml in depth

dbt_project.yml is the single file that answers more cert questions than any other. Most of those questions are not about what a key means — they are about which of three places a config was set in, and which of the three wins.

### Top-level keys you will see on the exam

```yaml
name: 'my_project'
version: '1.0.0'
profile: 'my_project'
require-dbt-version: ">=1.11.0"

model-paths: ["models"]
seed-paths: ["seeds"]
test-paths: ["tests"]
macro-paths: ["macros"]
snapshot-paths: ["snapshots"]
analysis-paths: ["analyses"]
target-path: "target"
clean-targets: ["target", "dbt_packages"]

vars:
  start_date: '2022-01-01'

on-run-start:
  - "grant usage on schema {{ target.schema }} to role analyst"
on-run-end: []

models:
  my_project:
    staging:
      +materialized: view
    marts:
      +materialized: table

seeds:
  my_project:
    +schema: reference

snapshots:
  my_project:
    +schema: snapshots
```

Walking through each:

- **`name`, `version`, `profile`** — identity keys. `profile` is the pointer to `profiles.yml`. See `/reference/project-configs/name`, `/reference/project-configs/profile`.
- **`require-dbt-version`** — a version range; dbt refuses to run if the installed `dbt-core` is outside the range. Useful for locking teams to a tested minor version when a downstream upgrade is staged. Quote the value and leave no whitespace after the operator — `">=1.11.0"` — or YAML hands dbt something that is not a version range. The check is not scoped to your own project: an **installed package** whose `require-dbt-version` excludes your version fails the whole project at read time, before a single model is parsed. `--no-version-check` bypasses both. See `/reference/project-configs/require-dbt-version`.
- **`*-paths` keys** — the six path lists from §2.3. Every one of them has a default, `analysis-paths` included: it is `["analyses"]`, and the reference page for that key is wrong to say it has none. Declaring a path key **replaces** its default rather than adding to it, so a project that retargets `analysis-paths` stops discovering anything left in `analyses/`.

`target-path`, which sets the directory for compiled artifacts, sits with them but is deprecated inside `dbt_project.yml`: any value other than the default `target` warns and points you at the `--target-path` flag or `DBT_TARGET_PATH`.

- `clean-targets` — directories that `dbt clean` is allowed to delete. If the key is omitted, the built-in default is just the project's `target-path/` (typically `target/`). `dbt init` ships starter projects with `clean-targets: ["target", "dbt_packages"]`, which is what most teams keep. Naming a configured source directory here is refused rather than obeyed: `dbt clean` aborts with a `Runtime Error` whose message reads `dbt will not clean the following source paths: [...]`, and deletes nothing at all, including the entries that were safe. The guard covers only the paths the project declares — `model-paths`, `seed-paths`, `snapshot-paths`, `analysis-paths`, `macro-paths`, `test-paths`, `function-paths` — so any other directory you list is removed without comment. See `/reference/project-configs/clean-targets`.

- `vars` — project-level variables readable from any model via `{{ var('start_date') }}`. By default, top-level entries under `vars:` are **global** — visible from any package and any model. If you want to scope a variable to this project only, nest it under the project name:

```
vars:
  <project_name>:
    var1: xx
    var2: yy
```

  Five levels resolve a `var()` call, most specific first: a `--vars` value on the command line; a block keyed to a package name inside the **root** project's file; a global entry in the root project's file; the entry in the **package's own** project file; and the fallback in `var('name', default)`. The root project beating the package is what makes `vars:` the supported way to configure an installed package (Ch 8).

  The subtlety is **scope**: a variable resolves in the scope of the node that *consumes* it, not the package that defines the macro doing the reading. A macro shipped inside a package that calls `var('lookback_days')` reads your root project's global value when one of your models calls it, and reads the value under that package's key when one of the package's own models calls the same macro. Changing any variable also invalidates the partial-parse cache for the next run, so a `--vars` sweep is slower than it looks.

- `on-run-start` / `on-run-end` — SQL statements that run at the beginning and end of six commands: `build`, `run`, `seed`, `snapshot`, `source freshness`, `test`. (`source freshness` is the one people miss: it builds nothing, but it runs project hooks like any other execution command.) `dbt parse` and `dbt clean` do **not** trigger the hooks, and neither do `dbt compile` or `dbt docs generate`, which the reference page still lists. Useful for grants, session-level settings, and audit logging. See `/reference/project-configs/on-run-start-on-run-end`.

- `models` / `seeds` / `snapshots` — per-resource-type config trees. Each tree nests by project name, then by folder, and uses `+` to mark configs.

## The + prefix — configs vs. properties

Inside `models:`, `seeds:`, `snapshots:` blocks, keys prefixed with `+` are **configs** (behaviour-affecting settings like `+materialized`, `+schema`, `+tags`). Unprefixed keys are **folder names** that nest deeper into the tree. Only folder and file names belong unprefixed: a config written without the `+` is **deprecated**. dbt still applies it and still builds the model, but it emits a deprecation warning naming the key.

That warning is adapter-gated, which matters chiefly so you do not read its absence as approval. dbt runs its **deprecation** JSON-schema pass over `dbt_project.yml` on Snowflake, Databricks, BigQuery and Redshift only; on Postgres the unprefixed config applies with nothing printed. The rule is identical on every adapter — only the diagnostic differs. Write `+` on every config and the ambiguity never arises.

The distinction is not only about where the `+` goes. Configs can be set in three places — `dbt_project.yml`, a properties `.yml`, or an in-file `{{ config() }}` block — but **properties can only ever be written in a properties `.yml` file.** There is no `{{ config(description='...') }}`, and writing one does not describe the model; it is not an error either, which is why this is worth knowing rather than discovering.

The YAML-only list is short enough to hold: `description`, `columns`, `data_tests` and `quote` — plus the entries that *define* a source (`loaded_at_field`, `database`, `schema` under `sources:`) or an exposure (`type`, `maturity`, `owner`). Two that look like they belong on that list are **not** on it: `docs` and `freshness` are both genuine configs. `{{ config(docs={'show': false}) }}` and `+docs:` in `dbt_project.yml` bind identically, and `freshness` binds on both surfaces too — which surface you reach for depends on the resource. A source has no `.sql` file to carry a config block, so its freshness is written as `+freshness:` under `sources:` in the project file or in the source's own `.yml`; a model carries `freshness.build_after` in `dbt_project.yml` or inline, as `{{ config(freshness={'build_after': {'count': 6, 'period': 'hour'}}) }}`. The rule of thumb that gets you the rest: a **config** changes how dbt *builds* the thing; a **property** describes or tests the thing it built. Materialization, schema and tags change the build. A description does not.

## Config precedence — the one rule

dbt has three places a model's config can be set, and the precedence is **most-specific wins** — highest first:

1. `{{ config(materialized='table') }}` inside the `.sql` file.
2. A YAML properties file — typically `_models.yml` — with a `config:` block under the model.
3. `dbt_project.yml` under `models:` with a `+config` key.

Within category 3, a deeper folder path wins over a shallower one. So a `+materialized: table` under `models: my_project: marts: finance:` beats a `+materialized: view` under `models: my_project:`.

One case sits outside that ladder entirely. A config written with **no resource path at all** — `models: +enabled: false`, straight under the resource type — applies to every model dbt knows about, **including the models inside installed packages**. Nesting the config under your project name is what excludes them. That is what the project-name level in the tree is for, and why deleting it as boilerplate is a mistake. See `/reference/define-configs` for the standard treatment. This precedence is a frequently-tested place to hide a gotcha — if a question shows you two or three config sources and asks which one wins, work from specific to general.

**One additive-vs-overwrite nuance.** "Most-specific wins" is the rule for **scalar** configs only. Lists accumulate instead — the frequently-tested trap is a multi-step "what tags does this model end up with?" question — and dict configs split three ways rather than two, one of which does not merge at all.

| Config type | Examples | What the deeper value does |
|---|---|---|
| scalar | `materialized:`, `+schema:` | replaces the shallower value |
| list | `tags:`, `pre-hook:`/`post-hook:` | is *added* to it |
| dict, **shallow-merged** | `meta` | merges per top-level key — a key set at both levels is replaced whole, and the nested keys inside the loser are lost |
| dict, merged **per key** | `freshness` | a `warn_after` set on a source survives an `error_after` set on one of its tables |
| dict, replaced outright | `persist_docs` | replaces the less specific dict whole, keys the winner does not mention included |

So a `+tags: ['mart']` under `marts:`, plus a `+tags: ['finance']` under `marts: finance:`, plus an SQL-level `config(tags=['q_close'])`, gives the model **all three** tags — not just the SQL one.

> **Configs vs. properties.** *Configs* (runtime behaviour flags like `materialized`, `grants`, `persist_docs`, `freshness`) and *properties* (YAML-structural keys like `description`, `columns`, `constraints`, `versions`, `data_tests`) live in separate trees in the docs — configs under `/reference/resource-configs/*`, properties under `/reference/resource-properties/*`.

## Custom schemas and aliases

Two configs decide where a model lands and what it is called when it gets there. Both are routinely half-remembered, and the half that gets dropped is the half the exam asks about.

`+schema:` is the one §2.3 introduced: it routes through the built-in `generate_schema_name` macro, which concatenates by default. Overriding that macro in your own `macros/` directory is the supported way to change the rule — and dbt **ignores** a `generate_schema_name` that ships inside an installed package when it names *your* models: a package's copy governs only the nodes that package itself owns, so it can never change where your project's models land.

The macro compiles in a **restricted context**, because it runs while dbt is still deciding what to name things:

- **Available** — `target`, `env_var`, `log`, `exceptions`, and your project's and packages' macros.
- **Partly available** — `var()`, but it reaches only globally-scoped variables and anything passed with `--vars`.
- **Not available at all** — relations and the database.

`generate_schema_name_for_env` inverts the rule by environment: the custom schema is used verbatim in production and ignored everywhere else, leaving dev and CI models in the target's own schema. It ships with dbt but is **disabled** — you turn it on by writing a `generate_schema_name` that calls it, and it behaves as advertised only when the production target is named `prod`. See `/docs/build/custom-schemas`.

`+database:` looks like its twin and behaves like its opposite. Where a custom schema is *appended* to the target's, a custom database **replaces** the target's outright: `generate_database_name` returns the value you wrote, verbatim, with no combination of any kind. Set `+schema: marketing` against target schema `analytics_prod` and the model lands in `analytics_prod_marketing`; set `+database: reporting` against target database `analytics` and it lands in `reporting`, not `analytics_reporting`.

The asymmetry is the point, and it is worth saying out loud before you meet it in a stem: **schema concatenates, database substitutes.** It bites hardest in development, because a hard-coded `+database:` ignores the target and every developer writes to the same place — the collision the custom-schema default exists to prevent. See `/docs/build/custom-databases`.

`alias:` moves the identifier dbt writes to the warehouse, and moves nothing else:

```
models:
  my_project:
    marts:
      dim_customers:
        +alias: customers
```

The relation becomes `<database>.<schema>.customers`. **`ref()` still takes the filename** — `{{ ref('dim_customers') }}` — because the node in the graph is still `model.my_project.dim_customers`, and the alias never becomes a second name you can look the model up by. Write `{{ ref('customers') }}` and dbt fails at compile with `depends on a node named 'customers' which was not found`. An ephemeral model is the one place the alias shows through into compiled SQL: its inlined CTE is named `__dbt__cte__customers`, after the alias rather than after the file.

The failure worth recognising is the collision. Because `alias` moves a relation without moving the node, two resources can end up pointing at one address — a `dim_customers.sql` aliased to `customers`, and a `customers.sql` that lands in the same schema. dbt catches that while it is building the graph, not while it is running:

```
Compilation Error
  dbt found two resources with the database representation ""analytics"."dbt_dev"."
     customers"".
  dbt cannot create two resources with identical database representations. To fix this,
  change the configuration of one of these resources:
  - model.my_project.dim_customers (models/marts/dim_customers.sql)
  - model.my_project.customers (models/marts/customers.sql)
```

Nothing is overwritten and nothing half-builds; the run stops before any DDL is sent, and the message names both offenders and their paths. See `/docs/build/custom-aliases`.

## The other collision — two nodes, one name

The alias error above is about two nodes landing on one *address*. There is a second collision, about two nodes sharing one *name*, and it is the stricter of the two: **a ref-able name has to be unique across the whole project, not merely within its own resource type or folder.** Two models called `orders` in different directories collide. So do a model `orders` and a seed `orders`, even though nothing about `seeds/orders.csv` and `models/marts/orders.sql` looks like a conflict — `{{ ref('orders') }}` has no way to say which one you meant.

The two cases are enforced differently. **Different-type duplicates are governed by a behaviour flag**, off by default:

```
# dbt_project.yml
flags:
  require_unique_project_resource_names: true
```

Turn it on and a shared NAME is a parse-time error. Leave it off — the 1.11 default — and the shared name is a deprecation warning, `DuplicateNameDistinctNodeTypesDeprecation`, and the build proceeds.

**That is only half the answer, and the half that decides most stems is the other one.** The flag governs the *name*; it does nothing about the *address*. A model `orders` and a seed `orders` resolve to the same `database.schema.identifier` by default, so they also trip the alias collision above — and that one is a hard `Compilation Error` whatever the flag is set to. Executed on stock 1.11 with nothing else configured, a project holding `models/orders.sql` and `seeds/orders.csv` prints the deprecation warning, then stops with *"dbt found two resources with the database representation"* and exits 2 having built nothing. Give one of them a distinct `alias:` and the same project parses to exit 0 with the warning alone.

So the exam-shaped rule is a pair, not a single fact: **at the 1.11 default the shared name warns, and the build survives only if the two resolve to different relations.**

### `dbt_project.yml` vs. `profiles.yml` — separation of concerns

One-line mental model: **`dbt_project.yml` is versioned, shared, warehouse-agnostic. `profiles.yml` is machine-local, personal, warehouse-specific.**

| Lives in `dbt_project.yml` | Lives in `profiles.yml` |
|---|---|
| Project name, version | Warehouse type (Postgres / Snowflake / BigQuery / Databricks) |
| Default materializations per folder | Account / host / server addresses |
| `vars` shared across environments | User / role / password / service-account |
| Hooks | Target schema and database **defaults** (can be overridden by dbt configs) |
| Test paths, macro paths, seed paths | `threads` setting |
| `models:` config tree | `target:` currently-active output |

A useful litmus test: if the value would be the same on your teammate's laptop, it belongs in `dbt_project.yml`. If it is secret or machine-specific, it belongs in `profiles.yml`.

---

## 2.5 A model's life cycle

Every model on the exam goes through the same four stages. Recognizing where you are in the sequence is most of debugging.

### 1. SQL file

Your hand-written `.sql` file under `models/` — with Jinja expressions still in place (`{{ ref() }}`, `{{ config() }}`, `{{ var() }}`). At this point, it is inert — dbt hasn't looked at it yet.

### 2. Parse & compile

When you run any command, dbt parses every project file into an in-memory graph (the **manifest**, written to disk after parsing as `target/manifest.json` — the same file that Ch 12's state and `--defer` machinery later reads back). For each model, it then **compiles** the SQL: Jinja expressions are rendered into literal SQL, `ref()` and `source()` calls resolve to fully-qualified warehouse-relations, and the compiled text is written to target/compiled/<project-name>/<path>/<model>.sql. The Jinja substitution itself is pure text substitution — no DDL is sent. (Compile may still open a warehouse connection for introspective queries such as relation cache or `dbt_utils.get_column_values`; it just doesn't materialise anything.)

You can do just this step with `dbt compile`. It is invaluable for debugging: when a model fails, the first question is "did it compile to the SQL I expected?" — and the answer sits on disk under `target/compiled/`. `dbt compile --inline 'select * from {{ ref("stg_orders") }}'` even lets you compile ad-hoc SQL without adding a file.

### 3. DDL wrapping

For each compiled model, dbt wraps the rendered `select` in the DDL appropriate to its materialization:

- `view` → `create or replace view <relation> as (<compiled sql>)`
- `table` → `create or replace table <relation> as (<compiled sql>)`
- `incremental` → either `create table` (first run / `--full-refresh`) or an adapter-specific merge/upsert pattern on subsequent runs. Which pattern you get depends on the adapter and on whether a `unique_key` is set; Ch 4 §4.3 carries the strategy catalogue and the per-adapter defaults.
- `ephemeral` → not materialised at all; the compiled SQL is inlined as a CTE into downstream models
- `materialized_view` → the adapter's own materialized-view DDL, on the adapters that implement it (Ch 4 §4.1)

The wrapped DDL is written to `target/run/<project-name>/<path>/<model>.sql`. This is the SQL dbt actually sends to your warehouse.

### 4. Execute

`dbt run` sends the wrapped DDL to the warehouse, in dependency order derived from the DAG. Threads (configured in `profiles.yml`) control how many models can execute in parallel — siblings at the same DAG level run concurrently up to the thread limit. The execution results (success / error / row counts / timing) land in `target/run_results.json`.

### When compilation fails

If `{{ ref('stg_orders') }}` points to a model that doesn't exist — typo, missing file, or `enabled: false` — dbt fails at **compile** time, before anything touches the warehouse. That is a gift: the cycle is 1 second, not 60 seconds, and the error message tells you the exact compile-time dependency that couldn't resolve.

Two error shapes to recognise:

- **Compile-time errors** (the dbt layer) — missing `ref`, unknown macro, YAML parse error. The traceback points at a specific line in a `.sql` or `.yml` file, and nothing was sent to the warehouse. Fix it from the compiler message alone.
- **Runtime errors** (the warehouse layer) — the compiled SQL is legal dbt but the warehouse rejected it. Typical causes: `select a_column_that_doesnt_exist`, a column whose type has been changed upstream (e.g. `varchar` → `int`) so a downstream cast now fails, permissions, or an out-of-memory join. The error comes back with a warehouse stack trace; the compiled SQL under `target/compiled/<project>/.../model.sql` is the first file to open.

---

## 2.6 In practice: the Credora project-file pattern

> *This section is an "in practice" sidebar — the first of the book's recurring set. It draws on the public dbt-project structure guidance at `/best-practices/how-we-structure/1-guide-overview`. Credora is a fictional consumer-fintech project (`credora`) — a multi-market consumer fintech, over 1,000 models across roughly a dozen Databricks catalogs; see Ch 14's opening note for the composite-project disclaimer.*
>
> **Illustrative only.** The YAML below is Databricks-specific (catalog routing, `+databricks_tags`) and does **not** run on the Postgres companion repo. Read it for the shape; run the companion repo for the concepts that execute on your laptop.

Beyond the two-folder toy project, real-world `dbt_project.yml` files can grow past a thousand lines. The shape of the growth is almost always the same: more nesting under `models:`, driven by per-market or per-domain catalog / schema assignments. Here is a redacted, fictional version showing the pattern.

```
# dbt_project.yml - condensed fictional excerpt
name: 'credora'
version: '1.0.0'
profile: 'credora'
require-dbt-version: ">=1.11.0"

model-paths: ["models"]
seed-paths: ["seeds"]
test-paths: ["tests"]
macro-paths: ["macros"]
snapshot-paths: ["snapshots"]
clean-targets: ["target", "dbt_packages"]

vars:
  raw_catalog: "{{ env_var('RAW_CATALOG', 'cr_partner_ingest_dev') }}"
  run_date: "{{ run_started_at.strftime('%Y-%m-%d') }}"

on-run-start:
  - "{{ require_select_arg() }}"

models:
  credora:

    # Shared cross-market models ---------------------------
    cr_global:
      +database: cr_global
      staging:
        +schema: staging
        +materialized: view
      intermediate:
        +schema: intermediate
        +materialized: ephemeral
      marts:
        +schema: analytics
        +materialized: table
        +databricks_tags:
          domain: "global"

    # UK market ------------------------------------------
    cr_uk:
      +database: cr_uk
      +databricks_tags:
```

```
        market: "uk"
        owner: "@analytics-uk"
      staging:
        +schema: staging
        +materialized: view
      marts:
        +schema: analytics
        +materialized: table

    # US market -----------------------------------------
    cr_us:
      +database: cr_us
      +databricks_tags:
        market: "us"
        owner: "@analytics-us"
      staging:
        +schema: staging
        +materialized: view
      marts:
        +schema: analytics
        +materialized: table

    # APAC and EMEA follow the same shape ------------------
    cr_apac_1: { +database: cr_apac_1, +databricks_tags: { market: "apac_1" } }
    cr_apac_2: { +database: cr_apac_2, +databricks_tags: { market: "apac_2" } }
    cr_emea_1: { +database: cr_emea_1, +databricks_tags: { market: "emea_1" } }

seeds:
  credora:
    +schema: reference
    +quote_columns: true
```

## What this snippet shows

- **Per-market `+database` routing.** Each top-level folder under `models: credora:` maps to a different warehouse catalog (on Databricks, "catalog" = "database" in dbt's terminology). A staging model under `models/cr_uk/staging/` materialises into `cr_uk.staging.*`; the same file path under `cr_us/` routes to `cr_us.staging.*`. This is how one project ships the same logical shape to many isolated markets.
- **Folder-cascading materializations.** The §2.3 staging/intermediate/marts convention, applied at the folder level. A single `{{ config(materialized='incremental') }}` inside an individual marts model would override the folder default per §2.4's precedence rule.
- **Adapter-specific configs pass through +-prefixed keys.** `+databricks_tags:` is passed to the Databricks adapter at materialization; the pattern is the same for `+snowflake_warehouse:`, `+bigquery_labels:`, etc. The exam does not test adapter-specific keys, but it does expect you to recognise that `+foo:` nested under `models:` is a config, not a folder.
- `require-dbt-version: ">=1.11.0"` — the §2.4 guard in production use: it stops a laptop with a stale `dbt-core` install from producing a subtly different build.

### What this snippet does NOT show

- **No SQL.** Credora's actual models are not shown; this is project file only. Every model is authored from scratch against the conventions this chapter teaches.
- **No production secrets.** `profiles.yml` is deliberately not shown. Database, host, and credentials are machine-local.
- **No exact scale figures.** Credora runs "over 1,000 models" and "roughly a dozen catalogs" — both ranges, not exact counts. (The exam doesn't care about scale figures; real production projects care deeply.)

### Dual source — this pattern is not unique to Credora

The multi-catalog-nesting pattern under `models:` is public and widely documented:

- dbt Labs' own *How we structure our dbt projects* shows the same nesting shape on smaller projects.
- dbt Labs' resource-path reference documents the same folder-cascading `+config` nesting under `models:`.

If you would like to see the pattern in a small project you can clone, use the companion repo: `https://github.com/snowleafbooks/dbt-analytics-engineer-certification`. The Credora sketch above is a composite — it picks the same structural moves those references make, with fictional catalog names chosen to anchor the multi-market framing.

---

## Summary

- A dbt project is a directory, and `dbt_project.yml` is the only file it requires. `profiles.yml` is machine-local and belongs outside the project — but dbt searches the working directory before `~/.dbt/`.
- **`ref()` is how models reference each other.** Hard-coded schemas break CI, break the DAG, and make refactoring unsafe. The rule: dbt-managed tables → `ref()`; raw tables → `source()` (Ch 3); nothing else.
- The **DAG is inferred from `ref()` calls.** dbt topologically sorts at run time; `dbt ls --select +model` inspects what would run.
- The standard project structure is **staging → intermediate → marts**, with prefixes `stg_`, `int_`, `fct_`, `dim_`. Staging files are named `stg_[source]__[entity]s`; intermediates are named `int_[entity]s_[verb]s` and drop the double underscore. Folder-level configs in `dbt_project.yml` cascade to every model in the folder.
- A healthy DAG **narrows to the right**: many parents into one model is expected, many children out of one is the smell. Folders are the primary selection mechanism; tags are for sets that cut across folders.
- **`dbt_project.yml` top-level keys** to memorise: `name`, `version`, `profile`, `require-dbt-version`, `model-paths`, `seed-paths`, `test-paths`, `macro-paths`, `snapshot-paths`, `analysis-paths`, `clean-targets`, `vars`, `on-run-start`, `on-run-end`, and the per-resource-type trees (`models`, `seeds`, `snapshots`).
- **Config precedence:** `{{ config() }}` in SQL > YAML `config:` block > `dbt_project.yml +config`. More-specific folder path wins inside `dbt_project.yml`, and a config with no resource path at all reaches installed packages too. A config written without the `+` is deprecated, and the warning it raises is adapter-gated.
- **`alias` moves the relation, not the node.** `ref()` still takes the model's filename; two resources aliased onto one address fail at compile time, not at run time.

- **Model life cycle:** SQL file → parse & compile (`target/compiled/`) → DDL wrap (`target/run/`) → execute against the warehouse.

## Learning-goal checklist (self-assess)

- ☐ I can create a dbt project from empty directories — `dbt_project.yml`, `models/`, a `.sql` model, a `profiles.yml` entry — and run `dbt run` end-to-end.
- ☐ I use `ref()` for every dbt-managed table and can explain why hard-coding a schema is wrong in at least three ways.
- ☐ I can name the staging → intermediate → marts layers, their prefixes (`stg_`, `int_`, `fct_`, `dim_`), and the role of each.
- ☐ I can read a `dbt_project.yml` top-to-bottom, identify every top-level key, and recite the config-precedence rule from memory.
- ☐ I can read a DAG fragment and say whether its shape is healthy, place a given transformation in staging, intermediate or marts, and justify the materialization that layer expects.
- ☐ I can say what `alias` changes and what it leaves alone, spell a staging and an intermediate model name from the convention, and recognise the two-resources-one-relation compile error.
- ☐ I can resolve a `var()` call through its five levels and say which project's `vars:` block a package macro reads.
- ☐ I can trace a single model through its four life-cycle stages (SQL → compile → DDL → execute) and name the `target/` sub-directory that holds each artifact.

---

## Practice questions

Thirty-three questions covering every sub-topic from §2.1–§2.5 at least twice (§2.6 is a sidebar — not drilled); `dbt_project.yml` snippet-reading appears in Q7, Q11, Q14, Q17, Q23; `ref()` vs hard-coded schema in Q4 and Q18, at apply and analyze level respectively; the structure conventions of §2.3 in Q2, Q9, Q10, Q24, Q25 and Q26.

**1.** What does the `{{ ref('stg_orders') }}` Jinja expression return when a dbt model is compiled?
A. A fully-qualified relation reference to the `stg_orders` model, resolved against the current target
B. The path `models/stg_orders.sql`
C. The string `'stg_orders'` literally
D. The raw SQL body of the `stg_orders` model inlined into the current query

**2.** A model in `models/marts/finance/` is read directly by three BI dashboards through the working day, and one other mart `ref()`s it. Which description matches the marts layer as the structure guide defines it?
A. Name it for the source system it derives from, materialise it as a table, and have the other mart re-derive the logic rather than `ref()` it
B. Name it for the business entity, materialise it as ephemeral so the consuming mart absorbs the build cost, and point the dashboards at that mart
C. Name it for the business entity, materialise it as a view so the dashboards read current rows without waiting on a rebuild, and let the other mart `ref()` it
D. Name it for the business entity, materialise it as a table or incremental, and let the other mart `ref()` it

**3.** You clone a repository containing a `models/` directory full of `.sql` files, a `packages.yml`, and a `README.md`, then run `dbt run` from its root. dbt exits immediately with `Runtime Error: No dbt_project.yml found at expected path ....` What does that tell you?
A. `dbt deps` has not been run, so the packages named in `packages.yml` are not yet installed
B. `profiles.yml` is missing from `~/.dbt/`, so dbt cannot resolve a connection
C. `model-paths` was never declared, so dbt did not discover the `.sql` files under `models/`
D. The directory is not a dbt project — `dbt_project.yml` is the file that makes one, and no project-loading command will run without it

**4.** A model `marts/finance/fct_payments.sql` contains the line:

```
from analytics_dev.staging.stg_payments
```

When the project is promoted to the `ci` target, `dbt build --target ci` fails on this model. What is the most likely cause?
A. The `ci` target lacks permission to create tables in the schema the model writes to
B. CI runs require `--full-refresh`, and without it the model cannot resolve the relation it selects from
C. `dbt build` cannot be combined with `--target`, so the invocation itself is invalid
D. The schema `analytics_dev.staging` exists in dev but not in CI; `ref()` would have resolved to the CI schema automatically

**5.** How does dbt determine the execution order of models in a project?
A. By topologically sorting a graph inferred from `ref()` and `source()` calls
B. By the order models appear in `dbt_project.yml`
C. Alphabetically by filename
D. By the order the user specifies in `--select`

**6.** A project's `dbt_project.yml` declares `name`, `version` and `profile` and nothing else. One file sits at `analyses/adhoc.sql`. What does `dbt ls --resource-type analysis` print?
A. The analysis node — `analysis-paths` defaults to `["analyses"]`, so the file is found with the key absent
B. Nothing — `analysis-paths` has no default, so dbt looks for analyses in no directory until the key is declared
C. Nothing — an analysis is not a graph node, so `dbt ls` does not list one; `dbt compile` is what renders it
D. An error — `analysis-paths` is a required key, and a project file that omits it fails validation

**7.** A project running on Snowflake has this in `dbt_project.yml`, and the models under `models/marts/` carry no `{{ config() }}` block and no YAML `config:` entry:

```
models:
  my_project:
    marts:
      materialized: table
```

What does `dbt run` do?
A. Builds the marts as views, warning that `materialized` was read as a folder name
B. Builds the marts as tables and prints nothing — the `+` is optional on a leaf key
C. Builds the marts as tables, warning that a config written without `+` is deprecated
D. Fails during parsing with a validation error naming `materialized` as an unexpected key under `marts`

**8.** Which of the following is true about `profiles.yml`?
A. It is part of the dbt project and should be committed to Git alongside `dbt_project.yml`
B. It defines model configurations
C. It is generated by `dbt run` and should not be edited
D. It holds warehouse connection details and is typically stored in `~/.dbt/`, outside the project directory

**9.** In the dbt Labs "How we structure our dbt projects" guide, what is the purpose of the **staging** layer?
A. To store the project's unprocessed CSV files, which are loaded into the warehouse before any modelling happens
B. To contain the reusable macros called across the project, so transformation logic lives in one place rather than in each model
C. To hold the fact and dimension tables that BI tools query, joined and aggregated into their final reporting shape
D. To provide one-to-one models over each source table, with light cleanup and renaming; the only place `source()` is called

**10.** According to the standard structure, what does a model prefixed with `int_` represent?
A. A purpose-built intermediate transformation between staging and marts, typically materialised as a view or ephemeral
B. An internal table dbt creates for its own bookkeeping, which the project should not edit or materialise itself
C. A model that must not be referenced by other models, since it exists only as a staging step for one mart
D. An "integration" model that writes its result out to an external system rather than into the warehouse

**11.** Given the top of a `dbt_project.yml`:

```
name: 'sales_project'
version: '1.0.0'
profile: 'sales_warehouse'
```

Where does dbt look for the warehouse connection details when `dbt run` is executed?
A. In `profiles.yml` (by default at `~/.dbt/profiles.yml`), under a top-level key named `sales_warehouse`
B. In an environment variable `DBT_PROFILE`, which holds the connection details for the profile the project names
C. In `dbt_project.yml` itself, under a `connections:` block keyed by target name alongside `name:` and `version:`
D. In a `.env` file in the project root, which dbt loads automatically before it resolves the profile

**12.** Which `dbt_project.yml` key changes the directory dbt scans for CSV files loaded by `dbt seed`?
A. `model-paths` B. `csv-paths`
C. `seed-directory` D. `seed-paths`

**13.** Which directories does `dbt clean` delete?
A. The directories listed under `clean-targets` in `dbt_project.yml`
B. `logs/` and `target/`
C. `target/` plus any project subdirectory dbt wrote to during the last invocation
D. `target/compiled/`, leaving `target/run/` in place so the last invocation stays inspectable

**14.** The file `models/marts/fct_orders.sql` has `{{ config(materialized='table') }}` at the top. A `_models.yml` file in the same folder has:

```
models:
  - name: fct_orders
    config:
      materialized: view
```

And `dbt_project.yml` has:

```
models:
  my_project:
    marts:
      +materialized: incremental
```

Which materialization does `fct_orders` get?
A. `incremental` B. `view`
C. `table` D. The parse fails due to conflict

**15.** In a `dbt_project.yml`, what does the `+` prefix on a key inside a `models:` block indicate?
A. The key is required (not optional)
B. The key is an alias for an environment variable
C. The key makes the config additive, merging with any value set at a broader scope instead of replacing it
D. The key is a config (behaviour-affecting setting), not a folder name that nests deeper

**16.** After `dbt compile`, where does dbt write the rendered SQL for each model?
A. Back into the original `.sql` file
B. `target/compiled/<project-name>/<model-path>.sql`
C. `logs/compiled-sql.log`
D. Directly to the warehouse as a temporary table

**17.** Consider:

```
on-run-start:
  - "create schema if not exists {{ target.schema }}"
```

Which of these commands executes that statement?
A. `dbt clean` B. `dbt source freshness`
C. `dbt run-operation` D. `dbt deps`

**18.** A team is investigating why their `fct_orders` model "works in dev but breaks in CI." An engineer points out that the model's SQL contains:

```
from analytics_dev.staging.stg_orders
join analytics_dev.staging.stg_customers using (customer_id)
```

Which of the following is the **best** remediation, considering CI correctness, DAG integrity, and future-proofing?
A. Add `if target.name == 'ci'` branches around each hard-coded schema
B. Rewrite both clauses as `{{ ref('stg_orders') }}` and `{{ ref('stg_customers') }}` so dbt resolves schemas per target and registers the dependencies
C. Set `target: ci` as the default in `profiles.yml`
D. Add both schemas to `on-run-start` as `create schema if not exists` statements

**19.** Model A uses `{{ ref('B') }}`; model B uses `{{ ref('C') }}`; a developer then adds `{{ ref('A') }}` inside model C. They run `dbt run`. What happens?
A. dbt runs them in the order the files were parsed — A, B, C — and each reads whatever its upstream held before the run
B. dbt drops the edge that was added last, runs C, B, A, and warns that the graph was modified
C. dbt fails before sending any SQL to the warehouse, reporting `Found a cycle:` and naming the models involved
D. dbt runs all three to completion, warning that the rows inside the cycle may be one run behind

**20.** A model ran successfully yesterday; today it fails with a "table not found" error mentioning an upstream model. What is the *first* file to inspect?
A. `dbt_project.yml`, where the model's materialization is configured
B. `profiles.yml`, where the target's schema and database are set
C. The failing model's compiled SQL, under `target/compiled/`
D. `~/.dbt/logs.json`, where dbt records each invocation

**21.** `models/marts/dim_customers.sql` begins with `{{ config(alias='customers') }}`. Another mart in the same folder has to read it. Which pairing is correct?
A. `{{ ref('customers') }}`, and the relation dbt builds is named `customers`
B. `{{ ref('dim_customers') }}`, and the relation dbt builds is named `dim_customers`
C. `{{ ref('dim_customers') }}`, and the relation dbt builds is named `customers`
D. Either spelling resolves, and the relation dbt builds is named `customers`

**22.** A project has `models/marts/dim_customers.sql` carrying `+alias: customers`, and a second model `models/marts/customers.sql` with no alias. Both land in the same schema. What happens on `dbt run`?
A. Both build; whichever runs second replaces the first, and nothing in the run output flags it
B. dbt builds the aliased model and skips the other, warning that its relation is already claimed
C. dbt fails while building the graph, reporting that two resources share one database representation
D. dbt fails at run time on the second model, when the warehouse rejects the duplicate relation name

**23.** Your project installs a package named `finance_macros`. Both project files set the same variable:

```
# your dbt_project.yml
vars:
  lookback_days: 30
  finance_macros:
    lookback_days: 7
```

```
# the package's own dbt_project.yml
vars:
  lookback_days: 90
```

The package ships a macro whose body is `{{ var('lookback_days') }}`. One of **your** models calls that macro, with no `--vars` on the command line. What value does the macro read?
A. `7` — a macro from a package reads the block keyed to that package's name
B. `30` — a var resolves in the scope of the node that consumes it, and that node is a model in your project
C. `90` — a macro reads the `vars:` block of the project file it is defined in
D. dbt fails at parse — the variable is declared in two project files and the conflict has to be resolved

**24.** Reviewing a project's graph you find two shapes. In the first, six staging models feed a single intermediate model. In the second, one intermediate model is `ref()`-ed by nine marts, each of which adds one column to it. Which shape is the warning sign, and why?
A. The first — that many parents means the model is doing too much and should be split into several
B. The second — the DAG should narrow as it moves right, so many children is where the widening was skipped
C. Both — a post-staging model should carry a similar number of edges in each direction
D. Neither — edge counts reflect how the source system is shaped, not a modelling defect

**25.** A project's staging files are named `stg_shopify__orders.sql` and `stg_stripe__charges.sql`. What do the two underscore runs in those names separate?
A. Single: the layer prefix from the entity. Double: the entity from the source system
B. Single: the layer prefix from the source system. Double: the entity from its grain
C. Single: the layer prefix from the source system. Double: two words inside one entity name
D. Single: the layer prefix from the source system. Double: the source system from the entity

**26.** A mart model has grown to bring together seven concepts, and the heavy window function that weaves three of them together is written out again in two other marts. What does the structure guidance say to do about it?
A. Materialise it as `incremental`, so the cost of the joins is paid once and then amortised
B. Extract the reusable part of the join into an intermediate model, so the mart joins fewer inputs
C. Move the joins up into the staging models that feed it, so each one arrives pre-joined
D. Split it into one mart per grain and let the BI layer join them back together

**27.** A model is configured +schema: marketing and +database: reporting. The active target sets database: analytics and schema: dbt_alex. Which relation does dbt build?
A. reporting.dbt_alex_marketing.<model>
B. analytics_reporting.dbt_alex_marketing.<model>
C. reporting.marketing.<model>
D. analytics_reporting.marketing.<model>

**28.** A developer's target schema is dbt_alex. Models under models/staging/ are configured +schema: staging. Which schema does dbt build them in?
A. staging
B. dbt_alex_staging
C. staging_dbt_alex
D. dbt_alex — a custom schema only applies when the target is named prod

**29.** You install a package that ships its own generate_schema_name macro. Your root project does not define one. What decides where your models are built?
A. The package's macro — installed macros are dispatch candidates like any other
B. Neither — dbt raises an ambiguous-macro error at parse time
C. dbt's built-in default concatenation; a package's generate_schema_name is ignored
D. Whichever macro sorts first by package name

**30.** You need to join orders, customers and payments into one customer-order grain that three different marts will each consume. Which layer does that model belong in?
A. Staging — it is the first place the three sources meet, so the join belongs at the layer that reads them
B. Intermediate — it is a purpose-built join that exists to be consumed by the marts downstream, not by a BI tool directly
C. Marts — it produces a business-facing customer-order grain, which is what a mart is for
D. None of these — make it a macro so each of the three marts can call the same join logic where it needs it

**31.** A project contains both seeds/country_codes.csv and models/staging/country_codes.sql. Nothing else is configured. On stock dbt 1.11, what does dbt build do?
A. Warns that two resources share the name, then fails before building — both resolve to the same relation
B. Builds both, emitting a DuplicateNameDistinctNodeTypesDeprecation warning and nothing else
C. Builds both silently; ref('country_codes') resolves to the model
D. Builds the model and skips the seed as shadowed

**32.** That seed/model name clash also collided on one relation; give the model an alias: and the build succeeds, leaving the shared **name** reported only as a deprecation warning. You want that name itself to fail parsing instead. What do you add to dbt_project.yml?
A. flags: require_unique_project_resource_names: true
B. +unique: true on the seed
C. flags: restrict_direct_pg_catalog_access: true
D. Nothing — there is no flag; rename one of the two resources

**33.** Which of these can **not** be set from an in-file `{{ config() }}` block?

A. `materialized`
B. `tags`
C. `description`
D. `schema`

## Answer key

**1. A.** `ref()` resolves at compile time to a schema-qualified database reference (e.g., `"analytics"."staging"."stg_orders"`), using the schema and database of the active target. It also registers a dependency edge so dbt can order the DAG correctly. Source: `/reference/dbt-jinja-functions/ref`.

**2. D.** Marts are the business-facing end of the line, and the guide's prescription has three parts. Name the model for the entity in plain English, because source-conformed naming is what the project leaves behind at the staging boundary. Materialise it as a table — or incremental, once a full rebuild costs more than the added complexity — because a mart is read many times a day and the transformation should be paid for once. And let other marts `ref()` it; mart-to-mart references are expected, and the only prohibition is the cycle the DAG rejects anyway. A gets the naming and the reuse both backwards: re-deriving logic instead of ref-ing it is exactly what the DAG exists to prevent. C mistakes a view for freshness — a view re-runs its SQL on every dashboard query, which is the read cost the marts layer exists to remove. B leaves nothing for a BI tool to query at all, because an ephemeral model produces no relation. Sources: `/best-practices/how-we-structure/4-marts`, `/best-practices/best-practice-workflows`.

**3. D.** `dbt_project.yml` is what makes a directory a dbt project, and dbt looks for it before it looks at anything else — the failure is at project load, not during the run, which is why no model is even listed. Run `dbt run` in a directory of `.sql` files with no `dbt_project.yml` on dbt 1.11 and you get exactly this: `Runtime Error: No dbt_project.yml found at expected path <cwd>/dbt_project.yml`. Verified against dbt 1.11.14. `packages.yml` is optional and `dbt deps` never runs first by itself (A); a missing profile produces a *different* error, and only once the project has loaded (B); `model-paths` defaults to `["models"]` and is not required (C). Source: `/reference/dbt_project.yml`.

**4. D.** The query hard-codes a dev-specific schema. `ref('stg_payments')` would resolve against whatever target is active (`ci` → CI schema, `prd` → prod schema). The fix is to replace the `from` clause with `{{ ref('stg_payments') }}`. Source: `/reference/dbt-jinja-functions/ref`.

**5. A.** Every `ref()` or `source()` call inside a model's SQL adds an edge to the dbt internal graph (the manifest). dbt topologically sorts the graph and runs upstream models first. `--select` filters which subset runs but does not set ordering. Source: `/docs/build/models`, `/reference/dbt-jinja-functions/ref`.

**6. A.** `analysis-paths` defaults to `["analyses"]`, and the reference page that says it has no default is wrong — dbt 1.11.14 refutes it. Executed against a project file holding `name`, `version` and `profile` and nothing else, `dbt ls --resource-type analysis` reports `Found 1 model, 1 analysis, 477 macros` and prints `<project>.analysis.adhoc`, exit 0. One run disposes of the other three: the directory was scanned with no key present (B), `dbt ls` did list the node (C), and the project loaded without the key (D) — `name` and `profile` are the only keys `dbt_project.yml` requires. What the key controls is *which* directory. Add `analysis-paths: ["custom_analyses"]` to that same project and the count falls to `Found 1 model, 477 macros`, then `No nodes selected!`: declaring a path key **replaces** its default rather than adding to it. Source: `/reference/project-configs/analysis-paths`.

**7. C.** The config applies. Executed on dbt 1.11.14 against Postgres, an unprefixed `materialized: table` under a folder key is honoured — `dbt ls --output json --output-keys "name config.materialized"` reports `"config.materialized": "table"` for every model beneath the folder — so A, which has dbt reading `materialized` as a folder name and falling back to the default, and D, which upgrades a deprecation to a parse failure, are both out. What separates B from C is the adapter. Writing a config without the `+` is deprecated, but dbt runs its **deprecation** JSON-schema pass over `dbt_project.yml` on Snowflake, Databricks, BigQuery and Redshift only; on Postgres the same file applies the config and prints nothing. The stem names Snowflake, so the warning is raised. Read the silence on the other adapters for what it is: the `+` is not optional, the diagnostic is just missing. Source: `/reference/resource-configs/plus-prefix`.

**8. D.** `profiles.yml` is the connection-config file — it defines how dbt connects to your warehouse (type, host, credentials, threads) and is looked up by name via `profile:` in `dbt_project.yml`. By default it lives at `~/.dbt/profiles.yml` (machine-local), outside the project directory. Option A is the one worth thinking about rather than dismissing: teams do check a profile in, and dbt will read it — the working directory is searched before `~/.dbt/` (§2.1). But it can only be committed by writing `{{ env_var('VAR_NAME') }}` over every secret, and *committable under conditions* is not the same as being part of the project — `profile:` names a block, never a path, and nothing in `dbt_project.yml` binds the file to the repo. Source: `/docs/local/profiles.yml`.

**9. D.** Staging models have a one-to-one relationship with source tables, apply column renames and light casting, and avoid joins. They are the only layer that calls `source()`; everything downstream refs the staging model. Source: `/best-practices/how-we-structure/2-staging`.

**10. A.** `int_` denotes an intermediate model — a reusable transformation step (e.g., a join of multiple staging models, a re-graining, a pivot) that sits between staging and marts. They are usually materialised as views or ephemeral because they are not meant to be consumed by end users. Source: `/best-practices/how-we-structure/3-intermediate`.

**11. A.** The `profile:` key in `dbt_project.yml` is the name of the block dbt looks up in `profiles.yml`. The default location is `~/.dbt/profiles.yml` but can be overridden with the `--profiles-dir` flag or the `DBT_ENGINE_PROFILES_DIR` environment variable (the legacy `DBT_PROFILES_DIR` still resolves). Source: `/docs/local/profiles.yml`, `/reference/project-configs/profile`.

**12. D.** `seed-paths` is the list of directories dbt searches for seeds; default is `["seeds"]`. `model-paths`, `test-paths`, `macro-paths`, `snapshot-paths`, and `analysis-paths` are the siblings that control other resource types. Source: `/docs/build/projects`, `/reference/dbt_project.yml`.

**13. A.** `dbt clean` deletes each directory listed in `clean-targets`. Two separate defaults to keep straight: (1) the **built-in default** — when `clean-targets` is omitted entirely from `dbt_project.yml`, `dbt clean` deletes only the `target-path` directory; (2) the **`dbt init` starter-project default** — projects bootstrapped with `dbt init` ship with `clean-targets: ["target", "dbt_packages"]` already in `dbt_project.yml`, which is why most projects clean both. You can add more entries — but naming a configured source directory (`models/`, `seeds/`, `macros/`, `snapshots/`, `analyses/`, `tests/`) does not delete the code: `dbt clean` refuses the whole run with `dbt will not clean the following source paths: [...]` and removes nothing, including the entries that were safe. C and D both describe a `clean` that reasons about what the last run produced; it does not reason at all, and it does not read `run_results.json` — it deletes the directories the config names, whether or not anything ran. Source: `/reference/project-configs/clean-targets`.

**14. C.** Config precedence is most-specific wins: `{{ config() }}` in SQL beats a YAML `config:` block, which beats `dbt_project.yml` `+config`. The SQL sets `table`, so `table` wins; the other two are overridden silently. Source: `/reference/define-configs`.

**15. D.** Inside `models:`, `seeds:`, and `snapshots:` trees, `+`-prefixed keys are configs; unprefixed keys are folder names that nest further. The `+` is mandatory when a key could otherwise be mistaken for a folder name. Option C is the trap worth knowing: `+` *does* mean "add to, don't replace" in one other place in dbt — on a `grants` privilege key, where `'+select'` appends grantees instead of clobbering them (Ch 13). That is a different `+`, in a different position, and it is the only place the character carries that meaning. A resource-config `+` never changes how the value merges; list-typed configs such as `tags` accumulate across every level that sets them, outermost first. Sources: `/reference/resource-configs/plus-prefix`, `/reference/resource-configs/grants`.

**16. B.** `dbt compile` renders Jinja and writes the result to `target/compiled/<project-name>/<model-path>.sql`. This is where you inspect the compiled SQL when debugging. The wrapped DDL (what is actually sent to the warehouse) goes to `target/run/<project-name>/<model-path>.sql`. Source: `/reference/commands/compile`.

**17. B.** `dbt source freshness` builds nothing, which is why it surprises people — but the `source_freshness_run_project_hooks` behaviour flag defaults to `true` at 1.11, so a freshness check runs the project's `on-run-start` and `on-run-end` hooks like any other execution command. Executed on dbt 1.11.14: `dbt source freshness` wrote both a start and an end row to a hook-logging table; `dbt clean`, `dbt run-operation` and `dbt deps` wrote none. The other three are the shapes to reason past: `clean` and `deps` never open a warehouse connection at all, and `run-operation` opens one and really executes SQL — but it invokes a single macro outside the node graph, and project hooks are bound to the graph run, not to the connection. Verified against dbt 1.11.14. Sources: `/reference/project-configs/on-run-start-on-run-end`, `/reference/global-configs/behavior-changes`.

**18. B.** `ref()` resolves schemas per target automatically, registers DAG edges so dbt orders the run correctly, and fails at compile time on typos. Option A hides the problem with conditionals; C changes defaults but doesn't fix the hard-coded names; D creates empty schemas but still reads from the wrong place. Source: `/reference/dbt-jinja-functions/ref`.

**19. C.** The graph is linked before any node is scheduled, and that is where dbt detects cycles: a cyclic graph has no valid topological sort, so there is no order to run the models in and dbt refuses rather than picking one. Executed on dbt 1.11.14, `dbt run` on exactly this three-model cycle exits 2 with `RuntimeError: Found a cycle: model.my_project.A --> model.my_project.C --> model.my_project.B` — a chain in the linker's traversal order, not necessarily the order the refs were written in, so do not expect the message to close the loop for you. Ch 10 §10.1 files this under dependency errors, the graph-validation family. A and B both presuppose that an order exists, and B additionally credits dbt with editing your graph, which it never does. D downgrades a structural impossibility to a warning you could ship past. This is also why hard-coding is unsafe: dbt cannot detect a cycle you have written as a string schema. Source: `/docs/build/models`, `/reference/dbt-jinja-functions/ref`.

**20. C.** The life cycle is SQL → compile → DDL wrap → execute. A "table not found" at runtime means the compiled SQL is pointing at a relation that doesn't exist in the target, so the fastest move is to read what dbt actually rendered; almost always the clue is there (wrong schema resolved, missing upstream, typo in a `ref`). Reading a config file instead tells you what *should* have happened, not what did: A and B are where the wrong relation was *configured*, and you can only tell which one after you have seen the resolved name. D is not a file dbt writes — run logs go to `logs/dbt.log` inside the project, not to `~/.dbt/`. Source: `/reference/commands/compile`, `/guides/debug-errors`.

**21. C.** `alias` moves the identifier dbt writes to the warehouse; the node in the graph keeps the filename, so `ref()` keeps taking the filename. Executed on dbt 1.11.14: with `alias='customers'` set on `dim_customers.sql`, a downstream `{{ ref('dim_customers') }}` compiles to `"analytics"."dbt_dev"."customers"`, and `dbt ls --output json` reports the pair `{"name": "dim_customers", "alias": "customers"}`. Swapping the call to `{{ ref('customers') }}` fails with `Compilation Error: Model 'model.<project>.fct_orders' (models/marts/fct_orders.`

`sql) depends on a node named 'customers' which was not found`. That one run rules out A and D together: the alias is not a lookup name, not even an additional one. B is the reading in which `alias` is cosmetic — a label on the docs site — but the identifier is the only thing it moves. Source: `/docs/build/custom-aliases`.

**22. C.** The two resources resolve to one address, and dbt refuses to build either. Because `alias` moves the relation without moving the node, the graph is legal right up to the point where dbt works out what each node will be called — which happens while the graph is being built, before any DDL is composed. Executed on dbt 1.11.14, the run exits 2 with `Compilation Error: dbt found two resources with the database representation ""analytics"."dbt_dev"."customers"". dbt cannot create two resources with identical database representations`, followed by both offending nodes and their file paths. A and B are the two silent-damage readings — an overwrite and a skip — and neither happens; nothing is built. D is the tempting one, because a duplicate name *is* something a warehouse would reject, and this item is really a question about which layer catches it. dbt never gets that far: it never sends SQL it already knows is ambiguous. Source: `/docs/build/custom-aliases`.

**23. B.** A variable resolves in the scope of the node that consumes it, not the package that defines the macro doing the reading. The consuming node here is one of your models, so the lookup runs against your project's scope and finds the global `lookback_days: 30`. Executed on dbt 1.11.14 with exactly this arrangement: a root model calling the package's macro compiled to the root project's global value, and a model *inside the package* calling the same macro compiled to the value under the package's key — same macro, two answers, decided by the caller. That is what makes A wrong: the package-keyed block is not "the block the package reads", it is the block that applies when a node in that package is doing the consuming. C describes lexical scope, which is how a programming language would resolve it and is not how dbt does. D imports the two-files conflict error from a later version; at 1.11 declaring the same variable in a root project and a package is ordinary, and the root project simply wins. Source: `/docs/build/project-variables`.

**24. B.** The guidance is *narrow the DAG, widen the tables.* Several inputs converging on one post-staging model is what a model is for, so the first shape is unremarkable. Several outputs fanning out of one model is the signal, and the stem says why: nine consumers each adding one column means the widening that should have happened once was deferred nine times, and the columns belong in the intermediate model. A reads fan-in as complexity, which inverts the rule and would push a project back toward one model per source table. C asks for symmetry, which is the one thing the guide rules out: the two directions are not equivalent, and a graph that looked the same read either way would mean no conforming had happened. D denies that graph shape carries any modelling information, which is the position the structure guide exists to argue against. Source: `/best-practices/how-we-structure/3-intermediate`.

**25. D.** The convention is `stg_[source]__[entity]s`. The single underscore after `stg` separates the layer prefix from the source system; the **double** underscore separates the source system from the entity. `stg_shopify__orders` is therefore the Shopify system's `orders` table, one staging model to one source table. A inverts the two halves, which produces `stg_orders__shopify` and loses the property that makes the convention useful — that files from one system sort together. B attaches grain to a layer that has no grain to declare: a staging model is one-to-one with its source table. C is the reading to be careful with, because multi-word entities really do exist — they keep *single* underscores inside the entity half, as in `stg_shopify__order_items`, which is exactly what keeps the double unambiguous. Source: `/best-practices/how-we-structure/2-staging`.

**26. B.** Seven concepts is past the four-or-five the structure guidance names as the point to stop and look, but the count on its own never settles it — the guidance is explicit that this is not a hard rule, and cuts both ways: eight staging models joined simply might be fine, while four woven with heavy window functions could already be too much (§2.3). What settles this one is the complexity and the repetition, and the documented remedy is to lift the reusable part of the join into an intermediate model. The mart then joins fewer, wider inputs, and the extracted step is available to the next mart that needs the same shape. A treats a structural problem as a cost problem: `incremental` changes how often the joins run, not how many there are, and it adds state to a model that was already hard to reason about. C is the more attractive mistake, because it does reduce the mart's join count — but joins in staging are the documented anti-pattern; staging is one-to-one with its source table and does renaming and casting only. D pushes the joins past the end of the project into a BI tool, where they are neither tested nor versioned, which is the situation the marts layer exists to prevent. Sources: `/best-practices/how-we-structure/4-marts`, `/best-practices/how-we-structure/3-intermediate`.

**27. A.** The two configs are asymmetric and that is the whole item. `generate_schema_name` **appends** the custom schema to the target's, giving `dbt_alex_marketing`; `generate_database_name` **returns the custom database verbatim**, giving `reporting` rather than any combination with `analytics`. B and C each get one half right and carry the other half's rule across. D reverses both. The phrase to hold is *schema concatenates, database substitutes* — and the practical consequence is that a hard-coded `+database:` ignores the target, so every developer writes to the same place.

**28. B.** `+schema:` routes through the built-in `generate_schema_name`, which **concatenates** `<target.schema>_<custom>`. So the developer gets `dbt_alex_staging` and CI, on target schema `analytics_ci`, gets `analytics_ci_staging` — which is the point of the default: two people building the same model never collide. A is what you get only after overriding the macro in your own `macros/`. D describes `generate_schema_name_for_env`, which does use the custom schema verbatim in production and ignore it elsewhere, but ships **disabled** — you turn it on by writing a `generate_schema_name` that calls it.

**29. C.** `generate_schema_name` does not resolve by ordinary dispatch. dbt builds one resolver per package and picks by the *node's own* package: a node in your root project gets the root project's macro, or dbt's built-in concatenation when there is none. An installed package's copy is never a candidate for that choice, so with no root-project definition you get the built-in concatenation whatever the package ships. A is the trap, because it states the rule that holds for every other macro — a package's macros really are dispatch candidates, which is why this exception is worth knowing rather than deducing. Nothing warns you: the package's macro sits in `dbt_packages/` looking effective, and it is not dead code — it names the nodes that package itself owns — but it has no say over yours.

**30. B.** Intermediate is the layer defined by exactly this shape: a step that joins across staging models, is not itself business-facing, and exists because more than one downstream model needs it. A fails on the staging rule — one staging model per source table, light transforms, no cross-source joins. C fails on audience: a mart is what a person queries, and this is consumed by three marts. D is the most tempting wrong answer because it does remove the duplication, but a macro re-runs the join inside every caller, so you pay three times and there is no single tested relation to point at.

**31. A.** Two things fire here and you need both. The shared **name** is only a warning at the 1.11 default — `require_unique_project_resource_names` is `false`, so dbt emits `DuplicateNameDistinctNodeTypesDeprecation` (*"Found resources with the same name 'country_codes'"*) and carries on. But "nothing else is configured" means the model and the seed also resolve to the same `database.schema.identifier`, and that **address** collision is a separate, unconditional `Compilation Error`: *"dbt found two resources with the database representation"*. Executed on dbt 1.11.14, this exact project prints the warning, then exits 2 having built nothing. B is the trap, and it is what you get only if the two land on different relations — give the model an `alias:` and the same project parses to exit 0 with the warning alone. D invents a shadowing rule dbt does not have. Note what the flag does and does not reach: turning it on makes the *name* an error too, but it was never what stopped this build.

**32. A.** At the 1.11 default, `require_unique_project_resource_names` is `false`, so a different-type name clash is a warning; setting it `true` turns the clash into a parse-time error. C is not a flag at all — `restrict_direct_pg_catalog_access` appears nowhere in the installed 1.11.14 tree, is absent from the fifteen behaviour flags `dbt/contracts/project.py` enumerates, and a project setting it runs clean with no warning, because an unrecognised key under `flags:` is simply ignored (§2.4). It is there to be rejected on that basis, not recognised. D is the honest workaround and would be right if the flag did not exist, which is what makes it the strongest distractor.

**33. C.** `description` is a **property**, not a config, and properties live only in a properties `.yml` file. Writing `{{ config(description='...') }}` does not document the model — and does not error either, which is why it is worth knowing rather than discovering. The separating question is what the key does: a config changes how dbt **builds** the thing (`materialized`, `tags`, `schema` all do), while a property describes or tests the thing that was built. The same rule puts `columns`, `data_tests` and the entries that define a source or an exposure in YAML only. Note two that look like properties and are not: `docs` and `freshness` are genuine configs, and both bind from `config()` and from `dbt_project.yml`.

# Chapter 3

# Sources, `source()`, and source freshness

> **Scope.** Ch 2 taught you half the "how tables enter a dbt project" picture — `ref()`, which points at tables dbt itself produced. Ch 3 teaches the other half: `source()`, which points at tables *someone else* loaded into your warehouse. By the end of the chapter you will have a `sources.yml` that dbt understands, a staging layer that calls `source()` instead of hard-coded schemas, and a freshness contract that tells you when your upstream has gone stale. You will also know the exam's source-counting trap: the answer is not one source per table.

**Prerequisites.** Ch 2. In particular: `ref()` discipline (§2.2), the staging → intermediate → marts layering (§2.3), and `dbt_project.yml`'s folder-cascading configs (§2.4). If `ref()` is not yet a reflex, go back and fix that first — sources only make sense once `ref()` does.

**Cheat-sheet pointer.** Front-of-book cheat sheet §7 (Topic 6 — external dependencies) is the one-line version of source freshness. Use it for spaced recall; use this chapter for the "why" that makes the one-liner memorable.

---

## 3.1 Declaring a source in `sources.yml`

A **source** in dbt is a named pointer to a raw table that somebody else — Fivetran, Airbyte, a custom ingestion script, a stored-procedure pipeline — landed in your warehouse. dbt did not create these tables, does not own them, and cannot rebuild them. But it can reference them, document them, test them, and monitor how fresh they are. All of that starts in a single YAML file.

### The minimum viable `sources.yml`

Create a file under `models/staging/` named `_sources.yml` (the leading underscore sorts it above the `.sql` files; the name is otherwise conventional):

```
version: 2

sources:
  - name: stripe
    database: raw
    schema: stripe
    tables:
      - name: customers
      - name: charges
```

That is a legal, complete source definition. Only `name:` and at least one entry under `tables:` are strictly required; every other key defaults.

- `version: 2` — **optional**, and the docs' own examples typically omit it. dbt does not validate the value (`version: 3` parses without a warning) and assumes the modern schema when the key is absent, so `2` is a convention, not a constraint. The book keeps it in examples for parity with what most existing projects look like.
- `sources:` — the top-level list of source declarations.
- `name: stripe` — the *source name*, and the first argument to `source(...)`. A dbt identifier, not a warehouse identifier: it does not have to match the schema name, though it often does.
- `database: raw` and `schema: stripe` — where the raw tables actually live in the warehouse. Omit `database:` and dbt falls back to the target's database (per `profiles.yml`); omit `schema:` and it falls back to the source's `name:` (here, `stripe`).
- `tables:` — the list of table references. `name: customers` points at `raw.stripe.customers`; add an `identifier:` sub-key when the warehouse name differs (e.g., `identifier: customer_t`).

So `source('stripe', 'customers')` resolves to `raw.stripe.customers`.

See `/reference/source-properties` for the full property surface and `/docs/build/sources` for the concept page.

## Descriptions and tests — the other reason sources exist

A raw-table pointer is only half the value of a source declaration. The other half is that sources participate in dbt's documentation and testing machinery the same way models do:

```
version: 2

sources:
  - name: stripe
    description: "Fivetran-synced Stripe data; refreshed every 30 minutes."
    database: raw
    schema: stripe
    tables:
      - name: customers
        description: "One row per Stripe customer."
        columns:
          - name: id
            description: "Stripe customer ID (prefix `cus_`)."
            data_tests:
              - unique
              - not_null
      - name: charges
        description: "One row per Stripe charge event."
        columns:
          - name: id
            data_tests:
              - unique
              - not_null
          - name: customer_id
            data_tests:
              - relationships:
                  arguments:
                    to: source('stripe', 'customers')
```

```
            field: id
```

Three things worth noticing.

1. **`description:` attaches at three independent levels — the source, the table and the column.** None inherits from the one above: a table that declares no description of its own carries an empty one, not its source's. All three are written into `manifest.json` at parse time and appear in the catalog `dbt docs generate` builds.
2. **`data_tests:` on a source column works the same as on a model column.** `unique`, `not_null`, `accepted_values`, and `relationships` are the four built-in generics; `relationships:` can point at another `source(...)` via the `to:` argument — nested under `arguments:`, exactly as on a model column (Ch 7 §7.2) — which is how you express "this charge's `customer_id` must be present in the customers source." See `/reference/resource-properties/data-tests`. These are real test nodes: their names carry a `source_` prefix that distinguishes them from the model-side test of the same generic, and they run under `dbt build` alongside everything else. They are also selectable without being named — `dbt test --select source:stripe.charges` selects the table, and the indirect selection of Ch 7 §7.6 takes the tests from there. Its default, `eager`, takes a test whenever **any** of its parents is selected, which cuts both ways: selecting `charges` runs the `relationships` test above even though `customers` was not, and selecting `customers` runs it even though it is declared under `charges`. Under `--indirect-selection cautious`, neither selection runs it.
3. **`tests:` remains valid as a backward-compatible alias**, so you will meet both spellings in existing projects and in package YAML — but a single resource cannot carry both keys. `data_tests:` is what the reference pages use, and it is the spelling that distinguishes data tests from unit tests.

## A note on the nested `config:` block

The reference page documents `freshness:`, `loaded_at_field:`, `meta:`, and `tags:` under a nested `config:` block on a source or on an individual table, and that is the layout to reach for in new YAML:

```
sources:
  - name: stripe
    tables:
      - name: customers
        config:                         # nested form
          meta: {owner: finance}
          tags: [pii]
```

The same keys are also still accepted at the **top level** of a source or table block — that spelling parses and binds identically — which is why `/reference/source-properties` shows both layouts in places and why you will meet both in real projects. Whether it also *warns* is adapter-gated. dbt runs its JSON-schema property validation on Snowflake, Databricks, BigQuery and Redshift only, so on those four a top-level `freshness` or `loaded_at_field` raises `PropertyMovedToConfigDeprecation`, and on Postgres the identical YAML is silent. Same behaviour on every adapter, different diagnostic — do not read the silence as approval. Most of this chapter's examples use the top-level spelling; read either form confidently when a question puts a YAML snippet in front of you.

### Which source properties resolve the relation, and which are metadata

Of everything you can write under a source, only a handful of keys decide which warehouse object `source()` compiles to. The rest is documentation that lands in the manifest and changes nothing about resolution.

| Key | Declared on | Resolves the relation? | Behaviour |
|---|---|---|---|
| `database` | source | yes | The catalog the raw table sits in — the *project* on BigQuery. |
| `schema` | source | yes | The schema — the *dataset* on BigQuery. |
| `identifier` | table | yes | The physical table name. Defaults to the table's `name:`. |
| `quoting` | source, table | no — decides how the name is written | Three sub-keys: `database`, `schema`, `identifier`. A table's block overrides its source's. `true` by default on most adapters, `false` on Snowflake. |
| `loader` | source | no | Names the tool that landed the table (`loader: fivetran`). In the reference page's words, "for documentation purposes only — dbt does not meaningfully use this." A table-level `loader:` parses and is then discarded — only the source's value reaches the manifest. |
| `external` | table | no | An extensible dictionary — `location`, `file_format`, `row_format`, `tbl_properties`, `partitions`, plus any additional keys you invent. dbt Core never acts on it. |

Four consequences of that split.

- **`database` and `schema` belong to the source, and that is the trap.** Writing `schema:` under a `tables:` entry is neither an error nor an override — dbt ignores it, and the source falls back to resolving the schema from its own `name:`. The YAML parses, the model compiles, and the relation is wrong. Pointing `database:` anywhere other than the target database also requires a warehouse that permits cross-database queries in the first place.
- **`identifier` is the rename mechanism §3.5 turns on.** On BigQuery it also carries a sharded-table wildcard — `identifier: "events_*"` — so a downstream model can filter shards with `where _table_suffix > '20200101'`.
- **`quoting` here is the read-side setting: it governs how the relation `source()` *reads* is written.** dbt also accepts a project-level `quoting:` in `dbt_project.yml` that governs the relations it *builds*; this book does not teach that one, because the exam asks about the source-side key. Reach for the reference page below if you meet the project-level form. The consequence is case sensitivity, and how far that goes is the adapter's business, not dbt's. On Snowflake a quoted identifier *is* case-sensitive — `"Orders"` and `"ORDERS"` are two different tables, which is why the adapter defaults `quoting` to `false` there. Databricks Unity Catalog resolves names case-insensitively, so quoting a mixed-case name protects the special characters in it without making the case load-bearing. Reach for it when a raw table's name is a reserved word, is mixed-case, or contains special characters; leave it alone otherwise, and check your adapter before assuming what quoting buys you.
- **`external` is inert in dbt Core, not inert everywhere.** It lands in `manifest.json` and in `graph.sources`, where a package such as `dbt-external-tables` reads it and turns it into DDL. Recognise `loader` and `external` precisely because a question can offer them as the mechanism for something they do not do.

See `/reference/resource-properties/database`, `/reference/resource-properties/identifier` and `/reference/resource-properties/quoting`.

---

## 3.2 `source()` — the other half of `ref`

Ch 2 pounded a single rule: if a table was produced by a dbt model, `ref()` it. Ch 3's counterpart is symmetric and just as absolute: **if a table was produced by anything *other* than a dbt model, `source()` it.** There is no third option — no legitimate reason to hard-code a `database.schema.table` anywhere in a dbt model's SQL.

### What `source()` does

`source()` is a Jinja function that takes two arguments and returns a schema-qualified relation reference:

```
-- models/staging/stripe/stg_stripe__customers.sql
select
    id          as customer_id,
    email       as customer_email,
    created     as created_at
from {{ source('stripe', 'customers') }}
```

At compile time, `{{ source('stripe', 'customers') }}` is replaced by `raw.stripe.customers` (or whatever database + schema the `sources.yml` declares). The compiled SQL under `target/compiled/.../stg_stripe__customers.sql` contains the fully-qualified relation, no Jinja. You can inspect it with `dbt compile` and then read the file; no warehouse round-trip is involved in that resolution. Whether the three parts arrive quoted follows §3.1's `quoting` row and nothing about `source()`: the bare `raw.stripe.customers` shown here is what an adapter with quoting off produces, and on one that quotes, the same model compiles to `"raw"."stripe"."customers"`. One resolution, two spellings — read past the quotes to the three parts.

Three properties of `source()` that `/reference/dbt-jinja-functions/source` is explicit about:

1. **Two positional arguments.** First is the source name (`stripe`); second is the table name (`customers`). Both must be declared in a `sources.yml` somewhere in the project — see `/docs/build/sources` — and dbt raises a compile-time error if either is missing.
2. **`source()` registers a DAG edge.** dbt records "this model depends on source `stripe.customers`" in the manifest. On the lineage graph, source nodes appear as green rounded rectangles upstream of the models that ref them.
3. **`source()` compiles to the full object name — database, schema, and table.** That is the central fact behind §3.4's trap.

### Why staging models are the only place `source()` appears

In the structure convention from Ch 2 §2.3, **staging models are the one and only layer that calls `source()`.** Intermediate and mart models call `ref()` against the staging models, never `source()` against the raw tables directly. The payoff is that if a raw table is renamed, moved to a different schema, or deprecated, you change the `source()` call (or the `sources.yml`) in exactly one place — the `stg_` model. Everything downstream keeps working because it refs the staging model, not the source.

This is the load-bearing reason the staging layer exists at all. The prefix `stg_` is a promise: this model is the project's only knowledge of what the raw table looks like, and everything downstream is insulated from raw-table churn.

### `source()` vs. `ref()` — the one-line discipline

- **Raw table (not dbt-managed)** → `{{ source('system', 'table') }}` — only in `stg_*.sql`.
- **dbt model** → `{{ ref('other_model') }}` — everywhere else.
- **Hard-coded `database.schema.table`** → wrong. Always — in a `join` clause exactly as in a `from` clause, so a rewrite that converts only the `from` leaves the joined table's dependency unrecorded.

The easiest way to build a DAG that runs in the wrong order is a trio of models that hard-code schemas: dbt has no way to infer the dependencies, so the compile graph is flat even though the SQL is chained.

---

## 3.3 Source freshness

A staging model that runs cleanly against a six-hour-old snapshot of the raw table is still a bug if nobody noticed the six hours. Source freshness is dbt's answer: a declarative contract about how often each raw table is expected to receive new rows, and a command that checks it.

## Configuring freshness on a source

```yaml
version: 2

sources:
  - name: stripe
    database: raw
    schema: stripe
    loaded_at_field: _fivetran_synced    # source-level default
    freshness:
      warn_after: {count: 12, period: hour}
      error_after: {count: 24, period: hour}
    tables:
      - name: charges
        loaded_at_field: created          # overrides source-level default
        freshness:
          warn_after: {count: 1,  period: hour}
          error_after: {count: 3, period: hour}
      - name: customers
        # inherits the source-level loaded_at_field and freshness block
      - name: disputes
        freshness: null                   # opt this table out of freshness checks
```

Five keys do all the work.

| Key | Effect |
|---|---|
| `loaded_at_field` | The timestamp column dbt reads: it issues `max(loaded_at_field)` and compares the result to the current time. Typically an ingestion-tool field like `_fivetran_synced` or `_airbyte_emitted_at`, or an app-level `created_at`/`updated_at`. Required only conditionally — see "Freshness without a `loaded_at_field`" below. |
| `warn_after: {count: N, period: ...}` | The lower threshold. If the most recent row is older than `N` of the given period, `dbt source freshness` reports the table as `warn`. Period values: `minute`, `hour`, `day`. |
| `error_after` | The upper threshold. Older than this and the check returns `error`, which makes the command exit non-zero in CI. |
| `freshness: null` (table level) | Opts a single table out of freshness checks even when the source-level block is set — for tables you know won't update on a schedule, such as a reference dimension refreshed quarterly. |

| Key | Effect |
|---|---|
| filter: (optional) | A SQL predicate that constrains the max(loaded_at_field) query, and only that query; it does not reach any other use of the source. On a table partitioned or clustered on that column — BigQuery, Databricks Delta — filter: "_partition_date >= current_date - 1" is what lets the engine prune to one partition instead of reading the history. The predicate always narrows the rows *evaluated*; whether it narrows the bytes *read* depends on the table layout, its statistics and the plan, so a filter on an unpartitioned column buys you much less than it looks like it should. It has one blind spot, covered below. |

max(loaded_at_field) only measures freshness if the column advances when **new** rows arrive. loaded_at_field: created on an immutable charges table does; loaded_at_field: updated_at on a table whose old rows get back-dated does not, and the table reads fresh because it was touched rather than because it was loaded.

Source-level settings cascade to each table; table-level settings override. See /docs/build/sources#source-data-freshness for the discussion and /reference/source-properties for the property surface.

> **URL-tree tripwire.** The reference page at /reference/resource-configs/freshness describes a *different* freshness: config — the one for **model** freshness (state-aware orchestration). It documents build_after, not warn_after/error_after, and applies to models, not sources. For source freshness, cite /docs/build/sources and /reference/source-properties, never /reference/resource-configs/freshness. The configs-vs-properties split runs through the whole docs site; this is a particularly easy place to land on the wrong page.

### Freshness without a loaded_at_field

loaded_at_field is the usual way dbt learns when a table last received data. It is not the only one, and it is not unconditionally required. Three paths exist, and dbt takes the first one it finds.

1. **loaded_at_query:** — SQL you supply, whose single value dbt treats as the load timestamp. It replaces loaded_at_field rather than refining it, and declaring both at the same level is a parse error: **Cannot specify both loaded_at_field and loaded_at_query at source level.** The exclusion is checked per level, so a table-level loaded_at_field still wins over a source-level loaded_at_query — most-specific still applies, quietly.
2. **loaded_at_field:** — the column, as this section has used it so far. dbt issues select max(<field>) against the table.
3. **Warehouse metadata** — on Snowflake, Redshift and BigQuery the adapter reads a table's last-modified time out of the warehouse catalog, so a freshness: block with neither of the first two keys still computes. One catalog query covers every such table in the invocation, and the source table itself is never scanned. target/sources.json comes back with the same fields either way — max_loaded_at, snapshotted_at, max_loaded_at_time_ago_in_s, criteria, status — so nothing downstream, source_status:fresher+ included, can tell which path produced it.

On an adapter that cannot read that metadata — Postgres among them — the same YAML warns at parse time and the table fails at run:

```
The configured adapter does not support metadata-based freshness. A loaded_at_field must
      be specified for source 'stripe.customers'.
...
  Runtime Error in source customers (models/_sources.yml)
  Could not compute freshness for source customers: no 'loaded_at_field' provided and
     postgres adapter does not support metadata-based freshness checks.
```

So the rule is conditional: `loaded_at_field` is optional where the warehouse answers the question itself or where `loaded_at_query` answers it for you, and required everywhere else. See `/reference/resource-properties/freshness`. Which adapters expose the metadata is adapter-documentation territory and moves between releases; the fact to carry into the exam is that the requirement is conditional at all.

`filter:` belongs to the second path alone. Put a `filter:` on a table that uses `loaded_at_query` and the query you wrote is issued exactly as written — the predicate is neither applied nor rejected, and the status you get back is computed unfiltered.

**Both thresholds are optional, and each is all-or-nothing.** Supply neither `warn_after` nor `error_after` anywhere in the chain and dbt calculates no freshness for that table at all — a second route to the same place as `freshness: null`, reached by omission rather than by declaration. Supply half a threshold, a `count` with no `period` or the reverse, and the result is worse than either: the YAML parses, the incomplete object is recorded in `sources.json` under `criteria` as `{count: null, period: null}` — the half you did supply is dropped at parse too — and the threshold is discarded at evaluation. Written on its own, that half-threshold takes the table out of the run altogether — `Nothing to do, results: []`, exit 0, and no freshness computed for it at all. Written beside a well-formed `warn_after`, the table is checked, but no amount of lag can reach `error`. Either way the gate you thought you wrote never fires.

The same block written under `config:` — the layout §3.1 recommends for new YAML — behaves identically and cascades identically:

```
sources:
  - name: stripe
    database: raw
    schema: stripe
    config:
      loaded_at_field: _fivetran_synced
      freshness:
        warn_after: {count: 12, period: hour}
        error_after: {count: 24, period: hour}
    tables:
      - name: charges
        config:
          loaded_at_field: created
          freshness:
            warn_after: {count: 1, period: hour}
            error_after: {count: 3, period: hour}
      - name: customers
```

## Running `dbt source freshness`

The command is `dbt source freshness`, not `dbt freshness` and not `dbt source --freshness`. A typical invocation:

```
$ dbt source freshness
23:14:02  Running with dbt=1.11.14
23:14:02  Found 42 models, 118 data tests, 3 seeds, 9 sources, 418 macros
23:14:03  Concurrency: 4 threads (target='prd')
23:14:03  1 of 9 START freshness of stripe.charges .................. [RUN]
23:14:03  1 of 9 PASS freshness of stripe.charges ................... [PASS in 0.41s]
23:14:03  2 of 9 START freshness of stripe.customers ................ [RUN]
23:14:03  2 of 9 WARN freshness of stripe.customers ................. [WARN in 0.38s]
...
23:14:05  Done.
```

Each source table returns one of four statuses: `pass`, `warn`, `error`, or `runtime error` (the query itself failed — missing column, permission issue, etc.). The docs prose sometimes spells `warn` as "warning"; the literal status string in `sources.json` is `warn`. The command supports the standard selection flags — `--select source:stripe` to check a single source, `--select source:stripe.charges` for a single table, and `--output path/to/file.json` to write the artifact somewhere other than the default. That last flag still works and still writes where you point it, but every use of it raises `CustomOutputPathInSourceFreshnessDeprecation`, which puts it in the same recognise-it-do-not-write-it category as the `overrides:` property in §3.5. (`--exclude` is inherited from the global selection surface; the `dbt source` command page does not enumerate it explicitly.) See `/reference/commands/source`.

Two behaviours worth memorising:

- **`dbt source freshness` does not run any models.** It issues `select max(loaded_at_field)` against each source table that declares one — and, because `source_freshness_run_project_hooks` defaults to `true`, it runs the project's `on-run-start` and `on-run-end` hooks around them. Cheap, but not read-only: a hook that writes will write here too.
- **The command's exit code reflects the worst status.** If any table is `error`, the command exits non-zero. If the worst is `warn`, it exits zero. That distinction is what lets CI pipelines fail on staleness thresholds without failing on every flaky minute-late sync.

## Stale source, or wrong source?

Two different failures both surface as a red source, and they take opposite fixes. Read the status label and the error body, not the colour.

A **stale** source is pointing at the right object, and the object has stopped receiving rows. dbt reaches the table, computes a load timestamp, compares it to `error_after` and reports `ERROR STALE`. The result lands in `sources.json` with a real `max_loaded_at` and a real `max_loaded_at_time_ago_in_s`. Every model downstream still builds, and builds green — on old data. The fix is upstream: the sync, the ingestion job, the partner feed.

A **mis-declared** source is pointing at an object that is not there. The freshness query never completes, so there is no timestamp to compare and no criteria to compare it against; the status is a plain `ERROR` carrying the warehouse's own message, and the result does not reach `sources.json` at all:

```
2 of 2 ERROR freshness of stripe.customers ............ [ERROR in 0.03s]

  Database Error in source customers (models/_sources.yml)
  relation "raw.stripee.customers" does not exist
```

The fix is in `sources.yml`: a `database:`, a `schema:` or an `identifier:` naming something the warehouse does not have. Confirm the diagnosis by running the models — every one that calls `{{ source('stripe', 'customers') }}` fails with the same relation in the same message, because the compiled SQL carries the literal that `sources.yml` produced.

**A build runs no freshness check.** `dbt build` executes models, tests, seeds and snapshots; it runs no freshness node and writes no `sources.json`. A green nightly build is evidence that the SQL ran, not that the data arrived — a source that stopped syncing on Monday keeps a build green all week. Freshness has to be its own invocation: a separate step whose exit code the job honours, or the producer of the `--state` artifact that `source_status:fresher+` reads.

### The `sources.json` artifact

After `dbt source freshness` completes, dbt writes `target/sources.json` — a structured summary of every freshness check. See `/reference/artifacts/sources-json`. The fields that matter for the exam and for day-to-day use:

- `results[].unique_id` — the source's fully-qualified dbt ID (e.g., `source.my_project.stripe.charges`), matching entries in `manifest.json`.
- `results[].max_loaded_at` — the max value of `loaded_at_field` the check found.
- `results[].snapshotted_at` — the wall-clock time dbt ran the check.
- `results[].max_loaded_at_time_ago_in_s` — the gap between the two, in seconds.
- `results[].criteria` — the `warn_after` / `error_after` thresholds at the time of check.
- `results[].status` — `pass`, `warn` or `error`. Only those three: a table whose freshness query itself failed is dropped from `results[]` entirely (above), so the run's fourth status, `runtime error`, never reaches the artifact.

This artifact is the *input* to the `source_status:fresher+` selector below, and the thing your CI's next job reads to decide whether to short-circuit.

### `source_status:fresher+`

After `dbt source freshness` has been run twice (once earlier, once now), you can compare the two `sources.json` artifacts and select only the sources that have fresh data in the newer artifact — i.e., sources whose `max_loaded_at` increased between runs. The selector is:

```
dbt build \
  --select source_status:fresher+ \
  --state ./prior-artifacts
```

`source_status:fresher` selects source nodes that are fresher in the current run than in the `--state` reference. The `+` suffix extends to everything downstream of those sources in the DAG. Combined with `--defer`, this is the classic slim-CI recipe: on every schedule tick, check freshness, only rebuild the downstream of sources that actually got new data. Full treatment is in Ch 12; for Ch 3's purposes, know that the selector exists and that it requires a prior `sources.json` in the `--state` directory. See `/reference/node-selection/methods`.

---

## 3.4 Modeling sources from a SQL snippet — the classic trap

The exam tests **modeling**: a question hands you a SQL snippet that references several `db.schema.table` triples and asks how many sources and tables to declare in `sources.yml`. The answer it wants is one source per distinct `(database, schema)` pair; counting one source per table overshoots.

dbt does not enforce that grouping. A source is identified by its YAML `name` — `database` and `schema` say *where* the source lives, not what makes it a distinct source — so nothing stops you declaring two sources on the same `(database, schema)` with different `names`. The collapse is convention, and the exam grades against the convention.

### The convention, spelled out

A `sources:` declaration requires a `name`; `database` and `schema` are optional (each defaults — see §3.1). Two tables that share the same `(database, schema)` belong, by convention, to **one** source with **two** tables. Two tables in different schemas — even of the same database — are **two different sources**. Two tables in different databases are obviously two different sources.

Turning that into a deduplication checklist when you see a SQL snippet:

1. List every `database.schema.table` reference in the snippet.
2. Collapse repeated triples (the same table referenced twice is one table, not two).
3. Group the remaining distinct triples by `(database, schema)`.
4. **Each group is one source. Each triple inside a group is one table under that source.**

### Worked example

Suppose the legacy SQL you are migrating is:

```
select
    u.user_id,
    u.signup_date,
    sub.plan_code,
    sub.status,
    geo.country_code
from analytics.billing.users        u
left join analytics.billing.subscriptions sub
    on sub.user_id = u.user_id
left join analytics.billing.subscriptions sub_latest
    on sub_latest.user_id = u.user_id
   and sub_latest.is_latest
left join analytics.geo.countries   geo
    on geo.country_iso = u.country_iso
where u.user_id in (
    select user_id
    from ops.events.signup_events
    where event_date >= '2025-01-01'
)
```

Walk the checklist.

1. Distinct `database.schema.table` triples referenced: `analytics.billing.users`, `analytics.billing.subscriptions` (appears twice as `sub` and `sub_latest` — same table, one entry), `analytics.geo.countries`, `ops.events.signup_events`.
2. Distinct triples after deduplication: **four**.
3. Group by `(database, schema)`:
    - `(analytics, billing)` → `users`, `subscriptions`
    - `(analytics, geo)` → `countries`
    - `(ops, events)` → `signup_events`
4. Therefore **3 sources with 4 tables total.**

The corresponding `sources.yml`:

```
version: 2

sources:
  - name: billing
    database: analytics
    schema: billing
    tables:
      - name: users
      - name: subscriptions

  - name: geo
    database: analytics
    schema: geo
    tables:
      - name: countries

  - name: signup_events
    database: ops
    schema: events
    tables:
      - name: signup_events
```

The trap is to count four sources ("one per distinct table") or one source ("it's all one project"). Neither matches the convention. **One source per distinct `(database, schema)` pair** is the modeling rule the exam tests against.

### Two subtleties

- **The source `name:` is an arbitrary dbt identifier, not the schema name.** The first source above could be `billing`, `analytics_billing`, `finance_billing`, or anything else — as long as `source(...)` is passed the same string. The convention, used by `dbt-utils` and the dbt Labs structure guide, is to name a source after its upstream source system (`stripe`, `fivetran_stripe`, `hubspot`), not its warehouse schema.
- **A table's warehouse identifier can differ from its dbt name.** `name: customers` with no `identifier:` means the warehouse table is called `customers`; adding `identifier: customer_latest_v3` resolves the source to `database.schema.customer_latest_v3` while `source('...', 'customers')` stays as it was. That buys clean logical names over a messy upstream, and it lets you repoint a source at a new warehouse table without touching any staging SQL; §3.5 Pattern 1 works it through.

---

## 3.5 Handling raw-catalog changes

Over the life of a project, upstream will rename tables, move them to different schemas, and occasionally shift the whole catalog under you. dbt has two patterns for absorbing the change in exactly one file.

### Pattern 1 — rename in `sources.yml` only

If the raw `customers` table is renamed to `customer_v2` in the warehouse, you don't touch any staging SQL. You add one line to `sources.yml`:

```
tables:
  - name: customers          # dbt-side logical name - unchanged
    identifier: customer_v2  # warehouse-side physical name - new
```

Every `{{ source('stripe', 'customers') }}` call keeps working. The compiled SQL now reads from `raw.stripe.customer_v2`, and no downstream model file changes. This is the day-to-day payoff of the abstraction.

## Pattern 2 — multi-environment catalogs via `env_var()`

Most mature projects run the same dbt project against different raw catalogs in different environments: dev reads from a dev-scale snapshot, CI reads from a CI fixtures catalog, prd reads from the real raw catalog. Hard-coding `database: raw` in `sources.yml` paints you into a corner. The idiomatic escape hatch is `env_var()`:

```
version: 2

sources:
  - name: stripe
    database: "{{ env_var('RAW_CATALOG', 'raw_dev') }}"
    schema: stripe
    tables:
      - name: customers
      - name: charges
```

Three properties of `env_var()` — see `/reference/dbt-jinja-functions/env_var` — that make it a good fit for raw-catalog routing:

1. **It resolves at parse time.** By the time dbt builds the manifest, the `database:` field is already the literal string `raw_dev` (or whatever the env var says). No run-time indirection.
2. **The optional second argument is a default.** `{{ env_var('RAW_CATALOG', 'raw_dev') }}` falls back to `raw_dev` when the env var is unset, which is what lets a developer run the project locally without setting it.
3. **A bare `{{ env_var('RAW_CATALOG') }}` fails loudly.** With no default, an unset variable raises a parse error rather than resolving to something dangerous — which is exactly what you want in prod.

The CI pipeline then exports `RAW_CATALOG=raw_ci` before it runs dbt; prod exports `RAW_CATALOG=raw`. Same `sources.yml`, three environments, zero merge conflicts.

## Two edges of the source boundary

**Turning off a source that arrived with a package.** A package can ship its own `sources.yml`, and you will not always want every table in it. `sources:` is a config block in `dbt_project.yml` exactly like `models:`, and `+enabled: false` under it switches sources off. The length of the path sets the scope — package name alone for all of a package's sources, package plus source name for one source, package plus source plus table name for a single table:

```
sources:
  events:             # the package
    clickstream:      # the source
      pageviews:      # the table
        +enabled: false
```

The trap is the resource path. A source declared in a properties file inside a subfolder needs that subfolder in the path too, between the package name and the source name; get it wrong and the config binds to nothing, silently, with no error to tell you so. See `/reference/source-configs`. The older `overrides:` property does a different job, is deprecated, and is not the mechanism to reach for — recognise it, do not write it.

**When a "data input" is not a source.** A small static CSV that lives inside the dbt repo and changes only by hand — ISO country codes, a tax-rate lookup, a list of internal test-account email domains — is a **seed**, not a source. Seeds have a separate lifecycle (loaded by `dbt seed`, not by an upstream tool) and a separate teaching home in **Ch 5**. The cert occasionally tests the seed-vs-source decision; the rule of thumb is *who owns the data and how does it get into the warehouse?* If the answer is "the dbt project's team, via a CSV in the repo", it's a seed.

---

## 3.6 In practice: multi-environment `env_var()` sources

*This section is an "in practice" sidebar. It draws a composite pattern from (a) the canonical `env_var()` reference at `/reference/dbt-jinja-functions/env_var` and (b) the multi-environment configuration guidance at `/docs/build/environment-variables`. Credora is fictional (`credora`); Ch 14's opening note has the composite-project disclaimer.*

Credora applies §3.5's Pattern 2 across a whole market catalog:

```
# models/cr_uk/_sources.yml
version: 2

sources:
  - name: uk_raw_events
    description: >
      Partner ingestion for UK market events - credit checks, offer views,
      application submits. Loaded by the partner ingestion pipeline.
    database: "{{ env_var('RAW_CATALOG', 'cr_partner_ingest_dev') }}"
    schema: uk_events
    loaded_at_field: _ingested_at
    freshness:
      warn_after:  {count: 1, period: hour}
      error_after: {count: 6, period: hour}
    tables:
      - name: credit_check
        description: "One row per UK credit-check event."
      - name: offer_view
```

```
        description: "One row per UK offer-view event."
      - name: application_submit
        description: "One row per UK application-submit event."
        freshness:
          warn_after:  {count: 30, period: minute}
          error_after: {count: 2,  period: hour}

  - name: uk_reference
    description: "Slow-moving reference data (FX rates, country codes, product SKUs)."
    database: "{{ env_var('RAW_CATALOG', 'cr_partner_ingest_dev') }}"
    schema: uk_reference
    loaded_at_field: _ingested_at
    freshness:
      warn_after:  {count: 2, period: day}
      error_after: {count: 7, period: day}
    tables:
      - name: fx_rate
        description: "One row per currency per day; inherits the 2-day warn."
      - name: country_lookup
        freshness: null       # quarterly refresh - cancel the inherited block
      - name: product_sku
        freshness: null
```

Three patterns visible above.

- **Same `env_var()` routing applied to multiple sources.** Every source in the UK market catalog points at `{{ env_var('RAW_CATALOG', 'cr_partner_ingest_dev') }}`. In prd, CI exports `RAW_CATALOG=cr_partner_ingest`; in dev, the default fallback kicks in. Adding a new market (`cr_us`, `cr_apac_1`) is one more `_sources.yml` with the same `env_var(...)` line.
- **Source-level defaults with per-table overrides.** The `uk_raw_events` source declares a 1-hour warn / 6-hour error default. Every table inherits it, except `application_submit`, which has a tighter 30-minute warn / 2-hour error because it feeds the real-time lending-offer pipeline. §3.3's cascade rule in action.
- **Opt-outs for slow-moving tables.** `uk_reference` declares a 2-day warn / 7-day error that `fx_rate` picks up by omitting the key. `country_lookup` and `product_sku` refresh quarterly, so they write `freshness: null` to **cancel** that inherited block; without the cancellation they would sit in `error` for most of every quarter. The key is doing work here only because there is an inherited block for it to cancel — §3.3 has the other route to the same place.

## Dual source — this pattern is not unique to Credora

Using `env_var()` inside `sources.yml` for multi-environment raw-catalog routing is a public, documented pattern:

- The dbt Labs reference for the function itself is `/reference/dbt-jinja-functions/env_var`, which explicitly lists `sources.yml` as a supported call site.
- The `database` config reference documents the knob itself — an overridable `database` whose default is `{{ target.database }}` — and the `var()` function reference the equivalent when a team chooses project variables instead of environment variables.

The Credora snippet above is a composite that picks the same structural moves those references make, with fictional catalog names chosen to anchor the multi-market framing.

## Summary

- A **source** is a named pointer to a raw table dbt did not create, declared in a `sources.yml` under `models/` with `name`, `database`, `schema`, and a list of `tables:`.
- `source('src_name', 'table_name')` is the only legal way to reference a raw table in a model. It resolves at compile time to the full `database.schema.table`, registers a DAG edge, and lets descriptions and tests attach to raw columns.
- **Staging models are the one layer that calls `source()`.** Everything downstream refs the staging model.
- **Source freshness** is configured with a `freshness: {warn_after, error_after}` block plus some way for dbt to find the load timestamp — `loaded_at_field`, `loaded_at_query`, or warehouse metadata on the adapters that expose it. `dbt source freshness` runs `select max(loaded_at_field)` against each source table that declares one, returns `pass/warn/error/runtime error`, and writes `target/sources.json`. `dbt build` runs no freshness check at all.
- **A stale source and a mis-declared source are different failures.** Stale means dbt reached the table and the data is old: `ERROR STALE`, a real `max_loaded_at`, and every downstream model still green. Mis-declared means the relation does not exist: a plain `ERROR` carrying the warehouse's message, no `sources.json` entry, and every downstream model failing on the same relation.
- **`database`, `schema` and `identifier` resolve the relation; `loader:` and a table's `external:` block do not** — dbt Core records them and acts on neither. Source and table `quoting` decide whether the resolved name is written quoted; what quoting then implies for case is the adapter's rule — case-sensitive on Snowflake, case-insensitive resolution under Unity Catalog.
- **Source-modeling convention:** group tables sharing `(database, schema)` under one source declaration with N tables; one source per distinct `(database, schema)` pair is the conventional answer to "how many sources?" questions. dbt does not enforce this — see §3.4.
- **Raw-catalog changes** are absorbed with `identifier:` (for renames) or `env_var()` (for multi-environment routing), both edited in `sources.yml` without touching any staging SQL.
- `source_status:fresher+` is the state-aware selector that bridges into Ch 12 — it picks sources whose `max_loaded_at` advanced between two `sources.json` artifacts and extends to everything downstream.

## Learning-goal checklist (self-assess)

- ☐ I can define a source in `sources.yml` with `name`, `database`, `schema`, and a `tables:` list, and I know `version: 2` is optional (still conventional in existing projects).
- ☐ I replace every hard-coded raw-table reference with `{{ source(...) }}` and know that staging is the only layer where `source()` appears.
- ☐ I can configure `warn_after` / `error_after` on a source or table, I know `loaded_at_field` is required only where neither `loaded_at_query` nor warehouse metadata supplies the timestamp, and I can explain what `target/sources.json` contains.
- ☐ I can tell a stale source from a mis-declared one by its status label and its error body, and I know `dbt build` runs no freshness check, so a green build proves nothing about staleness.
- ☐ I know which source properties resolve the relation (`database`, `schema`, `identifier`) and which are inert metadata (`loader`, `external`), and that a source's `quoting` governs what `source()` reads rather than what dbt builds.

- ☐ I can count sources and tables from a SQL snippet using the "source = (database + schema)" rule without tripping on repeated or same-schema tables.
- ☐ I know how `env_var()` in a source's `database:` field lets one project run against dev / CI / prd catalogs without code changes, and how `identifier:` absorbs a raw-table rename in one file.

---

## Practice questions

Twenty-five questions covering every sub-topic from §3.1–§3.5 (§3.6 is sidebar — not drilled). Source declaration and `source()` resolution are drilled by Qs 2, 3, 4, 19 and 24; the source-modeling skill ("how many sources per (database, schema)") by Q17; freshness configuration and diagnosis by Qs 5, 6, 7, 8, 9, 13, 16, 18, 20, 21, 22 and 23; raw-catalog changes by Qs 10 and 25; `source_status:fresher+` by Q12; the seed-vs-source decision by Q14; and source documentation, tests and test selection by Qs 1, 11 and 15.

**1.** Which statement about `description:` in a `sources.yml` is correct?
A. It attaches at three levels, but a table or column that declares none inherits the nearest declared value above it.
B. It attaches at three levels — source, table and column — and no level inherits: a table that declares none carries an empty description, not its source's.
C. It attaches at three levels, and only the source-level value reaches `manifest.json`; the table and column values are read straight from the YAML.
D. It attaches to tables only. A `description:` on the source itself is rejected at parse time, because a source names a namespace rather than a relation.

**2.** A staging model reads `from raw.stripe.customers` — the literal relation, hard-coded. You replace that one clause with `{{ source('stripe', 'customers') }}`, declare the source, and change nothing else. What has the project gained?
A. dbt records a dependency on the source node, so run ordering and source-status selection work, and the table's physical location moves in one YAML file.
B. dbt now manages `raw.stripe.customers`, and rebuilds it as part of the run whenever the staging model that reads it is built.
C. The relation is resolved when the model runs rather than when it compiles, so a rename in the warehouse takes effect without re-parsing or recompiling the project.
D. The staging model can now be reached by `--select source:stripe`, because calling `source()` registers the model itself as a member of that source's node group.

**3.** Which of the following is the minimum set of keys required to declare a source that resolves to a specific `(database, schema, table)` without relying on defaults?
A. `sources[].name`, `sources[].database`, `sources[].schema`, `sources[].tables[].name`
B. `version`, `sources[].name`, `sources[].tables[].name`
C. `version`, `sources[].name`, `sources[].database`, `sources[].schema`, `sources[].tables[].name`
D. `sources[].name`, `sources[].tables[].name`, `sources[].tables[].identifier`

**4.** According to dbt Labs' "How we structure our dbt projects" guide, which layer is the only one that should call `source()`?
A. `intermediate/` B. `marts/`
C. `staging/` D. `tests/`

**5.** Which command runs a freshness check against the sources defined in `sources.yml`?
A. `dbt source freshness` B. `dbt test --freshness`
C. `dbt freshness` D. `dbt build --select source_status:fresher+`

**6.** In a source freshness configuration, what is the relationship between `warn_after` and `error_after`?
A. They are synonyms; only one is needed, and setting both simply repeats the same threshold twice.
B. `warn_after` is a subset of `error_after` — once the warn threshold fires, the error threshold is skipped and the check reports `warn`.
C. `warn_after` applies to `dbt test` and `error_after` to `dbt source freshness`, so the two halves of the block are read by different commands.
D. `warn_after` is a lower (earlier) threshold; `error_after` is a higher (later) one. A source older than `warn_after` but younger than `error_after` returns `warn`; older than `error_after` returns `error`.

**7.** You configure freshness on a `stripe.charges` source with `loaded_at_field: updated_at`. The `updated_at` column is updated every time the row is re-synced by Fivetran, which re-syncs the entire table nightly. What is the most likely problem?
A. Freshness will report `error` on every run, because a column re-stamped by the sync reads as older than the threshold allows.
B. `dbt source freshness` will detect that the field is unsuitable and fall back to `CURRENT_TIMESTAMP` for the comparison.
C. `loaded_at_field` does not support a column named `updated_at`, because the name collides with the field dbt uses internally.
D. Freshness will always pass, because every row's `updated_at` is stamped nightly — the check cannot tell "data is fresh" from "data was last touched recently."

**8.** Which of the following is a legal value for `period` inside a `warn_after:` or `error_after:` block?
A. `second` B. `hour`
C. `week` D. `month`

**9.** After `dbt source freshness` completes, where does dbt write its structured result, and what is the top-level key of the per-source entries?
A. `target/run_results.json` — key `nodes` B. `target/manifest.json` — key `sources`
C. `target/sources.json` — key `results` D. `target/freshness.json` — key `checks`

**10.** You are told the raw table `raw.stripe.customers` has been renamed to `raw.stripe.customer_latest_v3` in the warehouse, and you must absorb the change without touching any staging SQL. What is the correct edit?
A. Rename `stg_stripe__customers.sql` to `stg_stripe__customer_latest_v3.sql`.
B. Change the `schema:` on the source to `customer_latest_v3`.
C. Add `identifier: customer_latest_v3` under the `customers` table entry in `sources.yml`.
D. Use `{{ ref('customer_latest_v3') }}` in the staging model.

**11.** In the §3.1 `sources.yml`, `stripe.customers` carries `unique` and `not_null` on `id`, and `stripe.charges` carries a `relationships` test on `customer_id` whose `to:` is `source('stripe', 'customers')`. You run `dbt test --select source:stripe.customers` with dbt's default settings. Which tests run?
A. Two — the `unique` and the `not_null` declared on `customers`. A test declared under `charges` belongs to `charges`, so this selector leaves it out.
B. Three — those two plus the `relationships` test declared under `charges`, because the default `eager` mode takes any test with a selected parent, and `customers` is one of its parents.
C. Three — those two plus a reverse `relationships` test dbt generates on `customers`, since a declared relationship is checked from both ends.
D. Zero — `source:` matches source nodes, which `dbt test` skips; raw tables are gated by `dbt source freshness` instead.

**12.** What does `--select source_status:fresher+` select, and what does it require?
A. Every source defined in `sources.yml`, whether or not its data moved; it needs no prior artifacts because nothing is being compared.
B. Every source whose `max_loaded_at` advanced between the prior `sources.json` (supplied via `--state`) and the current freshness check, plus everything downstream in the DAG.
C. Every source that returned `pass` in the current freshness check, plus its downstream; it needs only the current run's freshness results.
D. Every model tagged `fresher:+` in its config, which requires the tag to be declared on each model you want selected.

**13.** One table in a source updates quarterly during a manual refresh and needs no freshness monitoring. Its sibling tables must keep the source-level freshness checks. What is the simplest correct persistent table-level configuration?
A. Set `warn_after: {count: 100, period: day}`.
B. Delete the source declaration.
C. Set `freshness: null` at the table level.
D. Exclude the source from every `dbt source freshness` invocation with `--exclude`.

**14.** A data-team member says they want to "load a CSV of ISO country codes into the warehouse so the finance models can join against it." The CSV has 249 rows and changes a few times per year. Which dbt resource is the right home for this data, and why?
A. A source, because the data is external to dbt and something outside the project is responsible for landing it in the warehouse.
B. A seed, because the data is small, rarely changes, and belongs under project version control alongside the code that reads it.
C. A snapshot, because the file changes over time and the finance models will need the version of each row that was current when a report ran.
D. A model, because it is queried by analytics and should be built by the same `dbt run` that builds everything else downstream of it.

**15.** Which of the following is true of descriptions and data tests declared on a source?
A. A `relationships` test on a source column has to point at a model with `ref()`; `to: source(...)` is rejected, because a source cannot be the target end of a relationship.
B. Source tests run under `dbt test` but are skipped by `dbt build`, which confines itself to the models, seeds and snapshots it has been asked to build.
C. The built-in generics apply to a source column with nothing installed, and the resulting test node carries a `source_` prefix in its name.
D. A source table takes a `description:`, but its columns do not — column-level descriptions are a model property and are ignored under a source's `columns:`.

**16.** Which invocation checks freshness only on the `stripe` source's `charges` table, without touching any other source?
A. `dbt source freshness --models stripe.charges`
B. `dbt source freshness --select source:stripe.charges`
C. `dbt test --select source:stripe.charges`
D. `dbt source freshness stripe charges`

**17.** A junior analyst has already started on a `sources.yml` and writes:

```
sources:
  - name: sales_orders
    database: analytics
    schema: sales
    tables: [{name: orders}]
  - name: sales_customers
    database: analytics
    schema: sales
    tables: [{name: customers}]
```

dbt parses this without complaint and both tables resolve. Which single edit brings it into line with the source-modeling convention of §3.4?
A. Give the second entry a `schema:` of its own, so that no two sources in the file declare the same `(database, schema)` pair.
B. Rename both entries to match their schema exactly, so that each one is called `sales` and the naming is consistent with the warehouse.
C. Collapse the two entries into one source named `sales` on `(analytics, sales)`, with `orders` and `customers` under a single `tables:` list.
D. Move `database:` and `schema:` down onto each `tables:` entry, so that the shared pair is declared once per table rather than once per source.

**18.** A CI job runs `dbt source freshness` on every schedule tick. One source table returns `warn`, two return `pass`, and none return `error`. What is the command's exit code, and should the CI job consider this a failure?
A. Exit code 1; CI should fail.
B. Exit code 2; CI should retry the check.
C. Exit code 0; CI should pass (unless the job explicitly converts warn into failure).
D. Exit code is undefined when `warn` is present.

**19.** A developer runs `dbt compile` on a model that contains `from {{ source('stripe', 'customers') }}`. They then inspect `target/compiled/my_project/models/staging/stg_stripe__customers.sql` and see:

```
from raw.stripe.customers
```

Which of the following statements is MOST accurate?
A. The compiled SQL has been cached from a previous run; rerun `dbt compile --no-cache`.
B. `source()` resolves to `database.schema.table` at compile time, using the `database:` and `schema:` values from `sources.yml`. The compiled file reflects the documented resolution.
C. dbt queried the warehouse to verify the table exists before writing the compiled file.
D. The compiled file is wrong; `source()` should resolve to `{{ source('stripe', 'customers') }}` literally.

**20.** A nightly job runs `dbt build` and has been green for a week. An analyst reports that a dashboard's numbers stopped moving last Monday; the upstream sync that lands `raw.stripe.charges` has been dead since then. Which change to the job would have caught it?
A. Run `dbt source freshness` as a step before the build, and let that step's exit code fail the job when a source breaches `error_after`.
B. Add `--fail-fast` to the build, so that the first source dbt finds in a stale state stops the run before any downstream model is built.
C. Declare a `freshness:` block on each source in `sources.yml`, so that `dbt build` evaluates the thresholds before it builds the models that read from them.
D. Add `--select source_status:fresher+` to the build, so that the job rebuilds the part of the DAG whose sources actually received new rows.

**21.** `dbt source freshness` reports:

```
1 of 2 PASS  freshness of stripe.charges ................ [PASS in 0.41s]
2 of 2 ERROR freshness of stripe.customers ............ [ERROR in 0.03s]

  Database Error in source customers (models/_sources.yml)
  relation "raw.stripee.customers" does not exist
```

What has gone wrong, and where does the fix belong?
A. The customers table has breached its `error_after` threshold; loosen the threshold, or chase the upstream sync that has stopped writing to it.
B. The column named by `loaded_at_field` is missing from the customers table, so the freshness query failed; add the column upstream or name a different one.
C. The `loaded_at_field` on customers moves whenever an existing row is re-synced, so the check is measuring the wrong thing; switch to an ingestion timestamp.
D. The source is mis-declared rather than stale: no table was reached, so `sources.yml` names an object the warehouse does not have.

**22.** A source declares `warn_after` and `error_after` thresholds and no `loaded_at_field`. What happens when `dbt source freshness` runs?
A. The project does not parse: `freshness:` and `loaded_at_field` have to be declared together, and dbt rejects a block that carries one without the other.
B. The table is dropped from the run without comment, in exactly the way a table carrying `freshness: null` is dropped from it.
C. The check runs and reports `warn` for that table, because dbt has no timestamp to compare against and falls back to the softer of the two statuses.
D. On an adapter that reads last-modified times from the warehouse catalog it computes normally; on one that cannot, dbt warns at parse and errors at run.

**23.** A source table sets `filter: "loaded_at >= current_date - 7"` alongside its freshness thresholds. Under which declaration does that `filter:` make no difference to the status it reports?
A. When the table inherits `loaded_at_field:` from its source rather than declaring one of its own.
B. When the `freshness:` block is written under a `config:` key instead of at the top level of the table.
C. When both `warn_after:` and `error_after:` are declared, since a `filter:` narrows the warn evaluation and not the error one.
D. When the table supplies `loaded_at_query:` in place of `loaded_at_field:` — that query is issued as written.

**24.** A source's `quoting` sub-keys are left unset. On which adapter do they default to `false` rather than `true`, and what is the consequence of that default?
A. BigQuery — unquoted names let a sharded-table wildcard resolve
B. Redshift — unquoted names are folded to lower case on read
C. Snowflake — an unquoted name is case-insensitive, so raw tables stay selectable without matching their stored case
D. Databricks — Unity Catalog rejects quoted three-part names

**25.** A source table is declared `name: orders` with no `identifier:`. The raw table is later renamed to `orders_v2`, and someone adds `identifier: orders_v2` to the table's YAML entry. What must the twenty models that call `{{ source('jaffle_shop', 'orders') }}` be changed to?
A. `{{ source('jaffle_shop', 'orders_v2') }}` — the second argument is the physical table
B. Nothing — `source()` still takes `orders`, and only the compiled relation changes
C. `{{ source('jaffle_shop', 'orders', identifier='orders_v2') }}`
D. `{{ ref('orders_v2') }}` — a renamed source is no longer ref-able as a source

## Answer key

**1. B.** `description:` is declarable on the source, on each table under it, and on each column under a table, and the three are independent. Executed on dbt Core 1.11.14: a table added with no `description:` under a documented source parsed clean, and its manifest node came back with `description` empty while `source_description` still carried the source's text — the table inherits nothing (A). The same dump shows every table and column description present in `manifest.json`, which refutes C. A source-level `description:` is ordinary YAML and parses (D). Source: `/reference/source-properties`, `/reference/resource-properties/description`.

**2. A.** Three things change at once: dbt records `source.<project>.stripe.customers` in the model's `depends_on`, which is what gives the run an order and makes `source_status:fresher+` possible; the call resolves to the literal `raw.stripe.customers` at compile time; and the physical location now lives in `sources.yml` alone. C is backwards — resolution happens at compile time, which is exactly why the compiled file holds a literal (§3.2). B credits `source()` with building something: it builds nothing, and the raw table stays owned by whatever pipeline loaded it. D confuses the two node types — `source:stripe` selects source nodes, and the staging model is a model node that depends on one; reaching the model needs `source:stripe+` or the model's own name. Source: `/docs/build/sources`, `/reference/dbt-jinja-functions/source`.

**3. A.** Per `/reference/source-properties`, only `name` is strictly required on a source — omitting `database` falls back to the project's target database, and omitting `schema` falls back to the source's `name`. Because the stem rules out relying on those defaults, `database` and `schema` must both be declared explicitly, plus at least one entry under `tables:` with a `name`. `version: 2` at the top of the YAML is **optional** (see §3.1), so options that include `version` over-specify the minimum. `identifier:` remains optional (defaults to the table's `name`). Source: `/reference/source-properties`.

**4. C.** Staging models are defined as "one-to-one with source tables" and are the only layer where `source()` appears. Intermediate and mart models ref the staging models, which insulates them from raw-table churn. Source: `/best-practices/how-we-structure/2-staging`.

**5. A.** The command is `dbt source freshness` — `source` is the parent command and `freshness` is the subcommand, and it reports `pass/warn/error/runtime error` per table. C uses the subcommand as though it were top-level; there is no `dbt freshness`. B invents a flag on a command that runs data tests, which is a different check writing a different artifact. D is the interesting one: it is a real, valid invocation, but it runs no freshness of its own — `dbt build` never does — and the selector reads a *prior* `sources.json` supplied through `--state`, so with no preceding `dbt source freshness` there is nothing for it to compare against. Source: `/reference/commands/source`; command forms confirmed against dbt Core 1.11.14.

**6. D.** The two thresholds are ordered: warn is the soft alarm, error is the hard alarm. `dbt source freshness` exits non-zero only when at least one source is in `error`. Setting `warn_after` > `error_after` is a configuration bug. Source: `/docs/build/sources#source-data-freshness`; exit status confirmed against dbt Core 1.11.14.

**7. D.** `max(loaded_at_field)` only signals freshness if the field monotonically advances when **new** rows arrive. A column that also moves when old rows are touched will make a stale table look fresh. The idiomatic field is an ingestion-tool field (`_fivetran_synced`, `_airbyte_emitted_at`) or an append-only `created_at`, not a row-level `updated_at`. Source: `/docs/build/sources#source-data-freshness`.

**8. B.** The enum is a closed three-member list — `minute`, `hour`, `day` — and `hour` is the only member in the option list. The other three are rejected at parse time with `is not valid under any of the given schemas`, and the message names the whole `freshness` object rather than the offending key, so reading the error does not hand you the enum. `second` is the trap: it is the natural neighbour of `minute`, and it is not there. Source: `/reference/resource-properties/freshness`; `second`, `week` and `month` each rejected on dbt Core 1.11.14.

**9. C.** `dbt source freshness` writes `target/sources.json` with top-level keys `metadata`, `elapsed_time`, and `results`. Each entry in `results` carries `unique_id`, `max_loaded_at`, `snapshotted_at`, `max_loaded_at_time_ago_in_s`, `criteria`, and `status`. `manifest.json` and `run_results.json` are different artifacts. Source: `/reference/artifacts/sources-json`.

**10. C.** `identifier:` is the warehouse-side physical name; `name:` is the dbt-side logical name. Setting `identifier: customer_latest_v3` keeps every existing `source('stripe', 'customers')` call working while dbt resolves it against the new warehouse table. Option D (`{{ ref('customer_latest_v3') }}`) fails because `ref()` only resolves dbt-managed models — there is no model named `customer_latest_v3` in the project; the table is raw, so it must be reached via `source()`. Source: `/reference/source-properties`.

**11. B.** Source tests are ordinary test nodes, so `source:<name>.<table>` reaches them through the indirect selection of Ch 7 §7.6, and the default mode is `eager`: a test is selected when **any** of its parents is. The `relationships` test is declared under `charges` but has `customers` among its parents, so it comes along — the pull runs in both directions, which is what A misses. Executed on dbt Core 1.11.14: selecting one source table ran the tests declared on it **plus** the `relationships` test declared on the child table that points at it, and the identical selection under `--indirect-selection cautious` ran only the tests declared on the table that was selected. C invents a reverse test — a `relationships` test exists only where it is written. D is refuted by that run: gating raw data with `dbt test --select source:...` is exactly what source tests are for, and freshness answers a different question (§3.3). Source: `/reference/node-selection/methods`, `/reference/global-configs/indirect-selection`.

**12. B.** `source_status:fresher` compares the current `sources.json` to the one in `--state`, picking sources whose freshness timestamp increased. The `+` suffix extends the selection to every downstream node. It requires a prior `dbt source freshness` run whose artifact is in the `--state` directory. Source: `/reference/node-selection/methods`.

**13. C.** `freshness: null` at the table level overrides the source-level cascade for this table and opts it out of freshness checks entirely. It is the persistent table-local configuration while sibling tables keep inheriting source-level checks. Deleting the source (B) breaks every staging model that refs it; a huge threshold (A) still configures monitoring and can leave an inherited error threshold; `--exclude` (D) forces every invocation to remember the exclusion. Source: `/reference/source-properties`.

**14. B.** The seed/source decision hinges on ownership: seeds are small static reference CSVs that live *inside* the dbt project (under `seeds/`, loaded by `dbt seed`); sources are tables loaded into the warehouse by *something else*. 249 slowly-changing ISO codes owned by the analytics team is a textbook seed. A source would be right only if the CSV were already being loaded into the warehouse by a separate ingestion process. Ch 5 covers seeds in detail. Source: `/docs/build/seeds`, `/docs/build/sources`.

**15. C.** `unique`, `not_null`, `accepted_values` and `relationships` apply to a source column with no package installed, and the node dbt builds is named `source_<generic>_<source>_<table>_<column>` — the prefix is what distinguishes it from the model-side test of the same generic. A is refuted by §3.1's own example: `relationships:` takes `to: source('stripe', 'customers')`, which is how a raw foreign key is expressed. B is false in the other direction — source tests are ordinary test nodes and run under `dbt build` like any other. D denies column-level descriptions, which sources take exactly as models do and which flow into the generated catalog. Source: `/reference/source-properties`, `/reference/resource-properties/data-tests`; test-node naming and execution confirmed on dbt Core 1.11.14.

**16. B.** `dbt source freshness` supports the standard `--select` flag with the `source:` method; `source:stripe` selects every table under `stripe`, `source:stripe.charges` selects just that one table. `dbt test` (C) runs data tests, not freshness checks. Positional arguments (D) are not supported. Source: `/reference/commands/source`.

**17. C.** The stem concedes what execution shows — dbt parses two source entries on one `(database, schema)` without a word, and both relations resolve. The defect is in the modelling, and the convention of §3.4 collapses them into one source with two tables. The source `name:` is an arbitrary dbt identifier, so renaming to `sales` costs nothing. A fixes the symptom by breaking the project: those tables really are in `analytics.sales`, and pointing them at an invented schema compiles clean and fails at the warehouse. B asserts a naming rule dbt does not have, and would leave the file with two sources called `sales`. D is the most instructive wrong answer — `database:` and `schema:` are source-level properties, and dbt neither honours nor rejects them on a `tables:` entry; it ignores them and falls back to resolving the schema from the source's own `name:`, so the edit silently repoints `orders` at a schema called `sales_orders`. Source: `/reference/source-properties`; parse behaviour and the table-level fallback both confirmed on dbt Core 1.11.14.

**18. C.** `dbt source freshness` exits non-zero only when at least one source is in `error` or `runtime error`. `warn` keeps the exit code at 0. The practical CI recipe is: let the command determine pass/fail, set tight enough `error_after` thresholds for anything critical, and use `warn_after` for early-warning telemetry that surfaces in dashboards rather than in CI failures. Source: `/reference/commands/source`.

**19. B.** `source()` is pure Jinja resolution — dbt substitutes the function call with the fully-qualified relation string at compile time, using only information from `sources.yml` (and any `env_var()`s it contains). The substitution itself does not require a warehouse round-trip; the `from raw.stripe.customers` literal in the compiled file is exactly what is then wrapped in DDL and sent to the warehouse at run time. (Note: `dbt compile` as a command may still issue introspective queries — relation cache, `dbt_utils.get_column_values`, etc. — so the broader "compile never touches the warehouse" claim is not quite right; what is right is that *resolving* *source()* does not.) Source: `/reference/dbt-jinja-functions/source`, `/reference/commands/compile`.

**20. A.** `dbt build` executes models, tests, seeds and snapshots and runs no freshness node at all — it writes no `sources.json`, and a dead sync leaves it green indefinitely. What catches staleness is a `dbt source freshness` invocation whose exit code the job honours, which is non-zero as soon as one table breaches `error_after`. C is the belief the scenario punishes: declaring thresholds is necessary but not sufficient, because nothing in a build evaluates them. B misreads `--fail-fast`, which aborts on the first *node failure* in a run — and there is no freshness node in that run to fail. D is a real selector but the wrong instrument: it narrows the build to the downstream of sources that *did* receive rows, needs a prior `sources.json` in `--state` to make the comparison, and would have made the job quieter rather than louder. Source: `/docs/deploy/source-freshness`; `dbt build` confirmed to run no freshness and write no artifact on dbt Core 1.11.14.

**21. D.** The status is a plain `ERROR` carrying the warehouse's own message, and that message names a relation — not a column, not a threshold. dbt never reached a table, so there was no timestamp to compare and no staleness to report. `raw.stripee.customers` is a typo in `sources.yml`, in the `schema:` or in an `identifier:`, and the fix belongs there. A describes the other failure entirely: a breach of `error_after` prints `ERROR STALE`, records a real `max_loaded_at`, and leaves every downstream model building green. B and C are both real freshness faults — a `loaded_at_field` that is not on the table, and one that moves whenever an existing row is re-synced (Q7) — but each of them presupposes a table dbt could reach. Source: `/docs/build/sources`.

**22. D.** `loaded_at_field` is conditionally required, not required. dbt looks for `loaded_at_query`, then `loaded_at_field`, then the adapter's ability to read a last-modified time out of the warehouse catalog, and only then raises. On Snowflake, Redshift and BigQuery the third branch computes; on an adapter without that capability — Postgres among them — the same YAML produces a parse-time warning naming metadata-based freshness and a runtime error per table (§3.3). A overstates the requirement into a parse rule; B confuses an omitted key with the `freshness: null` opt-out, which is a declaration rather than an omission; C invents a soft fallback that does not exist. Source: `/reference/resource-properties/freshness`; both branches executed on dbt Core 1.11.14.

**23. D.** `filter:` constrains the `max(loaded_at_field)` query and reaches nothing else. Under `loaded_at_query` there is no such query to constrain — dbt issues the SQL you wrote, exactly as you wrote it, and computes the status from an unfiltered result. Nothing warns and nothing fails, which is what makes it worth knowing. A and B both propose that a `filter:` changes meaning with layout: inheritance from the source level and nesting under `config:` are cascade and spelling respectively, and neither touches which query the predicate joins. C invents a split between the two thresholds, which are evaluated against the same computed timestamp. Verified by execution on dbt Core 1.11.14: the same `filter:` produces `WARN` under `loaded_at_field` and `PASS` under `loaded_at_query`. Source: `/reference/resource-properties/freshness`.

**24. C.** Snowflake is the one documented adapter-level exception: source `quoting` defaults to `false` there and to `true` on most others. The reason is the point of the item — quoting an identifier makes it **case-sensitive**, and Snowflake stores unquoted identifiers upper-cased, so quoting a raw table by the lower-case name written in YAML would stop it resolving. Leaving it unquoted keeps the name case-insensitive and selectable. A is the attractive wrong answer because BigQuery genuinely does have a source-side special case, the `identifier: "events_*"` wildcard of §3.1, which has nothing to do with quoting. Reach for `quoting: true` when a raw name is a reserved word, is mixed-case, or carries special characters; leave it alone otherwise.

**25. B.** `name:` is the symbolic key `source()` looks up; `identifier:` is the physical table dbt queries, and it **defaults to `name`** when omitted. Adding `identifier: orders_v2` makes the two diverge, and divergence is the whole feature: the twenty call sites keep saying `orders`, and the compiled SQL quietly starts pointing at `orders_v2`. That is the rename mechanism of §3.5 — one line of YAML absorbs a raw-layer rename that would otherwise be a twenty-file change. A is the trap for anyone who reads the second argument as a table name. The cost is that the two can now drift far enough apart that the YAML is the only place the real table name appears, which is why the entry is worth a `description`.

# Chapter 4

# Materializations: view, table, incremental, ephemeral (+ Python models sidebar)

> **Scope.** A **materialization** is just a way dbt turns a `select` into warehouse DDL — the difference between "rebuild this as a view" and "merge only new rows into this table" is one config line in your model. Ch 4 teaches the four standard choices — `view`, `table`, `incremental`, `ephemeral` — and drills the one that the exam really wants you to understand: `incremental`. By the end you can pick the right materialization for a given scenario, write a correct incremental model with `unique_key`, `is_incremental()`, `on_schema_change`, and a strategy, and explain what `--full-refresh` does and when to reach for it. The Python-models sidebar is a recall-only page: adapter support + `dbt.ref` vs Jinja `ref` is almost always the trap.

**Prerequisites.** Ch 2 (especially §2.4 on `dbt_project.yml` config precedence) and Ch 3 (enough `source()` fluency to recognise the pattern). If you haven't internalised that `{{ config() }}` in a SQL file beats a YAML `config:` which in turn beats `dbt_project.yml` `+config`, re-read §2.4 before you hit §4.2 — we'll use materialization as the worked example there.

**Cheat-sheet pointer.** Front-of-book cheat sheet §2 (Topic 1 — Developing and optimizing models) has the one-line version of every materialization in this chapter. Use it for spaced recall; use the chapter for the reasoning that makes "pick the right one" feel obvious under timed conditions.

---

## 4.1 The four standard materializations

Every model in a dbt project is a `select` statement plus a decision about what dbt should build from it. That decision is the model's **materialization**. The dbt materialization catalog at `/docs/build/materializations` lists five built-in materializations: four — `view`, `table`, `incremental`, `ephemeral` — that work on every supported warehouse, plus `materialized_view`, which is implemented on Postgres, Redshift, BigQuery, and Databricks but not on Snowflake (Snowflake users reach for Dynamic Tables instead).

Hold one sentence in your head first: **a materialization is a trade-off between freshness, cost, and complexity.** Views are cheap to build but slow to read; tables are fast to read but expensive to rebuild; incrementals are cheap *and* fast but the most fiddly to get right; ephemerals don't exist in the warehouse at all. Every exam question in this chapter is ultimately about which corner of that trade-off matches the scenario.

### `view` — the default

If you write a model file and never set `materialized`, dbt builds it as a **view**. Running `dbt run` compiles the model's `select` into a `CREATE OR REPLACE VIEW ...` statement. No rows are persisted; the view re-computes every time a downstream query reads from it.

Views are the right default because they have two useful properties. First, they're instantly consistent with their upstream — if you change the SQL or the upstream data, the next query sees the change without a rebuild. Second, they're cheap to build: the warehouse only stores the definition, not the result. They pay for themselves at read time instead.

The flip side is that a view's read cost equals the cost of its entire upstream chain every time it's queried. A view over a view over a view over a 1 TB fact table is a 1 TB scan every time someone opens a dashboard tile.

### `table` — materialized DDL

Setting `{{ config(materialized='table') }}` tells dbt to emit `CREATE OR REPLACE TABLE ... AS (<your select>)`. Rows are written to the warehouse and read cheaply afterward.

Tables are the right choice when:

- The model is read more often than it's rebuilt (e.g. a small `dim_customers` read by twenty dashboards).
- The upstream transformation is expensive enough that paying it once per build beats paying it once per read.
- The model is a final mart consumed by a BI tool that cannot handle view-read latency.

Every `dbt run` rebuilds every `table` model in full. That's fine for small lookups. It's painful for anything measured in hundreds of millions of rows — which is where `incremental` comes in.

### `incremental` — materialize-then-upsert

An **incremental** model is a table that dbt rebuilds in full the *first* time it runs, and then updates with only new or changed rows on every subsequent run. The mechanism is the `is_incremental()` Jinja macro, which returns `True` when a model already exists in the warehouse and the run is not in full-refresh mode — being run non-destructively — and `False` on a first run or whenever `--full-refresh` is passed.

Incrementals have more moving parts than the other three combined, and the exam drills them directly; §4.3 is most of this chapter.

### `ephemeral` — inlined CTE, no warehouse object

Setting `materialized='ephemeral'` tells dbt *not* to write anything to the warehouse at all. Instead, the model's SQL is inlined as a CTE inside every downstream model that `ref()`s it. Ephemerals are useful when you want the modularity of a separate model file — a named CTE you can reuse across marts — without the cost of materialising its intermediate result.

The cost is debuggability: you can't `select * from my_ephemeral` in the warehouse, because there's nothing there to select from. We'll come back to the trade-off in §4.6.

### `materialized_view` — adapter-specific

A materialized view is a warehouse-managed object that stores query results, and each adapter exposes it under its own config name: Snowflake uses `materialized='dynamic_table'`;

BigQuery, Databricks, Redshift and Postgres use `materialized='materialized_view'`. Each adapter adds its own refresh configs.

For the exam, you need to know two things and no more: (1) it is a materialization in its own right, and only its implementation is adapter-specific; (2) if a question asks you to pick between `view`, `table`, `incremental`, `ephemeral`, and `materialized_view` for a typical scenario, `materialized_view` is almost never the right answer because the scenario won't mention adapter-specific refresh behaviour. Eliminate it on what the scenario says, not because it isn't a real materialization.

### Materialized views are a deploy target, not a refresh schedule

`dbt run` on a materialized view is a **deploy** action: dbt asks the adapter what has changed between the object in the warehouse and the model, and acts on the answer. Where nothing has changed it still issues the platform's refresh — a no-change run reports `REFRESH MATERIALIZED VIEW` and the data moves — so the run is a deploy *and* a refresh. Only `on_configuration_change: continue` reaches a path that does neither.

**How much the adapter actually looks at is per-adapter, and on dbt-postgres it is very little.** `postgres__describe_materialized_view` fetches the object's *indexes* and nothing else — the macro says so in a comment: `for now just get the indexes, we don't need the name or the query yet`. So a changed `select` produces no detected change at all. Edit the SQL, run the model, and you get `REFRESH MATERIALIZED VIEW`, exit 0, a green build — and the warehouse still holds the OLD definition; the columns you added are not there. Only `--full-refresh` reaches the replace path. This is the trap worth carrying out of the section: on Postgres your edited SQL does not reach the warehouse until you force it, and nothing in the output says so. What Postgres lacks is refresh machinery of its own **between** runs: no auto-refresh, no scheduled recompute, so between deploys a Postgres materialized view holds whatever your last `dbt run` put in it. See `/docs/build/materializations`.

What dbt does on divergence is set by `on_configuration_change`:

| Value | Behaviour when a config has changed |
| --- | --- |
| `apply` | The default. dbt alters the object in place where the adapter can, and falls back to a full refresh where it cannot. |
| `continue` | dbt warns and leaves the object exactly as it was. Your project and the warehouse now disagree, which is how a downstream model starts failing on a column that was never added. |
| `fail` | dbt stops the run. |

`--full-refresh` replaces the relation regardless of the setting. See `/reference/resource-configs/on_configuration_change`.

The trap is how much "alter in place" covers. A materialized view's **SQL** is never altered in place on any adapter. What follows from that is per-adapter, and it is where Postgres differs: an adapter that *compares* the query replaces the object when it changes — on Snowflake dynamic tables a query change sets `requires_full_refresh` — while dbt-postgres never compares it, so the change is neither applied nor reported and `on_configuration_change` never comes into it. Only a subset of *configs* is alterable, and which ones is per-adapter: on BigQuery `enable_refresh`, `refresh_interval_minutes` and `max_staleness` alter while `partition_by` and `cluster_by` force a drop-and-create; on Snowflake dynamic tables `target_lag`, `refresh_mode` and `cluster_by` alter while `transient` and `copy_grants` force a full refresh. Read those two lists as illustrations of where the boundary falls, not as a matrix to memorise. See `/reference/resource-configs/bigquery-configs` and `/reference/resource-configs/snowflake-configs`.

Snowflake's `dynamic_table` carries two required configs — `snowflake_warehouse` and `target_lag` — defaults `refresh_mode` to `AUTO`, and does not support model contracts.

### The decision table

| Scenario | Right materialization | Why |
|---|---|---|
| Small lookup table (< a few MB) read by many downstream models | `table` | Cheap to rebuild; reads are instant; no incremental complexity warranted. |
| Frequently changing upstream with no reliable update key, queried rarely | `view` | Always consistent with upstream; avoids rebuild cost when reads are rare. |
| Append-heavy fact table with a `loaded_at` column and millions of new rows per day | `incremental` | Full rebuild is wasteful; only new rows matter; `is_incremental()` + `unique_key` handle the delta. |
| A named CTE you want to reuse across two or three marts but never query directly | `ephemeral` | Modularity without materialisation cost; inlined into downstreams at compile time. |
| Staging layer with light transformation over a small source table | `view` (the default) | Freshness matters more than read performance for stage models; rebuild cost is near-zero. |
| Final mart consumed by a BI tool that times out on view reads | `table` | Read-performance wins; rebuild cost amortised across many reads. |
| Large fact table where 95% of rows are new per run and 5% are late-arriving updates | `incremental` with `merge` strategy + `unique_key` | Captures late-arriving updates without full rebuild. |

Memorise the shape of this table. The exam asks "given X, pick the materialization" questions in several slightly different wordings; the underlying decision is always one of the seven rows above.

---

## 4.2 `{{ config(materialized='...') }}` in context

Ch 2 §2.4 introduced dbt's three-level config precedence. Here it is again, with materialization as the worked example:

1. **`{{ config() }}` in the model's SQL file** — highest precedence. Wins over everything.
2. **YAML `config:` in the model's `.yml` properties file** — middle. Overridden by an SQL-level `config()` on the same model.
3. **`dbt_project.yml` `+config` by folder path** — lowest. The default that SQL and YAML configs override.

"More specific wins" is the one-sentence summary. The `materialized` key follows exactly that rule.

> **What about SCD2 history?** The four materializations above all overwrite or append; none track *every historical version* of a row. For SCD2 — capturing every change to source rows with `valid_from/valid_to` columns — dbt provides **snapshots**, a separate resource type with its own command (`dbt snapshot`) and its own teaching home in **Ch 5**. If a question asks "which dbt construct gives me every prior version of every customer row?" the answer is *snapshot*, not *incremental.*

## Folder-level default + per-file override

Here's the pattern you'll see in every non-trivial project: set a folder default in `dbt_project.yml`, then override in individual SQL files as needed.

```
# dbt_project.yml
name: 'credora'
version: '1.0.0'
profile: 'credora'

models:
  credora:
    staging:
      +materialized: view       # all staging models are views by default
    intermediate:
      +materialized: ephemeral  # int_ models are inlined unless individually overridden
    marts:
      +materialized: table      # all marts are tables by default
      finance:
        fct_transactions:
          +materialized: incremental  # one file in finance overrides to incremental
```

The `+` prefix is dbt's signal that the key is a *config* (applies to resources inside this folder) rather than a *property* (applies to the folder itself). Folder paths nest: `models.credora.marts.finance.fct_transactions` matches only the `fct_transactions.sql` file inside `models/marts/finance/`. See `/reference/resource-configs/materialized` for the documented shape of the key.

## Overriding from the SQL file

A single model can override the folder default by setting `{{ config() }}` at the top:

```
-- models/marts/finance/fct_transactions.sql
{{ config(
    materialized='incremental',
    unique_key='transaction_id',
    on_schema_change='sync_all_columns',
    incremental_strategy='merge'
) }}

select
    transaction_id,
    customer_id,
    amount,
    loaded_at
from {{ ref('stg_transactions') }}

{% if is_incremental() %}
where loaded_at > (select max(loaded_at) from {{ this }})
```

```
{% endif %}
```

The SQL-level `config()` wins over the YAML override and the `dbt_project.yml` default. If two sources disagree on the same key, the SQL file is authoritative — always. This is a common "why isn't my config taking effect?" trap, and it's an easy exam question target.

### The YAML middle layer

You can also set `materialized` in a model's `.yml` properties file:

```
# models/marts/finance/_finance_models.yml
version: 2

models:
  - name: fct_transactions
    config:
      materialized: incremental
      unique_key: transaction_id
```

The YAML `config:` block sits between `dbt_project.yml` and the SQL file. In practice, teams pick one of two conventions — "all config in SQL" or "structural config in YAML, tactical config in SQL" — and stick with it. Either works; inconsistency within a single project is what causes the debugging pain.

---

## 4.3 Incremental models in depth

An incremental model has five concerns. Memorise the checklist:

1. **The materialization keyword** — `materialized='incremental'`.
2. **The `is_incremental()` guard** — a Jinja `{% if %}` block that filters the `select` to only new rows when the model already exists.
3. **A `unique_key`** — how dbt identifies which rows in the target are the same row as an incoming row.
4. **An `on_schema_change` policy** — what dbt does when the model's columns diverge from the target table's columns.
5. **An `incremental_strategy`** — how dbt physically combines new rows with existing rows (`merge`, `append`, `delete+insert`, `insert_overwrite`).

Get any one of these wrong and the model either silently drops rows, silently duplicates them, or fails on the next schema change. The rest of this section is each concern in turn.

### 4.3.1 The `is_incremental()` guard

`is_incremental()` is a Jinja macro that returns `True` exactly when:

- The model is configured as `materialized='incremental'`, AND
- The model's target table already exists in the warehouse (i.e. not a first run), AND
- The run is NOT in full-refresh **mode**. Note the wording: this is not "the flag was not passed". `full_refresh: false` configured on the model overrides `--full-refresh`, so the flag is on the command line and `is_incremental()` is still `True`; `full_refresh: true` puts the run in full-refresh mode with no flag at all (§4.5).

The macro is documented in the incremental-models guide at `/docs/build/incremental-models#understand-the-is_incremental-macro`, where the standard usage pattern is also illustrated.

The standard pattern:

```
{{ config(
    materialized='incremental',
    unique_key='order_id'
) }}

select
    order_id,
    customer_id,
    order_total,
    ordered_at
from {{ ref('stg_orders') }}

{% if is_incremental() %}
where ordered_at > (select max(ordered_at) from {{ this }})
{% endif %}
```

Read this carefully:

- On a **first run**, the table does not exist. `is_incremental()` returns `False`. The `{% if %}` block compiles away. dbt executes `CREATE TABLE AS (select ... from stg_orders)` — a full rebuild.
- On every **subsequent run**, the table exists. `is_incremental()` returns `True`. The `where` clause is compiled in, restricting the `select` to rows newer than the most recent row already in the target. dbt then merges those new rows per the configured strategy.
- If you run `dbt run --full-refresh` on a model whose `full_refresh` config is unset, dbt drops and recreates the existing table from scratch — `is_incremental()` returns `False` even though the table existed before the run started. Set `full_refresh: false` on the model and the same command leaves it on the incremental branch (§4.5).

The `{{ this }}` variable, documented at `/reference/dbt-jinja-functions/this`, resolves to the fully-qualified name of the current model's target relation. It's how you reference the model's own warehouse identity inside its own SQL — essential for the "newer than what's already there" self-query pattern above.

### 4.3.2 `unique_key`

`unique_key` tells dbt which column (or expression, or list of columns) identifies a row as "the same row" across runs. It's used by the `merge` and `delete+insert` strategies to find which rows in the target to update when an incoming batch contains late-arriving changes.

The standard shapes:

```
-- Single column
{{ config(materialized='incremental', unique_key='order_id') }}

-- Composite key (list syntax)
{{ config(materialized='incremental', unique_key=['market', 'order_id']) }}
```

See `/reference/resource-configs/unique_key` for the full reference, including the composite-key and expression forms.

Two exam gotchas:

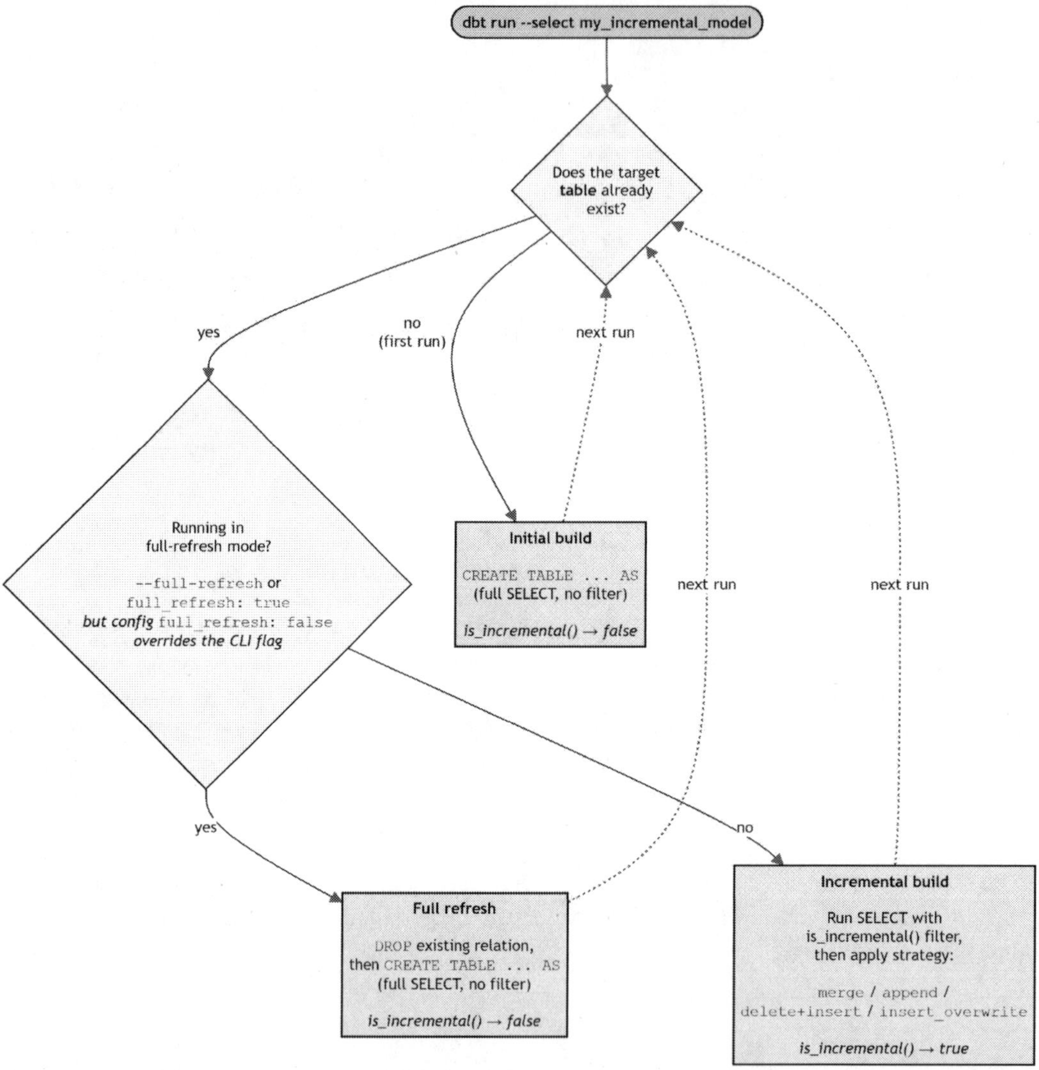


Figure 4.1: Decision tree for an incremental model run. The two questions dbt answers internally — *does the target table already exist?* and *is the run in full-refresh mode?* — determine which of the three branches executes and what `is_incremental()` returns inside the model SQL. Note the second one is not simply "was `--full-refresh` passed": a model configured `full_refresh: false` overrides the CLI flag and stays on the incremental branch. **`microbatch` does not follow this tree** — its body carries no `is_incremental()` guard and dbt runs one statement per batch rather than one per run; §4.4 has that path.

- If you **omit** `unique_key` under the `append` strategy, dbt will blindly insert every incoming row — you'll get duplicates for any row that was already in the target.
- If your `unique_key` column actually has duplicates in the incoming batch, the strategies that rely on uniqueness do not agree on what to do about it. On Snowflake, `merge` fails outright with a nondeterministic-merge error rather than picking a winner; the documented way out is to switch the model to `delete+insert`, which deletes and reinserts whole key groups and so tolerates a key that is not truly unique. A `unique` test tells you the duplication is there. The strategy is what lets the model build.

### 4.3.3 on_schema_change

Incremental models live with a tension: the warehouse table's column list was frozen at the last run, but your model SQL may have since added or removed columns. `on_schema_change` tells dbt what to do when it detects that divergence at the start of a run.

Four values, documented at the `/docs/build/incremental-models#what-if-the-columns-of-my-incremental-model-change` section "What if the columns of my incremental model change?":

| Value | Behaviour | Choose it when |
|---|---|---|
| `ignore` | The default. dbt does nothing for added columns (they are silently dropped from the insert). If a column is removed from the SQL, the run fails. | Rarely on purpose — it is what you get by not choosing, and it is behind the classic "my new column is always NULL" report. |
| `fail` | dbt raises an error if the column set differs. Forces you to either fix the SQL or run `--full-refresh`. | A schema change should be a deliberate human decision, not an automatic migration. |
| `append_new_columns` | dbt runs `ALTER TABLE ADD COLUMN` for any new columns in the SQL; does not remove columns that were removed from the SQL. The added column is **not backfilled** — and that is true of the whole config: none of the four values revisits a row already in the target, so every pre-existing row holds `NULL` in the new column until something reprocesses it, which means `--full-refresh`. | The safest default for production data: old historical columns stay readable and new ones arrive without a full rebuild. |
| `sync_all_columns` | dbt adds new columns AND removes columns that are no longer in the SQL. The target's schema follows the model's SQL exactly. | You trust the SQL to be the schema of record and accept losing historical columns when they are removed. |

### 4.3.4 Incremental strategies, and choosing one

An incremental model is the one materialization where re-running is not automatically safe. A `table` is rebuilt by `create or replace`, a `view` is redefined, and both land in the same state whether you run them once or fifty times. An incremental model carries state across runs — its result depends on what is already in the target — which makes it the easiest place in a dbt project to break **idempotence**, the expectation that a second run leaves the warehouse where the first one did. The overview page raises idempotence before it explains a single config, and that is the right frame for everything below: see `/docs/build/incremental-models-overview` and `/best-practices/idempotence`.

The **incremental strategy** is the mechanism — how dbt combines the new-rows result set with the rows already in the target. You set it with `incremental_strategy='...'`. Five ship in dbt Core. See `/docs/build/incremental-strategy`.

| Strategy | What it does | Key config |
|---|---|---|
| `append` | `INSERT INTO target (select ... new rows)`. No dedup; no update of existing rows. Fast, simple, and duplicates anything the delta filter lets through twice. | none |
| `merge` | `MERGE INTO target USING (new rows) ON unique_key WHEN MATCHED UPDATE ... WHEN NOT MATCHED INSERT` .... Updates late-arriving rows in place. | `unique_key` |
| `delete+insert` | Delete from the target every row whose `unique_key` appears in the incoming batch, then insert the batch. Same net effect as `merge`; different mechanism. | `unique_key` |
| `insert_overwrite` | Replace whole partitions of the target with the incoming batch's partitions. | `partition_by` |
| `microbatch` | Split the load into independent, time-bounded batches driven by an `event_time` column, one query per batch. Its own section — §4.4. | `event_time`, `begin`, `batch_size` |

`merge` and `delete+insert` are less far apart than the table makes them look. Where the warehouse has a native `MERGE`, dbt issues one; where it does not, dbt deletes the matching rows and inserts the batch — the `delete+insert` mechanism under the `merge` name. That fallback is the durable fact, with one carve-out worth carrying: BigQuery offers no `delete+insert` at all, so on that adapter the pair is not a pair. Which strategies a given adapter offers is not durable — availability is uneven and moves between releases — so read the adapter's own config page (`/reference/resource-configs/bigquery-configs`, `/reference/resource-configs/databricks-configs`, and the equivalents) rather than a memorised snapshot of the matrix.

What the exam expects is narrower and more stable: which strategies exist, that you select one with `incremental_strategy='...'`, that availability is adapter-dependent, and what each one does to a row already sitting in the target.

**Choosing between them is a question about the data, not about the adapter.** Read the shape of the dataset first; the strategy follows.

| Dataset shape | Strategy | Why |
|---|---|---|
| Append-only events at volume; rows are never revised once loaded | `append` | Nothing to match on and nothing to update. Matching would be pure cost. |
| Late-arriving updates to rows already loaded, keyed on a stable identifier | `merge` — or `delete+insert` where `MERGE` is not native | Only an upsert keeps the target correct when yesterday's row changes today. |
| Partitioned table where a whole partition is recomputed at once | `insert_overwrite` | Replacing a partition is one cheap operation; row-level matching inside it is wasted work. |
| Time-series events at a scale where one statement per run is too big to run, retry, or reason about | `microbatch` (§4.4) | Turns one statement into many independent, individually retryable ones. |
| Rows update often and unpredictably, or the table rebuilds inside the run window anyway | not incremental at all — `table` | Incremental complexity has to buy something. Where a rebuild is affordable, buy correctness instead. |

When a stem gives you row volume, arrival pattern and update rate in the same breath, it is asking you to run that table.

**Narrowing what a merge updates.** By default a `merge` overwrites the whole matched row with the incoming values. Two configs cut that down, and both are read only by the `merge` strategy: `merge_update_columns` takes a list and updates *only* those columns, keeping the stored value of every other one; `merge_exclude_columns` takes the complement, updating everything *except* the columns you name. Use one or the other, and use them when a column has to survive a merge intact — a first-seen timestamp, an originally quoted price, a manually corrected value:

```
{{ config(
    materialized='incremental',
    unique_key='customer_id',
    incremental_strategy='merge',
    merge_exclude_columns=['first_seen_at']
) }}
```

Both are documented on `/docs/build/incremental-strategy`. Set either one under any other strategy and it is dropped without a warning: `delete+insert` and `append` write whole rows on the way in, so there is no update statement for a column list to narrow. A column config is only as good as the `incremental_strategy` sitting beside it — and §4.3.5 shows how easily that goes unnamed.

`incremental_predicates` is the neighbouring config, and it is nearer than its name suggests. Its expressions are `and`-ed into the same `MERGE`'s `on` clause, alongside the generated key match, using the `DBT_INTERNAL_DEST` and `DBT_INTERNAL_SOURCE` aliases; dbt does not check them. What matters is what they narrow. A predicate narrows what counts as a *match* — it does not filter the incoming rows — so a row the predicate excludes takes the `when not matched` branch and is inserted a second time. On a model with no other de-duplication, a predicate is a duplicate generator for every row outside its window.

**The `unique_key` dependency.** `merge` and `delete+insert` are meaningful only with a `unique_key`. Leave it out and the adapter falls back to `append`, per `/reference/resource-configs/unique_key` — no error, no warning, and a duplicate for every row the delta filter re-processes. BigQuery is the exception: `MERGE` requires an `ON` clause, so a missing `unique_key` there surfaces as a failure rather than a silent append. `append` and `insert_overwrite` do not use `unique_key` at all; `insert_overwrite` partitions on `partition_by` instead.

### 4.3.5 Which strategy runs when you name none

`incremental_strategy` has no universal default. Leave it out and the **adapter** picks, and the adapters do not agree: `merge` on Snowflake, BigQuery and Databricks; `append` on Spark; and on Postgres and Redshift the pick turns on your own config — `append` with no `unique_key`, `delete+insert` with one. See `/reference/resource-configs/postgres-configs` and the equivalent page for whichever adapter you sit on. Learn the rule rather than the table: the adapter decides, and a `unique_key` can change its mind.

Read the Postgres row twice, because it is the one the companion project runs on. A model that sets `unique_key='customer_id'` and `merge_exclude_columns=['first_seen_at']` and names no strategy is not running a merge. It is running `delete+insert`; the exclusion is discarded without a word, and `first_seen_at` is overwritten on every matched row. The model builds, the run reports OK, and the column the config existed to protect is gone. Name the strategy.

**When the key is not unique.** `merge` needs one target row per key, and §4.3.2's warning has a strategy-level answer: `delete+insert` deletes every target row whose key appears in the incoming batch and reinserts the batch whole, so a duplicated key produces duplicated rows rather than a failed run. That is a decision about which mechanism you want, not a data-quality fix — the duplicates are still there.

**`insert_overwrite` is not one operation.** On BigQuery and Spark it replaces whole partitions and wants a `partition_by`; Spark without one replaces the entire table. On Snowflake it is not partition-based at all — it truncates and reinserts, with `overwrite_columns` deciding which columns take part. Carry the BigQuery meaning to Snowflake and you will predict the wrong thing.

**What each one costs.** The docs are direct about this, and §4.3.4's decision table leaves it out. `merge` scans the entire destination table to find its matches, which is what makes it a better fit for smaller targets than for enormous ones; `delete+insert` may be less efficient for larger datasets; `append` checks nothing, which is both why it is the cheapest and why it duplicates. Target size is a characteristic of the dataset exactly as much as arrival pattern is. When a stem gives you both, use both.

**A strategy name is a macro lookup, with one guard in front of it.** dbt resolves `incremental_strategy: X` by looking for a macro called `get_incremental_X_sql`. The only list it checks the token against first is the **builtin** set — the five in §4.3.4's table — and a builtin the adapter has not declared valid stops there: on dbt-postgres, `incremental_strategy='insert_overwrite'` fails with `The incremental strategy 'insert_overwrite' is not valid for this adapter`. That check is the only thing stopping it, too, because dbt Core does ship a `get_incremental_insert_overwrite_sql` and the lookup would otherwise find it. A token that is **not** a builtin skips the guard altogether, which is why a typo does not report itself as an invalid strategy, and does not report itself at parse time either — `dbt parse` and `dbt compile` both exit 0 on `incremental_strategy='megre'`, and the run then fails with `dbt could not find an incremental strategy macro with the name "get_incremental_megre_sql"`. Two different messages, and which one you get tells you whether you mistyped a name or named a real strategy this adapter does not offer. The same convention is what lets a project define a strategy of its own, though not on BigQuery or Spark, which do not support custom strategies. See `/docs/build/incremental-strategy`.

### 4.3.6 A fully-configured incremental model

Pulling it all together:

```
-- models/marts/core/fct_orders.sql
{{ config(
    materialized='incremental',
    unique_key='order_id',
    on_schema_change='append_new_columns',
    incremental_strategy='merge'
) }}

select
    order_id,
    customer_id,
    status,
    order_total,
    ordered_at
from {{ ref('stg_orders') }}

{% if is_incremental() %}
where ordered_at > (select max(ordered_at) from {{ this }})
{% endif %}
```

Every line matters. Drop `unique_key` and `merge` can't find matching rows. Drop the `{% if is_incremental() %}` block and dbt re-reads the entire upstream on every run (functionally equivalent to a `table` materialization that pays the merge cost on top). Change `append_new_columns` to `ignore` and a new column added to `stg_orders` will silently arrive as NULLs. Forget to run `--full-refresh` after a backfill in `stg_orders` and the incremental will never pick up the backfilled rows, because they're older than `max(ordered_at)`.

### 4.3.7 `event_time`

`event_time` is the name of a **config**, not of a column. Its value is the name of a column in your own relation, and dbt neither expects nor enforces any convention about what that column is called — `ordered_at`, `session_began_at`, `occurred_at` and `last_loaded_ts` are all legal values, which is why the examples in this section deliberately use a different name each time. Two things about the column do matter. It has to be a **date or a timestamp**, because dbt filters on it by inlining a UTC timestamp literal, and a column the warehouse cannot compare against one fails — not always loudly. And it should record **when the row's event actually happened**, a choice this section returns to after the examples.

Setting it changes nothing about how a model is built. What it changes is that the relation becomes time-aware, and three dbt features read it — but not in the same way, and the difference is assessable:

- **microbatch** filters every upstream `ref()` and `source()` that declares it, once per batch (§4.4). **Required**: without it there is no column to filter on.
- `--sample` narrows a run to a time window on the relations that declare it (Ch 11). **Required**, for the same reason — a relation without `event_time` is passed through whole.

- **Advanced CI's compare-changes** uses it to line up the same slice of time in CI and in production. **Recommended, not required**: the comparison runs without it and is simply less like-for-like.

So "removing `event_time` breaks three features" is too strong. It disables two and degrades the third.

Reference: `/reference/resource-configs/event-time`.

Four resource types accept it — **models, seeds, snapshots and sources**. Sources are the entry most often left off that list, and the one worth committing to memory.

It is a config, so it takes the same three surfaces §4.2 established for `materialized`, with the same precedence:

```
# dbt_project.yml - folder default
models:
  credora:
    marts:
      +event_time: ordered_at
```

```
# models/staging/_staging_sources.yml - on the source, not only on the model reading it
sources:
  - name: raw_ecom
    config:
      event_time: created_at
    tables:
      - name: orders
```

```
-- models/marts/fct_orders.sql - inline, highest precedence
{{ config(materialized='incremental', event_time='ordered_at') }}
```

**Prefer a real event timestamp over an ingestion column.** `account_created_at` and `session_began_at` are events: they happened once, at a fixed moment, and they never move. `_fivetran_synced` is not — it records when your loader wrote the row. `last_updated_at` is not — it moves when the row is edited, so the same row falls into a different batch on a later run. The docs allow ingestion timestamps where they are genuinely the only timestamps you have, and are direct about the price: with `loaded_at` or `last_updated_at` you can accumulate duplicate rows across runs, and a `lookback` window shrinks that without eliminating it; with an `ingested_at` column, a connector resync moves rows onto a new date and reprocesses them.

The *type* is not negotiable in the way the *name* is. dbt never inspects the column: it rewrites the upstream reference as `where <your column> >= '<batch start>' and <your column> < '<batch end>'` with both bounds inlined as **UTC timestamp strings**, and leaves the comparison to the warehouse. Verified at 1.11.14 on dbt-postgres with one source, six batches and `event_time` pointed at four different columns carrying the same instant: the `timestamp` and `date` columns each loaded the day's row; a `bigint` of epoch seconds failed the first batch outright with `invalid input syntax for type bigint` and skipped the other five; and a `text` column did not error at all — which is the dangerous case, because it does not fail cleanly either. Both sides are compared as strings, so most rows land in the right batch and the ones on a boundary do not: a stored `2026-09-04 00:00:00` is *shorter* than the inlined `2026-09-04 00:00:00+00:00` and therefore sorts before it, so a row stamped exactly midnight falls into the previous batch — or out of the run altogether when that boundary is `begin`. A row at 09:15 on the same day is filtered correctly, which is exactly why this survives a casual test: the fixture that first exposed it happened to stamp every row at midnight, so every batch came back empty and the failure looked total. It is not total; it is a silent, boundary-only misplacement, which is harder to notice and harder to trust. A date loaded as a string is the ordinary way to meet this, and the fix is to cast it in staging rather than to declare `event_time` on the raw text.

In practice the expensive mistake is declaring `event_time` on the model doing the reading rather than on the relation being read. Running `--sample` against a source with no `event_time` — the model had the config, the source did not — succeeded, reported OK, and processed the whole table; adding `config: {event_time: created_at}` to the source cut the same command to the rows inside the requested window. Nothing in the output distinguished the two runs. The rule generalises past `--sample`: the config has to sit on the relation dbt is being asked to filter.

---

## 4.4 Microbatch — one model, many independent batches

Every incremental model in §4.3 runs as a **single statement**. dbt compiles one `select`, wraps it in one merge or insert, and the whole node either succeeds or fails. That holds up until the table is large enough that one statement is too slow to run, too expensive to retry, and too coarse to reason about — at which point you want the same load broken into pieces that succeed and fail on their own.

That is what `microbatch` does. It is an incremental strategy like the other four, configured the same way, and it changes the unit of work: instead of one query over "everything new", dbt plans a series of time-bounded batches and issues **one query per batch**. Each batch is atomic and idempotent — reprocessing it produces exactly the rows it produced the first time — which is what lets dbt run batches concurrently and retry only the ones that failed. Reference: `/docs/build/incremental-microbatch`.

> **Runnable locally.** Unlike §4.7 and §4.8, every claim in this section runs on the Postgres companion repo. Run them. The `unique_key` behaviour in §4.4.5 is one you will only believe after you have watched batch 1 go green.

### 4.4.1 Three required configs, and two that matter

| Config | What it sets | Default |
|---|---|---|
| `event_time` | The column that says when the row occurred. Required on the microbatch model, and on any parent you want filtered. | none — required |
| `begin` | The beginning of time for this model: where the first build, and any full refresh, starts from. | none — required |
| `batch_size` | Batch granularity — `hour`, `day`, `month`, or `year`. | none — required |
| `lookback` | How many batches back from the current time to reprocess on an incremental run, to catch late arrivals. | `1` |
| `concurrent_batches` | Override for dbt's parallel-batch auto-detection. | unset |

Two of those are recall drills waiting to happen. **`batch_size` has no `week`** — the four values in the table are the whole set. And `lookback` accepts any integer greater than or equal to zero; see `/reference/resource-configs/lookback`.

### 4.4.2 The model body carries no guard

```
-- models/marts/fct_orders_microbatch.sql
{{ config(
    materialized='incremental',
    incremental_strategy='microbatch',
    event_time='order_created_at',
    begin='2024-01-01',
    batch_size='month',
    lookback=1,
    unique_key='order_id'
) }}

select
    order_id,
    customer_id,
    order_total,
    order_created_at
from {{ ref('stg_orders') }}
```

That is the entire model. There is no `{% if is_incremental() %}` block and no date predicate, and writing either would be a mistake. dbt supplies the filter itself, rewriting each upstream reference per batch. `stg_orders` declares an `event_time` of its own — `created_at` — and that is the column dbt filters it on, so the compiled SQL for the March 2024 batch reads:

```
select
    order_id,
    customer_id,
    order_total,
    order_created_at
from (
    select * from "credora"."dev"."stg_orders"
    where created_at >= '2024-03-01 00:00:00+00:00'
      and created_at <  '2024-04-01 00:00:00+00:00'
) _dbt_et_filter_subq_stg_orders
```

You write the model as though it processes exactly one batch, because it does — and that assumption is the point of the strategy. §4.3.1 installed the habit of hand-writing the delta filter; microbatch is the one place you must not. In practice, on Postgres, an unguarded `select` over `stg_orders` partitions the whole table cleanly across every monthly batch without a single predicate in the model SQL.

The same simplification is why a microbatch model previews sensibly: a compiled batch is a complete, bounded query you can read and run.

### 4.4.3 Where a row on the boundary lands

Read the predicate dbt generated for the March batch once more: `created_at >= '2024-03-01 00:00:00+00:00' and created_at < '2024-04-01 00:00:00+00:00'`. Every batch window is **half-open** — inclusive at its start, exclusive at its end — so a row stamped exactly `2024-04-01 00:00:00` UTC is not the last row of March. It is the first row of April. No batch ever claims a row twice, and no row between `begin` and now falls through the gaps.

The same bounds are readable from Jinja while a batch is running, through `model.batch`:

| Attribute | What it holds |
| --- | --- |
| `model.batch.id` | The batch's identifier, derived from the start of its window. |
| `model.batch.event_time_start` | The window's lower bound — **inclusive**. |
| `model.batch.event_time_end` | The window's upper bound — **exclusive**. |

Outside batch execution `model.batch` is `None`, so anything that reads it needs a guard: a macro that reaches for `model.batch.id` unconditionally breaks the first time it is called from a model that is not a microbatch batch. See `/reference/dbt-jinja-functions/model`.

### 4.4.4 How many batches dbt runs

dbt does not look at your data to decide. It derives the batch list from `begin`, `batch_size` and the current time, and it has no idea what your earliest row is.

The consequence catches people out. A model with `begin='2024-01-01'` and `batch_size='month'` plans one batch for every month from January 2024 up to and including the current one — a plan that grows by one every month, whatever the data does. The months your source never reached are not a bug: they run, they select nothing, they write nothing, and they report OK. Batch count is a function of `begin`, granularity, and the clock.

`begin` is therefore the only thing standing between you and a batch plan reaching back to the beginning of time, and it is not a filter on your data — it is the model's declared starting point. Set it to the earliest date the model should ever cover, and no earlier. Whatever you set, the value must parse as an ISO date or date-and-time: `2024-01-01`, `2024-01-01 06:30:00` and `2024-01-01T06:30:00` all parse, while `begin='3 days ago'` — or a non-ISO `01/01/2024` — stops the run at parse with `must provide a 'begin' config of valid datetime (ISO format)`. So there is no natural-language relative literal, but there *is* a documented relative form: compute the ISO string in Jinja, as in `begin=(modules.datetime.datetime.now() - modules.datetime.timedelta(1)).isoformat()`. Reach for it deliberately or not at all — a computed `begin` slides the whole batch plan forward with the clock, which is the opposite of what a table meant to cover a fixed history needs. See `/reference/resource-configs/begin`.

**When dbt actually reads `begin`, and the pattern that follows from it.** `begin` is consulted only when the plan has to be built from scratch — the first build, and any `--full-refresh`. A plain incremental run never looks at it: move `begin` from three days back to thirty and an incremental run still plans the same two batches, while a full refresh goes from four to thirty-one. And `--event-time-start` is not floored by it — with `begin` at three days back, a backfill window twenty days earlier runs its five batches without complaint.

That combination is worth exploiting. Set `begin` to a computed recent value — `begin=(modules.datetime.datetime.now() - modules.datetime.timedelta(3)).isoformat()` — and a full refresh rebuilds three days instead of three years, in seconds, with no date hard-coded in the model that somebody has to remember to move. Then load whatever history you actually want as a separate, deliberate job:

```
dbt run --select fct_orders --full-refresh                          # cheap: rebuilds the
    last 3 days
dbt run --select fct_orders \
        --event-time-start "2024-01-01" --event-time-end "2026-09-01"   # then the
    history you want
```

**The second command is not optional.** A full refresh does not merge into what is already there; it rebuilds the model over the batches it plans, and everything outside them is gone. A table holding thirty-one days, full-refreshed with `begin` at three days back, comes out holding four — exit 0, no warning. So this pattern trades a slow full refresh for a fast one *plus a backfill you must actually run*, and it is the right trade only where a full refresh is an operational event somebody is watching, not something a scheduler does unattended. Where the model is meant to hold a fixed history and be refreshed by a job nobody reads the output of, keep `begin` at the earliest date the model should ever cover.

`lookback` reprocesses the last N batches *counting back from now* on each incremental run, so a row that arrives late still lands in the batch it belongs to. dbt keeps no high-water mark for a microbatch model: the plan is built from the current time backwards, and neither `begin` nor the last successful run is an input to it.

**So an incremental run never catches up, and this is the config's sharpest edge.** If the job stops for longer than `lookback` — a paused scheduler, a broken credential, a week of failed runs — the batches in that gap are simply never planned again. The next successful run processes its `lookback` window, reports OK, and leaves a hole in the middle of the table that nothing will ever fill on its own. There is no error and no warning; the run is green.

Filling it is a deliberate act:

```
dbt run --select fct_orders --event-time-start "2025-09-01" --event-time-end "2025-10-01
    "
```

`--event-time-start` is inclusive and `--event-time-end` is exclusive, so the window above is September and nothing else; §4.4.7 has the rest of the flag rules. Only `dbt run` and `dbt build` accept them: `dbt retry` does not, because it reruns what *failed*, and a run that silently skipped a window did not fail.

One more detail worth committing: dbt plans `lookback + 1` batches, not `lookback`. `lookback: 3` on daily batches plans four — the current, partially-elapsed batch plus the three behind it. This is not a special case that fires on a boundary; it is what every incremental microbatch run does.

### 4.4.5 How a batch is replaced — and the `unique_key` trap

Microbatch uses the most efficient full-batch replacement mechanism each adapter offers, under the one config name:

| Adapter | Replacement mechanism |
|---|---|
| dbt-postgres | `merge` |
| dbt-redshift | `delete+insert` |
| dbt-snowflake | `delete+insert` |
| dbt-bigquery | `insert_overwrite` |
| dbt-spark | `insert_overwrite` |
| dbt-databricks | `replace_where` |

You do not choose the mechanism. You choose `microbatch`, and the adapter decides — which is exactly why the *key* requirement is adapter-specific. On dbt-postgres the mechanism is `merge`, and a merge needs something to match on, so **`unique_key` is required**. On BigQuery and Spark the mechanism replaces a partition wholesale, matches on the batch's time bounds, and needs no key at all; those two require `partition_by` instead.

In practice, on Postgres, the failure does not arrive where you would look for it. A microbatch model configured with `event_time`, `begin` and `batch_size` and **no** `unique_key` ran like this — and note the batch count, which is derived from `begin`, `batch_size` and **the clock at run time**, never from the data, so it is one higher every month you re-run this:

```
Batch 1 of 33 OK created batch 2024-01 ........................ [SELECT 0 in 0.10s]
Batch 2 of 33 ERROR creating batch 2024-02 .................... [ERROR in 0.04s]

Compilation Error in model fct_orders_microbatch
  dbt-postgres 'microbatch' requires a `unique_key` config
```

Every batch after the first failed identically. Batch 1 succeeded because a full refresh *creates* the relation on the first batch without taking the incremental code path — there is nothing to merge into yet, so the missing config cannot surface, and it succeeds even selecting zero rows. Adding `unique_key='order_id'` took the same model to a green run on every batch and a fully populated target. **One green batch is a false positive.** That is the trap in full, and the assumption behind it is the natural one: that microbatch, planning its own batches, supersedes `unique_key`.

Both absolutes are wrong, and an exam item will offer you one of them. "Microbatch never needs a `unique_key`" is false on Postgres. "Microbatch always needs one" is false on BigQuery. Answer the adapter, not the strategy.

### 4.4.6 Upstream `event_time`, and opting out

dbt can only time-filter an upstream `ref()` or `source()` that declares an `event_time` of its own. An upstream without one is not an error — dbt reads the whole relation, **once per batch**, so that parent is scanned in full as many times as the plan has batches, and the run reports OK throughout. It is silent too, as long as *some* input declares `event_time`; when **no** `ref()` or `source()` input has one, parse warns `The microbatch model '<name>' has no 'ref' or 'source' input with an 'event_time' configuration`, because then no filtering happens at all. The failure mode is a bill, not a stack trace.

The rule from §4.3.7 therefore applies twice over here: declare `event_time` on every parent you want filtered, at the parent. A dimensional parent with no meaningful event timestamp — a `customers` table whose old rows change as readily as its new ones — is simply scanned in full each batch, and that is documented, expected behaviour rather than a misconfiguration.

Where you want an exemption deliberately, `{{ ref('customers').render() }}` opts a single reference out of auto-filtering. Use it sparingly: most relations that declare `event_time` are large, which is why they declare it. It is not a microbatch keyword: the same method exempts a reference from more than this one rewrite, and Ch 11 §11.11 owns the family.

### 4.4.7 Backfilling a window

Reprocessing a stretch of history — bad source data, or a business-logic change that has to be applied retroactively — is a pair of flags:

```
dbt run --select fct_orders_microbatch \
        --event-time-start "2024-09-01" --event-time-end "2024-09-04"
```

Three things to hold on to. The two flags are **mutually necessary**: specify one and you must specify the other. Every time value in the microbatch surface — the `event_time` column, `begin`, and both flags — is interpreted as **UTC**, with no per-model timezone config. And `--full-refresh` is *not* a window backfill: on a microbatch model it reprocesses everything from `begin`, which is a rebuild. If you meant "reload September", the flags above are the tool; §4.5 covers what `--full-refresh` is for.

Because a rebuild from `begin` is rarely what anyone wants on a table large enough to need microbatching in the first place, the docs recommend setting `full_refresh: false` on microbatch models so they ignore the flag outright.

### 4.4.8 Retry, and running batches in parallel

Batches fail independently, so they recover independently: `dbt retry` reruns **only** the failed batches. Contrast a conventional incremental, which is a single node — one failure fails the whole model, and a retry redoes all of it. Ch 12 covers `dbt retry` in full.

**A custom strategy has to opt into batching, and at 1.11 it does not have to say so.** If your project defines its own `get_incremental_microbatch_sql` macro — inherited from a pre-microbatch codebase, say — dbt hands it one batch at a time only when `require_batched_execution_for_custom_microbatch_strategy` is on. That flag is **off by default at 1.11**, and with it off the macro is called once for the whole range: the per-batch `event_time_start` and `event_time_end` it never reads are simply not applied, and the model reprocesses everything on every run. It does not error, and the run still reports success — but it is not silent: dbt emits a deprecation at parse time on **every** invocation, naming the flag and the fix outright — `[WARNING]: The use of a custom microbatch macro outside of batched execution is deprecated.` The console line carries no code; under `--log-format json` the same event is `D020`, `MicrobatchMacroOutsideOfBatchesDeprecation`. Scroll past that line and the only remaining symptom is a microbatch model whose cost never falls after the first backfill — so when batching "isn't working", read the deprecations at the top of the run before you re-read the configs, and look for a project-level override of that macro.

Batches can also *run* in parallel, and dbt decides for itself whether they may. The detection is mechanical: if the model's SQL references `{{ this }}`, batches run **sequentially**, because concurrent writers against the relation being written conflict. Otherwise they may run in parallel, bounded by the thread count. `concurrent_batches` is an override on that decision rather than a gate — set it `false` for cumulative metrics, or any logic where one batch depends on another having finished, and `true` to force parallelism dbt declined to infer. See `/docs/build/parallel-batch-execution#how-parallel-batch-execution-works` and `/reference/resource-properties/concurrent_batches`.

Parallel *execution* is narrower than the override suggests, and this is the part worth reading twice. It requires **Snowflake or BigQuery**, and even there **the first batch and the last batch never run in parallel**. That is a different list from the six-row replacement table in §4.4.5, and the two resemble each other closely enough to be confused on purpose: Spark replaces a batch by `insert_overwrite` exactly as BigQuery does, and Spark is not on the parallel-execution list. See `/docs/build/parallel-batch-execution`.

---

## 4.5 `--full-refresh` and when to reach for it

Before that, one thing dbt never does. **Deleting a model does not drop its relation.** dbt creates and replaces objects for the nodes in the DAG; a node that has left the DAG is not visited, so the table or view it built stays in the warehouse holding whatever it held on the last run. The same goes for a model switched from `table` or `view` to `ephemeral` — ephemeral models build no relation, and the one it used to build is left behind.

Neither case warns you, and both are worse than clutter. The orphan is still queryable, still appears in the BI tool, and is now frozen at a date nobody recorded, so a dashboard pointed at it keeps returning plausible stale numbers indefinitely. Dropping it is manual, and it belongs in the same pull request as the deletion.

`dbt run --full-refresh` — documented at `/reference/commands/run` — tells dbt to drop and rebuild incremental models from scratch for this one run. The materialization stays `incremental`; what changes is that `is_incremental()` returns false, so the `where ordered_at > (select max(...) from {{ this }})` guard is omitted and the model rebuilds from the full upstream.

When to use it:

| Situation | Why an incremental run leaves it broken |
|---|---|
| Schema drift past `on_schema_change`'s automatic handling | Under `ignore` or `fail`, new upstream columns never reach the target without a rebuild — and even `sync_all_columns` can be defeated by a drastic type change. |
| A backfill in the upstream | The delta guard hides the backfilled rows: they are older than the `max(ordered_at)` already in the target. Editing the guard temporarily is the alternative. |
| Corrupted target contents | Duplicate, stale or partial rows. A run that failed after writing part of its batch leaves a `max(ordered_at)` the next delta filter will happily start above; `--full-refresh` is the blunt reset. |
| The first run after a logic change | A new window function, a changed join condition, a renamed grouping: the historical rows already in the target are no longer what the model *would* produce. One rebuild brings them in line. |

When NOT to use it:

- On a 6-hour daily incremental, because "it might be wrong." Diagnose first — an unjustified `--full-refresh` on a large model doubles your job's runtime and warehouse spend.
- As a routine part of CI. CI should run `--defer --state` against a prior build (Ch 12), not `--full-refresh`.

You can also pin `full_refresh: false` on specific models via `/reference/resource-configs/full_refresh` — a useful guard on a model that's too expensive to rebuild accidentally. The config has a mirror: `full_refresh: true` rebuilds the resource from scratch on every invocation whether or not the flag is passed, and it applies to seeds as well as models. Neither value can be overridden from the CLI — `dbt run --full-refresh` does not lift a `false` — which is why the documented escape is to make it a variable: `full_refresh = var('force_full_refresh', false)` in the config, then `--vars '{force_full_refresh: true}'` on the one run that needs it.

The `--full-refresh` flag changes behaviour for four resource kinds: an incremental model rebuilds from scratch, a seed is dropped and recreated instead of truncate-and-inserted (Ch 5 §5.4), a materialized view is replaced rather than refreshed or altered in place (§4.1), and `dbt clone` recreates a target relation that already exists instead of no-opping (Ch 12 §12.8). The `full_refresh` config two lines above reaches the first three of those and not the fourth: each of those three materializations resolves the mode through `should_full_refresh()`, which reads the resource's own `full_refresh` config first and only falls back to the flag, whereas `clone` reads the flag directly. On `view`, `table` and `ephemeral` models it has no incremental-vs-full effect: those are rebuilt either way, and ephemeral is not materialised at all. Ch 11 §11.10 carries the command-side detail, including that `dbt snapshot` does not register the flag at all.

## 4.6 Ephemeral — when to, when not to

An ephemeral model is not a warehouse object. Setting `{{ config(materialized='ephemeral') }}` tells dbt: "at compile time, inline this model's SQL as a CTE inside every model that `ref()`s it, and don't create anything in the warehouse."

### How it works mechanically

Given:

```
-- models/intermediate/int_orders_joined.sql
{{ config(materialized='ephemeral') }}

select o.order_id, o.customer_id, o.order_total, c.segment
from {{ ref('stg_orders') }} o
left join {{ ref('stg_customers') }} c using (customer_id)
```

And a downstream model that refs it:

```
-- models/marts/core/fct_orders.sql
{{ config(materialized='table') }}

select * from {{ ref('int_orders_joined') }} where order_total > 0
```

dbt compiles the downstream model as:

```
create or replace table analytics.core.fct_orders as (
  with __dbt__cte__int_orders_joined as (
    select o.order_id, o.customer_id, o.order_total, c.segment
    from analytics.staging.stg_orders o
    left join analytics.staging.stg_customers c using (customer_id)
  )
  select * from __dbt__cte__int_orders_joined where order_total > 0
);
```

The inlined CTE's name is always `__dbt__cte__` plus the model's identifier — the `alias` when one is set, the file name otherwise. A downstream compiled against `eph.sql` with `alias='my_alias_name'` reads `__dbt__cte__my_alias_name`, so the CTE names the alias, never the file.

Ephemeral models have no presence in the warehouse. They never get written to; they can't be `select`-ed directly; they don't appear in the catalog.

### When ephemerals are useful

- A **shared CTE** used by two or three downstream marts, where materialising an intermediate table would add cost and latency for no read-performance gain.
- A **logical group of column renames/casts** you want to keep in a separate file for review discipline but don't want to pay to materialise.
- A **very small, very fast transformation** that's cheaper to re-compute inline than to join to a persisted table.

### When ephemerals hurt

- **The warehouse cannot see them, so most of your tooling cannot either.** `select * from int_orders_joined limit 10` in your SQL editor fails, because there is nothing there — and that rules out the BI tool, the query profiler and every ad-hoc `select` you would normally reach for. dbt itself is not blind to it, though: `dbt compile --select int_orders_joined` writes its resolved SQL to `target/compiled/`, and `dbt show --select int_orders_joined` previews its rows, because dbt holds the SQL even though the warehouse holds no object. What you lose is everything downstream of the warehouse, not dbt's own view.

- **They fan out in the compiled SQL.** If an ephemeral is referenced by five downstream models, its SQL is inlined five times. The warehouse may or may not de-duplicate at query time. A large ephemeral used widely can bloat compiled SQL noticeably.
- **Python models can't ref ephemerals.** Python models (see §4.7) require materialised upstream tables; they can't consume a CTE.
- **`ephemeral` isn't available as a Python model materialization** either — see §4.7.
- **A macro run through `dbt run-operation` can't `ref()` one.** `run-operation` executes outside any model's compilation, so there is no downstream `select` for the CTE to be inlined into.
- **Ephemeral doesn't support model contracts.** A contract is enforced against a relation dbt builds, and this materialization builds none.

Rule of thumb: **if you'd want to query the intermediate result directly during debugging, it's not an ephemeral.** Make it a `view` — the cost is near-zero and the debuggability is dramatically better. Reserve `ephemeral` for genuine shared-CTE cases where the model exists purely to keep SQL DRY across two or three downstreams.

---

## 4.7 Python models — key points to remember

> *Sidebar — exam-skippable.* The current study guide (dbt Core 1.11) lists "Creating Python models" as a sub-bullet of Topic 1, but real-exam coverage is low-probability. You will not need to write a Python model on the exam. You will need to recognise one when you see it and know where the traps are. The recall list below is enough.
>
> **Illustrative only.** Python-model code in this section is **not runnable on the Postgres companion repo** — dbt-postgres implements no Python submission path. Read for shape and traps; don't try to `dbt run` them locally.

- **File type and entry point.** A Python model is a `.py` file under `models/`. It must define a function with exactly this signature:

```
def model(dbt, session):
    # return a DataFrame
    ...
```

  The return value is a DataFrame — Snowpark, PySpark, or BigQuery DataFrames, depending on adapter. Reference: `/docs/build/python-models`.

- **Adapter support is a frequently-tested exam trap.** Python models are supported on **Snowflake (via Snowpark)**, **Databricks (via PySpark)**, and **BigQuery (via BigQuery DataFrames, or PySpark on Dataproc — Serverless or cluster)** — the three platforms dbt Labs documents. Capability is two separate things: the **materialization macro** must declare `supported_languages=['sql', 'python']`, and the **adapter class** must implement `submit_python_job`. The macro is the gate you hit first — ask dbt-postgres for a Python model and the run fails with `Materialization "materialization_table_default" only supports languages ['sql']; got "python".`

dbt-redshift ships neither half; dbt-duckdb ships both and does run Python models, so answer the documented three rather than "no other adapter can".

- **`ref` and `source` are Python calls, not Jinja.** Inside the `model()` function, use `dbt.ref("model_name")` and `dbt.source("source_name", "table_name")`. Jinja `{{ ref() }}` does not work inside a `.py` file — this is the second-most-common exam trap.
- **The code does not run on your machine.** dbt ships the `model()` function to the platform and it executes there — in Snowpark, on a Databricks cluster, in BigQuery DataFrames or on Dataproc. Nothing in the function runs inside the local dbt process, which is why the DataFrame API is the platform's rather than pandas by default, why a library has to be available *to the warehouse* rather than to your virtualenv, and why network access from the function is the platform's to grant.
- **`print()` output does not reach the dbt logs.** This follows from where the code runs, and it is the debugging trap people lose an afternoon to: the statement executes, the string goes to the platform's own stdout capture, and `dbt run` prints nothing. Debug by writing what you want to see into the returned DataFrame as a column, by logging through the platform's own facility, or by reading the query history in the warehouse UI. A model that appears to run without executing your `print` is behaving correctly.
- **Configs are set with `dbt.config()`, or in YAML.** `dbt.config(materialized="table", packages=["scikit-learn"])` as the first line of the function body is the in-file surface; the Jinja `{{ config() }}` block is the one form that has no Python equivalent. The `packages=` argument is how you declare Python library dependencies — dbt ships them to the warehouse's compute environment.
- **Only `table` and `incremental` materializations are allowed.** Python models cannot be `view` or `ephemeral`. If a question asks "can you materialize a Python model as a view?", the answer is no.
- **Typical use case.** ML feature engineering, statistical transforms, model scoring — anything that's awkward in pure SQL but natural in a DataFrame library. For typical analytics transformations, stay in SQL.
- **Upstream is SQL, downstream can be either.** A Python model can `dbt.ref()` a SQL model, and a SQL model can `ref()` a Python model. They share the same DAG. The only constraint is the materialization and adapter-support rules above.

### The `dbt` class is the context

Everything a SQL model reaches through Jinja, a Python model reaches through the `dbt` object handed to `model()`. The list above states the negatives — `{{ ref() }}` does not work, `{{ config() }}` does not work — so here are the positives in one place:

| In a `.py` model | Its SQL counterpart |
|---|---|
| `dbt.ref("stg_orders")` | `{{ ref('stg_orders') }}` |
| `dbt.source("raw_ecom", "orders")` | `{{ source('raw_ecom', 'orders') }}` |
| `dbt.this`, with `.database`, `.schema`, `.identifier` | `{{ this }}` |
| `dbt.is_incremental` | `is_incremental()` |
| `dbt.config.get("key")` | `{{ var('key') }}`, `{{ env_var('KEY') }}`, `{{ target }}` |

| In a `.py` model | Its SQL counterpart |
|---|---|
| `dbt.config.meta_get("key")` | `{{ config.get('meta') }}` |

Read the fourth row twice. **`dbt.is_incremental` is an attribute, not a call.** The SQL macro takes parentheses; the Python attribute does not, and that pair of characters is the whole discrimination.

The last two rows answer the question the negatives leave open: if Jinja never renders in a `.py` file, how does a `var` reach the model at all? By being templated into the model's YAML `config:` block — which *is* Jinja — and read back with `dbt.config.get()`. The same route carries `env_var()` and `target`; custom `meta` values come back through `dbt.config.meta_get()`. Reference: `/docs/build/python-models`.

That route exists because of what `dbt.config()` cannot do. It accepts **literal values only** — strings, booleans, numbers — since dbt reads those arguments by statically analysing the file at parse time, without ever executing your Python. Anything computed, and anything structured, has to live in one of the other two surfaces.

An incremental Python model filters itself, because there is no `{% if %}` block to compile away:

```
def model(dbt, session):
    dbt.config(materialized="incremental", unique_key="order_id")
    df = dbt.ref("stg_orders")
    if dbt.is_incremental:
        bookmark = session.sql(f"select max(ordered_at) from {dbt.this}").collect()
    [0][0]
        df = df.filter(df.ordered_at > bookmark)
    return df
```

Two limits are easy to confuse with the materialization limit above. Python is not supported for non-model resource types, so there is no Python test and no Python snapshot — a limit on the resource, not on the materialization, and separate again from the ephemeral restriction §4.6 covers.

On BigQuery the runtime is chosen with `submission_method` — `serverless`, `cluster` or `bigframes` — with `gcs_bucket` and `dataproc_region` required, and `dataproc_cluster_name` required only under `cluster`. See `/reference/resource-configs/bigquery-configs`.

On **Databricks** the same config names where the code runs, and the choice is a cost and latency trade rather than a capability one: `all_purpose_cluster` is the default and is the fastest to start because the cluster is already warm, and the most expensive to leave running; `job_cluster` spins up per run, which is cheaper for scheduled work and slower to start; `serverless_cluster` removes the cluster management at the platform's own pricing; and `workflow_job` submits the model as a Databricks workflow, which is what you want when the run has to appear in that platform's own orchestration rather than only in dbt's. Development on all-purpose and scheduled runs on job or serverless is the usual split.

---

## 4.8 In practice: Credora's Delta merge incremental pattern

> *This section is an "in practice" sidebar. It draws a composite pattern from (a) the dbt incremental-strategy reference at `/docs/build/incremental-strategy` and (b) the Databricks adapter's Delta-merge guidance at `/reference/resource-configs/databricks-configs`. Credora is a fictional consumer-fintech project (`credora`) running on Databricks + Delta Lake + Unity Catalog; see Ch 14's opening note for the composite-project disclaimer.*
>
> **Illustrative only.** This snippet is Databricks-specific and **does not run on the Postgres companion repo**. The companion implements the equivalent idea with Postgres `MERGE` and `delete+insert` — see its incremental examples for a runnable version.

Credora runs a fact model called `fct_lending_offer_clicks_uk` in the `cr_uk` catalog's gold layer. It tracks user clicks on lending-product offers — append-heavy at volume, but late-arriving events and corrections are common enough that a pure `append` strategy would leave stale rows. The team uses Databricks' Delta `merge` incremental strategy:

```
-- models/cr_uk/gold/fct_lending_offer_clicks_uk.sql
{{ config(
    materialized='incremental',
    incremental_strategy='merge',
    unique_key='click_event_id',
    on_schema_change='sync_all_columns',
    tblproperties={
        'delta.enableChangeDataFeed': 'true',
        'delta.autoOptimize.optimizeWrite': 'true'
    },
    meta={'owner': '@analytics-engineering'}
) }}

with source_events as (
    select * from {{ ref('stg_offer_click_events_uk') }}

    {% if is_incremental() %}
    where event_received_at > (
        select coalesce(max(event_received_at), '1900-01-01'::timestamp) from {{ this }}
    )
    {% endif %}
)

select
    click_event_id,
    user_id,
    offer_id,
    event_received_at,
    clicked_at,
    source_campaign,
    _loaded_at
from source_events
```

Five choices worth reading carefully:

| Choice | Why the team made it |
|---|---|
| `incremental_strategy='merge'` | Delta's native `MERGE INTO` is efficient on Databricks and is the idiomatic choice there. See `/reference/resource-configs/databricks-configs`. |

| Choice | Why the team made it |
|---|---|
| `unique_key='click_event_id'` | Single-column, guaranteed unique at the ingestion layer — `merge` needs it to find matching rows. |
| `on_schema_change='sync_all_columns'` | `stg_offer_click_events_uk` adds and removes columns as event schemas evolve, and the team decided the gold table should follow SQL-as-schema-of-record. `append_new_columns` would have kept removed columns instead. |
| `tblproperties` including `delta.enableChangeDataFeed` | Databricks-specific: it makes the Delta table's row-level changes readable as a stream by downstream consumers — a real-time feature store, a Kafka bridge. See the Databricks Change Data Feed docs. |
| The `is_incremental()` guard inside the `source_events` CTE | Style, not semantics. Identical to guarding the final `select`, and easier to read once the guard grows — a lookback window, say. |
| `coalesce(max(...), '1900-01-01')` rather than a bare `max()` | An empty target makes `max()` return `NULL`, and `x > NULL` is `UNKNOWN` — so a bare watermark admits no rows at all and the run appends nothing, successfully and silently. Ch 14 §14.3 sets out this and the two other assumptions a watermark of this shape rests on. |

The pattern isn't Credora's invention: `/reference/resource-configs/databricks-configs` marks `merge` as the default incremental strategy on Databricks — "Specifying `merge` as the incremental strategy is optional since it's the default strategy used when none is specified" — and describes `unique_key` as the recommended companion, the key dbt matches on to update old records. Credora applies it the way any mature team does.

**Scale note.** Credora runs this incremental daily against multiple millions of new rows; a full refresh of the same table — if the team ever runs one to pick up a backfill — takes hours and is reserved for quarterly schema migrations or recovery from an upstream corruption. Between those, `--full-refresh` is not part of the routine job.

---

## Summary

- A materialization is how dbt turns your `select` into warehouse DDL. The four standard choices — `view`, `table`, `incremental`, `ephemeral` — trade off freshness, cost, and complexity in different directions.
- `view` is the default. `table` materialises full rebuilds. `incremental` materialises-then-upserts. `ephemeral` is a compile-time inlined CTE, always named `__dbt__cte__<identifier>` in the compiled downstream.
- `dbt run` on a materialized view is a deploy action that also refreshes: where nothing has changed it issues the platform refresh, and where a *config* has, `on_configuration_change` — `apply` by default, then `continue` and `fail` — decides what happens. The SQL is never altered in place on any adapter, and how much the adapter even looks at is per-adapter: **dbt-postgres inspects only indexes, so a changed `select` is**

**not detected**, the run reports OK and the old definition stays until a `--full-refresh`. Postgres also provides no auto-refresh between runs, so there `dbt run` is the only thing that refreshes it.

- Set materialization via `{{ config(materialized='...') }}` in SQL, a YAML `config:` block, or a `dbt_project.yml +materialized:` folder default — SQL beats YAML beats `dbt_project.yml`.
- Incremental models have five concerns: the materialization keyword, the `is_incremental()` guard, `unique_key`, `on_schema_change`, and `incremental_strategy`. Each has a failure mode if misconfigured.
- Five incremental strategies ship in dbt Core — `append`, `merge`, `delete+insert`, `insert_overwrite`, `microbatch`. Availability is adapter-dependent and moves between releases; the durable rule is that dbt issues a native `MERGE` where the warehouse has one and a delete-then-insert where it does not.
- Name a strategy. There is no universal default — the adapter picks, and on Postgres and Redshift the pick turns on whether a `unique_key` is set (`append` without, `delete+insert` with). `merge_update_columns` and `merge_exclude_columns` are read by `merge` alone and are discarded without a warning under anything else, so an unnamed strategy quietly disarms them.
- Choose a strategy from the shape of the dataset, not from the adapter: append-only at volume → `append`; late-arriving updates on a stable key → `merge`; whole-partition recomputation → `insert_overwrite`; time-series at retry-hostile scale → `microbatch`; frequent unpredictable updates or an affordable rebuild → not incremental at all. Without a `unique_key`, `merge` and `delete+insert` fall back to `append` silently — BigQuery excepted, where `MERGE` needs an `ON` clause and the run fails instead.
- `event_time` names the column recording when a row's event happened. It is settable on models, seeds, snapshots and **sources**. It is **required** for microbatch's upstream filtering and for `--sample`, and **recommended** for Advanced CI compare-changes. Declare it on the relation being filtered, not only on the model reading it. The column's *name* is yours — dbt enforces no convention — but its *type* is not: a date or timestamp filters correctly, a numeric column errors, and a text column silently matches nothing. Prefer a true event timestamp over an ingestion or load column — the docs allow an ingestion timestamp where it is the only one the table carries, and the cost is that a late-arriving row is filtered into the batch it landed in rather than the one it happened in.
- `microbatch` splits an incremental load into independent, individually retryable time batches. `event_time`, `begin` and `batch_size` (`hour`, `day`, `month`, `year` — no `week`) are required; the model body carries no `is_incremental()` guard and no date predicate. Batch count derives from `begin`, `batch_size` and the clock, never from the data.
- Batch windows are half-open — `>=` the batch start and `<` the next one — so a row stamped exactly on a boundary belongs to the later batch. `model.batch.event_time_start` is inclusive, `.event_time_end` exclusive, and `model.batch` is `None` outside batch execution.
- How a microbatch batch is replaced is adapter-specific, and so is the key requirement: on dbt-postgres `unique_key` is required and batch 1 succeeds without it, so one green build proves nothing. Back-fill a window with `--event-time-start` and `--event-time-end` — mutually required, UTC — not with `--full-refresh`.
- `--full-refresh` forces a rebuild of incremental models; use it for schema drift beyond `on_schema_change`'s handling, backfills, corrupted state, or first-run-after-logic-change — not routinely.
- Python models are `.py` files with a `model(dbt, session)` function. dbt Labs documents Snowflake, Databricks and BigQuery — answer with those three — while adapter capability is a separate question and other adapters do implement it (§4.7). Use `dbt.ref` not Jinja `{{ ref() }}`; only `table` or `incremental`.

- The `dbt` object is the Python model's whole context: `dbt.ref()`, `dbt.source()`, `dbt.this`, `dbt.is_incremental` — an attribute, not a call — and `dbt.config.get()`, which is how a `var` templated into the YAML `config:` block reaches a file Jinja never touches.

## Learning-goal checklist (self-assess)

- ☐ **Pick the right materialization per scenario.** §4.1 decision table; §4.6 ephemeral trade-off; practice Qs 1, 4, 12, 16.
- ☐ **Say what `dbt run` does to a materialized view, and what `on_configuration_change` decides.** §4.1 — deploy *and* refresh, `apply` / `continue` / `fail`, the SQL that is never altered in place, that dbt-postgres does not detect a changed `select` at all so only `--full-refresh` applies it, and that Postgres has no auto-refresh between runs.
- ☐ **Write `{{ config(materialized='...') }}`.** §4.2 worked example with folder-default + per-file override; practice Qs 2, 3.
- ☐ **Write a correct incremental model with `unique_key`, `is_incremental()` guard, `on_schema_change`, and a strategy.** §4.3.1–§4.3.6; §4.8 full example; practice Qs 5–7, 9, 10, 15, 17.
- ☐ **Choose an incremental strategy from the shape of the dataset, and say what each does to a row already in the target.** §4.3.4 strategy table and decision table, including the `unique_key` fallback and the adapter's own valid-strategy list; practice Qs 4, 6, 10, 19 and 38.
- ☐ **Name the strategy that runs when you set none, and say what the `merge`-only configs do beside it.** §4.3.5 — the adapter decides, a `unique_key` can change its mind, and a column config under the wrong strategy is discarded in silence; practice Qs 18, 20.
- ☐ **Configure `event_time`, and say which of the three features it is REQUIRED for.** §4.3.7 — required for microbatch filtering and `--sample`, recommended for Advanced CI compare-changes; four resource types including sources; three config surfaces; any column name you like but it must be a date or timestamp, event timestamp preferred over an ingestion column, and a column of the wrong type fails loudly or silently depending on the type; practice Qs 21, 30, 31 and 36.
- ☐ **Write a microbatch model and predict its batch plan.** §4.4 — the three required configs, the unguarded body, half-open batch windows, batch count from `begin` plus the clock, the per-adapter replacement mechanisms, and why one green batch on Postgres proves nothing; practice Qs 22, 23, 33 and 37.
- ☐ **Back-fill and retry a microbatch model.** §4.4.7–§4.4.8 — `--event-time-start` / `--event-time-end` versus `--full-refresh`; failed batches retry alone; parallel execution is Snowflake and BigQuery only, and never for the first and last batch; practice Qs 24, 25, 28 and 32.
- ☐ **Understand `--full-refresh` and when to use it, and that deleting a model never drops its relation.** §4.5; practice Qs 11, 13 and 29.
- ☐ **Recognise what a Python model file looks like, and what the `dbt` object gives it.** §4.7 recall list and the context table; practice Qs 8, 26, 27, 34 and 35.
- ☐ **Recognise when the right answer is not a materialization at all.** §4.2's SCD2 note; practice Q 14.

## Practice questions

Thirty-five questions across materialization choice, config precedence, incremental mechanics and strategy, `event_time` and microbatch, `--full-refresh`, Python models, and one production diagnostic.

---

**1.** An analytics engineer needs to reference a 3-row join of two staging models from exactly two downstream marts, never queries the intermediate result directly, and wants to avoid creating a new warehouse object. Which materialization fits?
A. `view` B. `table`
C. `ephemeral` D. `materialized_view`

**2.** Which of these locations for setting `materialized` has the highest precedence?
A. `dbt_project.yml` under `models:`, with `+materialized:` on the folder that holds the model
B. A YAML properties file under `models/**/_schema.yml`, with `config: materialized:`
C. An SQL model file, with `{{ config(materialized='...') }}`
D. `dbt_project.yml` under `models:`, with `+materialized:` keyed on the model's own name

**3.** Given this `dbt_project.yml` fragment:

```
models:
  my_project:
    marts:
      +materialized: table
      finance:
        +materialized: view
```

What materialization will `models/marts/finance/fct_revenue.sql` have, assuming no `{{ config() }}` in the file itself and no YAML config block?
A. `table`
B. It will fail to compile because of the conflict.
C. `ephemeral`
D. `view`

**4.** A dbt model reads an append-only event table that has accumulated several billion rows and gains a few million more each day. Rows are never revised once inserted. The only timestamp on the table is `loaded_at`, written by the ingestion tool; nothing on it records when the event itself occurred. Which materialization and strategy fit?
A. `table` — rebuilt nightly, so there is no delta filter and no strategy to choose.
B. `incremental` with `incremental_strategy='merge'` and `unique_key='event_id'`.
C. `incremental` with `incremental_strategy='append'` and a `loaded_at` delta filter.
D. `incremental` with `incremental_strategy='microbatch'`, plus `begin` and `batch_size`.

**5.** What does the `is_incremental()` Jinja macro return on the very first run of an incremental model, before the target table exists in the warehouse?
A. `False`
B. `True`
C. It raises an error because the table doesn't exist.
D. It returns `None`.

**6.** An incremental model on Snowflake (or Redshift / Databricks / Postgres) is configured with `incremental_strategy='merge'` but no `unique_key`. What happens on a run where rows in the new batch match rows already in the target?
A. dbt updates the matching rows in place.
B. dbt skips the run with a "missing required config" warning and writes nothing.
C. dbt raises a compilation error at parse time.
D. dbt appends the new rows; existing rows are unchanged, so you get duplicates.

**7.** Which value of `on_schema_change` causes dbt to add any new columns from the model SQL to the target table AND remove any columns that are no longer in the SQL?
A. `ignore` B. `fail`
C. `append_new_columns` D. `sync_all_columns`

**8.** In a Python model file, how do you reference an upstream dbt model called `stg_orders`?
A. `{{ ref('stg_orders') }}` B. `dbt.ref("stg_orders")`
C. `from models.stg_orders import df` D. `session.table("stg_orders")`

**9.** An incremental model has this config:

```
{{ config(
    materialized='incremental',
    unique_key='order_id',
    incremental_strategy='merge'
) }}
```

The model SQL adds a new column `promo_code` that wasn't present on the last run. The model's `on_schema_change` is left at its default. What happens on the next `dbt run`?
A. dbt raises an error because of the schema change.
B. dbt runs `ALTER TABLE ADD COLUMN promo_code` and inserts values into it.
C. dbt silently drops `promo_code` from the insert; new rows have no `promo_code` column written.
D. dbt forces a full refresh of the model.

**10.** Which of the following is **NOT** a built-in `incremental_strategy` on any adapter?
A. `merge` B. `append`
C. `replace` D. `delete+insert`
E. `insert_overwrite`

**11.** What does `dbt run --full-refresh` do?
A. The flag is what causes every model in the project to be rebuilt from scratch, regardless of materialization.
B. Runs only the models that have changed since the last run.
C. Drops and rebuilds incremental models from scratch; leaves all view, table, and ephemeral models unaffected in behaviour.
D. Validates the project without executing any SQL.

**12.** A team has a staging model that does a light cast-and-rename over a source table with ~1 GB of raw data. The model is rebuilt nightly and is read by three downstream marts that re-aggregate the data heavily. Which materialization is the best default?
A. `view` — the rebuild is cheap and the downstream marts materialise the heavy work themselves.
B. `incremental` — 1 GB is too big for a view.
C. `ephemeral` — inline it into the three marts.
D. `materialized_view` — adapter-native always wins.

**13.** A production incremental model has `full_refresh: false` set in its config. An engineer runs `dbt run --full-refresh` at the CLI. What happens to this model?
A. It is rebuilt from scratch, because a CLI flag is more specific than a config in the model file and so takes precedence.
B. It is skipped in terms of full-refresh behaviour — the model-level `full_refresh: false` overrides the CLI flag, so the run proceeds incrementally.
C. dbt raises a configuration error, because a model-level `full_refresh: false` and `--full-refresh` on the same run are mutually exclusive.
D. The model is rebuilt and the config is cleared, so later runs without the flag also ignore `full_refresh: false`.

**14.** A data team wants to model an SCD2 history table — every historical version of every customer row, with `valid_from` and `valid_to` columns. Which of the following is the right dbt construct?
A. An incremental model with `unique_key='customer_id'` and `merge` strategy.
B. A dbt snapshot.
C. A table materialization that selects from a warehouse-native history feature.
D. A view over the source table.

**15.** A 6-hour daily incremental job just broke in production. The database error names a column that does not exist on the temporary relation dbt built for the run. The model's `on_schema_change` is `ignore`, and a contributor recently dropped a column from the model's `select`. What's the best diagnostic order for the team?
A. Rerun with `--full-refresh` first, then read the compiled SQL to see which columns moved.
B. Read the compiled SQL to see which columns the model now selects, check `on_schema_change`, then pick between `sync_all_columns` and one `--full-refresh`.
C. Switch `on_schema_change` to `fail`, rerun so the divergence is named explicitly, then decide.
D. Restore the dropped column to the model's `select`, rerun, and raise the removal as a ticket.

**16.** A team has a large mart model that is materialised as a `view` because rebuilds used to be too expensive. Dashboards over the mart now time out because every read recomputes the full view. The team is considering three options: (a) switch to `table`, (b) switch to `incremental`, (c) switch to `materialized_view`. Which statement is most accurate?
A. Switch to `incremental`: it stores rows the way a `table` does but rebuilds fewer of them, so it is the cheaper of the two on a mart this size.
B. Switch to `table`: read cost is the problem and this is the smallest change that removes it; whether `incremental` then beats it turns on the mart having a reliable delta column.
C. Switch to `materialized_view`: the platform refreshes it on its own, so reads stay fast without the team scheduling a rebuild.
D. Keep the `view` and move the aggregation into the BI layer, where the tool's own cache absorbs the repeated reads.

**17.** An incremental model on Databricks writes to a Delta table with column mapping enabled, and uses `incremental_strategy='merge'` with `on_schema_change='sync_all_columns'`. A contributor removes a column from the model's `select`. After the next `dbt run`:
A. dbt issues DDL to drop the column from the target Delta table; no future runs write to it.
B. The column is kept in the Delta table but no new rows write to it.
C. dbt raises an error.
D. dbt automatically switches to `append_new_columns` to preserve the column.

**18.** A model on dbt-postgres is configured `materialized='incremental'` with `unique_key='order_id'`, and sets no `incremental_strategy`. Which strategy does dbt use on an incremental run?
A. `append` — the adapter's default, which setting a `unique_key` does not change.
B. `delete+insert` — the adapter's default once a `unique_key` is set.
C. `merge` — Postgres has a native `MERGE`, so dbt issues one unprompted.
D. `insert_overwrite` — with no strategy named, dbt replaces the relation wholesale.

**19.** An incremental model on Snowflake uses `incremental_strategy='merge'` with `unique_key='customer_id'`. An upstream change means some batches now carry two rows per `customer_id`, and the run fails with a nondeterministic-merge error. Which change is the documented remedy?
A. Add a `unique` test on `customer_id` so the duplication is caught before the merge runs.
B. Remove `unique_key` so that `merge` no longer has anything to match on.
C. Switch the model to `incremental_strategy='delete+insert'`, which tolerates a key that is not truly unique.
D. Add `merge_update_columns` so only the columns you name are written on a match.

**20.** A model sets `incremental_strategy='delete+insert'`, `unique_key='customer_id'` and `merge_exclude_columns=['first_seen_at']`. What happens to `first_seen_at` on an incremental run?
A. It keeps its stored value on matched rows — the exclusion is honoured.
B. It is overwritten with the incoming value — the exclusion is discarded and nothing is logged.
C. The run fails with a compilation error, because the config belongs to `merge`.
D. It is written as NULL, because the delete removes it and the insert has no value to restore.

**21.** A team adds `event_time: created_at` inside the `config:` block of an entry under `sources:`. Is that a valid place for the config, and what does it do?
A. Invalid — `event_time` is a model-level config; on a source it parses and is then silently ignored at run time.
B. Valid, but on a source it feeds `dbt source freshness`, standing in for `loaded_at_field`.
C. Invalid — dbt raises a parse error naming `event_time` as an unsupported source property.
D. Valid — sources are one of the four resource types that accept `event_time`, with models, seeds and snapshots.

**22.** A microbatch model sets `begin='2025-01-01'` and `batch_size='month'`. Its upstream holds rows only from March 2025 to May 2025. On a first full build in September 2025, how many batches does dbt plan?
A. 3 — one for each month that actually contains rows.
B. 5 — one per month from `begin` through the last month that holds rows.
C. 8 — one per month from `begin` up to but not including the current month.
D. 9 — one per month from `begin` through the current month.

**23.** A microbatch model plans thirty daily batches. It has two parents, and one of them declares no `event_time` of its own. What happens on the run?
A. dbt raises a compilation error naming the parent that has no `event_time`.
B. dbt warns once and skips the batches that would have needed to filter that parent.
C. dbt reads that parent in full on every batch, and the run reports OK throughout.
D. dbt falls back to filtering that parent on the microbatch model's own `event_time` column.

**24.** A microbatch model has `begin='2023-01-01'` and three years of history in its target. Bad source data means September 2025 has to be reprocessed, and nothing else. Which invocation does that?

A. `dbt run --select fct_orders --event-time-start "2025-09-01" --event-time-end "2025-10-01"`
B. `dbt run --select fct_orders --full-refresh`
C. `dbt run --select fct_orders --event-time-start "2025-09-01"`
D. `dbt retry --event-time-start "2025-09-01" --event-time-end "2025-10-01"`

**25.** A microbatch model on Snowflake plans forty batches, never references `{{ this }}`, and sets `concurrent_batches: true`. Which batches still run on their own?

A. None — the override forces all forty of them to run in parallel.
B. The first only, because it is the batch that creates the relation.
C. The first and the last, which are never parallelised whatever `concurrent_batches` says.
D. Every batch that falls inside the `lookback` window.

**26.** Inside a Python model's `model(dbt, session)` function, how do you branch on whether the model is running incrementally?

A. `if dbt.is_incremental:` B. `if dbt.is_incremental():`
C. `if is_incremental():` D. `if dbt.config.get("is_incremental"):`

**27.** A Python model needs the value of `var('run_region')`, and Jinja does not render inside a `.py` file. How does the value reach the model?

A. Call `dbt.var("run_region")`, the Python counterpart of the Jinja `var()` function.
B. Template it into the model's YAML `config:` block, then read it with `dbt.config.get("run_region")`.
C. Read it from the process environment as `os.environ["DBT_VAR_RUN_REGION"]` inside `model()`.
D. Declare it in the `dbt.config()` call in the `.py` file, then read it back with `dbt.config.get()`.

**28.** A project inherited a `get_incremental_microbatch_sql` macro written before batched execution existed. Its microbatch models run green, but cost never falls after the first backfill. On stock dbt 1.11, what is happening?

A. With `require_batched_execution_for_custom_microbatch_strategy` off — the 1.11 default — the macro is called once for the whole range and the per-batch window is never applied
B. dbt refuses to batch a custom strategy and aborts the run with an error until the macro is updated
C. The macro is called per batch, but `lookback` defaults high enough to cover the full range
D. Custom strategies ignore `begin`, so every run starts from the earliest row

**29.** A model file is deleted from the project and the change is merged. The next production `dbt build` is green. What is the state of the table that model used to build?

A. Dropped during the run, once dbt saw the node was gone
B. Dropped on the next `dbt clean`
C. Emptied but retained, so downstream queries return zero rows
D. Still there, still queryable, holding the rows from the last run that built it

**30.** A team removes `event_time` from a large source's YAML, believing it only mattered to one model. Which features **lose time filtering on that relation entirely**, as opposed to merely working less well?
A. Microbatch auto-filtering and `--sample`
B. Microbatch auto-filtering and `--full-refresh` targeting
C. `--sample` and `--empty` runs
D. Microbatch auto-filtering, `--sample`, and Advanced CI's compare-changes

**31.** Where can `event_time` be set?
A. Only in `dbt_project.yml`, as `+event_time:`
B. Only inside the model file, as `{{ config(event_time=...) }}`
C. In all three: `dbt_project.yml` as `+event_time:`, a properties `config:` block, or inline in `{{ config() }}`
D. Only on models — a source cannot declare it

**32.** A microbatch model runs 30 daily batches. Batches 12 and 19 fail; the rest succeed. You run `dbt retry`. What is reprocessed?
A. All 30 batches — the node failed, so the whole node is rerun from the start of its window
B. Batches 12 and 19 only — retry resumes at batch granularity, so the 28 batches that succeeded are not recomputed
C. Batches 12 through 30 — everything from the first failure onward, since later batches may depend on it
D. Nothing — `dbt retry` does not support microbatch models and reports no failed nodes to rerun

**33.** A microbatch model does not set `lookback`. What is the default, and what does the config control?
A. `1` — it reprocesses that many batches back from the current time on each incremental run, to pick up late-arriving rows
B. `0` — no reprocessing happens unless you ask for it
C. `1` — it moves `begin` back by one batch, widening the first full refresh
D. `3` — matching the three batches dbt runs in parallel by default

**34.** A Python model imports a library that is installed in the developer's local virtualenv but not registered with the warehouse. What happens?
A. It works — dbt executes the `model()` function locally and ships only the resulting DataFrame
B. It works — dbt bundles the local environment with the submitted job
C. It fails — the function runs on the platform, so the import must be available there
D. It fails at parse time, because dbt resolves imports while building the manifest

**35.** A developer adds `print(df.count())` to a Python model to debug it. `dbt run` succeeds and the output never appears. What is going on?
A. dbt suppresses model stdout unless `--debug` is passed
B. The function runs on the platform, so its stdout goes to the platform's capture, not to dbt's logs
C. `print()` is unavailable inside a `model()` function and is silently skipped
D. The statement ran, but dbt only surfaces stdout for models that fail

## Answer key

**1. C.** An `ephemeral` model is inlined as a CTE into every downstream model that `ref()`s it, with no warehouse object created. The "never queries it directly" and "only two consumers" criteria match exactly when ephemerals are appropriate. A `view` is the near miss — it is cheap, always fresh, and fine for two consumers — but it loses on the clause the stem states outright: a view IS a new warehouse object, so it does not satisfy "wants to avoid creating a new warehouse object". See `/docs/build/materializations`.

**2. C.** dbt's config precedence is SQL `{{ config() }}` > YAML `config:` > `dbt_project.yml +config`, and the surface decides before specificity does. A and D are both `dbt_project.yml` entries, so both sit at the bottom of that order however precisely they are targeted — D is the tempting one, because keying on the model's own name is the most specific thing that file lets you write and it still loses to the other two surfaces. Path specificity settles a contest *within* `dbt_project.yml`, which is Q3; it never lifts an entry above the file it lives in. See `/reference/define-configs` and `/reference/resource-configs/materialized`.

**3. D.** The more specific folder path wins. `marts.finance` is deeper than `marts`, so its `+materialized: view` overrides the `+materialized: table` set at the `marts` level. The path hierarchy does not conflict — it cascades. See `/reference/define-configs` and `/reference/resource-configs/materialized`.

**4. C.** Three clauses in the stem decide it. Rows are never revised, so there is nothing for `merge` to match and B pays for matching that never fires — and it names a `unique_key` the stem never gives you. Several billion rows make A's nightly rebuild an expensive answer to a cheap problem. And the table records only when the loader wrote the row, never when the event happened, which is what rules D out. Microbatch needs an `event_time`, and §4.3.7 is direct that an ingestion timestamp is *allowed* where it is the only timestamp you have — at a price it names: rows re-batch whenever the connector resyncs, so batches accumulate duplicates across runs. Paying that price to get batching you do not need, on a table nothing revises, is the wrong trade here. That leaves `append`, which inserts the delta and checks nothing, with `loaded_at` doing the one job it is fit for. See `/docs/build/incremental-strategy`.

**5. A.** `is_incremental()` returns `True` only when (a) the model is configured as incremental, (b) the target already exists in the warehouse, and (c) the run is not in full-refresh mode. On the first run, the target doesn't yet exist, so it returns `False` and the `{% if is_incremental() %}` guard compiles away — dbt performs a full CREATE TABLE AS. See `/docs/build/incremental-models`.

**6. D.** On most adapters (Snowflake, Redshift, Databricks, Postgres), `merge` without a `unique_key` has nothing to match on and dbt falls back to append-style behaviour — every incoming row is inserted, producing duplicates for keys that already exist. dbt does NOT raise an error at parse time (ruling out C) and does not skip the run (ruling out B); the trap is the silent degradation to append. (Adapter caveat: on BigQuery, where `MERGE` requires an `ON` clause, this can surface as a SQL error instead — but the answer that fits "what happens" across the supported-adapter family is still D.) See `/docs/build/incremental-strategy` and `/reference/resource-configs/unique_key`.

**7. D.** `sync_all_columns` makes the target's schema follow the model SQL exactly — new columns are added, removed columns are dropped. `append_new_columns` only adds, never removes. `ignore` is the default and does neither. `fail` raises an error on any schema divergence. See `/docs/build/incremental-models` section "What if the columns of my incremental model change?"

**8. B.** Inside a Python model, use `dbt.ref("model_name")` — a Python method call on the `dbt` object passed into the `model(dbt, session)` function. Jinja `{{ ref() }}` (A) does not render inside a `.py` file at all. C is the wrong mental model twice over: models are not importable Python modules, and the docs are explicit that functions cannot be shared across model files. D is the near miss worth knowing — `session.table()` is a real Snowpark call and it does return the relation, but it names a hard-coded object, so dbt sees no dependency, draws no DAG edge, and is free to build the two models in the wrong order. See `/docs/build/python-models`.

**9. C.** The default for `on_schema_change` is `ignore`. With `ignore`, dbt does nothing about the divergence: the new `promo_code` column is silently dropped from the insert, so even though the model's SELECT produces the column, it never reaches the target table. This is the classic "my new column is always NULL" trap. Fix by setting `on_schema_change='append_new_columns'` (or `sync_all_columns`) and optionally running `--full-refresh` once. See `/docs/build/incremental-models`.

**10. C.** dbt ships five incremental strategies — `append`, `merge`, `delete+insert`, `insert_overwrite`, and `microbatch` — and which of them a given adapter offers varies by platform. `replace` is not a strategy name under any of them. The near-miss worth knowing is Databricks' `replace_where`, a real strategy whose prefix collides with this distractor. See `/docs/build/incremental-strategy`.

**11. C.** `--full-refresh` changes behaviour for four resource kinds — incremental models, seeds, materialized views and `dbt clone` (§4.5) — and the one this question turns on is the incremental model: the flag puts the run in full-refresh mode, so `is_incremental()` returns `False` unless the model sets `full_refresh: false`, causing a full rebuild instead of an incremental upsert. View models are always rebuilt (they're cheap); table models are always rebuilt on a run; ephemerals don't materialise at all. The flag has no effect on those three. See `/reference/commands/run`.

**12. A.** Staging models are conventionally views: the transformation is light (rename, cast, basic filter) and the downstream marts materialise the heavy aggregation work. A view keeps staging code in step with the source table without rebuild cost. C loses on the two things the stem sets up: `ephemeral` builds no relation, so there is nothing in the warehouse to query when a cast comes out wrong, and it inlines the same staging SQL into all three marts instead of giving them one shared object. See `/best-practices/how-we-structure/2-staging`.

**13. B.** Per the `/reference/resource-configs/full_refresh` reference, a model-level `full_refresh: false` config tells dbt to never perform a full refresh on that model, even when the CLI flag is passed. This is a deliberate safety mechanism for expensive tables where an accidental rebuild would cost hours of compute. To rebuild the model, remove the config — or route it through `var()`, the escape §4.5 documents.

**14. B.** dbt **snapshots** are the purpose-built construct for SCD2 history — they track every change to source rows with `dbt_valid_from` / `dbt_valid_to` columns. An incremental model with `merge` updates rows in place, which is the opposite of SCD2. This is a Ch 5 topic, but it's worth recognising when *not* to reach for incremental. See `/docs/build/snapshots`.

**15. B.** The error is the signature of a **removed** column under `ignore`. With `on_schema_change='ignore'` dbt builds its column lists from the *target's* columns, so a column the model no longer selects is still named in the generated statement and is missing from the temporary relation dbt just built — which is exactly the error the stem reports. (An *added* column under `ignore` is the quiet case: it is dropped from the insert and the run succeeds. That is Q9.) Read the compiled SQL first because it costs seconds and says which columns actually moved; `on_schema_change` then explains why dbt did not adapt; only then is the fix a choice between `sync_all_columns` and one rebuild. A spends six hours before anyone knows what broke. C makes the next run fail earlier but no more informatively, and still costs a run. D restores the column and hides the divergence instead of resolving it. See `/docs/build/incremental-models` and `/reference/commands/compile`.

**16. B.** The immediate problem is read-time cost, and `table` removes it with one config change and the same SQL. A overstates the incremental case: an incremental model is cheaper than a `table` only when the mart has a reliable delta column and update semantics that suit a strategy, and the stem supplies neither — without them the rebuild happens anyway, with four more configs to design and maintain. C assumes the platform refreshes the object for you, which the adapter decides and the stem never names; on Postgres nothing refreshes a materialized view on its own, and a later edit to the mart's `select` would need a `--full-refresh` in any case. D moves the cost rather than removing it, and duplicates the mart's logic into a layer dbt cannot test. See `/docs/build/materializations`.

**17. A.** `sync_all_columns` makes the target schema match the model SQL exactly, so dbt issues the DDL to remove a column that is no longer in the SQL: it disappears from the target relation and no future run writes to it. The stem states that column mapping is enabled because on Delta it is a real prerequisite — `ALTER TABLE ... DROP COLUMN` requires the table to be in column-mapping mode, and without it the drop fails rather than silently doing nothing. What remains adapter-specific, and is not what the exam tests, is what happens to the values already in storage and how the drop interacts with time travel. One consequence worth carrying: a change-data-feed reader downstream of this table sees a non-additive schema change, which is the case CDF does not carry across cleanly. If the team wanted to keep the column — option B's outcome — they should have used `append_new_columns`, which adds new columns but never removes existing ones. Revisit §4.3.3 for when each value is the right choice. See `/docs/build/incremental-models`.

**18. B.** There is no universal default `incremental_strategy` — the adapter picks, and dbt-postgres picks by looking at your config: `append` when no `unique_key` is set, `delete+insert` when one is. A states the first half of that rule and then denies that the `unique_key` matters, which is the half the model here turns on. C is the belief most readers arrive with, and it is right on Snowflake, BigQuery and Databricks and wrong here — dbt-postgres will issue a `MERGE` if you ask for one by name, but it never reaches for one unprompted. D is not a Postgres strategy at all and would want a `partition_by`. The consequence matters more than the token: any `merge_update_columns` or `merge_exclude_columns` on this model is being discarded without a warning. See `/reference/resource-configs/postgres-configs` and `/docs/build/incremental-strategy`.

**19. C.** `merge` needs exactly one target row per key and will not choose between two source rows that claim the same one, so Snowflake raises rather than guessing. `delete+insert` is the documented way out: it deletes every target row whose key appears in the incoming batch and reinserts the batch whole, so a duplicated key becomes duplicated rows instead of a failed run — which is a decision about the mechanism you want, not a fix for the duplication. A is the right instinct on the wrong axis: a `unique` test reports the problem and the model still does not build. B does stop the error, by removing the only thing `merge` matches on, and the run then appends everything and duplicates far more. D narrows which columns a match writes; it does nothing about there being two candidate rows. See `/reference/resource-configs/snowflake-configs` and `/docs/build/incremental-strategy`.

**20. B.** `merge_update_columns` and `merge_exclude_columns` are read by the `merge` strategy alone. `delete+insert` has no update statement for a column list to narrow — it deletes the matching rows and reinserts the batch, and an insert writes every column — so the config is dropped without a warning, the run exits 0, and `first_seen_at` takes the incoming value. A is what the config promises and what it delivers only under `merge`. C would be the kinder behaviour and is not what dbt does; dbt does raise for one combination on this pair — setting *both* configs at once — but not for setting one under the wrong strategy. D describes a mechanism dbt never uses: the insert carries the full column list from the batch. See `/docs/build/incremental-strategy`.

**21. D.** `event_time` is settable on four resource types — models, seeds, snapshots and sources — and the source is the one readers leave off the list, which is a problem because it is often the one that matters. dbt filters a relation only if that relation declares the config, so putting it on the model that reads the source does nothing for the source, and A inverts that. B attaches it to the wrong feature: source freshness reads `loaded_at_field` or `loaded_at_query`, never `event_time`, and the two answer different questions — when the row was loaded, against when the event happened. C invents a parse error. See `/reference/resource-configs/event-time`.

**22. D.** dbt derives the batch list from `begin`, `batch_size` and the clock, and never looks at the data to do it. January through September inclusive is nine monthly batches. The four trailing ones select nothing, write nothing and report OK — legitimately empty, not a bug.

A is the answer you get from reasoning about the rows, which is the misconception under test. B stops at the last month that holds data, for the same reason. C is right about the mechanism and off by one on the current month, which the plan includes. See `/docs/build/incremental-microbatch` and `/reference/resource-configs/begin`.

**23. C.** dbt can only time-filter an upstream that declares an `event_time` of its own. One that does not is read in full, once per batch — thirty full scans of that parent across the run, every one of them reporting OK. A and B both assume a guard rail that does not exist: there is no error and no warning. D is the specific misconception §4.3.7 warns against — dbt will not borrow the consumer's column name to filter a parent that never declared one, because the config has to sit on the relation being filtered. Revisit §4.4.6. See `/docs/build/incremental-microbatch`.

**24. A.** `--event-time-start` and `--event-time-end` bound the run to one window, and they are mutually necessary — which is why C, giving only the start, is not a half-answer but an invalid invocation. Both values are interpreted as UTC. B is the trap: `--full-refresh` on a microbatch model is not a window backfill at all, it reprocesses everything from `begin`, so this one rebuilds three years to correct one month. D reaches for the wrong command — `dbt retry` reruns the batches that failed in the previous invocation, and nothing failed here; September's batches succeeded, with bad data. See `/docs/build/incremental-microbatch`.

**25. C.** Parallel batch execution is supported on Snowflake and BigQuery, and even there the first and last batch of a run never go in parallel with anything. `concurrent_batches: true` overrides dbt's auto-detection — the check for a `{{ this }}` reference, which is why the stem rules that out — and it does not lift the first-and-last rule, so A reads the override as more than it is. D borrows `lookback`, which decides which batches are reprocessed, not which run together. B is half the rule, and it is the half that sounds most reasonable if you are carrying §4.4.5's Postgres story across: batch 1 is special there because it creates the relation, but that is a different mechanism on a different adapter. See `/docs/build/parallel-batch-execution`.

**26. A.** On the `dbt` object it is `dbt.is_incremental`, an **attribute**, and the parentheses are the whole difference: `is_incremental()` (C) is the Jinja macro, which does not exist in a `.py` file because Jinja never renders there. B carries the SQL spelling onto the right object and calls something that is not callable. D invents a config key; `dbt.config.get()` is real and reads values templated into the model's YAML `config:` block, but nothing puts the incremental state there. An incremental Python model then has to write its own filter against `dbt.this` — there is no `{% if %}` block to compile away. See `/docs/build/python-models`.

**27. B.** Jinja renders in YAML, so the route in is the model's properties file: template the value into its `config:` block and read it back with `dbt.config.get("run_region")`. A invents a method — the `dbt` object exposes no `var`. C misplaces the process: the code runs on the warehouse's compute, not in the local dbt process, so dbt's environment is not there to read, and dbt sets no such variable anyway. D fails for the reason the YAML surface exists: `dbt.config()` accepts literal values only, because dbt reads those arguments by statically analysing the file at parse time without executing it, so `var('run_region')` has no point at which it could resolve. Revisit §4.7's context table for the rest of that surface. See `/docs/build/python-models`.

**28. A.** dbt hands a **custom** microbatch macro one batch at a time only when `require_batched_execution_for_custom_microbatch_strategy` is on, and that flag is off by default at 1.11. With it off, the macro is invoked once for the entire range: the `event_time_start` and `event_time_end` it was never written to read are simply not applied, and the model reprocesses everything every run. Nothing errors and the run reports success. It is not silent — a deprecation fires at parse time on every invocation, naming the flag and the fix (`[WARNING]: The use of a custom microbatch macro outside of batched execution is deprecated.`; event code `D020` in the JSON log, never on the console) — but past that warning the only symptom is the cost curve, which is why the diagnostic move is to read the deprecations and then look for a project-level override of that macro before re-reading the model's configs. It follows the usual behaviour-flag arc: new guard ships off, warns, defaults on later.

**29. D.** dbt creates and replaces objects for the nodes that are **in** the DAG. A node that has left the DAG is not visited, so nothing drops its relation and the table sits in the warehouse holding whatever it held on the final run that built it. The same is true of a model switched from `table` or `view` to `ephemeral`. This is worse than clutter: the orphan is still queryable, still appears in the BI tool, and is now frozen at a date nobody recorded, so a dashboard pointed at it keeps returning plausible stale numbers. B is the distractor to be sure about — `dbt clean` deletes the local directories named in `clean-targets` and never touches the warehouse. Dropping the object is manual and belongs in the same pull request as the deletion.

**30. A.** Three features read `event_time`, and the stem asks which two *require* it. **Microbatch** filters every upstream `ref()` and `source()` that declares it, once per batch; `--sample` narrows a run to a time window on the relations that declare it. Take the config away and neither has a column to filter on — the relation is read whole. That is why removing it from a *source* is more expensive than it looks: the config lives on the relation being read, not on the model doing the reading, so one deletion quietly widens every downstream batch.

D is the trap, and it is one letter from right. Advanced CI's compare-changes does use `event_time` — to line up the same slice of time in CI and in production — but the docs **recommend** it there rather than requiring it: the comparison still runs, it is just less like-for-like. "Gates three features" is the shorthand to distrust. B and C each pair one real feature with one that has no time awareness at all: `--full-refresh` rebuilds everything and `--empty` zeroes its *inputs*, and neither consults the column.

**31. C.** `event_time` is an ordinary config and takes all three config surfaces, with the usual precedence: in-file `{{ config() }}` beats a properties `config:` block, which beats `dbt_project.yml`. D is worth dismissing deliberately rather than by elimination, because a **source** is the highest-value place to declare it — microbatch filters upstream relations that declare it, so a source without `event_time` cannot be auto-filtered no matter what the reading model sets. The recurring mistake is declaring it on the model doing the reading and expecting the upstream relation to be narrowed.

**32. B.** Batches are independent units of work, so they fail independently and recover independently: `dbt retry` reruns **only** the failed batches. That is the operational argument for microbatch and the thing to be able to say out loud. Contrast a conventional incremental model, which is a single node wrapping a single statement — one failure fails the whole model and a retry redoes all of it, which is answer A. C is the plausible-sounding middle position, but batches are not a pipeline: 13 through 30 already succeeded and are not revisited.

**33. A.** `lookback` defaults to `1`, accepts any integer greater than or equal to 0, and reprocesses that many batches *counting back from the current time* on every incremental run. It exists for late-arriving data: a row that lands after its own batch has already been built would otherwise never be picked up. C is the discriminator worth being able to reject — `begin` is the fixed start of the model's history and `lookback` never moves it, so the two are independent knobs. B is a legal setting rather than a nonsense one, which is what makes it a fair distractor: setting `lookback: 0` is how you declare that late arrivals are impossible for this stream.

**34. C.** A Python model's `model()` function is shipped to the platform and executed there — in Snowpark, on a Databricks cluster, in BigQuery DataFrames, or on Dataproc. Nothing in it runs inside the local dbt process. That single fact explains most of the surprises: the DataFrame API is the platform's rather than pandas by default, a library has to be available *to the warehouse* rather than to your virtualenv, and outbound network access is the platform's to grant. D is worth rejecting explicitly: parsing builds the manifest and never executes the function body, so an import error surfaces at run time on the platform, not at parse time locally.

**35. B.** This follows directly from remote execution: `print()` runs, but the string goes to the platform's own stdout capture, and `dbt run` prints nothing. It is the debugging trap people lose an afternoon to, because the model appears to be ignoring the statement when it is in fact behaving correctly. The workable routes are to write the value you want into the returned DataFrame as a column, to log through the platform's own facility, or to read the query history in the warehouse UI. A is the tempting answer because `--debug` is the real remedy for *dbt's* own missing output, which is a different problem.

# Chapter 5

# Snapshots and seeds

> **Scope.** Topic 1's two narrow primitives. **Snapshots** turn a mutable source table into a type-2 slowly-changing-dimension history table, entirely inside dbt. **Seeds** load small, static CSV files from your repo into the warehouse as tables. Neither one is a high-frequency exam topic, and neither one is the reason anyone fails the exam — but misuse of both is common in real production projects, which is why the blueprint lists them and why this chapter insists on "when *not* to reach for each" as firmly as "how to write one." By the end you can declare a snapshot in either of its two forms, pick the right strategy for it, read its generated columns, use the `dbt snapshot` and `dbt seed` commands, and explain out loud why a CSV of "new orders this week" does not belong in `seeds/`.

**Prerequisites.** Ch 2 (`ref()`, the DAG, `dbt_project.yml` config-by-folder-path), Ch 3 (sources and `source()`), and Ch 4 §4.2 on config precedence. Snapshots and seeds have their own `snapshots/` and `seeds/` directories rather than living under `models/` — with one loosening §5.1 comes back to, but the config-resolution rules are exactly the same.

**Cheat-sheet pointer.** Front-of-book cheat sheet §2 (Topic 1 — Developing and optimizing models) carries both recall surfaces: the two snapshot strategies with the config each one requires and the four `dbt_`-prefixed columns dbt adds, then the three seed configs and what `--full-refresh` does to a seed but not to a snapshot. Use the chapter for the "when and why"; the cheat sheet entries are the recall lines.

---

## 5.1 Snapshots — the SCD2 primitive

A **snapshot** captures every observed version of every row of a mutable source table, with generated `dbt_valid_from` / `dbt_valid_to` columns saying which version was current when. An update to a raw `customers` table is destructive — the previous address, tier or email is gone the moment the new one is written — so the source table cannot answer "which email did this customer have on July 1st?" A snapshot can.

That pattern — one row per historical version, with validity-interval columns — is a **type-2 slowly-changing dimension**, usually abbreviated SCD2. You will see "SCD2" used interchangeably with "snapshot" in dbt writing, though they are not quite synonyms: SCD2 is the data-modelling pattern; a dbt snapshot is one specific implementation of it.

### Where snapshot definitions live

Snapshots live in their own top-level directory — by default `snapshots/`, configurable via the `snapshot-paths` key in `dbt_project.yml`.

Two declaration forms are current, and you will meet both. A snapshot is either an entry in a YAML file — the form the docs recommend for new work — or a `.sql` file wrapping the definition in a Jinja `{% snapshot %}` block. Both parse, both run, and both are examinable. What separates them is not a matter of taste: they differ in what they can express, and in where the resulting relation lands.

The directory rule is not quite identical for the two. A `.sql` file holding a `{% snapshot %}` block has to sit under `snapshot-paths`; the same file under `models/` is parsed as a model and fails with `Encountered unknown tag 'snapshot'`. A YAML entry is looser — dbt reads one from a `.yml` file under `models/` too — but keeping both forms under `snapshot-paths` is what makes the directory conventions and `resource_type:snapshot` selection line up.

Start with the YAML form:

```
# snapshots/customers_snapshot.yml
snapshots:
  - name: customers_snapshot
    relation: source('jaffle', 'customers')
    config:
      schema: snapshots
      unique_key: customer_id
      strategy: timestamp
      updated_at: updated_at
```

Four things to read off that block:

1. `name` — the snapshot's dbt identifier, and what you pass to `ref()` downstream. It is independent of the file name; one YAML file can declare several snapshots, and the file itself can be called anything.
2. `relation` — the object being snapshotted, written as a `source()` or a `ref()` call. This field takes the place of the `select` statement in the block form, and the substitution is less innocent than it looks; the next subsection is about that.
3. `config` — everything that governs how the snapshot behaves. Two keys are always required, `unique_key` and `strategy`, and the strategy then pulls in one more: `updated_at` under `timestamp`, `check_cols` under `check`. That is the *required* set, not the permitted one — `check` accepts an `updated_at` as well, for a purpose §5.2 sets out. Everything else is optional, including `schema` and `database`, the SCD2-shaping configs `hard_deletes`, `dbt_valid_to_current` and `snapshot_meta_column_names`, and the general configs (`tags`, `enabled`, `alias`, `pre-hook`, `post-hook`, `grants`, `persist_docs`) that every resource type accepts. The config table is on `/docs/build/snapshots`; the reference list is `/reference/snapshot-configs`.
4. **There is no `select`.** The YAML form gives you nowhere to put a query.

Memorise the required set as a pair plus one — **`unique_key` and `strategy` always, plus whichever column that strategy needs** — rather than as a flat list of four. `target_schema`, which the block form required and which still parses, is not part of it, and swapping it for `schema` is not the cosmetic rename it looks like.

**Watch out — `target_schema` → `schema` moves the table.** The two keys resolve differently:

| Key | Resolves through | Effect |
|---|---|---|
| `target_schema` | nothing — it hard-codes one schema | the same physical location in every environment |

| Key | Resolves through | Effect |
|---|---|---|
| `schema` | `generate_schema_name`, exactly as a model's does (Ch 2 §2.3) | environment-aware; the default macro concatenates the target's schema onto the custom name |

> Flipping the key **relocates the relation**. Nothing errors and nothing is deleted: on Postgres the first run after the change wrote a fresh table at the new address — `dev_snapshots`, where the macro prefixes the target schema — and left the original orphaned at the old one, frozen at the moment of the migration. Move the key and the existing data in the same change, or move neither. `target_database` → `database` is the same pair one level up, routing through `generate_database_name`.

## The rest of a snapshot's YAML entry

`config:` is the part of the entry that changes behaviour, so it is the part this chapter has spent its words on. It is not the whole entry. A snapshot is a resource like any other, and its YAML block takes the property surface a model's does: `description`, `meta`, a `docs:` mapping with `show` and `node_color`, `data_tests` at the snapshot level, and a `columns:` list whose entries carry their own `description`, `quote`, `data_tests` and `config`. Generic tests attach to a snapshot exactly as they attach to a model (Ch 7), which is the practical reason to write the fuller entry rather than the three-key minimum:

```
snapshots:
  - name: customers_snapshot
    description: SCD2 history for the raw customer table.
    relation: source('jaffle', 'customers')
    config:
      schema: snapshots
      unique_key: customer_id
      strategy: timestamp
      updated_at: updated_at
    columns:
      - name: customer_id
        description: Natural key carried from the source system.
        data_tests:
          - not_null
      - name: email
        description: Address as recorded at the time of this version.
```

See `/reference/snapshot-properties` for the property list and `/reference/snapshot-configs` for the config list.

Two more things belong with the four-key reading above: what `unique_key` will accept, and where a snapshot's config can come from.

**`unique_key` is a shape, not just a column name.** It takes a single column, a list of columns for a composite key — `unique_key: [order_id, line_number]` — or an expression the warehouse can evaluate. What it does not take is a guarantee. dbt never tests the key for uniqueness, so a key that turns out not to be unique produces wrong SCD2 output rather than an error: versions closed out against the wrong row, and a point-in-time query that fans out on the join. The documented remedy is a uniqueness test on the *source* relation, where a duplicate is visible before it reaches the history — not on the snapshot, where several rows per key are the normal shape. See `/reference/resource-configs/unique_key`.

**Config can come from three places, and one of them has a scope you did not choose.** The property file's `config:` block, a `snapshots:` block in `dbt_project.yml`, and a `{{ config() }}` call inside a block-form snapshot resolve by the precedence order Ch 4 §4.2 sets out for models — the rules do not change for this resource type. The one addition is scope: a bare `snapshots:` key in `dbt_project.yml` configures the snapshots in installed packages as well as your own, while `snapshots:` followed by your project name confines the block to it.

### `relation:` takes a relation, not a query

The block form ends in a `select`, so it can do whatever a `select` can: restrict the column list, alias a column, filter rows, join. The YAML form has no such affordance. `relation:` names an object, and dbt captures that object as it stands.

Usually this costs nothing, because the query in a snapshot is almost always a bare `select *` — a snapshot's job is to preserve *all* columns of *all* rows over time, so projecting and filtering are rare to begin with. When a block-form snapshot does project, though, converting it changes what gets captured, silently and without an error. In practice, on Postgres, a snapshot whose block selected six columns and aliased `name as product_name` was rewritten as a YAML entry pointing `relation:` straight at the source table. The next run captured all nine raw columns — `created_at` and `loaded_at` among them, and `name` un-aliased — and reported success.

The decision rule is therefore about the query, not about the syntax:

- **A snapshot whose `select` is `select * from {{ source(...) }}`** converts to YAML cleanly and loses nothing. The `check_cols: all` case belongs here too: if you want every column watched, you also want every column captured.
- **A snapshot that projects, filters, aliases or joins** either stays a `{% snapshot %}` block, or moves its transformation into an ephemeral model that the YAML `relation:` then references with `ref()`. The docs recommend the ephemeral route for both forms, because it puts the transformation somewhere you can test and run on its own.

Read "YAML replaced the SQL block" as shorthand for the common case, not as a general claim. The two forms are interchangeable in one direction only.

## The legacy `{% snapshot %}` block

The other form is a `.sql` file in `snapshots/` holding a Jinja block:

```
-- snapshots/customers_snapshot.sql
{% snapshot customers_snapshot %}

{{
    config(
        schema='snapshots',
        unique_key='customer_id',
        strategy='timestamp',
        updated_at='updated_at'
    )
}}

select * from {{ source('jaffle', 'customers') }}

{% endsnapshot %}
```

Three pieces inside the outer block, in order:

1. **{% snapshot <name> %} / {% endsnapshot %}** — the outer block. The name in the opening tag is the snapshot's dbt identifier, the same thing `name:` supplies in YAML.
2. **{{ config(...) }}** — the same configuration surface, spelled as keyword arguments rather than as a YAML mapping. The keys and their meanings do not change between the forms.
3. **The `select` statement** — the query dbt runs on each invocation to pull the current state of the source table; it uses `source()` just as a staging model would.

This form is documented and supported — `/reference/resource-configs/snapshots-jinja-legacy` exists to describe it, and offers it for use "in any dbt version". It is legacy in the sense that dbt Labs recommends YAML for new snapshots, not in the sense that it warns or breaks.

Two of its keys are worth learning as a pair, because each is the older spelling of something you have already met: `target_schema` (the warning above) and `invalidate_hard_deletes`, the boolean that `hard_deletes` replaced (§5.2). Every snapshot written before the YAML form existed uses those spellings, so they are what a mature repo will show you and what your muscle memory will offer under exam pressure.

See `/reference/commands/snapshot` for the command that executes snapshots in either form.

## The metadata columns dbt adds

By default, every row in a snapshot table carries four columns that dbt adds automatically:

| Generated column | Meaning |
|---|---|
| `dbt_valid_from` | Timestamp at which this version of the row first became current. Under the `timestamp` strategy it comes from the source record's `updated_at`, so the oldest snapshot of a row can be dated well before the first `dbt snapshot` run that observed it; under `check` with no `updated_at` configured (§5.2), it is the snapshot run's wall-clock time. |
| `dbt_valid_to` | Timestamp at which this version of the row stopped being current. `NULL` for the row version that is current *right now*; a concrete timestamp on every superseded version. |
| `dbt_scd_id` | A unique identifier generated by dbt for each snapshotted row version. Useful as a primary key for the snapshot table. |
| `dbt_updated_at` | Under the `timestamp` strategy, this is the `updated_at` timestamp from the source record that caused the snapshot row to be added or updated, and is typically equal to `dbt_valid_from`. Under the `check` strategy, unless an `updated_at` is configured as well (§5.2), there is no source-side update timestamp, so dbt sets `dbt_updated_at` to the snapshot run's wall-clock time. |

The validity-interval columns (`dbt_valid_from`, `dbt_valid_to`) are the point-in-time query hook: to answer "what did this customer look like on July 1st?", you `where dbt_valid_from`

`<= '2024-07-01' and (dbt_valid_to > '2024-07-01' or dbt_valid_to is null)`. Without snapshots you would have had to log row changes yourself; with snapshots the log is a first-class dbt table.

"By default" is load-bearing. Three configs change that picture, and each one changes something a downstream query depends on — which is why they are worth knowing even though none of them is required.

**`dbt_valid_to_current` changes what the current row holds.** Set it, and dbt writes the value you name into `dbt_valid_to` on the currently-valid version instead of `NULL`. The value is a string containing an expression the warehouse understands, conventionally a far-future date:

```
config:
  schema: snapshots
  unique_key: customer_id
  strategy: timestamp
  updated_at: updated_at
  dbt_valid_to_current: "to_date('9999-12-31')"
```

The reason to do this lives downstream. With the default `NULL`, the current row's interval is open at one end, so every point-in-time predicate needs the guard you saw above — `dbt_valid_to > '2024-07-01' or dbt_valid_to is null` — and every consumer has to remember it. With a sentinel, both ends are closed, `between` and plain range comparisons work unchanged, and the guard disappears. The cost is the idiom the guard replaced: `where dbt_valid_to is null` now returns **zero rows** rather than the current ones. Neither predicate errors; the wrong one just comes back empty. Read the config before you write a current-row predicate against someone else's snapshot. See `/reference/resource-configs/dbt_valid_to_current`.

**`snapshot_meta_column_names` changes what they are called.** It takes a dictionary mapping dbt's name to the name your team uses, and it accepts any of the metadata columns:

```
config:
  snapshot_meta_column_names:
    dbt_valid_from: start_date
    dbt_valid_to: end_date
```

That is a house-style convenience rather than an exam-heavy config, but it is the reason the table above describes a default rather than a guarantee: a snapshot with no column literally named `dbt_valid_to` is still a perfectly ordinary snapshot. See `/reference/resource-configs/snapshot_meta_column_names`.

**`hard_deletes: new_record` adds a fifth column.** That one belongs with the rest of the hard-delete story, in §5.2.

### Watch out — migrating a live snapshot

A snapshot cannot be rebuilt. Drop the table and the history is gone, because the history is the only place those observations were ever recorded and nothing upstream can regenerate them. That is the documented reason to give snapshots their own schema, their own privileges and on some platforms their own role — and it is why changing a config on a snapshot that already holds rows is a different operation from changing one on a model.

The two configs above fail in opposite ways when you set them on a built snapshot, and the direction is not the one you would guess.

**`snapshot_meta_column_names` errors and writes nothing.** The run reaches the snapshot materialization, finds the target relation does not carry the columns the config names, and stops:

```
Compilation Error in snapshot customers_snapshot
  Snapshot target is missing configured columns (missing "start_date", "end_date").
```

The failure lands at run time rather than at parse time, so a `dbt parse` will not catch it — but nothing is written, and the table is exactly as it was.

**`dbt_valid_to_current` succeeds and leaves the table inconsistent.** dbt does not adjust the current rows it already wrote, deliberately, so as not to modify data you did not ask it to modify. In practice, on Postgres, a four-row snapshot carrying real history took the new config, ran, and reported `INSERT 0 0` at exit 0 — no back-fill, no warning, no error. Rows that already had `NULL` keep `NULL`; only rows that change on some later run get the sentinel. A run or two later the current rows are split between the two conventions, and `where dbt_valid_to is null`, `where dbt_valid_to = '9999-12-31'` and a plain range predicate each return part of the answer. None of the three errors.

Migrating back is worse. With the config removed, dbt's current-row predicate narrows to `dbt_valid_to is null` again, so every sentinel-bearing row drops out of the comparison set and is never closed. The next change to such a row inserts a second open version beside the first — two overlapping validity intervals for one `unique_key`, at exit 0, which fans out on any join downstream.

So the config that errors is the safe one. The route out is the same for both and it is manual: back up the table, `alter table` it into the shape the new config expects — adding the renamed columns, or updating the current rows' `dbt_valid_to` to the sentinel — and rehearse the change in development before production. See `/reference/resource-configs/dbt_valid_to_current` and `/reference/resource-configs/snapshot_meta_column_names`.

One failure has a manual repair you should not reach for:

```
Snapshot target is missing configured columns (missing "dbt_scd_id", "dbt_valid_from", "
    dbt_valid_to")
```

Same message as the rename failure above, and from the same check — dbt looks for those three column *names* on the target relation and nothing else. So adding them by hand does clear the error, and the run then succeeds. Do not do it. What dbt is telling you is that the relation was not built by a snapshot at all, and a table that satisfies a column-name check without ever having been snapshotted holds NULL metadata on every row it already contains: no `dbt_scd_id` to match on, no closed interval behind it. The first change to one of those rows opens a second interval beside an unclosed first, and the history you were trying to keep is now wrong rather than missing. The honest route is to drop the relation and let `dbt snapshot` build it fresh — discarding whatever the table held. The route in is a legacy project where a snapshot was configured `materialized='table'`: correcting that config leaves a plain table sitting at the target. At 1.11 the door is shut at the front — `A snapshot must have a materialized value of 'snapshot'` is a parse-time error — so the mistake surfaces before anything is built rather than after, and you meet this only on a project that carried the misconfiguration forward.

## Watch out — the source query drifts, the snapshot table only half-follows

Add a column to a snapshot's `select` and dbt adds it to the destination on the next run. Widen a `varchar(50)` to `varchar(200)` and dbt expands the destination column to match. That is the whole of what it reconciles.

It never drops a column you removed from the query, and it never changes an existing column's type beyond that size expansion — `string` to `date` is not applied. Both are deliberate: dropping a column would destroy history, and retyping one could fail against the data already stored. The consequence is that a long-lived snapshot accumulates columns nobody selects any more, frozen at the values they held when they stopped being populated, alongside columns typed by a decision made two years ago. Nothing warns you. Once the drift matters, the fix is again manual: build the new shape alongside, migrate, cut over.

### When snapshots are the right tool

The blueprint expects you to recognise a snapshot scenario on sight. The signal is: **a slowly-changing source table without its own history, where downstream analytics needs to answer point-in-time questions.** Concretely:

- `customers` table whose `address`, `tier`, and `status` columns are updated in place — and finance needs "what was this customer's tier at time of each transaction?"
- `product_catalog` table that changes prices and descriptions over time, where marketing wants "what was this product's price the day each order was placed?"
- `employee_assignments` table that changes cost-centre mappings, where HR reporting needs "which cost-centre owned each time entry on the day it was submitted?"

Signal that snapshot is **not** the right tool:

- The source table is **append-only** — every update inserts a new row with a `created_at`. That's already SCD2 in the raw layer; you don't need dbt to re-derive it. Write an incremental model (Ch 4 §4.3) instead.
- The warehouse already records the change history — Delta Lake's Change Data Feed, Snowflake's Time Travel, BigQuery's change-history tables. If the raw layer already exposes row-level history, a snapshot re-derives it; read the history the source publishes instead. Check the retention window before you rely on it, though: all three are *retained* change data, not permanent history. CDF records nothing from before it was enabled and keeps records only as long as the table's history is retained, so where the requirement is history that outlives the retention window, something has to materialise it — a snapshot, or a downstream SCD2 table built from the feed. (§5.6 has a real-project example of this exact choice.) See the analyse-level question Q18 at the end of this chapter.
- **The arithmetic does not work.** A snapshot re-reads the entire source relation every run, so it costs rows × runs no matter how many rows actually changed. A 400-million-row table swept hourly to catch a few thousand daily edits pays for 9.6 billion row-reads a day to record a few thousand facts. When volume times update-frequency reaches that shape, the answer is a change feed from the source, not a better-tuned snapshot.

The rule of thumb: snapshots excel when the source is mutable and no upstream process is already capturing history. The docs state a purpose rather than a rate — dbt "provides a mechanism, **snapshots**, which records changes to a mutable table over time" (`/docs/build/snapshots`) — so the question is whether those changes are already recorded somewhere, not how fast they arrive. Where they are, reach for that instead.

---

## 5.2 Snapshot strategies — timestamp vs check

The `strategy` config is required; there is no default. It tells dbt *how* to decide whether a row has changed since the last snapshot run. Two built-in strategies — `timestamp` and `check` — cover essentially every real case. See `/docs/build/snapshots` for the recommended-strategy framing and `/reference/resource-configs/strategy` for the reference definition.

### `timestamp` — the preferred strategy

Set `strategy: timestamp` when the source table has a column that monotonically increases whenever a row is updated. The config pattern:

```
config:
  schema: snapshots
  unique_key: customer_id
  strategy: timestamp
  updated_at: updated_at
```

On each `dbt snapshot` run, dbt compares the incoming row's `updated_at` to the `dbt_valid_from` recorded on the current version of that row in the snapshot table. The comparison column is `dbt_valid_from`, not `dbt_updated_at`, and deliberately so: `dbt_valid_from` is always present, whereas a snapshot first built under `check` may hold historical rows that never carried the `updated_at` you have just configured. If the incoming value is newer, dbt closes out the old version (sets `dbt_valid_to` to the incoming row's `updated_at`) and inserts a new row version. If the values match, nothing happens.

Two properties make `timestamp` the preferred strategy when you can use it:

1. **It is cheap.** dbt only compares two timestamps per row, not the full row body. On a large table, that matters.
2. **Its change signal is narrow.** One column decides, so nothing else in the row can version it. Under `check`, anything in the watched set can — which is the `check_cols: all` trap below. Neither strategy drifts on its own: a second run over an unchanged table writes no new version under either.

The trap is the `updated_at` column itself — exactly the trap from Ch 3 §3.3 on source freshness. The column must advance *only* when a row is genuinely updated. An `updated_at` that every nightly re-sync bumps to `now()` (even when the underlying data is unchanged) will produce spurious new versions every run. See `/reference/resource-configs/updated_at`.

### `check` — the fallback when no `updated_at` exists

Set `strategy: check` when the source table has no reliable update timestamp. dbt compares the values of a specified list of columns — or all columns — between the incoming row and the current snapshot row, and considers the row changed if any value differs.

```
config:
  schema: snapshots
  unique_key: customer_id
  strategy: check
  check_cols:
    - email
    - address
    - tier
```

`check_cols` takes either a list of column names or the literal string `all`. The trade-off:

- **Specific columns** (`check_cols: [email, address]`) — fast, deterministic, explicit about what counts as a change. The cost is discipline: if you add a column to the source that you care about tracking, you have to add it to `check_cols` manually.
- `check_cols: all` — catches every column automatically, so you never miss a change. The cost is that *any* column change counts as a row change: a rename, a cast, a whitespace normalisation — and, far more often than those three, an audit or load timestamp

(`loaded_at`, `updated_at`, `_ingested_at`) sitting in the snapshotted relation, which an ETL re-load bumps on every row it touches. On a 50-row product table, a `loaded_at`-only re-load produces 50 spurious SCD2 versions under `all` and none under an explicit `check_cols` list. The rule to carry away: `all` is a statement about the *projection*, not about the table. It is safe when your `select` controls the column list, and unsafe over a raw relation whose shape you do not own. Also slower on wide tables — the comparison is column by column, not a single hash of the row, so `all` makes the change predicate as wide as the relation.

See `/reference/resource-configs/check_cols`.

The asymmetry with `timestamp` is the strategy's real maintenance cost. `timestamp` watches one column and therefore covers the whole row for free — add a column to the source query and it is tracked from the next run. `check` watches exactly what you listed. Add a column and it is invisible to change-detection until somebody edits `check_cols`, and nothing tells you: no error, no warning, no log line observing that the source has columns the snapshot is not watching. The rows change upstream and the snapshot reports no changes, which reads exactly like a quiet period.

### `check` with an `updated_at`, and what `check_cols` compares

The pairing in §5.1 is a rule about what each strategy *requires*, not about what it will accept. `check` takes an `updated_at` as well, and a config block carrying both keys is valid:

```
config:
  schema: snapshots
  unique_key: customer_id
  strategy: check
  check_cols: [email, address, tier]
  updated_at: source_modified_at
```

`check_cols` still decides *whether* a row changed. What `updated_at` decides is *when*: dbt stamps `dbt_valid_from`, `dbt_valid_to` and `dbt_updated_at` from that column, exactly as the `timestamp` strategy does, instead of from the snapshot run's clock. Reach for the combination when the source carries a modification timestamp you want the history dated by, but whose movement is broader than the change you want to capture — it advances for columns outside `check_cols` too, so `strategy: timestamp` would version rows on edits you do not care about.

**Write a column name, not an expression.** The value is interpolated into the generated SQL, so an expression compiles — and the strategies then diverge. Under `check`, a `coalesce(upd, created)` keeps running. Under `timestamp` it builds on the first run and fails on every later one, because dbt qualifies the interpolated value with the source alias — `source_data.coalesce(upd, created)` — which only parses for a bare column name: `column reference "upd" is ambiguous`. If the timestamp has to be computed, compute it in an ephemeral model and point `relation:` at that — the same escape hatch §5.1 gives a snapshot that needs to project. dbt also warns when the column's data type does not match the adapter's configured default, which is the signal that a snapshot is comparing a date against a timestamp. See `/reference/resource-configs/updated_at`.

It also has to be populated, and dbt does not check. Configure `updated_at` and dbt stamps from it unconditionally: a row whose value is null gets `NULL` in `dbt_valid_from`, `dbt_valid_to` and `dbt_updated_at` rather than a fall-back to the run clock — and because the current version is then never closed, that row's next change opens a second interval beside the first, two open versions on one `unique_key` at exit 0 with `WARN=0`. The wall-clock stamps in §5.1's table are the `check` snapshot with *no* `updated_at` configured, which is the other case entirely. A nullable modification timestamp is the ordinary shape of a source you reached for `check` to handle, so coalesce it in the ephemeral model above rather than pointing `updated_at` straight at it.

One property of the comparison itself is worth knowing before you put a nullable column in `check_cols`. dbt does not compare the two values with a bare `=`, which would make a null on both sides read as unknown rather than as unchanged; it tests each column for inequality *and* for a null on one side only. So a value that goes from populated to null, or from null to populated, counts as a change, and a column null on both sides does not.

## Which strategy to pick

A decision flow:

1. Does the source table have a column that monotonically advances whenever a row is updated *and does not move for unchanged rows*? → **`strategy: timestamp`** with that column as `updated_at`.
2. Otherwise, is there a small, stable set of columns whose changes you care about? → **`strategy: check`** with an explicit `check_cols` list.
3. Otherwise, you want to catch any change to any column and accept the cost? → **`strategy: check`** with `check_cols: all`.

**`timestamp`** is what the docs recommend, and schema-evolution robustness is the reason they give — be able to name it on demand.

## Hard deletes — the `hard_deletes` config

Real source tables sometimes hard-delete rows: a row is simply gone on the next sync. Left alone, a snapshot keeps the last observed version of that row as current, **`dbt_valid_to`** unset — the snapshot cannot tell a deleted row from a row that nobody has touched in a while. **`hard_deletes`** is how you tell it the difference. It is not a fourth strategy; it is an opt-in that layers onto whichever strategy you already chose, and it takes three values:

| `hard_deletes` | What dbt does when a row disappears from the source |
|---|---|
| `ignore` | The default. Nothing. The last observed version stays current forever. |
| `invalidate` | Closes the row out — sets **`dbt_valid_to`** on the current version, exactly as if the row had been superseded. The history then has a gap where the row used to be, with no record of *why* it ended. |
| `new_record` | Inserts a new row version marking the deletion explicitly, and adds a **`dbt_is_deleted`** column to the relation to carry the marker. History stays continuous; a restore later shows up as a further row with **`dbt_is_deleted`** set back to false. |

```
config:
  schema: snapshots
  unique_key: customer_id
  strategy: timestamp
```

```
    updated_at: updated_at
    hard_deletes: new_record
```

The examinable detail is the column, and specifically what causes it. `dbt_is_deleted` **is added by `hard_deletes: new_record`, not by snapshots in general.** In practice, on Postgres, a snapshot configured `new_record` came back with `dbt_scd_id`, `dbt_updated_at`, `dbt_valid_from`, `dbt_valid_to` *and* `dbt_is_deleted`, while a snapshot in the same project configured `ignore` carried only the first four. It also comes back typed `text` rather than boolean, so treat it as a string in downstream predicates. A question that asks which columns a snapshot table carries is asking about the default configuration unless the stem shows you a `hard_deletes` setting; a question that shows you `dbt_is_deleted` has told you the setting.

Choose between the two active modes on what the gap costs you. `invalidate` is enough when a missing row is simply the end of the story and nobody will ask why the interval closed. `new_record` is what you want when deletions are themselves an event worth reporting on, or when a row can come back and you need the return visible in the history rather than inferred from a second `dbt_valid_from`.

One trap, and it is a naming trap rather than a behavioural one. The deprecated boolean `invalidate_hard_deletes: true` does what `hard_deletes: invalidate` does, and it still has a live reference page of its own — so the older name is the one you will read in existing repos and the one your fingers will type. There is no `hard_deletes: true`, and `invalidate_hard_deletes` has no `new_record` equivalent. Write `hard_deletes`; recognise `invalidate_hard_deletes`; and do not write both on one snapshot, which is an error rather than a redundancy — dbt raises `You cannot set both the invalidate_hard_deletes and hard_deletes config properties on the same snapshot.` See `/reference/resource-configs/hard-deletes` and, for the boolean, `/reference/resource-configs/invalidate_hard_deletes`.

**Turning `hard_deletes` on later is not a migration, and the two modes fail differently.** Switching a live snapshot to `new_record` does not produce a mixed table — it does not run at all. The next `dbt snapshot` stops with `Compilation Error ... Snapshot target is missing configured columns (missing "dbt_is_deleted")`, because `assert_valid_snapshot_target_given_strategy` is called before `create_columns` in the snapshot materialization, so the run can never add the column it is waiting for. You add it yourself, or you rebuild. Switching to `invalidate` does run — and it is not inert either: a row deleted from the source *before* the change is closed on the retrofit run, stamped with that run's own timestamp rather than with when the deletion actually happened. Neither mode leaves you where you were, and neither is a clean cutover. The remedy is the manual one from §5.1: back up, bring the existing rows into the new convention with your own `update`, and rehearse it outside production first.

---

## 5.3 The `dbt snapshot` command

`dbt snapshot` runs every snapshot in the project (or a selected subset) against the warehouse, in whichever form it is declared. The docs for the command are at `/reference/commands/snapshot`.

```
dbt snapshot                              # run every snapshot
dbt snapshot --select customers_snapshot  # run one
dbt snapshot --exclude legacy_snapshots+  # run all except a subtree
```

Selector semantics are the same as `dbt run` — `--select`, `--exclude`, `--selector`, and the graph operators. The full selector language lives in Ch 11.

### What the command actually does

For each snapshot, dbt:

1. Reads its config (`unique_key`, `strategy`, the strategy-specific column, and any of `schema`, `hard_deletes` or `dbt_valid_to_current` that are set) from wherever it is declared.
2. Queries the relation against the warehouse — the `select` in a block-form snapshot, the object named by `relation:` in a YAML one. This is the "current-state" query.
3. Compares the current-state result to the existing snapshot table (if it exists) using the configured strategy.
4. For each row that has changed, closes the previous version (sets `dbt_valid_to` to the new row's `updated_at` under `timestamp`, and to the snapshot run's timestamp under `check` — unless an `updated_at` is configured there too, which §5.2 covers) and inserts a new current row version, whose `dbt_valid_to` is `NULL` unless `dbt_valid_to_current` names a sentinel.
5. For each row that has not changed, does nothing.
6. On the first run, creates the snapshot table from scratch — every source row becomes its initial version.

One consequence of that sequence is worth carrying into a debugging session. At 1.11 a snapshot has no compiled **file**. `dbt compile` does render the SQL — it prints `Compiled node '<name>' is:` with the resolved SELECT, exit 0, in either declaration form — and the manifest carries `compiled_code` for a selected snapshot. What stays empty is `compiled_path`, which is `None` on every snapshot node, so nothing is written under `target/compiled/` to open in an editor. Read the config, then read the warehouse table.

### A snapshot sees only what was there when it ran

`dbt snapshot` is a point-in-time sweep, not change data capture. It reads the source as it stands at the moment it runs and compares that to the current versions already in the snapshot table. Anything that happened between two runs, and did not survive to the second one, was never observed — and never will be.

Run the snapshot nightly at 02:00, and suppose a customer's tier goes gold to platinum at 09:00 and back to gold at 16:00. The next run sees gold, compares it to gold, and writes nothing. There is no platinum row, no gap, and no warning: the history simply says the tier never changed that day. The same swallowing happens to any change superseded by a later one before the next sweep — only the last state of the interval is ever recorded.

So cadence is a modelling decision rather than an ops detail. **The run has to be more frequent than the changes you need to see.** If finance needs intra-day tier history, a nightly snapshot cannot supply it however correctly it is configured, and the answer is a tighter schedule or a source that publishes its own change feed (§5.1).

### Where `dbt snapshot` fits in the pipeline

Three practical points the exam leans on.

**It is part of `dbt build`.** Running `dbt build` executes snapshots alongside models, seeds, and tests, in DAG order with short-circuit-on-failure. For small projects this is fine — the snapshot runs on every `dbt build` tick.

**At scale, snapshots are usually isolated.** Because snapshots capture a point-in-time observation, you do **not** want to re-run them as often as you run models. The idiomatic large-project pattern is:

- A dedicated snapshot job runs `dbt snapshot --select tag:snapshots_hourly` on a fixed schedule (every hour, every few hours, daily), independent of the main build.

- The main build pipeline runs `dbt build --exclude resource_type:snapshot` so downstream models read the current state of the snapshot tables without re-triggering captures.

This separation matters because a snapshot's whole contract is "I observed the source at this moment." Running a snapshot on every CI build would pollute the validity-interval timeline with CI-scheduled captures, which is usually not what you want.

**Snapshots are not rebuilt by `--full-refresh`.** Unlike incremental models, snapshots ignore the `full_refresh` config, and the `--full-refresh` CLI flag does nothing to them — `dbt build --full-refresh` runs the snapshot normally, without dropping or recreating the snapshot table, and `dbt snapshot` does not register the flag at all: `dbt snapshot --full-refresh` exits with `Error: No such option: --full-refresh`. The history *is* the point; a routine CLI flag does not destroy it. If you ever need to rebuild a snapshot from scratch, drop the warehouse table manually and run `dbt snapshot` again; the next run creates the table fresh.

---

## 5.4 Seeds — loading CSV reference data

A **seed** is a CSV file in your project that dbt loads into the warehouse as a table. You write the CSV; `dbt seed` reads it, creates (or re-creates) a table with columns matching the CSV header, and inserts the rows. The created table is available downstream via `ref('seed_name')` just like a model.

Seeds live in `seeds/` by default, configurable via `seed-paths` in `dbt_project.yml`. The concept page is `/docs/build/seeds`.

```
seeds/
├── country_codes.csv
├── currency_codes.csv
└── risk_bands.csv
```

`country_codes.csv`:

```
country_code,country_name,region
US,United States,North America
GB,United Kingdom,Europe
AU,Australia,Asia Pacific
```

Running `dbt seed` creates a warehouse table `country_codes` with three columns — `country_code`, `country_name`, `region` — and three rows. A downstream model can then `{{ ref('country_codes') }}` to read it.

### The `dbt seed` command

```
dbt seed                                      # load every seed in seeds/
dbt seed --select country_codes              # load just one seed
dbt seed --select country_codes --full-refresh  # drop and recreate the table
```

One selector reads as if it would do more than it does. You edit `country_codes.csv`, want the models that depend on it rebuilt, and run `dbt run --select country_codes+`. The selector is valid — a seed is a graph node, so `+` resolves its children correctly and the right models run. What does not happen is the seed loading: `dbt run` executes models and nothing else, so the seed is selected, passed over as a non-model, and the downstream models read whatever rows are already sitting in the table. Exit 0, models green, mapping stale. dbt build --select country_codes+ is the invocation that does what you meant, because build runs seeds, models, snapshots and tests together in DAG order.

By default dbt seed uses a **truncate-and-insert** pattern — the existing table is truncated, then the CSV rows are inserted. Passing --full-refresh issues a drop and create instead, which is necessary whenever the CSV's column set changes (new columns added, types changed, columns removed). Documented at /reference/commands/seed and /faqs/Seeds/full-refresh-seed.

That default is a safety property, not just an optimisation. Truncate-and-insert leaves the table object in place, so anything built directly on it *outside* the DAG survives the load — a BI view, a grant, a materialized view a platform team created by hand. --full-refresh drops the table first, and the drop **cascades**: the BI view built on country_codes goes with it, and dbt reports success, because from dbt's side the seed rebuilt perfectly. Before reaching for --full-refresh on a seed that has been in production a while, know what is layered on top of it.

> **On --show.** --show *is* a dbt seed flag: after the load it prints a random sample of up to ten rows of each seed it wrote. What it is not is a selector — it takes no value, so dbt seed --show country_codes fails on the stray positional, and the working spelling is dbt seed --select country_codes --show. dbt show is a separate command, documented at /reference/commands/show: it previews the first N rows of a model, test, analysis, or inline SQL query (--inline) by compiling its SQL and running it with a limit. It previews a seed too, but by loading it first — so neither route reads a CSV without writing it. To read the file, open it; to read what landed, select * from <seed_name> limit 10 in the warehouse after dbt seed has run.

## Seed configs — column_types, quote_columns, delimiter, enabled

/reference/seed-configs splits these four: quote_columns, column_types and delimiter are listed under "Seed-specific configurations", and enabled under "General configurations" that seeds share with every other resource. They are set under a seeds: block in dbt_project.yml — or, equivalently, in a seed properties YAML file under seeds: - name: <seed-name>; config: {...} (the per-seed YAML form documented at /reference/seed-configs). Configuring from inside the CSV itself is not possible.

```
# dbt_project.yml
seeds:
  my_project:
    +schema: reference                        # all seeds write to the reference schema
    country_codes:
      +column_types:
        country_code: varchar(2)
        country_name: varchar(128)
    currency_codes:
      +quote_columns: true                    # keep column names exactly as written
    risk_bands:
      +delimiter: "|"                         # CSV is actually pipe-delimited
    legacy_regions:
      +enabled: false                         # keep the file but don't load it
```

What each one does:

| Config | What it does | Set it when |
|---|---|---|
| `column_types` | Maps a column name to an explicit warehouse data type, in place of dbt's inference from the CSV rows. | the inferred type is wrong or ambiguous — see the next subsection |
| `quote_columns` | `true` quotes every column name in the create-table DDL, preserving case and allowing special characters; `false` does not quote. The default is adapter-specific. | the CSV's column names need case preservation, or carry characters the warehouse would otherwise reject |
| `delimiter` | Names the CSV's field separator, default `,`; set `;`, `\t` or a pipe for a non-comma file. dbt has no auto-detection, so the config has to match the file. | the file is not comma-separated |
| `enabled` | `false` keeps the CSV in the repo but skips it on `dbt seed`. | a seed is temporarily retired, or loaded only under a specific run-time profile |

See `/reference/resource-configs/column_types` and `/reference/resource-configs/quote_columns`.

### Hooks on a seed add up; they do not override

Most seed configs behave the way `dbt_project.yml` trains you to expect: set `+schema: reference` at the project level and `schema: staging` on one seed, and the specific value wins. **Hooks are the exception.** A `post-hook` in `dbt_project.yml` and a `post-hook` in the seed's own config block are *cumulative* — both run. Write a project-level `grant select` hook, then add a per-seed hook granting to one more role, and you get both grants rather than the second one only.

The rule is the same for models, and it is the one config-precedence question where "more specific overrides" is the wrong answer. If you need the project-level hook not to run for one resource, narrow the project-level config; restating it on the resource adds, it does not replace.

### When column types are inferred vs explicit

Without `column_types`, dbt looks at the CSV rows and picks a warehouse type per column based on what it sees (integers if every value parses as an int, strings otherwise, floats if any decimals). That inference is fine for well-behaved data — product categories, department names, integer row counts — and wrong in two classic ways: a ZIP or postcode column with leading zeros may infer integer and drop the zero, and a `country_code` column holding only two-letter codes today may infer `varchar(2)` and then truncate a three-letter code like `'USA'` added later. Mixed-type columns fail the same way — a column where "N/A" is supposed to be a string but "42" turns up later in the file. The explicit `column_types` map is the reliable-in-production option; inference is the "quick start" default.

Two things about `column_types` surprise people, and both fail quietly.

**The keys are matched case-sensitively, and `quote_columns` does not change that.** A CSV whose header reads `Country_Name` is not configured by a key of `country_name`: the key matches no column, dbt falls back to inference for it, and there is no "unknown column" error to tell you. Copy the key from the CSV header, character for character.

**And the config only takes effect when the table is created.** Add or edit `column_types` on a seed that has already been loaded, run `dbt seed`, and the column keeps its old type — the default load truncates and re-inserts into the existing table, so the DDL that would have applied the new type never runs. Exit 0, no warning, wrong type still in place. `dbt seed --full-refresh` drops and recreates, and is what actually applies the change. Which is the trap doubling back on itself: the flag you need is the one that cascades.

### Size limits — the docs set a purpose, not a row count

Seeds load by insert — the sample run on `/docs/build/seeds` reports `OK loaded seed file analytics.country_codes...................... [INSERT 3 in 0.01s]`. The docs set no row limit. They set a purpose instead: seeds "are best suited to static data which changes infrequently", their listed good use cases are a country-code mapping, a list of test emails and a list of employee account IDs, and "Loading raw data that has been exported to CSVs" is listed as a poor use case. The seed-data FAQ is blunter: "Seeds should **not** be used to load raw data (for example, large CSV exports from a production database)" and "Loading CSVs using dbt's seed functionality is not performant for large files. Consider using a different tool to load these CSVs into your data warehouse." So the test is not a row count — it is whether the file is business-specific logic a human edits and commits, or an export. If it is an export, you're misusing the tool; see §5.5.

---

## 5.5 Seeds vs sources — a common confusion

The seed/source decision is one of the most commonly muddled topics in real dbt projects. The rule is short:

- **Seed** — small, static, version-controlled, human-edited, loaded from a CSV inside the dbt repo. Examples: ISO country codes; a hand-maintained list of internal test-account email domains to exclude from analytics; a finance team's manual product-category mapping; a fixed tax-rate lookup.
- **Source** — raw data already loaded into the warehouse by some *other* system (Fivetran, Airbyte, a stored procedure, a streaming pipeline). Examples: every production transaction; an application's user table; daily event streams from a product.

The five dimensions on which they differ:

| Dimension | Seed | Source |
|---|---|---|
| **Who owns the data?** | The dbt project's team (analytics engineers). | Upstream — an ingestion tool, a product team, a third party. |
| **Where does the data live before dbt touches it?** | A CSV file committed to the dbt repo. | Already a table in the warehouse. |
| **How does it get into the warehouse?** | `dbt seed` loads it. | An external process loads it; dbt never writes to it. |
| **How does it change?** | Edited by a human, reviewed via PR, loaded again on the next `dbt seed`. | Inserted / updated / deleted by the external loader. |

| Dimension | Seed | Source |
|---|---|---|
| **Scale?** | Hundreds to low thousands of rows. | Anywhere from a few rows to billions. |

### A worked scenario: "new orders this week"

A product-team Slack message says: "Can you add a CSV I exported from the orders database to dbt so my dashboard can use it? It's this week's orders — about 180,000 rows."

**Is this a seed or a source?**

Walk the table. *Who owns the data?* The orders database — so not analytics-engineering. *Where does it live before dbt?* In the application's orders table, which must already be syncing into the warehouse somehow (or should be). *Is it static?* No — next week there will be a new CSV. *How does it change?* Orders are created, updated, cancelled continuously upstream.

Every dimension points at **source**, not seed. Two further costs the table does not carry:

1. **Git is not a data-transport mechanism.** Checking a 180,000-row CSV into the repo bloats it, makes diffs unreadable, and breaks PR review. Every week adds another file; every merge conflicts on the CSV.
2. **Losing the upstream connection hides reality.** If orders have a `status` that changes after insert (shipped / delivered / cancelled), the weekly-export CSV freezes each order's status at export time. Meanwhile the real database has up-to-date statuses that the dbt project has no access to.

The right answer is: *"get the orders table loaded into the warehouse via Fivetran / a proper ingestion job, then declare it as a source in your `sources.yml`."* That is Ch 3 material; the seed is wrong for this data, not because seeds are technically incapable of loading 180,000 rows, but because every operational property of this data makes "seed" the wrong home.

### Common seed use cases

- ISO country / currency / region codes.
- A fixed tax-rate lookup.
- A mapping of internal email domains to department codes.
- An exclusion list of test accounts to filter from production analytics.
- A manual product-category taxonomy that the analytics team curates.
- Holiday calendars used for date-spine joins.

In all of these, *the analytics team owns the data*, *it changes a few times a year at most*, *it is small*, and *its history is captured fine in git*.

---

## 5.6 In practice: the Credora project uses seeds heavily, snapshots not at all

> *This section is an "in practice" sidebar. It draws a composite pattern from (a) the seeds reference at `/docs/build/seeds` and (b) the snapshots reference at `/docs/build/snapshots`. Credora is fictional (`credora`); Ch 14's opening note has the composite-project disclaimer.*

`credora` shows a pattern you will see repeatedly in mature dbt projects on modern lakehouse platforms: **seeds are used liberally for reference data across every market catalog, but the project declares zero snapshots — the `snapshot-paths` key points at a `snapshots/` directory that is genuinely empty.** SCD2 history is handled entirely outside dbt, by the underlying Delta Lake layer and an upstream CDC tool.

## Seeds across markets

Each of Credora's market catalogs (`cr_uk`, `cr_us`, `cr_apac_1`, etc.) ships a small library of reference seeds under per-market paths like `seeds/cr_uk/` and `seeds/cr_us/`. Typical contents:

```
seeds/cr_uk/
├── uk_currency_codes.csv         # ISO 4217 currencies relevant to UK market
├── uk_risk_bands.csv             # credit-risk band thresholds, set by risk team
├── uk_product_tiers.csv          # product-tier labels and their pricing plans
└── uk_internal_test_accounts.csv  # test accounts to exclude from analytics
```

The `dbt_project.yml` block governing seeds looks roughly like:

```
seeds:
  credora:
    +schema: reference
    +quote_columns: true
    cr_uk:
      +database: cr_uk
    cr_us:
      +database: cr_us
    cr_apac_1:
      +database: cr_apac_1
```

Three patterns visible there:

- **Per-market catalog routing.** The same folder-cascading `+database:` pattern from Ch 2 §2.6 applies — seeds under `seeds/cr_uk/` write to the `cr_uk` catalog, and so on.
- **A dedicated `reference` schema.** Every seed lands in the `reference` schema of its catalog, separate from the `staging`, `intermediate`, and `analytics` schemas used by models. That keeps the object namespace clean and makes grants simpler — the `reference` schema has different read-access rules from `analytics` in some markets.
- **`quote_columns: true` as the default.** Several Credora seeds have multi-word column names (`"Risk Band Label"`) or case-sensitive column identifiers required by the downstream BI tool. Setting `quote_columns: true` at the project level avoids surprises; specific seeds override it where appropriate.

## The missing `snapshots/` directory

`dbt_project.yml` declares:

```
snapshot-paths: ["snapshots"]
```

But the `snapshots/` directory declares nothing — no `.sql` blocks and no `snapshots:` YAML either, which is the check to make now that both forms live in that directory. `dbt snapshot` runs and finds nothing to execute. This is deliberate. SCD2 at Credora is handled two ways outside dbt:

1. **Delta Lake Change Data Feed (CDF).** Source tables on Databricks are Delta tables with CDF enabled; row-level changes are queryable as a stream, and the upstream ingestion layer has materialised SCD2-shaped history tables in the raw catalog. dbt models read those history tables as sources — they are already SCD2. Note where the durability actually comes from: the materialised history tables, not the feed. CDF starts at enablement and is bounded by the table's retention, so it is the mechanism that *feeds* permanent history rather than the thing that holds it.
2. **A vendored CDC tool** on the warehouse-adjacent raw layer captures and versions the mutable source tables that don't have CDF enabled. Its output tables carry the same SCD2 shape `dbt snapshot` would produce — one row per version, with a validity interval — under the tool's own column names rather than dbt's `dbt_`-prefixed ones, so downstream dbt models consume them as sources.

The pedagogical takeaway: *snapshots are not a failure of mature dbt projects; they are one of several SCD2 options, and a project whose lakehouse already records row-level change history can read that instead.* The decision is not "dbt or nothing" — it's "which layer owns SCD2, and which is cheapest to maintain at your scale?" Credora's scale (multiple markets, high-volume event data, existing lakehouse history) tips the decision away from dbt snapshots. A smaller project with one market, no CDF, and no CDC tool would tip the other way.

### Dual source — this choice is not unique to Credora

The mechanism Credora leans on instead of `dbt snapshot` is a documented platform feature, not a local invention:

- Databricks' Change Data Feed documentation describes CDF as tracking "row-level changes between versions of a Delta Lake table or Apache Iceberg v3 table", and states: "Each change record includes the row data along with metadata that indicates whether the row was inserted, updated, or deleted." That is row-level history recorded by the storage layer rather than by dbt, and the page lists "Audit trails that track data modifications for compliance and governance requirements" among its use cases — the same point-in-time need §5.1 gives as a reason to snapshot.

The Credora sketch above is a composite. The specific choice — `snapshot-paths` declared, `snapshots/` empty, SCD2 delegated to Delta + CDC — rests on the documented platform feature quoted above rather than on `dbt snapshot`. It is worth flagging in a book like this because readers encountering a project with no snapshots sometimes conclude the project is "missing something" — more often, the project has deliberately chosen a different SCD2 layer.

---

## Summary

- A **snapshot** is dbt's SCD2 primitive: a table that captures every historical version of every source row, with `dbt_valid_from`, `dbt_valid_to`, `dbt_scd_id` and `dbt_updated_at` added by default.
- **Two declaration forms, both current.** A YAML entry under `snapshots:` with `name`, `relation` and `config` is the recommended form for new snapshots; a `.sql` file wrapping a `{% snapshot %}` / `{% endsnapshot %}` block around a `{{ config(...) }}` and a `select` is legacy but fully supported. The block form has to live under `snapshot-paths`; a YAML

entry may also sit in a `.yml` file under `models/`. Both take the same required set — a pair plus one: `unique_key` and `strategy`, plus `updated_at` or `check_cols`. `schema` is optional and environment-aware; `target_schema` is the deprecated legacy key, and switching to `schema` **relocates the relation** rather than renaming a setting.

- **`relation:` is a relation, not a query.** The YAML form cannot project, filter or alias, so a block-form snapshot that does any of those changes what it captures when converted — silently, with no error. Move the transformation into an ephemeral model, or leave the snapshot as a block.
- **A snapshot's YAML entry is more than `config:`.** `description`, `meta`, `docs:`, snapshot-level `data_tests` and a `columns:` list all belong to it, and generic tests attach to a snapshot exactly as they do to a model. `unique_key` takes a column, a list of columns or an expression — and dbt never tests it, so the uniqueness test belongs on the source.
- **Two strategies.** `timestamp` uses an `updated_at` column and is preferred when one exists — cheap, and only that one column can version a row. `check` uses an explicit `check_cols` list or `check_cols: all`, and is the fallback when no reliable update timestamp is available.
- **`check` accepts an `updated_at` too.** `check_cols` decides *whether* a row changed; an `updated_at` under `check` decides *when*, stamping the validity columns from that column rather than from the snapshot run's clock. Write a column name: an expression is interpolated as SQL, survives under `check`, and breaks a `timestamp` snapshot on its second run.
- **Migrating a live snapshot is not a config change.** `snapshot_meta_column_names` errors and writes nothing; `dbt_valid_to_current` succeeds and leaves the current rows split between `NULL` and the sentinel, with the reverse migration opening a second interval on the same key. The config that errors is the safe one, and a snapshot cannot be rebuilt.
- **Three optional configs reshape the output.** `hard_deletes` layers onto either strategy — `ignore` (default), `invalidate` (close the row out, same as the deprecated `invalidate_hard_deletes: true`), or `new_record`, which adds a `dbt_is_deleted` column. `dbt_valid_to_current` replaces the current row's `NULL` in `dbt_valid_to` with a sentinel, so range predicates need no NULL guard and `where dbt_valid_to is null` returns zero rows. `snapshot_meta_column_names` renames the metadata columns — which is why the four above are a default, not a guarantee.
- `dbt snapshot` runs every snapshot (or a `--select`-ed subset) against the warehouse. At scale, snapshots are usually isolated from `dbt build` and run on their own schedule so that validity intervals align with observation windows. `--full-refresh` does **not** reset snapshot history — that is intentional.
- A **seed** is a CSV file in `seeds/` that `dbt seed` loads into the warehouse as a table. Seeds are for small, static, version-controlled reference data owned by the analytics team — country codes, risk bands, test-account exclusions, manual taxonomies.
- **Seed configs** in `dbt_project.yml`: `column_types` for explicit warehouse types (vs inference), `quote_columns` for case/character-preservation, `delimiter` for non-comma files, `enabled: false` to skip a seed. Configuration from inside the CSV is not possible.
- **`--show` is a `dbt seed` flag, but not a selector.** It takes no value and prints a sample of the loaded rows — `dbt seed --select <seed> --show`. `dbt show` is a separate command, and it previews seeds as well as models, tests and analyses.
- **Seed vs source.** Seeds are small, team-owned, version-controlled reference CSVs. Sources are raw tables loaded by an external process. A CSV of "new orders this week" belongs in the ingestion pipeline as a source, not in `seeds/`.
- A lakehouse project can declare `snapshot-paths` and ship no snapshots — SCD2 handled by warehouse-native history features (Delta CDF, Snowflake Time Travel) or by an external CDC tool; §5.6 sketches one. This is a choice, not an oversight.

## Learning-goal checklist (self-assess)

- ☐ I can state out loud when a snapshot is the right tool — mutable source, no upstream history, point-in-time analytics need — and when it isn't (append-only source, warehouse-native CDC available).
- ☐ I can read a snapshot in either form — a YAML `snapshots:` entry with `name` / `relation` / `config`, or a `{% snapshot %}` block with a `config()` and a `select` — and say which configs are required and which the strategy pulls in.
- ☐ I can say why a YAML snapshot takes a `relation:` rather than a query, name the kind of block-form snapshot that therefore cannot be converted, and give the ephemeral-model way around it.
- ☐ I can explain why switching `target_schema` to `schema` moves the snapshot table rather than renaming a setting, and what a developer sees when they query the old location afterwards.
- ☐ I can name what a snapshot's YAML entry holds besides `config:` — `description`, `meta`, `docs:`, `data_tests` and a `columns:` list — and say why a `unique_key`'s uniqueness test belongs on the source rather than on the snapshot.
- ☐ I can pick between `timestamp` and `check` given a scenario, and name the trade-offs (`check_cols: all` vs a specific list) within `check`.
- ☐ I can say what `strategy: check` does with an `updated_at` when one is configured, and why a block carrying both keys is valid rather than contradictory.
- ☐ I can name the three `hard_deletes` modes, say which one adds `dbt_is_deleted`, and recognise `invalidate_hard_deletes` as the deprecated boolean it replaced.
- ☐ I can name the four metadata columns dbt adds by default and explain what each one means — especially that `dbt_valid_to is NULL` marks the current version, that `dbt_valid_to_current` replaces that NULL with a sentinel and makes the `is null` test return nothing, and that `snapshot_meta_column_names` can rename any of them.
- ☐ I can say which of `dbt_valid_to_current` and `snapshot_meta_column_names` errors when applied to a snapshot that already holds rows, which one succeeds and leaves a mixed table, and why the one that errors is the safer failure.
- ☐ I can describe what `dbt snapshot` does and what it doesn't (it doesn't get reset by `--full-refresh`, and at 1.11 it leaves no compiled artefact to read).
- ☐ I can explain the seed-vs-source decision using the ownership / scale / update-frequency / repo-appropriateness dimensions, and I never reach for seeds as a substitute for a proper ingestion pipeline.
- ☐ I can name the three seed-specific configs (`column_types`, `quote_columns`, `delimiter`), place `enabled` among the general configs seeds share with other resources, and say when to override inference with an explicit `column_types` map.

---

## Practice questions

Thirty-four questions covering every chapter sub-topic; the configs that reshape a snapshot's output are drilled hardest (Q2, Q3, Q5, Q9, Q22) alongside seed-vs-source discrimination (Q13, Q15) and which definition syntax the docs now lead with (Q23).

---

**1.** What problem does a dbt snapshot solve?
A. It backs up the warehouse nightly in case of data loss.
B. It replicates a table from one warehouse to another.
C. It reads a source table's warehouse-native change history and exposes it as a dbt model.
D. It captures every historical version of a mutable source row, so downstream analytics can answer point-in-time questions.

**2.** A snapshot's history table carries `dbt_scd_id`, `dbt_updated_at`, `dbt_valid_from`, `dbt_valid_to` **and** `dbt_is_deleted`. Which config produced the fifth column, and how does a downstream model filter on it?
A. `hard_deletes: invalidate` — filter with `where dbt_is_deleted is false`.
B. `hard_deletes: new_record` — filter with `where dbt_is_deleted = 'False'`.
C. `strategy: check` — filter with `where dbt_is_deleted is false`.
D. `snapshot_meta_column_names` — filter with `where dbt_is_deleted = 'False'`.

**3.** You inherit a `{% snapshot %}` block whose config sets `invalidate_hard_deletes=true`. What does that key do, and what is its current spelling?
A. It closes the row out when it disappears from the source; today you write `hard_deletes: invalidate`.
B. It inserts a deletion-marker row version; today you write `hard_deletes: new_record`.
C. It removes superseded row versions from the snapshot table; today you write `hard_deletes: ignore`.
D. It is the legacy name of a snapshot strategy; today you write `strategy: invalidate`.

**4.** By default, which of the following columns does dbt generate on every row of a snapshot table?
A. `source_row_hash` B. `scd_row_version`
C. `dbt_valid_from` D. `last_seen_at`

**5.** A snapshot is built with default metadata configuration. How do you identify the row version that is currently valid?
A. `where dbt_valid_to = current_date`
B. `where dbt_valid_to is null`
C. `where dbt_scd_id = 'current'`
D. `where dbt_valid_to = '9999-12-31'`

**6.** In a legacy `snapshots/*.sql` file, which block delimiters wrap a snapshot definition?
A. `{% model %}` / `{% endmodel %}`
B. `{% materialization %}` / `{% endmaterialization %}`
C. {% snapshot <name> %} / {% endsnapshot %}
D. <<snapshot>> / <</snapshot>>

**7.** Which directory does `snapshot-paths` default to?
A. `snapshots/` B. `seeds/`
C. `models/` D. `macros/snapshots/`

**8.** Which command executes a project's snapshots against the warehouse?
A. `dbt run --snapshots` B. `dbt run --resource-type snapshot`
C. `dbt snapshot` D. `dbt seed --snapshot`

**9.** A project overrides `generate_schema_name` in the usual way, so a custom schema name is prefixed with the target's schema in development. A team edits a live snapshot's config from `target_schema='snapshots'` to `schema='snapshots'` and re-runs `dbt snapshot` in dev. What do they see?
A. The run succeeds and writes to `snapshots` exactly as before — the two keys name the same location.
B. The run succeeds and writes to `dev_snapshots`; the rows in `snapshots` are left where they are.
C. The run fails, because `schema` is a model config and a snapshot has to use `target_schema`.
D. The run succeeds and moves the existing history into `dev_snapshots`, leaving `snapshots` empty.

**10.** What does `dbt seed` do?
A. Creates an empty dbt project scaffold with example models.
B. Installs packages declared in `packages.yml`.
C. Generates sample data for development based on production table schemas.
D. Reads every CSV file under `seeds/` (or `seed-paths`) and loads each as a table in the warehouse.

**11.** Which of the following is a valid seed config that you can set under a `seeds:` block in `dbt_project.yml`?
A. `+rows_limit` B. `+compression`
C. `+column_types` D. `+refresh_interval`

**12.** A team adds a new column to `country_codes.csv`. They run `dbt seed --select country_codes`. What happens?
A. dbt issues a `DROP TABLE ... ; CREATE TABLE ...` and loads the new CSV, including the new column.
B. dbt's truncate-and-insert default does not add the new column; `--full-refresh` is needed to drop and recreate the table.
C. dbt automatically detects the new column and issues `ALTER TABLE ADD COLUMN`.
D. `dbt seed` always drops and recreates the table, so no flag is needed.

**13.** Which of the following is the best candidate for a dbt seed?
A. A 50-row CSV of ISO currency codes maintained manually by the finance team, updated a few times a year.
B. A production `orders` table synced hourly by Fivetran, with ~10M rows.
C. A Databricks Delta table produced by an upstream ingestion job.
D. The output of a previous dbt model you want to snapshot.

**14.** A `{% snapshot %}` block ends in `select product_id, sku, name as product_name, price_cents from {{ source('raw_ecom', 'product_catalog') }}`. A developer rewrites it as a YAML entry with `relation: source('raw_ecom', 'product_catalog')` and the same config. What changes about what the snapshot captures?
A. Nothing — `relation:` compiles to the same `select` the block held.
B. The run fails, because a YAML snapshot needs `check_cols` to stand in for the missing `select`.
C. It captures the same four columns, but dbt warns that the alias was dropped.
D. It now captures every column of the source relation, with `name` un-aliased.

**15.** Which of the following statements is correct?
A. Seeds and snapshots are the same resource with different inputs: a seed reads a CSV, a snapshot reads a `select`, and both write validity-interval columns.
B. Sources and snapshots are the same resource at different refresh rates: a source is a snapshot dbt re-runs on every `dbt run`, and both are declared in `sources.yml`.
C. Seeds, sources, and snapshots are three distinct dbt resource types: seeds load CSVs from the repo into the warehouse; sources are pointers to raw tables the warehouse already has; snapshots capture row-level history from a source or model over time.
D. Seeds and sources are two names for the same thing: both declare data the warehouse already holds, and `dbt seed` refreshes either one.

**16.** A developer types `dbt seed --show country_codes` expecting to preview the CSV's rows. What happens?
A. dbt prints the first five rows of the loaded table to the terminal.
B. dbt shows the compiled DDL that would be used to create the table, without running it.
C. dbt opens the CSV in the default text editor.
D. The command errors on the stray positional argument — `--show` takes no value, so the working spelling is `dbt seed --select country_codes --show`.

**17.** A product team's `customers` table has a reliable `updated_at` column and mutable `email`, `tier`, and `address` columns; updates happen a few times a day. Finance needs to answer "what tier was this customer on the day of this payment?" for audit. The `customers` table is already loaded into the warehouse by Fivetran. Which dbt resource(s) does the team need?
A. A seed containing customer history.
B. A source for `customers`, and nothing else.
C. A source declaration for `customers` plus a `timestamp`-strategy snapshot.
D. Two sources — one "current" and one "historical."

**18.** A team is considering a `dbt snapshot` on a high-volume source table: 500M rows, updated every few minutes by an upstream CDC process, running on Snowflake. The source already exposes row-level change history via the CDC tool. Which factor most argues *against* adding a snapshot here?
A. The CDC tool already publishes row-level change history, so the snapshot would re-derive history the source already exposes.
B. dbt snapshots are not supported on Snowflake and have to be replaced by an incremental model there.
C. A snapshot cannot read from a source; its `relation:` has to name a `ref()` to a staged model.
D. A snapshot re-runs as part of `dbt build`, so it cannot be scheduled independently of the main pipeline.

**19.** A team runs `dbt build --full-refresh` against a project containing three snapshots. What happens to the existing snapshot history?
A. The snapshots run normally and their history is preserved; `--full-refresh` rebuilds models and seeds only.
B. It is wiped, and each snapshot is rebuilt from the current state of its source query.
C. The command exits with `Error: No such option: --full-refresh` before anything runs.
D. dbt prompts for confirmation before it discards any snapshot history.

**20.** A snapshot's config sets `strategy: check`, `check_cols: [email, tier]` and `updated_at: source_modified_at`. What does dbt do with that block?
A. It runs, ignoring `updated_at`, which has no meaning outside the `timestamp` strategy.
B. It runs; `check_cols` decides whether a row changed and `source_modified_at` supplies the validity timestamps.
C. It fails, because `check_cols` and `updated_at` are mutually exclusive keys.
D. It runs as a `timestamp` snapshot, because `updated_at` takes precedence over `check_cols`.

**21.** An order-line source has no single-column primary key: `order_id` and `line_number` are unique only together. A team writes `unique_key: [order_id, line_number]` on the snapshot and asks what dbt will do if that assumption ever turns out to be wrong. What do you tell them, and where does the test belong?
A. dbt never tests a snapshot's `unique_key`; the test belongs on the source relation, not on the snapshot.
B. dbt validates the key at the start of every `dbt snapshot` run and fails the node on duplicates.
C. A composite `unique_key` is not supported, so the key must be one column and the situation cannot arise.
D. `dbt_scd_id` is unique per row version, so a duplicated `unique_key` cannot corrupt the history.

**22.** A team adds `dbt_valid_to_current` to one live snapshot and `snapshot_meta_column_names` to another, then runs `dbt snapshot`. Both snapshots already hold history. What happens?
A. Both runs succeed, and dbt back-fills the existing rows to match each new config.
B. Both runs fail — dbt refuses to change the metadata shape of a snapshot that already holds rows.
C. The `dbt_valid_to_current` snapshot errors and writes nothing; the `snapshot_meta_column_names` snapshot succeeds and renames the columns in place.
D. The `dbt_valid_to_current` snapshot succeeds and leaves its current rows split between `NULL` and the sentinel; the `snapshot_meta_column_names` snapshot errors and writes nothing.

**23.** A team is writing its first snapshot on dbt 1.11 and opens the snapshot reference to see how the docs define one. Which shape does the page lead with?
A. A top-level `snapshots:` YAML block whose `relation:` names the thing being snapshotted, with the settings under `config:`
B. A `.sql` file under `snapshots/` wrapping the SELECT in `{% snapshot %}` ... `{% endsnapshot %}` with a `{{ config(...) }}` call inside it
C. A model file with `materialized: snapshot` in its config, which replaced both older forms
D. Either form — the Jinja block and the YAML block are equal alternatives, and the docs present neither as primary

**24.** A snapshot uses `strategy: check` with `check_cols: [email, address]`. A `phone` column is added to the source query and starts changing weekly. What does the snapshot record?
A. New versions from the first run after the column appears — dbt re-reads the projection each run
B. Nothing, and it errors: `check_cols` no longer matches the relation's shape
C. Nothing, and it does not error — `phone` is outside `check_cols`, so those weeks look like a quiet period
D. New versions, but only once `dbt snapshot --full-refresh` rebuilds the table

**25.** A snapshot has been running for a year on the default `hard_deletes: ignore`. Someone sets `hard_deletes: new_record` and runs `dbt snapshot`. What is the result?
A. Consistent — dbt backfills `dbt_is_deleted` across the existing history on the first run after the change
B. Mixed — rows deleted before the change stay open forever, and only rows written after it carry a `dbt_is_deleted` value
C. The run fails: the target is missing the `dbt_is_deleted` column the config requires, and dbt will not add it
D. Consistent — dbt closes every previously deleted row as part of adopting the new mode

**26.** A seed's CSV header reads `Country_Name`. Its config sets `+column_types: {country_name: varchar(128)}` and `+quote_columns: false`. What type does the column get?
A. `varchar(128)` — with `quote_columns: false` the name is folded, so the key matches
B. Whatever dbt infers — the key is matched case-sensitively and matches nothing
C. `varchar(128)` — `column_types` keys are always case-insensitive
D. The run fails: `column_types` names a column that does not exist

**27.** A seed loaded months ago inferred `zip` as an integer, dropping leading zeros. A developer adds `+column_types: {zip: varchar(5)}` and runs `dbt seed`. What is the column's type afterwards?
A. `varchar(5)` — the config is applied on every load
B. `varchar(5)`, but only for rows inserted after the change
C. Still integer, and the run fails with a type-mismatch error
D. Still integer, at exit 0 with no warning at all

**28.** A BI team built a view directly on the `country_codes` seed table, outside the dbt project. An engineer runs `dbt seed --select country_codes --full-refresh`. What happens?
A. The seed reloads; the drop cascades and takes the view with it, and dbt reports success
B. The seed reloads and the view is untouched — dbt truncates rather than drops
C. dbt refuses to drop, reporting dependent objects on the relation
D. The view survives but returns zero rows until it is refreshed

**29.** `dbt_project.yml` sets a project-wide `post-hook` granting `select` to `reporter`. One seed's own config block adds a `post-hook` granting `select` to `auditor`. After `dbt seed`, which grants exist on that seed's table?
A. `auditor` only — the resource-level config overrides the project level
B. `reporter` only — project-level hooks cannot be extended per resource
C. Both — hooks are cumulative, and every level that declares one contributes it
D. Neither — two `post-hook` keys on one resource is a configuration error

**30.** A developer edits `country_codes.csv`, then runs `dbt run --select country_codes+` to rebuild what depends on it. The run is green. What was actually built?
A. The seed and its downstream models — `+` selects the node and its children
B. The downstream models only, against the rows already in the seed table
C. Nothing — `dbt run` rejects a selector that resolves to a seed
D. The downstream models, after dbt automatically loaded the changed seed first

**31.** A snapshot runs nightly at 02:00. A customer's tier goes gold to platinum at 09:00 and back to gold at 16:00 the same day. What does the snapshot hold afterwards?
A. Two new versions — one for each transition
B. One new version recording the platinum period
C. One new version, with `dbt_valid_from` and `dbt_valid_to` both set to the 02:00 run time
D. No new version at all, and no warning — the history says the tier never changed

**32.** Between two runs, a snapshot's source query gains a `region` column, drops a `fax` column, widens `notes` from `varchar(50)` to `varchar(200)`, and changes `signup` from string to date. What does dbt do to the destination table?
A. Adds `region`, drops `fax`, widens `notes`, and retypes `signup`
B. Adds `region`, widens `notes`; leaves `fax` in place and `signup` as a string
C. Adds `region` only — every other change requires a rebuild
D. Fails the run and reports a schema mismatch against the target

**33.** `dbt snapshot` fails with `Snapshot target is missing configured columns (missing "dbt_scd_id", "dbt_valid_from", "dbt_valid_to")`. The target holds two years of rows that no snapshot ever wrote. What is the sound fix?
A. Add the three meta-columns to the existing table — the check passes and the next run succeeds
B. Set `snapshot_meta_column_names` to the names the table already uses
C. Drop the table and let `dbt snapshot` rebuild it — which discards whatever history it held
D. Run `dbt snapshot --full-refresh`, which rebuilds the target in snapshot form

**34.** A snapshot reads a raw `products` relation the team does not own, with `strategy: check` and `check_cols: all`. The nightly ETL re-loads the relation and bumps every row's `loaded_at` audit column; the fifty product rows are otherwise unchanged for weeks. The snapshot table grows by fifty rows a night. What is happening, and what stops it?
A. `all` compares every column the snapshot's `select` projects, `loaded_at` included; naming the business columns in `check_cols` stops it.
B. The snapshot has no `unique_key`, so dbt cannot match a row to its previous version; adding one stops it.
C. `check` re-versions unchanged rows by design; only `strategy: timestamp` with `updated_at: loaded_at` stops it.
D. dbt compares its own `dbt_updated_at` column too; renaming it via `snapshot_meta_column_names` stops it.

## Answer key

**1. D.** A snapshot is dbt's type-2 slowly-changing-dimension primitive: it observes a mutable source on each run and records one row per historical version, with validity-interval columns. It is not a backup (A) and not cross-warehouse replication (B). C is the real alternative §5.1 weighs a snapshot against — reading Delta Change Data Feed or a CDC tool's output as a source — but that history is produced upstream, and a snapshot builds its own. Source: `/docs/build/snapshots`.

**2. B.** `hard_deletes: new_record` is the only setting that adds a column: it records a deletion as a further row version and needs `dbt_is_deleted` to carry the marker, so the column is caused by the setting rather than by snapshots generally (§5.2). It comes back typed `text` rather than boolean, which makes the predicate a string comparison and rules out the `is false` spellings. A is the mode that closes the row out and adds nothing; C confuses change detection with deletion handling, and the strategy governs only whether a row changed; D renames metadata columns and cannot create one. Source: `/reference/resource-configs/hard-deletes`.

**3. A.** `invalidate_hard_deletes: true` is the deprecated boolean that `hard_deletes` replaced, and it maps onto exactly one of the three modes — `invalidate`, which sets `dbt_valid_to` on the current version when the row disappears from the source. It has no `new_record` equivalent, which is what makes B the strongest distractor. C describes something no snapshot does: superseded versions *are* the history and are never removed, and `ignore` is the do-nothing default. D promotes deletion handling to a strategy; it is not one, and layers onto whichever of `timestamp` or `check` you already chose — though writing it beside `hard_deletes` is an error rather than a redundancy (§5.2). Source: `/reference/resource-configs/hard-deletes`, `/reference/resource-configs/invalidate_hard_deletes`.

**4. C.** The four snapshot columns dbt generates by default are `dbt_valid_from`, `dbt_valid_to`, `dbt_scd_id`, and `dbt_updated_at`. "By default" is doing work in the stem: `snapshot_meta_column_names` can rename any of them, and `hard_deletes: new_record` adds a fifth (Q2). The other three names in this question are plausible-sounding inventions not present on real snapshot tables. Source: `/docs/build/snapshots`.

**5. B.** With default metadata configuration `dbt_valid_to` is `NULL` on the current version of a row and a concrete timestamp on every superseded version, so `dbt_valid_to is null` returns the current-state view. A stamps the current row with today's date, which never happens — the column records when a version *stopped* being current. C invents a status literal for `dbt_scd_id`, which identifies a row version rather than flagging one. D is the predicate you would need on a snapshot configured with `dbt_valid_to_current`; on a default snapshot it returns nothing, and on a configured one B returns nothing instead (§5.1). Source: `/docs/build/snapshots`.

**6. C.** A legacy `snapshots/*.sql` file holds a Jinja block named between `{% snapshot <name> %}` and `{% endsnapshot %}`, with a `{{ config(...) }}` and a `select` statement inside. Both declaration forms are current: YAML is what the docs recommend for new snapshots (§5.1), and this block is supported, not deprecated. Source: `/reference/resource-configs/snapshots-jinja-legacy`.

**7. A.** `snapshot-paths` in `dbt_project.yml` defaults to `["snapshots"]`, so an unconfigured project keeps its snapshot definitions in `snapshots/` at the project root. `seeds/` is the `seed-paths` default, and there is no `macros/snapshots/` convention. `models/` is not the `snapshot-paths` default — though a snapshot declared in YAML may sit in a file under `models/`, which is why this question asks about the path config rather than about where a definition can live. Source: `/reference/project-configs/snapshot-paths`.

**8. C.** `dbt snapshot` is the standard command. Option B is invalid — `dbt run` does not run snapshots; the snapshot resource type is selected by `dbt ls --resource-type snapshot` and executed by `dbt build` or `dbt snapshot`. Option A's `--snapshots` flag does not exist, and `dbt seed` is the CSV loader, not a snapshot runner. Source: `/reference/commands/snapshot`, `/reference/commands/run`.

**9. B.** `target_schema` bypasses `generate_schema_name` and hard-codes one physical location for every environment; `schema` routes through the macro exactly as a model's does, so a project whose macro prefixes the target schema builds `dev_snapshots` in development — the run recorded in §5.1. A is the belief the swap invites, and the reason the trap works. C has the deprecation backwards: `schema` is the current spelling and `target_schema` the legacy one. D is wrong in the direction that matters most — dbt writes a fresh table at the new address and never moves, copies or drops the old one, so the history is orphaned rather than migrated. Source: `/reference/snapshot-configs`.

**10. D.** `dbt seed` loads CSV files from `seed-paths` (default `seeds/`) into the warehouse as tables, creating one table per file. The other options describe different commands — `dbt init` (A), nothing dbt does by default (C), `dbt deps` (B). Source: `/reference/commands/seed`.

**11. C.** `column_types` is a standard seed config — a map from column name to warehouse data type, used when dbt's automatic inference is wrong or ambiguous (leading-zero IDs, mixed-type columns). The other options are invented. Source: `/reference/seed-configs`, `/reference/resource-configs/column_types`.

**12. B.** By default `dbt seed` truncates the existing table and re-inserts the rows, which leaves the existing DDL untouched — so the insert names a column the table does not have and the run fails with a database error: `column "region" of relation "country_codes" does not exist`. A CSV column addition requires `--full-refresh` to drop and recreate the table with the new column set; the docs' own FAQ is titled "The columns of my seed changed, and now I get an error when running the seed command". Forgetting `--full-refresh` after a CSV column change is a common real-project trap. Source: `/reference/commands/seed`, `/faqs/Seeds/full-refresh-seed`.

**13. A.** Seeds are for small, static, version-controlled, team-owned reference data. 50 rows edited a few times a year by the analytics / finance team is the documented shape. Option B belongs in sources (ingested by an external tool); option C is already in the warehouse and should be a source; option D should be a `ref()` to the upstream model, not a seed. Source: `/docs/build/seeds`.

**14. D.** `relation:` names an object; it is not a place to put a query. dbt captures the relation as it stands, so every column the source carries lands in the snapshot and the alias is gone — §5.1 records the rewrite that turned six projected columns into all nine raw ones. A is the assumption that makes the conversion dangerous; the two forms are interchangeable in one direction only. B invents a requirement, since `check_cols` belongs to the `check` strategy and has nothing to do with projection. C is wrong in the half that matters: the run reports success and issues no warning, which is why the change is easy to ship. Source: `/docs/build/snapshots`.

**15. C.** The three resource types do different jobs with different ownership models. Confusing any two of them leads to architectural mistakes — putting transactional data in seeds, expecting sources to produce history automatically, and so on. The best way to internalise the distinction is the ownership / scale / update-frequency / repo-appropriateness table in §5.5. Source: `/docs/build/seeds`, `/docs/build/sources`, `/docs/build/snapshots`.

**16. D.** `--show` *is* a `dbt seed` flag, but it is a boolean rather than a selector: the trailing `country_codes` is an unexpected positional, and dbt exits with `Error: Got unexpected extra argument (country_codes)`. The working spelling is `dbt seed --select country_codes --show`. `dbt show` is a separate command and it does cover seeds, by loading them first (§5.4). Source: `/reference/commands/seed`, `/reference/commands/show`.

**17. C.** The source declaration gives dbt a handle on the raw Fivetran-loaded table; the snapshot, which reads `from {{ source('...', 'customers') }}`, captures the SCD2 history that answers finance's question. Option B is wrong because sources do not capture history — they are pointers to whatever the warehouse currently contains. Option A is wrong because seeds are for team-owned static data, not production customer records. Option D invents a dbt pattern that does not exist. Source: `/docs/build/snapshots`, `/docs/build/sources`.

**18. A.** The deciding factor is the upstream history that already exists. A snapshot, in the docs' own words, is the mechanism "which records changes to a mutable table over time"; a CDC tool already publishing row-level change history has done that job, so the snapshot re-derives what the source already exposes. The idiomatic choice is to read the CDC tool's history table as a dbt source and skip the snapshot entirely. Options B, C and D are false: dbt snapshots work on Snowflake, a `relation:` names a `source()` as readily as a `ref()` (§5.1), and the idiomatic large-project pattern is the independent snapshot schedule §5.3 describes — `dbt build --exclude resource_type:snapshot` beside a `dbt snapshot` job of its own. Source: `/docs/build/snapshots`.

**19. A.** The `full_refresh` config is scoped to models and seeds (per `/reference/resource-configs/full_refresh`), so a project-wide `dbt build --full-refresh` rebuilds those and leaves every snapshot table updated in place, with its historical rows intact. The asymmetry with incremental models is deliberate — a snapshot's history *is* its value, and no routine CLI flag destroys it. Option C is the trap, and it is true of a *different* command: `dbt snapshot` does not register the flag at all, so `dbt snapshot --full-refresh` exits with `Error: No such option: --full-refresh` before any node runs, and `dbt test` behaves the same way — while `build` and `run` both accept it. Source: `/reference/commands/snapshot`, `/reference/resource-configs/full_refresh`.

**20. B.** `check` *requires* `check_cols`; it does not forbid `updated_at`, and the two keys answer different questions — `check_cols` decides *whether* a row changed, `updated_at` decides *what* the validity columns are stamped from — that column rather than the snapshot run's clock (§5.2). A describes the *default* `check` snapshot, which is the reading this block is built to defeat. C borrows a real prohibition from the wrong pair — `hard_deletes` and `invalidate_hard_deletes` cannot coexist; `check_cols` and `updated_at` can. D inverts the relationship: `strategy` names the strategy, and no other key promotes a snapshot into a different one. Source: `/docs/build/snapshots`, `/reference/resource-configs/updated_at`.

**21. A.** A snapshot's `unique_key` takes a single column, a list of columns for a composite key, or an expression — so the pair is a legal key and C is false. What dbt does not do is check it: nothing validates uniqueness, so a non-unique key produces wrong SCD2 output rather than an error, and the documented remedy is a uniqueness test on the *source* rather than on the snapshot, where several rows per key are the normal shape (§5.1). B and D each assume a guard that does not exist — B a run-time validation, D a property of `dbt_scd_id`, which identifies a row *version* and says nothing about whether two source rows share a key. Source: `/reference/resource-configs/unique_key`, `/docs/build/snapshots`.

**22. D.** The two configs fail in opposite directions, and the direction is the point. `snapshot_meta_column_names` errors with `Snapshot target is missing configured columns`, and writes nothing. `dbt_valid_to_current` succeeds, because dbt deliberately does not adjust current rows it has already written: on Postgres it reported `INSERT 0 0` at exit 0 and kept every existing `NULL`, leaving two current rows on `NULL` against one on `9999-12-31` once a later run moved a row (§5.1). A and B assume dbt treats the two the same way. C has the asymmetry the wrong way round, which is the reading to unlearn — the config that errors is the safe one, because the one that succeeds leaves a table where three different current-row predicates each return part of the answer and none of them errors. Source: `/reference/resource-configs/dbt_valid_to_current`, `/reference/resource-configs/snapshot_meta_column_names`.

**23. A.** The snapshot page leads with a top-level `snapshots:` block: `relation:` names the thing being snapshotted — a `source()` or a `ref()` — and the settings sit under `config:`. B is the older Jinja-block form. It still parses, existing snapshots keep working, and the page still documents it, which is why it is the strongest distractor; it is simply no longer what the page leads with. C names a real materialization — dbt ships `{% materialization snapshot, default %}`, and a model carrying `materialized: 'snapshot'` *together with* `unique_key`, `strategy` and the strategy's companion config builds as `OK created sql snapshot model`; the materialization on its own fails with a Compilation Error — but it replaced nothing and the reference does not offer it as a way to define a snapshot. D is the answer of a reader who has met both forms in the wild and never checked the page; it is not neutral between them. Note that `config:` does not swallow everything: `description`, `meta`, `docs` and the column list stay its siblings (§5.1). Source: `/docs/build/snapshots`.

**24. C.** `check_cols` is a hand-maintained list, and nothing tells you when the source outgrows it — no error, no warning, no log line noting that the relation has columns the snapshot is not watching. The rows change upstream and the snapshot reports no changes, which reads exactly like a quiet period. That is the asymmetry with `timestamp`, which watches one column and therefore covers any column added to the query from the next run onward. D is worth rejecting on its own terms: `dbt snapshot` does not accept `--full-refresh` at all — the invocation exits on `No such option` (§5.3) — so it is not a remedy for anything here.

**25. C.** The run does not get far enough to write a mixed table. `dbt snapshot` stops with `Compilation Error ... Snapshot target is missing configured columns (missing "dbt_` is_deleted") at exit 1, and it cannot fix itself: the snapshot materialization calls assert_valid_snapshot_target_given_strategy **before** it calls create_columns, so the guard fires on the run that would otherwise have added the column. You add it by hand, or you rebuild. Note that invalidate behaves differently on the same retrofit — it runs, and it *does* touch history, closing a row deleted from the source before the change and stamping it with the retrofit run's own timestamp rather than the real deletion time. Neither mode is a clean cutover, which is the point of §5.2's manual-migration remedy. Ch 5 Q22 turns on the same guard from the other side. Revisit **Ch 5 §5.2**. Cognitive level: analyze.

**26. B.** column_types keys are matched **case-sensitively no matter how quote_columns is set**. country_name does not match a column named Country_Name, so the entry applies to nothing and dbt falls back to inference for that column — with no "unknown column" error to tell you. The two configs are easy to conflate because both are about column names, but they act at different moments: quote_columns decides whether dbt quotes names in the create-table DDL, and therefore whether they are case-sensitive in the *warehouse*; column_types matching happens before that, against the CSV header as written. Copy the key from the header, character for character.

**27. D.** column_types is applied in the create-table DDL, and the default dbt seed truncates and re-inserts into the **existing** table, so that DDL never runs. The column keeps its old type, the load succeeds, and nothing warns. dbt seed --full-refresh drops and recreates and is what actually applies the change. The related trap sits one line away in the same config: its keys are matched **case-sensitively** regardless of quote_columns, so a key of zip against a CSV header of ZIP matches nothing and silently falls back to inference — also with no error. Copy keys from the header character for character.

**28. A.** The default truncate-and-insert exists to avoid exactly this: it leaves the table object in place, so anything layered on it outside the DAG — a BI view, a grant, a hand-built materialized view — survives the load. --full-refresh drops and recreates, and the drop cascades. dbt reports success because from dbt's side the seed rebuilt perfectly; nothing in the run output mentions the view, because dbt never knew about it. The trap tightens when you meet it beside column_types: editing a seed's types has no effect without --full-refresh, so the flag you are told to reach for is the one that cascades. Know what is layered on a long-lived seed before using it.

**29. C.** Hooks are the exception to the precedence rule everything else in dbt_project.yml follows. A post-hook at the project level and a post-hook on the resource are **cumulative** — both run — so you get both grants. This is the one config-precedence question where "more specific overrides" is the wrong answer, and it holds for models as well as seeds. The practical consequence is that you cannot suppress a project-level hook by restating it on a resource: restating adds. If one resource must not run the project-level hook, narrow the project-level config so it does not select that resource.

**30. B.** The selector is valid — a seed is a graph node, so + resolves its children correctly and the right models run. What does not happen is the seed loading: dbt run executes models and nothing else, so the seed is selected, passed over as a non-model, and the downstream models read whatever rows are already sitting in the table. Exit 0, models green, mapping stale, and nothing in the output distinguishes this from having loaded the CSV. dbt build --select country_codes+ is the invocation that does what was meant, because build runs seeds, models, snapshots and tests together in DAG order.

**31. D.** dbt snapshot is a point-in-time sweep, not change data capture. It reads the source as it stands at the moment it runs and compares that to the current versions in the table. The next run sees gold, compares it to gold, and writes nothing — there is no platinum row, no gap and no warning. The same swallowing happens to any change superseded by a later one before the next sweep: only the last state of the interval is ever recorded. So cadence is a modelling decision rather than an ops detail: **the run has to be more frequent than**

**the changes you need to see.** If finance needs intra-day tier history, no amount of correct configuration will supply it from a nightly schedule.

**32. B.** dbt reconciles a snapshot's destination table only partially, and the boundary is the examinable part: it **adds** new columns and **expands** varchar-family sizes, and it never drops a removed column, nor changes an existing column's type beyond that widening. Both refusals are deliberate — dropping a column would destroy history, and retyping one could fail against the data already stored. The consequence is that a long-lived snapshot accumulates orphaned columns frozen at the values they held when they stopped being populated, alongside columns typed by a decision made years ago, with nothing warning you. Once the drift matters, the fix is manual: build the new shape alongside, migrate, cut over.

**33. C.** The message means the relation was not built by a snapshot at all. Note carefully what A gets right, because it is why A is the dangerous option rather than the silly one: dbt's check is pure column-NAME presence on the target, so adding `dbt_scd_id`, `dbt_valid_from` and `dbt_valid_to` by hand really does clear the error, and the next `dbt snapshot` really does succeed. What it cannot do is invent the observation times the two years of existing rows never carried. Those rows sit there with NULL metadata: nothing matches them on `dbt_scd_id`, no interval is closed behind them, and the first change to one opens a second interval beside an unclosed first. You have converted missing history into wrong history, which is worse and much harder to notice. The sound fix is to drop the table and let `dbt snapshot` build it fresh, discarding what it held. The route in is a legacy project that carried `materialized='table'` on a snapshot forward — correcting the config leaves a plain table sitting at the target. At 1.11 that misconfiguration is a parse-time error, `A snapshot must have a materialized value of 'snapshot'`, so you meet this state only where it predates the check. D is the reflex answer and is wrong twice over: `dbt snapshot` does not accept the flag — the invocation exits on `No such option` (§5.3) — and even if it did, the history would still be gone.

**34. A.** `check_cols: all` is a statement about the *projection*, not about the table: every column the snapshot selects is in the compared set, so a load timestamp the ETL touches on every row makes every row look changed. Fifty rows in, fifty new SCD2 versions a night, at exit 0 with nothing in the log to say the history is now noise. Replacing `all` with the columns you actually track — `check_cols: [name, price, category]` — is the fix, and it is why `all` is safe over a projection you control and unsafe over a raw relation whose shape you do not (§5.2). B is wrong twice over: `unique_key` is required for either strategy, so a snapshot without one does not run at all. C misstates `check`, which writes nothing when the compared values match — and points at a cure that is the same disease, since `updated_at: loaded_at` versions on exactly the column that is moving. D borrows a real config for an unreal purpose: `snapshot_meta_column_names` renames dbt's generated columns, which are not in the source projection and are never compared. Sources: `/reference/resource-configs/check_cols`, `/docs/build/snapshots`.

# Chapter 6

# Jinja, macros, and configuration

> **Scope.** Jinja is how dbt gets its SQL superpowers. Every `{{ ref() }}`, every `{% if is_incremental() %}`, every `{{ config(materialized='table') }}` you have met in the last four chapters was Jinja — we just hadn't slowed down to look at the machinery. This chapter does. By the end you can read any Jinja expression or statement and know what dbt will do with it at compile time, write a reusable macro and call it from a model, recite the config-precedence rule cold, place `pre_hook` / `post_hook` / `on-run-start` / `on-run-end` in the right slot, and use `{{ doc() }}` for reusable descriptions. Jinja and macros are one of the most heavily-tested clusters on the exam, and they lean toward the **apply** end of the cognitive-level spectrum: "given this macro, what does calling it with X produce?" more often than "name the function that does Y."

**Prerequisites.** Ch 2 in full — especially §2.4 (config precedence) and §2.5 (the SQL → compile → DDL → execute life cycle). Ch 4 §4.3 taught you to recognise `is_incremental()` and `{{ config() }}` in an incremental model without explaining the Jinja shape; this chapter unpacks that shape. Ch 5 showed you inline `{{ config(...) }}` inside a snapshot block; same thing.

**Cheat-sheet pointer.** Front-of-book cheat sheet §2 (Topic 1 — Developing and optimizing models) lists the Jinja context at one-line granularity: `ref`, `source`, `config`, `var`, `env_var`, `this`, `target`, `run_started_at`, `adapter`, `builtins`. Use it for spaced recall; use this chapter for the reasoning behind each.

---

## 6.1 Jinja in one page

Jinja is a templating language. Flask popularised it; dbt adopted it to let SQL authors interleave logic, variables, and reusable fragments into otherwise-plain SQL. There are exactly three pieces of Jinja syntax you will see in a dbt project, and the first thing to commit to memory is what each one does.

### The three delimiters

| Syntax | Name | Purpose |
| --- | --- | --- |
| `{{ ... }}` | **Expression** | Evaluate something and splice its string value into the rendered output. Everything you want to appear in the compiled SQL goes in `{{ }}`. |
| `{% ... %}` | **Statement** | Control flow or side-effecting declaration — `if`, `for`, `set`, `macro`, `call`. Statements produce no output on their own; they shape what the expressions around them render. |
| `{# ... #}` | **Comment** | Stripped from the rendered output entirely. Unlike a SQL `--` comment, a Jinja `{# #}` comment does not reach the warehouse. |

A quick worked example:

```
-- models/marts/fct_orders.sql

{# Rebuild the whole table in dev, merge incrementally elsewhere. #}
{{ config(
    materialized='incremental',
    unique_key='order_id'
) }}

select
    order_id,
    customer_id,
    amount,
    order_updated_at
from {{ ref('stg_orders') }}

{% if is_incremental() %}
where order_updated_at > (select max(order_updated_at) from {{ this }})
{% endif %}
```

Four Jinja moves are at work. The `{# ... #}` comment disappears. The `{{ config(...) }}` expression is evaluated for its side effect — registering the model's config — and renders to an empty string. The `{{ ref('stg_orders') }}` expression renders to `"analytics"."staging"."stg_orders"`. The `{% if is_incremental() %}...{% endif %}` statement either keeps or drops the `where` clause depending on whether the model already exists. See `/docs/build/jinja-macros` for the standard overview.

## Compile-time, not run-time

The fact about Jinja that everything else in this chapter depends on is that **all of it is resolved before the model's SQL reaches the warehouse** — during the parse and compile passes, never at query time. We covered this at a high level in Ch 2 §2.5; it bears repeating here because every Jinja question on the exam assumes you know it.

Concretely: when you dbt run, dbt parses your .sql files, renders every Jinja expression and statement into literal SQL, and writes the rendered text to target/compiled/<project>/<path>.sql. At that point there is no Jinja left — just a plain select. dbt then wraps it in DDL (create or replace view ..., merge into ..., etc.) and ships the resulting SQL to the warehouse. The warehouse never sees {{ or {%; by the time it gets the query, Jinja has already done its job and retired.

Three consequences worth internalising:

1. **A typo in a ref() fails at compile time, not runtime.** {{ ref('stg_ordrs') }} can't resolve, and dbt raises an error during the render step — a 1-second loop, not a 60-second warehouse round-trip.
2. **var('x') and env_var('FOO') are baked into the compiled SQL.** run and build recompile every invocation, so this only bites when you preserve target/compiled/ between commands — change a var after an isolated dbt compile and the artifact the next command reuses is stale.
3. **A Jinja branch is decided once, before the query runs.** It cannot test a value in the rows the model is about to return — there is no "if this row's amount is over 1 million". It *can* read the warehouse: run_query inside {% if execute %} issues a real query during compile and the branch is decided from what comes back (§6.2). Everything else a branch reads is render-time state — target.name, var(...), is_incremental(), execute.

Jinja compiles, SQL executes. Keep the two phases distinct in your head.

## What the parser sees before it renders

For most models dbt never renders the Jinja at all to work out the dependencies. A **static parser** reads the file with a tree-sitter grammar and lifts the ref, source and config calls straight out of the text — fast, and sufficient for a model whose Jinja is limited to those three calls. Put anything else in the file — an {% if %}, a {% for %}, a macro call — and that model drops back to a full render, where the calls are recorded as they evaluate. See /reference/parsing.

That has a consequence worth pinning down, because an exam item can turn on it. Whichever route a model takes, **its config() values are settled at parse** — before any SQL is rendered, and before dbt has opened a connection. Run a bare dbt parse on a project whose model carries {{ config(schema=build_schema_name()) }} and target/manifest.json already holds the resolved value in the node's config.schema, its schema, and the fully-qualified relation_name dbt will later write to — while compiled_code is still null. So a macro that hands back a hard-coded schema has already produced the wrong answer at parse; dbt compile is not where it first goes wrong, it is merely where most people first look. This is also why dbt parse earns its own CI step: it is the cheapest place to catch a config bug, and it needs no warehouse.

The wording deserves care, because dbt's own writing is loose here. "Compile time" is often used for all Jinja rendering, in the sense of *before the warehouse sees anything* — that usage is fine and this section opened with it. But dbt has two passes with two commands, and when a question offers **parse** and **compile** as separate answers it is asking which pass, not which side of the warehouse boundary.

Back to the parser, and to dependencies: a ref() that never evaluates is a ref() dbt does not know about. Put one inside a branch that renders false, or inside a {% call statement(...) %} block, and the edge is missing from the DAG: the model still compiles, and dbt simply builds it in the wrong order. The documented fix is to state the dependency in a **SQL** comment at the top of the file:

```
-- depends_on: {{ ref('stg_orders') }}
```

That is Jinja inside a SQL comment, not Jinja inside a Jinja comment. dbt renders `ref('stg_orders')`, registers the edge, and the leading `--` keeps the rendered relation name out of the query's meaning. Write the same line as `{# depends_on: {{ ref('stg_orders') }} #}` and nothing at all happens, because `{# #}` is stripped before any expression inside it is evaluated. Two characters apart; one registers a dependency and the other does not. See `/reference/dbt-jinja-functions/ref`.

---

## 6.2 The Jinja context

The "Jinja context" is dbt's name for the set of variables and functions that are available inside every `{{ ... }}` and `{% ... %}` you write in a model, snapshot, macro, or test. Some are functions you call (`ref()`, `source()`, `config()`, `var()`); others are values you read (`target`, `this`, `run_started_at`). Ten of them come up on the exam repeatedly.

### The exam ten — a concise table

| Name | Kind | One-line use | Reference |
|---|---|---|---|
| `ref('model_name')` | function | Qualified reference to a dbt-managed model; registers DAG edge. | `/reference/dbt-jinja-functions/ref` |
| `source('src', 'table')` | function | Qualified reference to a raw table declared in `sources.yml`; registers DAG edge. | `/reference/dbt-jinja-functions/source` |
| `config(...)` | function | Set per-model configs inline (e.g., `materialized`, `tags`). Settled at **parse**, not in the later compile pass (§6.1); renders to empty string. | `/reference/dbt-jinja-functions/config` |
| `var('name', 'default')` | function | Read a project variable declared under `vars:` or passed via `--vars`. | `/reference/dbt-jinja-functions/var` |
| `env_var('FOO', 'default')` | function | Read an environment variable from the host running dbt. | `/reference/dbt-jinja-functions/env_var` |
| `this` | value | The current model's relation object (`this.database`, `this.schema`, `this.identifier`). | `/reference/dbt-jinja-functions/this` |

| Name | Kind | One-line use | Reference |
|---|---|---|---|
| `target` | value | The active profile target's settings — `target.profile_name`, `target.name`, `target.schema`, `target.type` and `target.threads` on every adapter, plus adapter-specific keys. | /reference/dbt-jinja-functions/target |
| `run_started_at` | value | Python datetime — wall-clock time the current dbt invocation began (UTC by default). | /reference/dbt-jinja-functions/run_started_at |
| `adapter` | object | Wrapper around the active warehouse adapter, for reflective calls like `adapter.get_relation(...)`. | /reference/dbt-jinja-functions/adapter |
| `builtins` | dict | Holds the built-in `ref`, `source`, `config` — lets a macro override one of the three and still reach the original via `builtins.ref(...)`. | /reference/dbt-jinja-functions/builtins |

Two more honourable mentions, lightly drilled but worth recognising:

- `log('message', info=True)` — prints to the dbt log (or stdout with `info=True`). Handy for macro debugging. See /reference/dbt-jinja-functions/log.
- `return(value)` — returns a value (dict, list, int, string) from a macro without stringifying it. Written either way: `{% do return(value) %}` reads as a statement, `{{ return(value) }}` is the form the reference page's own example uses, and both short-circuit the macro identically. The caller consumes it with `{% set x = my_macro() %}`. See /reference/dbt-jinja-functions/return.

The `target` row hides an adapter split worth knowing. `profile_name`, `name`, `schema`, `type` and `threads` are present whatever you are connected to; the rest belong to one adapter family. Postgres and Redshift expose `dbname`, `host`, `port` and `user`; BigQuery exposes `project` and `dataset`; `target.database` is documented under Snowflake, and on Postgres it resolves too, returning the same value as `target.dbname`. Branch on `target.name` and `target.schema` when you want a rule that survives a warehouse migration, and treat the rest as connection detail.

`modules` is the whole of Python inside Jinja, and it is closed: `datetime`, `pytz`, `re`, `itertools`, and nothing else. No config widens it, and Jinja has no `import`. `modules.itertools` emits a deprecation warning when you reach for it. When a transformation genuinely needs Python, the escape hatch is a Python model (Ch 4 §4.7), not a bigger `modules`. See /reference/dbt-jinja-functions/modules.

### Three pairs of context functions that frequently get confused

Three question shapes recur:

**`ref` vs `source`.** If dbt built the table, `ref`. If something else built it, `source`. (Ch 2 §2.2 and Ch 3 §3.2 drilled this; it returns here because a Jinja-context question will often list both and ask which one is appropriate for a specific case.)

**`var` vs `env_var`.** Both return a string-ish value at compile time. `var('raw_catalog')` reads from `vars:` in `dbt_project.yml` (or from a `--vars` override on the command line); it lives in code you commit. `env_var('RAW_CATALOG')` reads from an environment variable set by the shell or CI system; it lives outside the project. The rule of thumb: **`var` for values the team agrees on and commits; `env_var` for values that differ per machine or per deployment and shouldn't be in Git.** Both accept a second positional argument as a default: `var('run_date', '2024-01-01')`, `env_var('RAW_CATALOG', 'raw')`.

**Where a `var` is read from, in order.** Once packages are in play a variable can be declared in several places at once, and dbt resolves them by a fixed ladder — first hit wins:

1. `--vars` on the command line
2. a package-scoped var in the root `dbt_project.yml`
3. a global var in the root `dbt_project.yml`
4. the package's own project file
5. the default argument in the `var()` call itself

Two things fall out of that order and both are worth holding. **The root project always outranks the package**, which is what lets you retune a package's behaviour without forking it — levels 2 and 3 both sit above level 4. And **the `var()` default is the last resort, not a floor**: it applies only when nobody declared the variable anywhere, which is why a default silently masks a variable somebody meant to set — the rule in the next paragraph. Package-scoped beats global inside the root project, so `vars: {dbt_utils: {surrogate_key_treat_nulls_as_empty_strings: true}}` overrides your own project-wide setting for that package alone.

**A `var()` with no default is a hard failure, not a null.** Ask for a variable nobody declared and dbt raises a compile error naming it — `Required var 'raw_catalog' not found in config`. It does not render empty, and it does not fall through to a null that quietly produces `where country = ''` in the compiled SQL. That is the behaviour you want, and it is why the two-argument form is a decision rather than a habit: `var('raw_catalog')` declares the variable mandatory and fails loudly when it is missing, while `var('raw_catalog', 'raw')` declares a default and can never tell you the variable was forgotten. Use the one-argument form for anything a run must not proceed without.

**`this` vs `target`.** `target` describes the *profile* — which warehouse, which schema, which account. `this` describes the *current model's relation* on that target — fully qualified. Inside `models/staging/stg_orders.sql`, `{{ this }}` renders to `analytics.staging.stg_orders`; `{{ target.schema }}` renders to `staging`. You will almost always reach for `this` inside an incremental `where` clause and `target` inside a hook or env-switch macro. Reaching for the wrong one is a classic compile-time bug.

### Reading environment variables safely

Two prefixes change what dbt *does* with an environment variable rather than what it returns.

| Prefix | What dbt does with it |
|---|---|
| `DBT_ENV_SECRET_<name>` | Scrubs the value to `*****` everywhere dbt writes a log or an artifact, whether or not anything read it. Legal in `profiles.yml` and `packages.yml`, rejected in `dbt_project.yml` and model SQL. Cannot be filtered, cast, concatenated or handed to a macro — one secret is one whole configuration value. |
| `DBT_ENV_CUSTOM_ENV_<name>` | Strips the prefix and carries the value out into `metadata.env` in the artifacts and `info.extra` in the structured logs — how a run gets stamped with the CI job that produced it. |

And remember what `env_var()` returns: a string, always. `env_var('STRICT_MODE', 'false')` is the string `false`, which is not empty, so `{% if env_var('STRICT_MODE', 'false') %}` is **true**. Compare the value explicitly rather than testing it for truthiness, and pipe it through `int` or `as_number` when you want arithmetic. See `/reference/dbt-jinja-functions/env_var`.

### `execute` — the flag for parse-only blocks

One context variable is rare in models but common in macros: `execute` is a boolean that is `False` during parsing and `True` during actual command execution. Code that introspects the graph (`graph.nodes`, `adapter.get_relation(...)`) must be guarded with `{% if execute %}` because the graph isn't populated during the initial parse:

```
{% if execute %}
  {% set rows = run_query('select count(*) from ' ~ this) %}
  {{ log("Row count: " ~ rows.columns[0][0], info=True) }}
{% endif %}
```

The name misleads in one direction worth pinning down. `execute` is `True` whenever dbt compiles with a warehouse connection, and that includes `dbt compile` and `dbt docs generate`, not only `dbt run`. So `{% if execute %}` guards against the *parse* pass and nothing else: a side-effecting `run_query` wrapped in it still fires when somebody regenerates the docs. When you need to branch on which command is running, the documented handle is `flags.WHICH` — the `require_select_arg` macro in §6.8 uses it for exactly that.

The exam rarely drills `execute` directly, but it appears in scenario questions where a macro mysteriously "works on `dbt run` but fails on `dbt parse`."

---

## 6.3 Writing your first macro

Jinja expressions are how dbt injects values into SQL. A **macro** is how you reuse the *expression logic* itself — the templating equivalent of a function. If three models all need to build the same "UTC timestamp cast with null-handling" fragment, you don't paste the fragment into each; you write it once as a macro and call it from each model.

### The shape

Macros live in `.sql` files under the `macros/` directory (configurable via `macro-paths` in `dbt_project.yml`, but `macros/` is the universal default). A macro is a named Jinja block:

```
-- macros/cast_timestamp_utc.sql
{% macro cast_timestamp_utc(column_name) %}
    cast({{ column_name }} as timestamp) at time zone 'UTC'
{% endmacro %}
```

Three things to notice.

1. **{% macro <name>(args) %} / {% endmacro %}** — the outer block, exactly like a function definition in Python. Positional args are the usual case; keyword args with defaults are also allowed (`{% macro foo(col, fmt='YYYY-MM-DD') %}`).
2. **The filename is conventionally the macro name.** dbt does not enforce this — you can put many macros in one `.sql` file, and dbt will discover all of them. But a `macros/cast_timestamp_utc.sql` file containing the `cast_timestamp_utc` macro is the house style, and the exam uses that convention.
3. **The macro's body is Jinja.** `{{ column_name }}` splices the argument into the output. The rendered result is raw SQL that gets interpolated wherever the macro is called.

### Calling it from a model

Call a macro from a model the same way you call any Jinja function:

```
-- models/staging/stg_orders.sql
select
    order_id,
    {{ cast_timestamp_utc('order_created_at') }} as order_created_at_utc,
    {{ cast_timestamp_utc('order_updated_at') }} as order_updated_at_utc
from {{ ref('raw_orders') }}
```

At compile time, each `{{ cast_timestamp_utc('order_created_at') }}` renders to `cast(order_created_at as timestamp) at time zone 'UTC'`. Look under target/compiled/<project>/models/staging/stg_orders.sql to see the fully-rendered SQL — no macro call, just the expanded output.

See `/docs/build/jinja-macros` for the macro authoring page.

### Returning SQL vs returning values

Most macros return SQL — a fragment that gets spliced into a compiled model. A minority return *values* (a dict, a list, an int) that the caller then uses programmatically. The shapes use different Jinja tags:

**Returning SQL (the usual case).** Whatever the macro body renders to is its return value. No explicit `return` is needed.

```
{% macro timestamp_cols(name) %}
    {{ name }}_created_at,
    {{ name }}_updated_at,
    {{ name }}_deleted_at
{% endmacro %}
```

Call with `{{ timestamp_cols('order') }}` and you get three column expressions inlined.

**Returning a value.** Use `{% do return(value) %}` at the end of the macro to return a typed value usable by `{% set x = my_macro() %}`. This is how you build helper macros that compute a value consumed by another macro or by a Python-style context variable. (`{{ return(value) }}` is the same call written as an expression, and it is the form the reference page shows; both short-circuit the macro and hand the value back. Pick one and be consistent.)

```
{% macro list_of_markets() %}
  {% set markets = ['uk', 'us', 'apac_1', 'apac_2', 'emea_1'] %}
  {% do return(markets) %}
{% endmacro %}
```

Calling `{% set ms = list_of_markets() %}` makes `ms` a Python list; `{% for m in ms %}...{% endfor %}` iterates it. See `/reference/dbt-jinja-functions/return` for the semantics.

**Returning a value the warehouse computed.** A third shape sits between the two: a `{% call statement(...) %}` block runs SQL from inside a macro and hands the result back through `load_result`.

```
{% macro max_order_date() %}
  {% call statement('probe', fetch_result=True) %}
    select max(order_updated_at) from {{ ref('stg_orders') }}
  {% endcall %}
  {% do return(load_result('probe')['data'][0][0]) %}
{% endmacro %}
```

`statement(name, fetch_result=False, auto_begin=True)` names the result; `load_result(name)` returns a dict with exactly three keys — `response`, `data` and `table`. `data` is a list of row-lists and `table` is the Agate table. `run_query(sql)` is a thin wrapper over the same machinery for the one-statement case: it returns an Agate table whatever the SQL was — empty of rows for anything that is not a `select`, not the `none` the reference page describes — and opens no transaction of its own. Both need `{% if execute %}` around them, and both hide their `ref()` from the parser — §6.1 has the fix. See `/reference/dbt-jinja-functions/statement-blocks`.

## Don't nest your curlies

Once a `{{ ... }}` is open, a second `{{ ... }}` inside it is not an expression — it is text. dbt raises no error and prints no warning; the inner call is stored as its own source characters and the model builds around them:

```
-- wrong: alias is set to the literal text {{ var('table_alias') }}
{{ config(alias="{{ var('table_alias') }}") }}

-- right: you are already inside Jinja, so just call it
{{ config(alias=var('table_alias')) }}
```

Hooks are the sole documented exception, and only because a hook is stored rather than evaluated. dbt keeps the hook string as the config value and renders it a second time when the hook actually runs, which is why `post_hook="grant select on {{ this }} to role analyst"` in §6.5 works and has to be written that way — `{{ this }}` means nothing until there is a model being built. Everywhere else the rule is one set of curlies deep. See `/best-practices/dont-nest-your-curlies`.

## A worked example — `cast_timestamp_utc` with a null-safe cast

Putting the pieces together. We want a macro that takes a column name, casts it to `timestamp` at UTC, and returns `NULL` (not an error) when the source value is unparseable. The macro lives at `macros/cast_timestamp_utc.sql`:

```
{% macro cast_timestamp_utc(column_name, default='NULL') %}
    coalesce(
        try_cast({{ column_name }} as timestamp),
        {{ default }}
    ) at time zone 'UTC'
{% endmacro %}
```

Call it from a staging model:

```
-- models/staging/stg_payments.sql
select
    payment_id,
    {{ cast_timestamp_utc('raw_paid_at') }} as paid_at_utc,
    {{ cast_timestamp_utc('raw_refunded_at') }} as refunded_at_utc
from {{ source('stripe', 'payments') }}
```

Four wins: the logic is defined once, every staging model spells "UTC cast" the same way, schema changes propagate through one file, and the rendered SQL is still transparent — read `target/compiled/...` and the cast is right there.

### Raising your own errors

A macro that detects a bad argument should say so rather than render broken SQL. The `exceptions` namespace holds more than the handful you will use; the four below are the ones worth knowing, and the one that matters most is the one that does *not* fail:

| Call | What it does |
|---|---|
| `exceptions.warn(msg)` | Logs the message and carries on. The node is reported `PASS`. |
| `exceptions.raise_compiler_error(msg)` | Fails the node at compile time. |
| `exceptions.raise_fail_fast_error(msg)` | Stops the invocation immediately. |
| `exceptions.raise_not_implemented(msg)` | The signal an adapter or package author raises for an unsupported operation. |

Wrap all four in `{% if execute %}`, or a `dbt parse` trips them.

`warn` is escalatable, and that is the half a scenario question turns on. `--warn-error` promotes every warning in the run to an error; `--warn-error-options '{"error": ["JinjaLogWarning"]}'` promotes only the ones `exceptions.warn` raises, `JinjaLogWarning` being the event name dbt gives them. Under either flag the node that passed a moment ago fails with a compilation error carrying your own message. Ch 10 §10.9.3 covers the flag pair and how it is configured. See `/reference/dbt-jinja-functions/exceptions`.

### Documenting a macro

Macros are documented the way models are, with one restriction that gets tested. A macro's properties live in a `.yml` file under `macro-paths` and nowhere else — there is no `macros:` block in `dbt_project.yml` for this, and no `config()` call inside the macro body. dbt calls them *special properties* for that reason.

```
# macros/_macros.yml
version: 2

macros:
```

```
- name: cast_timestamp_utc
  description: "Casts a column to timestamp at UTC, returning NULL when the value is
  unparseable."
  config:
    docs:
      show: true
    meta:
      owner: analytics_engineering
  arguments:
    - name: column_name
      type: string
      description: "The column to cast."
    - name: default
      type: string
      description: "SQL literal substituted when the cast fails."
```

`config:` carries `docs:` and `meta:`; `arguments:` documents each parameter with `name`, `type` and `description`. The supported `type` vocabulary is `string` / `str`, `boolean` / `bool`, `integer` / `int`, `float`, `any`, `list[T]`, `dict[K, V]`, `optional[T]`, `relation` and `column`. Those types are documentation: nothing checks a call against them, and a mismatch costs you a docs-site inaccuracy rather than a build. See `/reference/macro-properties` and `/reference/resource-properties/arguments`.

### Where macros live in the DAG

Macros are not nodes in the DAG the way models and sources are. They are text-substitution units: dbt knows every macro by name, renders them into their calling models at compile time, and does not track per-macro lineage. There is no `macro` value for `dbt ls --resource-type`, and no "which model depends on macro X" query dbt supports — you grep the project for `{{ x(` to find call sites. The only lineage the DAG records is the models-and-sources graph derived from `ref()` / `source()` edges. Rename a macro and nothing in dbt tells you what you broke until the render fails.

One counterweight, and it is dbt Labs' own: favour readability over DRY-ness. Not every repeated line earns a macro, and a project where every model is three macro calls is harder to read than the duplication it replaced. Before you write one, check whether `dbt_utils` — or dbt Core's own `dbt` namespace, §6.7 — already ships it. See `/best-practices/how-we-style/4-how-we-style-our-jinja`.

---

## 6.4 Config precedence, with Jinja

Ch 2 §2.4 introduced the three places a model's config can live. Ch 4 §4.2 used materialization as the worked example. This section closes the loop by naming the *Jinja phase* each one is resolved in — because that's where a certain class of exam question hides its gotcha.

### The three sources, restated

1. **`{{ config(materialized='table', ...) }}`** inside the model's `.sql` file — resolved during the **parse** phase, when dbt builds the manifest (§6.1).
2. **YAML `config:` block** under the model in a `_models.yml` properties file — rendered during the **parse** phase with the properties-file Jinja context.
3. **`dbt_project.yml` `+config` keys** under the `models:` tree — resolved during the **parse** phase.

**Spelling follows the file, not the config.** Where you misspell a key decides whether you ever hear about it:

| Misspelled key | What dbt does |
|---|---|
| A top-level `dbt_project.yml` key, underscored — `on_run_start:`, `analysis_paths:` | Refuses to load the project: `at path []: Additional properties are not allowed ('on_run_start' was unexpected)`, exit code 2, nothing built. |
| A top-level key that is *supposed* to be underscored, dashed — `data-tests:`, `unit-tests:` | The same refusal, in the opposite direction: `Additional properties are not allowed ('data-tests' was unexpected)`. Of the 27 multi-word top-level keys, 25 are dashed and exactly **two** are underscored — `data_tests:` and `unit_tests:`. Learn the pair; the general rule will mis-spell them. |
| An unrecognised `+` resource config under `models:` — `+persist-docs:` | Discards it without a warning. Parsed on 1.11.14, `+persist_docs: {relation: true, columns: true}` resolves to `{'relation': True, 'columns': True}` and `+persist-docs:` with the identical value resolves to `{}` — exit 0 both times, nothing logged. |
| A dashed key in a properties `config:` block or a `config()` call — `unique-key: id` | Drops it in silence: `unique_key` stays `None`, and the incremental model loses the key it merges on. |

So one typo class fails in opposite directions, and the loud half cannot reach production while the quiet half can, and does. `+pre-hook` and `+pre_hook` both fire, but **that is a property of those particular keys, not of the `+` prefix** — `dbt/hooks.py` names the *dashed* form as canonical, so `pre-hook` and `post-hook` are the one pair safe on every surface, and reading them as a general rule is how a silent defect ships. `+persist-docs:` is an alias of nothing. See `/reference/dbt_project.yml`.

## The rule is still "most specific wins"

The precedence is, from highest to lowest:

1. `{{ config() }}` in SQL.
2. YAML `config:` block.
3. `dbt_project.yml +config`.

Within `dbt_project.yml`, a deeper folder path wins over a shallower one (`marts.finance.+materialized: incremental` beats `marts.+materialized: table`). And if no config is set at any of the three layers above, dbt's built-in default applies (e.g., a model with no `materialized` config anywhere materializes as `view`, because `view` is the field's default in dbt Core itself) — that implicit fallback is the fourth, lowest-priority layer. A few of those defaults are the adapter's rather than core's: leave `incremental_strategy` unset and dbt dispatches the choice per adapter — and a `unique_key` can change its mind again, which is why an unconfigured incremental model appends on one warehouse and merges on another (Ch 4 §4.3). See `/reference/define-configs` and `/reference/model-configs`.

### Why the Jinja angle matters

Two classes of bug only make sense once you know which phase a config is resolved in.

**Dynamic `config()` calls are still parse-time.** You can write `{{ config(materialized=var('default_mat', 'view')) }}` and it works — `var(...)` is evaluated as the config is resolved, so `materialized` gets set to whatever `var` returned. But you *cannot* write `{{ config(materialized=run_query('select ...')) }}` — `run_query` requires an active warehouse connection, which doesn't exist during the parse-time pass dbt uses to discover configs.

**YAML configs can render simple Jinja values.** Properties YAML goes through dbt's Jinja renderer, so `config: {materialized: "{{ var('default_mat', 'view') }}"}` resolves before dbt validates the config. Quote the whole Jinja string so the YAML parser sees a string first, then let dbt render it. If the variable is missing and you did not provide a default, dbt raises a compilation error during parse. SQL `{{ config() }}` still wins the precedence contest and is usually the clearer home for model-local branching.

**`dbt_project.yml` also supports a limited Jinja pass.** `env_var()`, `var()`, and a few built-ins are available, but arbitrary project macros are not; dbt is still constructing the project when this file is rendered. You can write `vars: {run_date: "{{ env_var('RUN_DATE', '2024-01-01') }}"}` and it works. What each YAML file gets is not the same, because dbt reads them at different moments:

| File | The Jinja it gets |
|---|---|
| `profiles.yml` | `env_var`, and `var` for `--vars`-supplied values only |
| `packages.yml` | `env_var`, `var`, `builtins`, `dbt_version` — no `target` |
| `dbt_project.yml` | `env_var`, `var`, `target`, `builtins`, `dbt_version` — no project macros |
| Properties YAML (`_models.yml`, `_sources.yml`, ...) | the same five, plus `doc()` inside description fields |

`profiles.yml` is the restricted one for a reason worth holding: dbt has not read `dbt_project.yml` when it renders your connection details, so there are no project `vars:` in scope yet. See `/reference/dbt-jinja-functions/profiles-yml-context` and its three siblings.

The exam pattern: a question shows you a `{{ config() }}` block, a YAML `config:` block, and a `dbt_project.yml` `+config` entry that disagree, and asks which wins. The answer is always the SQL `config()`, provided it's reachable (i.e., you didn't put it inside an `{% if %}` that renders to false).

### Reading a config back

`config()` writes; `config.get()` and `config.require()` read. `config.get('key')` returns `None` when the key is unset and never raises, and `config.get('key', default='x')` supplies the fallback. `config.require('key')` raises a compilation error instead — *does not define a required config parameter* — which is what you want in a macro that cannot do anything sensible without the value. Neither reads `config.meta`: set `owner` under `meta:` and `config.get('owner')` still comes back `None`. The meta-scoped forms are `config.meta_get('owner')` and `config.meta_require('owner')`. See `/reference/dbt-jinja-functions/config`.

## 6.5 Hooks and operations

Hooks are SQL statements that dbt runs around model materialization. There are two varieties, distinguished by scope.

### Per-resource hooks: `pre_hook` and `post_hook`

`pre_hook` runs immediately before a specific model's DDL; `post_hook` runs immediately after. Both are configured per-model, either inline or via YAML / project-file:

```
-- models/marts/fct_orders.sql
{{ config(
    materialized='table',
    pre_hook="set query_tag = 'fct_orders_build'",
    post_hook=[
        "grant select on {{ this }} to role analyst",
        "analyze table {{ this }} compute statistics"
    ]
) }}

select ...
```

Three things worth remembering about per-resource hooks:

1. **The value is either a string (one statement) or a list of strings (several).** The list form above runs the two statements in order, both after the model's DDL.
2. **Jinja is available inside the hook string.** `{{ this }}` resolves to the fully-qualified relation for the current model — exactly what you want for grants and table maintenance. This is the one place a `{{ }}` nested inside an already-open `{{ config() }}` behaves: dbt stores the hook string as the config value and renders it a second time when the hook runs (§6.3).
3. **Hooks can call macros.** `post_hook="{{ refresh_materialized_view_downstream(this) }}"` runs the macro, the rendered SQL from which then gets executed against the warehouse. This is the bridge between macros (which produce SQL) and operations (which execute it).

On an adapter that wraps dbt's DDL in a transaction — Postgres and Redshift — hooks run *inside* that transaction by default. That is what you want for a `grant` and what you do not want for a `vacuum`. Three opt-outs move a statement out: wrap it in `before_begin("…")` to run it before the transaction opens, in `after_commit("…")` to run it once the transaction has closed, or write the hook as a dict, `{"sql": "…", "transaction": false}`. On adapters with no transaction semantics the modifiers parse and change nothing.

When more than one hook applies to the same model, the order is fixed rather than arbitrary: hooks contributed by dependent packages run before the active project's; `dbt_project.yml` hooks run before the model's own `config()` hooks; and within a single level dbt keeps the order you wrote them in. Hooks are additive, not overriding — a project-level `pre_hook` and a model-level one both run.

See `/reference/resource-configs/pre-hook-post-hook`.

### Project-level hooks: `on-run-start` and `on-run-end`

These are declared at the top of `dbt_project.yml`, not on individual resources. They fire once per dbt invocation — `on-run-start` before any model runs, `on-run-end` after all of them:

```
# dbt_project.yml
on-run-start:
  - "create schema if not exists {{ target.schema }}"
  - "{{ require_select_arg() }}"
on-run-end:
  - "{{ upload_dbt_artifacts() }}"
  - "analyze schema {{ target.schema }}"
```

Use cases: schema bootstrap, audit logging, CI safety gates, artifact uploads. See `/reference/project-configs/on-run-start-on-run-end`.

Three context variables exist inside an `on-run-end` hook, and their absence everywhere else is the part worth memorising:

- `schemas` — the schemas dbt wrote to during the run, as a list of names.
- `database_schemas` — the same list as `(database, schema)` pairs, for a project that spans databases.
- `results` — one `Result` object per node dbt executed, carrying `status`, `execution_time` and `adapter_response`.

A model, a macro and a `post_hook` do not have them, and neither does `on-run-start` — where the absence hides, because the names render empty, a loop over them turns zero times, and the hook reports no error. The standard use is a grant loop — iterate `schemas` at the end of a run and issue `grant usage` on each. A fourth variable is broader: `selected_resources` holds the node IDs the current command selected, is available in all four hook types, and is empty during parse. See `/reference/dbt-jinja-functions/on-run-end-context` and `/reference/dbt-jinja-functions/selected_resources`.

## What commands trigger hooks?

A frequently-tested gotcha. Hooks fire on the six commands that run the node graph against the warehouse:

- `dbt build`
- `dbt run`
- `dbt seed`
- `dbt snapshot`
- `dbt source freshness`
- `dbt test`

`dbt source freshness` is the surprising one — it builds nothing, only issuing `select max(loaded_at_field)` per source, but the `source_freshness_run_project_hooks` flag defaults to `true` at 1.11, so the run reports `Finished running 2 project hooks, 1 source`. Set that flag `false` and the hooks are skipped, with a deprecation warning.

Three commands do **not** trigger them:

- `dbt parse` — parses the project and writes `target/manifest.json` without opening a warehouse connection.
- `dbt clean` — purely file-system cleanup; no warehouse involvement.
- `dbt run-operation` — opens a warehouse connection, but it invokes one macro outside the node graph, and project hooks are bound to the graph run.

`dbt compile` and `dbt docs generate` are the pair to be careful with: the reference page lists both as triggers, and at 1.11 neither fires a project hook. Reason from the graph — a command that does not run nodes does not run project hooks.

### `dbt run-operation` — run a macro without a model

The counterpart to hooks is the `dbt run-operation` command, which invokes a single macro directly:

```
dbt run-operation grant_select_on_mart --args '{schema: analytics, role: analyst}'
```

dbt renders the macro against a live connection. It does **not** run what the macro renders: the rendered text is discarded, so a macro whose body is a bare `grant select …` statement grants nothing and the command still reports success. The macro has to issue the SQL itself — `run_query(sql)` or a `{% call statement %}` block — which is why the reference's own grant example wraps the statement in `{% set %}` and `{% do run_query(sql) %}`. Useful for: one-shot admin tasks (grants, role creation), custom data-loading procedures, invoking utility macros that don't need to be tied to a model's hook. See `/reference/commands/run-operation`.

`run-operation` does not fire `on-run-start` / `on-run-end` unless you explicitly invoke them inside the macro — it's a narrow-scope command.

---

## 6.6 Doc blocks and `{{ doc() }}`

Descriptions in YAML are useful but repeat themselves. If every `uk_market_id` column in twenty models has the same description, copying the description into each `_models.yml` is fragile. Doc blocks solve this exact problem.

### Defining a doc block

A **doc block** is a named chunk of Markdown wrapped in `{% docs %}` / `{% enddocs %}` tags, living in a `.md` file under any path `docs-paths` covers — which by default is every resource path in the project, `macros/` as much as `models/`:

```
<!-- models/_shared_descriptions.md -->

{% docs uk_market_id %}
The market identifier for UK-originated records. Values conform to ISO-3166-1
alpha-2 codes; the master list lives in the `dim_markets` table.
{% enddocs %}

{% docs user_status_values %}
Possible values for `user_status`:

- `active` - user has signed in within the last 30 days
- `dormant` - user has not signed in for -30180 days
- `churned` - user has not signed in for more than 180 days
{% enddocs %}
```

The block name (`uk_market_id`, `user_status_values`) is a dbt identifier — not the column name, though they often match for readability.

### Referencing the block with `{{ doc() }}`

In a `_models.yml` properties file, replace a literal string description with a call to `doc()`:

```
version: 2

models:
```

```
- name: dim_users_uk
  description: "UK users dimension. {{ doc('user_status_values') }}"
  columns:
    - name: user_id
      description: "Primary key - opaque UUID."
    - name: market_id
      description: "{{ doc('uk_market_id') }}"
    - name: user_status
      description: "{{ doc('user_status_values') }}"
```

At parse time, each `{{ doc('block_name') }}` is replaced by the Markdown inside the matching `{% docs %}` block — a bare `dbt parse` is enough to put the substituted text into the node's `description` in `manifest.json`. Every model that references `user_status_values` now inherits the same description; updating the reference definition updates every usage. Two constraints come with that. Within one project a doc block's name has to be unique — a one-argument `doc('name')` resolves by name alone, and there is no path qualifier that would let two blocks in the same project share one. The only qualifier there is disambiguates across *packages*, not across directories: `doc('a_package', 'name')` pins the lookup to that package, which is how an installed package and your own project can each define a block called `uk_market_id`. And `doc()` is usable only in a `description:` field of a properties file; it is not a general-purpose include. See `/reference/dbt-jinja-functions/doc` and `/docs/build/documentation`.

### What renders where

Running `dbt docs generate` writes two artifacts to `target/`: `manifest.json` (the parsed project graph) and `catalog.json` (warehouse-introspected metadata). `dbt docs serve` spins up a local web server that reads those two files and renders the documentation site. Doc blocks appear on the model's detail page, on its column descriptions, and on any other model that `{{ doc(...) }}`s the same block. Ch 9 is the dedicated documentation chapter; for now, the payoff is: **write a description once, reference it anywhere a description field accepts Jinja.**

### Subtlety: descriptions are not Jinja-evaluated in every surface

`description:` fields in YAML properties files (`_models.yml`, `_sources.yml`, etc.) accept `{{ doc() }}`. Source descriptions belong in those YAML files — they are not declared inside `dbt_project.yml`. Custom `meta:` fields render through a context with no `doc` in it, so a `{{ doc() }}` there stops the parse with `Compilation Error … 'doc' is undefined` rather than surviving as a plain string. If you want to put a long note under `meta: {runbook: "..."}`, keep it literal.

---

## 6.7 Cross-adapter macros — `dispatch`

Most macros are warehouse-agnostic. A few are not: a macro that truncates a table, or one that reads the current user's role, looks different on Snowflake vs. BigQuery vs. Databricks. dbt's answer is **dispatch** — a way to write one macro interface and have it resolve to an adapter-specific implementation at compile/render time.

### What dbt Core already ships

Before you write a dispatched macro, check whether dbt Core has already written it. Core ships around thirty **cross-database macros** in its own `dbt` namespace — `dbt.dateadd`, `dbt.datediff`, `dbt.date_trunc`, `dbt.last_day`, `dbt.safe_cast`, `dbt.cast`, `dbt.hash`, `dbt.concat`, dbt.split_part, dbt.listagg, dbt.except, dbt.intersect, dbt.any_value, dbt.bool_or, dbt.escape_single_quotes, dbt.string_literal, and the dbt.type_* family. Every one of them is dispatched, so {{ dbt.dateadd('day', 7, 'order_date') }} renders the right syntax on whichever warehouse you point it at, and no package install is involved. See /reference/dbt-jinja-functions/cross-database-macros.

## The pattern

Two pieces. First, the dispatching macro — the one users call:

```
-- macros/my_macro.sql
{% macro my_macro(arg) %}
    {% do return(adapter.dispatch('my_macro')(arg)) %}
{% endmacro %}
```

Second, one or more adapter-specific implementations, each prefixed with the adapter's name plus a double underscore:

```
-- macros/my_macro.sql (continued)
{% macro default__my_macro(arg) %}
    -- a safe default that works on most adapters
    select {{ arg }}
{% endmacro %}

{% macro snowflake__my_macro(arg) %}
    -- Snowflake-specific variant
    select {{ arg }}::variant
{% endmacro %}

{% macro databricks__my_macro(arg) %}
    -- Databricks-specific variant
    select cast({{ arg }} as string)
{% endmacro %}
```

At compile time (when the Jinja in my_macro is rendered into SQL), adapter.dispatch('my_macro') inspects target.type, looks for <target.type>__my_macro, falls back to default__my_macro if none exists, and returns the matching macro object. {% do return(...) %} hands the result back to the caller. The chosen implementation is baked into the compiled SQL before the warehouse ever sees it. See /reference/dbt-jinja-functions/dispatch.

The chain is longer than two steps on an adapter that inherits from another. dbt-redshift is built on dbt-postgres, so on Redshift dispatch tries redshift__my_macro, then postgres__my_macro, then default__my_macro; on Databricks it tries databricks__my_macro, then spark__my_macro, then default__my_macro. A macro that defines only a postgres__ variant therefore still fires on Redshift — convenient in practice, and the trap in any stem that shows you two implementations and a third warehouse.

## Why package authors use it

dbt_utils, dbt_expectations, and most widely-used dbt packages rely on dispatch so one package install works on every warehouse. When you read dbt_utils.deduplicate(...), the package's deduplicate macro is dispatching to snowflake__deduplicate, postgres__deduplicate, and so on — you don't see the choice, but it's happening. Dispatch runs even where only one implementation exists: dbt_utils.date_spine(...) dispatches too, and lands on default__date_spine every time, because that is the only variant the package ships.

### Overriding dispatch order: `dispatch:` in `dbt_project.yml`

Sometimes you want to *override* a package's implementation of a dispatched macro with your own. The `dispatch:` block in `dbt_project.yml` tells dbt where else to look:

```
# dbt_project.yml
dispatch:
  - macro_namespace: dbt_utils
    search_order:
      - my_project
      - dbt_utils
```

That block says: when `dbt_utils.some_macro` is dispatched, search **my__project** before `dbt_utils`. This is how teams shim package behaviour without forking the package. See `/reference/project-configs/dispatch-config`.

What the block does not do is switch that behaviour on. Whenever the namespace you name is a package you installed, root-project-first is already dbt's order for it, so a correctly-named override sitting in your own `macros/` directory wins with no configuration at all. What `dispatch:` buys you is a *different* order — the package ahead of you, or a third namespace in the chain — and a declaration of the intent that the next reader of `dbt_project.yml` can see.

### What `dispatch` actually searches

The search is easy to read as "find my adapter's implementation wherever it lives, then fall back to a default". It works the other way round. dbt walks the namespaces in order — the one you listed, or the default one above — and **exhausts each one before moving to the next**:

1. `my_project.postgres__some_macro`
2. `my_project.default__some_macro`
3. `dbt_utils.postgres__some_macro`
4. `dbt_utils.default__some_macro`

Package specificity outranks adapter specificity. A `default__some_macro` in your own project therefore beats `postgres__some_macro` in `dbt_utils`, even though the package's implementation is the one written for your warehouse — which is precisely what you want when you are deliberately shimming a package, and precisely what surprises you when you are not. Reverse the two entries in `search_order` and the package wins instead.

One thing `search_order` will not tell you is that an entry has been ignored. **A package listed there is dropped from the search space entirely if it ships no macros.** It installed fine, its models and seeds and docs are all present and usable, and dispatch simply never considers it — silently, because from dispatch's point of view a package with nothing to dispatch to is not a candidate. The symptom is a `search_order` that reads correctly and behaves as though the entry were absent, which sends you looking at adapter prefixes and namespaces rather than at the package's contents. When a dispatch override does not take, check that the package you named actually has a `macros/` directory before checking anything else.

Two boundaries come with it. The `dispatch:` block is honoured **only in the root project**: a package cannot rearrange the search order for a project that installs it. And it routes macros, not materializations — Ch 8 §8.6 covers what happens when a package tries to replace `table`.

Recognise the pattern when a multi-adapter scenario shows you two `snowflake__` / `bigquery__` macros next to a plain `foo` wrapper, and read the search order carefully whenever a stem supplies one. One older spelling is worth recognising in an option list: `adapter_` macro('foo') is deprecated and superseded by adapter.dispatch('foo'), as are already_exists() and get_columns_in_table().

---

## 6.8 In practice: Credora's global macros

> *This section is an "in practice" sidebar. It draws a composite pattern from (a) the dbt hooks reference at /docs/build/hooks-operations and (b) the query_comment reference at /reference/project-configs/query-comment. Credora is fictional (credora); Ch 14's opening note has the composite-project disclaimer.*

Three project-level macros cover most of what a mature production dbt project wants to do beyond the per-model surface: (a) stamp every compiled query with observability metadata, (b) guard against accidental full-project builds, and (c) apply warehouse-side security controls. Credora implements all three.

### Macro 1 — query_comment for JSON telemetry

dbt ships a built-in query-comment config that attaches a SQL comment to every query it sends to the warehouse. On Snowflake the comment appears at the *end* of the query, which stops it being stripped during processing; on every other adapter it appears at the *beginning*. That is what the reference states, and it states nothing about how — append: true is the config that puts it at the end explicitly, anywhere. The default is already a JSON payload of five keys — app, dbt_version, profile_name, target_name, node_id — and teams at scale replace it with a macro that renders more: run start time, invocation ID, whatever the observability stack keys on. query-comment: null switches it off entirely.

```
-- macros/query_comment.sql
{% macro query_comment(node) %}
    {% set comment_dict = {
        'app': 'dbt',
        'dbt_version': dbt_version,
        'target_name': target.name,
        'target_type': target.type,
        'run_started_at': run_started_at.isoformat(),
        'node_id': node.unique_id if node else none
    } %}
    {% do return(tojson(comment_dict)) %}
{% endmacro %}
```

> **Watch out.** dbt_version is documented as part of the query_comment context's variable list (alongside invocation_id, node, tojson, etc. — see /reference/project-configs/query-comment), and that guarantee is scoped to this macro. Before reaching for any of them inside a post_hook or a run-operation macro, check the reference for the context you are actually in.

Wired in at the project level:

```
# dbt_project.yml
query-comment:
  comment: "{{ query_comment(node) }}"
  append: true
```

The dict form takes `comment`, `append`, and on BigQuery `job-label`. One trap lives inside it: `var()` called from a query-comment macro reads `--vars` **only**. A `vars:` block in `dbt_project.yml` is invisible there, so `var('run_id', 'unset')` in a query comment comes back `unset` on any run that did not pass `--vars`, whatever the project file says. That is a genuine exception to §6.2's `var` rule, and not the only one: `var()` called from `dbt_project.yml` itself reads `--vars` only in exactly the same way at 1.11, which is why `+schema: "{{ var('env_schema', 'analytics') }}"` in that file silently takes its default on any run without `--vars`. The reference scopes the restriction to this release. Properties YAML is the contrast that makes the shape clear — `materialized: "{{ var('default_mat') }}"` in a `_models.yml` *does* resolve from the project's `vars:` block. It is the context that decides, not the release.

Now every query Credora compiles carries a JSON header identifying the run. Snowflake's Query History, Databricks' Query History and its `system.query.history` table, and BigQuery's `INFORMATION_SCHEMA.JOBS` all let you filter on comment substrings — a one-line change turns opaque warehouse usage into dbt-attributed telemetry. Note which surface does which on Databricks: you **find** the query in Query History or `system.query.history`, searching the statement text for your comment; you then open **Query Profile** on that one query to see how it executed. Query Profile analyses a single selected query and is not where you search across them. The `/reference/project-configs/query-comment` reference page walks through the same pattern with different payload shapes.

## Macro 2 — `require_select_arg` as an on-run-start safety gate

A project of Credora's scale has a blast-radius problem: `dbt build` with no `--select` rebuilds the entire project — a long and expensive operation that nobody wants running by accident, least of all via a typo'd CI parameter. A short macro called from `on-run-start` can refuse to proceed unless a selector was explicitly set:

```
-- macros/require_select_arg.sql
{% macro require_select_arg() %}
    {% if flags.WHICH in ('run', 'build', 'test') %}
        {% set args = invocation_args_dict %}
        {% if not (args.get('select') or args.get('exclude') or args.get('selector')) %}
            {% do exceptions.raise_compiler_error(
                "Refusing to run without --select/--exclude/--selector. " ~
                "Pass --select state:modified+ for CI, " ~
                "or --select tag:daily for scheduled runs."
            ) %}
        {% endif %}
    {% endif %}
{% endmacro %}
```

`flags` exposes `WHICH` alongside the global config flags — `FULL_REFRESH`, `STORE_FAILURES`, `DEBUG` — but not `--select`, `--exclude` or `--selector`; an attribute that is not there is falsy, so a guard written against `flags.SELECT` refuses every run, selector or not. `invocation_args_dict` holds the parsed command line and is the handle that works.

Wire it at the top of `dbt_project.yml`:

```
on-run-start:
  - "{{ require_select_arg() }}"
```

Now `dbt build` with no selector raises at run start with a helpful error and the run exits non-zero; `dbt build --select state:modified+` proceeds.

**Two ways an `on-run-start` hook can fail, and only one of them is a gate.** This macro raises with `exceptions.raise_compiler_error`, so the failure is a **Compilation Error**:

dbt abandons the invocation before it builds anything and exits **2**. Executed on Core 1.11.14, a bare `dbt build` against the wiring above prints `Compilation Error in operation ...-on-run-start-0` naming the macro, and nothing is created. That is a real gate, and it works at the 1.11 default with no flag set.

The other failure mode is a hook whose **SQL the warehouse rejects**. That one is a node-level hook error, and it is what `skip_nodes_if_on_run_start_fails` governs — at its 1.11 default of `false` the error is reported and the selected models build anyway, exit `1`. So a guardrail built on a warehouse statement rather than a raised compiler error needs the flag set `true` to actually stop the run. Ch 10 §10.9.2 has both run summaries side by side, and §10.9.3 has the flag. The pattern — using `on-run-start` as a safety valve — is described in several community posts on the dbt Discourse forum; the dbt Labs hooks & operations documentation is the reference for the surface this macro builds on.

## Macro 3 — `generate_masking_functions` for Unity Catalog column masks

Databricks Unity Catalog supports column-level masking via ALTER TABLE <table> ALTER COLUMN <column> SET MASK <function> — the `ALTER COLUMN` clause is required when the column already exists, and is the half most often dropped when the statement is quoted from memory. A SQL function is applied to specific columns at read time, returning a masked value (hash, truncation, NULL) unless the reader has a designated role. Credora keeps the list of mask functions in a YAML config file and regenerates them at the start of every dbt run:

```
-- macros/generate_masking_functions.sql
{% macro generate_masking_functions() %}
    {% set masks = var('column_masks', {}) %}
    {% for mask_name, spec in masks.items() %}
        create or replace function {{ target.schema }}.{{ mask_name }}(val string)
        returns string
        return case
            when is_account_group_member('{{ spec.reader_group }}') then val
            else {{ spec.masked_expression }}
        end;
    {% endfor %}
{% endmacro %}
```

Wire it at the top of `dbt_project.yml`:

```
on-run-start:
  - "{{ generate_masking_functions() }}"
```

Each run refreshes the catalog of mask functions before any model builds. Individual models then reference these functions via a `post_hook` that issues ALTER TABLE <table> ALTER COLUMN <column> SET MASK <function>. This is pattern territory rather than exam territory — the `dbt-databricks` GitHub repository ships production examples of Unity Catalog integration, and the Databricks column-mask SQL reference is the external reference for the syntax. The dbt-side scaffolding — an `on-run-start` hook calling a macro — is exactly what `/docs/build/hooks-operations` describes.

## What the three patterns have in common

Each is a macro wired in once at the project level — two from `on-run-start`, one from the `query-comment` config — a dozen lines of dbt-native code in place of bespoke tooling.

---

## Summary

- **Jinja has three delimiters.** `{{ ... }}` for expressions, `{% ... %}` for statements, `{# ... #}` for comments.
- **Jinja is compile-time.** Every `ref`, `var`, `env_var`, `config`, and macro call is resolved before the warehouse sees any SQL. A branch cannot see a row the query is about to return; it can read a warehouse *value*, but only through `run_query` under `{% if execute %}`, and it is decided once for the whole model.
- **A `ref()` that never evaluates registers no edge.** Force the dependency with the SQL comment `-- depends_on: {{ ref('x') }}`; the Jinja form `{# depends_on: … #}` is stripped before it can render and does nothing.
- **The Jinja-context ten:** `ref`, `source`, `config`, `var`, `env_var`, `this`, `target`, `run_started_at`, `adapter`, `builtins`. Plus `log` and `return` as honourable mentions and `execute` as the parse-vs-execute guard.
- **Macros live under `macros/`.** Define with `{% macro name(args) %}`, call with `{{ name(args) }}`. Most macros return SQL; use `{% do return(value) %}` to return a Python value (list, dict, int, string) from a helper macro, and `{% call statement(...) %}` plus `load_result` when the value has to come from the warehouse.
- **Never nest curlies.** A `{{ }}` inside an already-open `{{ }}` is stored as literal text, silently. Hooks are the sole exception, because the hook string is re-rendered when the hook runs.
- **`exceptions.warn()` leaves the node passing**; `raise_compiler_error`, `raise_fail_fast_error` and `raise_not_implemented` all fail. `--warn-error`, or a `JinjaLogWarning` entry in `--warn-error-options`, escalates the warning to an error.
- **A macro's properties live in a `.yml` under `macro-paths`** — never in `dbt_project.yml`, never in a `config()` block — with `description`, `config:` (`docs:`, `meta:`) and `arguments:` (`name`, `type`, `description`).
- **Config precedence:** `{{ config() }}` in SQL > YAML `config:` > `dbt_project.yml` `+config` > dbt's built-in default (the implicit fallback when no layer sets the config — e.g., `view` for `materialized`; a few defaults, `incremental_strategy` among them, are dispatched per adapter instead). More-specific folder path wins inside `dbt_project.yml`. All three resolve during parse — SQL `config()` as dbt builds the node (§6.1), YAML and project-file configs with their own limited Jinja contexts. `dbt_project.yml`'s own top-level keys are dash-spelled and an underscore refuses to load the project; an unrecognised `+` resource config is dropped in silence, and only a key registered under both spellings — `pre-hook`, `post-hook` — takes either.
- **Hooks are per-resource or project-level.** `pre_hook` / `post_hook` fire around a specific model's DDL. `on-run-start` / `on-run-end` fire once per invocation, at the top of `dbt_project.yml`. Both accept strings or lists of strings and can call macros. On Postgres and Redshift they run inside the model's transaction unless `before_begin`, `after_commit` or `{"transaction": false}` moves them out.
- **`schemas`, `database_schemas` and `results` exist only in `on-run-end`** — absent everywhere else, `on-run-start` included. `selected_resources` is available in all four hook types.
- **Hook triggers:** `build`, `run`, `seed`, `snapshot`, `source freshness`, `test`. Not `parse`, `clean` or `run-operation` — and not `compile` or `docs generate`, whatever the reference page says.
- **dbt run-operation <macro>** runs a macro without a model run; does not fire project hooks.
- **Doc blocks** live in `.md` files under any path `docs-paths` covers (by default, every resource path in the project), defined with `{% docs block %}...{% enddocs %}`. Reference them from YAML descriptions with `{{ doc('block') }}`. Rendered by `dbt docs generate`.

- **Dispatch** routes a macro call to an adapter-specific implementation (`snowflake__foo`, `databricks__foo`, `default__foo`), inheriting through the adapter family — Redshift tries `redshift__`, then `postgres__`, then `default__`. dbt Core ships around thirty cross-database macros in the `dbt` namespace already dispatched.
- **`dispatch:` search order exhausts each namespace before the next**, so a root-project `default__foo` beats a package's `postgres__foo`. The block is honoured only in the root project.

## Learning-goal checklist (self-assess)

- ☐ I can read a Jinja expression or statement and say what dbt will compile it to, including distinguishing `{{ }}` / `{% %}` / `{# #}`.
- ☐ I can name the ten Jinja-context entries (`ref`, `source`, `config`, `var`, `env_var`, `this`, `target`, `run_started_at`, `adapter`, `builtins`) and distinguish `var` vs `env_var` and `this` vs `target` cold.
- ☐ I can write a macro in `macros/`, call it from a model, and decide between returning SQL and returning a value via `{% do return(...) %}`.
- ☐ I can recite the config-precedence rule from memory — SQL `config()` > YAML `config:` > `dbt_project.yml` `+config` > dbt's built-in default — and explain where YAML configs can safely use `var(...)` or `env_var(...)`.
- ☐ I can place a `pre_hook`, `post_hook`, `on-run-start`, and `on-run-end` in the right slot and name the six commands that trigger hooks (and the three that don't).
- ☐ I can say which spellings `dbt_project.yml` accepts — dash-only for its own top-level keys, either form only where a key is registered twice — and what dbt does with the wrong one, on each half of the file.
- ☐ I can explain why a `ref()` inside an unrendered branch or a `{% call statement %}` block creates no DAG edge, and write the `-- depends_on:` comment that fixes it.
- ☐ I can say what a `{{ }}` nested inside an already-open `{{ }}` passes, and name the one config where that construct is correct.
- ☐ I can name the four `exceptions` functions worth knowing, say which one leaves the node passing, and name the two ways that warning gets escalated to an error.
- ☐ I can write a `.yml` block documenting a macro and say where that block is *not* allowed to live.
- ☐ I can trace `adapter.dispatch` through a two-namespace `search_order` and say why a root-project `default__` beats a package's `postgres__`.
- ☐ I can write a doc block, reference it with `{{ doc('name') }}` from a YAML description, and explain when it renders.

---

## Practice questions

Twenty-seven questions covering Jinja & macros overview (Qs 1, 2, 3), Jinja context functions (Qs 4, 5, 6, 7, 8, 9, 27), macro definition and invocation (Qs 10, 11, 12, 13), config rendering and hierarchy (Qs 14, 15), static parsing and hidden dependencies (Qs 16, 17), project-file key spelling (Qs 18, 25), running a macro outside a build (Q19), doc blocks (Qs 20, 21), dispatch (Qs 22, 23, 26), and one analyze-level parse/compile/run triage (Q24).

**1.** Which Jinja delimiter is used for a statement like `if`, `for`, or `set` that produces no output of its own?
A. `{{ ... }}` B. `{{# ... #}}`
C. `{# ... #}` D. `{% ... %}`

**2.** What happens to the text inside a Jinja comment `{# this is a note #}` when dbt compiles a model?
A. It becomes a SQL -- comment in the compiled file
B. It is stripped from the output entirely; the warehouse never sees it
C. It is logged to `logs/dbt.log` but removed from the SQL
D. It causes a compile error

**3.** When is a `{{ ref('stg_orders') }}` expression resolved?
A. At warehouse query-plan time
B. When the model's view is first queried by a user
C. When `dbt debug` is called
D. At compile time, before the model's own SQL is sent to the warehouse

**4.** A team wants to parameterise the **raw ingestion catalog** so dev reads from `raw_dev` and production reads from `raw_prd`. The value is set by the CI system and should not be committed to the repo. Which Jinja function is the right choice?
A. `var('raw_catalog')` B. `env_var('RAW_CATALOG')`
C. `config(raw_catalog='...')` D. `target.raw_catalog`

**5.** A model wraps a `run_query('select count(*) …')` call in `{% if execute %}` and branches on the number it returns. What does `dbt compile` do?
A. Nothing is queried — `compile` opens no warehouse connection, so the branch falls to its parse-time default
B. It raises an error — `run_query` is valid in a macro or a hook, not in a model body
C. The branch is left in the compiled SQL for the warehouse to resolve when the query runs
D. The count is queried during the render, and `target/compiled/` holds the branch that number selected

**6.** A model at `models/marts/fct_orders.sql` builds the relation `analytics.marts.fct_orders`. Ignoring the identifier quoting the adapter adds, what does `{{ this }}` render to inside that model?
A. `analytics` B. `marts.fct_orders`
C. `analytics.marts.fct_orders` D. The literal text `this`

**7.** What value does `run_started_at` carry inside a Jinja expression?
A. A Python datetime object with the wall-clock time at which the current dbt invocation began, defaulting to UTC
B. The SQL `now()` evaluated per row
C. The last time the model was built, read from the warehouse
D. A string constant set at project install

**8.** A team wants to express "route queries to a different schema depending on which target is active." The decision is based on the dbt target, not on an OS environment variable. Which Jinja expression is correct?
A. `{{ env_var('TARGET') }}` B. `{{ var('target') }}`
C. `{{ target.name }}` D. `{{ this.target }}`

**9.** What does `{{ config(materialized='table') }}` render to in the compiled SQL output?
A. `CREATE TABLE ...`
B. A SQL comment documenting the materialization
C. The literal text `materialized='table'`
D. An empty string; the call sets the model's config as a side effect and produces no text

**10.** Where should a new macro named `cast_timestamp_utc` be saved so dbt discovers it automatically?
A. `macros/cast_timestamp_utc.sql` (or any `.sql` file under `macros/`)
B. `models/macros/cast_timestamp_utc.sql`
C. `dbt_project.yml`, under a `macros:` block
D. `~/.dbt/macros/`

**11.** Given the macro definition:

```
{% macro prefix_columns(cols, prefix='c') -%}
  {%- for c in cols -%}
    {{ prefix }}.{{ c }}{%- if not loop.last %}, {% endif -%}
  {%- endfor -%}
{%- endmacro %}
```

What does `{{ prefix_columns(['id', 'name'], 'u') }}` render to?
A. `u.id u.name` B. `u.id, u.name`
C. `c.id, c.name` D. `['id', 'name']`

**12.** A helper macro needs to produce a Python list of market codes that three different models will each iterate with `{% for m in markets %}`. Which construct does the macro need?
A. A bare `select` statement returning the codes as rows
B. `config(markets=[...])`
C. `{% set markets = ['uk', 'us', 'apac_1'] %}` at the top of each caller
D. `{% do return(['uk', 'us', 'apac_1']) %}` inside the macro body

**13.** A macro validates its argument and reports the problem without stopping the build. On a plain `dbt run` — no `--warn-error`, no `--warn-error-options` — which `exceptions` call prints the message and still leaves the node reported as `PASS`?
A. `exceptions.raise_compiler_error(msg)` B. `exceptions.raise_fail_fast_error(msg)`
C. `exceptions.warn(msg)` D. `exceptions.raise_not_implemented(msg)`

**14.** A model's config block reads:

```
{{ config(
    materialized='table',
    alias="{{ var('table_alias') }}",
    post_hook="grant select on {{ this }} to role analyst"
) }}
```

`vars:` sets `table_alias: fct_orders_uk`. What does dbt do with the two inner `{{ ... }}` expressions?
A. Both resolve, because `config()` renders its argument values before storing them
B. Neither resolves, and the model builds with the literal alias `{{ var('table_alias') }}` and a grant naming no real relation
C. `alias` keeps the literal text; the `post_hook` is re-rendered at run time and grants on the real relation
D. The parse fails — a `{{ }}` opened inside an already-open `{{ }}` is a Jinja syntax error

**15.** A developer defines `vars: {default_mat: table}` in `dbt_project.yml`, then writes this in `_models.yml`:

```
models:
  - name: fct_orders
    config:
      materialized: "{{ var('default_mat') }}"
```

What happens when dbt parses the project?
A. dbt raises a YAML syntax error because quoted Jinja is illegal in properties YAML
B. `materialized` is the literal string `"{{ var('default_mat') }}"`
C. dbt returns a warning and defaults to `view`
D. `materialized` is set to `table`, the rendered value of `default_mat`

**16.** A model's only `{{ ref('stg_returns') }}` sits inside `{% if var('include_returns', false) %}`, and the project never sets `include_returns`. The project parses, the model compiles, and `dbt build` sometimes builds `stg_returns` *after* it. Why does dbt not see the dependency?
A. With the variable unset the branch never renders, so the `ref()` never evaluates and no edge exists
B. `var()` is resolved after the graph is built, so an edge behind one is deferred to a later pass
C. dbt records the edge but drops it during selection, because `stg_returns` was not in the same command
D. A `ref()` inside any `{% %}` block is invisible to the parser; edges come from top-level calls

**17.** A model reads its upstream table only inside a `{% call statement('probe', fetch_result=True) %}` block, so dbt records no edge and the two models build in the wrong order. Which line, added at the top of the model file, registers the dependency?
A. `-- depends_on: {{ ref('stg_orders') }}`
B. `{{ config(depends_on=['stg_orders']) }}`
C. `-- depends_on: stg_orders`
D. `{# depends_on: {{ ref('stg_orders') }} #}`

**18.** A team adds two hooks to `dbt_project.yml`, both spelled with underscores: `on_run_start:` at the top level, and `+pre_hook:` under the `models:` tree. What happens on the next `dbt run`?
A. Both take effect — dbt treats dashes and underscores as interchangeable in this file
B. dbt refuses to load the project, reporting `Additional properties are not allowed ('on_run_start' was unexpected)`; the `+pre_hook` entry would have been valid
C. Both keys are ignored without comment, the run proceeds, and neither hook fires
D. The project loads and the start hook fires, but `+pre_hook` is rejected, because resource configs under `models:` must be dash-spelled

**19.** A team wants to invoke the `grant_select_on_mart` macro once, outside of any model build, passing it two arguments. Which command is appropriate?
A. `dbt run --macro grant_select_on_mart`
B. `dbt run-operation grant_select_on_mart --args '{schema: analytics, role: analyst}'`
C. `dbt macro grant_select_on_mart`
D. `dbt compile --inline '{{ grant_select_on_mart(...) }}'`

**20.** Where must a doc block (`{% docs my_block %} ... {% enddocs %}`) be written for dbt to register it?
A. In a `.sql` file under `macros/`
B. In a `docs:` key inside `dbt_project.yml`
C. In a `_models.yml` properties file, as a YAML string
D. In a `.md` file under any of the project's resource paths

**21.** A `_models.yml` has:

```
models:
  - name: dim_users_uk
    columns:
      - name: market_id
        description: "{{ doc('uk_market_id') }}"
```

A `.md` file under `models/` contains:

```
{% docs uk_market_id %}
The market identifier for UK-originated records.
{% enddocs %}
```

What does the `market_id` column's description look like on the docs site rendered by `dbt docs generate / dbt docs serve`?
A. The literal text `{{ doc('uk_market_id') }}`
B. Empty — `doc()` is only valid inside macros
C. "The market identifier for UK-originated records."
D. The docs command fails with a resolution error

**22.** In a cross-adapter package, what is the purpose of writing a macro in the form `snowflake__my_macro(arg)` alongside `bigquery__my_macro(arg)` and a dispatching wrapper `my_macro(arg)`?
A. To speed up compile time
B. To let `adapter.dispatch('my_macro')` resolve to the `<target.type>__` implementation, falling back to `default__`
C. To declare the macro private to the package
D. To register the macro in the package's `dispatch:` search order

**23.** A project running on Postgres installs `dbt_utils` and adds:

```
dispatch:
  - macro_namespace: dbt_utils
    search_order:
      - my_project
      - dbt_utils
```

`my_project` defines `default__deduplicate` and nothing else. `dbt_utils` ships both `postgres__deduplicate` and `default__deduplicate`. Which implementation does `{{ dbt_utils.deduplicate(...) }}` render?
A. Neither — dbt raises a compilation error, because the first namespace has no `postgres__` variant
B. `dbt_utils.postgres__deduplicate`
C. `dbt_utils.default__deduplicate`
D. `my_project.default__deduplicate`

**24.** A junior engineer writes this macro, saves it at `macros/build_schema_name.sql`, and calls it from a model:

```
{% macro build_schema_name() %}
    {% set schema = 'analytics_prd' %}
    {% do return(schema) %}
{% endmacro %}
```

The model has `{{ config(schema=build_schema_name()) }}`, and the project overrides `generate_schema_name` to return the custom name verbatim. In every environment — dev, CI, prod — the model ends up writing to `analytics_prd`, breaking the CI schema. At what phase does the bug first produce a wrong result?
A. Parse — the macro is loaded and called while dbt builds the manifest, so the hard-coded `'analytics_prd'` is already recorded as the node's schema before any SQL is rendered
B. Compile — the config is carried through parse unresolved and `build_schema_name()` is not called until the model's SQL is rendered
C. Run — the warehouse rejects the DDL
D. None of the three — the macro is fine, and the CI target's `schema:` in `profiles.yml` is what is misconfigured

**25.** A project sets `+persist_docs: {relation: true, columns: true}` under `models:` in `dbt_project.yml`, and a teammate later retypes the key as `+persist-docs:` with the same value. `dbt parse` is run. What happens?
A. The project parses at exit 0, nothing is logged, and the model resolves `persist_docs` to `{}` — the config is silently absent
B. The project parses at exit 0 and the config still applies, because dash and underscore are interchangeable for `+` keys under `models:`
C. dbt refuses to load the project: `at path []: Additional properties are not allowed`, exit 2
D. The project parses but emits a warning naming `persist-docs` as an unrecognised config

**26.** A project lists `my_shims` first in a `dispatch: search_order` so its implementation wins over `dbt_utils`. `dbt deps` succeeded and `my_shims` models and seeds are all usable, but the packaged `dbt_utils` macro still runs. What is the most likely cause?
A. `search_order` is read bottom-up, so `dbt_utils` wins as written
B. The shim is named `default__` and adapter-specific implementations always outrank it
C. `my_shims` ships no macros, so dispatch drops it from the search space and never reports the empty namespace
D. `dispatch` only applies to cross-database macros in dbt's own `dbt` namespace

**27.** A model contains `{{ var('raw_catalog') }}`. No `vars:` block declares it and no `--vars` is passed. What happens?
A. It renders empty, and the compiled SQL contains a blank where the value would be
B. dbt raises a compile error naming the variable, and nothing runs
C. It renders `None`, which the warehouse reads as SQL `NULL`
D. dbt warns and falls back to the variable's name as a literal string

## Answer key

**1. D.** `{% ... %}` wraps control-flow and declaration statements — `if`, `for`, `set`, `macro`, `call` — which shape what surrounding expressions render but produce no output themselves. `{{ ... }}` is for expressions whose value is spliced into the output. `{# ... #}` is a comment stripped before rendering. `{{# ... #}}` is not Jinja at all — the `{{#` section-open belongs to Mustache and Handlebars, and a reader arriving from front-end templating is the one it is there for. Source: `/docs/build/jinja-macros`.

**2. B.** `{# ... #}` is a Jinja comment and is removed during the render step; nothing about it reaches the compiled SQL or the warehouse. A SQL `--` comment, by contrast, survives compilation and is sent to the warehouse as part of the query. Source: `/docs/build/jinja-macros`.

**3. D.** `ref()` is resolved during the compile phase, when dbt renders Jinja into literal SQL and writes the result to `target/compiled/`. By the time the warehouse receives the model's query, `ref` has been replaced with a fully-qualified relation. Note the scope of "before": rendering settles the model's SQL before that SQL is submitted, but compilation is not warehouse-free — dbt opens a connection for the relation cache and for any `run_query` inside `{% if execute %}` (Ch 10 §10.2). What D rules out is A and B, which put the resolution *after* submission. Source: `/reference/dbt-jinja-functions/ref`, `/reference/commands/compile`.

**4. B.** `env_var()` reads from the host's environment variables — ideal for values that differ per deployment and live outside the repo (CI secrets, per-machine overrides). `var()` reads from `vars:` in `dbt_project.yml` or a `--vars` CLI argument; the value is committed. `config()` sets per-model config; `target` exposes the active profile. Source: `/reference/dbt-jinja-functions/env_var`, `/reference/dbt-jinja-functions/var`.

**5. D.** `compile` renders the model with a live warehouse connection, so the `run_query` inside the `execute` guard really runs: the count comes back during the render, and the compiled file in `target/compiled/` carries the branch that number selected — the whole decision is made before anything is materialised. A is the belief the item exists to break. *Compile never touches the warehouse* is false: the relation cache and every `run_query` are introspective queries issued during compile, which is why an opt-out flag exists at all. C misplaces the phase — no `{% %}` survives the render, so the warehouse is handed a branch already taken, never a choice. B invents a restriction: `run_query` is legal in a model body, and the `execute` guard is what stops it firing during the parse pass, where neither the connection nor the graph exists yet (§6.2). Source: `/reference/commands/compile`, `/reference/dbt-jinja-functions/execute`, `/reference/dbt-jinja-functions/run_query`.

**6. C.** `this` is the relation the materialization will write to, qualified all the way down: database, schema, identifier. A is the database alone and B the schema-and-identifier pair — two partial slices, reached for by a reader who thinks `this` drops the database or keeps only the leaf. D is the "Jinja leaves it alone" misconception. On a real adapter the render carries identifier quoting (`"analytics"."marts"."fct_orders"`), which is why the stem sets quoting aside. Use `this` inside an incremental `where` clause: `where updated_at > (select max(updated_at) from {{ this }})`. Source: `/reference/dbt-jinja-functions/this`, `/reference/dbt-jinja-functions/target`.

**7. A.** `run_started_at` is a Python datetime captured at the start of the dbt command; it's constant across the entire run, so every model in the same invocation sees the same value. UTC is the default; you can convert with `pytz` if needed. Useful for stamping audit columns so every row loaded in one run carries the same timestamp. Source: `/reference/dbt-jinja-functions/run_started_at`.

**8. C.** `target.name` is the name of the currently active target in `profiles.yml` (`dev`, `ci`, `prd`, etc.). `env_var` reads from the shell environment; `var` reads from `vars:`; `this.target` is the trap: it does not error, it renders to an empty string, because `this` exposes `database`, `schema` and `identifier` and nothing else. A silently empty schema name is worse than a crash. Source: `/reference/dbt-jinja-functions/target`.

**9. D.** `config()` inside a `.sql` file is a side-effect call: dbt records the config settings — at parse, when the node is built into the manifest (§6.1) — and `config()` itself returns nothing. The compiled `.sql` file has an empty line where the call used to be. The DDL wrapper applies `create table ...` later, not `config()` itself. Source: `/reference/dbt-jinja-functions/config`, `/reference/commands/compile`.

**10. A.** Macros live under the directory named by `macro-paths`, which defaults to `macros/`. dbt discovers every macro defined in every `.sql` file under that directory, regardless of file name. `macros/` is a top-level project directory — not a sub-directory of `models/`. C is the near-miss worth knowing: `dbt_project.yml` never holds macro *code*, and it does not hold macro *properties* either — those go in a `.yml` under `macro-paths`, per §6.3. Source: `/docs/build/jinja-macros`, `/reference/project-configs/macro-paths`.

**11. B.** The macro iterates the list, prefixing each column with the string `u` (overriding the default `c`), and joining with commas via the `loop.last` check. Option A omits the comma — that is the discriminator vs B, and without it the rendered text would be a SQL syntax error. The `-%}` and `{%-` controls on every tag strip the surrounding whitespace, so the render is exactly `u.id, u.name` with nothing around it. The default `'c'` is only used when the caller omits the second argument. Source: `/docs/build/jinja-macros`.

**12. D.** `{% do return(value) %}` makes the macro return a Python object — a list, dict, int, string — instead of SQL text. Without `return()`, whatever the macro renders is the rendered string, which isn't iterable as a Python list. The caller then does `{% set markets = list_of_markets() %}` and `{% for m in markets %}` iterates the list. C is the option worth pausing on: a caller-side `{% set %}` genuinely works, and it works in exactly one file — write it at the top of each of three models and you have three copies of the list to keep in step, which is the duplication the macro exists to remove. The `{{ return(value) }}` expression form short-circuits identically; both are current, and the choice between them is style. Source: `/reference/dbt-jinja-functions/return`.

**13. C.** `exceptions.warn()` is the only one of the four that fails nothing: dbt logs the message and the node is reported `PASS`. That is also why the stem rules out the escalation flags: `--warn-error`, or a `JinjaLogWarning` entry in `--warn-error-options`, reverses it, and the node that passed a moment ago fails with a compilation error carrying your own message (§6.3). A fails the node at compile time; B stops the whole invocation on the spot; D is the signal an adapter or package author raises for an operation the warehouse cannot perform, and it fails too. All four want `{% if execute %}` around them, or a bare `dbt parse` trips them. Source: `/reference/dbt-jinja-functions/exceptions`, `/reference/global-configs/warnings`.

**14. C.** A `{{ ... }}` opened inside an already-open `{{ ... }}` is not a second expression; it is text inside a string argument. So `alias` is set to the characters `{{ var('table_alias') }}` exactly as written — no error and no warning, which is what makes it dangerous, and A generalises the one exception to every config. Hooks are that exception, and only because a hook is stored rather than evaluated: dbt keeps the string as the config value and renders it again when the hook runs, so `{{ this }}` resolves to the fully-qualified relation at run time. That is why §6.5's grant example is written the way it is, and why B is wrong about the second half. D expects an error dbt does not raise. Source: `/best-practices/dont-nest-your-curlies`, `/reference/resource-configs/pre-hook-post-hook`.

**15. D.** Properties YAML is rendered through dbt's Jinja context (during the parse phase) before config validation. Because `default_mat` is defined as `table`, the quoted Jinja string resolves to `table` and dbt applies that as the YAML-level model config. If the variable were missing and no default were supplied, parsing would fail with a required-var compilation error. Source: `/reference/configs-and-properties`, `/reference/dbt-jinja-functions/var`.

**16. A.** dbt learns a model's dependencies from the `ref()` calls that actually evaluate. A branch that renders false renders nothing inside it, so the `ref('stg_returns')` never runs, no edge reaches the manifest, and the two models are unordered relative to each other — which is why the failure is intermittent rather than a build error. D over-generalises the same idea into something false: a `ref()` inside a `{% for %}` that does render, or inside a rendered `{% if %}` branch, registers perfectly well; it is evaluation that matters, not nesting. B has the phases backwards — `var()` resolves during parse, which is when the graph is being built. C describes selection, which prunes what dbt runs and never edits the edges. The fix is the `-- depends_on:` comment in §6.1. Source: `/reference/dbt-jinja-functions/ref`, `/reference/parsing`.

**17. A.** The `-- depends_on:` form is Jinja inside a *SQL* comment: dbt renders `ref('stg_orders')` like any other expression, registers the edge, and the leading `--` keeps the resulting relation name out of the query's meaning. D puts the same call inside a *Jinja* comment, and `{# #}` is stripped before anything inside it is evaluated — the call never happens, so nothing is registered. C drops the `ref()` and leaves a bare name, which is just text in a comment; dbt reads relation names out of `ref()` calls, never out of comment prose. B invents a config: `depends_on` is an exposure property, and passing it to `config()` parses without complaint and registers nothing, which is the worst of the three failure modes because it looks deliberate. Source: `/reference/dbt-jinja-functions/ref`, `/reference/dbt-jinja-functions/statement-blocks`.

**18. B.** `dbt_project.yml`'s own keys are validated against a schema that knows the dash spellings only, so `on_run_start:` is not a mis-set hook — it is an unknown key, and dbt stops at project load with `at path []: Additional properties are not allowed ('on_run_start' was unexpected)` and exit code 2. Nothing is built, which is the mercy in it. The `+pre_hook` entry in the same file is fine: `+`-prefixed resource configs carry the names a `config()` call uses, and `+pre-hook` and `+pre_hook` both fire. That asymmetry is what makes A and D each half-right and wholly wrong — A generalises the tolerant half to the whole file, D generalises the strict half. C is the failure this file does not commit: an unknown top-level key is refused, not ignored (§6.4). The two hooks differ in scope as well as spelling: `on-run-start` fires once per invocation, `pre_hook` before each selected model's DDL. Source: `/reference/dbt_project.yml`, `/reference/resource-configs/pre-hook-post-hook`.

**19. B.** `dbt run-operation` is the command for invoking a macro without a model run, and the only one of the four that takes an `--args` mapping — YAML or JSON — to carry the two values. It invokes the macro and stops there: what the macro *renders* is discarded, so `grant_select_on_mart` has to issue the grant itself with `run_query` (§6.5). A is not an option `dbt run` has, and there is no `dbt macro` command; both exit before they reach the macro. D is the near-miss, and it fails on what the command produces rather than on whether it touches the warehouse: `dbt compile --inline` renders the string and prints the compiled node, and it refuses the very flag the stem's two arguments need — `No such option: --args`. Compile is not inert, as §6.2 says; a compiled node is simply not an invoked operation. Source: /reference/commands/run-operation.

**20. D.** Two requirements, and both have to hold. The extension must be .md, because dbt's documentation parser reads Markdown files and nothing else — the same block in a .sql file is invisible no matter which directory it sits in, which is what kills A. And the file must sit somewhere dbt already looks: docs-paths defaults to the project's resource paths, so a .md file under models/, macros/, seeds/, snapshots/, analyses/ or tests/ is scanned during parse, while one in a directory named by no path config is never found. B and C put the block in structured YAML — a project-config key and a properties file — and a doc block is neither a config nor a YAML string. Source: /docs/build/documentation, /reference/project-configs/docs-paths, /reference/dbt-jinja-functions/doc.

**21. C.** {{ doc('block') }} inside a YAML description is resolved during **parse**: dbt looks up the matching {% docs uk_market_id %} block and writes the substituted Markdown into that column's description in manifest.json, which a bare dbt parse is enough to prove. dbt docs generate then writes catalog.json, and the site renders a description that was already resolved. A missing block is a parse-time failure, not a docs-time one. This is the mechanism that lets one shared description be reused across many models. Source: /reference/dbt-jinja-functions/doc, /docs/build/documentation.

**22. B.** Dispatch is dbt's multiple-dispatch mechanism: the wrapper macro calls adapter.dispatch('my_macro'), which looks for <target.type>__my_macro in the active namespace and falls back to default__my_macro when no adapter-specific variant exists. That is what the naming convention buys — one interface, one call site, a different body per warehouse, so a package installs unchanged everywhere. D is the near-miss worth understanding: the dispatch: block in dbt_project.yml is real and is taught in §6.7, but it overrides *where* dispatch searches; the <adapter>__ prefix is what registers an implementation, and no block registers anything. Nothing about the convention affects compile speed (A) or macro visibility (C). Source: /reference/dbt-jinja-functions/dispatch, /reference/project-configs/dispatch-config.

**23. D.** dbt exhausts one namespace before it looks at the next, so the order tried is my_project.postgres__deduplicate, my_project.default__deduplicate, dbt_utils.postgres__deduplicate, dbt_utils.default__deduplicate — and the second entry is the first that exists. Package specificity outranks adapter specificity, which is the whole point of the override: your default__ implementation is meant to win, or shimming a package would be impossible. B reads the search order the intuitive way round and loses; C assumes the macro's own package supplies the fallback, when the only thing search_order changes is which namespace is consulted first; A expects a miss inside the first namespace to be fatal, when it simply moves the search on. Reverse the two search_order entries and B becomes correct. Source: /reference/dbt-jinja-functions/dispatch, /reference/project-configs/dispatch-config.

**24. A.** The bug is in the macro's body — it hard-codes 'analytics_prd' instead of deriving the schema from target or env_var — and it lands earlier than most readers expect. {{ config() }} is evaluated while dbt builds the manifest, so build_schema_name() is called during **parse** and its constant is written into the node there. Executed on dbt 1.11.14 against a profile pointing at port 1 with unusable credentials, a bare dbt parse --no-partial-parse exits 0 and target/manifest.json already carries config.schema = analytics_prd, schema = analytics_prd, and relation_name = "unused"."analytics_prd"."example" — while compiled_code is still null. The wrong relation is settled before a line of SQL is rendered and without a warehouse to ask. B is the belief this item exists to correct: dbt's public writing does often call all Jinja rendering "compile time", but parse and compile are two passes with two commands, and this value is fixed in the first of them — dbt parse alone is enough to reveal it, which is why it belongs in CI. C is not run: the warehouse would happily create analytics_prd if permissions allowed. And D misplaces the fault: the macro returns a constant, so no edit to profiles.yml can make it hand back a different value. The fix is to make the macro target-aware, e.g., `{% set schema = target.schema + '_analytics' %}`. Sources: `/reference/parsing`, `/reference/dbt-jinja-functions/config`, `/reference/artifacts/manifest-json`.

**25. A.** An unrecognised `+` key beneath `models:` is discarded without a warning. Parsed on 1.11.14: `+persist_docs: {relation: true, columns: true}` resolves to `{'relation': True, 'columns': True}`, and `+persist-docs:` with the identical value resolves to `{}` — exit 0 both times, nothing logged. **B is the discriminator and it is the belief §6.4 exists to correct:** `+pre-hook` and `+pre_hook` really do both fire, but that is a property of those keys, which dbt registers under both spellings, not of the `+` prefix. `persist-docs` is an alias of nothing. C is the behaviour of a misspelled **top-level** key — `model_paths:` or `on_run_start:` do fail exactly that way, which is what makes C so plausible and why the two halves are worth holding apart: the loud failure cannot ship, and the quiet one can. D describes the warning dbt does not emit; the whole hazard is the silence. Source: `/reference/project-configs/model-paths`; settled by execution.

**26. C.** A package named in `search_order` is dropped from the candidate search space entirely if it contains **zero macros**. It installed fine and its non-macro content is all present and usable, so nothing looks wrong — and dispatch simply never considers it, because a package with nothing to dispatch to is not a candidate. The absence is silent, which sends people to check adapter prefixes and namespaces rather than the package's contents. B is worth being able to reject on the rule rather than by elimination: package specificity really does outrank adapter specificity, so a `default__` in your own project beats a `postgres__` in `dbt_utils`. Executed on dbt 1.11.14: a project whose `search_order` names a macro-less package first compiles clean — exit 0, no warning — and the macro resolves from the next entry in the order; name that package alone and the failure reads `In dispatch: No macro named 'star' found within namespace`, listing the candidate names it tried rather than reporting the package. When an override does not take, check that the package you named actually has a `macros/` directory first. Source: `/reference/dbt-jinja-functions/dispatch`; settled by execution.

**27. B.** A `var()` with no default is a hard failure: dbt raises a compile error naming the variable — `Required var 'raw_catalog' not found in config` — and nothing is sent to the warehouse. It does not render empty and it does not become a null, which is the behaviour you want, because a blank rendered into a predicate produces valid SQL that quietly returns the wrong rows. That makes the two-argument form a decision rather than a habit: `var('x')` declares the variable mandatory and fails loudly when it is missing, while `var('x', 'default')` can never tell you it was forgotten. Use the one-argument form for anything a run must not proceed without. Source: `/reference/dbt-jinja-functions/var`, `/docs/build/project-variables`; settled by execution.

# Chapter 7

# Testing (and unit-tests sidebar)

> **Scope.** Data tests are the contracts between a dbt model and reality. They ride shotgun with every `dbt build`, every explicit `dbt test` run, every PR, and every CI job, and they are how you know — before a consumer does — that a primary key is no longer unique, a foreign key has dangled, or the payments table went empty overnight. This chapter teaches every test taxon dbt offers, the configs that shape test behaviour, and how tests slot into a real branch → test → merge workflow. Unit tests get their own section so readers can recognise the YAML on sight without confusing them with data tests.

**Prerequisites.** Ch 2 (`ref()`, the DAG, YAML property files under `models/`), Ch 3 (sources — tests attach to sources as well as models), Ch 4 §4.3 (incremental models — the "how do I test an incremental without rescanning the whole table" question is a Ch 7 concern dressed as a Ch 4 question), and Ch 6 in full (custom generic tests are macros with a `{% test %}` wrapper; the Jinja context and precedence rules from Ch 6 apply here unchanged).

**Cheat-sheet pointer.** Front-of-book cheat sheet §6 (Topic 5 — Tests) is the one-line recall version of this chapter: four test types, the test config keys, `dbt test --select tag:foo`, the four indirect-selection modes. Use it the morning of the exam; use this chapter for the reasoning that makes the lines stick.

---

## 7.1 The four test types

Most of the test surface is **data tests**, which come in three shapes. Unit tests are the fourth taxon and get their own treatment in §7.8.

| Kind | Where defined | What it asserts |
|---|---|---|
| **Built-in generic** | `data_tests:` block in a YAML properties file, pointing at a column or model | A pre-packaged assertion shipped with dbt — `unique`, `not_null`, `accepted_values`, `relationships` |
| **Custom generic** | `{% test my_test(model, column_name, ...) %}` macro under `macros/` or `tests/generic/`; called from YAML | A reusable, parameterised assertion you wrote yourself |
| **Singular** | A standalone `.sql` file under `tests/` containing a `select` | A one-off assertion that fails if the `select` returns ≥ 1 row |

| Kind | Where defined | What it asserts |
|---|---|---|
| **Unit test** (§7.8) | `unit_tests:` YAML block declaring mock inputs and expected outputs | An assertion about the **SQL logic** of a model, not the data — runs against mocked inputs, so no production warehouse data is consumed |

The mental model that saves you on the exam: a **data test is a query** that passes when it returns zero rows. Each failing row is an assertion violation. Read that as the *default-config* rule, because it is one — it holds while `fail_calc` is `count(*)` and the severity thresholds are `'!= 0'`, which is how tests arrive out of the box. §7.5 covers what changes when you move either, and it is the only place in this book that does. A **unit test is a mocked re-execution of a model's SQL** — you feed it fake inputs, tell it what outputs to expect, and the test passes when the model's logic produces the expected rows. See `/docs/build/data-tests`.

### Decision tree — which test do I reach for?

1. **Do I want to assert about the *values* of real data** — that `customer_id` is never null, or that `status` is one of `['active', 'cancelled']`? → **Data test.** Generic if the assertion is reusable across columns; singular if it is one-off.
2. **Do I want to assert about the *SQL itself*** — that my `case when` branch is unreachable if the input has no negative values, or that a window function partitions correctly on an edge case? → **Unit test.**
3. **Is the assertion reusable across many columns or models** — `valid_iso_country_code`, `ends_with_market_suffix`? → **Custom generic.**
4. **Is the assertion a specific cross-model invariant** — "the sum of `stg_orders.amount` equals the sum of `fct_order_totals.amount`"? → **Singular test.**

Built-in generics cover most assertions. Custom generics absorb the "we keep writing the same singular test shape" case. Singular tests mop up the rest. Unit tests are logic-assertions and do not overlap with the other three.

### The three failure modes

Any data test can fail in one of three ways, regardless of its taxon:

- **Error.** The test's SQL failed at the warehouse (syntax, permission, missing relation). Surfaces as a dbt error, not a test failure.
- **Fail (severity=error, default).** The test SQL ran and returned $\geq 1$ row. dbt exits non-zero; downstream work short-circuits under `dbt build`.
- **Warn (severity=warn).** The test SQL returned $\geq 1$ row, but severity is set to `warn`; dbt logs a warning and continues.

§7.5 unpacks `severity` and its `warn_if` / `error_if` thresholds. For now: all tests have a severity; the default is `error`.

---

## 7.2 Built-in generic tests

The four built-in generic tests are the workhorses of a dbt project: `unique` on primary keys, `not_null` on `_id` columns, `relationships` on foreign-key columns, `accepted_values` on enum-ish ones. See `/reference/resource-properties/data-tests`.

## The four, in order of how often you will use them

**`unique`.** Asserts that every non-null value in a column is distinct. Runs roughly `select col from model where col is not null group by col having count(*) > 1`.

**`not_null`.** Asserts the column has zero `NULL` values. Runs roughly `select col from model where col is null`.

**`accepted_values`.** Asserts every value is in a declared set. Takes a `values:` argument.

**`relationships`.** Asserts every value in this column exists in a referenced column of another model/source — a foreign-key check. Takes `to:` and `field:` arguments.

## Where the YAML lives, and two shapes

Tests attach to a model via a properties file (conventionally `_models.yml` or `schema.yml`) under `models/`. They can be placed at two levels.

The key is `data_tests:`. `tests:` remains valid as a backward-compatible alias, so you will meet both spellings in existing projects and in package YAML — but a single resource cannot carry both. Write both on one model and dbt refuses to parse the project. The same exclusion applies to the `dbt_project.yml` config tree.

**Column-level** — the common case:

```
# models/staging/_models.yml
version: 2

models:
  - name: stg_orders
    columns:
      - name: order_id
        data_tests:
          - unique
          - not_null
      - name: status
        data_tests:
          - accepted_values:
              arguments:
                values: ['placed', 'shipped', 'completed', 'returned']
      - name: customer_id
        data_tests:
          - not_null
          - relationships:
              arguments:
                to: ref('stg_customers')
                field: customer_id
```

**Model-level** — for assertions that span multiple columns or have no natural single-column home:

```
models:
  - name: stg_orders
    data_tests:
      - dbt_utils.unique_combination_of_columns:
          arguments:
            combination_of_columns: [order_id, order_version]
```

> **Null handling — load-bearing detail.** Neither `relationships` nor `accepted_values` fails on a `NULL`, and they get there differently. `relationships` carries an **explicit** `where <column> is not null` in the macro — deliberate, visible, adapter-independent — and `unique` does the same. `accepted_values` has no null handling at all: `NULL not in (...)` evaluates to `NULL`, and a `where` clause keeps only `TRUE` rows, so SQL drops the null, not dbt. Wrap the column in `coalesce()` and that free pass disappears. If you want `NULL` to fail the assertion, attach a separate `not_null` test on the same column — this is the null-handling trap the exam reaches for most.

Model-level tests are almost always custom generics (here, one from the `dbt_utils` package — Ch 8 material); the four built-ins are column-level by design.

## The 1.11 shape: `arguments:` and `config:` as siblings

Every generic test that takes inputs — `accepted_values`, `relationships`, and every custom generic — uses one YAML shape: the test name as a mapping key, and beneath it two sibling blocks that do different jobs.

`arguments:` carries the values passed *into* the test macro. `config:` controls *how* the resulting test node executes — `severity`, `where`, `store_failures` and the rest of §7.5's surface. Three properties stay at the top level beside them: `name`, which renames the test node; `test_name`, which names the generic being applied once `name` has taken the mapping key; and `description`. A config key written at that top level rather than inside `config:` still applies, and warns `PropertyMovedToConfigDeprecation`.

```
- name: status_is_one_of_the_five
  test_name: accepted_values
  description: "Order status is a closed set owned by the checkout service."
  arguments:
    values: ['placed', 'shipped', 'completed', 'returned']
    quote: true              # optional; defaults true
  config:
    severity: warn
    where: "created_at >= current_date - 30"
```

Read the split as *inputs versus execution.* `values` and `quote` are parameters of the `accepted_values` macro. `severity` and `where` are instructions to dbt about the node the macro produces. The two mistakes are not symmetric: dbt lifts the recognised config names back out of `arguments:` before calling the macro, and nothing puts a macro input back where it belongs.

| What you wrote | What dbt does |
|---|---|
| A config key under `arguments:` | Lifts it back into the config and honours it — `severity: warn` written there works, with no warning of any kind |
| A macro input under `config:` | Parses; the test then fails at run time with a database error from the SQL the macro built without it |
| An unrecognised key, under `arguments:` or flat beside the test name | Fails at parse — *takes no keyword argument* |
| The same config key in both blocks | Fails at parse — *Test cannot have the same key at the top-level and in config* |

Both blocks are optional. A test that takes no inputs and needs no configuration stays a bare string — `- unique` is complete YAML — and the shorter form, the test name as the mapping key with only `arguments:` beneath it, is what the examples above use.

`relationships` is worth internalising argument by argument: `to:` takes a `ref()` or `source()` — no hard-coded table names — and `field:` names the column in the referenced relation that the current column must join to. The test fails if any value in the current column is not present in that target column.

### The flat form, and the two deprecations that name it

Older projects and package documentation write the macro's inputs as bare siblings of the test name:

```
# Deprecated. This parses at 1.11 and warns.
- accepted_values:
    values: ['placed', 'shipped', 'completed', 'returned']
```

That form still parses, and it emits `MissingArgumentsPropertyInGenericTestDeprecation` — *"Arguments to generic tests should be nested under the `arguments` property."* The behaviour flag behind the requirement, `require_generic_test_arguments_property`, is on by default at 1.11 (Ch 10 §10.9.2 covers the flag lifecycle), so nesting is what a project expects unless someone has turned the flag off in `dbt_project.yml`.

Turning it off does not silence the warning; it inverts it. With the flag `false`, an `arguments:` block raises `ArgumentsPropertyInGenericTestDeprecation` instead — and then fails, because the flag is also what tells dbt to unwrap `arguments:` before calling the macro, so the block arrives as a keyword the test does not accept. The two warnings are named for the property rather than for the shape, which is why the prefix is the thing to read: `Missing...` means you wrote the flat form under the modern default, and the bare name means you wrote the nested form with the flag off. See `/reference/global-configs/behavior-flags/require_generic_test_arguments_property`.

### What a `data_tests:` block can attach to

Generic tests attach to **models, sources, seeds and snapshots**, at the resource level or the column level. Analyses are the exception, and the way they are excluded is the part worth holding on to: a `data_tests:` block under `analyses:` parses with no error and no warning, the analysis picks up the `description` and `columns` declared beside it, and no test node is created. Nothing in the run output says the assertion is missing, because as far as dbt is concerned there is no assertion. When a test you are sure you wrote never appears in a run, check the resource type you attached it to before you start suspecting the selector.

One more placement is easy to misread. A `data_tests:` key at the *top level* of a properties file, a sibling of `models:`, is not a project-wide attachment point — it is where **singular** tests are given properties: a `name` matching the `.sql` file, plus `description` and `config`. An entry there that names a generic instead fails to parse.

### How tests run

When you `dbt test` (or `dbt build`), dbt compiles each test to a `select` statement and executes it. A passing test returns zero rows; a failing test returns the offending rows. By default dbt doesn't persist the failing rows — it just counts them and reports. To persist them to a warehouse table for debugging, use `store_failures: true` (see §7.5).

---

## 7.3 Singular tests

A **singular test** is a `.sql` file containing a single `select` statement, living under `tests/` — which is the DEFAULT, set by `test-paths:` in `dbt_project.yml` and movable like any other path config (Ch 2 §2.4). The test passes if the `select` returns zero rows; it fails otherwise. No YAML declaration is needed — dbt discovers every `.sql` file under the configured test paths and runs it during `dbt test`. The shape is what distinguishes it from a generic test: one `select`, taking no arguments. See `/docs/build/data-tests`.

### Shape

```
-- tests/assert_order_amount_is_non_negative.sql
select
    order_id,
    amount
from {{ ref('stg_orders') }}
where amount < 0
```

Four things to notice.

1. The file name *is* the test name as far as dbt is concerned; `dbt test --select assert_order_amount_is_non_negative` runs this one and nothing else.
2. Jinja works: `{{ ref(...) }}`, `{{ source(...) }}`, `{{ var(...) }}`, any macro you have defined, and `{% if ... %}` all render the same way they do in a model.
3. The `select` is *declarative of failure.* It should find rows that violate the invariant, not rows that confirm it. A common rookie mistake is writing `where amount >= 0` — that returns all the passing rows, causing the test to fail on a healthy dataset.
4. The test file cannot itself be `ref()`-ed by a model. Singular tests are leaves in the DAG — nothing depends on them.

### When singular tests earn their keep

- **Cross-model invariants.** "The sum of `stg_orders.amount` equals the sum of `fct_order_totals.amount`." No built-in covers this; a custom generic would be overkill for a one-off.
- **One-off referential assertions.** "Every `shipment_id` in `fct_shipments` appears in exactly one row of `fct_orders`." More complex than `relationships` offers.
- **Business-rule assertions that are hard to express generically.** "For every row in `fct_subscriptions` with `status = 'cancelled'`, there exists a row in `stg_events` with `event_type = 'cancellation'` and a timestamp within 60 seconds of `cancelled_at`."

The rule of thumb: if you would write the same SQL three times with different table names, make it a custom generic (§7.4). If you would write it once, a singular test is the right home.

### Configuring a singular test

Singular tests accept the same configs as generic tests, set via a top-of-file `{{ config() }}` call:

```
-- tests/assert_order_amount_is_non_negative.sql
{{ config(severity='warn', store_failures=true) }}
```

```
select
    order_id,
    amount
from {{ ref('stg_orders') }}
where amount < 0
```

That turns the test into a warn-level check that persists its failing rows. Configuration keys are the same surface as §7.5.

---

## 7.4 Custom generic tests

A **custom generic test** is a reusable, parameterised assertion that looks like a built-in generic to anyone writing YAML. You define it once as a macro with a `{% test %}` wrapper; you call it from every column-level or model-level `data_tests:` block. The official guide is `/best-practices/writing-custom-generic-tests`.

### Shape

A custom generic test is a macro that lives under `macros/` (or the dedicated `tests/generic/` subdirectory — either works; dbt discovers them either way). The wrapper tag is `{% test %}` / `{% endtest %}` rather than `{% macro %}` / `{% endmacro %}`:

```
-- tests/generic/valid_iso_country_code.sql
{% test valid_iso_country_code(model, column_name) %}

    select {{ column_name }}
    from {{ model }}
    where {{ column_name }} is not null
      and length({{ column_name }}) != 2

{% endtest %}
```

Four structural rules.

1. **`model` and `column_name` are conventional first arguments.** When a custom generic is attached to a column in YAML, dbt passes the resource the column belongs to as `model` and the column's name as `column_name`. You can add any additional named arguments after those two. The first parameter is *always* spelled `model` — attach the test to a source, a seed or a snapshot and the relation still arrives as `model`, and a signature that renames it to `source` or `relation` binds nothing.
2. **The body is a `select` that returns failing rows.** Exactly like a singular test — zero rows means pass.
3. **File location is flexible.** `macros/valid_iso_country_code.sql` or `tests/generic/valid_iso_country_code.sql` both work. The `tests/generic/` convention is tidier once you have more than a handful.
4. **Reusing a built-in's name overrides it, project-wide and silently.** A `{% test unique %}` block in your project replaces dbt's built-in `unique` everywhere an unqualified `unique` appears in YAML — models and sources alike — and dbt reports nothing: no warning at parse, no note in the run output, just a different query where you expected the shipped one. The built-in stays reachable under its namespace as `dbt.unique`. The same precedence applies to a package's test, but only for the unqualified name: `dbt_utils.unique_combination_of_columns` still runs the package's version, because the namespace decides. The one case that errors is two blocks of the same test name inside one project,

and it errors at parse: dbt reports that it found *multiple macros named `test_unique`* in the project it names, then lists both files.

## Calling a custom generic from YAML

Once defined, it shows up in YAML the same way a built-in does:

```
# models/staging/_models.yml
models:
  - name: stg_customers
    columns:
      - name: country_code
        data_tests:
          - not_null
          - valid_iso_country_code
```

If the test takes extra arguments, pass them as a mapping:

```
-- tests/generic/value_in_range.sql
{% test value_in_range(model, column_name, min_value, max_value) %}
    select {{ column_name }}
    from {{ model }}
    where {{ column_name }} < {{ min_value }}
       or {{ column_name }} > {{ max_value }}
{% endtest %}
```

```
- value_in_range:
    arguments:
      min_value: 0
      max_value: 120
```

## Worked example — `valid_iso_country_code`

Suppose the staging layer has five models that each carry a `country_code` column. The business rule: every non-null value is a two-letter upper-case ISO-3166-1 code. You could write five near-identical singular tests, one per model — or write one custom generic and attach it five times:

```
-- tests/generic/valid_iso_country_code.sql
{% test valid_iso_country_code(model, column_name) %}

    with invalid as (
        select {{ column_name }} as code
        from {{ model }}
        where {{ column_name }} is not null
          and (length({{ column_name }}) != 2
               or {{ column_name }} != upper({{ column_name }}))
    )

    select * from invalid

{% endtest %}
```

```
# models/staging/_models.yml
models:
  - name: stg_customers
    columns:
      - name: country_code
        data_tests:
          - valid_iso_country_code
  - name: stg_addresses
    columns:
      - name: billing_country_code
        data_tests:
          - valid_iso_country_code
  # ... three more models, same test
```

One definition, five attach points. If the rule changes — say, ISO-3166-1 alpha-3 replaces alpha-2 — you edit one file.

### When custom generics shine

Custom generics are the right answer when you catch yourself about to copy-paste a singular test. They are also the idiomatic way to enforce *conventions* — a test that asserts every model's name ends in a recognised market suffix, or that every timestamp column is in UTC. The rule is: one definition, many attach points.

### `equals()` and the null that is not equal to itself

dbt ships an `equals()` macro for comparing two expressions, and it is worth knowing precisely because the obvious reading of it is wrong. It follows **standard SQL three-valued logic**: `NULL = NULL` is `UNKNOWN`, not `TRUE`, so two null values do not match. A test built on `equals()` over a nullable column therefore excludes exactly the rows people assume it covers, and reports zero failures while doing so.

`enable_truthy_nulls_equals_macro` flips it to `IS NOT DISTINCT FROM` semantics, where two nulls do match. It is **off by default**, so the exam's default is three-valued logic. Reach for the flag only when you genuinely want null-equals-null across the whole project; otherwise write the null handling into the test itself, where the next reader can see it.

---

## 7.5 Test configuration — the keys that shape every test

Every data test — generic, custom generic, or singular — accepts the same set of configuration keys. They are documented together at `/reference/data-test-configs`, with dedicated pages for `severity` (`/reference/resource-configs/severity`) and `store_failures` (`/reference/resource-configs/store_failures`). The `where:` key is the one Topic 5 questions reach for most often, and this set of keys together is what the rest of them turn on.

### The config keys

| Key | Effect | Example |
|---|---|---|
| severity | 'error' (default) fails the test and, under dbt build, short-circuits downstream. 'warn' logs a warning and proceeds. | severity: warn |
| warn_if | Threshold expression; the test warns when true. Reached only when error_if has not fired, and it is the only threshold checked under severity: warn. Default '!= 0'. | warn_if: '>10' |
| error_if | Threshold expression; the test errors when true. Checked first, and only under severity: error. Default '!= 0' — so at the defaults a single failing row meets both thresholds and the test takes its configured severity. Used with warn_if to tier responses. | error_if: '>100' |
| store_failures | true persists failing rows to a warehouse table in a schema named <schema>_dbt_test__audit by default (suffix on the active schema; configurable) so you can inspect them after the fact. | store_failures: true |
| store_failures_as | table, view or ephemeral. Names the shape the persisted failures take, and overrides store_failures wherever both are set. | store_failures_as: view |
| where | A SQL predicate that wraps the resource in a filtered subquery (select * from (select * from <resource> where <predicate>) dbt_subquery) before the test runs. Use this to restrict the test to a subset — recent rows, one market, only production. | where: "created_at >= current_date - 7" |
| limit | Integer cap on rows returned by the failing-rows query. Does *not* reduce what the warehouse scans; it caps what gets counted. | limit: 500 |

| Key | Effect | Example |
|---|---|---|
| `fail_calc` | The expression dbt evaluates to get the number it compares against the thresholds. Default `count(*)`. | `fail_calc: "sum(exposure)"` |

The keys attach to the test query at three points. `where` narrows what the query reads, by wrapping the resource in a filtered subquery. `limit` and `fail_calc` sit on the counting layer: dbt wraps the test's own SQL in a subquery, applies `limit` inside it, and evaluates `fail_calc` over what survives. `severity` plus `warn_if` / `error_if` then classify the number that comes back. The ordering has a consequence worth knowing — because `limit` sits *inside* the counted subquery, it caps the number `warn_if` and `error_if` see, not merely the number you are shown.

`fail_calc` is the key that changes what "failing" counts as. Its default is `count(*)`, so the number dbt compares against the thresholds is a row count. Swap in an aggregate — `sum(amount_over_limit)`, say — and the test reports that instead, which is how you express "warn when total exposure crosses a line" rather than "warn when more than N rows are bad". The edge is the healthy case: a `sum()` over zero rows returns `NULL`, dbt requires an integer there, and the test **errors** on exactly the data that should have passed it. Wrap the aggregate — `coalesce(sum(...), 0)` — so that a clean run returns a number. See `/reference/resource-configs/fail_calc`.

### `store_failures_as`, and what an unset `store_failures` defers to

`store_failures` is a boolean; `store_failures_as` is the enum that says what shape the persisted failures take. It accepts `table`, `view` and `ephemeral`, and wherever both are set, **`store_failures_as` wins** — in both directions:

- `store_failures: true` with `store_failures_as: ephemeral` persists **nothing**. `ephemeral` is not a third storage format; it is the value meaning *do not store*, and it exists so that one test can switch persistence off underneath a `dbt_project.yml` setting that turned it on for everything.
- `store_failures: false` with `store_failures_as: view` persists a **view**. The boolean does not veto the enum.

With `store_failures: true` and `store_failures_as` left unset, the failures land as a **table**. That is the pairing to hold on to, because the intuition that the enum carries its own independent default pulls the other way.

Leave `store_failures` unset altogether and the decision moves to the command line: the test defers to `--store-failures`, so `dbt test --store-failures` persists failing rows for every test that has not made the choice itself, while a test that set the config keeps what it set. That is the flag to reach for when you want the rows once, for one debugging run, without editing YAML you then have to remember to edit back. See `/reference/resource-configs/store_failures_as`.

### Setting configs — the five placements, and which one wins

There are five places a test config can be written, and they resolve as two chains rather than one, because a generic test and a singular test do not have the same surfaces available to them.

1. **On a generic test's instance in a properties file** — the `config:` block of §7.2's shape:

```
- name: customer_id
  data_tests:
    - not_null:
        config:
          severity: warn
          where: "created_at >= current_date - 7"
```

2. **Inside a custom generic's own definition**, as a `{{ config() }}` call at the top of the `{% test %}` block. This sets the default for every attach point of that test.

3. **At the top of a singular test's `.sql` file**, as a `{{ config() }}` call — see §7.3's example.

4. **On a singular test's entry under a properties file's top-level `data_tests:`** — the `config:` block beside the `name` that matches the `.sql` file (§7.2):

```
# models/_properties.yml
data_tests:
  - name: assert_order_amount_is_non_negative
    config:
      severity: warn
```

5. **In `dbt_project.yml` under `data_tests:`** — project-wide defaults:

```
# dbt_project.yml
data_tests:
  +severity: warn            # every test is warn-by-default in this project
  +store_failures: true      # every test persists failing rows
```

For a **generic test**, the chain runs instance `config:` in the properties file > the generic definition's own `{{ config() }}` > `dbt_project.yml`. Read it as specificity: one attach point beats the definition it was made from, and the definition beats the project default.

For a **singular test** there is no instance-versus-definition split — the file *is* the test — so its in-SQL `{{ config() }}` is the most specific surface it has: it beats the `config:` on its properties-file entry, and both beat `dbt_project.yml`.

The middle term is where this gets misread. It belongs to a generic's *definition*, not to a singular test, and paraphrasing the rule as "for a test the YAML always beats the SQL" gets the singular case backwards — a singular test is the one place where the SQL wins.

## Why `where` is the documented answer for incremental tests

The pattern every certified engineer should recognise on sight is the interaction between `not_null` tests and incremental models. The naive configuration attaches `not_null` to a primary-key column on an incremental model:

```
models:
  - name: fct_events          # incremental, tens of billions of rows
    columns:
      - name: event_id
        data_tests:
          - not_null
```

On every `dbt test`, the `not_null` test query is roughly `select event_id from fct_events where event_id is null`. The warehouse has to *scan the whole table* — every partition, every day of history — to prove there's no null anywhere. On a model that is incrementally inserting a thin new slice every hour, that is perverse: you only added today's rows, but you are re-testing the entire history.

Two standard fixes exist, and both are worth knowing because the exam skill here is recognising that these are *the* two fixes out of a field of plausible-but-orthogonal distractors.

**Fix 1 — `where` restricts the scan.** Pass a predicate; dbt rewrites the test query so the resource is wrapped in a filtered subquery (`select * from (select * from <resource> where <predicate>) dbt_subquery`), so the warehouse only scans the filtered slice:

```
- name: event_id
  data_tests:
    - not_null:
        config:
          where: "event_date >= current_date - interval '1 day'"
```

The test now evaluates only the latest day of rows. Whether that also means the warehouse *reads* only the latest partition depends on the table being partitioned or clustered on `event_date` — which is the point of choosing that column for the predicate. Given that layout the cost is bounded by the size of the new increment rather than the whole table; on a column the table is not organised by, the row count drops but the scan may not.

**Fix 2 — push the assertion into a warehouse-level `not_null` constraint.** On adapters that support contracts with `constraints:` (Ch 13), a `not_null` constraint is enforced by the warehouse at insert time. If a null were about to be inserted, the warehouse would reject the insert and dbt would surface the error immediately — no separate test scan needed. With a contract-enforced `not_null`, the invariant is *pre-checked* by the warehouse on every insert, making a redundant dbt `not_null` test unnecessary.

Both fixes buy the same property — testing stays proportional to the size of the new data — by different means. `where` keeps the test in dbt and restricts the query; a `not_null` constraint moves the check out of dbt entirely.

**What the config `limit` does *not* do.** A recurring distractor: "set `limit` on the `not_null` test to avoid scanning the whole table." `limit` caps the rows the test's query returns, not the rows it scans. The warehouse still has to find the nulls before it can decide what to limit. `limit` is useful when a failing test returns millions of rows and you just want a sample for debugging — it is not a scan-reduction tool. Nor is `store_failures`: that adds cost (a write of the failing rows), not subtracts it.

## `warn_if` / `error_if` — tiered severity

The `warn_if` and `error_if` keys let you express thresholds other than "one failing row is bad":

```
- name: status
  data_tests:
    - accepted_values:
        arguments:
          values: ['placed', 'shipped', 'completed', 'returned']
        config:
          severity: error
          warn_if: '>10'
          error_if: '>100'
```

Interpretation: 1–10 bad rows pass; 11–100 rows warn; >100 rows error. The logic follows the docs order: with `severity: error`, `error_if` is checked **first** — if its condition is met, the test errors. Otherwise `warn_if` is checked — if met, the test warns. With `severity: warn`, only `warn_if` is checked (a `warn` test never escalates to `error`). Default `warn_if` and `error_if` are both `'!= 0'`, meaning any failing row triggers the test's configured `severity`. **An explicit `warn_if` / `error_if` replaces the `'!= 0'` default** — that's why 1–10 failing rows pass under `warn_if: '>10'`: the explicit threshold supersedes the implicit "any failure" floor. Customise them when a handful of failures is known-tolerable but a flood is actionable.

---

## 7.6 Running tests — `dbt test` and `dbt build`

The command that runs tests is `dbt test`. See `/reference/commands/test`. Selection syntax is the same as `dbt run` and is covered in depth in Ch 11 — this section covers only what's test-specific.

### `dbt test` vs `dbt build`

`dbt test` runs tests only. It does not build models first, so tests run against whatever state the warehouse is currently in.

`dbt build` runs every buildable resource type together in DAG order — Ch 11 §11.2 has the full list — so a model is built and its tests are run immediately after; if any test fails with `severity: error`, the model's downstream subtree short-circuits — none of the dependent models build. This is the recommended CI command. Ch 11 §11.2 covers `dbt build` in depth.

For exam purposes, the distinction that matters: `dbt test` tests existing state; `dbt build` builds-and-tests in one pass with failure propagation.

### Selecting tests

```
dbt test                                 # every test in the project
dbt test --select stg_orders             # every test that touches stg_orders
dbt test --select tag:critical           # tests tagged 'critical'
dbt test --select test_type:generic      # only generic tests
dbt test --select test_type:singular     # only singular tests
dbt test --select test_type:unit         # only unit tests
dbt test --select test_type:data         # generic and singular together, no unit tests
```

The `test_type:` selector is useful when a project has a mix of generic and singular tests and you want to run one side only — say, during an exploration where singular tests are slow but generics are cheap. `data` is the parent of `generic` and `singular` rather than a fourth sibling, so reach for it when the line you want to draw is against unit tests, not between the two data-test shapes.

### Indirect selection — the four modes

When you select a *model*, dbt decides which tests to run based on **indirect selection**. The four modes are documented at `/reference/global-configs/indirect-selection`.

| Mode | Behaviour |
|---|---|
| `eager` (default) | Runs a test if *any* of its referenced models is in the selection — even if other referenced models are unselected. Most inclusive. |
| `cautious` | Runs a test only if *all* of its referenced models are in the selection. Most exclusive. |
| `buildable` | Middle ground: runs a test if every referenced model is either selected or an ancestor of a selected model. Useful when you want tests to run even if their second inputs are "ambient" upstream context. |
| `empty` | Runs *no* tests. The selection is taken literally — only the selected nodes, nothing adjacent. |

Set the mode globally with `--indirect-selection`:

```
dbt test --select fct_orders --indirect-selection cautious
```

Or set it away from the command line, on any of three other surfaces: the `DBT_ENGINE_INDIRECT_SELECTION` environment variable (Ch 10 §10.9.1 owns the naming convention and the precedence chain every global config follows), `indirect_selection:` under `flags:` in `dbt_project.yml` for a project-wide default, and `indirect_selection:` inside a `selectors.yml` definition, which applies to that one selector and nothing else. The question the modes answer is: "I selected one model; should I run tests that reference it *and* reference other models I didn't select?"

`--exclude` runs through the same mode. Excluding a model under `eager` therefore drops every test that touches it, including tests whose other parents are still selected; under `cautious` that same test survives, because exclusion reaches only tests all of whose parents are excluded.

The exam has been known to drill the difference between `eager` (default, inclusive) and `cautious` (exclusive). Remember the direction: eager pulls tests *in*; cautious pushes tests *out*.

---

## 7.7 Testing in the workflow

A test that runs only in production, after a bad merge, is a liability rather than an asset. The recommended workflow pushes testing as close to the code change as possible.

### The branch → test → merge loop

1. **Branch.** Cut a feature branch from `main`. No changes to shared schemas yet.
2. **Change.** Edit the model, add a column, rewrite a CTE.
3. **Test locally.** Run `dbt build --select state:modified+` (Ch 12 material — the `state:modified+` selector only rebuilds models you changed and their downstreams, using a prior manifest as the state anchor). `dbt build` runs the models *and* their tests; any failure short-circuits the dependent subtree.
4. **Commit and push.** CI picks up the PR and runs `dbt build` (or at minimum `dbt test --select state:modified+`) against a CI schema, optionally with `--defer --state <prior-manifest>` to skip rebuilding unchanged upstreams.
5. **Review and merge.** PR review is about SQL correctness and documentation; tests catch the mechanical regressions. CI is green → merge to `main`.

6. **Production run.** Scheduled `dbt build` in production rebuilds and re-tests on fresh data.

The principle that ties this together: **tests run as close to their cause as possible.** A failing `unique` test in CI means the reviewer knows the primary key broke; a failing `unique` test only in production means the reviewer didn't know, and downstream consumers learn with a broken dashboard. The fix is always "push the test earlier" — never "add more production alerting."

### What changes in CI vs local

Locally you run `dbt build --select state:modified+` — your change and its downstream, for fast feedback. CI runs the full `dbt build` over the whole project, because CI has time you do not; it is the safety net.

Ch 12 covers the state-and-defer mechanics in full. For this chapter the *shape* is what matters: tests ride next to model changes in the same PR, not separately.

### Tests and `severity`

Some teams set `severity: warn` on tests that cover known-imperfect data — a legacy source with ~0.01% nulls that accounting won't fix — so CI doesn't block on the known-bad rows. The trap is that a warn-level test in production is a silent test: if nobody reads the warning logs, it might as well not exist. Use `severity: warn` as a staging tier — "I care about this column but it's not blocking-grade yet" — not as a permanent hiding place for known bugs. A `not_null` test that passes locally under the default `error` but appears to "fail" in CI — it is actually warning — usually means a config override somewhere in the chain.

---

## 7.8 Unit tests

### What a unit test is

A **unit test** asserts about a model's **SQL logic** by supplying mock input rows and stating the output those rows should produce. dbt renders the model's SQL, substitutes the mock rows for every `ref()` and `source()` call the model makes, executes the result, and diffs it against an `expect` block. Matching output passes; a difference fails and prints the diff. See `/docs/build/unit-tests`.

The axis is the thing to hold on to. A data test runs SQL against **real warehouse data** and passes when it returns zero rows. A unit test runs SQL against **mocked inputs** and passes when the output matches a stated expectation. Neither displaces the other. Unit tests catch logic regressions before a model is materialized; data tests catch data regressions after. A production project runs both.

"Runs against mocked inputs, not warehouse data" is worth stating precisely, because the careless reading of it is wrong. The mocks replace the model's *inputs*. The model's compiled SQL still executes on the warehouse, over those mocks — which is why a unit test costs a query (a trivial one, over a handful of literal rows) and why the model's direct parents must exist as relations before the test can run. What a unit test never reads is the *contents* of those parents. Change every row in `stg_customers` and the unit tests on `dim_customers` return exactly the same verdict.

### Where they live

`unit_tests:` blocks belong in a `.yml` file under `model-paths` — `models/`, by default — declared alongside the models they test. That is the convention, not a constraint the parser enforces: a `unit_tests:` block in a YAML file under `tests/` is discovered, selected and run exactly as one under `models/` is. Keep them in `models/` anyway, because `tests/` is where a reader goes looking for data tests.

### The `unit_tests:` schema

`/reference/resource-properties/unit-tests` carries the full property list. Four keys are required and four are optional:

| Key | Required | What it does |
|---|---|---|
| `name` | yes | Unique test identifier — what `--select <name>` matches |
| `model` | yes | The model under test, named as a bare string |
| `given` | yes | Mocked inputs, one entry per `ref()` / `source()` the model calls |
| `expect` | yes | The rows the model's SQL should produce from those inputs |
| `description` | no | Free text; surfaces in the docs site |
| `versions` | no | `include:` / `exclude:` lists of versions. Omit it and the test runs against **every** version of a versioned model |
| `config` | no | `meta`, `tags`, `enabled`, `static_analysis` |
| `overrides` | no | `macros`, `vars`, `env_vars` — covered below |

Note what is *not* there. No `severity`, no `where`, no `store_failures`: the configuration surface of §7.5 shapes data tests, and none of it applies to a unit test. A unit test either matches or it does not.

### `given:` and `expect:`

```
# models/marts/_unit_tests.yml
unit_tests:
  - name: test_dim_customers_lowercases_email
    model: dim_customers
    given:
      - input: ref('stg_customers')
        rows:
          - {customer_id: 1, email: 'ALICE@example.com'}
          - {customer_id: 2, email: 'BOB@example.com'}
    expect:
```

```
    rows:
      - {customer_id: 1, email: 'alice@example.com'}
      - {customer_id: 2, email: 'bob@example.com'}
```

Five rules govern the pair.

1. **One `given` entry per direct input.** Every `ref()` and `source()` the model calls needs its own entry, or compilation fails with a node-not-found error. `input:` takes the call as a string — `ref('stg_customers')`, `ref('dim_customers', v='2')`, `source('stripe', 'customers')`.
2. **Mock only the columns the logic touches.** A column the model never references may be left out under **all three** formats. Under `dict` and `csv` you may go further and omit a column the model *does* reference — dbt null-fills it from the parent — whereas under `sql` the projection is the input and a referenced column must be there. So you declare the columns you care about and leave the rest out — two columns of mock data for a test about email casing, not the model's full forty-column surface.
3. **`rows: []` is a legal input** — the empty-input case, and the cheapest way to assert what a model does with nothing.
4. **A seed input's `rows:` may be omitted, not its entry.** Keep the `given` entry and drop `rows:`, and dbt reads the seed file from disk. Drop the entry itself and rule 1 applies, seed or not.
5. **`expect` takes no `input:`.** It describes an output, so it carries only `format`, and then `rows` or `fixture`.

One structural gotcha with join logic: table names must be **aliased** in the model for a unit test to exercise the join. Mock rows are injected in place of the `ref()`, and an unaliased relation reference has nothing left to bind to.

## The three input formats

`format:` sits on each `given` entry and on `expect`, set independently. It takes one of three values.

| `format:` | Where the data lives | Shape |
|---|---|---|
| `dict` (default) | Inline, under `rows:` | A YAML list of mappings — the form above |
| `csv` | Inline block string under `rows:`, or a fixture file named by `fixture:` | A header line, then comma-separated rows. An empty value (`,,`) reads as `null`, not as an empty string |
| `sql` | Inline block string under `rows:`, or a fixture file named by `fixture:` | A `select` statement returning the mock rows |

Fixture files live in a `fixtures` subdirectory of a test path — `tests/fixtures/` under the default layout — and `fixture:` names the file without its extension:

```
given:
  - input: ref('stg_customers')
    format: csv
    rows: |
      customer_id,email
      1,ALICE@example.com
```

```
        2,BOB@example.com
    - input: ref('top_level_email_domains')
      format: sql
      rows: |
        select 'example.com' as tld
        union all
        select 'gmail.com' as tld
  expect:
    format: csv
    fixture: dim_customers_email_casing    # -> tests/fixtures/<fixture>.csv
```

Reach for `dict` by default, `csv` once a fixture outgrows a handful of rows and a spreadsheet becomes the better editor, and `sql` when a column's *type* matters to the logic under test — `sql` is the only format where you cast explicitly instead of letting dbt infer types from the model's own projection. `sql` also carries conditions the other two do not. The projection **is** the input, so any column the model references must appear in your `select` or the test errors at run time with `column "…" does not exist`; `dict` and `csv` null-fill an undeclared column from the parent instead. A column the model never references may be left out under all three formats. Jinja is unsupported inside a SQL fixture file, and a model that depends on an **ephemeral** model can only be unit-tested by giving that input `format: sql`. See `/reference/resource-properties/data-formats`.

## Overrides — what they replace, and the two that are mandatory

`overrides:` swaps out three things for the duration of one unit test — macro return values, project `vars`, and `env_vars`:

```
overrides:
  macros:
    is_incremental: false
    dbt_utils.star: col_a, col_b, col_c
  vars:
    lookback_days: 3
  env_vars:
    MARKET_CODE: uk
```

**What an override actually replaces.** An override does not patch the model's text. It replaces one entry in the context the model's SQL is rendered against, for the duration of that one unit test: `macros:` swaps a macro's return value, `vars:` and `env_vars:` swap what `var()` and `env_var()` return. Because the substitution lives in the render rather than in the file, an override on 1.11 also reaches a macro or a `var()` resolved inside a macro the model calls — though `/reference/resource-properties/unit-test-overrides` states the reach more narrowly, as covering only what the model references directly. Design to the narrower rule regardless. A unit test whose verdict depends on an override travelling three macros deep is a test the next reader cannot check by reading the model.

Two overrides are not optional.

- `is_incremental`. Unit-testing an incremental model requires an explicit boolean override. Leave it out and the failure is a **parsing error**, before anything runs — dbt refuses to guess which branch of the model you meant to test. Set it to `false` to test the full-refresh path, `true` to test the incremental path. With `true` you must also supply a `- input: this` entry standing in for the current contents of the target relation; omit that and you get a second parsing error. Then read the assertion carefully: for an incremental model, `expect` describes **what the materialization would merge or insert**, not what the table looks like afterwards.

- **`dbt_utils.star`.** A model that calls `star()` needs `dbt_utils.star` overridden to an explicit column list. `star()` takes a relation for its `from` argument, and the unit test has replaced that relation with injected rows, so the macro has nothing left to introspect.

### Where unit tests sit in a run

Three facts, and the exam pressure is on the first.

**`dbt test` runs unit tests.** An unselected `dbt test` executes unit tests alongside data tests — it is not a data-test-only command, and there is no flag to add. `/reference/commands/test` says so outright, and the run output confirms it: unit tests appear in the same numbered node list and the same `PASS=… ERROR=…` tally as everything else. Narrow with `--select test_type:data` or `--select test_type:unit` when you want one side only.

**`dbt build` interleaves them per model, in lineage order:** run the model's unit tests → materialize the model → run the model's data tests. That ordering is what makes unit tests pay in CI, because a logic regression is caught before the bad SQL is allowed to write a relation. A unit-test failure stops the sequence there — the model is skipped rather than built, so its data tests never run either.

**Production runs should exclude them.** Unit-test inputs are static, so re-running them on production compute buys nothing. Drop them with the resource-type flag, or with the `DBT_ENGINE_EXCLUDE_RESOURCE_TYPES` environment variable:

```
dbt build --exclude-resource-type unit_test
DBT_ENGINE_EXCLUDE_RESOURCE_TYPES=unit_test dbt build
```

See `/reference/global-configs/resource-type` for the flags and `/reference/global-configs/environment-variable-configs` for the `DBT_ENGINE_` form. Note the shape: `--exclude-resource-type` is a CLI flag taking a resource type, not a graph selector method. `--exclude unit_test` is a different mechanism and does not do this.

One operational note that catches people the first time. A unit test needs its model's direct parents to **exist** as relations, even though it reads none of their rows. Building them with `--empty` satisfies that requirement for the price of a `create table … as select … where false`:

```
dbt run --select "stg_customers top_level_email_domains" --empty
```

Ch 11 covers `--empty` in full.

### Selecting unit tests

```
dbt test --select test_type:unit                          # every unit test
dbt test --select "dim_customers,test_type:unit"          # unit tests on one model
dbt test --select test_dim_customers_lowercases_email # one test, by name
```

`test_type:unit` is disjoint from `test_type:data` and from `data`'s two narrower values, `generic` and `singular`. A unit test is not a kind of data test, so no `test_type:` value matches both. Ch 11 §11.6 owns the full method catalog, including the separate `unit_test:` method, which selects unit-test nodes by name and is a different thing from the `unit` *value* of `test_type:`.

### What unit tests cannot do

The limits are a plausible source of "which of these models can you unit test" items, and they are short enough to memorise. Unit tests support **SQL models only**, in **your**

**own project only** — not models pulled in from a package. They do not support models materialized as a **materialized view**, models using **recursive SQL**, or models running **introspective queries**. And they attach to models and nothing else: there is no unit test on a source, a seed, a snapshot or an exposure.

### Exam trap — unit test vs data test

The trap, if it appears, is framing. "A test that asserts the model's join logic handles nulls correctly" is a unit test (logic, over mocks). "A test that asserts the model's output has no nulls in `customer_id`" is a data test (values, over real rows). The words "assert" and "test" are overloaded; read for *what is being asserted* — logic or values — and route to the right taxon.

The second-order version of the trap swaps the axis for the artefact. **`unit_tests:`**, **`given:`** / **`expect:`**, mock rows and a **`models/`** YAML file all point one way; **`data_tests:`**, a zero-rows-pass query, **`severity`** and **`where`** all point the other. An option that mixes the two vocabularies — a **`where:`** on a unit test, a **`given:`** block under **`data_tests:`** — is wrong on shape alone, before you read the rest of it.

---

## 7.9 In practice: custom generic tests at Credora's scale

> *This section is an "in practice" composite. It draws a composite pattern from (a) the custom-generic-test guidance at `/best-practices/writing-custom-generic-tests` and (b) the test-configuration reference at `/reference/resource-properties/data-tests`. Credora is a fictional consumer-fintech project (`credora`) running on Databricks; see Ch 14's opening note for the composite-project disclaimer.*

### Shape 1 — custom generic tests as convention enforcers

When a project has ten market catalogs, naming conventions stop being a matter of politeness and become an actual constraint: a model named `fct_offers` in the `cr_uk` catalog has to be `fct_offers_uk`, or cross-catalog queries get ambiguous. Writing a code-review rule is one approach; writing a *test* is better, because tests run in CI and don't rely on a reviewer remembering.

```
-- tests/generic/valid_market_suffix.sql
{% test valid_market_suffix(model, column_name=None, allowed_suffixes=None) %}
    {# This is a model-level test; column_name is unused but the signature
       keeps dbt's call convention. #}
    {% set suffixes = allowed_suffixes or ['_uk', '_us', '_apac_1', '_apac_2', '_emea_1',
      '_global'] %}
    {% set model_name = model.identifier %}
    {% set matches = namespace(found=false) %}
    {% for s in suffixes %}
        {% if model_name.endswith(s) %}
            {% set matches.found = true %}
        {% endif %}
    {% endfor %}

    {% if matches.found %}
        select 1 as dummy where false    {# zero rows = pass #}
    {% else %}
        select '{{ model_name }}' as invalid_model_name    {# one row = fail #}
    {% endif %}
```

```
{% endtest %}
```

Apply it to every model whose name should follow the convention. The mechanism here is *attachment* — `dbt_project.yml`'s `data_tests:` tree configures **defaults** for tests that already exist (severity, where, store_failures), but it cannot itself *attach* a test to every model in the project. So a project-wide convention enforcer takes one of two shapes:

```
# Pattern A - explicit per-model attachment via a YAML properties file.
# Best when you can list every model that should be checked.
version: 2
models:
  - name: fct_lending_offer_clicks_uk
    data_tests:
      - valid_market_suffix
  - name: dim_offers_global
    data_tests:
      - valid_market_suffix
```

Two things will bite you here. A properties entry attaches by **model name**, so pointing one at a versioned model's `defined_in` filename attaches nothing: dbt warns twice, drops the test from the graph, and exits 0 — a convention gate that is green because it is empty. And a versioned model's relation is <model_name>_v<v> by default (Ch 13 §13.4), so a suffix rule read off the relation name fails on one unless the version carries an `alias:` that puts the suffix back. Exempt versioned models from this test, or write the rule against `node.name` as Pattern B does.

```
-- Pattern B - a singular test that iterates the graph (under tests/).
-- Best when "every model" really means every model and you want one test file.
{% set own = graph.nodes.values()
     | selectattr('resource_type', 'equalto', 'model')
     | selectattr('package_name', 'equalto', project_name)
     | list %}
{% for node in own %}
  select '{{ node.name }}' as offending_model
  where not exists (
    select 1 where regexp_like('{{ node.name }}', '_(uk|us|apac_[12]|emea_1|global)$')
  )
  {% if not loop.last %}union all{% endif %}
{% endfor %}
```

The `package_name` filter is load-bearing, and the recommendation two sentences down is why: `graph.nodes` holds every node in the manifest, installed packages included, so an unfiltered loop tests somebody else's models against your naming convention and fails the build on models nobody on your team wrote. Restricting to `project_name` keeps the rule pointed at the project it belongs to (Ch 14 §14.5 shows the same test at scale).

Either way, a mis-suffixed model breaks CI before the PR is reviewed. The dbt Labs package `dbt-project-evaluator` bundles a large set of tests in this style — naming conventions, documentation coverage, unused sources — using the singular-over-graph pattern (Pattern B). It is worth browsing as a public reference for the pattern: custom generics and graph-iterating singulars applied at scale as a lint-style guardrail. See `/best-practices/writing-custom-generic-tests` for the authoring surface this builds on, and `/reference/data-test-configs` for what `dbt_project.yml`'s `data_tests:` tree *can* do (it sets defaults like `+severity: error` for already-defined tests).

### Shape 2 — a handful of singular tests for cross-model invariants

A multi-market project has a small but crucial set of invariants that don't factor into a generic: "every offer appearing in `fct_offers_uk` is also present in the cross-market `dim_offers_global` with the same `offer_id`"; "the sum of market totals equals the global total"; "no market-specific model references a model from another market's catalog." Each of these is written once as a singular test under `tests/`, often with `severity: warn` until the codebase is clean and then `severity: error` to prevent regression. The count is small — maybe four or five files — but the payoff is specific guarantees that hold across the whole project.

### Shape 3 — moving from a home-grown harness to native unit tests

Credora's dbt project carries a home-grown harness under `macros/unit_tests/`: macros that create a temporary view from mock rows, execute the model's SQL against the view, and compare the output to expected rows. It covers logic assertions such as "does this case-when handle the null-market edge case correctly?" but remains a custom maintenance burden with bespoke YAML syntax.

`unit_tests:` provides a first-class feature with native syntax. Migrate a bespoke harness to native unit tests when it covers the same logic, then retire the custom framework.

---

## Summary

- **Four test taxa.** Built-in generic, custom generic, singular (the three data-test shapes) — and unit tests, which assert about logic, not data.
- **Built-in generics:** `unique`, `not_null`, `accepted_values` (with `values:`), `relationships` (with `to: ref(...)` and `field:`). Placed column-level (usual case) or model-level (for cross-column assertions).
- **The 1.11 YAML shape:** macro inputs nest under `arguments:`, execution settings under `config:`, and `name`, `test_name` and `description` stay top-level. The flat form warns with `MissingArgumentsPropertyInGenericTestDeprecation`; with `require_generic_test_arguments_property` turned off, the nested form warns with `ArgumentsPropertyInGenericTestDeprecation` instead. Generic tests attach to models, sources, seeds and snapshots — attach one to an analysis and it parses silently and produces no test node.
- **Singular tests** are `.sql` files under `tests/` — at the default `fail_calc` and thresholds, pass on zero rows returned and fail otherwise. Jinja and macros work. Use for one-off cross-model invariants.
- **Custom generic tests** are macros wrapped in `{% test name(model, column_name, ...) %}` / `{% endtest %}`. Reusable — one definition, many attach points. Can take extra arguments. The first parameter is always spelled `model` whatever resource it binds to, and a block reusing a built-in's name shadows that built-in project-wide and silently — `dbt.unique` still reaches the shipped one.
- **Test configs:** `severity` (`error` default, `warn`), `warn_if` / `error_if` (thresholds, default `'!= 0'`), `store_failures` (persist failing rows), `store_failures_as` (`table` / `view` / `ephemeral`, and it overrides `store_failures` in both directions), `where` (predicate to narrow the test's scan), `limit` (caps the rows the query returns, and so what gets counted — not scan size), `fail_calc` (what gets counted, default `count(*)`). An unset `store_failures` defers to `--store-failures`; a `sum()`-based `fail_calc` errors on zero rows unless wrapped.

- **Config precedence:** for a generic test, instance `config:` in the properties file > the generic definition's `{{ config() }}` > `dbt_project.yml`. A singular test has no instance/definition split, so its own in-SQL `{{ config() }}` is its most specific surface.
- **The incremental-test pattern:** to avoid re-scanning an incremental on every `not_null` test, use `where` to restrict to new data, or push the assertion into a warehouse `not_null` constraint (Ch 13). `limit` and `store_failures` do not reduce scan cost.
- **`dbt test` vs `dbt build`:** `test` runs tests against current warehouse state; `build` interleaves model builds with their tests in DAG order and short-circuits downstreams on `severity: error` failure.
- **Selection:** `--select tag:foo`, `test_type:generic`, `test_type:singular`, `test_type:unit`. Selecting models pulls in tests via **indirect selection** — `eager` (default, inclusive), `cautious` (exclusive), `buildable` (middle), `empty` (no tests).
- **Workflow:** branch → `dbt build --select state:modified+` locally → commit → CI runs tests → merge. Tests run close to changes, not in isolation.
- **Unit tests** assert model *logic*, not data. A `unit_tests:` block lives in a `models/` properties YAML by convention (the parser also accepts `tests/`), requires `name`, `model`, `given` and `expect`, and takes optional `description`, `versions`, `config` and `overrides`. One `given` entry per `ref()` / `source()` the model calls; `format:` is `dict` (default, inline `rows:`), `csv` or `sql`, either inline or from a fixture under `tests/fixtures/`. The mocks replace the model's inputs — the compiled SQL still executes on the warehouse.
- **Unit-test overrides and placement:** `overrides:` (`macros`, `vars`, `env_vars`) replace entries in the render context for one test, and the reference page describes their reach as covering only what the model references directly — design to that. An incremental model will not parse without an explicit `is_incremental` override, and with `is_incremental: true` it also needs an `- input: this` entry. Plain `dbt test` runs unit tests alongside data tests; `dbt build` orders them per model as unit test → materialize → data test; production runs drop them with `--exclude-resource-type unit_test`.

## Learning-goal checklist (self-assess)

- ☐ I can name the four test taxa and route a given assertion to the right one.
- ☐ I can write built-in generics in YAML at column- and model-level and pass the argument forms for `accepted_values` and `relationships`.
- ☐ I can write a generic test in the 1.11 shape — what stays top-level, what nests under `arguments:`, what nests under `config:` — and name the deprecation each of the two argument shapes raises.
- ☐ I can name the resource types a `data_tests:` block attaches to, and say what happens when one is attached to an analysis.
- ☐ I can write a singular test under `tests/` and explain why the `select` should return *failing* rows, not passing ones.
- ☐ I can define a custom generic test with `{% test name(model, column_name, ...) %}` and call it from YAML with extra arguments.
- ☐ I can say what a project-local block reusing a built-in's name does to that built-in, how to reach the built-in anyway, and which duplication is the one that errors.
- ☐ I can apply `severity`, `warn_if`, `error_if`, `store_failures`, `where`, `limit` and `fail_calc` to a test and explain which reduce scan cost (only `where`) and which do not.
- ☐ I can predict which of `store_failures` and `store_failures_as` wins when they disagree, and say what an unset `store_failures` defers to.
- ☐ I can name the five placements for a test config and give the precedence chain for a generic test and for a singular test.

- ☐ I can describe the `dbt test` vs `dbt build` distinction and name the four indirect-selection modes.
- ☐ I can place testing in a branch → test → merge workflow and explain why tests must run close to the code change.
- ☐ I can write a `unit_tests:` block with `given` and `expect`, put it in the directory the convention names, and name every `ref()` / `source()` the model calls as an input.
- ☐ I can choose between `format: dict`, `csv` and `sql` for mock data, and say where a fixture file has to live for `fixture:` to find it.
- ☐ I can say what an `overrides:` block actually replaces, and why unit-testing an incremental model fails at parse time without an `is_incremental` override — and what a second parse error then asks for.
- ☐ I can place unit tests in a run — what plain `dbt test` does with them, where they fall in `dbt build`'s per-model order, and how to keep them out of production.

---

## Practice questions

Twenty-seven questions covering built-in generics (Qs 1–5), custom generics (Qs 6–8), singular tests (Qs 9–10), test configs (Qs 11–12), selection by test type (Q13), unit tests (Q14), workflow (Q15), a CI severity override (Q16), a shadowed built-in (Q17), tiered severity (Q18), failure persistence (Q19), `fail_calc` (Q20), where tests can attach (Q21), unit-testing an incremental model (Q22), an override reaching a macro the model never names (Q23), the argument-property deprecation pair (Q24), why `dbt test` errors against unbuilt models (Q25), a bare test config that is accepted and deprecated rather than refused (Q26), how `equals()` treats two nulls (Q27), the key that makes a renamed test entry parse (Q28), and what becomes of a macro input written under `config:` (Q29).

**1.** Which four tests are shipped as built-in generic tests in dbt?

A. `unique`, `not_null`, `positive`, `relationships`
B. `unique`, `not_null`, `accepted_values`, `relationships`
C. `unique`, `primary_key`, `accepted_values`, `relationships`
D. `unique`, `not_null`, `accepted_values`, `foreign_key`

**2.** A column `customer_id` on `stg_orders` should be a valid foreign key to `stg_customers.customer_id`. Which YAML test definition is correct?

A.

```
- relationships:
    arguments:
      to: stg_customers
      field: customer_id
```

B.

```
- relationships:
    arguments:
      model: ref('stg_customers')
      column: customer_id
```

C.

```
- relationships:
    arguments:
      to: ref('stg_customers')
      field: customer_id
```

D.

```
- foreign_key:
    arguments:
      ref: stg_customers.customer_id
```

**3.** The `accepted_values` test fails when:
A. The column has any `NULL` values
B. Any row has a value that *is* in the `values:` list
C. The column's distinct-value count exceeds the length of `values:`
D. Any row has a value that is not in the configured `values:` list

**4.** A `not_null` assertion applies to one column of one model. Where in a `_models.yml` properties file does it attach?
A. Under the properties file's own top-level `data_tests:` key, a sibling of `models:`
B. Under that column's `data_tests:` list inside its model's `columns:` block
C. In `dbt_project.yml`, under the `data_tests:` config tree
D. In a separate `tests/generic/not_null.yml` file

**5.** Which statement about the built-in `unique` test is true?
A. It asserts every non-null value in the column is distinct; nulls do not fail the test
B. It asserts the column has no null values
C. It asserts both uniqueness and not-nullness in one test
D. It runs only against the primary key declared in a model's contract

**6.** Which tag-pair wraps a custom generic test definition?
A. `{% macro %}` / `{% endmacro %}` B. `{% assertion %}` / `{% endassertion %}`
C. `{% generic %}` / `{% endgeneric %}` D. `{% test %}` / `{% endtest %}`

**7.** Given the custom generic test:

```
{% test value_in_range(model, column_name, min_value, max_value) %}
    select {{ column_name }} from {{ model }}
    where {{ column_name }} < {{ min_value }}
       or {{ column_name }} > {{ max_value }}
{% endtest %}
```

Which YAML invocation is correct to assert `age` is between 0 and 120 in `dim_customers`?

A.

```
- value_in_range(0, 120)
```

B.

```
- value_in_range:
    arguments:
      min_value: 0
      max_value: 120
```

C.

```
- value_in_range: [0, 120]
```

D.

```
- value_in_range:
    args:
      min_value: 0
      max_value: 120
```

**8.** A team has written the same "column matches a regex pattern" singular test as four separate `.sql` files, one per model. What is the idiomatic refactor?
A. Move all four into a single `.sql` file under `tests/` that references all four models
B. Add a `regex_check` macro under `macros/` that is invoked from each singular test
C. Promote the logic to a custom generic test under `tests/generic/regex_check.sql` and call it from every model's YAML with the regex as an argument
D. Move all four to a package and install via `dbt deps`

**9.** A singular test's `select` statement, with `fail_calc` and the severity thresholds left at their defaults, passes when:
A. It returns at least one row B. It returns zero rows
C. It returns exactly one row D. It returns any `NULL`-only result

**10.** Where must a singular test's `.sql` file be placed for dbt to discover and run it automatically?
A. In `models/` alongside the models it tests
B. In `macros/`, wrapped in `{% test %}` tags
C. In the directory named by `test-paths` (default `tests/`)
D. In `analyses/`

**11.** What is the default `severity` for a dbt test?
A. `warn` B. `strict`
C. `debug` D. `error`

**12.** What does `store_failures: true` do when set on a test?
A. Persists the failing rows from the test's query into a warehouse table so they can be inspected after the run
B. Causes the test to be skipped if any row previously failed
C. Prevents the test from failing — it only warns
D. Increases the test's `limit` to return all failing rows

**13.** A project keeps its singular tests under `tests/` and declares dozens of generic tests in YAML. Which expression, passed to `dbt test --select`, runs the singular tests and no generic ones?
A. `tag:singular` B. `test_type:singular`
C. `test_type:data` D. `type:singular`

**14.** What does a unit test assert, as distinct from a data test?
A. That real warehouse rows satisfy a value-level invariant, evaluated against whatever the table holds at the moment the test runs
B. That the model's SQL compiles without error, so a broken `ref()` or Jinja block is caught before the model is built
C. That the model's SQL logic produces expected output rows when given mocked input rows — asserting logic, not data
D. That the test harness itself is functioning, by checking dbt's own behaviour rather than the project's models

**15.** In the standard dbt testing workflow, when should tests first run on a feature-branch change?
A. In production, on the first scheduled run after the merge
B. In CI, once the pull request has been opened
C. Locally before the commit, via `dbt build --select state:modified+`, and again in CI before merge
D. On the nightly schedule, alongside the rest of the project

**16.** A team sees `not_null` tests pass locally when a developer runs `dbt test` but "fail silently" — logging warnings rather than errors — in CI. Local config is default; CI has an override. What is the most likely cause?
A. CI's dbt version is newer than local, and the newer version classifies `not_null` failures differently
B. CI is running `dbt build` instead of `dbt test`, and `build` evaluates test severity more leniently than `test` does
C. CI's `dbt_project.yml` is setting `+severity: warn` project-wide, and test-level overrides that would restore `error` aren't being applied
D. The underlying data differs between local and CI, so more rows fail the test in CI than they do on the developer's machine

**17.** A project adds a `{% test unique(model, column_name) %}` block under `macros/`, with a body of its own. The project's YAML already carries dozens of `- unique` entries, on models and on sources alike. What happens on the next `dbt test`?
A. Parsing fails with a duplicate-macro error, because `unique` is already defined
B. The model-level `unique` tests pick up the project's body, while source-level ones keep the built-in
C. The block is ignored until `dispatch:` in `dbt_project.yml` puts the root project ahead of dbt's global macros
D. Every unqualified `unique` test runs the project's body, on sources as well as models, with no warning from dbt

**18.** A test is configured as:

```
- not_null:
    config:
      severity: error
      warn_if: '>10'
      error_if: '>100'
```

A run produces 50 failing rows. What happens?
A. The test passes silently because 50 is between the thresholds
B. The test warns — 50 is `>10` (warn_if triggers) but not `>100` (error_if does not)
C. The test errors — the default `severity: error` wins unconditionally
D. The test warns and errors simultaneously

**19.** A project sets `+store_failures: true` under `data_tests:` in `dbt_project.yml`. One noisy test is then given `store_failures_as: ephemeral` in its own `config:` block. What does that test do when it fails?
A. It persists nothing — `store_failures_as` overrides `store_failures`, and `ephemeral` is the value meaning do not store
B. It writes its failing rows to the audit schema anyway, because `store_failures: true` is the setting that decides whether rows are persisted
C. It persists nothing, and dbt raises a compilation error because `ephemeral` is not a valid `store_failures_as` value
D. It writes its failing rows to a relation that is dropped again at the end of the run

**20.** A test carries `fail_calc: "sum(amount_over_limit)"` so that it reports total exposure rather than a row count. The data is cleaned up, and the test's query now returns no rows at all. What does dbt report?
A. `ERROR` — `sum()` over zero rows returns `NULL`, and dbt requires an integer for the failure count
B. `PASS` — zero rows is the pass condition for every data test, and `fail_calc` changes just the number printed beside it
C. `WARN` — with nothing to aggregate the threshold expressions evaluate to `NULL`, which dbt treats as a warning
D. `ERROR` — `fail_calc` takes `count(*)` or a bare column name, so the expression is rejected at parse time

**21.** An engineer attaches `not_null` and `unique` to a column of an analysis, in a properties file under `analyses/`. `dbt parse` exits zero and prints no warning, but neither assertion ever runs. Why?
A. Analyses are built by `dbt build` rather than `dbt test`, and their tests run after that materialization
B. Analyses are compiled but never executed, so their tests are reported as `NO-OP` and skipped
C. The properties file has to sit under `models/` before dbt will discover the tests it declares
D. `data_tests:` is not implemented for analyses: the block is read for `description` and `columns`, but no test node is created

**22.** `fct_events` is materialized as `incremental`, and its SQL guards a filter with `{% if is_incremental() %}`. A `unit_tests:` entry for it declares `name`, `model`, `given` and `expect`, and nothing else. dbt refuses to parse the project. What is the entry missing?
A. A `config:` block setting `materialized: table`, so that the test compiles the full-refresh branch
B. A `where:` config narrowing the mock rows to the model's incremental window
C. A second `expect:` block, one per branch, so that both paths through the `if` are asserted
D. An `overrides:` block giving `is_incremental` an explicit `true` or `false`, since dbt will not choose the branch

**23.** A model's SQL calls `{{ order_label() }}`. That macro calls `{{ region_code() }}`, which returns `REAL`. The model itself never names `region_code`. A unit test for the model declares `overrides:` with `macros: {region_code: "MOCK"}`. What value does the rendered model produce under that test?
A. `MOCK` — an override replaces an entry in the render context, so it applies at every point the macro resolves, including inside `order_label()`
B. `REAL` — overrides reach only macros the model references directly, so `region_code` is untouched
C. A parsing error — dbt rejects an override naming a macro the model under test does not call
D. `MOCK`, but only if `order_label` is listed under `overrides.macros` as well

**24.** A project leaves `require_generic_test_arguments_property` at its 1.11 default and writes `accepted_values` with its `values:` list as a bare sibling of the test name. `dbt parse` exits zero. What does dbt emit?
A. `ArgumentsPropertyInGenericTestDeprecation` — the flat form is the shape that property deprecates
B. `MissingArgumentsPropertyInGenericTestDeprecation` — the inputs are not nested under `arguments:`
C. `PropertyMovedToConfigDeprecation` — a key written flat beside a test name is read as a config
D. Nothing — the flat form parses clean, and the warning arrives once the flag is turned off

**25.** A developer cuts a feature branch, edits `stg_orders`, and runs `dbt test --select stg_orders+` against an empty personal schema without building anything first. Every test errors with a relation-not-found message. Why?
A. `dbt test` materializes nothing — it runs assertions against relations it expects to exist already, so the models have to be built first
B. `dbt test` builds the models its selected tests depend on, but `+` pulled in downstream models it does not build
C. Indirect selection at its `eager` default pulled in tests with an unselected parent, and an unselected parent errors
D. Test nodes are compiled from the manifest, so `dbt parse` has to run on the branch before `dbt test` can resolve `ref()`

**26.** A `not_null` test is written with `severity: warn` as a bare sibling of the test name rather than under a nested `config:` key. The column does contain a NULL. What does `dbt test --no-partial-parse` report?
A. `ERROR=1` — the bare key never reaches the test's config, so `severity` keeps its `error` default
B. `WARN=1`, plus `PropertyMovedToConfigDeprecation` naming `severity` and where it belongs
C. A parse failure — the schema rejects any key beside a test name that is not `config:` or `arguments:`
D. `WARN=1` and nothing else — the two spellings are interchangeable at 1.11 and neither is deprecated

**27.** A test built on dbt's `equals()` macro compares a nullable `promo_code` column between two models. Several thousand rows are null on both sides. On stock dbt 1.11, how are those rows treated?
A. As matches — `equals()` exists precisely to make two nulls compare equal
B. As failures — an unmatched null is reported as a failing row
C. As matches, but only after `enable_truthy_nulls_equals_macro` is set to `false`
D. As non-matches — `NULL = NULL` is `UNKNOWN`, so those rows are excluded from the match

## Answer key

**1. B.** The four built-in generics are `unique`, `not_null`, `accepted_values` (which takes a `values:` list), and `relationships` (which takes `to:` and `field:`). `primary_key` and `foreign_key` are *constraints* under contracts (Ch 13), not generic tests. `positive` isn't a built-in; it would be a custom generic or a singular test. Source: `/reference/resource-properties/data-tests`.

**2. C.** `relationships` takes two arguments: `to:` (the referenced model or source, via `ref()` or `source()`) and `field:` (the column in that relation). Hard-coding the model name (A) bypasses `ref()` and does not register the dependency in the DAG; `model` / `column` (B) are not valid keys; `foreign_key` (D) is a constraint keyword, not a test. Source: `/reference/resource-properties/data-tests`.

**3. D.** `accepted_values` asserts that every value in the column falls inside the configured set. A row with a value outside the set causes a failure. NULL handling is independent — `accepted_values` does not by itself fail on nulls; combine with `not_null` if that is also required. Source: `/reference/resource-properties/data-tests`.

**4. B.** A single-column built-in attaches under the column's own `data_tests:` list, inside its model's `columns:` block — that is what tells `not_null` which column it applies to. Option A names a section that genuinely exists, but a top-level `data_tests:` key is where **singular** tests are given properties: a `name` matching the `.sql` file, plus `description` and `config`. An entry there naming a generic instead does not silently attach anything; it fails to parse, with `Entry did not contain a name`. C sets project-wide defaults for tests that are *already* attached — the config tree configures tests, it cannot attach one. D invents a per-test YAML file convention; `tests/generic/` holds custom generic *definitions*, not attachments. Source: `/reference/resource-properties/data-tests`.

**5. A.** `unique` ignores nulls — multiple null rows do not fail `unique`. To require both, combine `unique` and `not_null` on the same column. `unique` is not tied to contracts; it runs on any column you attach it to, regardless of whether the model has a contract declared. Source: `/reference/resource-properties/data-tests`.

**6. D.** Custom generic tests use `{% test name(model, column_name, ...) %}` / `{% endtest %}`. The file can live under `macros/` or `tests/generic/` — dbt discovers both. `{% macro %}` is for regular macros (Ch 6); the other two tags don't exist. Source: `/best-practices/writing-custom-generic-tests`.

**7. B.** A custom generic's extra arguments are named keys nested under `arguments:`, one level below the test name. `model` and `column_name` are supplied implicitly by dbt from the attach point; `min_value` and `max_value` come from the YAML. The other three fail differently. A's Jinja-style call parses — dbt reads the test name off the front and discards `(0, 120)` — then dies at run time on SQL built without the bounds. C is rejected at parse: *test arguments must be a dict.* D's `args:` is one token off the property dbt reads, so `args` reaches the macro as a keyword and parse fails: *takes no keyword argument 'args'.* Source: `/best-practices/writing-custom-generic-tests`, `/reference/resource-properties/data-tests`.

**8. C.** Repeated test logic across multiple models is a classic case for a custom generic: one `{% test %}` definition with a `pattern` (or similar) parameter, invoked from each column's YAML `data_tests:` list. Option A bundles the queries but doesn't parameterise; B introduces indirection without reducing call-site count; D is overkill for in-project reuse — packages are for cross-project reuse. Source: `/best-practices/writing-custom-generic-tests`.

**9. B.** At the defaults the stem pins — `fail_calc: count(*)`, `severity: error`, `error_if: "!= 0"` — a data test passes when its compiled query returns zero rows. The returned rows are the *failing* cases, so "no failing rows" is the pass condition. Writing a singular test that returns the passing rows is the classic rookie inversion: the test then fails on healthy data. Those defaults are why the stem states them. Override `fail_calc` and the test is scored on whatever that expression computes rather than on a row count; raise `error_if`/`warn_if` and a non-zero count can still pass (§7.5). A test written to assert that something *is* present — a `fail_calc` of `case when count(*) = 0 then 1 else 0 end` — inverts the rule entirely, and an empty input makes it fail. Source: `/docs/build/data-tests`.

**10. C.** Singular tests live under the `test-paths` directory (default `tests/`), not `models/`, not `macros/`, not `analyses/`. dbt scans `tests/` and runs every `.sql` file there as a singular test during `dbt test` or `dbt build`. `tests/generic/` is a subdirectory convention for custom generic tests; singular tests typically sit at the `tests/` top level. Source: `/docs/build/data-tests`.

**11. D.** A test with no explicit `severity` config fails with severity `error`, which both exits `dbt test` non-zero and — under `dbt build` — short-circuits downstream models in the DAG. `warn` is the opt-in alternative for known-imperfect data; `debug` and `strict` are not valid severity values. Source: `/reference/resource-configs/severity`.

**12. A.** `store_failures: true` writes the failing rows to a warehouse table in a schema named `<schema>_dbt_test__audit` by default (the suffix is appended to the active profile schema; configurable). The test still reports a failure; `store_failures` adds a debugging surface — you can `select *` from the failures table to see which rows tripped the assertion. It does not reduce scan cost and does not change severity. Source: `/reference/resource-configs/store_failures`.

**13. B.** The `test_type:` method takes one of `data`, `generic`, `singular`, or `unit`, and `singular` matches exactly the `.sql` files under `tests/`. `test_type:data` (C) is the parent category over `generic` and `singular`, so it runs every YAML-declared generic test as well — the ones the stem asks you to leave out. `tag:` (A) filters on tags someone applied deliberately; no tag is derived from a test's taxon, so `tag:singular` matches nothing unless every singular test was tagged by hand. `type:` (D) is not a method name at all, and the selector fails with `'type' is not a valid method name`. There is no per-taxon flag either — `dbt test --singular` exits on `No such option` — because taxon selection goes through `--select`. Source: `/reference/node-selection/methods`, `/reference/commands/test`.

**14. C.** A unit test supplies mock rows for each `ref()` and `source()` the model uses, runs the model's SQL against those mocks, and compares the result to an `expect` block. It asserts about logic — how the SQL handles the inputs — not about real data. Data tests (A) assert about values on real rows. Compilation checks (B) are implicit in any `dbt compile`; they are not what unit tests add. The selection for unit tests is `test_type:unit`. Source: `/docs/build/unit-tests`, `/reference/resource-properties/unit-tests`.

**15. C.** The principle is "tests run as close to their cause as possible." Locally before commit gives the developer fast feedback; CI before merge gives the team a safety net; the scheduled production run is the final trip-wire. A pushes the first check past the merge, so a preventable failure reaches a shared environment before anyone knew it was coming. B drops the fast local loop and makes the developer wait on a pipeline to learn what a local build would have said. D detects the regression a full cycle after the merge that caused it. Source: `/best-practices/best-practice-workflows`, `/docs/build/data-tests`.

**16. C.** The symptom — tests running and emitting a non-blocking warning instead of failing — matches the behaviour of `severity: warn`. Combined with "works locally" vs "silent in CI," the most likely cause is an environment-scoped override in `dbt_project.yml` or a `--vars`-passed flag that sets `+severity: warn` for the whole project, with no per-test override escalating specific tests back to `error` — an inline `config:` on the test would have won if one existed (§7.5; Ch 6 §6.4). Version drift (A) does not produce this symptom; `dbt build` (B) runs tests with the same severity logic as `dbt test`; differing data (D) would produce different *counts* of failures but not a systematic warn-vs-error flip. Source: `/reference/resource-configs/severity`, `/reference/data-test-configs`.

**17. D.** A `{% test unique %}` block in your project takes precedence over dbt's built-in wherever `unique` is written unqualified, and the reach is project-wide: model-level and source-level tests alike compile the project's body. dbt announces none of it — parse is clean, the run output looks ordinary, and the only sign is that tests which used to pass now behave differently. A names the one duplication that *does* error, but it takes two blocks of the same test name inside one project; a project block and a built-in are not a collision. B invents a split that does not exist — the override is not scoped by resource type. C borrows the protection that applies to built-in *materializations*, which a package cannot replace without an explicit root-project override (Ch 8); test names carry no equivalent guard, and `dispatch:` sets a search order for macros rather than reserving names. The built-in stays reachable under its namespace, as `dbt.unique`. Source: `/best-practices/writing-custom-generic-tests`.

**18. B.** Per the docs evaluation order: with `severity: error`, `error_if` is checked **first** — `>100` is false at 50 failing rows, so the test does not error. `warn_if` is then checked — `>10` is true at 50, so the test warns. The thresholds tier severity by failing-row count — 1–10 rows: passes (the explicit `>10` raises the default `!= 0` floor); 11–100 rows: warn; >100 rows:

error. The configured `severity: error` is the baseline severity used when `error_if` is met — here it is not, so the test warns instead. Source: `/reference/resource-configs/severity`, `/reference/data-test-configs`.

**19. A.** `store_failures_as` overrides `store_failures` wherever both are set, so this test persists nothing: `ephemeral` is not a third storage format but the value meaning *do not store*, which is exactly why it exists — so that one test can opt out of a project-level setting that turned persistence on for everything (§7.5). B has the precedence the wrong way round. C is wrong about the enum — `ephemeral`, `table` and `view` are the three accepted values, and dbt names all three in the error it raises for anything else. D reads `ephemeral` as the materialization of the same name: nothing is created, so nothing is dropped. Source: `/reference/resource-configs/store_failures_as`.

**20. A.** `fail_calc` names the expression dbt evaluates to get the number it compares against `warn_if` and `error_if`, and the default — `count(*)` — returns `0` over an empty result. `sum()` does not: over zero rows it returns `NULL`, dbt requires an integer for the failure count, and the node errors on the healthiest possible data. Wrap the aggregate as `coalesce(sum(...), 0)` and the clean run reports zero. B states the pass rule correctly and then assumes `fail_calc` changes only what is *printed*; it changes what is *evaluated*. C invents a warning dbt does not emit. D treats `fail_calc` as a closed enum — it takes any expression the counting query can evaluate. Source: `/reference/resource-configs/fail_calc`.

**21. D.** Generic tests attach to models, sources, seeds and snapshots. Analyses are the documented exception, and the failure mode is silence: the YAML block is read — the analysis picks up the `description` and `columns` declared beside the test — and no test node is created, so there is nothing for `dbt test` to select, skip or report. A and B both assume a node exists and is being deferred or short-circuited, and neither is true; `dbt build` does not run analyses either. C blames file placement, but a properties file is discovered under its own resource's path, and this one was found — that is how the `description` landed. Source: `/reference/resource-properties/data-tests`.

**22. D.** dbt will not guess which branch of an incremental model a unit test meant to exercise, so the test fails at parse until `is_incremental` is overridden to an explicit `true` or `false` — and, with `true`, again until an `- input: this` entry is supplied (§7.8). A reaches for a materialization change, but `config:` on a unit test carries `meta`, `tags`, `enabled` and `static_analysis` — not `materialized`. B borrows `where` from the data-test config surface, none of which applies to unit tests. C misreads the schema: one unit test has one `expect`, and exercising both branches means writing two unit tests with opposite overrides. Source: `/reference/resource-properties/unit-test-overrides`, `/docs/build/unit-tests`.

**23. A.** An override does not patch the model's text — it replaces one entry in the context the SQL is rendered against, for the duration of that test. So the substitution applies wherever the name resolves, however deep in the macro chain, and the model does not have to name the overridden macro itself. Executed on 1.11.14: a model calling only `probe_outer()`, which calls `probe_inner()`, failed its unit test against an un-overridden expectation and passed against the overridden one; the `vars:` arm behaves identically for a `var()` read inside a nested macro. **B is the discriminator, and it is what the docs say** — the reference page describes the reach as covering only direct references. §7.8 and the cheat sheet both record the gap and advise designing to the narrower rule, because a promise the runtime exceeds today can be narrowed tomorrow. C invents a validation dbt does not perform: an override naming a macro that is never resolved is simply inert. D adds a requirement that does not exist — only the macro whose return value you want to change needs listing. Source: `/reference/resource-properties/unit-test-overrides`; settled by execution, which the docs page does not.

**24. B.** At the 1.11 default the flat form still parses — `dbt parse` exits zero — and warns `MissingArgumentsPropertyInGenericTestDeprecation`: *"Arguments to generic tests should be nested under the `arguments` property."* A names the opposite warning, which fires the other way round: set the flag to `false` and an `arguments:` block raises `ArgumentsPropertyInGeneric`

`TestDeprecation` and then fails, because the flag is also what tells dbt to unwrap the block before calling the macro. C is a real deprecation aimed at a different mistake — a *config* key such as `severity` written flat beside the test name is lifted into the config, honoured, and warned about under that name. D reads the flag backwards: the default is what makes nesting expected, so the flat form is exactly what warns under it (§7.2). Source: `/reference/global-configs/behavior-flags/require_generic_test_arguments_property`.

**25. A.** `dbt test` runs assertions and nothing else: it materializes no models, seeds or snapshots, and assumes every resource under test is already in the warehouse. On a fresh schema there is nothing to assert against, so each test fails at the warehouse rather than on its data. Build first — `dbt run`, or `dbt build`, which is why the local loop in §7.7 is `dbt build --select state:modified+` and not `dbt test`. B invents a build step `dbt test` does not have. C describes `eager` correctly and then invents a failure: running a test whose other parent is unselected is exactly what `eager` is for, and it errors only if that parent does not exist. D is the wrong layer — `dbt test` parses the project itself; a stale manifest is not what is missing here, the relations are. Source: `/reference/commands/test`.

**26. B.** The setting works: `Done. PASS=0 WARN=1 ERROR=0 SKIP=0 TOTAL=1`, byte-identical to the nested form — which it could only be if `severity` reached the test's config, so A is out. And dbt is not silent about it, which is what disposes of D: it raises `[WARNING] [PropertyMovedToConfigDeprecation]`, *"Found `severity` as a top-level property of `data_tests.not_null.severity` ... The `severity` top-level property should be moved into the `config` of `data_tests.not_null.severity`."* C is the belief worth killing — a bare test config is accepted, not rejected. Note how this differs from Q24: `severity` is a **config** and moves under `config:`, so it raises `PropertyMovedToConfigDeprecation`; `values:` is an **argument** and moves under `arguments:`, so it raises `MissingArgumentsPropertyInGenericTestDeprecation`. Two deprecations for two different kinds of key, which is why Q24's option C is wrong there and this one is right here. The stem pins `--no-partial-parse` deliberately: the message is emitted during parsing, so a warm cache can swallow it on a re-run and leave you with the tally alone. Source: `/reference/data-test-configs`.

**27. D.** `equals()` follows standard SQL three-valued logic by default: `NULL = NULL` evaluates to `UNKNOWN`, not `TRUE`, so two nulls do not match and those rows fall out of the comparison. The practical danger is that they fall out **quietly** — the test reports zero failures while covering none of the rows people assumed it covered. `enable_truthy_nulls_equals_macro` switches the macro to `IS NOT DISTINCT FROM` semantics, where two nulls do match, and it is **off** by default, so the exam's default is three-valued logic. C is the discriminator: it names the right flag and inverts its sense.

# Chapter 8

# Packages and code reuse

> **Scope.** Packages are how dbt escapes the fate of every analytics team writing their own `generate_schema_name` macro, their own surrogate-key hash, their own regex-match generic test. A dbt package is just another dbt project — someone else's — that you install as a dependency and whose macros, tests, seeds, and models become part of your compile graph. This chapter covers the four things the exam will ask you about packages: how `packages.yml` is shaped, how to pin versions and what `package-lock.yml` is for, the four community packages you should be able to recognise on sight (`dbt_utils`, `dbt_expectations`, `audit_helper`, `codegen`), and how to override a packaged macro with your own implementation via **dispatch** when you need to. There is also a fork-the-package procedure for when a maintainer has gone quiet, and a walkthrough of a production-scale `packages.yml` at the end.

**Prerequisites.** Ch 2 (project layout — packages land in a sibling directory to `models/` and `macros/`). Ch 6 in full, especially §6.7 on `adapter.dispatch` and the `dispatch:` config block: §8.6 here *is* §6.7 applied to the specific case of overriding a package's macro. If dispatch still feels abstract, drill Ch 6 §6.7 first; this chapter will cement it.

**Cheat-sheet pointer.** Front-of-book cheat sheet §2 (Topic 1 — Developing and optimizing models) reduces this chapter to four lines: `packages.yml` + `dbt deps`, pinning with `version: "x.y.z"`, `package-lock.yml` commits the resolved pins, and the five package-source shapes (Hub / Git / local / private / tarball). Use it for recall; use this chapter for the reasoning, especially around the lockfile and dispatch.

---

## 8.1 What a dbt package is

A **dbt package** is a dbt project you install as a dependency. That is the whole concept. The package's maintainer laid out `models/`, `macros/`, `tests/`, `seeds/` — the same directories you know from Ch 2 — and shipped the whole thing as a git repository or Hub entry. When you list the package in your `packages.yml` and run `dbt deps`, dbt copies the files into `dbt_packages/` in your project root, and from that moment on the package's contents are part of your project's compile graph. See `/docs/build/packages`.

Three consequences follow from "a package is a dbt project":

1. **Macros in the package are callable from your models**, with one wrinkle: you prefix the call with the package name. `dbt_utils.generate_surrogate_key(['a', 'b'])` reaches into the `dbt_utils` package's `generate_surrogate_key` macro. A same-named macro in your own `macros/` directory would be called without a prefix. Name collisions are resolved by the namespace.

2. **Tests shipped by a package work like yours.** dbt_expectations.expect_column_values_to_match_regex is a custom generic test from the dbt_expectations package; attach it to a column in your _models.yml just as you would a built-in generic (Ch 7 §7.2).

3. **Seeds and models shipped by a package are built by dbt build.** Most packages are macros + tests only; if a package ships models (say, dbt_artifacts ships models that normalise dbt's run artifacts), dbt run materialises them in your warehouse alongside your own models — in your target schema, unless the package's own project file sets a +schema: suffix (§8.5).

dbt_packages/ is created for you on first dbt deps. It belongs in .gitignore — the contents are reproducible from packages.yml and package-lock.yml, so you do not commit the downloaded artifacts themselves. You can rename the directory via packages-install-path: in dbt_project.yml, documented at /reference/project-configs/packages-install-path, but the default is near-universal. Note the dashes. dbt_project.yml's own top-level keys are dash-spelled (Ch 6 §6.4 has the rule and its one exception), and the underscored spelling is not tolerated: packages_install_path: makes dbt deps exit 2 with Additional properties are not allowed ('packages_install_path' was unexpected), installing nothing.

### What a package is not

A package is **not** a Python package. pip install dbt-utils is wrong; dbt packages are downloaded by dbt deps, not by pip. dbt adapters (dbt-snowflake, dbt-databricks, dbt-bigquery) *are* Python packages, installed with pip, and are a separate concept — they are the warehouse driver, not the reusable-code-library concept this chapter covers.

A package is also **not** a substitute for your own code where the logic is specific to your business. dbt_utils.star pulling every column except the ones you list is a re-use win; a bespoke lending-risk score is model code, and no public package ships it.

---

## 8.2 packages.yml — the five source shapes

packages.yml sits at your project root, next to dbt_project.yml. It lists every external dependency in one of five shapes. The shape you pick depends on where the package lives.

> **dependencies.yml.** dependencies.yml is a sibling file that can also list packages, and additionally declares **cross-project dependencies** for dbt Mesh. For a pure-package project, packages.yml is the standard file and is what the current study guide assumes. Mesh and cross-project refs sit outside the exam's scope. One difference between the two files is worth carrying anyway: packages.yml is rendered as Jinja, so {{ env_var('GIT_TOKEN') }} inside a git URL resolves before the entry is read; dependencies.yml renders nothing, so the token-in-the-URL pattern is not available there — a private repository is declared with the private: shape below, or with a git: entry whose SSH URL needs no rendering.

### Hub — package:

The most common shape. The dbt Package Hub is a package registry maintained by dbt Labs. Every Hub package has a stable identifier of the form <org>/<package_name>.

```
# packages.yml
packages:
  - package: dbt-labs/dbt_utils
    version: 1.1.1
```

Hub installs require a version pin — `version:` is not optional for Hub entries. The Hub resolves the identifier to the underlying git repository, applies the version constraint, and downloads the matching tag. Use this shape when the package is on the Hub; it is the easiest to read, the easiest to version-constrain, and the only shape that surfaces compatibility signals (the Hub publishes each package's supported `dbt-core` version range).

### Git — `git:` with `revision:`

For packages not on the Hub, or for cases where you need to install from a branch/SHA the Hub does not track (most commonly: a fork of your own — see §8.7).

```
# packages.yml
packages:
  - git: "https://github.com/dbt-labs/dbt-utils.git"
    revision: 1.1.1
```

`revision:` accepts a branch name, a tagged release, or a full 40-character commit SHA. A tag is the usual choice for production pins; a SHA is the tightest possible pin and is what you reach for when the repository owner re-tags releases (which breaks tag-based pins). A branch name is the loosest — `revision: main` means "whatever main points at when the commit is RESOLVED," which is almost never what you want in a committed `packages.yml`. Note when resolution actually happens, because it is the half people get wrong: an install from an unchanged, committed `package-lock.yml` reinstalls the SHA already locked there and is perfectly reproducible whatever `revision:` says. The drift is on the first `dbt deps` for a project with no lock file, and on `dbt deps --upgrade`, which re-resolves. §8.3 covers the lock file that draws that line. See `/docs/build/packages`.

One key belongs to the two git-backed shapes. `subdirectory:` names the folder inside the repository that holds the package's `dbt_project.yml`, for a package that lives inside a monorepo rather than at the root of its own. dbt sparse-checks out that path, so the machine running `dbt deps` needs a recent `git`. The two published bounds differ, so know both: dbt itself checks for `>= 2.25.0` — the release that introduced `git sparse-checkout` — and raises *Please update your git version to pull a dbt package from a subdirectory* below it, while the packages reference page asks for `>= 2.26.0`. Install 2.26 or newer and both are satisfied. The key itself is accepted under `git:` and under `private:`, and the `packages.yml` schema rejects the entry outright under `package:`, `local:` and `tarball:` — *The packages.yml file in this project is malformed.*

### Local — `local:`

For monorepo setups where one dbt project references another dbt project in the same repository, or for iterating on a package locally before publishing.

```
# packages.yml
packages:
  - local: ../my_shared_dbt_package
```

Path is relative to the project root. `dbt deps` symlinks (or copies, on platforms without symlink support) the target directory under `dbt_packages/`. The local package is not versioned; its contents are whatever is on disk when `dbt deps` runs. Use this shape for rapid iteration — change the shared package, re-run `dbt deps` (or skip it and just re-compile, since the symlink picks up the new files), re-run your models. For anything crossing a repository boundary, prefer Git or Hub.

### Private — `private:`

The shape for packages hosted on private git repositories, where the authentication lives with the git provider integration (not a token in `packages.yml`).

```
# packages.yml
packages:
  - private: my-org/my_private_package
    provider: "github"
    revision: 1.0.0
```

`private:` works like a Git install but uses your configured git-provider credentials rather than a baked-in URL — which means it carries a prerequisite the shape itself does not show. The git-provider integration has to already exist: on the dbt platform that is a GitHub, GitLab or Azure DevOps connection configured under **Account settings → Integrations**. On dbt Core 1.11 there is no such integration to read, so a `private:` entry parses and then stops at resolution — *Cannot resolve private package* *`<org>/<repo>`* *because git provider integration is missing. Please use a "git" package instead.* Know the key, and know that it is the platform's shape. `provider:` names which git-provider integration to authenticate through — the three accepted values are `"github"`, `"gitlab"`, and `"ado"` (the docs use the short form for Azure DevOps). At 1.11 it is accepted but not required; from 1.12 it is required. `revision:` is optional and accepts the same values as `git:`. Treat `private:` as the modern way to install a private package **where that integration exists** — it is the documented path, and it keeps every credential out of the file. The older `git:` + SSH pattern still works, you will see it in older projects, and on dbt Core alone it is the shape that actually installs. See `/docs/build/packages`.

### Tarball — `tarball:`

For packages distributed as a pre-built archive — typically a fixed release downloaded from a release page or internal artifact store. Less common than Hub or Git, but documented as a supported fifth shape.

```
# packages.yml
packages:
  - tarball: https://codeload.github.com/dbt-labs/dbt-utils/tar.gz/1.2.1
    name: 'dbt_utils'
```

`tarball:` points at the archive URL; `name:` is required so dbt knows what directory to create under `dbt_packages/`. The archive is downloaded and extracted on `dbt deps`. No version resolution happens — the URL itself is the pin. Use this shape when a package isn't published to the Hub and isn't in a git repo you can reach (e.g., a vendor ships you a dated `.tar.gz` over SFTP that you re-host internally).

### One packages.yml, many entries

`packages.yml` is a list; you can mix shapes freely. A real project might have three Hub packages, one Git fork of a fourth package, and one private shared-macros package:

```
# packages.yml
packages:
  - package: dbt-labs/dbt_utils
    version: 1.1.1
  - package: metaplane/dbt_expectations
    version: 0.10.10
```

```
  - package: dbt-labs/audit_helper
    version: 0.12.0
  - git: "https://github.com/our-org/codegen.git"
    revision: v0.12.1-our-patch
  - private: our-org/internal_shared_macros
    revision: 2.3.0
```

The order of entries does not affect dispatch resolution or import priority — dbt treats package contents as a union, with name-collision rules covered in §8.6.

---

## 8.3 Pinning, version ranges, and `package-lock.yml`

Every Hub entry requires a `version:` key; a Git entry's `revision:` is optional. The choice of pin style has operational consequences, and the choice of whether to commit `package-lock.yml` is a downstream consequence of that.

### Three pin styles for Hub packages

**Exact — `version: "1.1.1"`.** Resolves to precisely `1.1.1`. Deterministic in the cleanest sense: rerun `dbt deps` on any machine, at any time, and you get the same files. Production pins are almost always exact.

**Range — `version: [">=1.0.0", "<2.0.0"]`.** Resolves to the latest version satisfying every constraint at the time `dbt deps` runs. Useful when you want to absorb patch releases without re-editing `packages.yml` but still block a breaking major version. The constraint follows a semver-style syntax documented on the packages page. A **single comparator** is the same style with one bound: `version: ">=1.0.0"` is legal, and it is a range with no ceiling — it takes the newest release the registry offers, so it pins nothing and is the shape behind most "it worked last week" CI breakages.

**Unpinned — `version:` omitted.** Not a legal Hub entry: package validation raises on the missing key before `dbt deps` downloads anything.

For Git entries, `revision:` plays the same role with the same trade-offs: a tag is the "exact"-like pin; `main` (or any branch name) is the loose equivalent. An omitted `revision:`, though, behaves the opposite way to an omitted Hub `version:` — it is legal. `dbt deps` installs the default branch's HEAD and warns:

```
WARNING: The git package "https://github.com/dbt-labs/dbt-utils.git"
  is not pinned, using HEAD (default branch).
  This can introduce breaking changes into your project without warning!
```

The resolved SHA still lands in `package-lock.yml`, so the build stays reproducible until somebody re-resolves it. `warn-unpinned: false` on the entry silences the warning; the docs advise against it, and so does every incident that began with a package moving under a CI job.

**Prereleases are excluded unless you ask for them.** Version resolution skips prerelease versions, so a range like `[">=1.0.0", "<2.0.0"]` will not pick up `1.5.0-rc1` however well it fits. Two things override that: writing the prerelease out in full as an exact pin, or adding `install_prerelease: true` beside the range. The key takes an underscore — the hyphenated spelling is rejected by the `packages.yml` validator, which reports the whole entry as `not valid under any of the given schemas` and installs nothing.

### `package-lock.yml` — what it is, what it does

When you run `dbt deps`, dbt resolves every entry in `packages.yml` to a specific concrete version and writes the result to `package-lock.yml` at the project root. The lockfile records:

- the package identifier (Hub, Git, or local),
- the **resolved** version (the exact tag or SHA dbt ended up installing), and
- a SHA1 hash of your `packages.yml` content, so dbt can detect "has the declaration changed since the lockfile was last written?"

On subsequent `dbt deps` runs, dbt reads `package-lock.yml` first. If the hash matches your current `packages.yml`, dbt installs the exact versions recorded in the lockfile — even when `packages.yml` uses a range like `[">=1.0.0", "<2.0.0"]` that *could* resolve to a newer release today. The lockfile locks the resolution. See `/reference/commands/deps`.

### When to commit `package-lock.yml`

The docs' recommendation, and near-universal practice, is **commit it, always**, for the same reason `package-lock.json` and `Cargo.lock` belong in source control: two developers on the same branch, and a CI run today against one from last week, install the same versions unless someone on the team bumped a pin.

Short exceptions:

- **Experimentation.** If you are writing a small one-off analysis and do not care that a patch-level drift might happen next week, you can leave it out. But nothing is lost by committing it.
- **Template repositories.** A starter project may ship without the lockfile so downstream users generate their own on first `dbt deps`.

The failure mode of not committing the lockfile is the one the Q16 scenario plays out: a range pin silently adopts a new minor release, a macro's signature shifts, your CI breaks on Monday for a change no one in your team made.

### Upgrading — `dbt deps --upgrade`

If you want to move to the latest resolution — for a range pin — run `dbt deps --upgrade`. dbt re-resolves every range pin against the latest available versions, rewrites `package-lock.yml`, and re-downloads into `dbt_packages/`. Commit the new lockfile as a deliberate dependency bump. The `--upgrade` flag exists precisely so the default `dbt deps` stays conservative; opt-in to moves rather than absorbing them accidentally. `dbt deps --lock` is the related flag that rewrites `package-lock.yml` without downloading — useful in CI for checking lockfile drift.

---

## 8.4 `dbt deps` — what it does, when to run it

Before that, one failure that looks like your project's fault and is not. **`config-version: 2` is required in every installed package's own `dbt_project.yml`, not just in yours.** A package still declaring `config-version: 1` breaks every command that has to **parse** the project — `parse`, `ls`, `compile`, `run`, `seed`, `build` — with `Internal Error / Got an unexpected project version=1, expected 2` at exit 2. Two details make it hard to diagnose. `dbt deps` and `dbt debug` both still succeed, so the two commands you reach for first report everything fine. And the message names **neither the package nor a file** — there is nothing in it to grep for. The check is per **node**, at `initial_config`, which takes the minimum of the node's own project version and the root's; a package shipping only macros therefore parses cleanly, because it contributes no node. It is the classic symptom of installing an unmaintained package against a modern dbt: the install succeeds, and the next command cannot load the project at all. The fix is to upgrade the package, pin to a version that declares `config-version: 2`, or fork it (§8.7) and change the one line.

`dbt deps` is the command that turns `packages.yml` + `package-lock.yml` into files on disk under `dbt_packages/`. It is documented at `/reference/commands/deps`. The full flow on a fresh clone:

1. Read `packages.yml`.
2. Read `package-lock.yml` if it exists. Compare its `packages.yml` hash with the current file.
3. If the hash matches, install the exact versions from the lockfile. If not, re-resolve every entry, update the lockfile, and install.
4. Fetch each package by the method its shape implies: a **git clone** for `git:` and `private:`; a **tarball download** for Hub packages, which resolve to `metadata.downloads.tarball` rather than to a clone; and, for `local:`, a **symlink where the platform supports one and a copy where it does not** — which decides whether an edit is picked up. Verified on a copying platform: editing the source package left the installed one unchanged, so there an edit needs `dbt deps` to take effect. Where the install is a symlink the edit is visible immediately (§8.2). Re-running `dbt deps` is the habit that works either way, and is what CI should do regardless.
5. Place the downloaded tree under `dbt_packages/<package_name>/`.
6. If `--add-package` was passed, append the new package to `packages.yml` and write the lockfile.

No models are run. `dbt deps` is inert with respect to your warehouse — it only touches local files.

## When to run it

- **First clone.** Before `dbt run`, `dbt test`, or anything else. A cloned repo has `packages.yml` but no `dbt_packages/` (that directory is git-ignored). Without `dbt deps` nothing compiles: the run stops at the package-count check with `dbt found N package(s) specified in packages.yml, but only 0 package(s) installed in dbt_packages`.
- **After editing `packages.yml`.** Adding, removing, or re-pinning any entry requires a fresh `dbt deps`.
- **After pulling a branch that changed `packages.yml` or `package-lock.yml`.** Same reason.
- **Before CI runs, always.** Most CI recipes make `dbt deps` the first step of any job, unconditionally. It is cheap when the lockfile is satisfied (just a hash check and an already-present `dbt_packages/`) and correct when it is not.

## Flags you might see

- `--upgrade` — re-resolves ranges past a matching lockfile, rewrites it, and installs what it finds.
- `--lock` — rewrites the lockfile without downloading; no `dbt_packages/` directory is created.
- `--add-package dbt-labs/dbt_utils@1.1.1` — append-style edit to `packages.yml`, then install. `--source` names the shape to write: the default `--source hub` produces a `package:`/`version:` pair, `--source git` takes a `<url>@<revision>` argument and produces a `git:`/`revision:` pair, and `--source local` produces a `local:` path.

Two behaviours around `dbt deps` catch people out. **The install is a rebuild, not a patch.** `dbt deps` removes `dbt_packages/` in full and re-creates it from the resolved list, so an entry you delete from `packages.yml` is off disk after the next run — and so is any edit you made to a file under there. The exception is a package another installed package depends on: it comes straight back as a transitive dependency, at whatever version the depending package pulls in rather than your deleted pin. And the **"Updated version available" notice is Hub-only.** dbt can compare your resolved version against what the registry currently publishes, so a Hub entry gets told when it has fallen behind; a git, tarball or local entry never does, because there is no registry to ask.

### The "why is my package missing" symptom

Overwhelmingly the cause of the package-count error on a freshly cloned or freshly pulled repo is: `dbt deps` has not been run since the last change. The fix is the command the message names. `'dbt_utils' is undefined` (or similar, for any package) arrives only once the counts agree, and points at the second cause: a typo in the package name. Inside `{{ }}` it is `dbt_utils`, not `dbt-utils` — and the Hub identifier is underscored too (`dbt-labs/dbt_utils`), not the hyphenated GitHub repo name (`dbt-labs/dbt-utils`).

---

## 8.5 The four packages you should know by name

Any production dbt project you encounter will have two or three of these installed, so "which package ships macro `X`?" is a recognition question rather than a trick. None of the four ships with dbt Core — every one is installed by `dbt deps` like any other package — but all are adopted widely enough to function as a de-facto standard library.

### `dbt_utils` — the Swiss Army knife

Hub slug: `dbt-labs/dbt_utils`. Hub URL: `https://hub.getdbt.com/dbt-labs/dbt_utils/latest/`. Maintained by dbt Labs. Every one of the top macros below dispatches per-adapter under the hood, which is why the package works identically on Snowflake, Databricks, BigQuery, Redshift, and Postgres.

The most-reached-for macros:

| Macro | What it does | Reach for it when |
|---|---|---|
| `generate_surrogate_key(['col1', 'col2', ...])` | concatenates the listed columns (with a separator and null-handling) and md5-hashes the result into one value | you need a composite key on a dimension |
| `star(from=ref('stg_orders'), except=['_etl_ts', '_raw_payload'])` | expands to every column in the source relation except the ones listed | you want "everything but a few" without the `select col1, col2, col3, ...` boilerplate |
| `unpivot(ref('metrics_wide'), cast_to='numeric', exclude=['date'], ...)` | reshapes wide columns into `(key, value)` row pairs | you would otherwise write vendor-specific `UNPIVOT` syntax |

| Macro | What it does | Reach for it when |
|---|---|---|
| `equality(compare_model= ref('expected'))` | a generic test that fails when two relations are not row-for-row equal; in YAML you write `- dbt_utils. equality:` | you are regression-checking a refactor |
| `generate_series(upper_ bound=30)` | produces a one-column relation of integers from 1 to the bound | you are backfilling a date spine, cross-joining a calendar dimension, or generating synthetic data |

`surrogate_key` is the legacy spelling of the first one. The file still ships, but its only implementation raises a compilation error pointing you at `generate_surrogate_key`: the two treat nulls differently, so the old name refuses rather than aliases, and any call site left on it breaks the run.

The `type_*` family reads like `dbt_utils` and is not. `type_string()`, `type_int()`, `type_timestamp()` and `type_numeric()` live in dbt Core's global project, so the call is `cast(x as {{ dbt.type_string() }})` — `text` on Postgres, `string` on Databricks and BigQuery. `dbt_utils.type_string()` is a compile error.

If a production project has exactly one dbt package installed, it is almost always `dbt_utils`. Treat recognising the top macros as table stakes.

### `dbt_expectations` — generic tests, Great-Expectations-style

Hub slug: `metaplane/dbt_expectations` — the slug moved with maintainership from Calogica to Metaplane, and `calogica/dbt_expectations` now warns with `PackageRedirectDeprecation` on `dbt deps`, when the resolver looks the slug up in the registry. Modeled after the Python `great_expectations` library; ports dozens of its assertions into dbt-native custom generic tests. Every macro in the package is a test you attach to a column (or a model) in YAML exactly like a built-in generic from Ch 7 §7.2.

A sample of what ships:

- `expect_column_values_to_match_regex` — argument: `regex: "..."`. Fails the test when any value in the column does not match the pattern.
- `expect_column_values_to_be_between` — arguments: `min_value`, `max_value`. A range assertion beyond what the built-in `accepted_values` can do (which requires an explicit list).
- `expect_column_pair_values_A_to_be_greater_than_B` — a two-column relational assertion: `ship_date >= order_date`, `end_ts > start_ts`. Singular tests that compare columns in the same row are a common use case.
- `expect_column_values_to_be_of_type` — asserts a column's SQL type matches the declared one. Softer than a contract, but useful pre-contracts.

Reach for `dbt_expectations` when the built-in generics (`unique`, `not_null`, `accepted_values`, `relationships`) do not cover the assertion shape you need and you do not want to write a custom generic from scratch. It is the most-installed second package after `dbt_utils`.

### `audit_helper` — diffing relations for migrations

Hub slug: `dbt-labs/audit_helper`. A small package built around a handful of comparison macros, but indispensable during a migration.

- `compare_relations(a_relation, b_relation, ...)` — compiles to a query that reports which rows exist in A but not in B, which exist in B but not in A, and which differ on non-key columns. The standard use case: you are migrating an Airflow DAG's output table into a dbt model and need to prove the new model produces the same rows as the old.
- `compare_queries(a_query, b_query, ...)` — same idea, but each side is a compiled SELECT rather than a table. Used during a model refactor when you cannot compare against the previous version's table (because the table has been overwritten).

Use `audit_helper` during migrations and refactors, archive the macro calls when done, and leave the package installed for the next one.

### `codegen` — scaffolding YAML and SQL

Hub slug: `dbt-labs/codegen`. Reduces the YAML-and-SQL tedium of starting a new source, a new model, or a new model's `columns:` block. It is a small package, intentionally so — the macros are meant to be run once (via `dbt run-operation`) to generate a block of text you paste into a file.

- `generate_source(schema_name='raw', database_name='my_db', ...)` — runs against the warehouse, introspects the schema, and prints a `sources.yml` block listing every table it found. Paste into a new `sources.yml`. Saves hours when you have 50 raw tables to declare.
- `generate_base_model(source_name='raw', table_name='orders')` — runs against the source table's metadata and prints a `select col1, col2, col3 from {{ source(...) }}` scaffold for a `stg_*` model. Paste into a new `.sql` file. Gives you every column in one pass, which you then edit.
- `generate_model_yaml(model_names=['dim_customers'])` — introspects an already-built model's columns and prints a `_models.yml` block listing each column under `columns:`. Paste and add descriptions.

Use `codegen` at project start-up or when adding a large batch of sources/models.

## Other packages you will see but may not need to memorise

- `dbt_artifacts` — captures dbt's run artifacts (manifest, run_results) into warehouse tables for observability.
- `dbt_date` — date-dimension utilities: calendar spines, holiday tables, fiscal-year arithmetic.
- `dbt_project_evaluator` — meta-tests about project health (unused sources, undocumented models, DAG shape).
- **Adapter-specific packages** — `dbt-external-tables` for query-over-object-store patterns, per-warehouse snapshot utilities.

For the exam, `dbt_utils`, `dbt_expectations`, `audit_helper`, and `codegen` are the four names that matter.

## Configuring an installed package from the root project

Whichever of these you install, you bend it to your project from your own `dbt_project.yml` — never from the package's. Nothing under `dbt_packages/` is yours to edit: the directory is build output, git-ignored, rewritten by the next `dbt deps`, and deleted by `dbt clean` on any project carrying the starter `clean-targets`, so a change made there survives exactly until the next person installs dependencies.

The lever is the package's name — the `name:` in the package's own `dbt_project.yml`, which is also the directory it lands in under `dbt_packages/`. Anywhere your project file takes a resource path, that name is a valid first level:

```
# dbt_project.yml - yours, not the package's
models:
  my_project:
    +materialized: view
  dbt_artifacts:
    +schema: dbt_meta           # the package's models land in <target_schema>_dbt_meta
    +materialized: table

seeds:
  internal_shared_macros:
    +enabled: false             # a reference seed this project does not want loaded

vars:
  internal_shared_macros:
    lookback_days: 30           # beats the package's own value for the package's nodes
```

**Your value wins.** Where your project and the package set the same key for the same resource, yours is the one that reaches the manifest. That is the whole point of the mechanism, and it is why needing a different schema name is never a reason to fork. The override is key by key rather than wholesale: set `+schema:` in your project and leave `+materialized:` to the package's file, and you get your schema and the package's materialization.

One shape looks close and is not. A config keyed under **your own** project's name reaches your resources only, so moving `+schema: dbt_meta` up under `my_project:` configures your models and leaves the package exactly where it was. The package name is not decoration; it is the selector. See `/docs/build/packages` and `/reference/define-configs`; Ch 2 §2.4 covers `vars` precedence in full.

---

## 8.6 Overriding a packaged macro via `dispatch`

Sometimes a package's macro is almost what you want, but not quite. `dbt_utils.generate_surrogate_key` hashes with md5; your platform needs sha256. `dbt_utils.star` excludes columns but does not preserve ordering; you need ordering preserved. The wrong reaction is to fork the package (§8.7 covers when fork is correct). The right reaction, most of the time, is to override the specific macro via **dispatch** — the same mechanism Ch 6 §6.7 introduced for cross-adapter macros, applied here to swap a *package*'s implementation for your own.

### The dispatch mechanic, recapped

A package's macros are written in dispatched form — `{% macro generate_surrogate_key(cols) %}{% do return(adapter.dispatch('generate_surrogate_key', 'dbt_utils')(cols)) %}{% endmacro %}`. At compile time, `adapter.dispatch('generate_surrogate_key', 'dbt_utils')` asks dbt: "find the best `generate_surrogate_key` implementation for the current adapter, searching the namespaces in the configured order." Because `dbt_utils` is a package you installed, that order already starts with your root project (Ch 6 §6.7) — so a correctly-named override in your own `macros/` directory already wins, with no configuration at all. You reorder or extend that list by editing `dbt_project.yml`.

## The override recipe

Three steps.

**Step 1.** In dbt_project.yml, pin the search order — your project's macros before the package's. That is already the default, so the block declares the intent rather than switching it on:

```
# dbt_project.yml
dispatch:
  - macro_namespace: dbt_utils
    search_order:
      - my_project      # the value of `name:` in your dbt_project.yml
      - dbt_utils
```

See /reference/project-configs/dispatch-config for the schema. The macro_namespace: value must match the name of the package whose macro you want to override — the value that appears in dbt_project.yml's name: inside the installed package, which for Hub packages matches the un-hyphenated form (dbt_utils, not dbt-utils).

**Step 2.** In your project's macros/ directory, write the override. The macro name must use dispatch's adapter-prefix format: <adapter>__<original_macro_name> for one adapter, or default__<original_macro_name> as the fallback for all adapters. The namespace comes from the package that contains the macro; it is not part of the macro's name:

```
-- macros/databricks__generate_surrogate_key.sql
{% macro databricks__generate_surrogate_key(field_list, null_placeholder='_dbt_null_') %}

    -- your platform-specific variant
    sha2(
        concat_ws(
            '-',
            {%- for field in field_list -%}
                coalesce(cast({{ field }} as string), '{{ null_placeholder }}')
                {%- if not loop.last %}, {% endif -%}
            {%- endfor -%}
        ),
        256
    )
{% endmacro %}
```

**Step 3.** Call the macro as you always would — {{ dbt_utils.generate_surrogate_key(['a', 'b']) }}. Dispatch consults the search_order, checks your project namespace first for databricks__generate_surrogate_key (or default__generate_surrogate_key), and uses it when it matches the active adapter. dbt_utils's own implementation is not touched; you did not patch the package. You shimmed it.

## When override is the right tool

- **A macro's output shape is fine; you want a different computation.** Swapping md5 for sha256 inside generate_surrogate_key is the classic case.
- **A macro's warehouse-SQL idiom needs changing.** dbt_utils.date_spine builds its spine by cross-joining a two-row table into a power-of-two range — if your platform ships a native generator function you would rather use, override the dispatched macro for that adapter.
- **A package's macro is broken on your adapter and the maintainer is slow.** An override unblocks you today; you can remove it once the upstream ships a fix.

### When override is the wrong tool

- **You need to change the macro's *interface*** (arguments, return shape). Override is for swapping implementations that share an interface; interface changes belong in a fork (§8.7) or in a different macro name.
- **You are overriding more than two or three macros from the same package.** At that point the fork is cheaper to maintain than the growing override surface.

See `/reference/dbt-jinja-functions/dispatch` for the `adapter.dispatch()` reference and Ch 6 §6.7 for the primer on how dispatch works before packages enter the picture.

### What `dispatch` does not reach

`search_order` is a macro mechanism, and only a macro mechanism. Two of the places a package's code meets yours are arbitrated by other rules entirely, and both are where a reader who has just learned dispatch reaches for the wrong lever.

**Materializations.** A package can ship one — `{% materialization table, default %}` is legal in anybody's `macros/` directory — but at 1.11 a package materialization whose name matches one dbt Core ships is dropped from resolution outright, and dbt runs its own. Naming the package in a `dispatch:` block changes nothing, because materialization resolution never consults `search_order`: it ranks candidates by where each one comes from — dbt Core, your root project, an installed package — and discards the package's whenever a Core implementation exists. The protected names are the materializations Core defines: `view`, `table`, `incremental`, `materialized_view`, `snapshot`, `seed`, `clone`, `test`, `unit`, and `function`, for user-defined functions.

The escape hatch is deliberately loud. Declare the materialization in your **own** project's `macros/`, where it outranks Core's, and call into the package's implementation from there; now the substitution is written down in the project that suffers it. The behaviour flag enforcing this, `require_explicit_package_overrides_for_builtin_materializations`, is already mature at 1.11, so a project inherits the strict behaviour without opting in — Ch 10 §10.9.2 has the lifecycle. Here it is enough to know that a package cannot quietly change what `materialized: table` means.

**A `ref()` written inside a package.** Suppose a package ships two models:

```
-- dbt_packages/shared_utils/models/orders.sql
select ...

-- dbt_packages/shared_utils/models/pkg_revenue.sql
select order_id, amount from {{ ref('orders') }}
```

The package's author wrote `ref('orders')` meaning their own `orders`. Your project then adds a `models/orders.sql` of its own — an ordinary name, and a likely collision. At 1.11 the package's `ref('orders')` resolves to **yours**: a one-argument `ref()` searches the root project first and the model's own package second. dbt says so at parse time and carries on building:

```
[WARNING]: The node 'pkg_revenue'in package 'shared_utils' depends on the root
project node 'model.my_project.orders'.This may lead to unexpected cycles
downstream. Please set the 'require_ref_prefers_node_package_to_root' behavior
change flag to True to avoid this issue.
```

Nothing errors, no SQL looks wrong, and a package model is now reading a table its author never saw. The block is quoted as 1.11.14 emits it, run-together spacing included and a trailing documentation link elided — and its third sentence is wrong: no flag named `require_ref_prefers_node_package_to_root` exists. Set it and dbt accepts the key silently, resolution stays root-first, and the same warning fires on the next parse. The flag that works is `require_ref_searches_node_package_before_root`, below. The remedy is the two-argument form, and its first argument is the `name:` the package declares in its `dbt_project.yml` — `shared_utils` — not the repository it was cloned from, `dbt-shared-utils`:

| Call written inside the package | Resolves to |
|---|---|
| `ref('orders')` | your root project's `orders` — the 1.11 default; the parse-time warning above is the only signal |
| `ref('shared_utils', 'orders')` | the package's own `orders`; the two-argument form pins the lookup to one package |
| `ref('dbt-shared-utils', 'orders')` | nothing — `depends on a node named 'orders' in package or project 'dbt-shared-utils' which was not found` |
| `ref('orders', package='shared_utils')` | your root project's `orders`, silently — `ref()` reads only `v` and `version` as keyword arguments, so `package=` is discarded and the call degrades to its one-argument form |

Setting `require_ref_searches_node_package_before_root: true` reverses the default and makes a package's `ref()` search its own package first. It sits at `false` on 1.11 and dbt Labs describe that default as a bug kept for compatibility; Ch 10 §10.9.2 covers why a flag stays where it is. Reference: `/reference/global-configs/behavior-flags/require_ref_searches_node_package_before_root`.

---

## 8.7 Forking a package when the maintainer has gone quiet

Override via dispatch covers "I want a different implementation of one macro." Forking covers everything else: a package has a bug the maintainer has not patched in months, you need adapter support the upstream lacks, you need a breaking-change fix that hasn't been merged, or the package has been effectively abandoned.

### The fork procedure

1. **Fork the repository** on your git host. Name the fork `my-org/<package_name>` so the origin is obvious.

2. **Clone it, check out a branch, make your fix.** Commit and push.

3. **Pin your project's `packages.yml` at the fork**, using the Git shape:

```
# packages.yml
packages:
  - git: "https://github.com/my-org/dbt-utils.git"
    revision: v1.1.1-my-patch
```

   The `revision:` should be a tag or SHA, not a branch name — you want reproducible builds (§8.3).

4. **Commit `packages.yml` and re-run `dbt deps`.** The lockfile now records your fork's SHA.

5. **Upstream the fix.** File a PR against the original repository. If it lands, you can switch back to the upstream pin and delete the fork.

### When to fork

- **Maintainer unresponsive** for a blocker bug — issues and PRs open for months with no response.
- **Adapter support missing.** The package dispatches for Snowflake, BigQuery, Postgres, Redshift; your warehouse is not one of them and you need to add a `<your_adapter>__<macro>` implementation.
- **Breaking-change fix** that the upstream refuses or has not yet accepted.
- **Private extension.** A one-off internal macro you want to bundle with the package's install (though at that point a separate private package is usually cleaner).

### When *not* to fork

- **You can solve it with a dispatch override** — do that first.
- **You want a version the Hub does not have** — use the `git:` shape against the original repo with a specific revision.
- **The package needs light configuration** — most community packages accept config via `vars:` in `dbt_project.yml`; read the README before assuming fork is necessary.

A fork is a maintenance burden. You now have to rebase on every upstream release, keep your fix relevant, and re-pin your consumers. Pay the cost only when dispatch override cannot reach.

---

## 8.8 In practice: a five-package setup at Credora

> *This section is an "in practice" sidebar. It draws a composite pattern from (a) the packages reference at `/docs/build/packages` and (b) the Hub listings of the five named packages. Credora is fictional (`credora`); Ch 14's opening note has the composite-project disclaimer.*

In our fictional `credora` project, `packages.yml` holds five entries — a typical production shape: every name widely adopted, each with one well-defined job. For a small public project with installed packages, see the companion repo: `https://github.com/snowleafbooks/dbt-analytics-engineer-certification`.

```
# packages.yml
packages:
  - package: dbt-labs/dbt_utils
    version: 1.1.1
  - package: brooklyn-data/dbt_artifacts
    version: 2.11.0
  - package: metaplane/dbt_expectations
    version: 0.10.10
  - package: dbt-labs/audit_helper
    version: 0.12.0
  - package: godatadriven/dbt_date
    version: 0.21.0
```

Five entries, all exact version pins, all from the Hub. `package-lock.yml` is committed to the repo — every CI job on every market branch reads the same lockfile, installs the same versions, compiles against the same macros, so a CI failure is never a package moving underneath the team.

The rationale for each package:

| Package | Why it is installed | What calls it |
|---|---|---|
| `dbt_utils` | the Swiss Army knife | `generate_surrogate_key` for composite keys in every staging model; `star(except=[...])` in every gold-layer model, to avoid spelling out every column |
| `dbt_artifacts` | normalises dbt's `manifest.json` and `run_results.json` into warehouse tables | the central data-platform team's internal "dbt health" dashboards — which models are growing slowest, which tests fail most often, which sources skip a freshness window |
| `dbt_expectations` | every generic test the built-ins cannot express | `expect_column_values_to_match_regex` for identifier formats; `expect_column_pair_values_A_to_be_greater_than_B` for temporal-order invariants |
| `audit_helper` | installed idle, activated during migrations | porting a legacy pipeline into `credora`: a temporary analysis under `analyses/` calls `compare_relations`, proves parity, and is deleted |
| `dbt_date` | date-dimension macros for the `dim_date` calendar used across every market | `date_spine(...)` for the date backbone; holiday-schedule macros for market-specific business-day calculations |

## The dispatch override for Databricks-native surrogate keys

Credora runs on Databricks and has settled on SHA-256 as its surrogate-key convention — a team standard about collision margin and consistency across markets, not a platform requirement. Databricks documents both `md5` and `sha2` as returning `STRING`, and neither Unity Catalog nor Delta expresses a preference between them. The point of the example is the mechanism: the team overrides `dbt_utils.generate_surrogate_key` via dispatch rather than rewriting every call site, and dispatch is what makes a project-wide hashing decision a one-file change:

```
# dbt_project.yml
name: credora
version: 1.0.0
config-version: 2

dispatch:
  - macro_namespace: dbt_utils
```

```
search_order:
  - credora
  - dbt_utils
```

```
-- macros/databricks__generate_surrogate_key.sql
{% macro databricks__generate_surrogate_key(field_list, null_placeholder='_dbt_null_') %}

    sha2(
        concat_ws(
            '||',
            {%- for field in field_list -%}
                coalesce(cast({{ field }} as string), '{{ null_placeholder }}')
                {%- if not loop.last %}, {% endif -%}
            {%- endfor -%}
        ),
        256
    )
{% endmacro %}
```

Call sites in models remain `{{ dbt_utils.generate_surrogate_key([...]) }}`. Dispatch routes Databricks runs to `credora.databricks__generate_surrogate_key` because the `credora` namespace is searched before `dbt_utils`. No fork, no monkey-patch — a pattern that survives every future `dbt_utils` upgrade as long as the macro signature does not change.

### Why no fork

Every one of the five packages is actively maintained; every macro does what the team needs. The one customisation — the Databricks-flavoured surrogate-key hash — is an override, not a fork. This is the steady-state picture: most production projects do not fork. Fork is reserved for the exceptional case a maintainer has gone quiet or an adapter is unsupported; in the absence of that exception, Hub + exact pin + dispatch override + committed lockfile is the full package story.

---

## Summary

- **A package is a dbt project you install as a dependency.** `dbt deps` copies its files into `dbt_packages/`; its macros, tests, seeds, and models become part of your compile graph.
- **Five source shapes in `packages.yml`:** Hub (`package:` + `version:`), Git (`git:` + `revision:`), local (`local:` + relative path), private (`private:` + optional `revision:`), tarball (`tarball:` URL). Hub is the default; the others handle forks, monorepos, private repositories, and tarball distributions.
- **Pin styles:** exact (`version: "1.1.1"`) for production, range for auto-absorbing patches — bounded (`[">=1.0.0", "<2.0.0"]`) or a single unbounded comparator (`">=1.0.0"`) — unpinned not allowed for Hub. For Git, prefer tag or SHA over branch name.
- `package-lock.yml` records the resolved version + a hash of `packages.yml`. Commit it always, for the same reason you commit `package-lock.json` in a Node project. `dbt deps --upgrade` deliberately re-resolves range pins; default `dbt deps` respects the lockfile.
- **Run `dbt deps`:** on fresh clone, after editing `packages.yml`, after pulling a branch that changed package state, and as the first step of every CI job.

- **Four packages to know by name:** `dbt_utils` (Swiss Army knife), `dbt_expectations` (Great-Expectations-style generic tests), `audit_helper` (diff relations for migrations), `codegen` (scaffold YAML and SQL).
- **Override a packaged macro via dispatch** (Ch 6 §6.7): add a `dispatch:` block in `dbt_project.yml` with `macro_namespace: <package>` and `search_order: [<your_project>, <package>]`, then define `<adapter>__<macro_name>` or `default__<macro_name>` under `macros/`. The package's call sites automatically route to your override when the active adapter matches.
- **Configure an installed package from your own `dbt_project.yml`**, keying `models:`, `seeds:` and `vars:` under the package's declared name. Your value wins key by key, which is why a schema name is never a reason to fork — and why nothing under `dbt_packages/` is ever edited.
- **Dispatch does not reach materializations or `ref()`.** A package materialization whose name matches one dbt Core ships is excluded from resolution, and `search_order` has no say; re-declare it in your own `macros/` to reach it. Inside a package, a one-argument `ref()` searches the root project first at 1.11, and `ref('<package_name>', '<model>')` — the *declared* name, not the repository's — is the fix.
- **Fork a package** when dispatch override cannot reach — typically an unresponsive maintainer, a missing adapter, or an unshipped breaking-change fix. Use the Git shape with a tag or SHA `revision:` so your consumers have reproducible builds.

## Learning-goal checklist (self-assess)

- ☐ I can read a `packages.yml` and identify which source shape each entry uses, and I can distinguish Hub from Git from local from private by their YAML keys.
- ☐ I can explain the trade-off between exact pins, range pins, and no pins — and I can explain why `package-lock.yml` belongs in source control.
- ☐ I can describe what `dbt deps` does (and does not do) and name the two or three moments in a developer workflow when it must run.
- ☐ Given a macro or generic test, I can match it to the correct package: `dbt_utils`, `dbt_expectations`, `audit_helper`, or `codegen`.
- ☐ I can walk through the three-step dispatch-override recipe (`dispatch:` in `dbt_project.yml`, `<adapter>__<macro>` or `default__<macro>` file in `macros/`, unchanged call sites) and explain when override is the right tool versus when to fork.
- ☐ I can set an installed package's schema, disable a seed it ships, and change a variable it reads — all from my own `dbt_project.yml` — and say why editing anything under `dbt_packages/` is not an option (§8.5, Q18).
- ☐ I can explain why a `dispatch: search_order` cannot make a package's `table` materialization win, and what re-declaring it in my own `macros/` does instead (§8.6, Q20).
- ☐ I know which `orders` a one-argument `ref('orders')` inside a package resolves to at 1.11, and I can write the two-argument form that overrides it (§8.6, Qs 19 and 21).

---

## Practice questions

Twenty-four questions across `packages.yml` syntax, pinning and `package-lock.yml`, `dbt deps` and its flags, `packages.yml` versus `dependencies.yml`, which of the four community packages a given job calls for, when a fork beats a dispatch override, dispatch override and the boundaries it does not arbitrate — the root-first `ref()`, its two-argument remedy, and built-in materializations — plus a package's own `config-version`.

**1.** Which YAML key installs a package from the dbt Package Hub?

A. `git:` B. `source:`
C. `hub:` D. `package:`

**2.** Which `packages.yml` entry installs `dbt_utils` from a specific tag of a git repository?

A.

```
- package: "https://github.com/dbt-labs/dbt-utils.git"
  version: 1.1.1
```

B.

```
- git: "https://github.com/dbt-labs/dbt-utils.git"
  tag: 1.1.1
```

C.

```
- git: "https://github.com/dbt-labs/dbt-utils.git"
  revision: 1.1.1
```

D.

```
- hub: "dbt-labs/dbt-utils"
  revision: 1.1.1
```

**3.** What does a `local:` entry in `packages.yml` point at?

A. A URL on the local file system's HTTP server
B. A package published privately on the Hub
C. A relative path from the project root to another dbt project's directory
D. A git repository on a local bare-clone

**4.** Which `packages.yml` key installs a package from a private git repository, taking its credentials from your configured git-provider integration rather than from anything written in the file?

A. `package:` B. `git:`
C. `private:` D. `tarball:`

**5.** Which `version:` specification pins a Hub package to exactly one release?

A. `version: "1.1.1"` B. `version: ">=1.1.1"`
C. `version: "latest"` D. `version:` omitted

**6.** What does `package-lock.yml` record?

A. The resolved versions of every package plus a SHA1 hash of `packages.yml`
B. The SHA1 hash of `dbt_project.yml`
C. The most recent `dbt deps` run's timestamp
D. The list of adapters each package supports

**7.** A project pins `version: [">=1.0.0", "<2.0.0"]` for `dbt_utils` and has committed `package-lock.yml` with resolved version `1.1.1`. A developer runs `dbt deps` on a fresh clone. Which version is installed?
A. The latest `1.x.x` release available at the moment `dbt deps` runs
B. `1.0.0`, the floor of the range
C. `1.1.1`, because the lockfile's resolved version wins while `packages.yml` is unchanged
D. `dbt deps` errors because ranges require `--upgrade`

**8.** Which best describes `dbt deps`?
A. Loads seed CSVs and runs data tests against the warehouse
B. Uploads your project to the dbt Package Hub as a published package
C. Renders model SQL and writes the result to `target/compiled/`
D. Resolves `packages.yml`, downloads each package into `dbt_packages/`, writes `package-lock.yml`

**9.** An engineer pulls a branch that changed `packages.yml` by adding `dbt_expectations`, then runs `dbt build`. It fails before any model compiles, with `dbt found 2 package(s) specified in packages.yml, but only 1 package(s) installed in dbt_packages`. What is the fix?
A. Run `dbt clean` and retry
B. Delete `dbt_packages/` and retry
C. Run `dbt deps` to install the new package, then re-run `dbt build`
D. Re-install dbt via pip with the `dbt_expectations` extra

**10.** By default, where does `dbt deps` install package contents?
A. `target/packages/`, beside the compiled SQL B. `packages/`, beside `models/`
C. `dbt_packages/`, at the project root D. `~/.dbt/packages/`, shared across projects

**11.** A team moves every entry out of `packages.yml` and into `dependencies.yml` without changing a character. One entry reads `version: "{{ env_var('PKG_VER') }}"`, and `PKG_VER` is exported. What does `dbt deps` do on dbt 1.11?
A. Nothing changes — both files are rendered as Jinja before they are parsed
B. It fails: `dependencies.yml` renders no Jinja, so the literal braces reach the version parser
C. It ignores the file's `packages:` block, because `dependencies.yml` declares cross-project references
D. It succeeds once `PKG_VER` is also declared under `vars:` in `dbt_project.yml`

**12.** A developer has added a package to `packages.yml` and wants the CI job to regenerate `package-lock.yml` so the resolved versions can be reviewed in the pull request — without downloading anything into `dbt_packages/`. Which `dbt deps` flag does that?
A. `--upgrade` B. `--lock`
C. `--add-package` D. `--source`

**13.** To override a dispatched `dbt_utils` macro named `generate_surrogate_key` from your own project for all adapters, what should the fallback override macro be named?
A. `dbt_utils__generate_surrogate_key` B. `default__generate_surrogate_key`
C. `my_project__generate_surrogate_key` D. `dispatch__generate_surrogate_key`

**14.** A project declares a `dispatch:` block for the `dbt_utils` namespace. Which form keeps `adapter.dispatch('generate_surrogate_key', 'dbt_utils')` preferring your project's implementation when one exists?

A.

```
dispatch:
  - macro_namespace: dbt_utils
    search_order: [dbt_utils, my_project]
```

B.

```
dispatch:
  - macro_namespace: dbt_utils
    search_order: [my_project, dbt_utils]
```

C.

```
dispatch:
  - package: dbt_utils
    override: my_project
```

D.

```
dispatch-config:
  - dbt_utils: my_project
```

**15.** A team wants a single `dbt_utils` macro to hash with sha256 instead of md5 on one adapter. Which approach is idiomatic?
A. Fork `dbt_utils`, change the macro body, pin `packages.yml` at the fork
B. Add a `dispatch:` entry in `dbt_project.yml` and write an `<adapter>__<macro>` override under `macros/`
C. Edit `dbt_packages/dbt_utils/macros/sql/generate_surrogate_key.sql` in place
D. Copy the macro into `macros/` with the same name as the package's version

**16.** A team has pinned `dbt_utils` with `version: ">=1.0.0"` in `packages.yml`, has not committed `package-lock.yml`, and has had a stable CI for months. On Monday, CI suddenly fails with `'dbt_utils.star' takes no keyword argument 'except'`. Local developers on existing clones still succeed. What is the most likely root cause, and what is the cleanest fix?
A. CI upgraded dbt-core itself and the macro's signature moved with it; pin the dbt version in the CI image and rerun the job
B. `dbt_utils` published a release the range accepts and CI's fresh-clone `dbt deps` resolved to it; commit `package-lock.yml` so CI and local install the same version
C. The branch has diverged from `main` and CI is building stale model code; rebase the branch on `main` and rerun the job
D. CI's cached `dbt_packages/` went stale between runs; delete the cache directory and let `dbt deps` reinstall from scratch

**17.** A developer adds `packages_install_path: vendor` to `dbt_project.yml` to move the install directory. `dbt deps` exits 2 with `Additional properties are not allowed ('packages_install_path' was unexpected)` and installs nothing. What is wrong?
A. Top-level keys in `dbt_project.yml` take dashes; the key is `packages-install-path:`
B. `packages_install_path` belongs in `profiles.yml`, not in `dbt_project.yml`
C. `vendor/` must already exist; `dbt deps` writes into it but does not create it
D. The key must sit under a top-level `packages:` block rather than at the root

**18.** An installed package's own `dbt_project.yml` sets `+schema: audit` for its models, and you need those models built into `pkg_audit` instead, in a way that survives the next `dbt deps`. The package declares `name: shared_utils`; your own project declares `name: my_project`. What do you change?
A. Add `models: shared_utils: +schema: pkg_audit` to your own `dbt_project.yml`
B. Add `models: my_project: +schema: pkg_audit` to your own `dbt_project.yml`
C. Edit `dbt_packages/shared_utils/dbt_project.yml` and re-run `dbt deps`
D. Add a `dispatch:` entry for the `shared_utils` namespace with `my_project` first in `search_order`

**19.** A package named `shared_utils` ships `models/orders.sql` and a second model whose SQL is `select * from {{ ref('orders') }}`. Your own project also has a `models/orders.sql`, and your `dbt_project.yml` gives the package a custom schema so the two relations do not collide. On dbt 1.11 with no behaviour flags set, which model does the package's `ref('orders')` resolve to?
A. The package's own `orders` — a `ref()` written inside a package is scoped to that package
B. Your project's `orders`, provided `require_ref_searches_node_package_before_root` is set to `true`
C. Neither — dbt raises a compilation error naming both candidates and refuses to parse
D. Your project's `orders` — a one-argument `ref()` searches the root project before the package

**20.** An installed package ships a `table` materialization of its own, and your `dbt_project.yml` declares a `dispatch:` entry for the `dbt` namespace with that package first in `search_order`. On dbt 1.11 with no behaviour flags set, you run a model configured `materialized: table`. Which implementation executes?
A. The package's — `search_order` names it ahead of `dbt`, and materializations resolve through the dispatch chain like any other macro
B. The package's — `require_explicit_package_overrides_for_builtin_materializations` is `false` at 1.11
C. Neither — dbt raises an ambiguous-materialization error and refuses to run the model
D. dbt's built-in — a package materialization matching a name dbt Core ships is excluded from resolution

**21.** Your project and an installed package each define a model named `orders`. The package is installed from `https://github.com/our-org/dbt-shared-utils.git`, and its `dbt_project.yml` declares `name: shared_utils`. From a model in your own project, which call resolves to the *package's* `orders`?
A. `{{ ref('shared_utils', 'orders') }}` B. `{{ ref('orders', 'shared_utils') }}`
C. `{{ ref('dbt-shared-utils', 'orders') }}` D. `{{ ref('orders', package='shared_utils') }}`

**22.** dbt deps installs an unmaintained package whose own dbt_project.yml still declares config-version: 1. The root project declares config-version: 2, and the package ships models. What happens next?
A. dbt deps and dbt debug both succeed; every command that parses the project then fails at exit 2, with a message naming neither the package nor a file
B. Every command fails at project load, dbt debug included, with an error naming the offending package
C. Only the package's models are skipped; the rest of the project builds, with one warning per run
D. Nothing — config-version is read only from the root project

**23.** A team is migrating a legacy Airflow pipeline into a new dbt model and needs to prove that the new model produces the same rows as the old output table. Which package provides the most direct macro for this check?
A. dbt_expectations B. codegen
C. dbt_utils D. audit_helper

**24.** Which scenario best justifies forking a dbt package rather than overriding a macro via dispatch?
A. One macro should log a debug line but otherwise behave exactly as it does today
B. One hashing macro should use sha256 instead of md5 on the adapter you run on
C. One macro should emit varchar rather than string for your warehouse's dialect
D. The maintainer has not answered an issue in months and a dozen macros lack your adapter

## Answer key

**1. D.** Hub entries use package: "<org>/<name>" with a mandatory version:. git: is the real rival and installs straight from a repository, skipping the Hub entirely. hub: and source: are not packages.yml keys at all: on dbt 1.11.14 each one makes dbt deps fail schema validation with "The packages.yml file in this project is malformed" before anything is downloaded. Source: /docs/build/packages.

**2. C.** The Git shape uses git: for the URL and revision: for the branch, tag, or commit SHA. package: with a URL (A) is the Hub shape misapplied — it parses, then fails with "Package https://github.com/dbt-labs/dbt-utils.git was not found in the package index", because package: takes a Hub identifier and not a URL. tag: (B) is the item's real discrimination: there is no tag: key, revision: covers tags, branches and SHAs uniformly, and a tag: entry is rejected by the packages.yml validator. hub: (D) is likewise not a key. All three failures reproduced on dbt 1.11.14. Source: /docs/build/packages.

**3. C.** local: installs a package from a directory on disk, specified as a path relative to the project root. This is the monorepo shape — one dbt project in the repo depends on another. dbt deps symlinks (or copies, on platforms that cannot symlink) the target under dbt_packages/. No HTTP server, no Hub, no git involved. Source: /docs/build/packages.

**4. C.** private: names the repository as <org>/<repo> and takes its credentials from the git-provider integration, so nothing secret is written into packages.yml. It is a current shape at 1.11, not a future one: a bare private: entry with an optional revision: passes schema validation and is carried to resolution. What it needs there is the integration itself — on dbt Core alone, with no git provider configured, resolution stops with *Cannot resolve private package ... because git provider integration is missing*, so private: is the platform's shape and git: is what installs without one. package: (A) resolves a Hub identifier and cannot reach a private repository at all. git: (B) is the strongest distractor: it does reach a private repository, but it authenticates through the remote you supply — an SSH URL, or a token you have to keep out of the file some other way — which is the older pattern private: exists to replace. `tarball:` (D) fetches a pre-built archive over HTTP and does no git authentication. Source: `/docs/build/packages`.

**5. A.** A plain version string pins to the exact release: on dbt 1.11.14, `version: "1.1.1"` reports `Installed from version 1.1.1` and writes `1.1.1` into the lockfile. A comparator like `>=1.1.1` (B) defines a resolvable window and takes the newest match — the same file resolved to `1.4.1` — so it pins nothing. `"latest"` (C) is not a version at all: dbt raises `SemverError: "latest" is not a valid semantic version`. An omitted `version:` (D) does not parse for a Hub entry; package validation raises on the missing key. Source: `/docs/build/packages`.

**6. A.** `package-lock.yml` captures the concrete versions (including commit SHAs for Git entries) that `dbt deps` installed, together with a `sha1_hash` of `packages.yml` so dbt can detect whether the declaration has changed since the last resolution. Both halves are visible in a real lockfile on dbt 1.11.14, and nothing else is: no run timestamp (C) and no adapter compatibility list (D), which is Hub metadata rather than lockfile content. B is the precise near-miss — the hash is of `packages.yml`, the file that declares the dependencies, not of `dbt_project.yml`. The two-part content is what makes `dbt deps` reproducible. Source: `/reference/commands/deps`.

**7. C.** When `package-lock.yml` is present and its hash matches the current `packages.yml`, `dbt deps` installs the exact versions recorded in the lockfile — even when `packages.yml` uses a range that could resolve to a newer release. Run on dbt 1.11.14 with exactly this setup, `dbt deps` prints `Installed from version 1.1.1` and then, as a note rather than an action, `Updated version available: 1.4.1`. A describes what happens only when the lockfile is absent or its hash no longer matches. B confuses a floor with a resolution — nothing ever installs the bottom of a range. D invents an error: ranges resolve fine without `--upgrade`, which is the opt-in for moving off the recorded resolution. This is why the lockfile belongs in source control: it locks the resolution across developers and CI. Source: `/reference/commands/deps`.

**8. D.** `dbt deps` is a local-only operation: it reads `packages.yml`, consults `package-lock.yml`, resolves versions, downloads each package, and places the results under `dbt_packages/`. It makes no warehouse calls — pointed at an unreachable host on dbt 1.11.14, `dbt deps` still exits 0 while `dbt debug` on the same profile reports a failed connection test. A is `dbt seed` plus `dbt test`, both of which do need the warehouse; C is `dbt compile`; B describes a publishing step dbt has no command for — Hub listings come from a repository registration, not from the CLI. Source: `/reference/commands/deps`.

**9. C.** Changing `packages.yml` requires a `dbt deps` run to download the new package into `dbt_packages/`. dbt counts the declared packages against the installed ones before it compiles anything, so the error arrives as a project-level Compilation Error naming the shortfall and the remedy — the message on dbt 1.11.14 ends "Run "dbt deps" to install package dependencies". `dbt clean` (A) installs nothing — it removes build output, and because the `dbt init` starter lists `dbt_packages` beside `target` in `clean-targets`, on most projects it takes out the one package that *was* there; the retry then fails naming a wider gap, `only 0 package(s) installed`. Deleting `dbt_packages/` (B) treats the symptom as a stale install rather than a missing one, and removes the package that is present. `dbt_expectations` is a dbt package installed by `dbt deps`, not a pip extra (D). §8.4 names the neighbouring symptom: once the counts agree, an unresolved package name gives the per-model `'dbt_expectations' is undefined`, which points at a typo rather than a missing install. Source: `/reference/commands/deps`.

**10. C.** The default install path is `dbt_packages/` at the project root — a sibling of `models/` and `macros/`, not a child of `target/`. A confuses it with build output, which `dbt clean` deletes and `dbt deps` does not write to. B is the directory name minus its `dbt_` prefix, and is the shape you get only by setting `packages-install-path: packages`. D imagines a machine-wide package cache; dbt keeps nothing shared under `~/.dbt/` but your `profiles.yml`. The path is configurable via `packages-install-path:` in `dbt_project.yml` but is almost never changed in practice; the directory is git-ignored, since its contents are reproducible from `packages.yml` plus `package-lock.yml`. Source: `/reference/project-configs/packages-install-path`.

**11. B.** `packages.yml` is rendered as Jinja before it is parsed; `dependencies.yml` is not. Executed on dbt 1.11.14 with `PKG_VER=1.3.0`, the identical entry in `packages.yml` reports `Installed from version 1.3.0` and exits 0, while in `dependencies.yml` it exits 2 with `dbt_common.exceptions.base.SemverError: "{{ env_var('PKG_VER') }}" is not a valid semantic version.` — the braces reached the version parser unrendered. A asserts the equivalence that run refutes. C is the plausible reading of what `dependencies.yml` is *for* — it is the file dbt Mesh cross-project refs need — but the `packages:` block was read, which is how the parse got as far as a semver error. D invents a declaration requirement: `env_var()` reads the process environment and needs no `vars:` entry, and no entry can help a file that renders nothing. The rule to carry: a version or a token fed from the environment forces `packages.yml`. Source: `/docs/build/packages`.

**12. B.** `--lock` is the resolve-but-do-not-install flag: because `packages.yml` has changed, its hash no longer matches the lockfile, so dbt re-resolves every entry and rewrites `package-lock.yml` — and on dbt 1.11.14 it creates no `dbt_packages/` directory at all. That is exactly a reviewable lockfile diff with no download. `--upgrade` (A) also rewrites the lockfile, but it re-resolves *past* a matching lockfile and installs what it finds, so it both moves pins the developer did not ask to move and downloads. `--add-package` (C) is for adding an entry from the command line, in `name@version` form; here the entry is already in the file, and it installs too. `--source` (D) only tells `--add-package` whether to look at the Hub, a git remote, or a local path; on its own it changes nothing. Sources: `/reference/commands/deps`, `/docs/build/packages`.

**13. B.** Dispatch macro names use adapter prefixes, not project-name prefixes. For an all-adapter fallback, the override is `default__generate_surrogate_key`; for one adapter, it would be something like `databricks__generate_surrogate_key`. The project name appears in `dispatch.search_order`, which tells dbt which namespace to search first. The project-name prefix (option C, `my_project__generate_surrogate_key`) is never used in dispatch macro names — it would be silently ignored by `adapter.dispatch`. Source: `/reference/dbt-jinja-functions/dispatch`, `/reference/project-configs/dispatch-config`.

**14. B.** The `search_order` list is consulted in order; putting `my_project` first means dispatch checks your project's macros before falling through to `dbt_utils`. Option A is not a cosmetic reversal — executed on dbt 1.11.14, the same `default__` override that fires under B compiles away to nothing under A, because the package's own implementation is found first. Declaring the block backwards is worse than declaring none at all, since the root project is searched ahead of a package namespace by default. Options C and D use keys (`package:`, `override:`, `dispatch-config:` at the top level) that are not the documented schema — the top-level key is `dispatch:` and the entry keys are `macro_namespace:` and `search_order:`. Source: `/reference/project-configs/dispatch-config`.

**15. B.** Dispatch override is the documented extension point for swapping one macro's implementation without forking the package. For one adapter, write that adapter's implementation (`databricks__generate_surrogate_key`, `snowflake__generate_surrogate_key`, etc.) and put your project first in the package namespace's `search_order`. Forking (A) is overkill for a one-macro change. Editing `dbt_packages/` (C) does compile — and the next `dbt deps` restores the file, so the fix survives until the first person reinstalls dependencies. A same-named bare macro in your own `macros/` (D) fails more quietly still: on dbt 1.11.14 it raises no collision error and simply never reaches a `dbt_utils.`-qualified call site, which keeps compiling the package's own implementation. Source: `/reference/dbt-jinja-functions/dispatch`.

**16. B.** The symptom trio — CI suddenly failing, local still succeeding, a keyword-argument error inside a packaged macro — is the textbook signature of a range pin silently absorbing a new release. CI typically runs `dbt deps` on a fresh clone with no `dbt_packages/`, so it re-resolves the range every time; local developers, by contrast, still have last week's `dbt_utils` on disk and have not re-run `dbt deps`. The fix locks the resolution, not the range: commit `package-lock.yml`, and CI, local and production all install the exact same version. Rolling the range back only delays the next move, and tightening it to `[">=1.0.0", "<2.0.0"]` — which excludes the breaking major — is defence in depth on top of the lockfile, not a substitute for it. A is the closest rival and fails on the evidence: a dbt-core bump would change the error's shape rather than a package macro's keyword arguments, and pinning dbt does not stop the range from moving. C explains neither the error string nor the local/CI split — stale model code does not change a packaged macro's signature. D reads the split backwards: the stale copies are the ones that still *work*, and clearing the cache re-triggers exactly the range resolution that broke the job. Sources: `/docs/build/packages`, `/reference/commands/deps`.

**17. A.** `dbt_project.yml`'s own top-level keys are dash-spelled and schema-validated (Ch 6 §6.4; the `+`-prefixed resource configs are the one exception, and this key is not one of them), so the accepted spelling is `packages-install-path:`; its default value is `dbt_packages`. Executed on dbt 1.11.14, the dashed key installs into `vendor/` and exits 0, creating the directory itself; the underscored key first warns `[WARNING][CustomTopLevelKeyDeprecation]: ... Unexpected top-level key packages_install_path` and then raises the runtime error quoted in the stem, exit 2, with nothing installed. B moves a project key into the connection file; `profiles.yml` carries credentials and targets and holds no path configs. C inverts what the run shows — the dashed key created the directory on its own. D confuses the two files: `packages:` is the list key inside `packages.yml`, while `packages-install-path:` is a top-level key of `dbt_project.yml`. Source: `/reference/project-configs/packages-install-path`.

**18. A.** An installed package is configured from your own `dbt_project.yml`, with the config keyed under the package's declared name. Run this setup on dbt 1.11.14 and the package's models land in `<target_schema>_pkg_audit`; the `+schema: audit` in the package's own file has no effect, because where both files set the same key for the same resource, yours is the one that reaches the manifest. B keys the config under your project's name, which is the selector for *your* models — the package is untouched and its schema stays `audit`. C works until somebody else runs the project: `dbt_packages/` is build output, git-ignored, rewritten by the next `dbt deps`, and deleted by `dbt clean` on any project carrying the starter `clean-targets`. D reaches for the wrong mechanism entirely — `dispatch` resolves macro implementations, and no `search_order` has ever set a schema. Sources: `/docs/build/packages`, `/reference/define-configs`.

**19. D.** A one-argument `ref()` written inside a package model is resolved against the root project first and the model's own package second, so the package's `ref('orders')` returns *your* `orders`. Executed on dbt 1.11.14, the package model compiles against your project's relation and dbt emits a parse-time warning that the package node "depends on the root project node" — a warning, not an error, so the build proceeds with a package model reading a table its author never saw. A is the intuition the package's author was writing under, and it is exactly what the default takes away. B inverts the flag: `require_ref_searches_node_package_before_root` is `false` at 1.11, so it is not something you switch on to get your model — switching it on is what gets you the *package's*. C reads a duplicate name as fatal; the error dbt raises for two models named `orders` fires only when both resolve to the same relation, which the custom schema in the stem prevents. Q21 is the remedy. Source: `/reference/global-configs/behavior-flags/require_ref_searches_node_package_before_root`.

**20. D.** Materialization resolution ranks candidates by origin — dbt Core, your root project, an installed package — and at 1.11 it discards the package's whenever Core ships one of that name, so the built-in `table` runs. Executed on dbt 1.11.14 with a package `table` materialization whose body raises on sight, the run completes normally and the raise never fires; adding the package to the `dbt` namespace's `search_order` changes nothing, which is A's error: `search_order` governs macro dispatch and materializations never consult it. B inverts the flag — `require_explicit_package_overrides_for_builtin_materializations` is `true` at 1.11, and it is setting it `false` that lets the package's implementation run, with a deprecation warning naming the package. C imagines an ambiguity error; the exclusion is silent, which is why the rule is worth knowing. The way to reach the package's implementation is to declare the materialization in your own `macros/`, where it outranks Core's. Source: `/reference/global-configs/behavior-flags/require_explicit_package_overrides_for_builtin_materializations`.

**21. A.** The two-argument `ref()` takes the package first and the model second, and the package argument is the `name:` declared in the package's `dbt_project.yml` — which is why C fails: the repository is `dbt-shared-utils`, the package is `shared_utils`, and on dbt 1.11.14 the repository spelling raises `depends on a node named 'orders' in package or project 'dbt-shared-utils' which was not found`. B has the arguments the wrong way round and fails the same way, having read `orders` as the package name. D is the quietest of the three: `ref()` reads only `v` and `version` as keyword arguments, so `package=` is discarded, the call degrades to its one-argument form, and — by Q19's rule — you get the root project's `orders` back with no error at all. Source: `/reference/dbt-jinja-functions/ref`.

**22. A.** `config-version: 2` is required in the `dbt_project.yml` of **every installed package**, not only the root project — but the failure is narrower and much quieter than "nothing works". `dbt deps` installs the package and exits 0. `dbt debug` runs its connection test and prints `All checks passed!`, because it never parses the project's nodes. Everything that does parse — `parse`, `ls`, `compile`, `run`, `seed`, `build` — stops with `Internal Error / Got an unexpected project version=1, expected 2` and exit 2. The message names no package and no file, which is what makes B tempting and wrong: there is nothing in the error to point you at the culprit, and the two commands you would reach for to find it are the two that pass. C and D invert the scope — the check is not scoped to the package's own nodes, and it is not limited to the root project. Mechanically it is per node: `initial_config` takes `min(node's project config_version, root config_version)` and raises unless the result is 2, which is also why a package shipping only macros parses cleanly — it contributes no node to take the minimum over. Revisit **Ch 8 §8.4**. Cognitive level: analyze.

**23. D.** `audit_helper.compare_relations` is the standard "are these two relations row-for-row equal" macro: it reports rows present in A but not B, rows present in B but not A, and rows whose non-key columns differ — an itemised diff you read, which is what proving parity needs. `dbt_expectations` (A) asserts on a single column's values, not on two relations. `codegen` (B) generates scaffolding text. `dbt_utils` (C) is the nearest miss: its `equality` generic test compares two relations, but as a pass/fail assertion rather than a report of which rows differ. Note the spelling — in YAML the test is `dbt_utils.equality`; `test_equality` is the internal dispatch target, not the name you write. Sources: `/docs/build/packages` and the `audit_helper` Hub listing.

**24. D.** Fork is the right answer when a dispatch override cannot reach — typically when the maintainer has gone quiet and multiple macros need adapter-specific additions, or when a breaking-change fix is not being accepted upstream. Scenario A is a single-macro behavioural tweak that dispatch handles cleanly (write an adapter-specific or `default__` override that wraps the original with an extra `log()` call). Scenarios B and C are also textbook dispatch-override cases: one macro, one implementation, no upstream cooperation required. The discriminator is *how many macros* and *whether you need the maintainer* — not how badly you want the change. Sources: `/reference/dbt-jinja-functions/dispatch`, `/docs/build/packages`.

# Chapter 9

# Documentation and lineage

> **Scope.** dbt's documentation site is the one deliverable data consumers — analysts, product managers, decision-scientists — actually open. The warehouse tables your models produce are for machines; the docs site is for humans. This chapter covers the two commands that produce it (`dbt docs generate` and `dbt docs serve`), where descriptions live in YAML, how `persist_docs` pushes those descriptions down into warehouse `COMMENT` metadata so SQL tools pick them up, how to read the generated graph, and — at the greatest depth, because it is where the exam looks hardest — exposures: the YAML declarations that promote dashboards, notebooks and ML jobs into first-class nodes at the downstream edge of your DAG. Documentation is no longer a domain of its own on this exam. Writing it is still the difference between a project a new analyst can use and one they have to reverse-engineer, so the material stays here, weighted the way the exam weights it.

**Prerequisites.** Ch 2 (YAML project structure and the DAG primitive). Ch 3 (source YAML — §9.2 extends its `description:` pattern to model columns). Ch 6 §6.6 (`{% docs %}` blocks and `{{ doc() }}`; §9.3 here points back at it rather than teaching it twice). Ch 11 §11.5 and §11.7 (selector methods and graph operators — §9.5.5 leans on both).

**Cheat-sheet pointer.** This chapter's recall lines sit under front-of-book cheat sheet §2 (Topic 01 — Developing and optimizing models), and exposures under §7 (Topic 06 — external dependencies). Between them they are this chapter in four lines: `dbt docs generate` writes `catalog.json` + `manifest.json` to `target/` and `dbt docs serve` renders the site over them; descriptions go under `description:` in YAML; `persist_docs: {relation: true, columns: true}` pushes descriptions into warehouse `COMMENT`; an exposure carries `name`, `type` and `owner`, and `+exposure:<name>` selects everything upstream of it. Use the cheat sheet for last-day recall; use this chapter for the reasoning, especially around exposures.

---

## 9.1 `dbt docs generate` and `dbt docs serve`

Two commands produce the dbt documentation site. `dbt docs generate` builds the artifacts; `dbt docs serve` renders them. They are documented together on a single page — `/reference/commands/cmd-docs` — because neither is useful without the other. `docs` is one of the commands the blueprint names by hand, alongside `build`, `run`, `test`, `show`, `snapshot` and `seed`, so read this section as command material.

### `dbt docs generate` — what it emits

`dbt docs generate` writes the docs site's two JSON inputs to the `target/` directory:

- `manifest.json` — the graph of your project. Every resource (model, source, seed, snapshot, test, exposure, macro, metric, semantic model) appears as a node, with its configs, its `description`, its `ref()`/`source()` dependencies, its column list, and its compiled SQL. `manifest.json` is produced by almost every dbt command that parses the project; `dbt docs generate` re-emits it with the docs pipeline's particular needs in mind. See `/reference/artifacts/manifest-json`.
- `catalog.json` — warehouse metadata for your project's tables and views. For each relation, catalog.json lists every column's name and data type, plus table-level statistics the adapter knows how to surface (row count, bytes, last-modified, clustering-key metadata on Snowflake, and so on). Unlike `manifest.json`, which is built from YAML and SQL parsing, `catalog.json` is built from live warehouse introspection: dbt queries the warehouse's information schema (or the adapter's equivalent) to populate it. See `/reference/artifacts/catalog-json`.

Together, the two files are the docs site's entire payload. The web app you see when you open the site is a static bundle of HTML and JavaScript that reads `manifest.json` and `catalog.json` at load time and renders them as the DAG, the model pages, the column tables, and the lineage graph.

### `dbt docs generate` needs warehouse access

This trips people up. `dbt run`, `dbt build`, and `dbt test` obviously need warehouse credentials — they execute SQL. `dbt parse` does not — it only reads project files. `dbt docs generate`, despite sounding like "it just renders YAML I already wrote," needs warehouse access too — because `catalog.json` is built by querying the warehouse. On a CI runner with no warehouse connectivity, `dbt docs generate` will fail at the catalog-introspection step.

Three flags on the page are worth knowing by name, and only one of them avoids the warehouse:

| Flag | Warehouse | What changes on disk | Reach for it when |
|---|---|---|---|
| `--no-compile` | still introspected — the run logs `Building catalog` | writes `catalog.json`; drops the compile step, and with it the `manifest.json` rewrite, which is compile-gated | you want a fresh catalog over an already-compiled project — never to produce a site without a warehouse |
| `--empty-catalog` | skipped | writes a structurally valid `catalog.json` with zero nodes and zero sources | the CI runner has no database credentials and the site's lineage matters more than its column types |
| `--static` | unchanged | adds `target/static_index.html`, with the manifest and catalog embedded in the page | that one file is the whole site — hand it over email or drop it on a share rather than host three files |

Run `dbt docs generate --help` against your installed version for the full list; flags move faster than the reference page does. For a local run, or a CI job that has warehouse credentials anyway (most do), run `dbt docs generate` plain.

### `dbt docs serve` — the local web server

`dbt docs serve` starts a local web server on `http://localhost:8080` (change it with `--port`) over the files in `target/` (`--target-path` reads them from somewhere else). It is a static-file server and nothing more: it drops dbt's packaged `index.html` into the target directory, then serves whatever is sitting there. No warehouse connection, no parse, no regeneration — delete `catalog.json` and `serve` will hand the browser a 404 for it rather than rebuild it. Rendering happens in the browser, which loads the two JSONs from the server.

Hold that boundary, because the reference page will push you the other way: `/reference/commands/cmd-docs` renders forward-looking content in places — it gives the default port as 8580, and it reads as though `serve` will refresh a stale site for you. The installed 1.11 CLI does neither. Where a page and the parser disagree, believe the parser — it is what your exam environment runs.

The common use is local development: run `dbt docs generate` once, then `dbt docs serve`, then navigate the project in the browser. For every subsequent change, re-run `dbt docs generate` and refresh; the serve command can keep running.

### Hosting the docs site in production

`dbt docs serve` is for local use only. In production, the two artifact files and the static web bundle are hosted somewhere everyone in the org can reach — typically an S3 bucket with a static-website front end, or the dbt platform's hosted docs surface, or a GitHub Pages deployment, or whatever static-hosting primitive your platform offers. The CI job that runs `dbt docs generate` uploads all three — `target/index.html`, `target/manifest.json` and `target/catalog.json` — to that host as its last step; users open the host's URL in their browser and see the latest docs.

The docs site does not need to sit behind your warehouse's auth perimeter for the same reason your repository does not: `manifest.json` and `catalog.json` carry your schema shape, your compiled SQL and your descriptions — not query results. Treat them like source code, and host them where the team can reach them. Do not upgrade that into a guarantee that they hold nothing sensitive, because what ends up in them is a property of your project rather than of dbt: a compiled `where` clause can embed a real identifier, a description can quote a real record, and column names and comments can themselves be the confidential part. Scope access to what your own artifacts actually contain.

### A common trap — stale docs

Because `manifest.json` and `catalog.json` are static, a hosted docs site is only as fresh as the last `dbt docs generate` run: rename a column and the site keeps showing the old name until someone regenerates. The fix is to make `dbt docs generate` part of the production deployment pipeline — every successful main-branch build re-generates and re-uploads the artifacts — so docs freshness matches deployment cadence.

---

## 9.2 Descriptions in YAML

Descriptions are the text content of the docs site. Every resource type — model, seed, snapshot, source, source table, column, macro, exposure — takes a `description:` key in its YAML properties block, and whatever you write there renders on that resource's page. See `/reference/resource-properties/description`, and `/reference/exposure-properties` for exposures.

A model description sits directly under the model's `name:`, at the same indentation as `columns:` and `data_tests:`, and describes the whole table. A column description sits under its own column entry, at the same indentation as `data_tests:`, and describes just that column:

```
# models/marts/core/_core__models.yml
version: 2

models:
  - name: fct_lending_offer_clicks
    description: "Click-level grain of lending-offer impressions across all markets. One
      row per offer card viewed by a signed-in user."
    columns:
      - name: event_id
        description: "Surrogate key, sha256 over (user_id, offer_id, client_event_ts)."
        data_tests:
          - unique
          - not_null
      - name: user_id
        description: "Credora member ID. FK to dim_users.user_id."
      - name: client_event_ts
        description: "Timestamp from the client-side event beacon. UTC. May lag server-
    side ingestion by up to 10 minutes."
```

Sources take descriptions at three levels, documented at `/reference/source-properties`: the source (the logical grouping), each table within the source, and each column of each table. The shape mirrors models — `description:` next to `name:` at whichever level you are describing. Populating all three levels is the ideal; populating only the source level is the minimum that does not look abandoned.

Every description is a YAML string, so multi-line content uses YAML's block scalars. `|` (literal) preserves newlines as written; `>` (folded) collapses them into spaces, which is what you want when the YAML wraps but the docs should show one paragraph. The site renders Markdown inside either — headings, lists, bold and italic, inline code, and links all work:

```
models:
  - name: fct_user_session_facts
    description: |
      Session-grain facts about authenticated users.

      **Grain.** One row per (user_id, session_id). A session starts at
      the first authenticated event and ends after a 30-minute idle gap
      or a logout, whichever comes first.

      **Known gaps:**
      - Sessions that cross the midnight UTC boundary are split into two
        rows (upstream partitioning limitation).
      - Mobile-app sessions lacking a server-side confirmation are
        excluded.
```

Neither block scalar is a dbt invention; both are ordinary YAML.

---

## 9.3 Doc blocks and `{{ doc() }}` — the DRY tool for long descriptions

Long or repeated description text does not have to live inline in YAML. Chapter 6 §6.6 covers the mechanic in full: define the text once inside a `.md` file under `models/` — or any path listed in `docs-paths:` — as `{% docs block_name %} … {% enddocs %}`, then pull it into any description with `{{ doc('block_name') }}`. The `description:` value is a Jinja expression, so the surrounding string is quoted:

```
models:
  - name: dim_users
    columns:
      - name: email
        description: '{{ doc("pii_column_email") }}'
      - name: alternate_email
        description: 'Recovery address. {{ doc("pii_column_email") }}'
```

Duplication is what justifies the indirection. The same 200-word compliance paragraph on twelve PII columns is twelve diffs to audit when the retention policy changes from 90 days to 180, and one diff when it is a doc block. For a single-sentence description on one column, stay inline. Block names live in a namespace of their own, and the case where two of them claim the same name is back in §6.6. See `/docs/build/documentation` and `/reference/dbt-jinja-functions/doc`.

---

## 9.4 `persist_docs` — pushing descriptions into the warehouse

The docs site is one audience for descriptions. The warehouse is another. Analysts working in SQL tools that surface object metadata — Snowsight, Databricks' Unity Catalog UI, the BigQuery console, Superset, DataGrip — see a `COMMENT` field on each relation and column, and by default it is empty: the warehouse knows the shape of your table but has no idea what `client_event_ts` means. `persist_docs` fills it. See `/reference/resource-configs/persist_docs`.

```
# dbt_project.yml
models:
  +persist_docs:
    relation: true
    columns: true
```

Two sub-keys, each settable on its own:

| Sub-key | Applies | Via |
|---|---|---|
| `relation: true` | the model's `description:` | `COMMENT ON TABLE` / `COMMENT ON VIEW` |
| `columns: true` | each column's `description:` | `COMMENT ON COLUMN` |

Set `persist_docs` at any of the usual config layers — globally or per path in `dbt_project.yml`, in a model's YAML `config:` block, or in an in-model `{{ config() }}` call. The reference page lists support on Postgres, Redshift, Snowflake, BigQuery, Databricks and Apache Spark, plus Starburst Galaxy through `dbt-trino`. Two adapter caveats: on Snowflake a mixed-case column name needs the `quote` config or uniform casing before its comment persists; on Databricks column comments need a `file_format` of `delta`.

That adapter list is not a formality. `persist_docs` reaches the warehouse through two dispatched macros — `alter_relation_comment` and `alter_column_comment` — and the `default__` implementation of each raises rather than doing nothing, with `alter_column_comment macro not implemented for adapter <name>`. An adapter that has not written its own pair fails at the first described relation rather than skipping it quietly. `COMMENT` being widespread SQL is beside the point; what the config needs is an adapter that implements the two macros.

The cost is DDL, and it is per column: one `COMMENT` statement per relation and one per described column, emitted after the main `CREATE` or `MERGE`, each a round-trip to the warehouse on every run. It scales with how many columns you have described, not with how much data you moved. Scope it rather than abandon it — leave `persist_docs` off across staging and intermediate, whose column comments nobody reads, and turn it on under `marts:`, where analysts do. Where even that is too expensive on a very wide table, `relation: true, columns: false` keeps the table description and drops the per-column sweep.

You will meet this config again in Ch 12: `state:modified.persisted_descriptions` (§12.2) is the state sub-selector that fires when a description that gets persisted has changed. `persist_docs` is what makes a description **comparable at all**. With it off, an edited `description:` matches neither that sub-selector nor the omnibus `state:modified`, so a docs-only PR selects nothing on a CI gate built on either — and with it on, the same edit matches both.

---

## 9.5 Exposures — documenting what consumes your models

### 9.5.1 What an exposure is, and which way it points

An exposure is a YAML declaration that something outside dbt — a dashboard, a notebook, an analysis, an ML job, an application — depends on named resources inside your project. Declaring one puts a node on the DAG at the downstream edge of the graph and gives you a selector that reaches the tree feeding it. Per `/docs/build/exposures`, that buys two things: you can run, test and list the resources that feed the exposure, and the exposure gets a page of its own in the generated docs site.

Hold the direction firmly, because it is the confusion an exam item reaches for first. A **source** is an upstream input dbt reads and does not build. An **exposure** is a downstream consumer dbt neither reads nor builds. Sources sit at the left edge of the graph, exposures at the right, and both are declared in YAML rather than in SQL — which is exactly what makes them easy to swap in an option list. Neither one executes anything: there is no `dbt run --exposure`, and selecting an exposure in order to build it is a category error.

Three payoffs, in the order teams usually discover them:

1. **The docs site shows downstream lineage.** Without exposures the DAG ends at your leaf models, and analysts cannot tell which models power which dashboards. With them the graph extends into BI, notebooks and ML, and the site answers "if I change this model, what breaks?"
2. **The selector enables targeted CI.** "Run every test upstream of the finance dashboard" becomes one flag on every PR that touches a finance-adjacent model. The declaration turns into an operational gate.
3. **Ownership is captured alongside the lineage.** When a model breaks and the on-call engineer needs to know who cares, the exposure's `owner:` block is the answer.

### 9.5.2 The shape

Exposures are declared under an `exposures:` key in a properties YAML file — conventionally somewhere under `models/`, alongside model and source properties. See `/docs/build/exposures` and `/reference/exposure-properties`.

```
# models/exposures/_exposures.yml
```

```
version: 2

exposures:
  - name: weekly_revenue_dashboard
    label: "Weekly Revenue (Exec)"
    type: dashboard
    maturity: high
    url: https://looker.credora.internal/dashboards/42
    description: "Weekly executive revenue dashboard. Refreshed Monday 06:00 UTC."
    depends_on:
      - ref('fct_orders')
      - ref('dim_customers')
      - source('raw_billing', 'invoice')
    owner:
      name: Finance Analytics
      email: finance-analytics@credora.internal
    config:
      tags: [finance, executive]
      meta:
        slack_channel: "#alerts-finance"
```

### 9.5.3 Required, expected, and optional properties

`/reference/exposure-properties` annotates its example with **three** requirement levels, not the usual two, and the middle one is easy to miss:

- **Required** — `name` and `type`. `name` is matched against `[\w-]+$`: letters, digits, underscores and hyphens, capitals included. Anything outside that — a space, a dot — is an `ExposureNameDeprecation` warning and the parse still succeeds, so snake_case is a convention here, not a rule. Uniqueness is among *exposures* only: an exposure may share a model's name without error, while two exposures sharing a name is a hard `Compilation Error`. It is the handle `+exposure:weekly_revenue_dashboard` reaches for.
- **Expected** — `depends_on`, and nothing else. "Expected" is dbt's own third category, and it is not enforcement: delete `depends_on` and the project still parses, with no error and no warning. What you lose is the point of the exposure. Without it the node renders as an orphan — visible, but attached to nothing, and out of reach of every selector that walks the graph.
- **Optional** — `url`, `description`, `maturity`, `label` and the `config:` block. `owner` is marked nothing at all. The page also prints `enabled: true | false` at this level, and that one is not a property at all: a top-level `enabled:` stops the parse with `at path []: Additional properties are not allowed ('enabled' was unexpected)`. It is a config, and it belongs under `config:` (§9.5.4).

That silence is the trap. Remove the `owner:` block and dbt Core 1.11 refuses to parse the project, failing with `'owner' is a required property` — the parser over the page again (§9.1). Treat `owner` as required, and note that it is enforced twice: the block must be there, and it must carry `name`, `email` or both. An `owner:` present but supplying neither fails separately, with `Exposure owner must have at least one of 'name' or 'email'`. Those two are the only sub-fields that satisfy the rule — any extra key parses silently and rides into `manifest.json` without counting. Read Required / Expected / Optional as three tiers of *intent* that line up only partly with enforcement.

The rest of the field list is short:

| Property | Required | Values | What it does |
|---|---|---|---|
| `type` | yes | `dashboard`, `notebook`, `analysis`, `ml`, `application` | classifies what the consumer *is*; it rides into `manifest.json` and drives nothing on the generated site. `ml` covers a training or inference job that consumes features; `application` is the catch-all for services reading dbt-produced tables — a pricing engine, a recommender, a feature-store consumer |
| `maturity` | no | `high`, `medium`, `low` | signals how much of the organisation leans on this consumer; teams prioritise on it and decide what CI gates on |
| `url` | no | a URL | renders as a link on the exposure's page, to the live dashboard, notebook or service |
| `description` | no | free text | Markdown, rendered like any other description |
| `label` | no | free text | the human-friendly display name the site shows, with spaces and capitals; `name` stays the identifier |

`type` and `maturity` are the pair to keep straight: two short enums hanging off the same exposure, which is exactly what a matching item swaps.

`depends_on` takes a list of `ref()`, `source()` and `metric()` calls — the same expressions you write in model SQL, quoted here as YAML strings. Any dbt-built node is fair game, seeds included: the reference schema shows `ref('seed')` beside `ref('model')`. The list is the only shape accepted — a dict keyed by resource type is rejected outright, `at path ['depends_on']: ... is not of type 'array'`. Bare names are the dangerous shape, because they are not rejected: `depends_on: [fct_orders, dim_customers]` parses clean, with no error and no warning, and the strings render to nothing. The exposure lands in the manifest with `refs: []`, `sources: []` and no edges, so `+exposure:<name>` walks back from it to nothing — the same orphan a missing `depends_on:` gives you, arrived at without a word of complaint. A `metric()` entry implies the Semantic Layer, which the exam leaves out of scope; recognise the call in an option list without feeling obliged to learn MetricFlow behind it.

One gap is worth naming so you do not read too much into it. The `ref()` reference documents a version argument — `ref('model_name', version=2)`, with `v=2` as the shorthand (`/reference/dbt-jinja-functions/ref`) — and the exposure properties page documents `depends_on`. No page shows the two together; the parser resolves it anyway. A versioned entry **pins the edge**: `depends_on: [ref('dim_users', v=1)]` attaches to the `dim_users.v1` node alone, so `+exposure:<name>` walks v1's tree and leaves v2's unguarded. A bare `ref('dim_users')` attaches to `latest_version`, which is not necessarily the highest `v:` declared — a group holding `v: 1`, `v: 2` and `v: 3` under `latest_version: 2` is three-way: v2 latest, v1 old, and v3 **prerelease**, a real buildable node that no unversioned reference reaches. See `/reference/resource-properties/latest_version`.

### 9.5.4 Where exposure configuration lives

An exposure has exactly three configs — `enabled`, `tags` and `meta` — and all three can be set in either of two places: inside the exposure's own `config:` block, or in an `exposures:` block in `dbt_project.yml` keyed by project and path, the same shape the `models:` block uses.

```
# dbt_project.yml
exposures:
  credora:
    +meta:
      review_cadence: quarterly
    +tags: [declared]
```

That reaches every exposure in the project that does not set the key itself. `+enabled: false` at that level drops every exposure out of the manifest at once, which is how you park a set of declarations without deleting them.

`/reference/exposure-properties` says none of that is possible. It opens by calling exposure properties "special properties" that cannot be configured in `dbt_project.yml`, then carves out `enabled` as the one project-level exception. Parse the block above and `+meta` and `+tags` land exactly as `+enabled` does — there was never an exception to carve, because those three keys are the whole config surface an exposure has. This is §9.5.3's discrepancy again, pointing the other way: there the page understates what the parser demands, here it understates what the parser accepts. Do not let the page talk you out of the behaviour your project actually gets.

Two things do not follow from that. There is no in-model `config()` route, because an exposure has no SQL file to put one in. And `depends_on:` is not a config — it is a property, it lives in the exposure's own YAML, and there is no project-level equivalent.

Inside the exposure, `tags` and `meta` belong under a `config:` block, as §9.5.2 shows:

```
    config:
      tags: [finance, executive]
      meta:
        slack_channel: "#alerts-finance"
      enabled: true
```

The top-level `tags:` and `meta:` you will find on exposures in older repositories are the earlier shape. They still parse at 1.11 on every adapter, and dbt hoists the values into `config` for you. Whether you are *told* is adapter-gated: dbt runs its JSON-schema property validation on Snowflake, Databricks, BigQuery and Redshift only, so on those four the top-level form raises `PropertyMovedToConfigDeprecation` and on Postgres it is silent. Do not read that silence as approval — the `config:` form is what to write and what to expect in a stem. Either way the values behave normally: `--select tag:finance` picks the exposure up, and `meta` rides into `manifest.json` for tooling to read (§9.7).

One failure mode is worth knowing because it is loud rather than silent. If depends_on: names a model that something has disabled, parsing stops:

```
Compilation Error
  Exposure 'exposure.credora.lending_risk_model_training' (models/exposures/
    _ml_exposures.yml)
  depends on a node named 'features_user_behaviour_90d' which is disabled
```

An exposure is a real edge in the graph, so a dangling one is a build-breaking error, not a cosmetic gap.

### 9.5.5 Selecting from an exposure

exposure:weekly_revenue_dashboard, bare, selects the exposure node and nothing else. That is legal and, under run or build, useless: an exposure has nothing to materialise. The method exists to be combined with the + prefix, which /reference/node-selection/methods states outright — use it in conjunction with the + operator:

```
dbt build --select "+exposure:weekly_revenue_dashboard"
```

The + prefix means "this node and everything upstream of it", so the command builds every model, seed and snapshot that feeds the dashboard, tests them on the way, and stops. A source upstream of the dashboard is selected too — + walks all the way back to it — but dbt build has no runner for one: it neither builds a source nor checks its freshness. Nothing unrelated runs. Chapter 11 covers the grammar in full; two consequences are exposure-specific:

- **A trailing + buys nothing.** exposure:name+ asks for descendants, and an exposure is a leaf — it has none — so it resolves to the same lone node the bare form does. The + has to go on the left.
- **Wildcards work.** dbt test --select "+exposure:*" tests everything upstream of every exposure in the project, and dbt ls --select "+exposure:*" --resource-type source lists the source tables any declared consumer ultimately depends on. Both are documented examples on the methods page.

This is the operational justification for declaring exposures at all. Pre-release CI recipes run dbt test --select "+exposure:<critical_exposure>" on every PR, so a change that breaks a dashboard's upstream tree is caught before it reaches main — and the list of models being guarded is the depends_on: block in source control, not a hand-maintained array in a CI script.

---

## 9.6 Reading the DAG

The docs site's centrepiece is the interactive lineage graph — the auto-generated DAG at the top of the site.

### What it shows

Every parsed node in your project renders as a bubble on the graph:

- **Sources** — styled apart from models to signal "raw input."
- **Seeds** — reference CSVs loaded via dbt seed.
- **Models** — staging, intermediate, marts; the bulk of the graph.
- **Snapshots** — SCD2 tables from dbt snapshot.

- **Exposures** — leaf nodes at the downstream edge, once declared (§9.5).

Edges are the `ref()` and `source()` dependencies dbt inferred from your SQL, plus the `depends_on:` edges you declared on exposures. The layout is produced automatically — left to right, upstream to downstream, sources on the left and exposures on the right.

### Navigating a node

Click a node and the docs site drills into its page:

- **Description** — the model's `description:` and any `{{ doc() }}` content.
- **Columns** — the column table, each with its name, data type (from `catalog.json`), and `description:`.
- **Depends on** — the list of upstream `ref()` / `source()` references.
- **Referenced by** — the inverse: the downstream models, exposures, and tests that depend on this node.
- **Tests** — every test attached to the node, with their configs.
- **SQL** — the raw SQL from the `.sql` file.
- **Compiled** — the compiled SQL, with `{{ ref() }}` and `{{ var() }}` expanded. Matches what `target/compiled/<path>.sql` contains.

An exposure's page is that anatomy minus the SQL: its `depends_on:` entries render as the depends-on list, and its `maturity` and `owner` render as details a consumer can act on, beside the exposure's own name. `type` is the one property that does not appear: it classifies the consumer in the YAML and in `manifest.json`, and the generated site never reads it. Note the naming, because the current docs will hand it to you unannounced — dbt's own browsing surface is now called **Catalog**, and `/docs/explore/explore-projects` is where the exposure detail page and its Healthy / Caution / Degraded health signal are documented. Catalog is a dbt platform product and sits outside the exam's scope; what you are examined on is the graph the generated site renders, where the load-bearing fact is that an exposure is a first-class node in it rather than an annotation hanging off one.

Filter controls at the top of the graph let you narrow by tag, resource type, path, or selector expression. Typing `+fct_orders` filters the graph to `fct_orders` and everything upstream — the same mental model as the CLI's `--select`.

### A common trap — a node disappears from the graph

If a model you expect to see is missing from the DAG, work down this list:

1. **The model is `enabled: false`.** It is parsed into the manifest's `disabled` collection rather than `nodes` — out of the graph and absent from the docs.
2. **The file is under a path not listed in `model-paths:`.** Add a sibling directory to `models/` without adding it to `model-paths:` in `dbt_project.yml` and dbt never sees it.
3. **The file is matched by `.dbtignore`.** A path listed there never enters the manifest.
4. **`dbt docs generate` last ran before the model was added.** Docs freshness lags the last generate run (§9.1).

The first three are also reasons the model would not appear in `dbt run` or `dbt build` — they are parse-scope problems, and Ch 10 is where you diagnose them. The fourth is specific to the docs surface, and it is the most common by a wide margin.

## 9.7 `meta:` — free-form metadata, and where it does not reach

The `meta:` dict is dbt's mechanism for stashing arbitrary metadata on a resource. See `/reference/resource-configs/meta`. dbt does not interpret the keys; it parses them, stores them on the node, writes them into `manifest.json`, and renders them on the resource's page in the docs site. Everything useful downstream — alert routers, access-control systems, governance dashboards, internal catalogues — is tooling somebody wrote to read the manifest.

```
models:
  - name: fct_lending_offer_clicks
    description: "..."
    meta:
      owner: "@analytics-engineering"
      layer: gold
      pii: false
      slack_channel: "#alerts-analytics-engineering"
```

The keys are whatever the team agrees on. `owner` is the most common — a team handle or an email, driving alert routing and review assignment. `layer` carries a medallion or staging/intermediate/mart taxonomy, `pii` a boolean governance tooling scans for, `sla` a freshness target in hours, `cost_centre` a warehouse chargeback key. None of these are dbt semantics.

For models, the scalable pattern is a folder-level default in `dbt_project.yml`:

```
# dbt_project.yml
models:
  my_project:
    marts:
      core:
        +meta:
          owner: "@analytics-engineering"
          layer: gold
```

Every model under `models/marts/core/` inherits both keys with no per-model YAML, and an individual model overrides a key in its own `config:` block or `{{ config() }}` call.

The pattern generalises further than the `models:` block. `exposures:` takes the same shape (§9.5.4) — the difference is only that an exposure's own copy belongs under `config:` rather than at top level.

Where `meta:` stops is at the edge of dbt's own artifacts. It lands in `manifest.json` and on the docs site, and that is all. It is not in `catalog.json`, whose per-node payload is `columns`, `metadata`, `stats` and `unique_id` and nothing else, because the catalog is warehouse-introspected and the warehouse has never heard of your `meta` keys. It is not in the warehouse's `COMMENT` fields either: those carry `description:` text, and only when `persist_docs` is on (§9.4). Anything you want acted on outside dbt has to be read out of the manifest by tooling somebody wrote.

One more edge, and it is the one CI trips over. `state:modified` and `state:modified.configs` both select on a **model-level `meta`** edit, and neither moves for a column-level `meta`, a column-level `tags` or a **model-level `tags`** edit. Model-level `meta` is the one cell of that grid that fires — Ch 12 §12.2 sets that result inside the wider matrix of what `state:modified` does and does not compare.

---

## 9.8 In practice: Credora's docs pipeline

> *This section is an "in practice" sidebar. It draws a composite pattern from (a) the* `persist_docs` *reference at* `/reference/resource-configs/persist_docs` *and (b) the exposures reference at* `/docs/build/exposures`*. Credora is fictional (*`credora`*); Ch 14's opening note has the composite-project disclaimer.*

In our fictional `credora` project, documentation is part of the deployment pipeline, not a weekly chore. Descriptions exist on every column a human will ever touch. `persist_docs: {relation: true, columns: true}` is set once at the top of the `models:` block in `dbt_project.yml`, because Databricks' Unity Catalog reads `COMMENT` fields off Delta tables and that is the surface SQL-only users discover tables through — the DDL overhead (§9.4) is real on column-heavy marts and has been accepted as the price of one descriptions surface instead of two. Ownership is a folder-level `+meta: {owner: ...}` under each mart directory (§9.7), scraped nightly out of `manifest.json` by an internal catalogue that routes a failed test on a `marts/core/` model to the `@analytics-engineering` on-call and a failure under `staging/` to `@data-platform-engineering`.

The part worth walking through is the exposures.

## Two ML-type exposures for downstream training

Two ML jobs consume features tables produced by `credora`:

```
# models/exposures/_ml_exposures.yml
version: 2

exposures:
  - name: lending_risk_model_training
    type: ml
    maturity: high
    description: |
      Weekly retraining job for the lending-risk scoring model.
      Consumes feature tables from the `marts/core/features/` tree.
      Retraining gates the Monday morning scoring batch.
    depends_on:
      - ref('features_user_behaviour_90d')
      - ref('features_credit_history_rollup')
      - ref('dim_users')
    owner:
      name: ML Platform
      email: ml-platform@credora.internal
    url: https://mlflow.credora.internal/experiments/lending_risk
    config:
      tags: [ml, weekly]

  - name: offer_recommender_training
    type: ml
    maturity: medium
    description: |
      Daily retraining of the offer-recommendation model.
    depends_on:
      - ref('features_offer_interaction_30d')
      - ref('dim_offers_global')
    owner:
      name: ML Platform
      email: ml-platform@credora.internal
    url: https://mlflow.credora.internal/experiments/offer_recommender
```

```
  config:
    tags: [ml, daily]
```

The docs site now renders both jobs as leaf nodes on the DAG, off the right edge of the `features_*` subtree. A reader browsing `features_user_behaviour_90d` can see — from the "Referenced by" section of that node's page — that the lending-risk training job consumes it. The lineage, previously opaque, is now navigable.

### Exposure-driven pre-release CI

The operational payoff lives in the CI pipeline. Before promoting a feature-engineering change to main, Credora's CI runs:

```
dbt build --select "+exposure:lending_risk_model_training,state:modified+" --defer --
    state ./prior-artifacts
```

The `+exposure:lending_risk_model_training` selector walks upstream from the exposure and reaches every model, seed and source that feeds the lending-risk training job; the comma intersects that with `state:modified+`, so the run covers only what is both upstream of the ML job and changed since the last promoted manifest. `--defer --state` (which Ch 12 covers in depth) resolves the rest against the promoted relations rather than rebuilding them. The effect is that every PR touching a feature-adjacent model is validated against the ML job's exact upstream dependency set — if a test fails, the job is blocked before it reaches the ML pipeline.

Without the exposures, the team would hand-maintain a list of upstream feature tables in a CI script, and that list would drift. With them, the `depends_on:` list on the exposure is the list, it is in source control, and the `+exposure:` selector reads it directly.

### Why this arrangement works

`persist_docs` pushes descriptions into Unity Catalog (§9.4). Folder-level `meta:` captures ownership without per-model YAML (§9.7). Exposures close the DAG's downstream edge and enable targeted CI (§9.5). That is the general shape of docs at production scale: a handful of dbt primitives, each small, arranged so the documentation surface maintains itself as the project evolves.

---

## Summary

- **`dbt docs generate`** emits `manifest.json` (the project graph) and `catalog.json` (warehouse-introspected column and table metadata) to `target/`; `--static` adds a single self-contained `static_index.html`, `--empty-catalog` skips warehouse introspection entirely, and `--no-compile` drops the compile step but still builds the catalog. **`dbt docs serve`** is a static-file server on port 8080 that regenerates nothing.
- **`dbt docs generate` needs warehouse access** because `catalog.json` is built from information-schema queries. Production docs live on a static host (S3, the dbt platform, Pages) that the CI pipeline re-uploads on every main-branch build, so docs freshness tracks deployment cadence.
- **Descriptions live under `description:`** in YAML, at the source / source-table / source-column / model / model-column / seed / snapshot / exposure level. Markdown renders; multi-line strings use YAML's `|` (literal) or `>` (folded) block scalars. Repeated text goes into a `{% docs %}` block and comes back through `{{ doc('block_name') }}` (Ch 6 §6.6).

- `persist_docs: {relation: true, columns: true}` writes relation and column descriptions into the warehouse's `COMMENT` metadata, at the cost of one `COMMENT` statement per relation and per described column on every run. Scope it to marts on large projects. It is also what makes a description **comparable** to `state:modified` at all — you meet it again as `state:modified.persisted_descriptions` in Ch 12.
- **Exposures** (`exposures:` in a properties YAML file) declare downstream consumers — dashboards, notebooks, analyses, ML jobs, applications — and render as leaf nodes at the right edge of the DAG. Sources are upstream inputs; exposures are downstream consumers; neither executes anything.
- **The property tiers are Required (`name`, `type`), Expected (`depends_on`) and Optional (everything else)** — but dbt refuses to parse an exposure with no `owner`, so treat `owner` as required despite the page marking it nothing at all. `type` is the required enum (`dashboard`, `notebook`, `analysis`, `ml`, `application`); `maturity` is the optional one (`high`, `medium`, `low`).
- **`depends_on:` takes `ref()`, `source()` and `metric()` calls**, seeds included; bare names parse but create no edge, leaving the exposure an orphan. A `v=` argument pins the edge to that version; without one the edge lands on `latest_version`, which need not be the highest `v:` declared. An exposure's three configs — `enabled`, `tags`, `meta` — sit under its `config:` block, and an `exposures:` block in `dbt_project.yml` sets all three project-wide.
- **`+exposure:<name>` selects the exposure and its whole upstream tree** — the `+` has to be on the left, because an exposure is a leaf and a trailing `+` selects nothing extra. Bare `exposure:<name>` is legal and useless under `run`/`build`; `+exposure:*` covers every declared consumer at once.
- **Read the DAG** by clicking nodes for their description, columns, depends-on, referenced-by, tests, raw SQL and compiled SQL. A missing node usually means `enabled: false`, a path outside `model-paths:`, a `.dbtignore` match, or stale docs.
- **`meta:` is free-form metadata** that ends up in `manifest.json` and on the docs site — never in `catalog.json` and never as a warehouse `COMMENT`. Folder-level `+meta:` under `models:` in `dbt_project.yml` is the scalable pattern; exposures need their own `exposures:` block, because the `models:` block never reaches them. `state:modified` compares it at model level only — a column-level `meta` edit is invisible, and so is a `tags` edit at either level.

## Learning-goal checklist (self-assess)

- ☐ I can run `dbt docs generate` and `dbt docs serve`, I know `generate` needs warehouse credentials because `catalog.json` comes from information-schema queries, and I can say what `--static`, `--empty-catalog` and `--no-compile` each drop or add — including that only `--empty-catalog` avoids the warehouse.
- ☐ I can write `description:` strings at the source, source-table, source-column, model, and model-column levels, use YAML block scalars for multi-line content, and reach for a `{% docs %}` block when the same text repeats.
- ☐ I can explain what `persist_docs` writes into the warehouse, what it costs per run, how to scope it so the cost lands only where analysts read the metadata, and what an adapter that has not implemented the comment macros does with it.
- ☐ I can say which end of the DAG an exposure attaches to, how that differs from a source, and why `dbt build` materialises nothing for one.
- ☐ I can write an exposure from scratch, sort its properties into Required, Expected and Optional, and say why `owner` behaves as required though the reference page marks it nothing at all.
- ☐ I can tell `type` from `maturity`, list both enums, and give the shape of `depends_on:`.

- ☐ I can put `tags` and `meta` in the right place on an exposure, name the three configs an exposure has, set all three from `dbt_project.yml` as well as from the exposure's own `config:` block despite what the reference page says, and predict what dbt does with a top-level `tags:` written in the older shape.
- ☐ I can select an exposure's upstream tree with `+exposure:<name>`, explain why the bare and trailing-`+` forms do not do it, and use `+exposure:*` across the project.
- ☐ I can read the auto-generated DAG — identify node types, navigate a node's depends-on and referenced-by lists, and diagnose why a model might be missing from the graph.
- ☐ I can say what `persist_docs` changes about state selection, which `meta:` edits `state:modified` compares and which it ignores, and which node an exposure's `depends_on:` entry attaches to when the model it names is versioned.

---

## Practice questions

Fifteen questions, all on stretches the 1.11 blueprint scores directly: the `dbt docs` command (Qs 1–4), exposures (Qs 5–12, 14), and the two places this chapter's material is scored under Topic 07 — `persist_docs` as the gate on `state:modified.persisted_descriptions` (Q13) and `meta:` under state comparison (Q15). Documentation is no longer an exam domain, so descriptions and doc blocks are taught above and drilled in the chapters the blueprint scores them under.

**1.** Which two JSON artifacts produced by `dbt docs generate` are the inputs that the dbt docs site renders?

A. `manifest.json` and `run_results.json` B. `catalog.json` and `sources.json`
C. `manifest.json` and `catalog.json` D. `dag.json` and `descriptions.json`

**2.** You delete `target/catalog.json` and then run `dbt docs serve`. What happens?

A. `catalog.json` is rebuilt from the warehouse before the server starts
B. The site is served from the manifest alone, with column types read live from the warehouse
C. `dbt docs serve` refuses to start and reports the missing artifact as an error
D. The server starts and the browser gets a 404 for `catalog.json`; nothing regenerates it

**3.** Why does `dbt docs generate` require warehouse credentials?

A. It materialises the project's models and snapshots as part of the generate step
B. It compiles every SQL file and sends the result to the warehouse for validation
C. It introspects the warehouse's information schema to populate `catalog.json` with column types and table statistics
D. It persists descriptions into warehouse `COMMENT` metadata as part of generation

**4.** A team wants the dbt docs site available to every analyst in the company, refreshed on every main-branch deployment. Which is the recommended production approach?

A. Add `dbt docs generate` to the main-branch CI job and upload the generated site to a shared static host
B. Install dbt on each analyst's machine and run `dbt docs serve` there as a startup service
C. Commit the `target/` directory to the repository and have each analyst clone and open it locally
D. Run `dbt docs generate --live`, which pushes the rendered site to the configured host automatically

**5.** An exposure's YAML is missing one property and `dbt parse` fails with `'owner' is a required property`. Which set of three does dbt Core 1.11 actually refuse to parse without?
A. `name, type, depends_on` B. `type, owner, maturity`
C. `name, owner, url` D. `name, type, owner`

**6.** Which list matches the valid values for an exposure's `type:` field?
A. `table, view, incremental, ephemeral`
B. `source, model, seed, snapshot`
C. `dashboard, notebook, analysis, ml, application`
D. `bronze, silver, gold`

**7.** Which values does an exposure's `maturity:` field accept?
A. `stable, unstable, deprecated` B. `green, yellow, red`
C. `high, medium, low` D. `production, staging, development`

**8.** What does the selector `+exposure:weekly_revenue_dashboard` select?
A. Only the exposure node itself
B. The exposure and every downstream node
C. The exposure and every upstream model, seed, snapshot, and source it depends on
D. Every exposure in the project whose name begins with `weekly_revenue`

**9.** Which is the correct shape for an exposure's `depends_on:` list?
A. A list of `ref()`, `source()`, and/or `metric()` Jinja expressions: `depends_on: [ref('fct_orders'), ref('dim_customers'), source('raw_billing', 'invoice')]`
B. A list of bare model and source names, unquoted: `depends_on: [fct_orders, dim_customers, raw_billing.invoice]`
C. A single comma-separated string that dbt splits on parse: `depends_on: "fct_orders,dim_customers,raw_billing.invoice"`
D. A dict keyed by resource type: `depends_on: {models: [fct_orders, dim_customers], sources: [raw_billing.invoice]}`

**10.** A team declares an exposure for their finance dashboard. Where does that node sit relative to the models the exposure names, and what does `dbt build` do with it?
A. Upstream of them, and dbt reads the dashboard's data the way it reads a source
B. Downstream of them, and dbt builds nothing for it — it materialises no relation
C. Downstream of them, and `dbt build` refreshes the dashboard through the exposure's `url:`
D. Beside them, outside the graph, because an exposure is documentation rather than a node

**11.** A project adds an `exposures:` block to `dbt_project.yml` setting `+meta`, `+tags` and `+enabled: true`, and no exposure sets any of the three in its own YAML. What reaches the manifest?
A. Every exposure carries all three — those three are an exposure's whole config surface
B. Nothing — the parse fails, because `exposures:` is not a block `dbt_project.yml` accepts
C. Every exposure carries `enabled`; the `meta` and `tags` keys are dropped with no warning
D. Every exposure carries `meta` and `tags`; `enabled` must be set on the exposure itself

**12.** An exposure declares `tags: [finance]` at its own top level rather than inside its `config:` block. Parsed on Postgres the project is silent; parsed on Snowflake the identical YAML raises `PropertyMovedToConfigDeprecation`. What is true at dbt Core 1.11?
A. Snowflake is reporting a failure — on the four adapters that validate properties against dbt's JSON schema the top-level form is rejected
B. Both parse, but only Snowflake applies the tag; on Postgres a top-level `tags:` is inert and `tag:finance` selects nothing
C. Both parse and apply the tag, and the top-level form warns on every adapter — the Postgres run simply omitted `--show-all-deprecations`
D. Both parse and apply the tag; only the diagnostic differs — dbt runs that JSON-schema validation on Snowflake, Databricks, BigQuery and Redshift only

**13.** A project has never set `persist_docs`. A PR edits one model's `description:` in YAML and changes nothing else. One CI job runs `dbt build --select "state:modified" --state ./prior-artifacts`; a second runs the same build with `state:modified.persisted_descriptions`. What do the two select?
A. Both select the model — a `description:` edit is a YAML change and `state:modified` compares the YAML
B. Neither selects anything — with `persist_docs` unset there is no persisted description to compare, and the omnibus does not compare descriptions either
C. The sub-selector selects it and the omnibus does not — `state:modified.persisted_descriptions` compares descriptions whether or not they are persisted
D. The omnibus selects it and the sub-selector does not — `state:modified` compares YAML properties wholesale, while the sub-selector needs `persist_docs`

**14.** Same version group — `v: 1`, `v: 2`, `v: 3`, `latest_version: 2`. A second exposure declares `depends_on: [ref('dim_offers_global')]` with no version argument. Which node carries that edge, and what is `v: 3`?
A. `.v3` — it is the latest, because the highest declared version wins and `latest_version` merely sets a deprecation floor
B. `.v2` — `v: 3` is a prerelease: a real, buildable node no unversioned `ref()` resolves to
C. `.v2` — `v: 3` is old, because any version other than `latest_version` is superseded
D. `.v1`, `.v2` and `.v3` — an unversioned `ref()` in `depends_on:` fans out across the whole group

**15.** A PR touches one properties file and no SQL. It adds `meta: {pii: true}` to a **column** entry under `dim_users`, and `meta: {owner: '@analytics'}` to `fct_lending_offer_clicks`'s **model-level** `config:` block. What does `dbt ls --select "state:modified" --state ./prior-artifacts` return?
A. Both models — a `meta` edit is a config change wherever it sits
B. `fct_lending_offer_clicks` only — `state:modified` compares model-level `meta` and does not compare column-level `meta` at all
C. `dim_users` only — column metadata is part of the compared column spec, while model-level `meta` is documentation
D. Neither — `meta` is metadata rather than configuration, so no `meta` edit ever reaches `state:modified`

## Answer key

**1. C.** The docs site renders from `manifest.json` (the graph of parsed resources, with descriptions and dependency edges) and `catalog.json` (warehouse-introspected column and table metadata). `dbt docs generate` also produces a normal invocation `run_results.json`, but that is not an input to the rendered docs site. `sources.json` is produced by `dbt source freshness`; `dag.json` and `descriptions.json` do not exist. You can watch the split directly:

delete `catalog.json`, start `dbt docs serve`, and the browser gets a 200 for `manifest.json` and a 404 for the file the site needs to render column types. Sources: `/reference/commands/cmd-docs`, `/reference/artifacts/run-results-json`; verified against dbt 1.11.14.

**2. D.** `dbt docs serve` copies dbt's packaged `index.html` into the target directory and serves that directory over HTTP on port 8080 by default (`--port` changes it). It opens no warehouse connection and runs no part of the generate pipeline, so a missing artifact stays missing: run with `catalog.json` deleted, the server starts normally, `index.html` and `manifest.json` return 200, and `catalog.json` returns 404. A and B both have `serve` reaching the warehouse, which it never does — A at start-up, B per request. C invents a pre-flight check; `serve` inspects nothing before binding the port. Rebuilding is `dbt docs generate`'s job, and it is the only half of the pair that needs credentials. Sources: `/reference/commands/cmd-docs`; verified against dbt 1.11.14.

**3. C.** `catalog.json` carries column data types and table statistics for every relation, and that data comes from live information-schema queries — the step the log announces as `Building catalog`. Point dbt at a warehouse it cannot reach and `dbt docs generate` fails there, exiting 1 with `Database Error` inside the catalog step; `manifest.json`, built from YAML and SQL parsing alone, would have been produced without complaint. A confuses generation with execution — no relation is created or refreshed. B describes a validation round-trip dbt does not perform; compilation is local string work. D names a real mechanism attached to the wrong command: `persist_docs` writes `COMMENT` DDL during `dbt run`, not during generation. If you want the catalog without the warehouse, that is `--empty-catalog`, and it gives you zero nodes. Sources: `/reference/commands/cmd-docs`; verified against dbt 1.11.14.

**4. A.** Generation belongs in the pipeline that already has warehouse credentials, and the output belongs on a host everyone can reach — S3 behind a static-website front end, the dbt platform's hosted surface, GitHub Pages, whatever your org already runs. Docs freshness then tracks deployment cadence for free. B puts a local development server in front of production readers and needs dbt, credentials and a checkout on every laptop. C ships a build artifact through source control; `target/` is conventionally `.gitignored` precisely because it is regenerated output. D is the fabrication: there is no `--live` on `dbt docs generate`, and no flag on it pushes anywhere — uploading is a pipeline step you write. Source: `/reference/commands/cmd-docs`.

**5. D.** Take each away in turn and parse. Drop `type` and dbt reports `'type' is a required property`; drop the `owner:` block and it reports `'owner' is a required property`; drop `name` and it fails earlier still, with `a list element for 'exposures' does not have a name attribute`. Those three, and only those three, stop the parse. Note the discrepancy this item is built on: `/reference/exposure-properties` marks `owner` nothing at all — neither required nor optional — and the parser enforces it. Where a page is silent and the parser is not, the parser is what your exam environment runs. A swaps `owner` for `depends_on`, which is the trap the page's third tier sets: `depends_on` is labelled **Expected**, and expected is not enforced — remove it and the project parses clean, leaving a useless orphan node but no error. B and C each drop one genuinely required property and substitute an optional one — `url` in C, `maturity` in B — so both fail on the substitution rather than on the count. Sources: `/reference/exposure-properties`; verified against dbt 1.11.14.

**6. C.** The exposure-properties page lists `dashboard`, `notebook`, `analysis`, `ml`, and `application` as the valid `type:` values. `ml` is the type for downstream ML jobs; `application` is the catch-all for services that consume dbt-produced tables. Option A lists materialisations; option B lists resource types (but not valid exposure types); option D lists a medallion-style layer convention. Source: `/reference/exposure-properties`.

**7. C.** The exposure-properties page documents `maturity:` as one of `high`, `medium`, `low` — a hint about how much of the organisation relies on the exposure. `maturity:` is optional and inert — no dbt Core behaviour keys on it. Teams prioritise on it and decide what CI gates on;

the docs site does nothing with it beyond printing it as one row of the exposure's detail table. None of A, B, or D are dbt-recognised values. Source: `/reference/exposure-properties`.

**8. C.** A leading `+` means "this node and everything upstream of it", and the walk is resource-type-agnostic: run against a real project it returns the exposure plus staging and mart models, the seed feeding one of them, and the source tables underneath. A describes the **bare** `exposure:<name>` form, which is legal and returns exactly one node — useless under `run` or `build`, since an exposure materialises nothing. B has the arrow backwards; an exposure is a leaf, and the trailing form `exposure:<name>+` returns the same lone node the bare form does. D reads the method as a prefix match on the name — `exposure:*` is the wildcard, and `+exposure:*` is how you cover every declared consumer at once. Sources: `/reference/node-selection/methods`; verified against dbt 1.11.14.

**9. A.** `depends_on:` is a YAML list whose entries are `ref()`, `source()` and `metric()` calls written as strings — the same expressions you write in model SQL. dbt renders each one, resolves it to a node, and draws the edge. B is the option to be careful with, because it does **not** raise an error: a list of bare names parses clean, and the damage is silent. The strings render to nothing, the exposure ends up with an empty `refs` and `sources` list, and `+exposure:<name>` walks back to nothing at all — a declaration that looks right in the file and is invisible in the graph. C fails on the list requirement and D fails on the type: a dict under `depends_on:` is rejected outright with `is not of type 'array'`. Sources: `/reference/exposure-properties`; verified against dbt 1.11.14.

**10. B.** An exposure attaches at the downstream edge of the graph: dbt draws an edge from every node in its `depends_on:` list to the exposure, and nothing flows back the other way. It also materialises nothing — there is no relation behind an exposure, so a `dbt build` that selects one runs no SQL for it. A has the direction inverted, which is the confusion the pair is built to catch: a **source** is the upstream input dbt reads and does not build, an exposure is the downstream consumer dbt neither reads nor builds (§9.5.1). C invents a refresh dbt has no mechanism for — `url:` is a link rendered on the exposure's page, and nothing dereferences it. D denies the node altogether: an exposure is a first-class node in the manifest and on the DAG, which is why a `depends_on:` naming a disabled model stops the run with `Compilation Error` instead of being ignored. Sources: `/docs/build/exposures`; verified against dbt 1.11.14.

**11. A.** An exposure's config surface is exactly three keys — `enabled`, `tags` and `meta` — so an `exposures:` block in `dbt_project.yml` reaches all of it, not a carve-out of it. Set the three at project level and every exposure that does not override a key inherits it. B and C are what `/reference/exposure-properties` tells you: B is its opening claim that exposure properties cannot be configured in `dbt_project.yml` at all, C its carve-out of `enabled` as the single exception. Neither survives a parse, and C is the sharper of the two because it is the version a careful reader carries away from the page. D inverts C without improving on it — `enabled` is no more special than the other two. Sources: `/reference/exposure-properties`; verified against dbt 1.11.14.

**12. D.** Top-level `tags:` and `meta:` are the earlier shape and dbt still accepts them on every adapter: the exposure parses, the values are hoisted into `config`, and the node carries them in both places in `manifest.json`. What the adapter decides is only whether you are told. `_can_run_validations()` in `dbt/jsonschemas` tests the invocation's adapters against `{bigquery, databricks, redshift, snowflake}` and skips the entire schema check otherwise, so those four raise `PropertyMovedToConfigDeprecation` and Postgres raises nothing. A reads a warning as a rejection — it is a `[WARNING]`, the parse exits 0, and the tag is applied. B invents a behavioural difference where there is none: on Postgres the tag still hoists and `dbt ls --select "tag:finance" --resource-type exposure` still returns the exposure. C is the assumption worth losing — a Postgres parse run *with* `--show-all-deprecations` prints nothing for this YAML while printing `PropertyMovedToConfigDeprecation` for a flat generic-test property in the same run. Read the silence as a gate that is closed, not as approval. Sources: `/reference/exposure-properties`; verified against dbt 1.11.14.

**13. B.** Executed on dbt-core 1.11.14 / dbt-postgres 1.11.0 against a baseline manifest of the same project. With the project's `+persist_docs` block removed, a one-line `description:` edit produced `The selection criterion 'state:modified.persisted_descriptions' does not match any enabled nodes` and `No nodes selected!` — and the omnibus `state:modified` said exactly the same. Put the block back, regenerate the baseline, make the identical edit, and both return the model. So `persist_docs` is not a precondition the sub-selector merely mentions; it is what makes a description **comparable** in the first place, and a docs-only PR on a project without it moves neither selector. A is the intuition that `state:modified` diffs the YAML file — it compares node contents, and an unpersisted description is not among them. C and D split the pair the wrong way in opposite directions: C makes the sub-selector independent of the config it is named for, D makes the omnibus wider than the sub-selector on this edit when the two in fact move together. §9.4; Ch 12 §12.2. Sources: `/reference/resource-configs/persist_docs`, `/reference/node-selection/methods`.

**14. B.** An unversioned `ref()` resolves to `latest_version`, which is a declaration, not an arithmetic maximum. Executed on dbt 1.11.14 with `v: 1`, `v: 2`, `v: 3` and `latest_version: 2`, the exposure's `depends_on.nodes` held the `.v2` node, and `+exposure:<name>` returned v2 and v2's upstream while v3 stayed out of the tree. All three parse as real nodes — `dbt ls` on the model name lists v1, v2 and v3 — so v3 is buildable and simply unreferenced: that is what **prerelease** names. A inverts the rule and is the arithmetic reading of a declarative key. C gets the node right and the label wrong, which is the whole discrimination: the state is three-way (old / latest / prerelease), not two-way, so a version above `latest_version` is not superseded by it. D fans the edge across the group, which no `ref()` does at any version. §9.5.3. Source: `/reference/resource-properties/latest_version`.

**15. B.** Executed on 1.11.14 against a baseline manifest of the same project: adding `meta:` to a **column** entry returned `The selection criterion 'state:modified' does not match any enabled nodes` / `No nodes selected!`, and `state:modified.configs` returned the same; adding `meta:` to a **model-level** `config:` block selected that model under both. Of the four edits in that grid — `meta` and `tags`, at model level and at column level — model-level `meta` is the only one that moves either selector. A generalises the model-level result one level down, which is the natural and wrong inference. C inverts the observation outright. D is what `/reference/node-selection/state-comparison-caveats` leads you to — it files `meta` as metadata that does not flag a node — and the runtime contradicts it at model level; where the page and the parser disagree, answer from the parser. §9.7; the rest of the matrix is Ch 12 §12.2. Source: `/reference/resource-configs/meta`.

# Chapter 10

# Debugging and error triage

> **Scope.** Debugging is the one domain where the exam and real life converge most directly. Every other chapter teaches you how to build the right thing; this chapter teaches you what to do when the thing you built does not work. The exam tests the triage loop: given an error message, which layer is the bug in — your YAML, dbt's compile stage, the SQL the warehouse rejected, or the connection? You will name that layer on sight, read the compiled SQL that settles it, recognise every member of the `ref()`, YAML and macro error families — including the one that raises nothing and compiles a hole into your SQL — read exit codes and log levels, and tell apart the four unrelated things dbt calls a flag. The chapter closes on the branch → fix → test → PR loop and a compile-as-CI-gate that catches contract drift before it merges.

**Prerequisites.** Ch 2 in full — the `ref()` / DAG / compile-vs-run mental model is load-bearing here, and almost every error in this chapter is ultimately a claim about the compile graph. Ch 4's incremental-config material informs §10.1's SQL-runtime bucket. Ch 6 §6.1–§6.4 (Jinja context, macros, dispatch) is essential for §10.5's macro-error family. Ch 7 re-appears in §10.8, where the test step is the verification point before a fix is merged. Ch 9's treatment of `manifest.json` is useful background for why a missing `ref()` target fails at parse time rather than run time.

**Cheat-sheet pointer.** Front-of-book cheat sheet §4 (Topic 3 — Debugging error families) reduces this chapter to four lines: YAML (tabs/indent/type/unknown property); compile (`ref()` missing / disabled / cyclic / typo); runtime SQL (cast / join key / NULL aggregation / window); and the triage path — run → failed? → logs → `target/compiled/<path>.sql` → warehouse query editor → fix → `dbt test`. Use the cheat sheet for last-day recall. Use this chapter for the reasoning, especially when the exam shows you an error message and expects you to pick the layer it belongs to.

---

## 10.1 The triage frame — YAML vs dbt vs SQL vs Connection

Every error dbt surfaces lives in exactly one of four layers. The fastest path from message to fix is to name the layer first, because each layer has a different toolkit.

- **YAML — parse-time failures.** dbt cannot even build its internal graph because a `.yml` file does not load. Causes: tabs instead of spaces, misaligned indentation, a key typo at the wrong nesting level, a value whose type does not match the config it is set on, or a property dbt does not recognise. The fix toolkit is a YAML linter and your editor's indentation guides. Nothing reaches SQL or the warehouse; dbt aborts before parsing your models.

- **dbt — compile-time failures.** dbt parsed your YAML successfully and is now resolving the graph: every `ref()` must point somewhere, every macro must be defined, every Jinja template must evaluate. If any of that fails, dbt raises a **Compilation Error** (for Jinja, macro and unresolvable-`ref()` problems) or a **Dependency Error** (for graph-validation failures, which at 1.11 means cycles and nothing else). The guide `/guides/debug-errors` names these two categories explicitly alongside Runtime and Database errors; Compilation and Dependency errors are both dbt-layer. Read *Dependency Error* as the guide's name for the category rather than a banner you will see on screen — an unresolvable `ref()` prints `Compilation Error`, and a cycle prints no category label at all.

- **SQL — runtime failures.** dbt has compiled your model into a valid SQL statement and sent it to the warehouse. The warehouse rejected it. Causes: a column cast the warehouse cannot perform, a join key that does not exist, a window function that references a column outside its PARTITION, NULL propagation that turns a predicate into a mystery, a numeric-overflow on a SUM, a datatype that the warehouse does not recognise. These are reported as **Database Errors** by dbt and their text is mostly the warehouse's own error text with a dbt wrapper.

- **Connection — environment failures.** dbt cannot reach the warehouse at all: bad credentials, expired token, missing `profiles.yml` entry, network/VPN issue, wrong target. Reported with the adapter's transport-level message attached ("could not connect", "auth failed", "timeout"). The fix toolkit is `dbt debug` (§10.6), `profiles.yml`, and the secret store. Connection errors rarely sit alongside model errors — if `dbt debug` reports a clean connection, you can rule the layer out and move on.

The triage question to ask on sight of any error is: *did dbt get far enough to produce a compiled SQL file?* If the error mentions YAML or "could not parse", you are in the YAML layer. If the error mentions a node name, a dependency, a macro, or Jinja, you are in the dbt layer. If the error contains warehouse-specific vocabulary (`ORA-`, Snowflake SQLSTATE codes, Databricks `AnalysisException`, BigQuery `Unrecognized name`), you are in the SQL layer. If the error mentions credentials, network, profile, or "could not connect", you are in the Connection layer. Once the layer is named, the right tool is obvious:

| Layer | Symptoms | First tool |
|---|---|---|
| YAML | Parse error; file path + line:column in the message; error before any model is selected | YAML linter; editor indent guides |
| dbt | Compilation / Dependency error; mentions a node name or Jinja context | `dbt compile --select <model>`, open `target/compiled/...` |
| SQL | Database error; quotes warehouse error text; mentions `CAST`, `JOIN`, column names | Open `target/compiled/<model>.sql`, paste into the warehouse query editor |
| Connection | Auth / network / profile / "could not connect" errors; no node-specific context | `dbt debug` (§10.6), `profiles.yml`, secret store |

The exam tests this directly: given a symptom, pick the layer. The practice bank opens with triage questions for exactly that reason.

### Why the frame matters

When a team debugs by pattern-matching on error text, they guess a lot. "The error said `column not found` — let me check my model's SELECT list" is a reasonable first guess but a bad second guess: the error could equally be a typo in a `ref()` that made dbt generate SQL pointing to a schema without the expected column, or a YAML config that disabled the upstream model and caused dbt to emit a stale identifier, or a warehouse-side schema change that invalidated the column. The four-layer frame forces you to answer *which layer emitted the message* before you touch anything. From there, the triage step in §10.2 either confirms the layer or reassigns it within a minute.

### A note on short-circuiting

When a run hits a model error on an upstream node — or, under `dbt build`, a test failure — every descendant is skipped rather than executed, and appears as `skipped` rather than `error`. This is useful to remember when triage looks at run results: if you see one `error` with many `skipped` below it, the root cause is the single `error`, not the skips. The `result:error+` selector (Ch 12) takes you directly to the upstream failure plus everything it blocked. `dbt build` documents this at `/reference/commands/build`.

### What the exit code tells the CI step

A CI step reads one number, and dbt gives it three. `/reference/exit-codes` sets them out; the artifact column below describes the commands that build nodes:

| Exit code | What it means | What is on disk afterwards |
|---|---|---|
| `0` | Success. Nothing errored; warnings may still have printed | `target/run_results.json`, with every node's final status |
| `1` | A **handled** error — dbt ran to completion and something inside the run failed | `target/run_results.json`, with the failing node's status recorded |
| `2` | An **unhandled** error — dbt did not complete, so there was no run to report on | Possibly nothing — a parse-stage exit `2` need not create `target/` at all |

The line between `1` and `2` is the one CI configuration gets wrong, and the misreading is a standing exam trap: *exit 1 means dbt crashed.* It does not. A model whose SQL the warehouse rejects exits `1` — the invocation finished, the other models built, the run artifact is there, and a state-aware retry (Ch 12) can read it. A typo'd `ref()` exits `2` — dbt never resolved the graph, no node ran, and a pipeline step that unconditionally uploads `run_results.json` fails on a missing file. Read `2` as "the project is broken" and `1` as "the project is fine and the data is not".

Those three numbers are not the only ones the `dbt run` reference carries. The same page lists a second set — queued `1`, starting `2`, running `3`, success `10`, error `20`, cancelled `30`, skipped `40` — and those are the statuses dbt Cloud's list-runs API reports for a whole run, not codes any process exits with. The overlap is what makes them confusable: `1` and `2` sit in both sets and mean nothing in common. Read `40` as a run status, never as an exit code; a run that skips eleven nodes still exits `1`. See `/reference/commands/run`.

### --fail-fast — ending the run at the first failure

--fail-fast (-x) is a global config, so §10.9.1's precedence chain applies in full — dbt run --fail-fast, DBT_ENGINE_FAIL_FAST=1 and fail_fast: true in the flags: block all produce the same run. dbt run --help puts it in five words — Stop execution on first failure. — and the exam asks about the mechanics behind them. The trigger is a node coming back error, fail or partial success, so a failing **test** under dbt build trips it as readily as a rejected model. dbt then terminates the thread pool, cancels every open adapter connection, and appends every node it has not already recorded — the in-flight ones included — to the results as **skipped**, with the message Skipping due to fail_fast.

Eight models on eight threads: one whose SQL the warehouse rejects, one model downstream of it, and six long-running siblings. That downstream model is the SKIP=1 in the first row.

| Invocation | Run summary | Elapsed | Exit code |
|---|---|---|---|
| dbt run --threads 8 | PASS=6 WARN=0 ERROR=1 SKIP=1 NO-OP=0 TOTAL=8 | 15.40s | 1 |
| dbt run --threads 8 --fail-fast | PASS=0 WARN=0 ERROR=1 SKIP=7 NO-OP=0 TOTAL=8 | 0.30s | 1 |

Three readings of that pair:

- **The exit code does not discriminate.** Both are 1. Only the run summary tells the two apart — the same trap skip_nodes_if_on_run_start_fails sets in §10.9.2.
- **CANCEL is a log line, not a node status.** Each terminated connection prints one — CANCEL query model.<project>.<model> .... [CANCEL] — but the node's recorded status is skipped. dbt's node statuses are success, error, fail, warn, skipped, partial success, pass, runtime error and no-op; there is no cancelled status, and the string cancel occurs zero times in the run_results.json that second run wrote. An option reporting the in-flight nodes as *cancelled* names something the artifact never holds.
- **It only ever ends a run earlier.** It cannot make a node build that would otherwise have been skipped; what it changes is how much of the graph is attempted after the first failure. That is why it is a CI policy choice (Ch 12 §12.4), not a correctness setting.

---

## 10.2 Inspecting compiled SQL — the highest-leverage triage step

The one habit that separates fast debuggers from slow ones is looking at the compiled SQL before guessing. dbt run produces a compiled SQL artifact for every model it attempts to execute, written to target/compiled/<project_name>/<path_to_model>/<model>.sql. That file is exactly what dbt sent to the warehouse, with every {{ ref() }}, {{ source() }}, {{ config() }}, and Jinja variable resolved to literal identifiers. Everything the warehouse saw is in that file, and nothing that the warehouse saw is anywhere else.

dbt compile — documented at /reference/commands/compile — regenerates these artifacts. Compile opens a warehouse connection to run introspective queries (populating the relation cache, resolving macros like run_query or dbt_utils.get_column_values), but it does **not** materialize anything; it is therefore much cheaper than dbt build. The usual invocation during triage is narrow:

```
dbt compile --select stg_orders
```

This writes target/compiled/<project>/models/staging/stg_orders.sql without re-compiling every other model. Open it, read the identifiers the ref() calls resolved to, then paste the compiled SELECT into the warehouse query editor and run it.

| What you find | Layer | Next move |
|---|---|---|
| An identifier you did not expect — wrong database, schema or table | dbt config | Look for a +database: nested wrong in dbt_project.yml, an env_var() returning the wrong value, or a {{ target }} check gated on the wrong target |
| Identifiers right, the warehouse rejects the SELECT | SQL | The bug is pure SQL; the warehouse's own message is the diagnosis |
| Identifiers right, the SELECT runs, dbt run still fails | Between compiled SQL and what dbt executed | Open target/run/<path>/<model>.sql — the same SQL inside the materialization's CREATE TABLE / MERGE wrapper. Rare; usually pre-hook/post-hook interactions or materialization-wrapper SQL |

The /guides/debug-errors guide calls out the target/compiled/ vs target/run/ split.

--select resolves against the same graph the run commands use, so the selection pulls in more than the model itself: dbt compile --select stg_orders also writes the compiled SQL for every generic test attached to stg_orders, under target/compiled/<project>/models/<the properties file>.yml/. That is the file to open when a test fails and the failure makes no sense — the test's own select is sitting there ready to paste into the warehouse. To reach tests directly, select them by type: resource_type:test takes all of them, test_type:generic and test_type:singular take one kind each. When dbt compile --select <name> answers The selection criterion '<name>' does not match any enabled nodes, dbt ls --resource-type test --select <model> prints what the graph actually calls the tests you were reaching for.

This step is mechanical and takes under a minute. It is the triage step the exam's Topic 3 sub-bullet "troubleshooting using compiled code" names specifically.

## What the compiled file shows

Consider a model fct_orders.sql with this body:

```
{{ config(materialized='table') }}

select
    o.order_id,
    o.customer_id,
    c.customer_name,
    o.amount_usd
```

```
from {{ ref('stg_orders') }} o
left join {{ ref('stg_customers') }} c on c.customer_id = o.customer_id
```

After `dbt compile --select fct_orders`, the file at `target/compiled/my_project/models/marts/fct_orders.sql` contains:

```
select
    o.order_id,
    o.customer_id,
    c.customer_name,
    o.amount_usd
from analytics_dev.staging.stg_orders o
left join analytics_dev.staging.stg_customers c on c.customer_id = o.customer_id
```

Three things to notice. The `{{ config() }}` call is gone — that config drives the materialization wrapper in `target/run/...`, not the SELECT itself. The `{{ ref() }}` calls resolved to fully-qualified identifiers that include the database and schema `target` is using right now. If any of those three parts (database, schema, table) are wrong, the bug is in the dbt layer, and you are one edit from a fix.

### When `dbt compile` itself fails

Compile does not always succeed. If a model has a missing `ref()`, a cyclic dependency, or a Jinja error, `dbt compile --select <model>` fails and no compiled SQL is written for that model. In that case you have already localised the problem to the dbt layer (the §10.1 frame), and the triage path moves to §10.3 (if it is a `ref()` error) or §10.5 (if it is a macro/Jinja error).

---

## 10.3 The `ref()` error family

Every `ref()` call is a claim that another node exists in your project. Four ways that claim can go wrong, each with a distinct error signature.

### 10.3.1 Missing model — typo in the referenced name

The most common form. `ref('stg_orderz')` when the model file is `stg_orders.sql`. dbt raises a Compilation Error:

```
Compilation Error
  Model 'model.my_project.fct_orders' (models/marts/fct_orders.sql) depends on a
  node named 'stg_orderz' which was not found
```

The fix is the typo. The error names both the offending model (`fct_orders`) and the node it could not find (`stg_orderz`), so there is no detective work. Note the bare banner: an unresolvable `ref()` is caught when dbt links the graph, before it renders the node, so the model and its path arrive inside the message rather than as an `in model ...` clause on the banner line. §10.5's undefined-macro error is raised while a node renders, and does carry it. This exact-string guarantee is what makes the `ref()` error family cheap to fix: dbt knows what it was looking for. The reference page for `ref()` semantics is `/reference/dbt-jinja-functions/ref`.

### 10.3.2 Disabled upstream — `enabled: false` somewhere above

Less obvious. The referenced model exists on disk — the file is there, the name is spelled correctly — but its config has set `enabled: false`. Once disabled, dbt does not consider the model part of the project, and any downstream `ref()` to it behaves as a missing node. The `/reference/resource-configs/enabled` page calls this out directly: "When a resource is disabled, dbt will not consider it as part of your project. Note that this can cause compilation errors." The error text tends to hint at the disablement ("disabled" appears in the message), which is the tell that distinguishes it from a plain typo.

`enabled: false` is set in several places:

- In `dbt_project.yml` under a path — for example `models: my_project: archive: +enabled: false`, which disables every model under `models/archive/`.
- In the model's own `{{ config(enabled=false) }}` at the top of the SQL file.
- Through a variable — `{{ config(enabled=var('enable_archive', false)) }}` — which turns a model on or off via `--vars`.

The fix depends on intent. If the upstream is disabled because it should be, the *downstream* should not be ref-ing it; remove the `ref()` or disable the downstream too. If the upstream is disabled by accident — most commonly by a path-level `+enabled: false` in `dbt_project.yml` that captured more models than the author intended — narrow the scope.

### 10.3.3 Typo on a versioned `ref()`

dbt's model versions (Ch 13) let you write `{{ ref('dim_users', v=2) }}` to pin a specific version. If you ask for a version that does not exist — `{{ ref('dim_users', v=3) }}` when only v=1 and v=2 exist — dbt raises a Compilation Error that names the version it could not find:

```
Compilation Error
  Model 'model.my_project.fct_orders' (models/marts/fct_orders.sql) depends on a
  node named 'dim_users' with version '3' which was not found
```

The phrase "with version '3'" is the tell — §10.3.1's missing-node error with a version clause spliced in, and dbt does not list the versions that do exist. Fix either by removing the `v=` kwarg (the long form `version=` is its documented alias; with neither, the ref resolves to `latest_version:`), correcting it to a version that exists, or releasing a new version on the upstream side. The `ref()` signature and its `v=` kwarg are documented at `/reference/dbt-jinja-functions/ref`.

### 10.3.4 Cyclic dependency

A ref-cycle: model A refs model B, and model B refs model A — directly, or through a chain A → C → D → A. dbt parses such a project but cannot build a graph from it: the cycle surfaces on the first command that compiles the DAG. The `/guides/debug-errors` guide names "Dependency errors" — acyclic validation failures — as one of the four primary error categories. The error names the cycle, printing the path without closing the loop back to the first node:

```
Found a cycle: model.my_project.a --> model.my_project.b
```

Fixes depend on why the cycle exists. In small projects a cycle is almost always a typo — one of the refs was meant to point at a staging equivalent. In larger projects it is usually a design break: two marts models have grown mutual dependencies, and one of them needs its shared logic refactored into an intermediate model that both of the offenders can ref instead. The DAG is a constraint, not an inconvenience; resolving a cycle is modelling work, not a dbt-config edit.

### Quick-reference table

| Family member | Error text tell | Fix |
|---|---|---|
| Missing | "depends on a node named 'X' which was not found" | Correct the typo in `ref('X')` |
| Disabled | Same shape, plus "disabled" | Re-enable the upstream or drop the `ref()` |
| Wrong version | Same shape, plus "with version 'N'" | Correct the `v=` kwarg or release version N |
| Cyclic | "Found a cycle: A --> B" | Break the cycle (usually by refactoring one leg into an intermediate model) |

---

## 10.4 YAML failure modes

YAML is unforgiving. When a YAML file fails to parse, dbt stops before it does anything else — no models compile, no tests run, no docs generate. The error message includes a file path and usually a line:column, which narrows the search to one file quickly, but the cause takes a little pattern-recognition because YAML's failure modes repeat across projects.

The definitive reference for what keys go where is `/reference/configs-and-properties`. Four failure modes cover almost every YAML bug you will encounter.

### Tabs vs spaces

YAML forbids tabs for indentation. Any tab character where YAML expects spaces is a parse error. Every text editor has a setting for "insert spaces instead of tabs"; set it on your `.yml` files or you will pay for it. The failure looks like:

```
Parsing Error
  Error reading credora: _models.yml - Runtime Error
    Syntax error near line 4
    ------------------------------
    1  | version: 2
    2  | models:
    3  |   - name: stg_orders
    4  |     description: "One row per order"

    Raw Error:
    ------------------------------
    while scanning a plain scalar
      in "<unicode string>", line 3, column 11
    found a tab character that violates indentation
      in "<unicode string>", line 4, column 1
```

The raw error names the tab outright, and the line:column pair points at the offending character. The banner above it is generic: the indentation error covered next produces the same `Parsing Error / Error reading <project>: <file> - Runtime Error` wrapper and the same `Syntax error near line N` excerpt, and differs only in the `Raw Error:` block, where a mis-indent reads `did not find expected key`. So read past the banner before deciding which of the two you have. An editor with visible whitespace guides prevents both.

### Indentation

YAML's block structure is entirely indentation-based. A key that is one space too deep becomes the child of the previous key; two spaces too shallow, and it becomes a sibling of its grandparent. dbt's YAML schemas are specific about what can be nested where. A common shape error is:

```
# WRONG - columns is at the wrong nesting level
version: 2
models:
  - name: stg_orders
    description: "One row per order"
      columns:
        - name: order_id
          data_tests:
            - not_null
```

The `columns:` key is indented under `description:` rather than as a sibling of `name:` and `description:`. That is not valid YAML, so dbt fails at the parse step and never reaches its schema validation. The fix is to dedent `columns:` by two spaces:

```
# RIGHT
version: 2
models:
  - name: stg_orders
    description: "One row per order"
    columns:
      - name: order_id
        data_tests:
          - not_null
```

### Wrong data type for a config's value

Every dbt config has an expected type. `materialized` takes a string; `enabled` takes a boolean; `columns:` takes a list of mappings; `meta:` takes a mapping. Supplying the wrong type is a parse-time error. Two common forms:

```
# WRONG - materialized is not a boolean
models:
  - name: stg_orders
    config:
      materialized: true
```

`materialized` must be `view`, `table`, `incremental`, `ephemeral`, or `materialized_view` (plus adapter-specific values). YAML parses `true` as a boolean; dbt rejects it because `materialized` expects a string. The error names the config and the expected type.

```
# WRONG - data_tests must be a list, not a mapping
columns:
  - name: order_id
    data_tests:
      not_null: {}
      unique: {}
```

`data_tests:` is a list of test invocations — `- not_null` and `- unique`, each prefixed with `-`. The mapping form above puts the tests at the wrong structural level. dbt's schema rejects it at parse time.

### Misplaced or unknown keyword

YAML does not mind if you put a key at the wrong level; it parses fine. Whether dbt *tells* you depends on your adapter.

| Adapter | What happens |
|---|---|
| BigQuery, Databricks, Redshift, Snowflake | Validates properties YAML against a schema and warns at parse time — `CustomKeyInObjectDeprecation` for a key it does not know, `PropertyMovedToConfigDeprecation` for a real config key sitting one level too high |
| Every other adapter, Postgres included | Skips that schema check entirely — parse is silent and exits 0 |

What dbt *does* is a separate question: it turns on the resource, not the adapter, and the three cases do not agree:

| Where the misplaced key sits | What happens to it, on every adapter |
|---|---|
| A model | Dropped — the reliable check is that the config is absent from `target/manifest.json` |
| An exposure or a source | Hoisted into `config` — a top-level `tags:` on an exposure is live and selectable, on Postgres too (Ch 9 §9.5.4) |
| A generic test | Hoisted **and** warned about — this path skips the schema check, so `PropertyMovedToConfigDeprecation` fires on Postgres as well (Ch 7 §7.2) |

Common cases: `materialized:` as a top-level key in a properties YAML where it belongs inside `config:`; `owner:` on an exposure at the wrong nesting. Move the key to its documented home — `/reference/configs-and-properties`. Nesting a key so that a list becomes a mapping — `description:` under `data_tests:` — is a different fault: it belongs to the wrong-type family above, and raises a `Parsing Error` on every adapter before anything is written to `target/`.

A subtlety worth internalising: broadly, dbt's reference splits these keys into two areas — YAML-structural keys (`description`, `columns`, `constraints`, `versions`, `data-tests`, `unit-tests`) tend to live under `/reference/resource-properties/`; resource configs (`enabled`, `materialized`, `grants`, `persist_docs`, `freshness`) tend to live under `/reference/resource-configs/`. A key in the wrong area fails quietly — at best a warning, on most adapters nothing at all — and then produces surprising behaviour when the config appears to be set but is not.

---

## 10.5 Macro errors

Macros and Jinja are rendered during parsing and again during compilation, so the family straddles both layers: a *known* macro called wrongly — bad arity, bad keyword — and a failed `adapter.dispatch` resolution both raise during `dbt parse`, while an unknown macro *name* becomes a Jinja `Undefined` that survives parse and fails at compile. Every banner below reads `Compilation Error` regardless: the label names the error class, not the stage that raised it. The family is small but distinctive, and its last member prints no banner at all. The concept page is `/docs/build/jinja-macros`.

### Undefined macro

The macro name you called does not resolve. Either you typed it wrong, you did not install the package that supplies it, or you forgot to qualify the name with the package namespace. The error:

```
Compilation Error in model fct_orders (models/marts/fct_orders.sql)
  'generate_surrogate_key' is undefined. This can happen when calling a macro that does
    not exist. Check for typos and/or install package dependencies with "dbt deps".
```

Three common causes:

- **Typo.** `generate_surrogat_key` when you meant `generate_surrogate_key`.
- **Not a missing `dbt deps` run — check this first and rule it out.** If `packages.yml` declares packages and `dbt_packages/` is absent, dbt never reaches a per-model macro error: it stops at project load with `dbt found N package(s) specified in packages.yml, but only 0 package(s) installed in dbt_packages. Run "dbt deps"`, exit 2. So an error naming *your model* and *one macro* means the package is already installed and something else is wrong — almost always the missing namespace below. §8.4 covers the package-count error itself.
- **Missing namespace.** The macro lives inside a package, and you called it bare. `dbt_utils.generate_surrogate_key(['a', 'b'])` is the namespaced call; `generate_surrogate_key(['a', 'b'])` looks at the project's own `macros/` first, and raises this error when nothing is there. Packages are covered in Ch 8.

### Wrong argument count

A macro defined with a single parameter, called with two:

```
Compilation Error in model fct_orders (models/marts/fct_orders.sql)
  macro 'dbt_macro__generate_surrogate_key' takes not more than 1 argument(s)
```

Pass a keyword the macro does not declare and you get the sibling message, `takes no keyword argument 'precision_level'`. Note the name in the error: dbt reports the internal `dbt_macro__`-prefixed form, not the `dbt_utils.generate_surrogate_key` you wrote, so the string in the banner is not one you can grep for in `dbt_packages/`. Read the macro's signature and adjust the call. If the macro's source is in `dbt_packages/`, open the file directly — macros are just Jinja in `.sql` files, perfectly readable, and the signature is the first line after `{% macro ... %}`.

### Dispatch miss — adapter-specific macro not defined for this adapter

`adapter.dispatch` (Ch 6 §6.7) lets a macro have adapter-specific variants: `snowflake__my_macro`, `databricks__my_macro`, and so on. The naming convention is `{adapter}__{macro}` — adapter prefix first. If the dispatch resolution cannot find a variant for the current adapter, dbt raises an error whose headline names the **bare** macro, with the adapter-prefixed names it looked for on a second line:

```
Compilation Error
  In dispatch: No macro named 'my_macro' found within namespace: 'None'
      Searched for: 'postgres__my_macro', 'default__my_macro'
```

Either add the missing variant, or add a `default__my_macro` that handles any adapter without a specific variant.

### Jinja compile error

A Jinja syntax error — unbalanced `{{ }}` braces, a missing `{% endfor %}`, a misspelled filter name. The error points at the offending line:

```
Compilation Error in model stg_orders (models/staging/stg_orders.sql)
  unexpected ')', expected ']'
    line 5
      select {{ var('cols', ['a', 'b') }}
```

Fix the brace or the punctuation. These are usually obvious once you look at the named line.

### Unquoted argument — the one that fails silently

The four failures above all print something. This one does not, and that is what makes it exam material. Jinja has no notion of a bare identifier: an argument written without quotes is read as the name of a *variable*, and a variable that is not in the rendering context resolves to `Undefined`, which renders as the empty string. Take a macro whose body interpolates its parameter:

```
{% macro max_of(col) %}
  max({{ col }})
{% endmacro %}
```

Call it with the column name unquoted:

```
select {{ max_of(order_id) }} as biggest from {{ ref('stg_orders') }}
```

`dbt compile` succeeds, exits 0, and prints no warning. The compiled file is:

```
select
  max()
as biggest from analytics_dev.staging.stg_orders
```

The argument is gone. There is no undefined-macro banner because the macro resolved perfectly well; it is the *argument* that did not. The bug surfaces one layer down and one step later, when the warehouse rejects `max()` as a Database Error — which sends a careless triage straight to §10.1's SQL bucket, where there is nothing to find. Quoting the argument, `max_of('order_id')`, compiles the same call to `max(order_id)`.

This is the failure that makes §10.2's habit non-negotiable. Every other member of this family names the macro and the line for you; this one hands you a syntactically valid query with a hole in it, and the only place the hole is visible is `target/compiled/`.

### The fix path for all of the above

`dbt compile --select <model>` is the right first move. The error messages are detailed; the corresponding compiled SQL, if compile succeeded, shows exactly what dbt resolved the Jinja to. For a macro that compiles but produces wrong SQL, `{{ log() }}` calls inside the macro print values to `logs/dbt.log` on every compile, which is how most dispatch and dynamic-reference bugs are pinned down.

## 10.6 `dbt debug` — connection issues

`dbt debug` is a separate tool from the compile-and-run triage path. It does not look at your models at all; it tests whether dbt can reach your warehouse and whether your project's configuration and environment hang together correctly. Think of it as the `ping` of the dbt CLI. The reference is `/reference/commands/debug`.

What it checks (per the docs page):

- **Database connectivity** — can dbt open a connection to the warehouse named in the active `target:` of your `profiles.yml`?
- **Project configuration** — is `dbt_project.yml` valid? Are paths named correctly?
- **System environment** — OS, Python version, installed dbt version.
- **Required dependencies** — is `git` available for `dbt deps`?
- **Adapter compatibility** — is the adapter version installed compatible with the dbt-core version?

`dbt debug --connection` runs only the database-connectivity check, which is faster when you already know the environment is otherwise fine and you just want to confirm warehouse reachability.

### When to reach for `dbt debug`

Not every time something goes wrong. A Compilation Error, a missing `ref()`, a YAML parse failure, a SQL cast error — these are all beyond `dbt debug`'s remit; `dbt debug` will happily report "All checks passed" while your `dbt run` fails with a Compilation Error. Reach for `dbt debug` specifically when:

- It is your first time setting up the project and you want to confirm `profiles.yml` is correctly pointed at the warehouse.
- Warehouse credentials were rotated and `dbt run` now fails with a connectivity-flavoured error (`authentication failed`, `role does not exist`, `cannot connect to host`, TCP timeouts).
- You changed `profiles.yml` or `~/.dbt/profiles.yml` and want to verify the change before running a full `dbt run`.
- A teammate reports "dbt just stopped working" and you do not know yet whether it is a code problem or a connection problem.

If `dbt debug` passes and `dbt run` still fails, the problem is upstream of warehouse connectivity — treat it as a §10.1 triage problem and open the compiled SQL. If `dbt debug` fails, fix that first; nothing downstream will work.

---

## 10.7 Logs and log levels

dbt produces two kinds of output: the console output you see while a command runs, and a rolling log file at `logs/dbt.log` (path relative to `dbt_project.yml`, configurable via `--log-path`). The reference pages are `/reference/events-logging` and `/reference/global-configs/logs`.

### The `--debug` flag

`dbt run --debug` (equivalently `dbt run -d`) redirects dbt's debug-level logs to standard output. The docs page warns this is verbose — a single model's run emits hundreds of debug-level events — but when the normal error text is not enough, `--debug` frequently surfaces the extra context you need. Typical wins: extra detail on exactly which query failed during a materialization, the full warehouse round-trip for each `ref()` resolution, the parse order, the compile order.

## Log levels

`LOG_LEVEL` supports five values: `debug`, `info`, `warn`, `error`, `none`. The two destinations carry different defaults, and the difference does real work.

| Destination | Default level | Set it at invocation with |
|---|---|---|
| Console — what you see without `--debug` | `info` | `--log-level`, which sets the file with it unless overridden |
| `logs/dbt.log` | `debug` | `--log-level-file`, which sets the file alone |

So `logs/dbt.log` already holds detail the console never printed: it runs an order of magnitude longer than the console output of the same invocation, per-query warehouse round-trips and parse order included. That is why a post-mortem on a run that has already finished starts with the file rather than with a re-run under `--debug`. Both flags accept `debug`/`info`/`warn`/`error`/`none`; the `/reference/global-configs/logs` page lists all five levels and the applicable CLI flags.

## Log formats — a different set of four

`--log-format` and `--log-format-file` read like siblings of the level flags and take a **different** vocabulary: `text`, `debug`, `json`, `default`. Neither default is `text` and neither is `json`, which is the pairing an exam item is likeliest to invert.

| Destination | Default format | Set it at invocation with |
|---|---|---|
| Console | `default` | `--log-format`, which sets the file with it unless overridden |
| `logs/dbt.log` | `debug` | `--log-format-file`, which sets the file alone |

The four differ in how much of the event they print, not in what dbt does. `default` and `text` both give the familiar `09:14:07 Running with dbt=1.11.14` line. `debug` prefixes every event with a microsecond timestamp, its level and its thread — `09:14:07.482913 [info ] [MainThread]: ...` — which is the shape `logs/dbt.log` already has, and the reason its default is `debug` rather than `default`. `json` emits one JSON object per event, each carrying `info.name`, `info.code`, `info.level` and the run's `invocation_id` alongside `msg`; those are the same event names §10.9.3's `warn_error_options` lists take. Reach for `json` when something downstream **parses** the log instead of reading it, and for `--log-format-file json` when only the durable copy needs to be machine-readable. The mirror-image flag, `--quiet`, suppresses non-error output on stdout without touching the file log at all; Ch 11 §11.10 has it, because on `dbt ls` it is the difference between output that parses and output that does not.

## When to reach for `--debug`

After you have read the normal error text, opened the compiled SQL, and read `logs/dbt.log` — which is already at `debug` — and none of the three was enough. Most bugs do not need `--debug`; the ones that do are usually materialization-wrapper bugs, hook-ordering bugs (`on-run-start` running in the wrong adapter namespace, a `pre-hook` silently failing), or dispatch-resolution bugs where you cannot tell which variant actually ran. `--debug` is a late-stage tool, not a first-resort one.

---

## 10.8 Fix-before-merge — the workflow

Finding the bug is half the job. The other half is fixing it on a branch, verifying the fix, and landing the change without breaking anyone else. The blueprint's Topic 3 sub-bullet "developing and implementing a fix and testing it prior to merging" is explicit about this, and it maps directly to git's branch → commit → PR loop. The primary dbt-Cloud-focused references for this workflow are `/docs/platform/git/version-control-basics` and `/docs/platform/git/pr-template`; the underlying mechanics apply equally to dbt Core projects hosted on GitHub, GitLab, or any other platform.

### The fix loop

A single fix cycle has six stages. Each one has a specific dbt command associated with it.

1. **Branch.** `git checkout -b fix/stg-orders-null-user-id` off your main development branch. The fix gets its own branch; `main` is protected on any serious project, so changes arrive by reviewed pull request rather than direct pushes. Git branching itself is prerequisite material at 1.11 rather than a domain bullet — Appendix A carries it. What Topic 3 assesses is the *ordering* of the five stages after this one.

2. **Edit.** Change the model, the YAML, the macro, the seed — whatever §10.1–§10.5's triage pointed you at.

3. **Compile.** `dbt compile --select <fixed_model>+` re-parses the project with your edit and regenerates compiled SQL. This is where YAML-level errors and compile-level errors reappear if your fix is incomplete. The `+` operator extends the selection to downstream, because a fix to model X may break models that depend on X.

4. **Run.** `dbt run --select <fixed_model>+` materialises the model and every downstream against the warehouse. If compile succeeded but run fails, you are now in the SQL layer — open the new compiled SQL from §10.2.

5. **Test.** `dbt test --select <fixed_model>+` runs every generic and singular test attached to the fixed model and its downstream. This is the checkpoint that the blueprint sub-bullet calls out: you do not merge a fix until the tests on the affected subgraph pass. Ch 7 covers the test mechanics; the point here is that the test step comes *before* commit, not after.

6. **Commit, push, open PR.** `git commit`; `git push origin fix/stg-orders-null-user-id`; open the pull request. The PR's CI pipeline then runs a broader validation — usually `dbt build` across a larger selection, often gated on state-aware selection (Ch 12) so CI rebuilds only the affected subset.

**Name the environment before asserting what is forbidden.** "You cannot edit files or run dbt commands against the production branch" is true, and it is a **dbt Studio IDE** behaviour rather than a universal rule. The version-control page states it of that surface and no other: in the Studio IDE the main branch is protected, so you cannot directly edit, format or lint files, nor execute dbt commands, on the protected primary branch — you branch first and commit there. Locally there is no such interlock; you can check out any branch and run whatever your warehouse permits, and the discipline in the six stages above is the only thing stopping you. A stem that states the prohibition without naming the surface is asking you which surface it belongs to.

The <model>+ selector is the workhorse of steps 3–5. It asks dbt to act on the model and everything downstream of it, because a fix in one place can break a consumer elsewhere. If your fix narrows a `NOT NULL` column back to `NULL`-accepting, a downstream test expecting `not_null` will fail — better to discover that before the PR is opened.

### `git fetch` vs `git pull` in a fix cycle

`git fetch` downloads remote refs without merging; `git pull` is `git fetch` followed by `git merge`. The exam tests that distinction, and it matters mid-fix: when teammates merge into the head branch while you are still working, `git pull` reconciles your branch with those merges, so stage 5's test step runs against the same upstream the PR will merge into. Appendix A has the git mechanics.

### When CI catches what local missed

A well-configured CI pipeline re-runs steps 3–5 on every push, plus a broader verification — typically `dbt compile --warn-error` and a subset `dbt build`. Two common "caught in CI, missed locally" cases:

- **YAML that parses in one YAML library but not another.** dbt's parser is consistent, but some editor YAML linters are more permissive than others. CI catches the mismatch because it runs a fresh `dbt compile`.
- **Environment variables set locally but not in CI.** A `ref()` that resolves with `env_var('ENV', 'dev')` to a model that exists in dev may resolve to a missing model when CI runs with `ENV=ci`. This is one of the high-payoff reasons to make `dbt compile --warn-error` part of CI (see §10.10).

---

## 10.9 Managing dbt behaviour with flags

"Flag" is the most overloaded word in dbt's vocabulary, and questions on this material trade on the overload rather than on any one mechanism. Four distinct things carry the name.

| What it is | Where you set it | What it controls |
|---|---|---|
| **Global config flags** | CLI option, environment variable, `dbt_project.yml`'s `flags:` block, `~/.dbt/user_settings.yml` | How one invocation runs — `--fail-fast`, `--log-level`, `--printer-width` |
| **Behaviour-change flags** | `dbt_project.yml`'s `flags:` block, and nowhere else | Whether this project has adopted a future dbt default early |
| `warn_error` / `warn_error_options` | The global-config surfaces above | Which of dbt's warnings are promoted to errors |
| `flags`, **the Jinja context object** | Nowhere — you read it, you do not set it | What macro code can learn about the invocation it is running inside |

The first three configure dbt; the fourth reports on it. {{ flags.WHICH }} returns the name of the command currently executing, which is how a macro behaves differently under dbt run than under dbt docs generate, and {{ flags.FAIL_FAST }} reads back whatever the precedence chain in §10.9.1 resolved. The Jinja side is Ch 6 §6.2's territory; what matters here is that a stem showing flags.WHICH and a stem showing a flags: block in dbt_project.yml are asking about two different mechanisms that happen to share a word.

FULL_REFRESH, STORE_FAILURES and EMPTY are members of that same Jinja object, and they are the tempting ones — branching a macro on {{ flags.FULL_REFRESH }} looks like a tidy way to vary its SQL. dbt Labs warns against exactly that, and the reason is partial parsing. flags, run_started_at and invocation_id all change from one invocation to the next, but a node whose file has not changed is not re-parsed, so a parse-time attribute driven from any of the three keeps whatever value the run that first parsed it happened to supply. Read them inside a materialization or a run-time expression, where they are re-evaluated; do not let one decide a config.

One thing that is *not* a flag in any of these senses is a resource config. enabled, materialized, grants and persist_docs (§10.4) configure a **resource**; flags configure an invocation, a project, or a project's migration posture. Reading enabled: false as "a flag" is the mistake that makes the behaviour-change exception in §10.9.1 look arbitrary.

### 10.9.1 Global config flags and the precedence chain

A global config can be set in four places, and the most specific setting wins. /reference/global-configs/about-global-configs states the order: CLI options take the highest precedence, then environment variables, then dbt_project.yml, and finally user_settings.yml.

| Precedence | Surface | Scope of the decision |
|---|---|---|
| 1 (highest) | CLI option — dbt run --fail-fast | This invocation only |
| 2 | Environment variable — DBT_ENGINE_FAIL_FAST=1 | This runtime environment (dev vs CI vs prod) |
| 3 | flags: in dbt_project.yml | Everyone who runs this project, under version control |
| 4 (lowest) | ~/.dbt/user_settings.yml | Every project on this machine — personal preference. **Documented; dbt Core 1.11 does not read it** |
| — | dbt's own default, if you set it nowhere | — |

Four surfaces, not three — that is the order the reference page states, and it is the order a precedence question is asking for. Rungs 1–3 resolve exactly as the table says; rung 4 does not resolve at all on dbt Core 1.11.14. A ~/.dbt/user_settings.yml holding flags: {fail_fast: true} leaves flags.FAIL_FAST at False, the string user_settings appears nowhere in the shipped package, and dbt Core has no login command to write the file. The page scopes itself to "the dbt Fusion engine or dbt Core engine" and does not split the claim; Core is the half that does not implement it. The rung that matters most on a team is the third: a value in dbt_project.yml is reviewed in a pull request, and a value in someone's shell is not.

**Environment-variable naming.** At 1.11 the convention is DBT_ENGINE_<CONFIG_NAME> — DBT_ENGINE_FAIL_FAST, DBT_ENGINE_LOG_LEVEL, DBT_ENGINE_LOG_PATH, and DBT_ENGINE_FAIL_

`FAST=1` is the form the reference page's own example uses. The bare `DBT_` spelling from an older runbook is still read, because each option registers both names — but `DBT_ENGINE_` is a reserved prefix, and a name dbt does not recognise inside it is ignored with a warning that it may collide.

**The second trap on the same page is the value type.** A boolean config takes the ordinary spellings, case-insensitively:

| Sets it | Clears it |
|---|---|
| `1, t, true, y, yes, on` | `0, f, false, n, no, off` |

Anything outside that set is refused rather than coerced — `DBT_ENGINE_FAIL_FAST=2` aborts the invocation with `Invalid value for '--fail-fast' / '-x': '2' is not a valid boolean`, naming the CLI option the environment variable feeds. The empty string is the near-miss worth carrying: the option's own recognised-value list begins with it, so it reads like a sixth way to clear a boolean, but an environment variable set to an empty value is treated as **unset**. `DBT_ENGINE_FAIL_FAST=` clears nothing — a `fail_fast: true` in the `flags:` block survives it untouched, and the resolution simply falls through to the next rung of the chain. See `/reference/global-configs/environment-variable-configs`.

**On the command line**, boolean global configs come as a pair — `--fail-fast` and `--no-fail-fast`, `--populate-cache` and `--no-populate-cache` — so a CLI option can turn a project-level `true` back off for one invocation. **One breaks the pattern.** `--warn-error` has no `--no-` form, so `dbt ls --no-warn-error` exits 2 with `Error: No such option: --no-warn-error`, and a `warn_error: true` in the `flags:` block cannot be lifted for a single run (`--warn-error-options` is refused alongside it: `warn_error_options: not allowed with argument warn_error`). §11.11's `--no-` table lists a second flag with no negative form, `--full-refresh`. Both are the fact Ch 11 Q15 turns on. Otherwise they are accepted on either side of the subcommand — `dbt run --no-populate-cache` and `dbt --no-populate-cache run` are the same invocation — which is not true of `--select`, a subcommand option only. Non-boolean configs take a value: `--printer-width=80`. That is documented at `/reference/global-configs/command-line-options`.

The counter-example is worth carrying, because it looks identical from the outside. `--introspect` / `--no-introspect` is spelled like a global config and is not one: it belongs to `dbt compile`, so `dbt compile --no-introspect` is accepted and `dbt --no-introspect compile` answers `Error: No such option: --no-introspect`. Position is the tell. A global config is accepted on either side of the subcommand; a subcommand option is accepted only on the right of it.

**Two exceptions, and they are mirror images.** Learn them as a pair, because a distractor that swaps them reads perfectly plausibly.

- **File-path configs cannot be set in `dbt_project.yml`.** `--log-path` and `--state` point at directories that depend on where and how the command is being run, so they are CLI-or-environment-variable only (`DBT_ENGINE_LOG_PATH`, `DBT_ENGINE_STATE`). The `--log-path` you met in §10.7 is one of these: a `log_path:` in the `flags:` block is accepted and then ignored — no error, no warning. This is a rule about the `flags:` block, not about the whole file — `model-paths`, `snapshot-paths` and their siblings are top-level `dbt_project.yml` keys precisely because they never vary by invocation.
- **Behaviour-change flags are set in `dbt_project.yml`'s `flags:` block.** They have no CLI option and no environment variable, which is the inverse of every other global config, and it is the answer to give. An option offering `dbt run --require_resource_names_without_spaces` is wrong twice over: the flag is not a command-line option, and the whole point of the mechanism is that adopting a new behaviour is a version-controlled,

peer-reviewed decision rather than something one engineer does in one shell. Two qualifications that do not change that answer: Core still reads a deprecated fallback from `profiles.yml` at 1.11 and warns when it does, and an adapter may surface its own flags by other routes. Neither makes the CLI or an environment variable a supported placement.

Not everything spelled with two leading dashes belongs to this system at all. `--empty` and `--sample` on `dbt run` and `dbt build` are build-time flags that change what data a model reads; they are neither global configs nor behaviour-change flags, and no precedence chain applies to them.

### 10.9.2 Behaviour-change flags

A behaviour change is a deliberate update where the same project code and the same command produce a different result than before — a new validation error, a changed built-in macro signature, a different artifact shape. Bug fixes and newly added warnings are not behaviour changes. dbt gates each one behind a boolean in the `flags:` block so that you choose when to adopt it:

```
# dbt_project.yml
flags:
  require_explicit_package_overrides_for_builtin_materializations: true
  require_resource_names_without_spaces: true
  source_freshness_run_project_hooks: true
  require_generic_test_arguments_property: true
```

`/reference/global-configs/project-flags` puts the restriction plainly: the `flags` dictionary is the only place you can opt out of behaviour changes while the legacy behaviour is still supported. That sentence explains the exception in §10.9.1 — there is nowhere else to set these, so there is nothing for a precedence chain to arbitrate.

**The lifecycle has three phases**, and the phase a flag is in tells you what its default is and what happens if you fight it. `/reference/global-configs/behavior-changes` names them:

1. **Introduced** — dbt ships both code paths. The new behaviour sits behind the flag, **disabled by default**, so upgrading changes nothing until you opt in.
2. **Mature** — the default flips to the new behaviour. The old behaviour is still reachable by setting the flag `false` explicitly, and you may now see a deprecation warning when you do.
3. **Removed** — the old code path is deleted from dbt. Most flags are supported indefinitely, none is guaranteed forever, and a removal comes with significant advance warning.

The practical read: **a flag's default is a fact about your dbt version, not about the flag.** Nothing in the name `state_modified_compare_more_unrendered_values` tells you whether it is on; the release you are running does.

**Four flags are mature — default `true` — at 1.11.** Setting them explicitly, as the block above does, changes no behaviour; it records that the project has finished the migration.

| Flag | Default at 1.11 | What setting it back to `false` restores |
|---|---|---|
| `require_explicit_package_overrides_for_builtin_materializations` | `true` | A package's materialization overriding a built-in one implicitly |

| Flag | Default at 1.11 | What setting it back to `false` restores |
|---|---|---|
| `require_resource_names_without_spaces` | `true` | Resource names that contain spaces |
| `source_freshness_run_project_hooks` | `true` | `dbt source freshness` not firing `on-run-start` / `on-run-end` (Ch 3) |
| `require_generic_test_arguments_property` | `true` | Generic-test inputs written flat instead of under `arguments:` (Ch 7 §7.2) |

**Seven flags are introduced but not yet mature, and are scheduled to flip at 1.12.** On 1.11 every one of them defaults to `false`, which is what a version-pinned question is asking about: `skip_nodes_if_on_run_start_fails`, `state_modified_compare_more_unrendered_values`, `require_yaml_configuration_for_mf_time_spines`, `require_batched_execution_for_custom_microbatch_strategy`, `require_nested_cumulative_type_params`, `validate_macro_args`, and `require_all_warnings_handled_by_warn_error`. The trap is a stem that describes the *matured* behaviour and asks what dbt does today — on 1.11 it does the old thing, unless the project opted in.

The remaining three — `state_modified_compare_vars`, `require_unique_project_resource_names`, `require_ref_searches_node_package_before_root` — sit at `false` with no maturity release announced. Four `true` plus ten `false` is the whole core list: `ProjectFlags.project_only_flags` holds exactly **14** entries at 1.11.14. The same table on the docs page also carries flags whose introduction is 1.12 or later; those are not part of 1.11 at all. Adapters publish their own behaviour-change flags under the same umbrella page — `enable_truthy_nulls_equals_macro` is one of those, declared by the adapter and read as `adapter.behavior.…`, not a Core project flag. They follow the same lifecycle and the same `flags:`-block restriction, and they are adapter documentation rather than Core material.

**One flag, end to end.** `require_generic_test_arguments_property` is the one behaviour change a 1.11 reader is already living inside, and it shows the shape of all of them: the flag shipped disabled, then matured to `true`, and by 1.11 a project that never touched it is already writing `arguments:` — with the flat form accepted and deprecated rather than refused. Its page is `/reference/global-configs/behavior-flags/require_generic_test_arguments_property`; the YAML shape it enforces is Ch 7 §7.2's.

## Five flags, and what each one actually changes

Names are not self-explanatory, and the exam trades on that. Five are worth knowing by their effect rather than their spelling.

`require_unique_project_resource_names` — `false` at 1.11. Models, seeds, snapshots, analyses, tests and functions share **one name namespace within a package** — that is the reference page's list, and it is the one to answer from; at 1.11 the check itself reaches only the relational three, models, seeds and snapshots (executed: a model, an analysis and a data test all named `sales` parse clean with the flag on; adding a seed of that name is what fails). So a project holding both `models/sales.sql` and `seeds/sales.csv` has made `{{ ref('sales') }}` ambiguous. At the 1.11 default dbt says so and carries on: it emits `DuplicateNameDistinctNodeTypesDeprecation` — *"Found resources with the same name 'sales' in package 'credora'"* — and parses to exit 0, provided the two resolve to different relations; a model and a seed of one name land on the same relation by default, and that collision raises a separate ambiguous-relation error whatever this flag is set to. Set the flag `true` and the shared name alone fails the parse, with dbt naming both resources and telling you to rename one. Note the scope word: the collision is *within a package*, so two packages may each have a `sales`.

**`require_ref_searches_node_package_before_root`** — `false` at 1.11. It changes which package a bare `ref()` inside an installed package searches first. The flag is the exam-facing half; the resolution mechanism it toggles is Ch 8 §8.6's.

**`require_explicit_package_overrides_for_builtin_materializations`** — mature, `true` at 1.11. A materialization defined in an installed package does not silently displace the built-in of the same name; overriding a built-in is something the project asks for by name. Ch 8 §8.6 has the mechanism.

**`skip_nodes_if_on_run_start_fails`** — `false` at 1.11, scheduled to flip at 1.12, and the one whose two values are easiest to state as a pair. At `false`, an `on-run-start` hook that errors is reported and the selected resources **build anyway**: a two-model run finishes `PASS=2 WARN=0 ERROR=1 SKIP=0 NO-OP=0 TOTAL=3`. At `true`, the same failure skips every one of them: `PASS=0 WARN=0 ERROR=1 SKIP=2 NO-OP=0 TOTAL=3`. Both invocations exit `1`, so the exit code does not tell the two apart — the run summary does. Ch 6 §6.5 covers what fires a project hook in the first place.

**`validate_macro_args`** — `false` at 1.11. It does **not** look at macro calls. With it on, dbt compares a macro's YAML `arguments:` block against the macro's own **Jinja signature** and warns where the two disagree — three messages: `Argument <name> in yaml for macro <macro> does not match the jinja definition.`, `The number of arguments in the yaml for macro <macro> does not match the jinja definition.`, and `Argument <name> in the yaml for macro <macro> has an invalid type.` `InvalidMacroAnnotation` is a **WarnLevel** event, so the run continues at exit 0. It therefore turns no §10.5 failure into anything: a wrongly-called macro already raises at parse (§10.5 above), and a call whose argument contradicts a declared `type:` is not checked at all — `{{ m(123) }}` against `type: string` compiles clean. This is the flag's whole purpose: keeping the generated documentation honest, which is what Ch 6 §6.3 says of those types — "nothing checks a call against them". The YAML shape it validates against is Ch 6 §6.3's.

### 10.9.3 `warn_error` and `warn_error_options`

`--warn-error` converts the warnings dbt routes through its warn-or-error handler into errors. That is nearly all of them — a `--select` that matched nothing, a deprecation, a config attached to no model, an `exceptions.warn()` raised by a macro, a test configured to warn — and it takes no warning name: it is a switch, not a filter, with no way to spell "promote this one warning". That is what makes §10.10's CI gate a single flag on a single command, and it is also the reason to think twice before putting it in a production job, where a warning introduced by a future dbt release starts failing the run.

**Nearly all, not all — and the gap has a name.** A handful of warn-level events are printed without passing through that handler, and `--warn-error` leaves them as warnings at 1.11. The one you are likeliest to meet is the warning that `--state` and `--target-path` resolve to the same directory (Ch 12): with `--warn-error` set, dbt still prints `Warning: The state and target directories are the same` and exits 0. **A source-freshness `WARN` is outside it too**, and that one is worth holding next to its near-twin: a `severity: warn` test result *is* promoted and fails the run, because the test task converts a warn-status result into a failure; the freshness task has no such branch, so a stale source still exits 0 under the flag — and under `--warn-error-options '{"error": "all"}'` as well. Two node statuses that look like a pair, and only one of them the flag can reach. `require_all_warnings_handled_by_warn_error` is the behaviour-change flag that closes the gap — `false` at 1.11, scheduled to mature at 1.12 — and with it `true` that same invocation dies with a `Compilation Error` quoting the warning text. Until then, "`--warn-error` fails the build on any warning" is a claim about 1.12, and a CI gate built on it has a seam.

Granularity lives entirely in `--warn-error-options`, which takes a JSON or YAML mapping with three keys, documented at `/reference/global-configs/warnings`:

- `error` — promote these. Set it to `"all"` or `"*"` for the `--warn-error` behaviour, or to an array of warning names.
- `warn` — keep these as warnings. It is the exception list when `error` is `"all"` or `"*"`; on its own it is a validation error, not a no-op. dbt states the precondition in the message it raises: `` `warn` can only be specified if `error` is one of ('all', '*') or Deprecations is in `error` or silence. ``
- `silence` — suppress these entirely, which is how a large project keeps one known-noisy warning out of the log without turning off the rest.

`Deprecations` is the name worth memorising out of that list, because it is a **bulk** name rather than a single warning: `--warn-error-options '{"error": ["Deprecations"]}'` escalates every deprecation warning at once. That is what you put in CI when the goal is "no new deprecations merge", as against `--warn-error`, which promotes everything and will fail your build on warnings that have nothing to do with deprecation.

```
# promote everything except one known-noisy warning
dbt run --warn-error-options '{"error": "all", "warn": ["NoNodesForSelectionCriteria"]}'

# promote exactly one
dbt run --warn-error-options '{"error": ["NoNodesForSelectionCriteria"]}'
```

`warn` and `silence` take arrays only, and the names are dbt's own event names — `NoNodesForSelectionCriteria`, `LogTestResult`, `JinjaLogWarning` — which the same page enumerates alongside their numeric event codes. Reach for that list when you need the exact string a `silence` entry has to match. One constraint is worth holding. `warn_error` and `warn_error_options` are **mutually exclusive**: set both, in any combination of surfaces, and dbt raises a usage error.

Both configs obey the ordinary precedence chain from §10.9.1, so the `flags:` block is a legitimate home for a project-wide policy:

```
# dbt_project.yml
flags:
  warn_error_options:
    error:
      - NoNodesForSelectionCriteria
    silence:
      - FreshnessConfigProblem
```

Older projects spell those two keys `include` and `exclude`. They still parse, and dbt tells you so through the `WEOIncludeExcludeDeprecation` event — "Deprecated `include` / `exclude` keys were used in `warn_error_options`; use `error` / `warn` instead." The legacy spelling is honoured, not merely tolerated: `include` does what `error` does and `exclude` does what `warn` does. So a stem showing `include: ["NoNodesForSelectionCriteria"]` behind a selection that matches nothing is a run that **fails** — `dbt ls --select nosuchmodel --warn-error-options '{"include": ["NoNodesForSelectionCriteria"]}'` prints the deprecation, then `Compilation Error / The selection criterion 'nosuchmodel' does not match any enabled nodes`, and exits 2; the same invocation without the flag exits `0`. What the legacy spelling changes is the output, never the promotion — you get the deprecation inline and again in a `Deprecations Summary`, and the modern spelling raises neither. The one case where the deprecation is itself the failure is `include: "all"`, which promotes every warning including the one the line just raised, so the setting fails on itself.

### `--no-version-check`, and what it does not fix

`require-dbt-version` in `dbt_project.yml` declares the dbt versions a project is willing to run under, and a mismatch stops every command with a version-incompatibility error. **`--no-version-check` is the sanctioned override** — equivalently the `VERSION_CHECK` config — and it suppresses that error and lets dbt run anyway.

What it does not do is make the project compatible. It suppresses the *diagnostic*, not the incompatibility, so whatever the pin was protecting you from is still there: a macro signature that changed, a config that means something else now, a materialization that behaves differently. Reach for it deliberately and briefly — to get a read on how much actually breaks before committing to the upgrade, or to unblock a single run while the real fix is in review — and treat a CI pipeline that carries it permanently as a pin nobody has maintained.

---

## 10.10 In practice: compile-as-CI-gate at Credora

> *Pattern from `credora`, the book's fictional teaching anchor. Cited public references inline.*

### The pattern

Credora's CI runs `dbt compile --warn-error` on every pull request before any other validation step. `--warn-error` promotes the warnings dbt routes through its warn-or-error handler (§10.9.3) to errors, so a pull request that introduces an unknown YAML key, a misconfigured `enabled:` config, or a path under `models:` that no longer matches any file fails CI at the compile step — early in the job, before any model is materialized. See `/reference/commands/compile`.

A failed compile in the CI job annotates the pull request with the offending file path, line number (where dbt surfaces one), and the exact error text, so the engineer sees the failure without leaving the PR UI.

**Contract drift is the one thing this gate does not catch, and it is worth knowing why.** Enforcement compares the columns the model's SQL actually produces against the `columns:` list in YAML, and dbt gets the first half by asking the warehouse — it wraps your `select` in an empty preflight query (`... where false limit 0`) and reads the column types back. That comparison lives in the macro that *creates the relation*, so it fires during `run`/`build` and not during a `compile`, which materializes nothing. A CI job that only compiles will pass a pull request whose contract no longer matches its SQL.

The cheap fix is `--empty`, which Ch 11 §11.11 covers: it limits every `ref()` and `source()` to zero rows but still executes the SQL and really creates the relations, so the contract check runs on a build that moves no data.

```
dbt compile --warn-error                        # shape: YAML keys, enabled:, dead paths
dbt build --empty --select state:modified+      # contracts: the check the compile misses
```

### Why `--warn-error` on the compile step

Three reasons.

- **Compile is cheap relative to build.** It runs introspective queries and materializes nothing (§10.2), so even on a large project it finishes in tens of seconds to low minutes — a whole class of mistakes caught for almost nothing.

- **Warnings are the early-signal layer.** dbt warns about things that do not break the graph but usually mean a bug: an unrecognised config key on an adapter that validates YAML, a deprecated syntax, an ignored freshness threshold, a persist_docs call on an unsupported adapter. In a sprawling project they scroll past unread; promoting them to errors makes them un-ignorable.
- **Contract drift is NOT catchable at compile.** Under contract: {enforced: true} the YAML columns: list *is* the contract, but dbt checks it by running an empty preflight query and comparing the result to the declaration — inside the macro that creates the relation. dbt compile creates nothing, so it never runs the check. Add dbt build --empty over the modified selection to catch drift before merge.

## The CI pipeline's shape

Credora's CI walks four stages on every PR:

1. **Install.** Fetch dbt and the project's packages.yml; run dbt deps.
2. **Compile gate.** dbt compile --warn-error. If this fails, the pipeline stops and posts the offending file + error text to the PR's comment stream. No model has been materialized — the only warehouse work is the introspective metadata queries compile uses to resolve macros and the relation cache.
3. **Test subset.** dbt build --select state:modified+ against a prior-artifacts manifest (the slim-CI pattern covered in Ch 12) — run + test of just the affected subgraph.
4. **Docs regen (main branch only).** On merge to main, a separate job runs dbt docs generate and uploads manifest.json + catalog.json to the static host.

The compile-gate step (step 2 above) is what this chapter focuses on; the test-subset step is Ch 12's state-aware selection, and the docs-regen step is Ch 9's documentation artifacts.

## Public attestation for the pattern

The dbt compile --warn-error CI pattern is documented community practice. dbt Labs' best-practice workflows guide argues for reviewing every change in a pull request and for building only the modified subgraph in CI; the /reference/commands/compile docs describe dbt compile as the right place to validate the graph without side effects. Every element of this pattern has a public reference; the Credora framing is a pedagogical composite, not a reproduction of any single team's pipeline.

## The ”posted to Slack” detail

Credora's pipeline also posts the compile-failure annotation to a team Slack channel. The content is the stderr of the failed dbt compile, and the plumbing is a built-in of every major CI tool — the pattern is not dbt-specific, the signal value is. A compile gate exists to fail *early*, and an early failure nobody notices is not much better than a late one.

---

## Summary

- The triage frame for turning a dbt error message into a fix has four layers — YAML, dbt, SQL, Connection — each with a different toolkit.
- Compiled SQL in target/compiled/ is the triage artifact you'll reach for most often; dbt compile --select <model> regenerates it. Compile opens a warehouse connection for introspective queries but materializes nothing, so it is much cheaper than dbt build.

- Four members of the `ref()` error family — missing, disabled, wrong version, cyclic — each with a distinct error text tell.
- Four YAML failure modes — tabs, indentation, wrong type, misplaced/unknown keyword.
- Five macro error modes — undefined, wrong arg count, dispatch miss, Jinja compile, and the unquoted argument, which raises nothing and compiles a hole into the SQL instead.
- `dbt debug` is the connection-level tool, separate from modeling-error triage.
- Log levels: `debug / info / warn / error / none`; the console defaults to `info` and the log file to `debug`, so `logs/dbt.log` already holds detail the console never printed, and `--debug` is a late-stage escalation rather than a first-resort tool. Log **formats** are a separate vocabulary — `text / debug / json / default`, defaulting to `default` on the console and `debug` in the file — so neither format default is `text` or `json`.
- Four things share the name "flag": global config flags, behaviour-change flags, the `warn_error` / `warn_error_options` pair, and the read-only Jinja `flags` object. A resource config such as `enabled` or `materialized` is none of them.
- Global configs resolve CLI > environment variable > `dbt_project.yml flags:` > `~/.dbt/user_settings.yml` > dbt's default — the documented order, whose fourth rung dbt Core 1.11 does not read — with two mirror-image exceptions: file-path configs cannot go in `dbt_project.yml`, and behaviour-change flags can go nowhere else. Environment variables are named `DBT_ENGINE_<CONFIG_NAME>`.
- Behaviour-change flags move through introduced (off by default) to mature (on by default) to removed, so a flag's default is a fact about your dbt version: four are mature at 1.11 and seven flip at 1.12.
- `--warn-error` promotes the warnings dbt routes through its warn-or-error handler and takes no warning name; a few warn-level events bypass that handler at 1.11 until `require_all_warnings_handled_by_warn_error` matures. `--warn-error-options` is the granular surface, with `error`, `warn` and `silence` keys.
- `--no-version-check` (`VERSION_CHECK`) is the sanctioned override for a `require-dbt-version` mismatch. It suppresses the diagnostic, not the incompatibility, so a pipeline that carries it permanently is a pin nobody maintains.
- The fix workflow: branch → edit → compile → run → test → commit → PR. The test step before commit is a blueprint-listed sub-skill.
- Exit codes are three, not many: `0` success, `1` a handled error with a run artifact to read, `2` an unhandled error with possibly no `target/` at all. dbt Cloud's run statuses (`10/20/40`) are a separate namespace and never appear as an exit code.
- `--fail-fast` (`-x`) stops on the first `error`, `fail` or `partial success`, cancels the in-flight queries and records every unbuilt node as `skipped`. CANCEL is a log line, never a node status. The same failing run exits `1` with the flag and without it; the run summary is what separates them.
- A compile-as-CI-gate pattern with `--warn-error` catches shape-level bugs before merge; contract drift needs `dbt build --empty` on top, because enforcement runs when the relation is created.

## Learning-goal checklist (self-assess)

- ☐ **Read a dbt error and classify it: dbt-side vs SQL-side vs YAML-side, and read a failed run's skips back to the one node that caused them.** §10.1 + practice Qs 1, 2, 3, 4.
- ☐ **Tell exit code `1` from exit code `2`, say what is on disk after each, and keep both out of dbt Cloud's run-status namespace.** §10.1 + practice Q 26.

- ☐ **Say what `--fail-fast` cancels, what it records as `skipped`, and what it leaves unchanged about the exit code.** §10.1.
- ☐ **Inspect compiled SQL in `target/compiled/` as the first triage step.** §10.2 + practice Qs 11, 12.
- ☐ **Recognize the `ref()` error family: missing, typo, cyclic, disabled upstream — and say which stage raises each.** §10.3 + practice Q 5; Mock 1 Q39.
- ☐ **Read the five macro error signatures — undefined, wrong arity, dispatch miss, Jinja syntax, and the unquoted argument that fails silently — and the log level that surfaces more; keep the five log LEVELS apart from the four log FORMATS and their differing defaults.** §10.5, §10.7 + practice Qs 13, 14, 17, 21, 22, 25.
- ☐ **Fix YAML failure modes: tab-vs-space, indentation, misplaced keyword, wrong data type — and tell a hard type violation from a merely unrecognised key.** §10.4 + practice Qs 9, 10.
- ☐ **Use `dbt debug` for connection issues.** §10.6 + practice Qs 15, 16.
- ☐ **Tell the four things dbt calls a flag apart, and set a global config on the right surface in the right precedence order — including the environment-variable name and the spellings a boolean value accepts** (§10.9.1) + practice Qs 7, 8, 19, 20, 23.
- ☐ **Explain the introduced → mature → removed lifecycle, read a behaviour-change flag's 1.11 default off it, and say what five named flags actually change** (§10.9.2) + practice Qs 6, 24.
- ☐ **Choose between `--warn-error` and `--warn-error-options`, and recognise the deprecated `include` / `exclude` keys** (§10.9.3) + practice Q 28.
- ☐ **Say what `--no-version-check` overrides and what it leaves in place** (§10.9.3) + practice Q 27.
- ☐ **Follow branch → fix → test → PR loop.** §10.8 + practice Q 18.

---

## Practice questions

The drills lean analyse-heavy — an error message, a run summary or a compiled file, and the question is what it means.

**1.** A `dbt build` run ends with one model reported as `error` and eleven downstream nodes reported as `skipped`. What do the eleven skips tell you?
A. Each of the eleven failed a test of its own and was rolled back by dbt
B. dbt skipped them because their code is unchanged since the previous run
C. dbt built all eleven successfully but skipped the data tests attached to them
D. They were never executed — a failed node's descendants are short-circuited, so the single `error` is the root cause

**2.** `dbt run` fails with: `Database Error: SQL compilation error: invalid identifier 'ORDER_I'`. The column in the model's SELECT is `order_id`. Which layer is this error in?
A. dbt — a `ref()` is typo'd
B. SQL — the warehouse rejected a column identifier
C. YAML — a schema property is misnamed
D. Connection — credentials are wrong

**3.** `dbt run` fails before any model is selected: `Runtime Error: Syntax error near line 7` with a file path ending `.yml`. Which layer is this error in?
A. YAML — the file did not parse  B. dbt — a macro is undefined
C. SQL — the warehouse rejected the statement  D. Connection — no profile found

**4.** An error reads: `column "customer_name" does not exist`. Two plausible root causes: (a) the upstream column was renamed and the model still types the old name, or (b) `dbt run` resolved through a `--target` whose schema points at an older copy of the upstream that lacks the column. What is the fastest single action to disambiguate?
A. Re-run `dbt debug` and inspect its output for the schema the run resolved through
B. Re-run `dbt run --full-refresh` and see whether rebuilding the relation from scratch makes the column appear
C. Open `target/compiled/<path>.sql` and read the resolved `FROM` identifier, then paste the SELECT into the warehouse query editor
D. Re-clone the repository to rule out a local edit that changed the model's column list without being committed

**5.** A model contains `select * from {{ ref('stg_customrs') }}`. The staging file is named `stg_customers.sql`. What error appears at `dbt run`, and what is the fix?
A. YAML parse error — add a space after the colon in the model's `name:` property
B. Connection error — fix by rotating credentials
C. Database Error — the warehouse cannot find the table; fix by re-running `dbt seed`
D. Compilation Error — "depends on a node named 'stg_customrs' which was not found"; fix by correcting the typo to `stg_customers`

**6.** `source_freshness_run_project_hooks` matured in a release before 1.11. `state_modified_compare_more_unrendered_values` is introduced and scheduled to mature at 1.12. Your project's `dbt_project.yml` has no `flags:` block. On dbt Core 1.11, which statement holds?
A. The first is active and the second is not — a flag's default is a fact about your dbt version
B. Neither is active — a behaviour change reaches a project once it names the flag in its `flags:` block
C. Both are active, because 1.11 is later than the release each of them was introduced in
D. The first is active and the second makes dbt raise a parse-time error until you declare a value

**7.** A CI job needs `--fail-fast` on for every dbt invocation it runs, without editing `dbt_project.yml`. Which environment variable does dbt Core 1.11 read for that global config?
A. `DBT_FAIL_FAST` — dbt ignores anything set in the reserved `DBT_ENGINE_` namespace
B. `DBT_ENGINE_FAIL_FAST`; the bare `DBT_FAIL_FAST` spelling now raises an unknown-config error
C. `FAIL_FAST`, since dbt strips its own prefix before matching an environment name to a config
D. `DBT_ENGINE_FAIL_FAST`, and the older bare `DBT_FAIL_FAST` spelling is read as well

**8.** A project sets a behaviour-change flag to `true` in its `dbt_project.yml` `flags:` block. For one invocation you want it off. Which of these turns it off for that run?
A. `dbt run --no-<flag_name>`, because a CLI option outranks every other surface
B. `DBT_ENGINE_<FLAG_NAME>=0` in the shell, because an environment variable outranks the project file
C. Nothing does — behaviour-change flags are read from the `flags:` block and from no other surface
D. `<flag_name>: false` in `~/.dbt/user_settings.yml`, because a user setting is the most specific surface

**9.** A model's config contains `materialized: true`. What is the problem?
A. `true` must be quoted as `"true"` before YAML will hand dbt a value it can use as a materialization
B. `materialized: true` is valid, and it makes the model rebuild on every run instead of materializing incrementally
C. The config key should be `materialization:`, not `materialized:` — the value is fine and the key is what dbt rejects
D. `materialized` expects a string value (`view`, `table`, `incremental`, `ephemeral`, `materialized_view`); a boolean is a type mismatch

**10.** A properties YAML has `description:` nested under `data_tests:` for a column. What happens?
A. dbt raises a hard `Parsing Error` on every adapter, because `data_tests:` must be a list and is now a mapping
B. The description is attached to the column, and `data_tests:` still runs the tests listed beside it
C. dbt warns on adapters that validate properties YAML and accepts the file silently on the rest
D. dbt moves the key up to the column level and records a deprecation for the misplacement

**11.** Which of the following is true about the files in `target/compiled/`?
A. They contain raw Jinja exactly as written in the model's `.sql` file, so a `ref()` still appears as a `ref()` call
B. They contain resolved SQL: every `ref()`, `source()`, `config()`, and Jinja variable has been expanded to literal identifiers and values
C. They contain the `CREATE TABLE` wrapper that `dbt run` executes, around the model's resolved SELECT statement
D. They are regenerated only by `dbt build`, never by `dbt compile`, which reads them rather than writing them

**12.** To regenerate compiled SQL for a single model `stg_orders` without materializing anything, which command do you run?
A. `dbt run --select stg_orders` B. `dbt build --select stg_orders`
C. `dbt compile --select stg_orders` D. `dbt ls --select stg_orders`

**13.** A model calls `{{ generate_surrogate_key(['a', 'b']) }}` and `dbt compile` fails with "'generate_surrogate_key' is undefined". The project's `packages.yml` lists `dbt-labs/dbt_utils`. What is the most likely **first** fix?
A. Run `dbt clean` to reset compiled artifacts
B. Call the macro namespaced as `dbt_utils.generate_surrogate_key([...])`
C. Re-install dbt via pip
D. Add `generate_surrogate_key` to the project's `macros/` directory as an empty stub

**14.** A project on Databricks calls a macro that dispatches on adapter. `dbt compile` fails with `In dispatch: No macro named 'my_macro' found within namespace: 'None'`, and a second line reading `Searched for: 'databricks__my_macro', 'default__my_macro'`. The macro has a `snowflake__my_macro` definition. What is the fix?
A. Change the project's adapter to Snowflake, so the `snowflake__my_macro` definition is the one dispatch looks for
B. Add a `databricks__my_macro` definition (or a `default__my_macro` fallback) so dispatch can resolve on the Databricks adapter
C. Rename `snowflake__my_macro` to `my_macro`, so the macro is found by name without dispatch having to prefix the adapter
D. Run `dbt debug` to repair the dispatch resolution, since the namespace reported as `None` points at an environment problem

**15.** You just rotated your warehouse password and updated `~/.dbt/profiles.yml`. Before running a full `dbt run`, you want to confirm that dbt can reach the warehouse with the new credential. Which command is the **most targeted** tool?
A. `dbt compile` B. `dbt run --select +stg_orders`
C. `dbt debug --connection` D. `dbt docs generate`

**16.** `dbt debug` reports "All checks passed." Immediately after, `dbt run` fails with `Compilation Error: Model 'fct_orders' depends on a node named 'stg_orderz' which was not found`. What does this tell you about the bug's location?
A. The warehouse connection is intermittent
B. `dbt debug` is stale and needs re-running
C. The bug is in the dbt layer, not the connection
D. `profiles.yml` is misconfigured

**17.** Which `LOG_LEVEL` value produces the most detailed log output?
A. `info` B. `debug`
C. `warn` D. `none`

**18.** You are on a fix branch and have just edited `stg_orders.sql` to correct a NULL-handling bug. Nothing is committed yet. Which sequence most closely matches the recommended loop for landing the fix?
A. commit → push → open PR → let CI run compile, run and test
B. `dbt compile --select stg_orders+` → `dbt run --select stg_orders+` → `dbt test --select stg_orders+` → commit → push → open PR
C. `dbt compile --select stg_orders+` → `dbt run --select stg_orders+` → commit → push → open PR → let CI run `dbt test`
D. `dbt compile --select stg_orders` → `dbt run --select stg_orders` → `dbt test --select stg_orders` → commit → push → open PR

**19.** An engineer wants every invocation of a project to write its log file to `audit_logs/` instead of `logs/`, and adds this to `dbt_project.yml`:

```
flags:
  log_path: audit_logs
```

The engineer then runs `dbt run` with no command-line options. Where does the log file end up, and why?
A. In `logs/` — `log_path` is a file-path config, which the `flags:` block accepts and then ignores
B. In `audit_logs/` — the `flags:` block is the project-wide surface for any global config
C. In `logs/` — dbt refuses the key with a parse error and falls back to the built-in default
D. In `audit_logs/`, but only for invocations that do not also pass `--log-path` on the command line

**20.** A teammate suggests "just set the `enabled` flag to `false` in your shell for this one run". Which correction fits dbt Core 1.11?
A. `enabled` is a global config like `--fail-fast`, so `DBT_ENGINE_ENABLED=0` sets it for that shell
B. `enabled` is a behaviour-change flag, so it belongs in the `flags:` block and nowhere else
C. `enabled` is a member of the Jinja `flags` object, so a macro can flip it while parsing
D. `enabled` is a resource config, not a flag — no environment variable reaches it

**21.** A macro is defined as `{% macro max_of(col) %} max({{ col }}) {% endmacro %}`. A model calls it as `select {{ max_of(order_id) }} as biggest from {{ ref('stg_orders') }}` — the column name unquoted. What does `dbt compile` do?
A. Succeeds, writing `max()` — the unquoted name resolved to `Undefined` and rendered as nothing
B. Fails with `'order_id' is undefined`, naming the missing variable and the line that used it
C. Succeeds, writing `max(order_id)` — Jinja reads a bare identifier in a call as a string literal
D. Fails with `macro 'max_of' takes not more than 1 argument(s)`, because `order_id` arrives unbound

**22.** A `dbt run` failed an hour ago. You did not pass `--debug`, the console output is long gone from your scrollback, and `logs/dbt.log` from that run is still on disk. What can you expect to find in it?
A. Exactly what the console printed, line for line — the file is a transcript of the console stream
B. Warnings and errors and nothing else — without `--debug`, dbt writes nothing below `warn` there
C. Debug-level detail for the failed node, with the rest of the run written at `info`
D. Debug-level detail, per-query round-trips included — the file log defaults to `debug`, the console to `info`

**23.** Four shells each export `DBT_ENGINE_FAIL_FAST` before invoking dbt: `yes`, `True`, `off`, and `2`. What does dbt Core 1.11 do with them?
A. The first three are honoured (`yes` and `True` on, `off` off); `2` is refused as not a valid boolean
B. `True` is honoured and the other three are not — the value must be spelled the way Python spells it
C. `1` and `0` are the accepted spellings, so these four shells leave the config at its default
D. Each of the four is honoured — dbt reads a non-empty string as true, an empty one as false

**24.** A project on dbt Core 1.11 declares an `on-run-start` hook whose SQL the warehouse rejects, and sets no behaviour-change flags. `dbt run` selects two models. What does the run summary report?
A. `PASS=0 WARN=0 ERROR=1 SKIP=2 NO-OP=0 TOTAL=3` — a failed `on-run-start` hook skips the selected nodes
B. `PASS=0 WARN=0 ERROR=3 SKIP=0 TOTAL=3` — the hook failure is charged to each model as its own error
C. `PASS=2 WARN=1 ERROR=0 SKIP=0 TOTAL=3` — a hook failure is a warning, and the invocation exits 0
D. `PASS=2 WARN=0 ERROR=1 SKIP=0 NO-OP=0 TOTAL=3` — the hook failure is reported and the models build anyway

**25.** A run is invoked as `dbt run --log-level warn`. Which destinations end up at `warn`, and what would `--log-level-file warn` have done instead?
A. Both the console and `logs/dbt.log`; `--log-level-file` sets the file alone, leaving the console at its `info` default
B. The console alone; `--log-level-file` sets both, because the file log is a superset of the console stream
C. Both, and `--log-level-file` is a synonym for it that changes nothing
D. Neither — `log_level` is settable only in the `flags:` block of `dbt_project.yml`, so there is no CLI option for it

**26.** A `dbt run` ends with one model `error` and eleven nodes `skipped`, and a CI step branches on the number the shell gives it. Which number is that, and where do `20` and `40` come from?
A. `1` — a handled error; `20` and `40` are dbt Cloud run statuses, a separate namespace that never appears as a process exit code
B. `0` — skips are not failures, and dbt reserves a non-zero exit for an invocation that could not complete
C. `2` — a run that leaves nodes unbuilt did not complete, so no `run_results.json` is written
D. `20` — dbt exits with the node-status code for `error`, and `40` is the exit it uses when a run only skips

**27.** A project pins `require-dbt-version: [">=1.9.0", "<1.11.0"]` and CI is running dbt 1.11, so every command stops with a version-incompatibility error. A developer adds `--no-version-check`. What is the state of the pipeline?
A. Correct — the flag relaxes the pin to the installed version and the project is now compatible
B. Running, but no more compatible than before — the flag suppresses the error, not the incompatibility
C. Still failing — `--no-version-check` applies to package versions, not to `require-dbt-version`
D. Running, and dbt rewrites `require-dbt-version` to match the installed version

**28.** You want CI to fail when a pull request introduces any deprecation warning, while leaving every other warning at warn level. Which invocation does that?

A. `dbt build --warn-error`
B. `dbt build --warn-error-options '{"warn": ["Deprecations"]}'`
C. `dbt build --warn-error-options '{"error": ["Deprecations"]}'`
D. `dbt build --warn-error-options '{"error": "all", "silence": ["Deprecations"]}'`

## Answer key

**1. D.** A failed node's descendants are not executed at all — dbt marks them `skipped` and moves on, so a run summary of one `error` above eleven `skipped` describes one failure and eleven consequences. Read the `error`; the skips carry no independent diagnostic information. That is also why `result:error+` (Ch 12) is the selector that re-runs the failure plus everything it blocked. A skipped node ran nothing, so it cannot have failed a test of its own (A), and nothing was built to roll back; `skipped` is not a test outcome (C); and dbt does not skip on the basis of unchanged code unless you ask it to with state selection (B). Source: `/reference/commands/build`.

**2. B.** The wrapper phrase is "Database Error" and the verbatim warehouse text ("SQL compilation error: invalid identifier") is warehouse-emitted — Snowflake's wording, in this case. The bug is in the SELECT list of the compiled SQL. Opening `target/compiled/<path>.sql` and pasting into the warehouse query editor will reproduce the failure immediately. Neither YAML (C) nor a ref-level dbt issue (A) produces Database-Error wording; connection errors (D) say so explicitly. Source: `/guides/debug-errors` ("database errors" category).

**3. A.** The error fires before dbt enters the compile stage — no model name is mentioned because dbt has not built the graph yet. YAML parse failures halt dbt at the parse step; the line:column in the message points at the offending `.yml` file. Option B requires the YAML to have parsed first. Option C requires the graph to have compiled and a query to have hit the warehouse. Option D would be reported by `dbt debug` or as a connection error, not a syntax error in a YAML file. Source: `/guides/debug-errors` ("Invalid YAML" section).

**4. C.** The compiled SQL shows the fully-qualified identifier that `ref()` resolved to and the exact SELECT list dbt sent. If the `FROM` identifier is wrong (root cause b), the wrong schema is visible immediately; if the identifier is right but the column name is a typo, pasting into the warehouse reproduces the error and you can inspect the upstream's actual column list. Neither `dbt debug` (A — connection-level only) nor `--full-refresh` (B — rebuilds state, does not diagnose) helps. Option D is a wasted round-trip. Source: `/reference/commands/compile`, `/guides/debug-errors`.

**5. D.** `ref()` is resolved against the project's manifest at compile time; a typo's target does not exist in the manifest, and dbt raises a Compilation Error that names the missing node verbatim — the exact phrasing ("depends on a node named 'X' which was not found") is the standard error string documented on the debug-errors guide. The fix is the typo. YAML (A), SQL (C), and connection (B) are the wrong layers. Sources: `/guides/debug-errors` (canonical error phrasing), `/reference/dbt-jinja-functions/ref` (`ref()` resolution semantics).

**6. A.** A behaviour-change flag's default is a fact about the release you are running, not about the flag. `source_freshness_run_project_hooks` reached the mature phase before 1.11, so on 1.11 it is `true` and its new behaviour is live whether or not the project mentions it. `state_modified_compare_more_unrendered_values` is still in the introduced phase and does not mature until 1.12, so on 1.11 it is `false` and the old behaviour is what you get. That is the whole point of the phase vocabulary in §10.9.2, and it rules out B, which describes the introduced phase and applies it to both flags, and C, which treats "introduced before my version" as "on". D invents a requirement that does not exist: an undeclared behaviour flag takes its default silently, and a project with no flags: block parses without complaint. Source: /reference/global-configs/behavior-changes.

**7. D.** At 1.11 the convention is DBT_ENGINE_<CONFIG_NAME>, so DBT_ENGINE_FAIL_FAST is the name to reach for — and the bare DBT_FAIL_FAST spelling is *also* still read, because each global config registers both names. Both halves matter: knowing only the new prefix makes an older runbook look broken (A, B); knowing only the old one leaves the current documentation unrecognisable. DBT_ENGINE_ is a reserved prefix rather than an ignored one — a name dbt does not recognise inside it is dropped with a warning that it may collide (A). Nothing is stripped: an unprefixed FAIL_FAST is not a dbt config at all (C). Sources: /reference/global-configs/environment-variable-configs; both spellings confirmed against dbt Core 1.11.14.

**8. C.** Behaviour-change flags are the one config in dbt that the precedence chain never arbitrates, because they have exactly one surface. There is no CLI option in either spelling — dbt rejects --<flag_name> and --no-<flag_name> alike as unknown options (A) — and no environment variable: a DBT_ENGINE_-prefixed name for a behaviour flag is not a recognised config at all, and dbt warns that you have put a custom variable in a reserved namespace before ignoring it (B). user_settings.yml is the *lowest*-precedence surface, not the most specific — and on dbt Core 1.11 it is not read at all (§10.9.1), so D is wrong twice over. The design intent is the whole point: adopting a new default is a version-controlled, peer-reviewed decision, not something one engineer does in one shell. Sources: /reference/global-configs/project-flags, /reference/global-configs/about-global-configs.

**9. D.** The materialized config takes one of the built-in materialization names as a string. A boolean true is a parse- or schema-validation error; dbt does not coerce. The key is materialized: (C is wrong) and the value is not a boolean (B is wrong). Source: /reference/resource-configs/materialized.

**10. A.** YAML will parse the structure, but dbt validates it against its schema for properties YAML. data_tests: is a list of test invocations; description: belongs at the column level, a peer of data_tests: and not a child of it. Nesting it there makes data_tests: a mapping where the schema requires an array, so dbt raises Parsing Error / at path ['columns'][0]['data_tests'] and stops. Option C is the trap, because it is true of a *different* fault: an unknown key sitting at a level dbt does not expect is a validation warning on BigQuery, Databricks, Redshift and Snowflake and silent everywhere else (§10.4). A type violation is not that — it is hard on every adapter, with no config that downgrades it. dbt never auto-moves keys (D), and the file does not load at all, so nothing is attached (B). Source: /reference/configs-and-properties; error text confirmed against dbt Core 1.11.14.

**11. B.** target/compiled/ contains the resolved SELECT — Jinja fully expanded, ref() calls resolved to fully-qualified identifiers, variables substituted. The raw Jinja is the source .sql file (A), not the compiled artifact. The CREATE TABLE / MERGE wrapper is in target/run/ (C), a separate directory. dbt compile is exactly the command that produces these artifacts without running them (D). Source: /reference/commands/compile, /guides/debug-errors.

**12. C.** dbt compile parses the project and writes compiled SQL to target/compiled/; --select narrows the operation to one model, and nothing is materialized. dbt run (A) and dbt build (B) both materialize, which the stem rules out. dbt ls (D) is the closest trap: it resolves the graph and prints the selected nodes, so it looks like a cheap compile — but it writes manifest.json and no per-model SQL, and target/compiled/ stays empty. Watch this one on the exam: dbt docs generate is *not* a safe distractor here, because it compiles the whole project as a side effect of building the catalog and does leave compiled SQL behind. Source: /reference/commands/compile; artifact behaviour confirmed against dbt Core 1.11.14.

**13. B.** This per-model undefined-macro error means the call lacks the package namespace (dbt_utils.generate_surrogate_key). The tempting alternative — "dbt deps has not been run" — is not reachable: with packages declared and dbt_packages/ absent, dbt stops at project load with the package-count error and never compiles a model at all (Ch 8 §8.4). Seeing this message therefore tells you the package IS installed. dbt clean (A) removes compile artifacts but does not install packages; pip reinstall (C) affects the dbt runtime, not dbt packages; a stub (D) hides the error but breaks the macro's logic. Source: /docs/build/jinja-macros.

**14. B.** adapter.dispatch resolves adapter-specific variants by looking for <adapter>__<macro> and then default__<macro>. With neither present, dispatch fails — and note the shape of the message, because it is the part candidates misread: the headline names the **bare** macro, and the adapter-prefixed names dbt looked for appear on the Searched for: line beneath it. Add the Databricks variant, or add a default__my_macro that covers every adapter without one. Switching adapters (A) is not a fix; renaming the Snowflake variant to my_macro (C) destroys the dispatch target and breaks Snowflake too; dbt debug (D) tests connectivity and has no bearing on macro resolution. Sources: /docs/build/jinja-macros, /reference/dbt-jinja-functions/dispatch; error text confirmed against dbt Core 1.11.14.

**15. C.** dbt debug --connection runs the database-connectivity subset of dbt debug's checks — the fastest, most targeted way to confirm credentials work before committing to a full run. dbt compile (A) does open a warehouse connection (for introspective queries to populate the relation cache), so it would surface a credential failure, but it is not the standard reachability check and it does extra work parsing and rendering the project that adds no diagnostic signal here; dbt run (B) also materializes models, which is more work than you need for a connectivity check; dbt docs generate (D) queries the warehouse for catalog metadata and would similarly surface an auth failure, but it is not the standard connectivity tool. Source: /reference/commands/debug.

**16. C.** dbt debug validates connectivity and environment only — the profile resolves, the credentials work, the adapter and Python versions are compatible. It never parses the project or resolves a single ref(), so a pass says nothing at all about the graph. The sequence in the stem is therefore normal and informative rather than contradictory: it places the bug above the connection layer, in this case at a missing ref() target. profiles.yml (D) is what dbt debug checks, so a pass rules that out. Options A and B are not what the debug pass implies. Source: /reference/commands/debug.

**17. B.** debug is the most verbose level — it captures every diagnostic event dbt emits, including per-query warehouse round-trips and parse-order detail. info (A) is the default, showing only run-level progress. warn (C) narrows to warnings and errors only. none (D) disables log output. Source: /reference/global-configs/logs.

**18. B.** The blueprint's Topic 3 sub-bullet on building and testing a fix before merge is this loop (§10.8), and the ordering is the sub-skill: verification sits *before* the commit, not after it. The + suffix extends each selection to downstream nodes because a local fix can break a consumer. Option A commits and pushes unverified and leaves CI to find out. Option C verifies that the fix compiles and builds, then ships it before anything is tested, so a not_null the fix broke surfaces in CI rather than on the branch. Option D runs the right three commands in the right order and drops the +, which confines every one of them to stg_orders itself and never exercises the consumers a NULL-handling change is likeliest to break. Source: /docs/platform/git/version-control-basics, /reference/commands/compile.

**19. A.** log_path is one of the two file-path configs — --log-path and --state — that point at directories depending on where and how a command is being run, so they are settable on the command line and through the environment (DBT_ENGINE_LOG_PATH) and nowhere else. Put one in the flags: block and dbt neither honours it nor complains: the run exits 0, audit_logs/ is never created, and the log goes to the default logs/. That silence is the whole exam point, which is why C is wrong in its mechanism even though it lands on the right directory — there is no parse error to fall back from. B applies the ordinary precedence chain to a config that is exempt from it, and D compounds the same mistake by inventing a tie-break between two surfaces that never both apply. The rule's scope is the flags: block, not dbt_project.yml as a whole (§10.9.1). Sources: /reference/global-configs/about-global-configs, /reference/global-configs/logs; silent-ignore behaviour confirmed against dbt Core 1.11.14.

**20. D.** `enabled` configures a **resource** — it decides whether a model is part of the project graph — and resource configs are set in YAML on the resource, in `dbt_project.yml` under a path, or in a `{{ config() }}` call. Flags are a different system entirely: they configure an invocation, a project, or a project's migration posture. Reading `enabled` as a flag is exactly the confusion that makes §10.9.1's behaviour-change exception look arbitrary. There is no `DBT_ENGINE_ENABLED`, because the environment-variable surface exists for global configs only (A); `enabled` is not on the behaviour-flag list and never was (B); and the Jinja `flags` object is read-only, so a macro reads the invocation's settings and cannot change one (C). Source: `/reference/global-configs/about-global-configs`, `/reference/resource-configs/enabled`.

**21. A.** Jinja has no bare identifiers: `order_id` inside the call is the name of a *variable*, nothing in the rendering context supplies it, and an undefined variable renders as the empty string. The macro itself resolved fine, so there is no undefined-macro banner (B) and no arity complaint — one argument was passed and one was expected (D). Jinja does not quote a bare name for you (C). What you get is a compile that exits 0 and a compiled file reading `max()`, and the failure only appears at run time when the warehouse rejects it as a Database Error — one layer below where the bug actually is (§10.5). Source: `/docs/build/jinja-macros`; compiled output confirmed against dbt Core 1.11.14.

**22. D.** The console and the log file have separate levels. The console defaults to `info`; the file defaults to `debug`, so `logs/dbt.log` holds the debug-level events the console never showed you — per-query warehouse round-trips, parse and compile order, macro resolution. That is the reason `--debug` is a late-stage escalation rather than something to re-run for: for a run that has already happened, the detail is on disk. A treats the file as a transcript of the console, which would make `--log-level-file` pointless; B and C both understate what is written, and neither matches a file that is an order of magnitude longer than the console output of the same run. Source: `/reference/global-configs/logs`.

**23. A.** A boolean global config accepts the ordinary spellings, case-insensitively — §10.9.1's table has the set. `yes`, `True` and `off` are all in it, so the first three shells set the config, two on and one off. `2` is not, and dbt refuses it rather than coercing it: the invocation aborts with `Invalid value for '--fail-fast' / '-x': '2' is not a valid boolean`, which also tells you that an environment variable is parsed as the CLI option it feeds. B mistakes the accepted set for Python's `repr`; C mistakes it for a numeric-only set, which would leave `DBT_ENGINE_FAIL_FAST=true` inert; D is the shell convention, under which `2` would mean true. Source: `/reference/global-configs/environment-variable-configs`; accepted values confirmed against dbt Core 1.11.14.

**24. D.** `skip_nodes_if_on_run_start_fails` is `false` at 1.11, so a project that sets no behaviour flags gets the old behaviour: the hook error is reported, and the selected models build regardless — `PASS=2 WARN=0 ERROR=1 SKIP=0 NO-OP=0 TOTAL=3`. A is the *same* run with that flag set `true`, which is what 1.12 will make the default, and it is the answer a candidate reaching for the newest documentation will give. Note what does not discriminate the two: both invocations exit `1`, so only the summary tells them apart. B invents an error status for nodes that never ran, and C misreads a failed hook as a warning — the run does not exit 0. Sources: `/reference/global-configs/behavior-changes`, `/reference/project-configs/on-run-start-on-run-end`; both flag values executed against dbt Core 1.11.14.

**25. A.** `--log-level` sets the minimum severity for **both** destinations at once — the option's own help says so — so `--log-level warn` quietens the console and `logs/dbt.log` together. `--log-level-file` is the narrower option: it overrides the file alone and leaves the console on whatever `--log-level` or the `info` default gave it (§10.7). B inverts the pair. C would make the file-specific option pointless. D is wrong twice: `log_level` is an ordinary global config with a CLI option, and the `flags:` block is the lowest-precedence of the three surfaces that resolve at 1.11, never the only one (§10.9.1). Source: `/reference/global-configs/logs`; option scoping confirmed against dbt Core 1.11.14.

**26. A.** Two number sets share the page and mean nothing in common. Process exit codes are `0`, `1`, `2`; a run that finishes and reports failures — which is what one `error` above eleven `skipped` is — is the handled case and exits `1`, with `run_results.json` on disk. `10`, `20`, `30` and `40` are the statuses dbt Cloud's list-runs API reports for a whole run; no process ever exits with one (§10.1). B is the reading that a red build is only red when dbt itself breaks. C is the standing exit-1-vs-2 trap inverted: `2` means dbt never got a run to report on, and this run reported one. D promotes a run status to an exit code, which is the confusion the two sets exist to create. Sources: `/reference/exit-codes`, `/reference/commands/run`; exit codes executed against dbt Core 1.11.14.

**27. B.** `--no-version-check` — equivalently the `VERSION_CHECK` config — is the sanctioned override for a `require-dbt-version` mismatch: it suppresses the version-incompatibility error and lets dbt run anyway. What it does not do is make the project compatible. It suppresses the *diagnostic*, not the incompatibility, so whatever the pin was protecting against is still present: a macro signature that changed, a config that means something else now, a materialization that behaves differently. Reach for it deliberately and briefly — to see how much actually breaks before committing to an upgrade, or to unblock one run while the real fix is in review — and read a CI pipeline that carries it permanently as a pin nobody has maintained. Source: `/reference/global-configs/version-compatibility`.

**28. C.** `Deprecations` is a **bulk** name rather than a single warning, so `--warn-error-options '{"error": ["Deprecations"]}'` escalates every deprecation warning at once and leaves the rest alone — documented as new in v1.10. That is the CI shape for "no new deprecations merge". A is the reflex answer and overshoots: `--warn-error` promotes everything, so the build fails on warnings that have nothing to do with deprecation. B puts the name in the wrong key: `warn` keeps a warning at warn level, which is the state the stem is trying to leave — and on its own it does not even run, because `warn` may only be specified when `error` is `"all"`/`"*"` or `Deprecations` is in `error` or `silence`. D inverts the requirement precisely, promoting all the warnings you wanted left alone and silencing the class you wanted to catch.

# Chapter 11

# The dbt CLI and node selection

> **Scope.** The CLI is where you actually use dbt. Every workflow in this book — local development, CI, scheduled deploys, incident response — terminates in a dbt command with some combination of `--select`, `--exclude`, `--selector`, and a handful of global flags. The cert tests this surface harder than any other single topic. §11.1 maps every invocable command into four functional groups. §11.2 carves out `dbt run` vs `dbt build` — the discrimination the exam asks about most. §11.3 does the same for `dbt compile` vs `dbt parse`, and closes on the parse cache that makes both of them fast and occasionally makes them lie. §11.4 walks `dbt ls`, which is how you introspect the project without touching the warehouse. §11.5 is the mental model for node selection — three orthogonal dimensions, which is the trick that reduces ten selector questions to one question repeated ten times. §11.6 catalogs every selector method. §11.7 drills the graph operators (`+`, `@`, `N+`, `+N`). §11.8 covers the three set operators (union, intersection, exclusion). §11.9 introduces `selectors.yml` for named, reusable selections. §11.10 enumerates the global flags every candidate should know. §11.11 and §11.12 cover the two build-time flags that change what data a run reads — `--empty` and `--sample`. §11.13 covers `.dbtignore`. §11.14 shows how Credora's CI glues all of this together into a slim-CI invocation.

**Prerequisites.** Ch 2 in full — you need the `ref()` / DAG mental model before the graph operators make sense, because every `+model` and `model+` expression is a traversal of the DAG you built in Chapter 2. Ch 10's triage frame reappears briefly in §11.3 and §11.14 (compile-vs-parse is a triage choice). §11.12 leans on `event_time`, which Ch 4 §4.3.7 introduces. No other hard prerequisites. Ch 11 feeds directly into Ch 12 (State, defer, and slim CI), which is selector syntax applied to the state artifacts in `target/`; the dependency map marks Ch 11 → Ch 12 as a hard arrow.

**Cheat-sheet pointer.** Front-of-book cheat sheet §9 (Commands reference grid) and §10 (Node-selection operators grid) are the one-line-per-command and one-line-per-operator distillations of this chapter. Use the cheat sheet for spaced recall; use this chapter for the reasoning that lets you pick the right command and the right selector when the exam gives you a scenario and four plausible-looking options.

---

## 11.1 The CLI surface

dbt's CLI groups naturally into four functional families. The table below is a map — one row per command, grouped by what the command is for.

### Build-time commands — execute models, tests, seeds, or snapshots

| Command | One-line purpose | Common flags | Doc ref |
|---|---|---|---|
| `dbt run` | Executes models against the warehouse. | `--select`, `--exclude`, `--full-refresh`, `--vars`, `--target`, `--threads` | `/reference/commands/run` |
| `dbt build` | `run` + `test` + `seed` + `snapshot` + functions — in DAG order, with short-circuit on failure. | Same as `run`; selection applies to all resource types. | `/reference/commands/build` |
| `dbt test` | Runs data tests and unit tests. | `--select`, `--exclude`, `--store-failures` | `/reference/commands/test` |
| `dbt seed` | Loads CSVs from `seeds/` into warehouse tables. | `--select`, `--full-refresh` | `/reference/commands/seed` |
| `dbt snapshot` | Executes snapshot SQL to capture SCD2 state. | `--select`, `--exclude` | `/reference/commands/snapshot` |
| `dbt compile` | Renders Jinja to SQL in `target/compiled/`; does NOT execute. | `--select`, `--inline` | `/reference/commands/compile` |
| `dbt retry` | Re-runs from the prior failure point using `run_results.json`. | `--threads`, `--vars`. NO `--select`. | `/reference/commands/retry` |

**Introspection commands — look at the project without touching the warehouse**

| Command | One-line purpose | Common flags | Doc ref |
|---|---|---|---|
| `dbt ls` (alias `dbt list`) | Lists resources matching a selector. | `--select`, `--resource-type`, `--output` | `/reference/commands/list` |
| `dbt parse` | Parses the project and writes `manifest.json` without rendering compiled SQL. | `--profiles-dir`, `--project-dir` | `/reference/commands/parse` |
| `dbt debug` | Validates connectivity, `profiles.yml`, project config, adapter. | `--connection`, `--config-dir` | `/reference/commands/debug` |
| `dbt show` | Previews a limited result set from a single model, test, analysis, seed, or snapshot. | `--select`, `--limit`, `--output`, `--inline` | `/reference/commands/show` |

### Artifact commands — produce docs or source-freshness artifacts

| Command | One-line purpose | Common flags | Doc ref |
|---|---|---|---|
| `dbt docs generate` | Writes `catalog.json` + `manifest.json` — the docs payload. | `--select`, `--no-compile` | `/reference/commands/cmd-docs` |
| `dbt docs serve` | Serves the docs site locally from the artifacts produced by `generate`. | `--port` | `/reference/commands/cmd-docs` |
| `dbt source freshness` | Queries configured sources for freshness; writes `sources.json`. | `--select`, `--exclude` | `/reference/commands/source` |

### Meta / lifecycle commands — manage the project itself

| Command | One-line purpose | Common flags | Doc ref |
|---|---|---|---|
| `dbt deps` | Installs packages declared in `packages.yml`; writes `package-lock.yml`. | `--upgrade` | `/reference/commands/deps` |
| `dbt clean` | Removes directories in `clean-targets`. If `clean-targets` is omitted from `dbt_project.yml`, the built-in default is just the project's `target-path/` (typically `target/`). `dbt init` writes starter projects with `clean-targets: ['target', 'dbt_packages']`. | (none) | `/reference/commands/clean` |
| `dbt init` | Bootstraps a project skeleton + profile entry. | (interactive prompts) | `/reference/commands/init` |
| `dbt clone` | Zero-copy clone of models from a prior `--state` manifest. | `--select`, `--state`, `--full-refresh` | `/reference/commands/clone` |
| `dbt run-operation` | Invokes a macro from the command line; useful for ad-hoc admin. | `--args '{key: value}'` | `/reference/commands/run-operation` |

Nineteen commands in total, across four families.

### `dbt show` — previewing rows without materialising a model

`dbt show` compiles one resource, runs the compiled SQL, and prints the first rows to the terminal. No model is materialised — though showing a seed loads it, because dbt runs the seed loader to have a table to read from. Three properties of the command are worth holding onto, because each one is a place the obvious guess is wrong.

**The preview is one node; the selection is not.** `--select` on `dbt show` resolves nodes exactly as it does on every other command — selector methods, graph operators, and indirect test selection (Ch 7 §7.6) all apply. `dbt show --select stg_orders` runs that model's attached tests too; `dbt show --select stg_orders+` runs every descendant model and their tests, and still previews `stg_orders` alone. So §11.5–§11.8 governs what the invocation *executes*, not what it prints — which is why a preview can fail inside a node you never named. What it prints is narrower still: dbt previews only the nodes whose name appears in the **first `--select` argument**. `dbt show --select path:models/staging` therefore compiles and executes every model under that directory — running their SQL without materialising anything, as the subsection says above — and prints nothing at all, exit 0 — a method or a path selector names no node, so every result is excluded from the output. `--select path:models/staging/stg_orders.sql` previews `stg_orders`, because now the name is in the argument. `--indirect-selection empty` narrows the invocation back to the one model. Previewing five models is five invocations.

**`--limit` rewrites the query.** The default is five rows, and `--limit 200` does not fetch the whole result and slice it in the terminal — dbt wraps your model's query and applies a SQL `limit` clause so the warehouse only processes and returns that many rows. That is why `show` stays cheap against a large table, and why the preview of an aggregate can surprise you: the limit lands on the outermost query, not on the inputs. Seeds are the exception: there is no query to rewrite, so a previewed seed prints in full.

**`--output` switches the format.** The default is `text`, the human-readable table you see in the terminal; `--output json` emits the same rows as JSON for piping into other tooling.

`--inline` skips resource selection altogether and runs an ad-hoc dbt-SQL string — `dbt show --inline "select * from {{ ref('stg_orders') }} where status = 'returned'"` — which is the fastest way to interrogate the DAG without adding a file to the project. Python models cannot be previewed. The reference page is `/reference/commands/show`.

### `dbt snapshot` — and the flag it ignores

`dbt snapshot` executes the project's snapshots and nothing else: no models, no tests, no seeds. `--select` and `--exclude` work normally against snapshot nodes. The trap is `--full-refresh`. `dbt snapshot` does not register the option, so the standalone command exits on a usage error. Inside a composite invocation the flag parses and produces a split worth memorising: `dbt build --full-refresh` rebuilds models and seeds from scratch and leaves snapshots intact, in the same pass, because the accumulated history *is* the value of the snapshot table. Ch 5 §5.3 owns the mechanics and the recovery path; the reference page for the command is `/reference/commands/snapshot`.

## What the `--select`-takes / doesn't-take pattern tells you

`dbt retry` is the outlier. It does **not** accept `--select` because its entire purpose is to consult `run_results.json` from the previous invocation and re-run whatever failed — the selection is implicit in the artifact. `dbt init` and `dbt clean` similarly do not take `--select` because they do not operate on nodes; neither do `parse`, `deps`, `debug`, `docs serve`, or `run-operation`. Every remaining command in the grid accepts `--select` and `--exclude`, and §11.5–§11.9 applies to them — `dbt show` included, though it previews only the one node you named. This is the single unifying pattern of the CLI: a command tells dbt *what to do*; `--select` tells dbt *which nodes to do it on*; the selector syntax is identical everywhere.

---

## 11.2 `dbt run` vs `dbt build`

The discrimination the exam asks about most. The two commands look similar and overlap in behaviour, but they have meaningfully different contracts.

`dbt run` executes *models only* — view, table, incremental, materialized_view, ephemeral (inlined into downstream models, not directly materialized). It does not run tests. It does not load seeds. It does not execute snapshots. If a model's upstream tests would have failed, `dbt run` runs the model anyway, because it is not looking at tests.

`dbt build` executes models, tests, seeds, snapshots and user-defined functions in a single DAG-ordered pass. The ordering matters: a model's tests run immediately after the model materializes, before any downstream model starts. If a model's tests fail, **`dbt build` short-circuits downstream work**: every node that depends on the failed model (directly or transitively) is marked `skipped` rather than executed. This is the property that makes `build` the recommended CI command. It means that when CI reports a failure, the failure is always the root cause, and the `skipped` downstream nodes are evidence of blast radius, not collateral damage.

The trade-off:

- `dbt run` is the right tool for local quick-loops. When you are iterating on a model and only care that it compiles and materializes, `run` is faster and doesn't require seeds/snapshots/tests to pass. Typical local usage: `dbt run --select stg_orders+`.
- `dbt build` is the right tool for CI, scheduled jobs, and any invocation where you want warehouse state to reflect a tested version of the DAG. Typical CI usage: `dbt build --select state:modified+ --defer --state ./prior-artifacts` (see §11.14).

On the exam, if the scenario emphasises testing, dependency-aware scheduling, or short-circuit-on-failure behaviour, the answer is `build`. If the scenario emphasises local development or "just materialize the models", the answer is `run`. The reference pages are `/reference/commands/build` and `/reference/commands/run`.

### What `dbt build` does NOT do

`dbt build` is a superset of `run/test/seed/snapshot`, not a superset of everything. It does not run `dbt deps` (packages must already be installed), it does not generate docs (`dbt docs generate` is separate), it does not `clone`, and it does not check source freshness. A CI pipeline that wants freshness gating typically runs `dbt source freshness` as a separate stage before `dbt build`.

---

## 11.3 `dbt compile` and `dbt parse`

Both commands validate the project without materializing anything. The difference is depth.

`dbt parse` — the lightest-weight project validation dbt offers. It reads every `.sql`, `.yml`, and `.csv` in the project, resolves `ref()` / `source()` dependencies into graph edges, and writes `manifest.json` into `target/`. It does **not** render compiled SQL. It does not hit the warehouse. It completes in seconds on most projects and in under a minute on huge ones. The docs page is `/reference/commands/parse`.

**dbt compile** — everything **parse** does, plus it renders every model's Jinja template into fully-resolved SQL and writes the result to **target/compiled/<project>/<path>/<model>.sql**. Compile does not execute the SQL. Depending on project size, compile takes seconds-to-minutes, because it has to render every template, not just resolve the graph. The reference page is /reference/commands/compile.

When to reach for each:

- **dbt parse** when you need **manifest.json** but not compiled SQL. The most common use is the first step of a state-aware CI job — generate the new manifest, diff it against the prior one, compute **state:modified+** — which only needs the graph, not the rendered SQL. **parse** is also a fast "does the project even load?" gate that CI can run on every commit.
- **dbt compile** when you need the rendered SQL in **target/compiled/** — most often during debugging (Ch 10 §10.2), or when you want to inspect what dbt would send to the warehouse without actually sending it. **dbt compile** is also the right command to run as a pre-merge gate in CI when you want **--warn-error** to turn deprecation warnings into failures (Ch 10 §10.10).

Both commands write **manifest.json**, and neither executes your models' SQL — but only one of them opens a warehouse connection. **dbt compile** connects: it runs introspective queries to populate the relation cache and to resolve whatever the templates ask the warehouse for, and **execute** is **True** while it renders. **dbt parse** connects to nothing, which is why the manifest it writes carries no compiled code. Ch 10 §10.2 owns that mechanism; what matters here is that "neither one touches the warehouse" is the wrong half of the distinction. The exam's Topic 3 debugging domain asks about **dbt compile** specifically; Topic 4's pipeline-troubleshooting sub-bullets occasionally touch **parse** as the fast-CI gate. Know both, and know that **parse** is the subset.

**dbt parse** also writes **target/perf_info.json** and prints its path on the way out — per-parser elapsed times and path counts for the invocation. It is the artifact you read when the *parse* is what got slow, as opposed to the run; **run_results.json** has nothing to say about parsing.

### Narrowing what you compile

**dbt compile** with no selector renders every node in the project, which on a large project is a lot of waiting for one answer. It takes the ordinary selection flags: **dbt compile --select fct_orders** renders that node alone, and the graph operators work as usual, so **--select +fct_orders** compiles it and everything it depends on.

**--inline** skips resource selection altogether and compiles an ad-hoc string against the project's context:

```
dbt compile --inline "select * from {{ ref('stg_orders') }} limit 5"
```

That is the fastest way to check what a **ref()** or a macro call resolves to without adding a file to the project. It compiles the string and prints the SQL; it does not execute it. **dbt show --inline** is the sibling that *does* run the query and print rows (§11.1).

### Partial parsing and the parse cache

Neither command re-reads the whole project every time. dbt caches the parsed manifest in **target/partial_parse.msgpack** and, on the next invocation, re-parses only the files whose contents changed. Partial parsing is on by default; **--no-partial-parse** turns it off for one invocation. It is what makes `dbt parse` a credible per-commit gate on a large project — and it is also what makes a stale project look like a broken one.

Six inputs invalidate the cache outright and force a full re-parse:

- `--vars` — any change to the values passed on the command line.
- `profiles.yml` — the connection fields of the *active* target. `threads`, and any output you are not running against, are not hashed and change nothing.
- `dbt_project.yml` — any change to the file at all, down to a comment.
- Installed packages — including a change to the `dbt_project.yml` of one already installed.
- The dbt version.
- A handful of macros dbt treats as overridable builtins — `ref`, `source`, `config`, `function`, and the `generate_schema_name` / `generate_database_name` / `generate_alias_name` family.

Everything else is incremental. Edit a model's SQL, add a `description:` to a properties file, write a new singular test, and dbt re-parses those files alone. The log tells you which of the two happened, because an invalidated cache prints its reason before parsing starts:

```
Unable to do partial parsing because a project config has changed
Unable to do partial parsing because config vars, config profile, or config target have
    changed
```

Environment variables are the middle case. A changed `env_var()` value re-parses only the files that read it — unless the variable is read from `profiles.yml` or `dbt_project.yml`, which puts you back on a full re-parse. One consequence is worth carrying into docs builds: while partial parsing is on, dbt does **not** re-render a `description:` that contains an `env_var()`, so the docs site keeps yesterday's value. `dbt docs generate --no-partial-parse` is the fix.

The same staleness is why dbt Labs discourage driving parse-time attributes — dependencies, configs, resource properties — from `run_started_at`, `invocation_id` or `flags`. Those change on every invocation, and a cached parse will not notice (Ch 10 §10.9).

When the cache itself is what is wrong, the symptom never says so. A node dbt insists does not exist, or a config that does not match what the YAML plainly says, is the shape of a stale or corrupt `partial_parse.msgpack`. Re-run with `--no-partial-parse`; if that clears it, `dbt clean` deletes the file outright. The reference page is `/reference/parsing`.

---

## 11.4 `dbt ls` — listing resources

`dbt ls` (alias `dbt list`) evaluates a selector and prints the matching nodes. It never queries the warehouse — though it does read and validate the connection profile on the way in, so it is not a command you can run in a checkout that has no `profiles.yml`. It is the most efficient way to answer "what models does `--select <expr>` actually include?" without guessing.

Two flags make `ls` useful beyond a flat model list.

`--resource-type` filters by node kind: `model`, `test`, `unit_test`, `source`, `seed`, `snapshot`, `exposure`, `analysis`, `function`, `metric`, `semantic_model`, `saved_query`, plus `all` (every kind) and `default` (the kinds the active command would already process). It does not accept `operation`, which the `resource_type:` *selector* does take (§11.6) — the flag's enumeration is the narrower of the two. Without this flag, `ls` lists every kind but `analysis`, and disabled nodes are never returned whichever flags you pass.

Both spellings work. The difference is **composability**. `resource_type:test` is a selector expression, so it takes graph operators and set operators like any other: `--select "resource_type:test,tag:nightly"` intersects, `+resource_type:exposure` walks upstream, and it can sit inside a `union:` in `selectors.yml`. `--exclude-resource-type test` is a flag: it filters the final node set and composes with nothing. Reach for the flag when you want a blunt whole-run exclusion, and for the method whenever the exclusion has to combine with anything else.

`--output` controls the format:

| Value | Prints |
|---|---|
| `selector` (default) | the project-qualified expression that would match the same set again, e.g. `my_project.staging.stg_orders` |
| `name` | just the node names |
| `path` | relative paths to files |
| `json` | full node metadata, useful for piping into `jq` |

Pair `--output json` with `--output-keys`, a space-delimited list of node properties, when the whole metadata blob is more than you want: `--output json --output-keys name resource_type materialized`.

And pair it with `--quiet` whenever something downstream has to read the result. `dbt ls --output json` on its own writes the version banner, the adapter line and the resource census to stdout ahead of the JSON, so a pipe into `jq` meets `Running with dbt=1.11.14` first and fails — zero lines parse. `dbt ls --output json --quiet` emits the JSON alone. This is the one place a logging flag is load-bearing rather than cosmetic: on `dbt run` it changes nothing that matters, and here it is the difference between a scripted selection that works and one that does not.

A few representative invocations:

```
# List every model tagged "daily"
dbt ls --resource-type model --select tag:daily

# Show the file paths of every test under the staging layer
dbt ls --resource-type test --select path:models/staging --output path

# Every source whose data advanced since the prior freshness run
# (run `dbt source freshness` first; --state holds the prior sources.json)
dbt ls --resource-type source --select source_status:fresher --state ./prior-artifacts --
    output json
```

The official reference is `/reference/commands/list`. Note the slug: the URL is `/list`, but the command is also invoked as `dbt ls`; both forms are supported.

### Using `dbt ls` to debug selectors

If a complex `--select` expression does not match what you expected, drop it into `dbt ls` first. The output is deterministic and costs no warehouse work, so you iterate in seconds instead of waiting for a `dbt run` to tell you what matched. Never run a production-costing command with a selector you have not first piped through `ls`.

---

## 11.5 Node selection — the three dimensions

Every node-selection expression answers three orthogonal questions. Read a selector by decomposing it into these three dimensions, and the exam's selector questions become mechanical.

1. **The thing.** Which nodes are you naming? By name (`fct_orders`), by tag (`tag:daily`), by path (`path:models/staging`), by config (`config.materialized:incremental`), by resource-type (`resource_type:test`), by state (`state:modified`), by test name (`test_name:unique`), by exposure, by package, by group, by access, by test type. The selector method (§11.6) answers this question.
2. **The graph.** Once you have named some nodes, which related nodes do you also want? Ancestors (`+fct_orders` — everything `fct_orders` depends on, plus itself), descendants (`fct_orders+` — everything that depends on `fct_orders`, plus itself), descendants plus the ancestors those descendants need (`@fct_orders`), depth-bounded (`2+fct_orders`, `fct_orders+3`), or degenerate (`fct_orders` — just the named node). The graph operators (§11.7) answer this question.
3. **The combiner.** When you have multiple (thing × graph) expressions, how do you combine them? Space-separated = union. Comma-separated within a single `--select` argument = intersection. `--exclude` = subtraction. The set operators (§11.8) answer this question.

### The 3x3 mental model

Laying the three dimensions side by side clarifies what any selector is actually asking for:

| Dimension | Example values | Answers the question |
|---|---|---|
| Thing (method) | `fct_orders`, `tag:daily`, `path:models/staging`, `config.materialized:incremental`, `state:modified` | **Which nodes?** |
| Graph (operator) | `model`, `+model`, `model+`, `2+model`, `model+3`, `@model` | **Which related nodes too?** |
| Combiner | space (union), comma (intersection), `--exclude` (subtraction) | **How do multiple expressions combine?** |

The exam tests all three dimensions, usually by varying one and holding the other two fixed.

### Worked reading of a complex selector

Take `--select tag:finance+ config.materialized:incremental --exclude tag:deprecated`.

- **Thing 1**: `tag:finance` — every node tagged `finance`.
- **Graph 1**: `+` suffix — include every descendant too.
- **Thing 2**: `config.materialized:incremental` — every incremental model.
- **Graph 2**: degenerate — just those nodes, no graph traversal.
- **Combiner** (for the two `--select` args, space-separated): **union**. The selected set is (`tag:finance+`) ∪ (`config.materialized:incremental`).
- **Subtractor**: `--exclude tag:deprecated` removes every node tagged `deprecated` from the union.

The full expression: "every `finance`-tagged node and all of its descendants, unioned with every incremental model, minus any node tagged `deprecated`." Read this way, the selector is parseable. Read as one blob, it is a memory test.

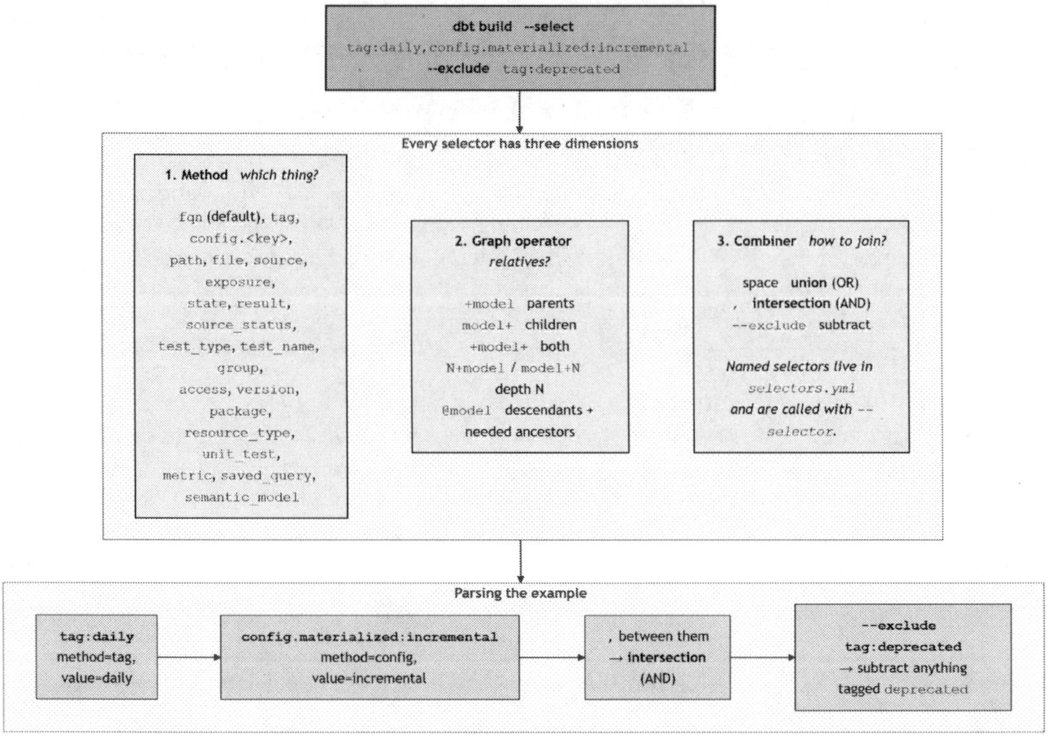


Figure 11.1: Anatomy of a `--select` expression. Every selector decomposes into three independent dimensions — the **method** picks which kind of attribute to match on, the **graph operator** decides whether relatives are pulled in, and the **combiner** controls how multiple selectors are joined. The worked example shows how the rules combine to resolve `tag:daily, config.materialized:incremental --exclude tag:deprecated`.

The reference for the selection grammar is `/reference/node-selection/syntax`.

---

## 11.6 Selector methods — the full catalog

Every method answers "which nodes?" in a different way. The default method is `fqn` — if a selector has no explicit method prefix, dbt treats it as a fully-qualified name lookup (which matches by model name, by project-qualified name, or by path fragment). Every other method requires an explicit `<method>:<value>` prefix. The catalog is **21 methods** (`fqn` + 20 named).

| Method | Syntax | Example | What it matches |
|---|---|---|---|
| `fqn` (default) | `fct_orders` or `my_project.staging.stg_orders` | `dbt run --select fct_orders` | Nodes by name or project-qualified name; also supports path fragments. |
| `tag` | `tag:<name>` | `--select tag:daily` | Every node whose `tags:` config contains `<name>`. |

| Method | Syntax | Example | What it matches |
|---|---|---|---|
| config | config.<key>:<value> | --select config.materialized:view | Nodes whose config matches the key/value. Works for any config — materialized, schema, alias, on_schema_change, etc. |
| source | source:*, source:<source_name> or source:<source_name>.<table> | --select source:raw_orders | Source nodes, at three granularities: source:* is every source in the project, the bare name is one source and all its tables, and the dotted form narrows to a single table. |
| path | path:<dir-or-file> | --select path:models/staging | Every node whose file lives under the given directory (or is the given file). |
| file | file:<filename> | --select file:stg_orders.sql | Nodes by file basename. |
| package | package:<package_name> | --select package:dbt_utils | Every node belonging to the named package (including installed packages). |
| group | group:<group_name> | --select group:finance | Nodes belonging to a YAML-declared group: (Ch 13). |
| access | access:public (or private/protected) | --select access:public | Models by access: config. |
| test_name | test_name:<name> | --select test_name:unique | Test nodes by generic-test name (unique, not_null, relationships, etc.). |
| test_type | test_type:data, test_type:generic, test_type:singular, or test_type:unit | --select test_type:data | Tests by category. data matches both generic and singular data tests; generic and singular narrow within data; unit matches unit tests and is disjoint from data (Ch 7 §7.8). |

| Method | Syntax | Example | What it matches |
|---|---|---|---|
| `resource_type` | `resource_type:<kind>` | `--select resource_type:snapshot` | Nodes by dbt resource kind — `model`, `test`, `unit_test`, `source`, `seed`, `snapshot`, `exposure`, `analysis`, `function`, `operation`, `metric`, `semantic_model`, `saved_query`. Note `operation`: the selector takes it, the `dbt ls --resource-type` flag does not, and the flag's enumeration differs in two further ways (§11.4). See `/reference/global-configs/resource-type` and `/reference/commands/list`. |
| `version` | `version:<spec>` | `--select version:latest` or `version:old` | Versioned models (Ch 13). Matches `latest`, `prerelease`, `old`, or `none` — those four are the whole vocabulary, and an exact version number is not one of them. |
| `state` | `state:modified`, `state:new`, `state:modified.body`, `state:modified.configs` | `--select state:modified+` | Compared against `--state <manifest-dir>` (Ch 12). |
| `result` | `result:error`, `result:fail`, `result:skipped`, `result:success` | `--select result:error+` | Compared against `run_results.json` from a prior run (Ch 12). |
| `source_status` | `source_status:fresher+` | `--select source_status:fresher+` | Compared against `sources.json` from a prior `dbt source freshness` run (Ch 12). |

| Method | Syntax | Example | What it matches |
|---|---|---|---|
| `exposure` | `exposure:<name>` | `--select +exposure: weekly_board_pack` | The named exposure and, with `+` prefix, every ancestor it depends on. An exposure is a graph leaf, so a *trailing* `+` reaches nothing new: `exposure:<name>+` returns the same lone node the bare form does. |
| `metric` | `metric:<name>` | `--select +metric: revenue` | Semantic-layer metrics by name; typically combined with `+` to pull in the semantic models and upstream physical models the metric resolves against. Semantic Layer — out of scope (Ch 1 §1.5). |
| `saved_query` | `saved_query:<name>` | `--select +saved_ query:weekly_exec_ summary` | Saved queries declared in the semantic layer; with `+` prefix, every metric and semantic model the saved query depends on. Semantic Layer — out of scope (Ch 1 §1.5). |
| `semantic_model` | `semantic_model: <name>` | `--select +semantic_ model:orders` | Semantic models by name; typically combined with `+` to include the physical model the semantic model is bound to. Semantic Layer — out of scope (Ch 1 §1.5). |
| `unit_test` | `unit_test:<name>` | `--select unit_test: test_order_totals` | Unit-test nodes by name (Ch 7 §7.8). Distinct from `test_type:unit`, which is a *value* of the `test_type` method and takes no name. |

The main reference for the full method catalog is `/reference/node-selection/methods`. Four common gotchas:

- `config.materialized:incremental` vs `tag:incremental`. The first asks "what is the model's materialization?"; the second asks "is the model tagged with the string `incremental`?". These are different questions and return different sets.
- `config.` **reaches configs only — properties are not selectable.** The method reads the config namespace, and the config/property split of Ch 2 §2.4 decides what is in it. `description:`, `columns:` and the other things a properties YAML *declares* are not configs, so `config.description:` has nothing to match — and, exactly like the `|` non-operator of §11.8, it says so by selecting nothing at exit **0** rather than by erroring. There is no such thing as a property selector; `dbt ls --select "config.description: foo"` is indistinguishable from a config nobody has set.
- `fqn` supports **wildcards inside path fragments**: `--select staging.*` matches every node whose fully-qualified name begins with `staging.`. See §11.7 for the wildcard story.
- `path:` **reaches resources `fqn` cannot.** A bare directory name usually works as a selector, because dbt retries an unmatched expression against the unscoped fully-qualified name — `--select staging` and `--select path:models/staging` return the same models and the same tests. They diverge on sources. A source has no file of its own and no fqn path to match, so only `path:` returns the sources declared in a YAML file under that directory.

---

## 11.7 Graph operators — deep dive

Once you have named some nodes with a method, graph operators let you expand the selection to related nodes.

### `+` — the ancestor / descendant operator

- `+model` (prefix): the node plus every ancestor (every node it depends on, transitively).
- `model+` (suffix): the node plus every descendant (every node that depends on it, transitively).
- `+model+` (both sides): ancestors AND descendants. Legal syntax, rarely the right tool — it tends to grab the whole DAG when the selector is anchored on a central model. Use it only when you know exactly why you want both directions at once.

Which one you reach for follows from what you are doing:

- **Local development** — `+model`. Build a mart and every staging and intermediate model it depends on, in one command.
- **Blast radius** — `model+`. You changed a model; re-run everything that could be affected. `dbt build --select stg_orders+` exercises every downstream consumer.

### `N+` and `+N` — depth-bounded traversal

The plain `+` operator traverses the graph to unbounded depth. Prefix a positive integer to bound it.

- `2+model`: the node plus the next two layers of ancestors (its direct ancestors and their direct ancestors, but no further).
- `model+3`: the node plus the next three layers of descendants.

The integer is the only depth control there is: **there is no `--max-depth` flag**, and asking for one is a `No such option` error. Depth is a property of the selector, not of the command.

Depth bounds matter when a project has a wide fan-out and unbounded traversal would select hundreds of models. Useful during debugging a specific slice of the DAG, or when writing a CI job that tests only the immediate neighbourhood of a change.

## `@` — descendants plus the ancestors they need

`@model` selects the model, all its descendants, and the ancestors needed to build those descendants. Read it as "descendants first, then pull in whatever upstreams those descendants require." The docs page for graph operators is `/reference/node-selection/graph-operators`.

**`@` is front-position only.** It has no suffix form and no both-sides form, so the symmetry the `+` bullets set up does not carry over. `+model+` is legal; `@model+` is rejected outright, with *"@ prefix and + suffix are incompatible"*. `model@` is the more dangerous of the two mistakes: dbt reads the trailing `@` as part of a *name*, finds no node called that, and reports only that the criterion matched nothing.

`@` is the operator you reach for in deferred / CI runs where the downstream models you want to exercise may depend on parents that have not yet been materialised in the CI schema. `+model` would only give you the model's ancestors; `model+` would give you descendants but not the extra parents those descendants pull in from elsewhere in the DAG. `@model` is the combination that guarantees every descendant has all its inputs available.

## Wildcard glob inside method values (orthogonal to graph operators)

The `*` character is a glob inside a method value, not a standalone operator. `--select fqn:staging.*` matches every node whose fully-qualified name starts with `staging.`; `--select path:models/staging/*` matches every node under the staging directory. The glob is not confined to those two. Every method that matches on a **name** runs its value through the same Unix-style matching, so `source:*`, `tag:d*`, `test_name:not_*` and `+exposure:*` all resolve, and `?` and `[abc]` character classes work alongside `*`. The methods that take **no** pattern are the ones whose values are a fixed vocabulary: `access:`, `version:`, `test_type:` and `resource_type:` compare the value exactly. Three of those four are strict about it — `version:`, `test_type:` and `resource_type:` abort the invocation with an `Invalid ... selector` runtime error on a value outside their enumeration. `access:` is the exception, and the trap: it matches nothing and says nothing, so a typo like `access:internal` is a green run over an empty selection rather than a complaint.

## Diagrammatic intuition

Imagine a small DAG:

```
stg_orders     stg_customers     stg_products
     \              /                /
      int_orders_enriched           /
               |                   /
            fct_sales ______/
                 |
            mart_revenue
```

Against this DAG:

- `+fct_sales` selects `stg_orders`, `stg_customers`, `stg_products`, `int_orders_enriched`, `fct_sales`. (All ancestors, plus the node itself.)

- `fct_sales+` selects `fct_sales`, `mart_revenue`. (The node itself and all descendants.)
- `@fct_sales` selects `fct_sales`, its descendants (`mart_revenue`), AND the ancestors those descendants need to build — `stg_orders`, `stg_customers`, `stg_products`, `int_orders_enriched`. On this small DAG `@fct_sales` happens to cover the whole graph; on larger projects the set is typically a strict subset, because only the ancestors of the *selected-plus-descendants* set are pulled in, not the ancestors of the entire DAG.
- `1+fct_sales` selects `int_orders_enriched`, `stg_products` and `fct_sales` only — one layer up, and that is *both* of `fct_sales`'s direct parents, not just the one on the main chain.

These four patterns cover almost every graph-operator question the exam asks.

---

## 11.8 Set operators — union, intersection, exclusion

Once you have multiple (method × graph) expressions, you need to combine them. dbt supports three combiners with distinct syntax.

- **Union (space-separated).** `--select tag:daily tag:hourly` selects every node in either set. dbt unions space-separated expressions whether they reach the parser as two separate `--select` arguments or as a single quoted argument with a space inside (`--select "tag:daily tag:hourly"`).
- **Intersection (comma-separated within a single argument).** `--select tag:daily,config.materialized:incremental` selects every node that is **both** tagged `daily` AND has incremental materialization. The comma is the intersection operator; it must sit inside a single shell-argument (no space around it).
- **Exclusion (`--exclude`).** `--exclude tag:broken` removes every node tagged `broken` from whatever `--select` produced. `--exclude` always applies **after** `--select`. If no `--select` is provided, dbt defaults to "everything"; `--exclude` then subtracts from the full project.

### Precedence — subtraction always wins

Combining all three:

```
dbt build --select tag:daily tag:hourly --exclude tag:broken
```

Reads as: `(tag:daily` ∪ `tag:hourly) \ tag:broken`. The exclusion happens last. This is the precedence rule: even if a node is `tag:daily` and explicitly named, a matching `--exclude` removes it. There is no "force-include" syntax that overrides exclusion.

The reference pages are `/reference/node-selection/set-operators` and `/reference/node-selection/exclude`.

### The `|` non-operator

A common mistake from other CLI surfaces: treating `|` as an "or" operator. **dbt does not use the pipe character** anywhere in the selection grammar. Union is space-separated; intersection is comma-separated. A `|` does not fail loudly either: dbt reads it as a literal character inside the method value, so `dbt ls --select "tag:a|tag:b"` exits **0** with `The selection criterion 'tag:a|tag:b' does not match any enabled nodes` and `No nodes selected!`. What you get is a silent empty selection, not an error. The cheat sheet §11 calls this out explicitly.

### The , gotcha in a shell

Because comma is the intersection operator **within a single argument**, it is sensitive to shell-side parsing. If you accidentally shell-escape the comma or put spaces around it, you will get two independent arguments (union) instead of one compound argument (intersection). Quote compound selectors when unsure:

```
# Intersection - one argument, no whitespace around the comma
dbt run --select 'tag:daily,config.materialized:incremental'

# Union - two arguments, space-separated
dbt run --select tag:daily config.materialized:incremental
```

The first invocation runs only nodes that are both `tag:daily` AND incremental. The second runs every node that is `tag:daily` OR incremental. Different commands, different node sets; the only syntactic difference is one character.

### Combining over the test surface

The combiners are method-agnostic, so everything above applies to tests exactly as it does to models. Practise it there deliberately: §11.6 introduces the test-facing methods one at a time, and the exam asks for them joined.

```
# Generic tests that are ALSO tagged nightly - intersection, one argument
dbt ls --select "test_type:generic,tag:nightly"

# Only the `unique` tests among the nightly-tagged nodes
dbt ls --select "test_name:unique,tag:nightly"

# The same selection, executed rather than listed
dbt test --select "test_type:generic,tag:nightly"
```

The intersection is strictly narrower than either half, and on tests it is dramatically narrower. `test_type:generic` alone also returns every untagged generic test; `tag:nightly` alone returns the singular tests, the unit tests, and the models and exposures carrying the tag, because a tag is not a test-only attribute. Swap the comma for a space and the same two methods produce the union instead — a far larger set from a one-character edit.

Check the selector with `ls` before you run it (§11.4). `dbt test` widens the resolved set afterwards through indirect selection (§11.9), so `dbt ls` is the honest place to see what the expression itself matched.

---

## 11.9 `--selector` and `selectors.yml`

A named selector, declared in `selectors.yml` at the project root, lets you reference a complex selection pattern by name. The benefits are concrete: the pattern lives in version control and gets code review.

Minimal `selectors.yml`:

```
selectors:
  - name: nightly_core
    description: "Every daily or hourly model, excluding deprecated tags; used by the
    nightly-build CI job."
    definition:
      union:
```

```
      - method: tag
        value: daily
      - method: tag
        value: hourly
      - exclude:
          - method: tag
            value: deprecated

  - name: finance_slim_ci
    description: "Modified nodes under models/finance/, plus all their descendants."
    definition:
      intersection:
        - method: state
          value: modified
          parents: false
          children: true
        - method: path
          value: models/finance
```

Referencing a named selector from the CLI:

```
dbt build --selector nightly_core
```

`--selector` replaces `--select` / `--exclude` with a named YAML selector, and "replaces" is literal: pass both and the `--select` is **discarded in silence**. `dbt ls --select a --selector nightly_only` returns exactly what `--selector nightly_only` returns on its own, with no error and no warning. That is the failure mode to watch for — a team that adds `--selector` to an existing command line leaves the old `--select` in place and never learns it stopped meaning anything. If a CI job needs both a named pattern AND a runtime tweak, the cleanest pattern is to refactor the selector YAML to express the variation, or fall back to `--select` / `--exclude` inline.

Named selectors shine when:

- **Reusability**: two CI jobs share a selection pattern. Define it once in YAML; reference from both.
- **Readability**: the selector has enough clauses that an inline expression would sprawl.
- **Self-documentation**: a selector with a `description:` field lets a new team member see what `nightly_core` means without decoding a 120-character `--select` string.

The reference page is `/reference/node-selection/yaml-selectors`.

## Indirect selection — how tests get pulled in

Selecting a model selects its tests too. *Which* tests, and when, is `--indirect-selection`, and it has four modes:

| Mode | A test is included when |
|---|---|
| `eager` | **the default** — any one of its parents is selected |
| `cautious` | *all* of its parents are selected |
| `buildable` | all of its parents are selected, or are ancestors of the selection |
| `empty` | never; only tests named directly |

The mode that bites is `eager` on a relationship test. Select one model and you pull in a test whose other parent is not in the run, so it executes against whatever that parent currently holds — which in a CI schema may be nothing. `cautious` is the conservative choice for a slim CI run, and it is the answer to "my CI keeps failing a test on a model I did not change".

**Exclusion is not mode-independent, whatever the reference page implies.** `/reference/node-selection/test-selection-examples` says *"test exclusion is always greedy: if ANY parent is explicitly excluded, the test will be excluded as well"*, with no mode qualifier — and that sentence is true of `eager`, the default, and of nothing else. Executed on Core 1.11.14 against the two-parent relationships test between `fct_orders` and `dim_customers`, with **both** parents selected:

| `--indirect-selection` | no exclusion | `--exclude dim_customers` | `--exclude fct_orders` |
|---|---|---|---|
| `eager` (default) | test runs | **dropped** | **dropped** |
| `cautious` | test runs | test runs | test runs |
| `buildable` | test runs | test runs | **dropped** |
| `empty` | no tests | no tests | no tests |

The reading that fits: `--exclude` is itself a selection, expanded by the *same* indirect-selection mode and then subtracted. Under `eager` the exclusion drags the test out with its parent; under `cautious` it does not, so the test stays in the set it was already in. `buildable` splits the two exclusions because `dim_customers` is an *ancestor* of `fct_orders` — losing it leaves the test's ancestry still closed by the surviving parent, while losing `fct_orders` does not. So the exam-safe form of the rule is: **greedy under `eager`; name the mode before you answer.**

**Tests inherit tags from some levels and not others.** A tag written at the **column** level, or at the **source** / source-table level, is inherited by the tests attached there, so `--select tag:pii` reaches those tests by direct selection. A tag written at the **model**, seed, or snapshot level is **not** inherited by that resource's tests. So `dbt test --select tag:nightly` against a model tagged `nightly` selects nothing **directly** — and the tests still run, because the default `--indirect-selection eager` pulls in the tests of any selected parent. `dbt test` applies indirect selection exactly as `dbt build` does; it is not a difference between the two commands. Add `--indirect-selection empty` and the same invocation selects only tests tagged in their own right (§7.6).

**A selector's own `indirect_selection` beats the flag.** Set `indirect_selection:` on a criterion inside `selectors.yml` and that value wins for that criterion; the `--indirect-selection` CLI flag does not override it and is silently ignored wherever the YAML has spoken. This is the opposite of the usual "CLI beats config" instinct, and it is deliberate: a named selector is meant to mean the same thing wherever it is invoked from. See `/reference/node-selection/yaml-selectors`, which carries the precedence rule, and `/reference/global-configs/indirect-selection` for the modes themselves.

## Referencing one selector from another

A selector can be reused inside another with `method: selector`:

```
selectors:
  - name: nightly_core
    definition:
      union:
        - method: selector
          value: core_models
```

```
        - method: tag
          value: nightly
```

**What comes back is that selector's node set, exactly as it defines it.** Wrapping the reference in `children:`, `parents:` or `indirect_selection:` does not extend or re-interpret it — the referenced selector's own definition is final, and those keys on the reference do not apply to it. If you need `core_models` plus its children, the graph operator belongs inside `core_models`, or you write a second selector. Reuse here is composition, not inheritance.

### Default selectors

A selector can be marked `default: true`, which means dbt applies it whenever the CLI does not provide `--select` / `--exclude` / `--selector`. Useful for "safe by default" invocations — e.g., a production project that never wants `dbt run` to execute deprecated models, even if a developer forgets to pass a selector. Default selectors are a nudge, not a hard gate; any inline selector override still works.

---

## 11.10 Global flags every candidate should know

Flags are not worth memorising as a block. What is worth knowing is which one answers the situation in front of you — the table below is the lookup, and this is the index into it.

| The situation | What you run |
|---|---|
| A column was added upstream and the incremental table still has the old shape | `dbt run --full-refresh --select the_model` |
| A PR must be tested without rebuilding production | `dbt build --select state:modified+ --defer --state ./prior-artifacts` (Ch 12 §12.4) |
| The nightly build died on node 400 of 600 | `dbt retry` — it resumes rather than restarting (Ch 12 §12.7) |
| You want to know the SQL compiles and the contracts hold, without waiting for data | `dbt build --empty` (§11.11) |
| A table is too large to develop against | `dbt run --sample='{"start": "…", "end": "…"}'` (§11.12) |
| dbt is running in a container with no `~/.dbt` | `--profiles-dir`, plus `--target` to pick the output |
| A deprecation must fail CI rather than scroll past | `--warn-error` (Ch 10 §10.9) |
| Another tool has to read the node list | `dbt ls --output json --quiet` — without `--quiet` the log lines reach stdout first and nothing parses (§11.4) |
| Two dbt projects in one repository | `--project-dir` |
| The run is slow and the warehouse is idle | `--threads` |

| Flag | Purpose | Common use |
|---|---|---|
| `--full-refresh` | Rebuilds instead of loading incrementally. Applies to the data-loading commands — `run`, `build`, `seed` — and goes after the subcommand. | Recovery after a schema change; first-time builds of a new incremental. |
| `--vars '{key: value, ...}'` | Overrides `vars:` from `dbt_project.yml` for this invocation. | Per-environment switches, e.g., `--vars '{run_date: "2024-01-15"}'`. |
| --target <name> | Selects which `profiles.yml` target to use. | `dev` vs `prod` runs; CI uses `--target ci`. |
| --profile <name> | Selects which *profile* in `profiles.yml` to load, overriding the `profile:` key in `dbt_project.yml`. | A monorepo whose projects share one `profiles.yml`. One level up from `--target`. |
| --profiles-dir <path> | Overrides the default `~/.dbt` location for `profiles.yml`. | Docker containers, CI runners, isolated test environments. |
| --project-dir <path> | Runs dbt against a project in a non-cwd directory. | Monorepos with multiple dbt projects. |
| --threads <N> | Parallelism — how many nodes dbt executes concurrently. | Set per target in `profiles.yml`; omit it and dbt uses 1. Override at invocation time for ad-hoc tuning against warehouse contention. |
| `--fail-fast` | Stops the run on the first failure instead of continuing. | CI jobs that want early termination on any error. |
| `--warn-error` | Treats every warning as an error. | Strict-CI gates; contract-drift annotations (Ch 10 §10.10). |
| `--no-partial-parse` | Forces a full project re-parse instead of using the partial-parse cache. | Stale-cache recovery, and docs builds whose descriptions embed env vars — see §11.3. |
| `--quiet` | Suppresses non-error logging on stdout, leaving only the command's own output. On `dbt run` that is cosmetic — errors still surface, the final summary does **not**, and nothing about the build changes. On `dbt ls`, `dbt show` and `dbt compile --inline` it is functional: it is what makes the output machine-readable. | Scripting a selection — `dbt ls --output json` alone writes log lines into stdout and nothing downstream can parse it. |

| | | |
|---|---|---|
| `--no-version-check` | Skips the `require-dbt-version` check at parse time. | Local debugging where the team is mid-upgrade and you do not want the parse to refuse to run. |

The main surface is `/reference/global-configs/*`, whose Available-flags table lists every flag with its type, default, environment variable and CLI spelling. Each flag also has its own page under that surface; when in doubt, search the global-configs area for the flag name.

### Precedence — which setting wins

Most global flags can also be set via environment variables (e.g., `DBT_ENGINE_TARGET=prod`), and the CLI option beats every other surface — which is what lets `--target ci` override a target hard-coded in `profiles.yml`. Ch 10 §10.9.1 owns the precedence chain in full, along with the two exceptions to it.

### `--full-refresh` is resource-specific, not project-wide

`--full-refresh` changes behaviour for four resource kinds: an incremental model rebuilds from scratch (Ch 4 §4.5); a seed is dropped and recreated instead of truncate-and-inserted (Ch 5 §5.4); a materialized view is replaced rather than refreshed or altered in place (Ch 4 §4.1); and `dbt clone` recreates a target relation that already exists instead of leaving it alone. That last one is the least-known of the four — without the flag, `clone` finds the existing relation, logs `Relation ... already exists` and no-ops, which is why a second clone into a warm CI schema appears to do nothing (Ch 12 §12.8). It is a no-op on `view`, `table` and `ephemeral` models — those are rebuilt every run anyway. `dbt snapshot` does not accept the flag at all — `Error: No such option: --full-refresh`, exit 2 — and inside `dbt build` it never reaches a snapshot: a full-refresh build over a snapshot that already holds history reports `INSERT 0 0` and leaves every version in place (§11.1). So `dbt run --full-refresh` on a project with neither incremental models nor materialized views is indistinguishable from `dbt run`.

---

## 11.11 `--empty` — dry-running schema and logic

`--empty` limits every `ref()` and `source()` in the run to zero rows. dbt still renders the Jinja, still sends the compiled SQL to the warehouse, and still creates the relation — it just does all of that over empty inputs, which is what makes the run cheap. The reference page is `/docs/build/empty-flag`.

```
dbt build --target ci --empty --full-refresh
```

Read the flag as *a dry run of your project against a real warehouse*, and everything else about it follows.

### `--empty` is not `dbt compile`

This is the discrimination worth drilling, because the two look like they occupy the same slot and do not. `dbt compile` (§11.3) renders SQL into `target/compiled/` and creates nothing; the warehouse never sees the query. `--empty` executes. Every selected model is really built, with its full column list. What `--empty` guarantees is the INPUT — every `ref()` and `source()` limited to zero rows — and the output follows from that, normally zero rows but not by decree: a model whose SELECT does not read its inputs, or aggregates without a GROUP BY, still returns a row. So an `--empty` build catches everything a compile catches — Jinja that does not render, a `ref()` that does not resolve — *plus* everything only the warehouse can tell you: a column that does not exist on the upstream table, a cast the platform rejects, a function name that is wrong for this adapter, a schema the run user cannot write to.

That is a real gate. It is also a narrow one, and the next two subsections are the boundaries of it.

### Default data tests can pass vacuously

`--empty` limits `ref()` and `source()` inputs to zero rows; it does not make every SQL model output empty. A model that emits literal or aggregate output can still return rows. For a table model whose SQL is `select order_id from {{ ref('stg_orders') }}`, the selected input is empty, so the relation has zero rows. Its default `unique` and `not_null` data tests then pass vacuously: `unique` finds no duplicates and `not_null` finds no nulls.

Two boundaries matter. A non-emptiness test can return a failing row when its input is empty, even with the default `fail_calc: count(*)`. Separately, a custom `fail_calc` such as the unwrapped `sum()` of Ch 7 §7.5 returns NULL over an empty failure query and errors unless you handle that case. Counting failures does not by itself guarantee vacuous success; the failure query must also return no rows, as the default built-in tests do over a zero-row relation.

A green `--empty` build validates the selected SQL execution and schema paths, not production row values. Vacuous success follows from the flag's input limit and the tests' failure queries; it is not a separate validation mode. See `fail_calc` for custom failure calculations.

### It limits rows, not dependencies

`--empty` does not exempt a model from needing its upstreams to exist. Select a model whose parent relation has never been built and the run fails with a missing-relation error from the warehouse, exactly as it would without the flag — dbt is still issuing a `select` against that parent, and a table that does not exist cannot be read, empty or otherwise. The flag limits input **rows**, not input **dependencies**.

The practical consequence: `--empty` is a dry run against a warehouse that already carries your schema, not a way to stand a project up from nothing. On a full-project selection this stays invisible, because each parent is built earlier in the same pass; it bites the moment you narrow the selection to a subset that skips one.

### `.render()` — when a reference must stay real

`--empty` does its work by rewriting each reference, not the model. Compile anything under the flag and the `ref()` comes back as a subquery that can only return nothing:

```
select o.order_id, c.customer_id
from (select * from "credora"."ci"."stg_orders" where false limit 0)
    _dbt_limit_subq_stg_orders o
left join (select * from "credora"."ci"."dim_customers" where false limit 0)
    _dbt_limit_subq_dim_customers c on c.customer_id = o.customer_id
```

That substitution is harmless wherever a relation and a subquery are interchangeable, which is most of a `select`. It is not harmless anywhere the statement needs a relation *name*. Hooks are the usual casualty:

```
models:
  - name: fct_orders
    config:
```

```
pre_hook: "grant select on {{ ref('stg_orders') }} to reporter"
```

On a normal run that grants. Under `--empty` the hook string renders with a subquery where the table name should be, and the warehouse refuses it:

```
Database Error in model fct_orders
  syntax error at or near "("
  LINE 2:        grant select on (select * from "credora"."ci"."stg_orders" wh...
```

`.render()` is the way out. It asks the reference for its relation name and nothing else, so that one reference is exempt from the zero-row rewrite while the flag stays on everywhere else:

```
pre_hook: "grant select on {{ ref('stg_orders').render() }} to reporter"
```

It is the same keyword as §11.12's opt-out from `--sample`, and as the microbatch auto-filter opt-out in Ch 4 §4.4.6 — one method, three mechanisms, and in every one of them it means *give me the plain relation*. Reach for it on the reference that breaks, not as a habit: a `.render()`ed reference under `--empty` reads the real table, which is the cost the flag exists to avoid.

### Where the flag applies

`run`, `build`, `snapshot`, and `compile` accept `--empty`. `dbt seed` does not, so `dbt seed --empty` is not an answer to reach for. Python models silently ignore it: no error, no warning, the model runs against its real inputs.

`--empty` registers an explicit negation. Not every boolean flag does, so read the negation off `--help` rather than assuming it.

| Flag | `--no-` form |
|---|---|
| `--empty` | `--no-empty` — legal, forces normal behaviour |
| `--partial-parse` | `--no-partial-parse` — the spelling §11.10 uses |
| `--version-check` | `--no-version-check` — the spelling §11.10 uses |
| `--full-refresh` | none. Exits 2 on a usage error: `Error: No such option: --no-full-refresh` |
| `--warn-error` | none — exits 2 the same way |
| `--select` | none — a flag that takes a value has nothing to negate; its opposite is a separate flag, `--exclude` |

Note also where the flag lives: `--empty` and `--sample` (§11.12) are documented under `/docs/build/`, not under the global-configs surface §11.10 catalogs. They are build-time flags that change what data a run reads, not configuration that changes how dbt behaves — a distinction the docs' own URL tree encodes and a plausible source of a wrong option.

That boundary is enforced by silence rather than by an error. Ch 10 §10.9 lists the four flag families and the surfaces each is settable from; `--empty` and `--sample` belong to none of them, so **`empty: true` in `dbt_project.yml`'s `flags:` block does nothing**. dbt does not schema-validate that block: the project parses at exit 0, no warning names the key, and the compiled SQL comes back without the zero-row rewrite — the same accepted-then-ignored behaviour §10.9 records for a `log_path:` set there. Reach for these two on the command line, and treat a `flags:` entry that changed nothing as the expected outcome rather than a bug.

## 11.12 --sample — running against a slice of the data

`--sample` runs the selected models over a *time window* instead of over the full history. It is what you reach for when `--empty` is too empty: you want real rows, enough of them to see whether the transformation is right, without scanning three years of events. Only `dbt run` and `dbt build` support it, and the rest do not merely ignore it — `dbt test --sample='3 days'` and `dbt snapshot --sample='3 days'` never reach the selection stage, exiting 2 on `Error: No such option: --sample`. The reference page is `/docs/build/sample-flag`.

Two ways to spell the window:

```
# Relative - counted back from the moment the command runs.
# Grain is hour, day, month or year, singular or plural.
dbt run --select stg_orders --sample="3 days"

# Static - an explicit start and end, date or timestamp. Pick a window inside
# your own data: one outside it is legal, exits 0, and lands nothing.
dbt run --select stg_orders --sample='{"start": "2024-07-01", "end": "2024-07-08
    18:00:00"}'
```

Nothing else is a grain: `--sample="3 weeks"` never reaches the warehouse, exiting 2 on `Invalid grain size 'weeks'. Must be one of ['hour', 'day', 'month', 'year', 'hours', 'days', 'months', 'years']`.

### The window is applied through `event_time`

dbt does not guess which column carries the event timestamp. It filters a relation only if that relation declares an `event_time` config — the same config the microbatch incremental strategy is built on (Ch 4 §4.3.7). It is available on models, seeds, snapshots, and sources:

```
sources:
  - name: raw_ecom
    tables:
      - name: orders
        config:
          event_time: created_at
```

Two things follow, and the second is the one that catches people.

**The config belongs on the relation being sampled, not on the model doing the reading.** If `stg_orders` selects from `source('raw_ecom', 'orders')`, sample mode filters `raw_ecom.orders` — so `event_time` has to sit on the source. Declaring it on `stg_orders` instead tells dbt how to filter `stg_orders` when something downstream reads it, which does nothing at all for the scan you were trying to shrink.

> **Watch out — `--sample` fails open.** If the sampled relation does not declare `event_time`, dbt does not error and does not warn. The command runs, reports OK, and quietly processes the full dataset. In practice, on Postgres, a static `--sample` window against a source with no `event_time` landed the WHOLE table — far outside the requested window. Adding `event_time: created_at` to that source and re-running the identical command landed only the rows inside the window. Nothing in the console output distinguished the two runs. That is the opposite of what someone reaching for `--sample` to save time or money expects, and it presents as "sample mode isn't working" rather than as a missing config.

### Opting a reference out

Append `.render()` to a `ref()` and that one reference is read in full while `--sample` stays active everywhere else:

```
select *
from {{ ref('fct_orders') }} o
join {{ ref('dim_customers').render() }} c on c.customer_id = o.customer_id
```

Use it for the small dimension a sampled fact table has to join against — sampling both sides of that join is a common way to get an empty result and conclude the model is broken.

### Sampling is an approximation, not a guarantee

- **Seeds build in full.** A seed is loaded normally and is sampled only when a downstream node references it.
- **Joins can come back under-populated.** Not every join will be populated. Sample a fact table to three days, join it to a relation that is not sampled on the same basis, and rows whose match falls outside the window drop out. The output is not a smaller copy of the real result; it is the result over less data.
- **Python models ignore the flag**, the same way they ignore `--empty`.

Treat a sample-mode run as a development convenience: the SQL runs, the shapes are right, and the row counts are wrong on purpose. Anything you would gate a merge on belongs in a real build.

---

## 11.13 `.dbtignore`

`.dbtignore` is a gitignore-style file at the project root that tells dbt which files to skip during parse. Syntax matches `.gitignore`: one glob pattern per line, `#` for comments, `!` for negation. The reference page is `/reference/dbtignore`.

A representative file:

```
# .dbtignore
models/_scratch/
models/**/_experimental/
*.bak
```

Files matching these patterns are invisible to dbt — they are not parsed, not compiled, not referenced from `ref()`, and not listed by `dbt ls`. This is different from `enabled: false`, which marks a resource as existing-but-disabled (Ch 10 §10.3.2); `.dbtignore` makes the resource genuinely invisible.

Common reasons to use it:

- **Work-in-progress models** that are not yet ready to enter the DAG but that you want to keep in the repo.
- **Non-SQL `.sql` files** that happen to live under `models/` (e.g., reference SQL snippets, DDL scripts for manual operations) that dbt should not try to parse as models.
- **Generated files** that tooling outputs into `models/` directories and that should not be treated as sources of truth.

`.dbtignore` vs `.gitignore`: one controls version control visibility, the other controls dbt's parse scope. A file can appear in one, the other, both, or neither. Typical pattern for an experimental directory: `.gitignore` excludes nothing (you want the work-in-progress in Git), `.dbtignore` excludes the directory so dbt doesn't try to parse it until the work is ready.

---

## 11.14 In practice: Credora's Makefile and slim-CI pattern

> *This section is an "in practice" sidebar. It draws a composite pattern from (a) the canonical `--defer --state` recipe documented at /reference/node-selection/defer, and (b) dbt Discourse community threads on slim CI. Credora is fictional (`credora`); Ch 14's opening note has the composite-project disclaimer.*

A mature dbt project needs exactly one standard way to invoke dbt for each workflow — local development, CI, scheduled deploys. Hand-rolled invocations drift into subtly different flag sets across machines, and the difference surfaces as a CI failure nobody can reproduce locally. The fix is a Makefile (or `justfile`, or `npm run` scripts — same idea) at the project root that encodes each workflow as a single target.

Below is a representative `Makefile` for the fictional `credora` project. Real ones add wrappers, secret-handling and logging; the dbt commands in each target are the load-bearing part.

```
# credora/Makefile

.PHONY: dev-compile dev-run dev-test build-all build-diff docs-serve retry clean

# -----------------------------------------------------------------
# Local development - fast feedback loop
# -----------------------------------------------------------------

# Compile only (fastest gate); use before committing
dev-compile:
	dbt compile

# Run a single model and every descendant
dev-run:
	dbt run --select $(MODEL)+

# Run tests only for the selected model and its neighbourhood
dev-test:
	dbt test --select $(MODEL)+

# -----------------------------------------------------------------
# Full build - scheduled nightly job. The selector is deliberate: this project
# wires require_select_arg() at on-run-start (Ch 6 §6.5), which raises a
# compiler error on a bare `dbt build`. "*" says "yes, all of it" out loud.
# -----------------------------------------------------------------
```

```
build-all:
    dbt build --select "*" --target prod --threads 8

# ----------------------------------------------------------------
# Slim CI - the standard PR-gate invocation
# ----------------------------------------------------------------

# Assumes ./prior-artifacts/ contains manifest.json from the most
# recent main-branch build, downloaded by the CI runner at job start.
build-diff:
    dbt build \
        --select state:modified+ \
        --defer --state ./prior-artifacts \
        --target ci \
        --fail-fast

# ----------------------------------------------------------------
# Recovery
# ----------------------------------------------------------------

# Retry inherits the failed invocation's target; do not pass --target here.
retry:
    dbt retry

# ----------------------------------------------------------------
# Docs + housekeeping
# ----------------------------------------------------------------

docs-serve:
    dbt docs generate && dbt docs serve --port 8080

clean:
    dbt clean
```

The `build-diff` target is the slim-CI workhorse. Expanded, the invocation is:

```
dbt build \
    --select state:modified+ \
    --defer --state ./prior-artifacts \
    --target ci \
    --fail-fast
```

Piece by piece:

| Piece | What it contributes | Taught in |
|---|---|---|
| `dbt build` | Models, tests, seeds and snapshots in DAG order, short-circuiting downstream work on failure. | §11.2 |
| `--select state:modified+` | Only nodes whose content or config has changed since the prior manifest, plus everything downstream of those nodes. | Ch 12 (`state`), §11.7 (`+`) |

| Piece | What it contributes | Taught in |
|---|---|---|
| `--defer --state ./prior-artifacts` | For every ancestor of a selected node that is itself unchanged, dbt resolves its `ref()` against that model's production relation from the prior run instead of rebuilding it into the CI schema. This is what makes the job "slim", and it assumes the fresh CI schema a PR gate normally gets — where a relation already exists in the target, deferral prefers it (Ch 12 §12.3). | Ch 12 |
| `--target ci` | Materialize into the CI target schema from `profiles.yml`, not production. | §11.10 |
| `--fail-fast` | Stop on the first failure. A slim-CI job has small blast radius, so failing fast puts the failure in front of an engineer in minutes. | §11.10 |

The effect is a PR gate that runs in seconds to low minutes instead of the tens of minutes a full rebuild costs. Nothing in it is new — a command (§11.1), a graph operator on a selector method (§11.5–§11.7), and two of §11.10's global flags. Ch 12 unpacks the rest: the `state:` method, `--defer` and `--state`.

---

## Summary

- The commands span four families: build-time (`run`, `build`, `test`, `seed`, `snapshot`, `compile`, `retry`), introspection (`ls`, `parse`, `debug`, `show`), artifacts (`docs generate`, `docs serve`, `source freshness`), and meta (`deps`, `clean`, `init`, `clone`, `run-operation`).
- The two discriminations the exam cares about most: `run` vs `build` (`build` adds tests, seeds, snapshots, and short-circuits downstream on failure), and `compile` vs `parse` (`compile` renders SQL and opens a connection for introspective queries, `parse` writes the manifest and connects to nothing).
- Node selection is three orthogonal dimensions: a method (what), a graph operator (how far), and a combiner (union, intersection, exclusion). Twenty-one selector methods, three graph operators (`+`, `N+`/`+N`, `@`), three set operators, plus `selectors.yml` for named reuse.
- Ten core flags every candidate should know, and they do **not** all sit on the same side of the subcommand. Accepted to the **left** of it, which is §10.9.1's discriminating test for a global config: `--target`, `--profile`, `--fail-fast`, `--warn-error`, `--no-partial-parse`. Accepted only to the **right**: `--vars`, `--threads`, `--profiles-dir`, `--project-dir`, and `--full-refresh`, whose effect is further scoped to incremental models and seeds (§11.10). Beware a second axis that does not coincide with the first: `--profiles-dir`,

--project-dir and --full-refresh all carry DBT_ENGINE_* environment variables and appear in the docs' available-flags table, while --vars and --threads carry neither. Placement is the reliable tell; the docs table is a different question. Two more (--quiet, --no-version-check) are situational.

- Partial parsing caches the manifest in target/partial_parse.msgpack and re-parses only changed files. Six inputs force a full re-parse — --vars, profiles.yml, dbt_project.yml, installed packages, the dbt version, and the widely-used name macros — and a stale cache presents as a node that does not exist rather than as a cache error.
- dbt show previews a **single** node — selection itself resolves normally, so graph operators and attached tests still pull nodes into the invocation — and --limit rewrites the query with a SQL limit rather than truncating the terminal output. dbt snapshot runs snapshots only and registers no --full-refresh; inside dbt build --full-refresh the flag leaves snapshots intact.
- --empty limits every ref() and source() to zero rows while still executing the SQL and really creating the relations: a compile/schema gate, not dbt compile and not a data gate. Default built-in data tests over zero-row relations pass vacuously, upstream relations must still exist, and Python models ignore the flag. .render() exempts one reference from the rewrite, which is what rescues a hook that needs a relation name rather than a subquery.
- --sample runs run and build over a time window, relative ("3 days") or static ({"start": ..., "end": ...}). It filters only relations that declare event_time, on the relation being sampled; without it the run succeeds and silently processes everything. .render() opts a single ref() out.
- .dbtignore makes files invisible to the parser.
- The slim-CI invocation dbt build --select state:modified+ --defer --state ./prior-artifacts is the production pattern this chapter ends on and the bridge to Chapter 12.

## Learning-goal checklist (self-assess)

- ☐ **Run every top-level command** and know what each one does (§11.1).
- ☐ **Distinguish dbt run from dbt build** and know which to reach for in each scenario (§11.2).
- ☐ **Use --select, --exclude, and --selector** with every selector method (§11.5–§11.9).
- ☐ **Apply every graph operator** — +model, model+, +model+, N+model, model+N, @model (§11.7).
- ☐ **Combine selections** with union (space), intersection (comma), and exclusion (§11.8).
- ☐ **Use the ten core flags, and say which are global configs.** — --target, --profile, --fail-fast, --warn-error, --no-partial-parse are accepted left of the subcommand; --vars, --threads, --profiles-dir, --project-dir and --full-refresh are not (§10.9.1, §11.10).
- ☐ **Name what partial parsing caches, what invalidates it, and how a stale cache presents** (§11.3).
- ☐ **Preview one model with dbt show** and explain why --limit changes the query rather than the output (§11.1).
- ☐ **State what a green --empty build proves and what it does not** — including why data tests pass over zero-row relations (§11.11).
- ☐ **Write both --sample window syntaxes**, say which relation needs event_time, and describe what happens when none does (§11.12).
- ☐ **Use** .render() to keep one reference real under either --empty or --sample, and say why a hook is where it usually matters (§11.11, §11.12).
- ☐ **Explain** .dbtignore and when to use it (§11.13).

☐ **Read a slim-CI invocation** and explain every flag (§11.14).

---

## Practice questions

Thirty-four questions across the chapter's command, selector, and flag surfaces, graded recall / apply / analyze.

**1.** `models/staging/` holds six models. You run `dbt show --select path:models/staging --limit 5`. What happens?
A. Only the first model in DAG order is previewed, and the other five are never executed
B. All six models are previewed in DAG order, five rows each
C. The command exits 2 — `dbt show` rejects a selection resolving to more than one node
D. All six models are compiled and executed, and no preview is printed — the command exits 0

**2.** Which statement is TRUE about `dbt retry`?
A. It accepts `--select` to choose which models to retry, narrowing the previous invocation's failures to the subset you name
B. It runs the entire project from scratch, ignoring which nodes succeeded in the previous invocation
C. It is equivalent to `dbt run --full-refresh`, rebuilding the failed models from their source data rather than incrementally
D. It reads `run_results.json` from the previous invocation and re-runs the nodes that failed or were skipped

**3.** A developer is iterating on a staging model locally. They want the fastest possible loop that re-materializes just the model, without running tests or reloading seeds. Which command fits?
A. `dbt run --select stg_orders` B. `dbt build --select stg_orders`
C. `dbt test --select stg_orders` D. `dbt compile --select stg_orders`

**4.** `fct_orders` joins `dim_customers`, and both relations declare `event_time`. `dim_customers` has to keep its config, because a microbatch model downstream relies on it. Under `dbt build --sample='3 days'` the join comes back nearly empty. Which edit keeps the window on `fct_orders` while `dim_customers` is read in full?
A. Append `.render()` to the `ref('dim_customers')` call in `fct_orders`
B. Add `--exclude dim_customers` to the invocation
C. Pass a second `--sample` argument carrying a wider window for `dim_customers`
D. Materialize `dim_customers` as a table so the sampled read hits a physical relation

**5.** In the selector `+fct_orders`, which nodes are selected?
A. `fct_orders` and every node it depends on (transitive ancestors)
B. `fct_orders` and every node that depends on it
C. `fct_orders` only
D. Every node in the project

**6.** You want to select `stg_orders` and the next two layers of descendants only — not the full downstream DAG. Which selector is correct?
A. `stg_orders+` B. `+stg_orders`
C. `stg_orders+2` D. `2+stg_orders`

**7.** Which selector matches nodes that are BOTH tagged `daily` AND have incremental materialization?
A. `--select tag:daily config.materialized:incremental`
B. `--select tag:daily|config.materialized:incremental`
C. `--select tag:daily,config.materialized:incremental`
D. `--select tag:daily +config.materialized:incremental`

**8.** For the invocation `dbt build --select tag:daily --exclude tag:deprecated`, what is the final node set?
A. Every node tagged `deprecated`
B. Every node tagged `daily` minus any that are also tagged `deprecated`
C. Every node tagged `daily`, including any that are also `deprecated`
D. Every node either tagged `daily` or tagged `deprecated`

**9.** Which selection returns `fct_sales`, every model downstream of it, and every upstream model those downstream models depend on?
A. `+fct_sales` B. `fct_sales+`
C. `@fct_sales` D. `+fct_sales+`

**10.** A model is tagged `incremental` in its YAML but materialized as a `view`. Does `--select config.materialized:incremental` include it?
A. Yes — a `config.` method matches any config or tag whose value is the given string
B. No — the selector is invalid, because `incremental` names an incremental strategy rather than a materialization
C. No — `config.materialized:` reads the `materialized` config value, which is `view`, not the tag literal
D. Yes — a tag that names a materialization sets the `materialized` config implicitly

**11.** A project declares its sources in `models/staging/_staging__sources.yml`, alongside the staging models' own properties file. Which selector returns every node whose file lives under `models/staging/` — those sources included?
A. `--select models.staging` B. `--select staging`
C. `--select path:models/staging` D. `--select dir:models/staging`

**12.** Which selector runs only the unit tests in a project?
A. `dbt test --select test_type:singular` B. `dbt test --select test_type:unit`
C. `dbt test --select test_type:generic` D. `dbt test --select test_type:data`

**13.** `stg_orders` selects from `source('raw_ecom', 'orders')`. The **model** `stg_orders` declares `event_time: created_at`; the **source** declares none. You run `dbt run --select stg_orders --sample='{"start": "2025-01-01", "end": "2025-03-01"}'`. What lands in `stg_orders`?
A. Only the rows whose `created_at` falls inside the window, filtered by the model's own `event_time`
B. Every row in the source table, with no error and no warning
C. No rows at all, because dbt cannot resolve a window without `event_time` on both relations
D. Nothing — the run fails with a missing-`event_time` error naming `raw_ecom.orders`

**14.** A team has a named selector `nightly_core` in `selectors.yml`. Which invocation runs a full `build` using that selector?
A. `dbt build --select nightly_core` B. `dbt build --select selector:nightly_core`
C. `dbt build --selector nightly_core` D. `dbt build --named nightly_core`

**15.** Each of these is a real boolean flag. For which one does dbt register no `--no-` form, so `dbt run --no-<flag>` exits 2 on `No such option`?
A. `--full-refresh` B. `--partial-parse`
C. `--version-check` D. `--empty`

**16.** A CI project should build over zero rows without anyone passing a flag, so the team adds `empty: true` under `flags:` in `dbt_project.yml`. What does the next `dbt run` do?
A. Builds every selected model over its real inputs — the key is accepted and does nothing
B. Builds every selected model over zero rows, exactly as `dbt run --empty` would
C. Fails at parse — `empty` is not a recognised key under `flags:`
D. Builds over zero rows only for the models that declare `event_time`

**17.** A project mixes SQL and Python models. The team adds `--empty` to their CI `dbt build` to get a cheap schema gate. What does the flag do to the Python models?
A. Nothing — they run against their real inputs, and nothing in the log says so
B. It fails them with a `--empty is not supported` error
C. It skips them silently, leaving their existing relations untouched
D. It builds them with their full column list and zero rows, like the SQL models

**18.** A team's CI is running too slowly. They are considering two approaches: (1) `dbt build --select state:modified+` with `--defer --state ./prior-artifacts`, or (2) `dbt build --select tag:critical` without `--defer`. Which statement best captures the trade-off?
A. Approach 1 rebuilds what changed and approach 2 reaches the same node set with less typing, so the two converge on one selection
B. Approach 2 is cheaper because `--defer` makes approach 1 rebuild every unchanged ancestor into the CI schema on each run
C. Approach 1 rebuilds changed nodes and their descendants, the shape a PR gate needs; approach 2 runs a fixed critical-path subset, good for a scheduled check but blind to changes elsewhere
D. Approach 1 needs a prior manifest and approach 2 does not, so approach 1 belongs in the nightly job rather than the PR gate

**19.** Which command lists every resource belonging to the installed `dbt_utils` package plus every source defined under the `raw_orders` source, but excludes any resource in the `finance` group?
A. `dbt ls --select package:dbt_utils,source:raw_orders --exclude group:finance`
B. `dbt ls --select package:dbt_utils source:raw_orders --exclude group:finance`
C. `dbt ls --select package:dbt_utils+source:raw_orders group:finance`
D. `dbt ls --select resource_type:package resource_type:source --exclude resource_type:group`

**20.** Between two `dbt parse` invocations you make exactly one change. Which one makes dbt discard the partial-parse cache and re-parse the whole project?
A. Editing the SQL body of one model under `models/staging/`
B. Adding a `description:` to a model in its properties file
C. Adding a new singular test under `tests/`
D. Adding a `+tags:` entry under `models:` in `dbt_project.yml`

**21.** In a schema that holds every upstream model but where `fct_orders` has never been built, you run `dbt compile --select fct_orders`, then `dbt run --select fct_orders --empty`. `fct_orders` is a plain `select` over its `ref()`s, with no aggregate and no literal-only branch. What exists in the warehouse after each?
A. Nothing after either — `--empty` renders the SQL and stops short of sending it
B. `fct_orders` after both, because `compile` executes the model's SQL to validate it
C. Nothing after `compile`; after the `--empty` run, `fct_orders` exists but with no columns, since there were no rows to infer them from
D. Nothing after `compile`; after the `--empty` run, `fct_orders` exists with its full column list and zero rows

**22.** A CI job runs `dbt run --select fct_orders --empty` against a freshly created schema. `fct_orders` reads `ref('stg_orders')`, which has never been materialized there. What happens?
A. The run fails with a missing-relation error from the warehouse — the flag limits input rows, not input dependencies
B. The run succeeds; with zero rows requested, dbt issues no query against `stg_orders`
C. The run succeeds, because `--empty` creates each missing parent as an empty relation first
D. The run fails at parse time, before any SQL is sent, because dbt verifies that its upstream relations exist

**23.** What does `--empty` change about the SQL dbt sends for a selected model?
A. It appends a `limit 0` to the model's own final `select`, leaving each `ref()` to read normally
B. It leaves the SQL untouched and truncates the target relation once the build finishes
C. It wraps each `ref()` and `source()` in a subquery returning no rows, and leaves the model's own `create` statement alone
D. It replaces each `ref()` with the plain relation name and skips the `create` statement

**24.** A model carries `pre_hook: "grant select on {{ ref('stg_orders') }} to reporter"`. It builds cleanly on a normal run, but `dbt run --empty` fails the model with `syntax error at or near "("`. Which edit fixes the hook and keeps the flag?
A. Append `.render()` to the `ref()` call inside the hook string
B. Wrap the hook string in `{% raw %}` / `{% endraw %}` so the `ref()` is left untemplated
C. Move the statement from `pre_hook` to `post_hook`, so it runs once the relation exists
D. Declare `event_time` on `stg_orders` so the flag narrows that relation by window instead

**25.** Which of these is rejected at 1.11 with `No such option`, because the command does not register `--empty`?
A. `dbt build --empty` B. `dbt compile --empty`
C. `dbt seed --empty` D. `dbt snapshot --empty`

**26.** A nightly job runs `dbt build --sample='3 days'`. An engineer splits it into `dbt run --sample='3 days'` followed by `dbt test --sample='3 days'`. What happens?
A. Both invocations succeed, and the tests run over the same three-day slice the models were built from
B. Both invocations succeed, but `dbt test` silently ignores the flag and tests the full relations
C. `dbt run --sample='3 days'` exits 2, because a sample window is legal only on `dbt build`
D. `dbt test --sample='3 days'` exits 2 on `No such option: --sample` — only `run` and `build` register it

**27.** A team switches its nightly job to `dbt build --sample='3 days'` to cut warehouse cost. The project includes a `country_codes` seed. What does the sampled run do with that seed?
A. Loads every row of the CSV; the window applies only where a downstream node reads the seed
B. Loads only the rows added to the CSV inside the window, going by the file's modification time
C. Skips the seed, because `--sample` narrows `dbt build` to models
D. Fails the seed, because a seed cannot declare `event_time`

**28.** A relationship test has two parents, `fct_orders` and `dim_customers`. A run selects **both** of them and then excludes one:

```
dbt test --select fct_orders dim_customers --exclude dim_customers \
    --indirect-selection cautious
```

What happens to the relationship test, and why?
A. It runs — under `cautious` the exclusion is expanded by the same mode, so it does not drag the test out with its parent
B. It runs — `cautious` ignores `--exclude` entirely and only ever narrows what `--select` widened
C. It is dropped, because `cautious` requires every parent of a test to be selected and one no longer is
D. It is dropped — the reference page says test exclusion is always greedy, whatever the indirect-selection mode

**29.** You need to exclude tests from a run, and later to exclude only the tests that are also tagged `nightly`. Which is true of the two `resource_type` surfaces?
A. `--exclude-resource-type test` can express both, since flags accept selector syntax
B. `--exclude "resource_type:test"` can express both, because it is a selector expression and takes set and graph operators
C. Neither can express the second without a `selectors.yml` file
D. Both express either, since the flag is an alias for the method

**30.** A run selects a mix of SQL and Python models with `--sample`. What happens to the Python models?
A. They are skipped, and the run reports them as skipped nodes
B. They build over the full input — the flag is silently ignored for them
C. The run fails: `--sample` is incompatible with Python models
D. They build over the sampled window, since sampling is applied to the upstream relation

**31.** A selector references another with `method: selector, value: core_models`, and wraps that reference with `children: true`. What node set comes back?
A. Exactly what `core_models` defines — `children:` on the reference never applies to it
B. `core_models` plus every descendant of its nodes
C. An error: `children:` is not valid alongside `method: selector`
D. Only the descendants, with `core_models`' own nodes excluded

**32.** A model is tagged `nightly` at the model level. Its columns carry `not_null` tests with no tags of their own. What does a plain `dbt test --select tag:nightly` run?
A. The model's tests — tests inherit their model's tags
B. The model and its tests
C. The model's tests — not by tag inheritance, which does not happen, but because the default indirect selection reaches the tests of a selected parent
D. Nothing — `dbt test` selects only nodes carrying the tag themselves

**33.** You want to run one unit test by name. Which selector does that, and why not the other?
A. `unit_test:test_order_totals` — `unit_test` is a method and takes a name; `test_type:unit` is a value and takes none
B. `test_type:unit:test_order_totals` — the value accepts a name suffix
C. Either; both accept an optional name argument
D. Neither; unit tests can only be selected as a whole class

**34.** A criterion inside `selectors.yml` sets `indirect_selection: cautious`. The job runs `dbt build --selector nightly --indirect-selection eager`. Which applies to that criterion?
A. `eager` — the CLI flag overrides project configuration, as everywhere else
B. Neither; dbt raises a conflicting-configuration error
C. `cautious` — the YAML value wins and the flag is silently ignored for that criterion
D. `eager`, with a warning that the selector's value was overridden

## Answer key

**1. D.** `--select` on `dbt show` resolves nodes like any other command, so all six staging models — and their attached tests — compile and execute. What `show` narrows is the **printing**: it previews only the nodes whose name appears in the first `--select` argument, and no node is called `path:models/staging`. In practice, on 1.11.14, the invocation exits 0 having printed nothing, and `--debug` shows `Excluded node 'stg_orders' from results` once per node. Substitute `--select path:models/staging/stg_orders.sql` and `stg_orders` previews, because now the name is in the argument. B is the natural expectation and the reason the silence is confusing. C is what "previews a single node" sounds like it should mean, but nothing is rejected and nothing exits 2. A is wrong twice over: no node is previewed, and every selected node ran. §11.1 has the rule. Source: `/reference/commands/show`.

**2. D.** `dbt retry` re-runs the prior invocation from the point of failure: it consults `run_results.json` and re-executes every node whose recorded status was `error`, `fail`, or `skipped` — i.e., the failure point and everything downstream that was skipped by DAG propagation. It does NOT take `--select` — its selection is implicit in the artifact (A is false). It is unrelated to `--full-refresh` (C). It does not re-run the whole project (B). Source: `/reference/commands/retry`.

**3. A.** `dbt run` executes models without running tests, seeds, or snapshots — the right tool for the local quick-loop. `dbt build` (B) adds tests and seed loads, slower and not what the scenario asks for. `dbt test` (C) runs only tests, not the model itself. `dbt compile` (D) renders SQL without executing — the model is not materialized. Source: `/reference/commands/run`.

**4. A.** .render() asks a reference for its relation name and returns it unwrapped, so sample mode passes that one reference over while every other relation in the run is still narrowed to the window. A small dimension joined against a sampled fact table is the case the opt-out exists for (§11.12). --exclude (B) governs which nodes the invocation builds, not how a surviving ref() reads them — and dim_customers is not being built here in any case. A sample window is one setting per invocation rather than a per-relation one, so a second --sample argument (C) buys nothing. Materialization (D) has no bearing on the flag: dbt narrows a relation because it declares event_time, not because of how it is stored. Source: /docs/build/sample-flag.

**5. A.** The + prefix selects the node plus all of its transitive ancestors — the upstream DAG. The + suffix (B) would select the node plus descendants. The degenerate expression with no + (C) selects only the named node. The full project (D) is what dbt run selects with no --select flag. Source: /reference/node-selection/graph-operators.

**6. C.** The integer goes on the side the traversal runs, so a *suffix* +N bounds descendants to N layers. stg_orders+ (A) traverses downstream to unbounded depth. +stg_orders (B) and 2+stg_orders (D) are both upstream — D is the same bound applied in the wrong direction, and it is a legal selector, so nothing about its syntax gives it away. Source: /reference/node-selection/graph-operators.

**7. C.** The comma operator (inside a single argument, no whitespace) is intersection. Option A uses a space, which is union — "daily OR incremental". Option B uses |, which is not a dbt selector operator. Option D uses a graph operator; it expands the incremental set upstream and unions it with tag:daily, which still does not require both criteria. Source: /reference/node-selection/set-operators.

**8. B.** --exclude subtracts its set from whatever --select produced. A node tagged both daily and deprecated is included by --select but removed by --exclude. There is no override for a force-include; exclusion wins. Source: /reference/node-selection/exclude.

**9. C.** @model selects the model, all its descendants, and the ancestors those descendants need to build. That is the exact shape the stem describes. +fct_sales (A) gives only ancestors and the node itself. fct_sales+ (B) gives only descendants and the node itself — it does **not** pull in extra ancestors those descendants depend on. +fct_sales+ (D) gives both directions from fct_sales itself but does not specifically chase down the ancestors of the descendant set. @ is the standard operator for deferred / CI runs where downstream models may need parents not yet materialised in the CI schema. Source: /reference/node-selection/graph-operators.

**10. C.** config.<key>:<value> matches on the config key's actual value. A model whose materialized config is view does not match config.materialized:incremental, however it is tagged; tag:incremental is the selector that returns it. A config. method does not fall back to tags (A), and a tag never writes a config (D) — the two namespaces are separate, which is the whole point of the discrimination. The selector in the stem is perfectly valid (B): incremental names both a materialization and an incremental strategy, and config.materialized: reads the materialization. The method's reach stops at the config namespace: a *property* such as description is not a config, so config.description: has nothing to match and returns an empty selection at exit 0 rather than an error (Ch 11 §11.6). Source: /reference/node-selection/methods.

**11. C.** The path: method matches every node whose *file* lives under the given directory, and a source declared in a YAML file there is one of them. Option B is the default fqn method, which returns the same models and the same tests — dbt retries an unmatched selector against the unscoped name, so a bare directory name usually does work — but it never returns a source, because a source carries no fqn path for the method to match. That is the discrimination the stem asks for. Option A's dotted notation is fqn-style too: a project qualifier, not a filesystem path. There is no dir: method (D). Source: /reference/node-selection/methods.

**12. B.** test_type:unit is the selector that matches unit-test nodes specifically. The four legal values for the test_type: method are data, generic, singular, and unit (per the §11.6 catalog and /reference/node-selection/methods). test_type:singular (A), test_type: generic (C), and test_type:data (D) are all valid selector tokens but match different categories — singular tests, generic tests, and the union of generic+singular respectively. Do not confuse test_type:unit with the unit_test: method: unit_test: takes a name and selects one unit test, while unit is a *value* of test_type and takes no argument. Source: /reference/node-selection/methods.

**13. B.** A sample window narrows a relation only if *that relation* declares event_time. Here the config sits on stg_orders, which is the relation being written, not the one being read; raw_ecom.orders declares none, so nothing is filtered. What makes it worth a question is that the flag fails **open**: the command succeeds, reports OK, and quietly processes every row — A is the reading most people bring to it. In practice, on Postgres, the identical invocation landed the whole table before event_time: created_at was added to the source, and only the in-window rows after, with nothing in the console output distinguishing the two runs. dbt does not write an empty relation (C), and there is no missing-event_time error to raise (D). Sources: /docs/build/sample-flag, /reference/resource-configs/event-time.

**14. C.** --selector <name> references a named selector from selectors.yml. It is distinct from --select, which takes inline selector expressions. Option A would attempt an fqn lookup for a node literally named nightly_core. Option B does not resolve at 1.11: selector: is not one of the selection methods §11.6 catalogs, so --select selector:nightly_core is a **usage error** — Runtime Error / 'selector' is not a valid method name, exit 2. That is the opposite of matching nothing: an unregistered method fails loudly, where an unmatched criterion prints No nodes selected! and exits 0 (§11.6). Option D (--named) does not exist. In practice --selector replaces --select / --exclude with a named YAML selector; they're typically not combined in the same invocation. Source: /reference/node-selection/yaml-selectors.

**15. A.** dbt registers most boolean flags as a --flag / --no-flag pair, which is where the --no-partial-parse (B), --no-version-check (C) and --no-empty (D) spellings come from. --full-refresh is not a pair: dbt run --no-full-refresh exits 2 on Error: No such option: --no-full-refresh, and --warn-error behaves the same way. Read the negation off --help rather than assuming it. Note also that a flag taking a *value* has nothing to negate, which is why there is no --no-select — --select's opposite is a separate flag, --exclude. Ch 4 §4.5 owns what --full-refresh does to an incremental model. Source: /reference/global-configs/command-line-options.

**16. A.** --empty is a build-time flag, not a global config: it is documented under /docs/build/, and flags: in dbt_project.yml sets global configs and behaviour-change flags only. dbt does not validate the key, so nothing pushes back — on 1.11.14 the project parses with exit 0, emits no warning naming empty, and the compiled SQL carries no zero-row rewrite; add --empty on the command line and the same model compiles with each ref() wrapped in a where false limit 0 subquery. B is the belief the stem is built on. C is the schema validation dbt does not perform here — an unrecognised flags: key is accepted in silence. D imports --sample's event_time mechanism into a flag that has none: --empty limits every reference to zero rows regardless of any config. Ch 10 §10.9 has the four flag families and the surfaces each one is settable from; §11.11 places --empty outside all of them. Source: /docs/build/empty-flag.

**17. A.** A Python model ignores --empty — no error, no warning, and it runs against its real inputs. That is the gap in the gate: the SQL half of the project is cheap and the Python half is not, so the job costs whatever the Python models cost and the log says nothing about it. B is the wrong generalisation to draw from dbt seed --empty, which is refused outright — Error: No such option: --empty, exit 2 (§11.11) — rather than run and failed. C confuses ignoring the flag with skipping the node. D is the assumption of uniformity the flag does not honour, and it is the discriminator: the SQL models really are built with their full column list, over inputs limited to zero rows, which is exactly why the Python exception is easy to miss. Source: `/docs/build/empty-flag`.

**18. C.** The two approaches answer different questions. `state:modified+ --defer --state` is the slim-CI strategy: it rebuilds only what changed plus everything downstream, and points unchanged ancestors at the prior run's materializations, so it catches change-driven regressions at minimal cost. `tag:critical` runs the same nodes every time regardless of what changed — useful as a scheduled critical-path sanity check, blind to a regression in any model outside the tag. The two do not converge on one node set (A). B inverts what deferral does: `--defer` is what *avoids* rebuilding unchanged ancestors into the CI schema. D is right that approach 1 needs a prior manifest and wrong about the consequence — fetching that manifest is a slim-CI job's first step, and the recipe is the standard PR gate. Ch 12 unpacks the `state:` selector and `--defer` semantics. Sources: `/reference/node-selection/defer`, `/reference/node-selection/methods`.

**19. B.** Three selector methods from the §11.6 catalog: `package:`, `source:` — here the plain form, which matches every table under the source — and `group:`. `dbt ls` is the right verb because the selected set includes source nodes, which are selectable but not runnable by `dbt run`. Space-separated `package:dbt_utils source:raw_orders` is **union** (§11.8); the comma in A is **intersection**, which would match only nodes that are simultaneously in `dbt_utils` AND under `raw_orders` — empty set. `--exclude group:finance` subtracts the finance group per §11.8. C misuses the `+` graph operator and drops `--exclude`. D abuses `resource_type:`, and its two halves fail differently: `resource_type:package` is rejected outright as an invalid selector, while `resource_type:group` is a legal token that simply matches nothing. Either way the intended sets are never selected — `package` and `group` are selector methods, not resource kinds. Sources: `/reference/node-selection/methods`, `/reference/node-selection/set-operators`, `/reference/node-selection/exclude`.

**20. D.** Partial parsing re-parses only the files whose contents changed, so a model body (A), a `description:` in a properties file (B) and a new singular test (C) are all handled incrementally. `dbt_project.yml` is one of the six inputs that invalidate the cache outright, alongside `--vars`, `profiles.yml`, installed packages, the dbt version and the widely-used name macros. dbt says so before parsing begins: `Unable to do partial parsing because a project config has changed`. Source: `/reference/parsing`.

**21. D.** `--empty` limits every `ref()` and `source()` to zero rows — that is the guarantee, and it is about the INPUTS. The stem pins `fct_orders` to a plain projection over those refs, so zero rows in means zero rows out; a model that aggregated without a `GROUP BY`, or selected a literal, would still return a row from empty inputs. `dbt compile` renders SQL into `target/compiled/` and creates no relation. It opens a warehouse connection for introspective queries, but it never executes the model's own SQL (B). `--empty` does execute it: every selected model is really built, with its full declared column list, holding zero rows. That is the entire difference between a compile gate and an `--empty` gate; §11.11 lists what only the warehouse can tell you. A denies the execution half. C misreads where the column list comes from: it is the compiled `select`, not the rows, so a zero-row build still produces a correctly-shaped relation. Source: `/docs/build/empty-flag`.

**22. A.** `--empty` limits input **rows**, not input **dependencies**. dbt still issues a `select` against `stg_orders`, and a relation that does not exist cannot be read, empty or otherwise — so the run fails with the warehouse's own missing-relation error. B is the intuition that fails here. The flag builds nothing it was not asked to build (C), and dbt learns nothing about the warehouse at parse time, so there is no existence check to fail there (D). Read the flag as §11.11 does — a dry run against a warehouse that already carries your schema, not a way to stand a project up from nothing. Source: `/docs/build/empty-flag`.

**23. C.** The rewrite lands on the references, not on the model. Each `ref()` and `source()` compiles to a subquery that cannot return anything — `(select * from "credora"."ci"."stg_` `orders" where false limit 0) _dbt_limit_subq_stg_orders` — while the model's own `create` statement is what it would be on any other run, which is why the relation is created with its full column list. A inverts that: a `limit 0` on the model's own `select` would return no rows and tell you nothing about the inputs. B describes a truncate-after-build dbt does not do. D describes the opposite of the rewrite — leaving a reference plain is precisely what `.render()` opts into. Source: `/docs/build/empty-flag`.

**24. A.** A hook is a string dbt renders and sends as written. Under `--empty` the `ref()` inside it renders to a subquery, and `grant select on (select ...)` is not valid SQL on any platform — hence a syntax error on a hook that is fine every other day. `.render()` returns the relation name alone, which is what the `grant` needs, and leaves the rest of the run empty. `{% raw %}` (B) suppresses the templating altogether, so the statement would carry the literal text `{{ ref('stg_orders') }}` and the model would lose its dependency edge into the bargain. The wrapping is a property of how the reference renders, not of when the hook fires, so `post_hook` (C) changes nothing. `event_time` (D) belongs to `--sample` and to microbatch; `--empty` does not read it. No dbt docs page states this; §11.11 derives it from the compiled output the flag produces.

**25. C.** `run`, `build`, `snapshot` and `compile` register `--empty`. `dbt seed --empty` is rejected outright — `Error: No such option: --empty`, exit 2. Reading the flag off its own docs page and assuming every build-time command accepts it is the trap: the command list is part of the fact. Source: `/docs/build/empty-flag`.

**26. D.** Only `dbt run` and `dbt build` register `--sample`. `dbt test` does not, so the flag never reaches selection: the invocation exits 2 on `Error: No such option: --sample` before a single node is resolved. Keep that separate from the flag's other silence — `--sample` does fail open when a relation declares no `event_time`, but a command that never accepted the option does not silently ignore it (B). A would require `dbt test` to honour a window it cannot parse. C reverses the pair: `dbt run` is one of the two commands that do register it. Source: `/docs/build/sample-flag`.

**27. A.** A seed is created normally under `--sample` and is narrowed only where a downstream node references it — the window applies to reads, not to the load. So the seed is neither skipped (C) nor filtered by file metadata (B): `--sample` filters on an `event_time` column in the data, and a seed is one of the four resource types that may declare one, which is what makes D false on both counts. This is the general shape of the caveat the section ends on: a sampled run's output is not a smaller copy of the real result, it is the result over less data. Source: `/docs/build/sample-flag`.

**28. A.** The test **runs**. `--exclude` is itself a selection, expanded by the *same* indirect-selection mode and then subtracted — so under `cautious` the exclusion of `dim_customers` does not pull the test out with it, and the test stays in the set `--select` had already put it in. Executed on Core 1.11.14 (§11.9): with both parents selected, the relationship test is listed under `cautious` after excluding *either* parent, and is dropped under `eager` after excluding either. `buildable` splits them — it survives losing `dim_customers`, the ancestor, and is dropped when `fct_orders` goes.

D is the answer to beat, and it is the reference page's own sentence: *"test exclusion is always greedy: if ANY parent is explicitly excluded, the test will be excluded as well."* It carries no mode qualifier and is true of `eager` — the default — and of nothing else. Read an exclusion question for the mode before you answer it. B invents a rule: `cautious` does not ignore `--exclude`; the exclusion is applied, it is simply not expanded onto the test. C states `cautious`'s *inclusion* rule correctly and then applies it to the wrong operation — that is the reasoning trap, because it reaches a confident answer that the node set contradicts.

**29. B.** `resource_type:test` is a **selector expression**, so it composes like any other: `--exclude "resource_type:test,tag:nightly"` intersects the two criteria, `+resource_type:exposure` walks the graph, and it can sit inside a `union:` in `selectors.yml`. `--exclude-resource-type test` is a **flag**: it filters the final node set and composes with nothing, so it can express the blunt exclusion (A's first half) and not the conditional one. C is wrong because the selector expression handles the second case inline — a YAML selector file is a convenience for reuse, not a requirement. D is the tempting simplification: the two do overlapping work on the simple case, which is exactly why the composable one is worth reaching for by default. Source: `/reference/node-selection/methods`. Revisit **Ch 11 §11.4**. Cognitive level: analyze.

**30. B.** `--sample` is silently ignored for Python models, exactly as `--empty` is. They build over their full input while the SQL models beside them build over the sampled window — at no warning and no non-zero exit. That mixture is the practical trap: a development run that looks cheap because most of it was sampled can still be dominated by one Python model reading everything, and the log gives you nothing to point at. D is the plausible-sounding answer, because sampling *is* applied by narrowing upstream relations that declare `event_time` — it just is not applied for these nodes.

**31. A.** Referencing a selector returns that selector's node set **as it defines it**. Wrapping the reference in `children:`, `parents:` or `indirect_selection:` does not extend or re-interpret it — the referenced definition is final, and those keys on the reference do not apply. The YAML parses and the run proceeds, so the only symptom is a node set smaller than expected. Reuse here is composition rather than inheritance: if you need `core_models` plus its children, put the graph operator inside `core_models`, or write a second selector that does.

**32. C.** Two mechanisms, and the item turns on keeping them apart. **Tag inheritance does not happen** at the model level: a tag written on a model, seed or snapshot is not inherited by that resource's tests, so `tag:nightly` matches the model and nothing else *directly*. That is what makes A wrong — right outcome, refuted reason. **Indirect selection then runs the tests anyway.** dbt's default is `--indirect-selection eager`, which pulls in the tests of any selected node, and `dbt test` applies it exactly as `dbt build` does. The discriminator is the flag: the same invocation with `--indirect-selection empty` selects only tests tagged in their own right, which is what D describes and is true only under that flag. B is wrong on the command — `dbt test` runs tests, not models, so the model is never built even though it is what the tag matched. Note the contrast with a **column**-level or **source**-level tag, which the tests attached there DO inherit, making them direct matches (§11.9). Revisit **Ch 11 §11.9** and **Ch 7 §7.6**. Cognitive level: analyze.

**33. A.** The two look interchangeable and are structurally different. `unit_test` is a selector **method**, so it takes an argument and supports name matching: `--select unit_test: test_order_totals`. `test_type:unit` is a **value** of the `test_type` method, which takes one of `data`, `generic`, `singular` or `unit` and no name — it addresses the whole class. Reach for `test_type:unit` to run every unit test and `unit_test:<name>` to run one, and note that `test_type:data` matches both generic and singular tests, which is the other place this method surprises people.

**34. C.** This inverts the usual "CLI beats config" instinct, and it is deliberate: a named selector is meant to mean the same thing wherever it is invoked from, so a criterion that sets `indirect_selection` keeps that value and the `--indirect-selection` flag is ignored for it. The flag still governs criteria that do not set their own. What makes it worth drilling is the silence — nothing warns you that the flag had no effect, so a team debugging a CI run can spend a long time changing a flag that was never being read. If you need the mode to vary by invocation, leave it out of the YAML.

# Chapter 12

# State, defer, and slim CI

> **Scope.** Every feature in this chapter exists to answer one question: *what is the smallest amount of work that still proves a change is safe?* State is how dbt answers it — a point-in-time record of the project, written to `target/` as JSON, that a later invocation can diff against. This chapter builds the standard slim-CI recipe — `dbt build --select state:modified+ --defer --state ./prior-artifacts` — one pressure at a time, and explains every flag in it.

## The problem this chapter solves

Open the companion repository and change three lines in `models/staging/stg_orders.sql`. Now prove the change is safe.

The honest answer is `dbt build`, and on the companion project that is every node in it — models, seeds, snapshots and tests alike, the whole graph green.

The entire project rebuilt to prove a three-line change — every node in it, on a project small enough to make that cheap. On a real one it is thousands of nodes and a warehouse bill. You have changed one staging model. Almost everything that just rebuilt could not possibly have been affected — but dbt rebuilt it anyway, because nothing told it otherwise.

Reach for the selectors from Ch 11 and you get closer: `dbt build --select stg_orders+` builds the changed model and its descendants, and skips the rest of the graph. Better. But it is still wrong in both directions. You had to *know* that `stg_orders` was the thing you changed — on a branch with eleven commits from four people, nobody knows that. And the run fails, because a descendant set is not a buildable set. `stg_orders+` selects a handful of models, and three of them have a parent it does not: `dim_customers` needs `stg_customers`, `fct_orders` needs `stg_currency_rates`, and `fct_order_items` needs `int_order_items_enriched`. None of those three was selected, so none of them exists in an empty CI schema, and the models that depend on them fail on a missing relation.

Those two failures are the whole chapter, and each has an answer:

| The pressure | The answer | Where |
|---|---|---|
| "I do not know what changed" | dbt compares this run to a saved one | §12.1 the artifacts, §12.2 `state:modified` |
| "The parents I did not build do not exist" | read them from the environment that already has them | §12.3 `--defer --state` |
| "Now assemble the two into a gate" | the slim-CI recipe | §12.4 |

| The pressure | The answer | Where |
|---|---|---|
| "It failed on node 400 of 600" | resume, do not restart | §12.7 `dbt retry` |
| "Two tests failed and I want just those" | select on the last run's results | §12.5 `result:` |
| "Nothing changed in code but the numbers are wrong" | select on source freshness | §12.6 `source_status:fresher+` |
| "I need a prod-shaped environment, cheaply" | clone rather than rebuild | §12.8 `dbt clone` |

§12.9 assembles all of it into one CI pipeline. Read that section last and it is a summary; read it first and it is a map.

One warning that the rest of the chapter keeps earning: **every one of these features fails silently when its inputs are wrong.** A stale baseline selects too much, a missing `--state` is a hard error but a *wrong* `--state` is not, and a deferred build that finds a leftover relation in the target schema will quietly read that instead. The failure mode is a green run that proved nothing, which is worse than a red one.

**Prerequisites.** Ch 11 in full — every selector in this chapter uses the syntax from §11.5–§11.9. Ch 3 (sources and freshness) for §12.6. Ch 4 (materializations) for §12.8's clone discussion. No other hard prerequisites. Ch 12 is the tightest selector-syntax application in the book; if the `+model` / `model+` distinction from Ch 11 is still fuzzy, go back and re-read §11.7 before continuing.

**Cheat-sheet pointer.** Front-of-book cheat sheet §8 (Topic 7 — State and defer) is the one-line distillation of this chapter. Use the cheat sheet for exam-morning recall; use this chapter for the reasoning behind each line.

---

## 12.1 The state artifacts

*You cannot diff against something you never saved. Before any of this works dbt has to have written down what the project looked like last time — and it already has, on every invocation you have ever run.*

Every dbt invocation that touches the graph writes one or more JSON files into the project's `target/` directory. Collectively these are the **state artifacts**.

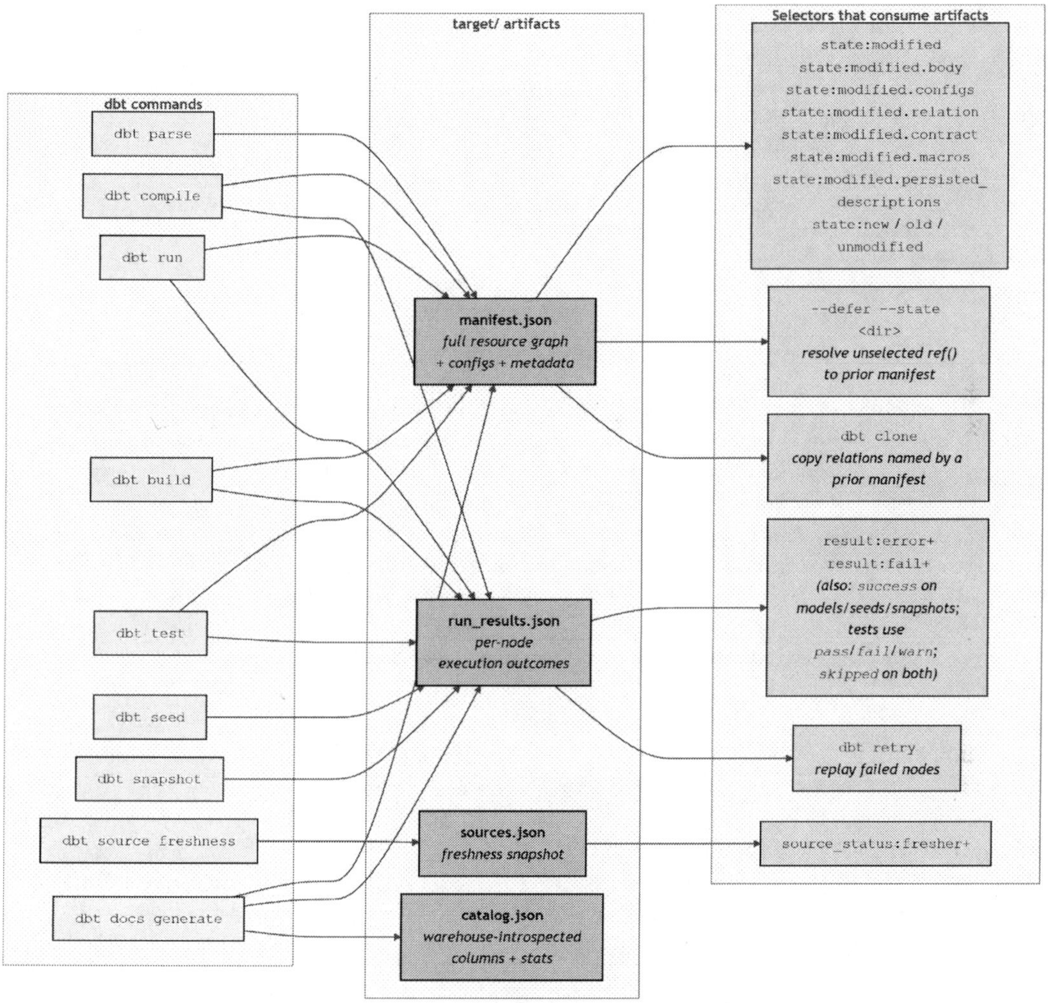


Figure 12.1: Commands → artifacts → selectors. The left column lists the dbt commands that write state; the middle column the four artifacts they emit into `target/`; the right column the selectors and flags that read those artifacts on a later invocation. Together this is the full state-aware execution loop the rest of the chapter unpacks.

| Artifact | What it contains | Produced by | Primary use |
|---|---|---|---|
| `manifest.json` | The full parsed graph — every model, test, seed, snapshot, source, exposure, macro; their `ref()` / `source()` edges; every resolved config; every YAML property; the compiled node hashes. | Any command that parses the project **and then writes its manifest**: `run`, `build`, `test`, `seed`, `snapshot`, `compile`, `parse`, `ls`, `docs generate`, `source freshness`, `run-operation`, `clone`, `retry`, `show`. Not `deps`, `clean`, `debug`, `init` or `docs serve` — and not `docs generate --no-compile`, which writes `catalog.json` alone. | State comparison (`state:modified`), docs-site rendering, external tooling. |
| `run_results.json` | Per-node status from the last command: `success` / `error` / `fail` / `warn` / `skipped` / `pass`, among others, plus timing, adapter response, and compiled SQL. | Commands that execute nodes: `run`, `build`, `test`, `seed`, `snapshot`, `compile`, `docs generate` (but not under `--no-compile`), `retry`, `clone`, `show`, `run-operation` (writes a results-shaped artifact even when no graph nodes execute). | Result-based selection (`result:error+`), `dbt retry`. |
| `sources.json` | Per-source freshness status: `pass` / `warn` / `error` / `runtime error`, last-loaded timestamp, time since last load. | `dbt source freshness`. | `source_status:fresher+` selection. |
| `catalog.json` | Warehouse-introspected metadata: column names/types, and adapter-dependent table stats (row counts, bytes). | `dbt docs generate`. | Powers the docs site's column-level metadata. |

A few points the cert likes to test:

- **All four live in `target/`** alongside the compiled SQL in `target/compiled/` and the DDL in `target/run/`. `target/` is project-local and gitignored by default.

- **`manifest.json` is produced by more commands than any other artifact**, but not by every command that parses the project: `dbt docs generate --no-compile` parses in full and still writes `catalog.json` alone. `parse` is the lightest-weight way to produce one — no compiled SQL, no warehouse round-trip.
- **`run_results.json` is overwritten on every command that executes nodes**. If a nightly `dbt build` completes and then you run `dbt docs generate`, the `run_results.json` from the build is gone. This matters for `dbt retry` — see §12.7. **`dbt docs generate --no-compile` is the exception**: it writes `catalog.json` only, leaving `run_results.json` and `manifest.json` byte-identical, so a pending `dbt retry` survives it.
- **`sources.json` is produced only by `dbt source freshness`.** Nothing else writes it. If you want `source_status:fresher+` to work in CI, a `dbt source freshness` step has to run first.
- **`catalog.json` requires warehouse access** — `dbt docs generate` introspects the warehouse to populate column types. This is why docs generation is slower than a plain `parse`.
- **State comparison never reads `catalog.json`.** The `state:` method, `--defer` and `dbt clone` read `manifest.json`; `result:` reads `run_results.json`; `source_status:` reads `sources.json`. The catalog feeds the docs site and nothing else, so a stale or missing `catalog.json` changes no selection.
- **Not everything in `target/` is a state artifact.** `partial_parse.msgpack` is dbt's parse cache and `perf_info.json` is a parse-timing report. Neither is compared, neither is versioned as an artifact, and neither belongs in the directory you hand to `--state`.

The reference pages:

- `/reference/artifacts/manifest-json`
- `/reference/artifacts/run-results-json`
- `/reference/artifacts/sources-json`
- `/reference/artifacts/catalog-json`

## Why artifacts matter

Every state-aware workflow — slim CI, selective retries, freshness-driven rebuilds — is the same recipe over one of these artifacts: save it from a prior invocation in a reference environment (typically production), diff against it on the next, and let dbt build only what changed.

## Keeping one step's artifacts from overwriting another's

Every invocation rewrites `target/`, which is a problem the moment a pipeline runs dbt more than once. A job that does `dbt compile` to produce a manifest and then `dbt run` gets the manifest overwritten by the second command before anything downstream can read the first.

`--no-write-json` (the `WRITE_JSON` config) is the answer: it stops dbt writing `manifest.json`, `run_results.json` and the other artifacts altogether, so the earlier step's files survive. Reach for it on the invocations whose artifacts you do not need, not on the one that produces the artifact you do.

It is worth separating from `--target-path`, which is the flag people reach for first. That relocates the output; this suppresses it. Relocating leaves you with a second set of artifacts somewhere else that the pipeline then has to reason about, which is usually not what you wanted.

## 12.2 `state:modified` — detecting what changed

*You have a saved manifest and a current one. Now: which nodes differ, and what counts as "differ"? The second question is the one that matters — get it wrong and the gate either rebuilds the world or, far worse, quietly skips the thing you broke.*

The `state:` selector method compares the project's *current* parse against the `manifest.json` in the directory you pass via `--state`. A node is "modified" if anything in its current representation differs from its representation in the prior manifest.

```
# Compare the current parse against the manifest in ./prior-artifacts,
# select every modified node plus its downstream descendants, and run them.
dbt run --select state:modified+ --state ./prior-artifacts
```

The `--state <path>` flag tells dbt where to find the comparison manifest. Typical values: `./prior-artifacts`, `./target-prod`, or whatever directory your CI runner has downloaded the prior artifact into. Without a `--state` flag, the `state:` method has nothing to compare against and dbt will error.

### Sub-methods — which kind of change?

`state:modified` is an omnibus selector that matches on *any* change. For tighter control, the method supports sub-selectors that match only specific categories of change:

| Sub-selector | Matches when... |
|---|---|
| `state:modified` | Any change — body, configs, relation, contract, persisted descriptions, or upstream macros. Also matches a brand-new model, seed, snapshot or test, which has no prior representation to differ from — but **not** a brand-new source or exposure: neither is a node, and the omnibus counts neither as a change. `state:new` is the selector to reach for; `state:modified.configs` matches both anyway, and `state:modified.relation` matches a new source, because a sub-selector treats a missing baseline as a difference. |
| `state:modified.body` | The node's **raw** SQL body has changed — the file text as written, before Jinja renders. Configs, YAML and macros are ignored, so a macro edit that changes every compiled byte selects nothing here (use `.macros`), while adding a Jinja comment that changes no compiled output does select the model. |
| `state:modified.configs` | A config value changed (e.g., `materialized`, `meta`, `unique_key`, `on_schema_change`), excluding `database` / `schema` / `alias` — and excluding `tags` and `group`, which no state selector compares at all. |
| `state:modified.relation` | `database`, `schema`, or `alias` changed — the node's warehouse identifier moved. |

| Sub-selector | Matches when... |
|---|---|
| `state:modified.persisted_descriptions` | A relation-level or column-level `description:` changed *and* `persist_docs` is enabled. With `persist_docs` off — the default — a description edit matches nothing, here or on the omnibus. |
| `state:modified.macros` | A macro the node depends on has changed — one it calls, or one further down that macro's own call chain, at any depth (even if the node itself is untouched). |
| `state:modified.contract` | The node's contract definition changed — column set, types, or constraints. |
| `state:new` | The resource exists in the current manifest but not in the comparison manifest. Not restricted to nodes: a brand-new source or exposure matches here, which is exactly what the omnibus above misses. |
| `state:old` | The resource exists in both manifests. |
| `state:unmodified` | The exact inverse of `state:modified`. For a node that means it exists in both manifests and nothing changed — but a brand-new source or exposure lands here too, because the omnibus does not count either as a change. |

These methods compare nodes, not models. A data test has its own body, config, and dependencies, so `state:modified` selects a test that is itself new or edited even when the model it points at is untouched — directly, not through the indirect selection of Ch 7 §7.6. Add one `unique` test to an unchanged model and `dbt test --select state:modified --state ./prior-artifacts --indirect-selection empty` runs that test and nothing else.

The reference documentation is `/reference/node-selection/methods`; `/reference/node-selection/state-selection` is the companion "About state in dbt" overview.

## Why the sub-methods matter

The omnibus `state:modified` is the right default for CI, because any change — SQL, config, relation, persisted description, macro, or contract — should trigger at least a re-parse of the affected nodes. It also matches too aggressively: a single-line config change in `dbt_project.yml` — a `+materialized:` switch, a shared `+pre-hook:` — can propagate as a `state:modified` hit on every model that inherits it, which in turn cascades through every `+` operator. When CI rebuilds 80% of the graph for a PR that touched two staging models, the usual culprit is a config-level change that pulled a large subtree into the match.

The fix is to narrow the selector. `state:modified.body+` matches only models whose SQL changed, plus downstream, ignoring YAML and config churn. That gives a tighter match but misses config-only regressions, so production pipelines typically layer both — a `body+` PR gate and a nightly full `modified+` build that catches config drift. The sub-methods are the knob; the omnibus is the default.

### + suffix — downstream propagation

The + graph operator (§11.7) applies to state selectors the same way it applies to any selector. `state:modified+` means "every modified node, plus every descendant of every modified node." This is the right default for CI because a downstream model can silently break when its ancestor's output changes, even if the downstream model's own SQL is unchanged.

`state:modified+` is the standard slim-CI selector. The alternative `state:modified` (no +) would miss every downstream model that consumes a changed upstream — it catches the fire but not the smoke detectors. You almost always want the +.

### When `state:modified` lies

State comparison is a diff between two manifests, and a diff is only as good as what the manifests recorded. Four cases matter, because in each of them the selector returns an answer that looks reasonable and is wrong.

**It compares rendered config values.** A config set on the model — in its `config()` block or in its YAML properties — is stored in the manifest as the value it rendered to, not as the expression you wrote. Write `{{ config(materialized=env_var('DBT_MATERIALIZATION', 'view')) }}`, set the variable to `table` in production and leave it unset in CI, and every model carrying that config differs from the production baseline on every comparison: baseline `table`, CI parse `view`. The gate rebuilds the whole mart layer for a one-line staging edit. The same mechanism hides the opposite change — replace that `env_var()` call with the literal `view` it already renders to and nothing matches, because the rendered value did not move. Configs set at project level in `dbt_project.yml` are stored as written and are unaffected either way.

The `state_modified_compare_more_unrendered_values` behaviour flag is the fix: with it on, dbt persists `unrendered_config` for models, and `unrendered_database` and `unrendered_schema` for sources, and compares those — the expression rather than its value. It is `false` at 1.11 and its default flips at 1.12; §10.9.2 covers how a behaviour flag's lifecycle is read. **Flipping it does not settle an old baseline.** The pre-flip manifest stored configs rendered and the post-flip parse stores them unrendered, so nodes compare unequal on configs nobody edited — and not only the nodes carrying Jinja: on 1.11.14 the flip alone matches models whose configs hold no Jinja at all. The first run after the flip is an oversized rebuild, and the noise clears only once the production job has regenerated the baseline under the flag.

**It is blind to data.** `state:modified` reads code, configuration and manifest-relevant metadata. Forty thousand new rows landing in `raw_ecom.orders` overnight change none of the three, so no node is modified and the job succeeds having built nothing. That is expected, not a fault, and it is the reason the selector belongs on CI and merge jobs rather than on a scheduled build. A nightly that must rebuild regardless of code drops the `state:modified` selector.

**It cannot read a manifest it has already overwritten.** dbt rewrites `target/manifest.json` during parsing, before selection runs. Point `--state` at `target/` and the comparison diffs the current manifest against itself. dbt warns — `Warning: The state and target directories are the same: 'target'. This could lead to missing changes due to overwritten state including non-idempotent retries.` — and then selects nothing. A warning is not an error, so the job goes green having built nothing, every run. Three recoveries: unpack the prior artifacts into a dedicated directory such as `state/`, give the build stage a distinct `--target-path`, or pass `--no-write-json` on a read-only command that only needs to reproduce a selection.

**It cannot diff a large seed.** dbt hashes seed contents below roughly 1 MiB. Above that it compares the file path alone and warns `Found a seed (…) >1MB in size at the same path, dbt cannot tell if it has changed: assuming they are the same.` Rewrite every row of a 4 MiB seed without moving the file and `state:modified` sees nothing.

Reference: `/reference/node-selection/state-comparison-caveats`.

**What else counts as a change.** The sub-selector table above is the documented core. `state:modified` also fires on metadata that no sub-selector names, and misses one edit the docs say it catches:

| Edit | Matches `state:modified`? |
|---|---|
| `access:` changed on a model | Yes, and `state:modified.configs` matches it too |
| `deprecation_date:` added or changed | Yes, on the omnibus only — it is a property, not a config |
| `latest_version:` bumped | Yes, and on *every* version of the model, not only the new latest |
| A source's `freshness:` or `quoting:` rules changed | Yes |
| An exposure's `maturity:` changed | Yes |
| A model reassigned from one `group:` to another | **No** |

The last row is a divergence worth carrying into the exam room. `/reference/node-selection/methods` states that changing a group flags the nodes involved; on 1.11.14 the reassignment matches neither `state:modified` nor `state:modified.configs`. The same page runs the opposite error on `meta`, calling it metadata-only and never a modification, when a **model-level** `meta` change matches both the omnibus and `.configs` — which is why the `.configs` row above lists `meta` among the configs it compares. Where the page and the runtime disagree, answer from the runtime: `tags` and `group` are excluded from state comparison, and a model-level `meta` change is not. Column level is the other half of that grid and behaves the opposite way — neither a column-level `meta` edit nor a column-level `tags` edit moves either selector; §9.7 works through it.

---

## 12.3 `--defer --state` — skipping upstream rebuilds

*`state:modified+` finally gives you the right set to build. It still will not run: as the chapter opening showed, three of those ten models have parents outside the selection, and an empty CI schema does not contain them. Deferral is how a subtree builds without its ancestors.*

Modifying a single downstream model and running it alone is a standard developer workflow. The problem: if `mart_weekly_revenue` references `int_order_summary` via `ref()`, and `int_order_summary` is not in the development schema, the run fails — the `ref()` compiles to a relation that does not exist.

`--defer` is dbt's answer. When `--defer` is passed alongside `--state <path>`, dbt rewrites every `ref()` in the running models as follows:

- If the referenced node is itself in the selected set (being built this invocation), the `ref()` compiles to the current target's relation, as normal.
- If the referenced node is **not** in the selected set and **does not exist** in the current target, the `ref()` compiles to the node's relation from the **prior-state environment** (typically production), as recorded in the `--state` manifest.
- If the referenced node is not in the selected set but **does exist** in the current target (maybe a prior run materialized it), the `ref()` uses the current-target relation.

The net effect: you build just the changed subset in your development / CI schema, and every unchanged ancestor is resolved against production's relations without rebuilding it. No CTAS, no warehouse cost, no wait.

```
# I'm working on mart_weekly_revenue. I don't want to rebuild its upstream.
dbt run --select mart_weekly_revenue --defer --state ./prod-artifacts
```

The reference is `/reference/node-selection/defer`.

## Prerequisites

- **A valid `manifest.json` must sit at the path given by `--state` or by `--defer-state`.** Defer reads that manifest to learn the prior-state relation names. Pass neither and the invocation stops with `--state or --defer-state are required for deferral, but neither was provided.`
- **The prior-state relations must actually exist** in the warehouse that your current target connects to. Defer rewrites `ref()` — it does not copy data. If the referenced production table has been dropped, the deferred query will fail at execution time.
- **Ephemeral models cannot be deferred**. Ephemeral is a pure CTE — there is nothing in the warehouse to defer to. dbt will materialize ephemeral ancestors inline, as normal.

`--state` sets one directory for two jobs: the comparison the `state:` method runs, and the relation lookup deferral runs. `--defer-state` overrides the second alone, and it satisfies deferral on its own — `dbt run --select mart_weekly_revenue --defer --defer-state ./prod-artifacts` runs with no `--state` flag at all. Splitting the two lets you compare against the logical state of one environment while resolving refs against the applied state of another: diff against last night's main-branch manifest, defer to the relations production actually has today.

All three have environment-variable equivalents — `DBT_ENGINE_STATE`, `DBT_ENGINE_DEFER` and `DBT_ENGINE_DEFER_STATE`. Set them once on the CI runner and the invocation stays short. Where a flag and its variable both appear, the flag wins. See `/reference/node-selection/configure-state`.

## `--favor-state` — when both exist, prefer the prior

By default, if a referenced node exists in both the current target and the prior-state, dbt uses the current target. `--favor-state` flips that default for **unselected** refs only — prefer the prior-state relation even when the current target has one. Selected nodes always materialize against the current target regardless of `--favor-state`. Rare in practice; useful when the current target has a stale materialization from an aborted run and you want deferred refs to point at production anyway.

## The multi-parent test trap

A `relationships` test has two parents: the model under test and the model named by `to:`. Under `--defer` those two can resolve to different environments. Change `fct_orders` and run `dbt build --select fct_orders --defer --state ./prod-artifacts` — the child side compiles to your CI relation, the `to:` side is unselected and absent from CI, so it compiles to production's:

```
with child as (
    select customer_id as from_field
    from "analytics"."ci"."fct_orders"              -- current target
    where customer_id is not null
),
```

```
parent as (
    select customer_id as to_field
    from "analytics"."prod"."dim_customers"          -- prior state
)
```

The test joins CI rows against production's dimension. A customer your branch adds to *both* models fails referential integrity on data that is perfectly consistent in the code you wrote, and it fails as a test failure rather than a database error — so it reads like your bug. Exclude those tests with `--exclude "test_name:relationships"`, or pass `--indirect-selection=cautious`, which drops any test whose parents are not all in the selected set. Single-parent tests — `not_null`, `unique`, `accepted_values` — read the current target only and are unaffected.

The `--exclude` route is the one `/reference/node-selection/state-comparison-caveats` recommends.

### Why defer matters

Defer is the mechanic that makes slim CI viable. Without it, a PR that changes a single downstream model would require rebuilding every one of its ancestors in the CI schema — because `ref()` on a non-existent relation fails. Defer lets the CI job rebuild *only what changed* while still letting downstream queries resolve against production's relations. On a thousand-model project, that is the difference between a two-minute PR gate and a fifty-minute one.

---

## 12.4 The slim-CI recipe

*Both halves are now in hand — work out what changed, and read what you deliberately did not build from the environment that already has it. This is what they assemble into, and it is the invocation the rest of your career in dbt will run most often.*

Assemble the primitives and you get the standard slim-CI invocation:

```
dbt build \
    --select state:modified+ \
    --defer --state ./prior-artifacts
```

Read flag by flag:

- **`dbt build`** — run models, tests, seeds, and snapshots in DAG order, short-circuit downstream on test failure (§11.2). This is the right verb for CI because it runs tests alongside models and treats test failures as hard stops.
- **`--select state:modified+`** — the thing × graph selector. *Thing*: nodes whose representation differs from the prior manifest. *Graph*: `+` suffix, include every descendant. The set is "changed nodes plus everything that depends on them."
- **`--defer`** — for unselected `ref()` targets, resolve against the prior-state relations rather than failing or rebuilding. This is what turns a downstream-heavy `state:modified+` selection into a bounded CI job. It assumes what a PR gate normally has: a **fresh CI schema**. Deferral prefers the current target wherever a relation is already there (§12.3), so in a warm schema an unselected `ref()` resolves to whatever that schema last built rather than to production — `--favor-state` is the flag that overrides it.
- **`--state ./prior-artifacts`** — the directory containing the comparison `manifest.json`. Both `state:` selection and `--defer` read it.

## The CI flow

A typical CI implementation wraps this invocation with two steps on either side:

1. **Before dbt runs:** download the prior `manifest.json` (and optionally `run_results.json`, `sources.json`) from an artifact store — S3, Databricks Volumes, Jenkins artifacts, GitHub artifacts — into `./prior-artifacts/`. The "prior" is usually the manifest from the most recent successful main-branch build.
2. **After dbt succeeds:** upload the fresh `target/manifest.json` (plus `run_results.json`) back to the artifact store, tagged with the commit SHA or branch name. Note what the next run should compare against, though: a PR job's manifest describes a partial build in the CI schema, so the baseline the next PR *defers* to has to come from a successful production build instead — §12.9 has the distinction.

The artifact store is the connective tissue between runs. Without it, the prior manifest is gone when the CI runner exits and state comparison has nothing to diff against.

## When the baseline is wrong

The comparison is only as trustworthy as the manifest step 1 downloaded. Two things make a baseline produce false positives — a gate that rebuilds far more than the PR touched, with no config change in the diff to explain it.

- **A baseline written by a different dbt version.** The manifest carries a schema version, and the comparison expects the one the running version writes. Regenerate the baseline on the version CI runs.
- **A baseline written under a different `state_modified_compare_more_unrendered_values` setting.** The flag changes what the manifest stores, so a manifest from before the flip cannot be compared against a parse from after it (§12.2).

Both have the same remedy: let the production job run once on the current version and settings, publish the manifest it writes, and compare against that. The cost is one oversized run, not a code change.

The mirror image is a `--state` that points at `target/`. That produces false *negatives* — a green gate that builds nothing — and §12.2 covers it.

## Variants

- **`dbt build --select state:modified+ --defer --state ... --fail-fast`** — stop on the first failure. A slim-CI job has a small blast radius; failing fast means engineers see the red build in seconds, not minutes.
- **`dbt build --select state:modified.body+ --defer --state ...`** — only SQL-body changes, ignore config churn. Useful for PR gates when config drift is noisy; pair with a nightly `state:modified+` build to catch the non-body changes.
- **`dbt run --select state:modified+ --defer --state ...`** then **`dbt test --select state:modified+ --defer --state ...`** — same idea but run and test as separate stages. Slightly more parse overhead than `build` (the project parses twice), but gives you clearer stage boundaries in CI dashboards.

## 12.5 Result selectors — re-running what failed

*The gate ran and two tests failed. Rebuilding the whole modified subtree to re-check two assertions is the same waste this chapter opened with, one level down.*

After any execution command, `target/run_results.json` contains a per-node status. The `result:` selector method queries that file, the same way `state:` queries the manifest.

| Selector | Matches nodes whose prior status was... |
|---|---|
| `result:success` | `success` — completed without error. |
| `result:error` | `error` — threw an error during execution (compile error, runtime error). |
| `result:fail` | `fail` — a test that returned failing rows. |
| `result:skipped` | `skipped` — did not run because an upstream dependency failed. |
| `result:warn` | `warn` — completed with a warning (e.g., test severity `warn`). |
| `result:pass` | `pass` — a test that returned no failing rows. |

A test that errors at runtime (e.g., a reference to a non-existent column in the test SQL, or warehouse timeout) is classified as `result:error`, not `result:fail` — `fail` is specifically for tests that returned failing rows.

The statuses are not interchangeable across resource types. `success` is what a model, seed or snapshot reports and never a test; `fail`, `warn` and `pass` are test statuses; `partial success` belongs to microbatch models alone (§12.7); `no-op` is what a node dbt walked but did not execute records, which in practice means an exposure (Ch 11 §11.2). `skipped` and `error` are the two every resource type can carry — anything a failed ancestor stopped is skipped, tests included — which is why `result:error` is the selector that spans the whole graph.

The reference page is `/reference/node-selection/methods`. The page primarily documents `result:error` (any non-test resource that returned an error) and `result:fail` (tests that returned failing rows); the `success`/`skipped`/`warn` tokens are accepted by the selector but less prominent in the reference. If a question hinges on a specific status name, anchor your answer to `result:error` and `result:fail` first.

### Typical use — surgical re-runs

```
# Re-run only the nodes that errored last time, plus their descendants
dbt run --select result:error+ --state ./prior-artifacts
```

The `result:` method reads `run_results.json` from the directory given by `--state` — there is no `target/` fallback. `dbt retry` is the command that defaults to `target/`; the two are easy to swap, and the exam likes that swap.

The `+` suffix does not transfer to a failed *test*. A test is a leaf — nothing in the DAG depends on it — so `result:fail+` returns the failed test and nothing else: not the model it tests, not anything built on that model. Reaching for it to rebuild what broke is the mistake the method invites. Walk upstream instead:

```
# Rebuild the model behind every test that failed last time, and re-run those tests
dbt build --select 1+result:fail --state ./prior-artifacts
```

`1+` is the one-generation ancestor operator from §11.7. `result:error+` keeps its trailing `+` because an errored *model* does have descendants; the asymmetry is a property of where tests sit in the graph, not of the selector.

### Combining state and result

The two selectors compose. A common CI pattern is:

```
# Re-run what failed, plus everything whose code has changed since
dbt build --select "result:error+ state:modified+" --defer --state ./prior-artifacts
```

Space-separated = union (§11.8). This re-runs failed-last-time nodes plus all-changed-since nodes, with deferral on the rest. Comma-separated = intersection, which narrows to "nodes that both failed AND were modified" — occasionally useful after a config change that you suspect caused a cascade of failures.

### When NOT to reach for `result:`

The `result:` method is for surgical re-runs after a known failure. It is not a substitute for `state:modified` in a PR gate, because a prior failure does not imply the code has changed. If the only thing that moved between runs is a transient warehouse error, use `dbt retry` (§12.7) instead — it reads `run_results.json` directly and does not require a selector.

---

## 12.6 `source_status:fresher+`

*Nothing in the code changed and the numbers are wrong anyway.* `state:modified` *cannot help here and never could — it is blind to data by design. What moved was upstream, in a source.*

After `dbt source freshness` runs, `target/sources.json` records which sources were refreshed since the comparison `sources.json`. The `source_status:fresher` selector matches those sources.

```
# Step 1: refresh source freshness and write sources.json
dbt source freshness

# Step 2: rebuild only the downstream of newly-fresher sources
dbt build --select source_status:fresher+ --state ./prior-artifacts
```

`source_status:fresher` by itself matches only the sources — which is not useful, because sources are not materialized by dbt. The `+` suffix extends the match to every descendant of those sources, which is what you actually want to rebuild.

The reference page is `/reference/node-selection/methods`.

### Why it matters — source-frequency-mismatched models

A lot of dbt projects have sources that refresh on different cadences: transactional sources update every few minutes; a slowly-changing reference source might update once a week. If your nightly `dbt build` rebuilds every downstream of every source, you are paying to rebuild models whose ancestors have not moved.

`source_status:fresher+` is the cost-saver: a cron that runs `dbt source freshness` every hour, compares against the prior `sources.json`, and triggers `dbt build --select source_status:fresher+` only when the freshness check actually detects a new load. Models whose sources are stable pay nothing; models downstream of a just-refreshed source get rebuilt. This is Chapter 3's source-freshness mechanism (§3.3) composed with Chapter 11's selector syntax.

### Running it on a schedule: the checkbox is not the run step

On the dbt platform the same command reaches a job two different ways, and they behave differently on failure. The **Run source freshness** checkbox in a job's execution settings *"will run `dbt source freshness` as the first step in your job and won't break subsequent steps if it fails."* Adding `dbt source freshness` to the run-step list instead gets you the opposite: *"if your source data is out of date — this step will "fail", and subsequent steps will not run."*

So the checkbox is telemetry and the run step is a gate. A team that ticks the box believing it has stopped stale data reaching the marts has bought a freshness graph and nothing else — the build after it runs regardless. Decide which one you actually want: if a stale source should halt the pipeline, it has to be a step. See `/docs/deploy/source-freshness`.

### Edge cases

- **Requires a prior `sources.json` in `--state`.** With no prior to compare against, the selector does not fall back to everything or to nothing — it stops with `Internal Error: No previous state comparison freshness results in sources.json`.
- **Does not fire for unchanged sources** — even if a downstream model changed since the last build. Use `state:modified+` in parallel to catch code changes.
- **Composable with `state:` and `result:`:** `--select "source_status:fresher+ state:modified+"` rebuilds anything that has a new source *or* new code.

---

## 12.7 `dbt retry` — the simplest state pattern

*The nightly build died on node 400 of 600, on a warehouse timeout that had nothing to do with the code. Starting again means paying for 399 nodes that already succeeded.*

`dbt retry` is a state-aware command with no selector syntax. It reads `run_results.json` from `target/` and re-runs exactly the nodes that did not complete successfully in the prior invocation — five statuses, in the four groups below.

```
# After a partial failure...
dbt build --target prod

# ... fix the bug in one model, then:
dbt retry
```

The reference page is `/reference/commands/retry`.

`dbt retry` supports nine commands: `build`, `compile`, `clone`, `docs generate`, `seed`, `snapshot`, `test`, `run` and `run-operation`. `source freshness`, `parse`, `ls` and `debug` are not among them, because none of them writes `run_results.json` — running one leaves the previous invocation's results in place, and a retry after it replays that invocation rather than the command you just ran. `dbt docs generate --no-compile` sits on the same side of the line for the same reason (§12.1), even though `docs generate` itself is retryable.

### What retry re-runs

- **Error nodes** — the ones that actually failed last time, `runtime error` included.
- **Fail nodes** — tests that returned failing rows.
- **Skipped nodes** — downstream nodes that were skipped because an ancestor failed.
- **Partial-success nodes** — a microbatch model whose run left some batches unbuilt.

Set `--warn-error` on the retry and warned nodes join that set as well. It does **not** re-run `success` nodes. If half a long `dbt build` completed before a connection blip, retry resumes at the failure point and runs the other half, not the whole job.

Retry has two different ways of doing nothing, and they are not the same condition. With no `run_results.json` in `target/` — nothing has executed nodes in this workspace yet, or `target/` was cleaned — retry stops with `Runtime Error: Could not find previous run in 'target' target directory`. With a `run_results.json` present in which every node succeeded, retry parses the project and reports `Nothing to do. Try checking your model configs and model specification args.` The first is a missing artifact; the second is an artifact with nothing left in it to do.

## The three flag behaviours

| Flags | What retry does with them |
|---|---|
| `--select`, `--exclude` | **Rejected outright** — not options on the command at all. `dbt retry --select fct_orders` exits immediately with `Error: No such option: --select`. The selection is implicit in `run_results.json`; accepting a selector would make retry something other than retry. |
| `--threads`, `--vars`, `--project-dir`, `--profiles-dir` | **Accepted and honoured** — the "small subset ... typically `--threads`, `--vars`, and related options" the reference page names. The path flags matter when you retry from a different working directory than the original. |
| `--target`, `--full-refresh` | **Accepted and silently discarded** — both parse without complaint, then are thrown away in favour of the failed invocation's own. `dbt retry --target ci` after a `dev` failure reports `target='dev'` and builds into the `dev` schema: no error, no warning, and the run lands somewhere other than where you asked. |

If you need a different target, a different refresh mode, or a different node set, run a fresh `dbt build --select ...` rather than `dbt retry`.

## When to use retry

- **Transient warehouse errors** — a connection timeout took down a subset of nodes, the fix is "run it again." Retry is the right tool because no code has changed. Retry repairs nothing by running, though: point it at the same failure without fixing the cause and it reproduces the identical failure, node for node.
- **Long-running builds that you don't want to restart** — a two-hour nightly failed in hour 1:45. Retry resumes from the failure, not from the start, and it re-parses first, so a fix to the failing model's SQL is picked up. What it does not recompute is *which* nodes to run.

### When NOT to use retry

- **After running any other node-executing command** — a subsequent `dbt compile`, `dbt docs generate` (unless you pass `--no-compile`), or `dbt test` will overwrite `run_results.json` and retry will re-run *those* results, not the failing build. See "The retry trap" below for the operational gotcha and the recovery path.
- **When the graph itself has changed since the failure** — retry re-runs the prior node list against the current code, and that list is frozen: a model added after the failure is invisible to it. Use `dbt build --select <the failing model>+` so dbt recomputes the selection from the current graph.
- **To re-run successful nodes** — retry does not re-run successes. For that, use a full `dbt build` or `dbt run` without a result selector.

### The same idea as a job button

The platform surfaces this command as a choice between **Rerun from start**, which reruns the entire job from the beginning, and **Rerun from failure**, which resumes from the previously failed step. The second one is `dbt retry` wearing a button, and it inherits the command's limits exactly: *"The job command that failed in the run must be one that supports the retry command."* A job whose failing step was `dbt source freshness` offers you no useful resume, for the same reason the CLI does not — the command wrote no `run_results.json` to resume from. Choosing it shows a modal listing which steps will be invoked, the failed step and any skipped ones, before anything runs. See `/docs/deploy/retry-jobs`.

### The retry trap

Any command that writes `run_results.json` between a failure and its retry destroys the retry. `dbt compile` is the trap, because it looks harmless: it materializes nothing, but it does write results — in which nothing failed — so `dbt retry` answers `Nothing to do. Try checking your model configs and model specification args` and the failed nodes are invisible. The rule: do not interleave commands between a failure and its retry; if you already have, point retry at a saved copy of the failed run's artifacts with `dbt retry --state ./failed-artifacts` rather than shuffling files back into `target/`.

---

## 12.8 `dbt clone` — zero-copy environments

*You need somewhere prod-shaped to develop against. Rebuilding production into a dev schema to get it is precisely the cost this chapter exists to avoid.*

`dbt clone` creates a copy of selected nodes from a prior-state environment into the current target, without re-running the SQL. It does that by building each selected node with the built-in `clone` materialization rather than the node's own — which is why the command needs no SQL execution and why an adapter can override the behaviour in one place. Where the warehouse supports zero-copy cloning — Snowflake, Databricks on Delta, BigQuery — and the source node is already a table, it issues the platform's native clone primitive. Everywhere else it creates a pointer view instead.

```
# Clone the modified nodes and their descendants from prior-state (production)
# into the CI target schema
dbt clone --select state:modified+ --state ./prior-artifacts
```

**`dbt clone` needs `--state`; it does not need `--defer`.** Deferral is not a flag you add to clone — it is what clone *is*, so the machinery runs unconditionally and the command reads the prior-state manifest either way. Executed on dbt Core 1.11.14: `dbt clone --select state:modified+ --state ./prior` reports `Done. PASS=1` and creates the relation, and adding `--defer` to the identical invocation changes nothing about the result. Drop `--state` instead and it stops — `Got a state selector method, but no comparison manifest`, or, with no selector to complain first, `--state or --defer-state are required for deferral, but neither was provided.`

Two environments add a wrinkle worth knowing, and neither contradicts the above. The reference notes that *"The `dbt clone` command in the dbt platform CLI automatically includes the `--defer` flag"* — on that CLI the flag is supplied for you, which is why you will see platform examples that never mention it. In the Studio IDE deferral is a setting rather than a flag: you enable **Defer to production** with a toggle before running the command. The reference page is `/reference/commands/clone`.

Two flags matter here. `--full-refresh` recreates a relation that already exists in the target, so you can re-point a stale clone. Raising `--threads` can reduce execution time because clone statements are independent; the gain depends on adapter and warehouse concurrency limits, not a guarantee of linear scaling.

## Flags clone accepts

- `--select` / `--exclude` — standard selector syntax, the same as any other command.
- `--state <dir>` — required, unless `--defer-state <dir>` already points deferral at a manifest. Tells clone where the prior-state relations live.
- `--full-refresh` — recreate pre-existing clones at the target. Without this, clone leaves a pre-existing relation alone: the node is a no-op reported as a success, not a skip.
- `--threads N` — concurrency.

## Why clone matters — zero-copy CI

On Snowflake and Databricks, a clone is a metadata operation: no data is copied, no storage is duplicated, the new relation is a reference to the source's underlying files. The cost is trivial and the time is seconds. That makes clone a viable alternative to `--defer` for a certain class of CI workflow:

- **Deferred runs** (§12.3) never materialize the unchanged ancestors in the CI target. Downstream SQL runs against production relations via rewritten `ref()`.
- **Cloned environments** materialize every ancestor as a zero-copy clone in the CI target. Downstream SQL runs against CI-local relations that happen to share data with production.

Each has trade-offs. Defer is lighter — no metadata operation at all, just the `ref()` rewrite. Clone is heavier setup but gives the CI schema a self-contained mirror of production, which is useful when other tools (BI, notebooks, ad-hoc queries) need to point at the CI environment. A blue/green deploy pattern often uses clone for the "green" environment, runs tests against it, and promotes on success.

## Zero-copy vs pointer view

The cert can ask about the fallback behaviour, which has two triggers rather than one. An adapter without zero-copy support (Postgres, Redshift, DuckDB) sends every node down the fallback path, and so does a source relation that is not a table — a `view` or `materialized_view` model gets a pointer view on Snowflake too. Either way `dbt clone` creates a view: `CREATE VIEW <target_relation> AS SELECT * FROM <source_relation>`. Functionally similar

— queries against the cloned view resolve to the source data — but semantically different: a zero-copy clone can diverge (you can write to it without affecting the source), a view cannot.

---

## 12.9 In practice: Credora's defer-state CI

> *This section is an "in practice" sidebar. It draws a composite pattern from (a) the recommended `--defer --state` recipe documented at `/reference/node-selection/defer`, and (b) dbt Discourse community threads on slim CI. Credora is fictional (`credora`); Ch 14's opening note has the composite-project disclaimer. Teams at scale commonly converge on some variation of this pattern — the steps below are not unique to any single company.*

Consider the CI pipeline that runs on every PR to Credora's main branch. The goal: a PR gate that rebuilds only what the PR changes, fails fast on a test regression, and finishes in low minutes rather than tens of minutes.

The pipeline has four steps:

```
1. Download prior-artifacts from the artifact store
2. dbt parse  (emit current manifest.json)
3. dbt build --select state:modified+ --defer --state ./prior-artifacts --fail-fast
4. On success: upload target/manifest.json back to the artifact store
```

Step by step:

**Step 1 — Download prior-artifacts.** The CI runner pulls a tarball from the artifact store (S3 in Credora's case; Databricks Volumes and Jenkins artifacts are common alternatives). The tarball contains `manifest.json`, `run_results.json`, and `sources.json` from the most recent successful build of the main branch, tagged with that build's commit SHA. Contents are unpacked into `./prior-artifacts/` in the CI workspace.

**Step 2 — `dbt parse`.** This is the cheapest way to produce a current `manifest.json`. It reads every `.sql`, `.yml`, and `.csv` in the project, resolves `ref()` and `source()` edges, and writes `target/manifest.json`. It does not render compiled SQL; it does not hit the warehouse. On a project with over a thousand models, it finishes in single-digit seconds. (Ch 11 §11.3 covers `parse` vs `compile`.)

**Step 3 — The slim-CI build.** This is the load-bearing step:

```
dbt build \
    --select state:modified+ \
    --defer --state ./prior-artifacts \
    --target ci \
    --fail-fast
```

- `state:modified+` diffs the current `target/manifest.json` against `./prior-artifacts/manifest.json` and selects every modified node plus its downstream descendants.
- `--defer --state ./prior-artifacts` tells dbt: for any `ref()` target that is not in the selection **and is not already present in the CI target**, resolve it against the prior-state relations (production) rather than building it in the CI schema. That second condition is not a detail — it is why the gate creates a fresh schema per PR. Against a warm schema an unselected `ref()` resolves to whatever that schema last built, unless `--favor-state` is passed (§12.3).
- `--target ci` materializes the selection into Credora's CI schema, not production.
- `--fail-fast` stops on the first failure. Slim-CI jobs tend to have small blast radius, and engineers much prefer a red build at minute 2 than at minute 12.

The effect: a PR that changes two staging models rebuilds those two plus their downstream (typically another handful), with every unchanged upstream resolved against production relations. A PR that changes a macro used by a hundred models rebuilds a hundred-model subtree. A PR that touches a project-level config that cascades through every model may still rebuild the graph, which is the signal to the engineer that the change is broad and warrants scrutiny.

**Step 4 — Upload on success.** If the build passes, the CI runner uploads `target/manifest.json` (and usually the full `target/` minus compiled SQL) back to the artifact store, tagged with the PR's commit SHA. Keep those for debugging that run.

**The next PR gate uses a different artifact.** A partial CI build's manifest retains the current project's node definitions, including unbuilt nodes, with relations resolved for the CI target. Deferral attaches prior-state relations at runtime; it does not replace those definitions, and the attached `defer_relation` is omitted from the written artifact. Promoting that manifest would make the next PR defer to CI relations that were never built or disappear when the schema is dropped. Publish `latest-main` from the **production** job's full, successful build instead. See Core's manifest merge and model serialization.

## What this pipeline is not

- **It does not run `dbt source freshness`.** Source-freshness checking is a separate cadence (Credora runs it on a cron, not on every PR). Integrating `source_status:fresher+` into the PR gate would be redundant — PRs change code, not source-load timing.
- **It does not use `dbt clone`.** Credora's CI uses defer rather than clone, because defer is lighter and the CI schema does not need a self-contained mirror of production. A team running blue/green deploys would layer clone in; Credora does not.
- **It does not use `dbt retry`.** Retry is for operational recovery from partial failures, not for CI. A failed CI build gets a red-X mark on the PR and the engineer fixes the code, not the build state.
- **`--fail-fast` is a policy choice**, not a requirement. Some teams prefer to let the build finish and report every failure at once; Credora chose fast-fail to keep engineer feedback tight.

## The pattern in context

The four-step flow — download artifacts, parse, build-with-state-and-defer, upload artifacts — is the shape slim CI converges on. The implementation details (artifact store, CI platform, shell wrapping) vary enormously; the dbt commands do not. If you can read this invocation as the sum of its parts — `build` from Ch 11 §11.2, `state:modified+` from §12.2 and §11.7, `--defer --state` from §12.3, `--fail-fast` and `--target` from Ch 11 §11.10 — you have the primitives. The pipeline is just wiring.

---

## Summary

- State is the mechanism by which dbt knows what has changed between runs. Four artifacts live in `target/`, and each feeds its own consumer: `manifest.json` (the graph) is what `state:`, `--defer` and `dbt clone` read; `run_results.json` (the last run's per-node status) is what `result:` and `dbt retry` read; `sources.json` (freshness results) is what `source_status:` reads; `catalog.json` (warehouse metadata) feeds the docs site and no selection at all.

- The `state:` selector method compares the current parse against a prior `manifest.json` supplied via `--state`; `state:modified+` is the standard PR-gate selector, with sub-methods (`.body`, `.configs`, `.relation`, `.persisted_descriptions`, `.macros`, `.contract`, plus `state:new` / `state:old` / `state:unmodified`) for narrower matches. It also fires on `access`, `deprecation_date`, `latest_version`, a source's `freshness` or `quoting` and an exposure's `maturity` — and not on a `group` reassignment.
- State comparison lies in four ways worth knowing: at the 1.11 default it compares rendered config values, so an environment-keyed config flags every model carrying it; it is blind to data changes, so a scheduled job succeeds having built nothing; it selects nothing when `--state` points at `target/`, because dbt overwrote the manifest first; and it cannot diff a seed above roughly 1 MiB.
- `--defer --state <dir>` rewrites unselected `ref()` calls to resolve against the prior-state relations rather than failing or rebuilding — the mechanic behind slim CI. `--defer-state` satisfies deferral on its own and can point at a different manifest from the one `state:` diffs against.
- Under deferral a multi-parent `relationships` test joins the current target against the prior state and can fail on internally consistent code; `--exclude "test_name: relationships"` or `--indirect-selection=cautious` drops it.
- The slim-CI recipe `dbt build --select state:modified+ --defer --state ./prior-artifacts` is the production PR gate this chapter ends on. A baseline written by a different dbt version, or under a different `state_modified_compare_more_unrendered_values` setting, is the usual cause of a gate that rebuilds too much.
- `result:` selectors re-query the `run_results.json` at `--state` for surgical re-runs: `result:error+` for an errored model and its descendants, `1+result:fail` for the model behind a failed test, because `+` after a test matches nothing.
- `source_status:fresher+` drives freshness-triggered rebuilds after `dbt source freshness`.
- `dbt retry` reads `run_results.json` and resumes from the failure point — `--select` and `--exclude` are rejected outright, and `--target` and `--full-refresh` are accepted and then silently discarded.
- `dbt clone` copies selected nodes from a prior-state environment into the current target using zero-copy clones (Snowflake / Databricks / BigQuery, and only where the source relation is already a table) or pointer views otherwise.
- The primitives assemble into a four-step CI flow: download prior artifacts, parse, build-with-state-and-defer, upload.

## Learning-goal checklist (self-assess)

- ☐ **Explain `manifest.json` and `run_results.json`** — what each contains, which commands produce each (§12.1).
- ☐ **Use `state:modified`, `state:modified+`, `state:modified.body`, `state:modified.configs`,** and name the metadata edits the omnibus catches that no sub-selector does (§12.2).
- ☐ **Name the four cases in which `state:modified` returns a wrong answer** — rendered config values, data changes, `--state` pointed at `target/`, and seeds above roughly 1 MiB (§12.2).
- ☐ **Say what `state_modified_compare_more_unrendered_values` changes, and why the baseline must be regenerated after the flip** (§12.2, §12.4).
- ☐ **Use `--defer --state`** to skip upstream rebuilds in CI, and distinguish `--defer-state` from `--state` (§12.3, §12.4).
- ☐ **Explain why a deferred `relationships` test can fail on correct code, and name both mitigations** (§12.3).

- ☐ **Use `result:error+`, `1+result:fail`, `result:skipped+`**, and say why `result:fail+` is not the selector you want (§12.5).
- ☐ **Use `source_status:fresher+`** after `dbt source freshness` (§12.6).
- ☐ **Run `dbt retry`** and know what it re-runs, what flags it accepts, and when not to use it (§12.7).
- ☐ **Understand `dbt clone`** for zero-copy CI environments (§12.8).

---

## Practice questions

Thirty-six questions covering every §12.1–§12.8 sub-topic, graded recall / apply / analyze.

**1.** Which statement best describes `manifest.json`?

A. The per-node success/error status from the last dbt invocation
B. The full parsed graph of every resource in the project, including edges, configs, and compiled node hashes
C. Warehouse-introspected column types and table statistics
D. The source-freshness status of every configured source

**2.** Which of the following commands does NOT write `run_results.json`?

A. `dbt run` B. `dbt test`
C. `dbt parse` D. `dbt build`

**3.** Which command produces `sources.json`?

A. `dbt source freshness` B. `dbt docs generate`
C. `dbt run` D. `dbt parse`

**4.** What does `--select state:modified --state ./prior-artifacts` match?

A. Every node whose current representation differs from its representation in `./prior-artifacts/manifest.json`, including brand-new nodes
B. Every node in the current project
C. Every node that errored in the prior run
D. Every node whose source has been refreshed since the prior freshness check

**5.** A team's slim-CI job uses `--select state:modified`. A PR changes one staging model, and CI rebuilds only that staging model — none of its downstream. What is the likely fix?

A. Add `--defer` to the invocation B. Use `state:new` instead of `state:modified`
C. Switch to `dbt run` from `dbt build` D. Add the `+` suffix: `--select state:modified+`

**6.** A model's `.sql` file and its YAML properties are byte-for-byte unchanged since the prior run, but a macro the model calls has been edited. Which sub-selector matches that model?

A. `state:modified.body` B. `state:modified.contract`
C. `state:modified.macros` D. `state:unmodified`

**7.** Several of a project's models set a config from `env_var()` in their own `config()` blocks. The team adds `state_modified_compare_more_unrendered_values: true` to the `flags:` block of `dbt_project.yml`, then runs the PR gate against the baseline manifest last week's production job published. What should they expect from that first run?
A. Nothing — the flag is accepted at 1.11 but takes effect only from 1.12, when its default flips to `true` and the comparison changes
B. Every one of those models matches `state:modified` on this run, and stops doing so once the baseline is regenerated under the flag
C. Nothing — dbt re-reads each manifest's configs unrendered at comparison time, so the setting under which the baseline was written does not matter
D. `state:modified` stops comparing configs altogether, leaving body, macro and contract changes as the only criteria the omnibus applies

**8.** A model selected for a CI run references an upstream model that is NOT in the selected set and does not exist in the CI target schema. With `--defer --state ./prior-artifacts`, how does dbt resolve the `ref()`?
A. It rewrites the `ref()` to point at the upstream's relation in the prior-state environment, as recorded in `./prior-artifacts/manifest.json`
B. It rebuilds the upstream in the CI schema before the selected model runs
C. It errors — the upstream does not exist
D. It falls back to compiling the `ref()` as a literal string

**9.** Which is a required prerequisite for `--defer` to work?
A. A valid `manifest.json` must always exist at the path given by `--state` or by `--defer-state`
B. The `dbt_project.yml` must declare `defer: true`
C. All deferred nodes must be ephemeral materializations
D. `--defer` can only be used with `dbt build`, not `dbt run` or `dbt test`

**10.** A CI job for a thousand-model project builds into a fresh CI schema using `dbt build --select state:modified+`, without `--defer --state`. A PR changes one staging model with many downstream dependents. On its own that invocation errors, and the team's fix is to widen the job so it builds the unchanged ancestors too — which is what makes it far more expensive than the equivalent invocation with `--defer --state`. What makes building those ancestors necessary?
A. `--defer` raises the effective thread count to match the number of deferred nodes, so the same set of models is built with more concurrency
B. Without `--defer`, every `ref()` has to resolve to a relation that already exists in the CI target, so the unchanged ancestors have to be built there before the changed subtree can run
C. Without `--defer`, `dbt build` runs every test twice — once against the CI relation and once against the prior-state relation it would otherwise have deferred to
D. `--defer` provisions each unchanged ancestor as a zero-copy clone in the CI schema, so the ancestors are still created, at metadata cost rather than compute cost

**11.** In `dbt build --select state:modified+ --defer --state ./prior-artifacts`, what is the role of `--state ./prior-artifacts`?
A. It is only used by `--defer`, which reads it to resolve unselected refs; the `state:` selector diffs against `target/` instead
B. It is only used by the `state:` selector, which diffs it against the current parse; `--defer` resolves unselected refs from the current run
C. Both the `state:` selector and `--defer` read the manifest at that path — every `state:` comparison diffs against it, and every deferred `ref()` resolves through it
D. It tells dbt where to write the new `manifest.json` on success, replacing the artifacts left in `target/` by the previous run

**12.** Which invocation re-runs the nodes that BOTH **errored** in the prior run AND have code changes since, together with their downstream?
A. `dbt build --select "result:error+,state:modified+" --state ./prior`
B. `dbt build --select "result:error+ state:modified+" --state ./prior`
C. `dbt build --select result:error+ --exclude state:modified+ --state ./prior`
D. `dbt retry --state ./prior`

**13.** A team has sources that refresh on different cadences; some update every few minutes, others once a week. They want a cron job that rebuilds only the downstream of sources that have actually received new data since the last run. Which approach is correct?
A. Run `dbt build --select state:modified+` on the cron, comparing against the prior run's manifest
B. Run `dbt build --select result:success+` on the cron, using the prior run's results to pick up where it left off
C. Run `dbt source freshness` first, then `dbt build --select source_status:fresher+ --state ./prior-artifacts`
D. Run `dbt retry` on the cron, so each invocation continues from the state the last one left behind

**14.** `dbt retry` rejects one of the following flags outright — it errors on the flag rather than parsing it and then ignoring it. Which one?
A. `--threads` B. `--vars`
C. `--select` D. `--target`

**15.** A developer runs `dbt build` and hits a failure on `fct_orders`. While fixing the SQL bug, they also add a new downstream dependency and want the rerun set computed from the current graph, not from the prior run's frozen failure list. Which is the best next step?
A. Run `dbt retry` — it re-parses the project and picks up the edited SQL, then rebuilds from the prior run's frozen result list
B. Run `dbt retry --full-refresh` — the flag is accepted, so the frozen list rebuilds from scratch and picks the new model up
C. Run `dbt build --select fct_orders+` — which re-parses the project and picks up the edited SQL, then rebuilds the failure point and its downstream
D. Delete `target/` and run `dbt build` from scratch — the current graph, reached by discarding every node that already succeeded

**16.** A CI pipeline runs `dbt clone --select fct_orders --state ./prior-artifacts` on a Databricks target. `fct_orders` exists in the prior-state environment as a Delta table. What does dbt create in the CI target schema?
A. A view that selects from the prior-state table
B. A zero-copy clone of the Delta table — a metadata reference with no data copied
C. A copy of every row from the prior-state table into a new table
D. Nothing — clone requires `--full-refresh`

**17.** A team's slim-CI job uses `dbt build --select state:modified+ --defer --state ./prior-artifacts`. The artifact store serves the manifest from the most recent successful main-branch build, produced by the same dbt version the CI job runs. They notice that most PRs — even small ones that touch two staging models — trigger a rebuild of roughly 80% of the graph. What is the likely cause and the most targeted fix?
A. `--defer` resolves each unselected `ref()` against its prior-state relation, and any node whose deferred relation differs from the CI one is added to the selection; drop `--defer`
B. `dbt build` selects a test as soon as one of its parents is modified, and each selected test then pulls its remaining parent models into the run; switch to `dbt run`
C. Config changes in `dbt_project.yml` or a shared YAML file are matching `state:modified` on every model that inherits them; narrow the PR gate to `state:modified.body+`
D. The artifact store is serving a manifest from a build older than the last main-branch run, so every node merged since then still reads as modified; clear the cache

**18.** A developer runs `dbt build`, sees three models fail, then runs `dbt compile` to inspect the rendered SQL, and finally runs `dbt retry`. Retry reports `Nothing to do` and re-runs none of the three failed models. What is the cause?
A. `dbt retry` requires `--state` to locate `run_results.json`, and the developer did not pass one
B. `dbt compile` overwrote `run_results.json` with its own per-node results; `dbt retry` consulted the post-compile `run_results.json`, not the failed-build one
C. The compile step silently succeeded the three failed models
D. `dbt retry` skips any node whose `manifest.json` entry has changed since the failure

**19.** Credora's mart models take their materialization from the environment — `{{ config(materialized=env_var('DBT_MATERIALIZATION', 'view')) }}` — with the variable set to `table` in production and left unset in CI. Two CI jobs run `dbt build --select state:modified+ --defer --state ./prior-artifacts` against the same PR, which edits one staging model's SQL and nothing else. Job A compares against the manifest from the nightly production build; job B compares against a manifest an earlier CI job on the same branch published. `state_modified_compare_more_unrendered_values` sits at its 1.11 default. Which job rebuilds every mart, and why?
A. Job A — the comparison holds each config's rendered value, so every mart's baseline `table` differs from its CI `view` and matches `state:modified`
B. Job B — a manifest published by a CI job is not a valid comparison baseline for a PR gate, so `state:modified` falls back to matching the whole project
C. Neither — `--defer` resolves the marts against production's relations, which removes them from the selection whatever the baseline happens to hold
D. Both — an `env_var()` call inside a `config()` block cannot be resolved at comparison time, so dbt marks every node carrying one as modified

**20.** A PR touches only YAML — no `.sql` file changes. Which of these edits does NOT match `state:modified`?
A. `dim_customers` gains `access: public`
B. `fct_orders` gains `deprecation_date: 2027-01-01`
C. The `raw_ecom` source's `warn_after` freshness threshold drops from 12 hours to 6
D. `stg_orders` moves from `group: finance` to `group: analytics`

**21.** A 4 a.m. scheduled job runs `dbt build --select state:modified+ --defer --state ./prior-artifacts` against the manifest the previous night's run published. Overnight the loader landed 40,000 new rows in `raw_ecom.orders`; nobody merged any code. The job finishes green in under a minute having built nothing. What has happened?
A. The comparison manifest is stale; a `state:modified` job needs its baseline regenerated after every source load
B. Expected — `state:modified` compares code, configuration and manifest metadata only, so new source rows never make a node modified
C. `--defer` resolved every model against the prior-state relations, which removed them from the selection
D. `state:modified` reads `sources.json` only when it is unioned with `source_status:fresher+`, and this job omits the freshness step that writes it

**22.** A CI job unpacks the prior artifacts straight into `target/` and runs `dbt build --select state:modified+ --state ./target`. dbt warns that the state and target directories are the same, and every run then reports that nothing was selected — even on PRs that change several models. What is happening, and what fixes it?
A. The warning is promoted to an error once parsing completes, so state selection is skipped for the rest of the invocation; demote it through `warn_error_options` and the comparison resolves
B. `--state` rejects a manifest written by a different dbt version than the one running; rebuild the baseline on the runner's version and point `--state` at that directory
C. dbt overwrites `target/manifest.json` during its own parse, before the comparison reads it, so the run diffs the current manifest against itself; unpack the prior artifacts into a separate `state/` directory
D. `state:` selection cannot resolve a relative path from the project root; pass an absolute path to `--state` and the comparison finds the manifest

**23.** A PR rewrites several thousand rows inside a 4 MiB seed file, leaving its path unchanged. CI runs `dbt build --select state:modified+ --state ./prior-artifacts`; the seed is not selected, and dbt warns that it cannot tell whether the file has changed. What is the rule?
A. Seeds are excluded from `state:modified` altogether; the only way to reload one in CI is an explicit `dbt seed --full-refresh` step
B. `state:modified.body` is the only sub-selector that covers seed contents, and the omnibus `state:modified` does not include it, so the gate has to name it
C. dbt compares a seed against the relation already in the warehouse rather than against the manifest, so a seed loaded in the CI schema is treated as unchanged
D. dbt hashes seed contents only below roughly 1 MiB; above that it compares the file path alone, so a content change at an unchanged path is invisible

**24.** A developer runs `dbt run --select fct_orders --defer --favor-state --state ./prod-artifacts`. Both `fct_orders` and its unselected parent `dim_customers` already exist in the developer's `dev` schema from an earlier run. What does `--favor-state` change?
A. `ref('dim_customers')` in `fct_orders` resolves to the prior-state relation instead of the existing `dev` one; `fct_orders` itself still builds into `dev` from its current code
B. Both models resolve to the prior-state relations, so the run reads production data and writes its output into the production schema as well
C. `dim_customers` joins the selection and is rebuilt in `dev` from its current code before `fct_orders` runs
D. Nothing — `--favor-state` restates the default, which already prefers the prior-state relation for an unselected `ref()`

**25.** A PR adds one new customer to both `dim_customers` and `fct_orders`. CI runs `dbt build --select fct_orders --defer --state ./prior-artifacts`. `fct_orders` builds into the CI schema, and then the `relationships` test on `fct_orders.customer_id` reports `Got 1 result, configured to fail if != 0`. Building both models into the CI schema and re-running the same test passes. What happened?
A. `--defer` does not apply to test nodes, so both sides of the join compiled against the prior-state relations and neither saw the CI build
B. `dbt build` orders tests by name rather than by DAG position, so the test ran against the CI relation before `fct_orders` had finished building
C. `dim_customers` is absent from the CI schema, so the join matched no rows at all and dbt reported the first unmatched one
D. The child CTE reads the CI relation while the `to:` side, unselected, resolves to `dim_customers` in the prior-state schema, so the join compares CI rows against production's dimension

**26.** A nightly `dbt build` ends with one failed `not_null` test on `fct_orders` and no other failures. The on-call engineer copies that run's artifacts to `./prior-run` and runs `dbt build --select result:fail+ --state ./prior-run`, expecting the model to rebuild and the test to re-run against fresh rows. dbt executes one node — the test — and it fails again on the same rows. Why did the `+` add nothing?
A. The `+` did expand, but `--state` filtered the descendants back out as unmodified since the prior run
B. A test is a leaf — nothing depends on it — so a trailing `+` has nothing to add; `1+result:fail` is the form that reaches the model
C. `--indirect-selection` defaults to `eager`, which runs a selected test without its parents; `--indirect-selection=cautious` would have pulled `fct_orders` in
D. The model was selected and then skipped: `dbt build` will not rebuild a model whose test failed in the prior run until that test passes

**27.** `dbt clone` is run into a target schema where several of the relations already exist. What happens to those, and what does `--threads` change?
A. They are recreated; `--threads` has no effect because clones run in dependency order
B. They are left as they are unless `--full-refresh` is passed; `--threads` controls concurrency among independent clone statements
C. They are dropped and skipped, and `--threads` is ignored for clone
D. The command fails on the first existing relation and reports a collision

**28.** A scheduled job fails midway. The platform offers **Rerun from failure**, but it is unavailable for this job. What is the most likely reason?
A. The job has more than one step, and the button only supports single-step jobs
B. The failure was a test failure rather than a model error
C. The job's command is not one that `dbt retry` supports
D. The previous run's artifacts expired, so there is no state to resume from

**29.** A CI runner exports `DBT_ENGINE_STATE=/artifacts/prod`, and the job's command passes `--state ./pr-base`. Which path is used, and what are these variables?
A. `/artifacts/prod` — environment variables are resolved last and therefore win
B. `/artifacts/prod`, because `DBT_ENGINE_STATE` replaces the flag
C. `./pr-base` — the flag beats the variable; the `DBT_ENGINE_*` variables are equivalents of their corresponding flags
D. Neither; dbt reports a conflict between the flag and the environment

**30.** A CI job runs `dbt build --select state:modified+ --defer --state ./pr-base --defer-state ./prod`. Which artifact answers which question?
A. `./prod` decides what is modified; `./pr-base` supplies the relations to defer to
B. `./pr-base` decides what is modified; `./prod` supplies the relations to defer to
C. `./pr-base` is used for both — `--defer-state` only takes effect when `--state` is absent
D. The two conflict and dbt raises a configuration error

**31.** A team wants a scheduled job to stop when a source is stale. They tick the job's freshness checkbox. A source goes stale. What happens?
A. The job fails at the freshness stage and the remaining steps are skipped
B. The job fails, but only if the source's `error_after` threshold is set
C. The job runs freshness and continues — the checkbox does not fail the job; an explicit `dbt source freshness` step does
D. The checkbox has no effect unless `--warn-error` is also set on the job

**32.** A pipeline runs `dbt compile` to produce a manifest, then a second dbt invocation that must not disturb it. What does `--no-write-json` on the second invocation do?
A. Stops dbt writing `manifest.json`, `run_results.json` and the other artifacts, leaving the first step's files intact
B. Stops dbt reading artifacts, forcing a full parse
C. Writes the artifacts to a temporary directory instead of `target/`
D. Suppresses only `run_results.json`, since the manifest is always written

**33.** Which statement about `result:<status>` selectors is correct?
A. `result:success` matches tests that passed, as well as models that built
B. `result:skipped` applies to models only; tests are never recorded as skipped
C. `result:fail` matches any resource whose last run errored
D. `result:success` applies to models, seeds and snapshots, never to tests

**34.** A run fails on a model with a SQL error. The engineer runs `dbt retry` immediately, without editing anything. What happens?
A. The same failure, in the same place — retry re-executes; it does not repair
B. The run succeeds, because retry rebuilds upstream dependencies first
C. dbt refuses, reporting that nothing has changed since the failed run
D. The failed node is skipped and the rest of the DAG completes

**35.** Which of these commands can `dbt retry` **not** resume?
A. `dbt clone`
B. `dbt docs generate`
C. `dbt run-operation`
D. `dbt source freshness`

**36.** A model's `schema:` is set in its `config()` block from an expression over `var('target_schema')`. The variable's value changes between the base manifest and the current run, but the expression renders to an identical schema name both times. The project is on the 1.11 defaults. Does `state:modified` select the model?
A. Yes — dbt compares the raw config, so any change to the variable is caught
B. No — the comparison sees the rendered value, which did not change
C. Yes, but only with `--defer-state` pointed at the same manifest
D. No, and there is no behaviour flag governing what `state:modified` compares

## Answer key

**1. B.** `manifest.json` is the full parsed graph — every model, test, source, exposure, macro, their `ref()`/`source()` edges, their resolved configs, and their compiled hashes. It is produced by most commands that parse the project — though not by `dbt docs generate --no-compile`, which parses in full and writes `catalog.json` alone. Option A describes `run_results.json`. Option C describes `catalog.json`. Option D describes `sources.json`. Source: `/reference/artifacts/manifest-json`.

**2. C.** `dbt parse` produces `manifest.json` only — it does not execute any nodes, so there are no results to record. `dbt run`, `dbt test`, `dbt build`, `dbt seed`, `dbt snapshot`, `dbt compile`, `dbt docs generate`, `dbt retry`, `dbt clone`, `dbt show`, and `dbt run-operation` all write `run_results.json`. Source: `/reference/artifacts/run-results-json`.

**3. A.** `dbt source freshness` is the only command that queries configured sources for their load timestamps and writes the result to `target/sources.json`. Other commands may read the file (e.g., selectors using `source_status:`) but do not write it. Source: `/reference/artifacts/sources-json`.

**4. A.** The `state:` method compares the current parse against the prior manifest and matches nodes whose representation differs, which includes brand-new nodes — a model, seed, snapshot or test with no prior representation compares as different. Note where that reasoning stops: sources and exposures are not nodes, and a brand-new one is matched by `state:new` but not by `state:modified` (§12.2). Option B would be no selector. Option C describes `result:error`. Option D describes `source_status:fresher`. Source: `/reference/node-selection/methods`.

**5. D.** `state:modified` matches only the changed nodes themselves. To include downstream descendants — which is what CI typically wants, since downstream models can break when upstream output changes — you need the `+` graph operator suffix. `--defer` (A) controls how unselected refs resolve, not which nodes are selected. Switching verbs (C) does not change the selection. `state:new` (B) matches only brand-new resources, which is fewer nodes than the current selector, not more. Source: `/reference/node-selection/graph-operators`, `/reference/node-selection/methods`.

**6. C.** `state:modified.macros` is the sub-selector for the indirect case: the node's own definition is untouched, but a macro it depends on changed — one it calls, or one further down that macro's own call chain — so the SQL it will compile to has changed. Verified on dbt 1.11.14 — editing a macro's body and re-selecting against the baseline manifest matches the calling model under `state:modified` and `state:modified.macros`, and matches nothing under `state:modified.body` (A), because the model's own body is byte-identical. `state:modified.contract` (B) tracks the contract block — column set, types, constraints — which the stem says is unchanged. `state:unmodified` (D) is the inverse of the whole family and excludes the model precisely because the macro edit did modify it. Source: `/reference/node-selection/methods`.

**7. B.** With the flag on, dbt persists `unrendered_config` at parse time and compares the expression rather than the value it rendered to. The published baseline was written before the flip, so it holds rendered values while the current parse holds unrendered ones, and every model whose own config carries Jinja compares unequal. Verified on dbt 1.11.14 with a model configured `materialized=env_var('DBT_MAT', 'view')`: flag off and the variable changed → the model matched `state:modified`; flag on against that same pre-flip baseline → it still matched; baseline regenerated under the flag → `No nodes selected!`. The extra matches cost one oversized run, not a code change (§12.2, §12.4). Option A confuses a default with a setting — a behaviour flag set explicitly takes effect on the version that carries it, and 1.11 carries this one (§10.9.2). Option C is what the false positives refute: the comparison reads what each manifest stored, and the two manifests stored different things. Option D describes no dbt behaviour — configs remain part of `state:modified` at either setting. Sources: `/reference/global-configs/behavior-flags/state_modified_compare_more_unrendered_values`, `/reference/node-selection/state-comparison-caveats`.

**8. A.** The defining behaviour of `--defer`: for unselected refs that do not exist in the current target, dbt consults the prior-state manifest and rewrites the `ref()` to point at the prior-state relation (typically production). Without `--defer`, option C would happen. Option B is what happens without `--defer` when you explicitly include upstream in the selection. Option D is not a dbt behaviour. Source: `/reference/node-selection/defer`.

**9. A.** `--defer` reads the prior-state `manifest.json` to learn the prior-state relation names. Without one — at `--state`, or at `--defer-state`, which satisfies deferral on its own — defer cannot rewrite `ref()` calls, and the invocation stops with `--state or --defer-state are required for deferral, but neither was provided`. There is no project-level `defer:` flag (B). Ephemeral models cannot be deferred — defer requires a materialized relation (C is backwards). `--defer` works with `run`, `test`, and `build` (D is wrong). Source: `/reference/node-selection/defer`.

**10. B.** Without `--defer`, every `ref()` must resolve to a relation that already exists in the current target. A fresh CI schema holds none of them, so the ancestors have to be built there before the changed subtree can run — which is why the job grows from "the changed subtree" to "the changed subtree plus everything it stands on". Note what B does *not* say: dbt never widens a selection to pull ancestors in. `state:modified+` selects the modified nodes and their descendants and stops there; getting the ancestors into the schema is the CI author's problem, and leaving it unsolved is a failed run rather than a slow one. With `--defer`, unselected refs resolve against the prior-state (production) relations, so the selection stays tight to "just the changed subtree." Option A invents a mechanism dbt does not have: thread count comes from `--threads` or the profile, and deferral changes how many nodes are built rather than how fast each one runs. Option C invents another: nothing in dbt executes a test twice, and under deferral a multi-parent test compiles to a single query whose two sides sit in different schemas (§12.3). Option D describes `dbt clone`, not `--defer` — deferral performs no metadata operation in the CI target at all (§12.8), which is exactly why the ancestors are missing from it. Source: `/reference/node-selection/defer`.

**11. C.** `--state <path>` supplies a single prior-artifacts directory that both the `state:` selector and `--defer` read. The selector uses the prior `manifest.json` to compute the diff that drives `state:modified`; defer uses the same manifest to learn prior-state relation names for unselected refs. One manifest, three consumers in total across the chapter — the `state:` selector, deferral, and `dbt clone` (§12.8), which reads it whether or not `--defer` is passed. Both A and B describe a partial use; C is complete. Option D is wrong — dbt always writes new artifacts to `target/`, not to `--state`. Sources: `/reference/node-selection/methods`, `/reference/node-selection/defer`.

**12. A.** Comma (with no whitespace) is the intersection operator (§11.8), so the invocation matches nodes in both sets: previously-errored AND modified, each set already widened by its own `+` to include descendants — which is what the stem's "together with their downstream" asks for. The stem says *errored* rather than *failed* on purpose: `result:error` selects nodes whose status was `error`, while `result:fail` selects tests that returned failing rows. They are different sets, and "failed" in casual speech covers both — read the selector, not the sentence. Both selectors read from the one `--state ./prior` directory — `state:` diffs its `manifest.json`, `result:` reads its `run_results.json` — and neither works without it. Verified on dbt 1.11.14 against a fixture where one model was modified only, one was both modified and errored: the space form returned both models, the comma form returned only the errored-and-modified one. Option B is that space form, which is union — nodes in either set, a strictly larger answer than the stem asks for. Option C keeps the errored nodes and then subtracts the modified ones, which is the complement of the intended filter. Option D is a legal invocation that answers a different question: retry re-runs the failed invocation's own node list and has no way to intersect it with a state diff. Sources: `/reference/node-selection/set-operators`, `/reference/commands/retry`.

**13. C.** `source_status:fresher+` matches sources whose `sources.json` status shows they have been refreshed since the comparison `sources.json`, plus their descendants. The prerequisite is a prior `dbt source freshness` run to produce the current `sources.json`. Option A matches code changes, not source-freshness changes. Option B matches previously-successful nodes (the opposite of new work). Option D retries prior failures, unrelated. Source: `/reference/node-selection/methods`.

**14. C.** Retry's flags fall into three groups, and the stem asks for the first. **Rejected outright:** `--select` and `--exclude` are not options on the command at all — `dbt retry --select m_b` exits immediately with `Error: No such option: --select`, verified on dbt 1.11.14. The selection is implicit in the prior `run_results.json`, so accepting `--select` would make the command something other than retry. **Accepted and honoured:** `--threads` (A) and `--vars` (B), the two flags retry lets you override on the re-run. **Accepted and discarded:** `--target` (D) parses without complaint and is then thrown away in favour of the failed invocation's own target — `dbt retry --target ci` after a `dev` failure reports `target='dev'` and builds into the `dev` schema. D is therefore a real trap rather than a free elimination, and the stem's "errors on rather than silently ignores" is what separates it from C. Source: `/reference/commands/retry`.

**15. C.** `dbt retry` re-runs the node list frozen in the prior `run_results.json`. It does re-parse, so it picks up an edited SQL body — but it never re-computes *which* nodes to run, so a node that did not exist at the time of the failure is invisible to it. Verified on dbt 1.11.14: repairing the failed model and adding a new downstream model, then running `dbt retry`, re-ran the two nodes from the prior run and not the new one. The stem asks for the rerun set to come from the current graph, so the selector-driven invocation is the right tool. Option A relies on the prior run's node list, which is exactly what the stem rules out. Option B is the trap the flag's acceptance sets: `dbt retry` takes `--full-refresh` without complaint and then **silently discards** it (§12.7). It changes neither which nodes are in the frozen list nor how they rebuild, so the new downstream model is still left out and nothing in the output says the flag did nothing. Option D reaches the right graph by rebuilding everything, discarding the 80 nodes that already succeeded. Source: `/reference/commands/retry`, `/reference/node-selection/graph-operators`.

**16. B.** Databricks Delta supports zero-copy cloning as a platform primitive. `dbt clone` issues the native clone operation, creating a new relation in the CI target that references the same underlying files as the source. No data is copied; the clone completes in seconds. (`dbt clone` runs the deferral machinery unconditionally, so the invocation needs `--state` but not `--defer` — verified on dbt Core 1.11.14, where `dbt clone --select … --state …` resolved the prior-state relation with no `--defer` flag, and dropping `--state` produced `Runtime Error: --`

`state or --defer-state are required for deferral, but neither was provided.`) Option A describes the fallback for adapters without zero-copy support (Postgres, Redshift, DuckDB). Option C describes a plain `CREATE TABLE AS` copy, which is not what clone does when zero-copy is available. Option D is wrong — clone works without `--full-refresh`; that flag is only for recreating existing clones. Source: `/reference/commands/clone`.

**17. C.** The omnibus `state:modified` matches any change — SQL body, config, relation, contract, upstream macro. A one-line edit to a shared config in `dbt_project.yml` (a `+materialized:` switch, a shared `+pre-hook:`) matches every model that inherits it, and the `+` operator then pulls each match's whole subtree in, which is how a two-model PR becomes an 80% rebuild. Not every YAML edit does this, and knowing which is the discriminator: verified on dbt 1.11.14, changing a model's `meta` matches `state:modified` and `state:modified.configs`, while changing its `tags` or its `group` matches neither, and a `description:` edit is invisible unless `persist_docs` is on. The fix is to narrow the PR-gate selector to `state:modified.body+`, paired with a nightly full `state:modified+` build so the config drift the gate now ignores is still caught somewhere. Option A misdiagnoses deferral: it rewrites unselected `ref()` calls to point at prior-state relations, and the selection is computed before any of that happens — a relation that differs between environments is not a selection criterion, and dbt never widens a selection to add nodes. Option B misreads indirect selection: at its default `eager` setting a test runs when any one of its parents is selected (Ch 7 §7.6), but a selected test never pulls its unselected parents into the run, so swapping `build` for `run` changes which resource types execute rather than which nodes the selector matches. Option D names a real failure mode, and the stem rules it out: the manifest being served is the current one from the last successful main-branch build, produced by the same dbt version, so it is not the source of the excess. Source: `/reference/node-selection/methods`.

**18. B.** `run_results.json` is overwritten by every command that walks the graph, `dbt compile` included — compile records a per-node result for each model even though it materializes nothing. The developer's sequence left `run_results.json` describing the compile, in which nothing failed, so retry found no non-successful node and stopped. Verified on dbt 1.11.14: a failed `dbt run` followed by `dbt compile` and then `dbt retry` prints `Nothing to do. Try checking your model configs and model specification args`. The recovery is `dbt retry --state <dir>`, pointing retry at a saved copy of the failed run's artifacts, or simply not interleaving commands between a failure and its retry (§12.7). Option A inverts the mechanism: retry defaults to `target/` and needs no `--state`; it is `result:` selection that errors without one. Option C would require compile to execute models, which it does not — it renders SQL and connects only to resolve the graph. Option D is wrong in both halves: retry's re-run set is the prior failed-node list recorded in `run_results.json`, and a changed `manifest.json` neither adds to it nor subtracts from it. Sources: `/reference/commands/retry`, `/reference/artifacts/run-results-json`.

**19. A.** At the 1.11 default, state comparison holds each config's *rendered* value. Production renders `materialized` to `table` and CI renders it to `view`, so every mart differs from the production baseline on a config the PR never touched, and the `+` then pulls each match's subtree in. Job B compares against a manifest produced in the same CI environment, where the variable renders identically on both sides, so only the staging model and its descendants match. Verified on dbt 1.11.14 with `materialized=env_var('DBT_MAT', 'view')` in a model's `config()` block: a baseline parsed with the variable set to `table` matched the model under `state:modified` when the current parse rendered `view`, and matched nothing when both parses rendered the same value. `state_modified_compare_more_unrendered_values` is the fix (§12.2, Q7). Option B invents a rule — any manifest written by the running version is a usable baseline; its provenance decides what the diff *means*, not whether a diff happens. Option C confuses resolution with selection: `--defer` rewrites unselected `ref()` calls and never removes a node from the selected set. Option D inverts the mechanism — the `env_var()` call resolves at parse time, and it is precisely because it resolves to two different values that the marts match. Sources: `/reference/global-configs/behavior-flags/state_modified_compare_more_unrendered_values`, `/reference/node-selection/state-comparison-caveats`.

**20. D.** Verified on dbt 1.11.14: a model reassigned from one declared group to another matches neither `state:modified` nor `state:modified.configs`. That is a divergence from `/reference/node-selection/methods`, which states that a group change flags the nodes involved; answer from the runtime (§12.2). Option A matches both the omnibus and `state:modified.configs` — `access` is a config. Option B matches the omnibus but *not* `.configs`, because `deprecation_date` is a property rather than a config; either way it matches, which is what the stem asks. Option C matches too: a source's `freshness` and `quoting` rules are among the extra criteria `state:modified` carries beyond the six sub-selectors, alongside an exposure's `maturity`. Source: `/reference/node-selection/methods`.

**21. B.** `state:modified` and `state:modified+` detect changes to code, configuration and manifest-relevant metadata — not changes to the data itself. New rows in a source table move none of those, so the selector matches nothing and the job succeeds having built nothing, which is documented as expected behaviour. The operational corollary the stem is built on: `state:modified` belongs on CI and merge jobs, and a scheduled job that must rebuild regardless of code drops the selector (§12.2). Option A misdiagnoses — a source load does not age the manifest, and regenerating it would change nothing about this run. Option C confuses deferral with selection: `--defer` only decides how an unselected `ref()` resolves, and here nothing was selected to begin with. Option D is a real selector applied to the wrong question — `source_status:fresher+` is how you *do* rebuild on new data (§12.6), but `state:modified` never reads `sources.json`, unioned or not. Source: `/reference/node-selection/state-comparison-caveats`.

**22. C.** dbt rewrites `target/manifest.json` during parsing, before node selection runs. With `--state ./target` the comparison therefore diffs the freshly written manifest against itself and finds nothing — a false negative, not an error, which is why the job stays green while building nothing on every run. Verified on dbt 1.11.14: the same edit returned two nodes under `dbt ls --no-write-json --select state:modified --state ./target` and `No nodes selected!` without the flag. Three recoveries: a dedicated `state/` directory, a distinct `--target-path` for the build stage, or `--no-write-json` on a read-only command (§12.2). Option A misreads the warning's severity — dbt prints it and carries on; `warn_error_options` promotes warnings to errors rather than the reverse (§10.9.3). Option B names a real cause of a *bad* comparison, the stale-baseline false positive of §12.4, but that produces too many matches rather than none. Option D is not a dbt behaviour — `--state` accepts relative paths, and every recipe in this chapter uses one. Source: `/reference/node-selection/state-comparison-caveats`.

**23. D.** dbt stores a content hash for seed files below roughly 1 MiB and includes them in `state:modified` when the contents change. Above that threshold it cannot diff the contents and falls back to the file path alone: move the file and the seed is modified, rewrite every row in place and it is not. Verified on dbt 1.11.14 against a 1.3 MB seed, which returned `Found a seed (…) >1MB in size at the same path, dbt cannot tell if it has changed: assuming they are the same` and selected nothing (§12.2). Option A overstates the carve-out — seeds under the threshold are compared by content like any other node. Option B misreads the sub-selectors: `state:modified.body` does cover seed values, but the omnibus is the union of every sub-selector, so naming `.body` narrows the gate rather than widening it. Option C describes a mechanism dbt does not have — state comparison is manifest-to-manifest and never queries the warehouse. Source: `/reference/node-selection/state-comparison-caveats`.

**24. A.** Deferral rewrites a `ref()` to the prior-state relation when the referenced node is unselected *and* absent from the current target. `--favor-state` drops the second condition, so an unselected ref resolves to prior state even though `dev` already holds a copy. What it does not do is reach a node inside the selection: `fct_orders` was named by `--select`, so it builds into `dev` from the code in the working tree regardless of the flag. Verified on dbt 1.11.14: with the parent present in the current target the deferred run passed, and adding `--favor-state` sent the compiled SQL back to the prior-state schema. Option B is the half of the asymmetry most summaries drop — selected nodes always materialize against the current target. Option C describes something no selector does: deferral never widens a selection to pull an ancestor in. Option D states the default backwards — resolving to prior state when the relation is missing is what plain `--defer` already does, and `--favor-state` exists precisely for the case where it is present. Source: `/reference/node-selection/defer`.

**25. D.** A `relationships` test has two parents, and under deferral they can land in different environments. `fct_orders` was selected, so its side of the join compiles to the CI relation; `dim_customers` was not selected and does not exist in CI, so the `to:` side compiles to the prior-state relation. The test then joins the branch's new customer in CI against production's dimension, which does not have it, and reports one failing row on code that is internally consistent. Verified on dbt 1.11.14: the compiled test SQL carried two schema qualifiers, the CI schema in the child CTE and the prior-state schema in the parent CTE, and building both models into one schema turned the same test green. Exclude these tests with `--exclude "test_name:relationships"`, or pass `--indirect-selection=cautious`, which drops any test whose parents are not all selected (§12.3). Option A has it backwards — deferral is exactly what resolved the `to:` side, and had both sides landed in prior state the test would have passed. Option B contradicts `dbt build`, which runs tests in DAG order behind the resources they depend on (§11.2). Option C would be a database error rather than a test failure, and it would strand every row rather than one. Source: `/reference/node-selection/state-comparison-caveats`.

**26. B.** A test sits at the end of the DAG — nothing depends on it — so `result:fail+` returns the failed test and nothing else: not the model it tests, not anything built on that model. The ancestor operator is what reaches back. `1+result:fail` selects the failed test plus its one-generation parent, so `dbt build` rebuilds the model and then re-runs the test against the new rows (§12.5). Verified on dbt 1.11.14: `result:fail+` returned the failed test alone, while `1+result:fail` returned the model and the test. Option A invents a filter — the invocation carries no `state:` selector, and `--state` here supplies the `run_results.json` that `result:` reads, nothing more. Option C inverts `--indirect-selection`, which decides whether a selected *model* pulls its tests in (Ch 7 §7.6); `cautious` DROPS a test whose parents are not all selected (§12.3) — it never adds a parent, so it would have removed the one node the run did execute. Option D describes no dbt behaviour: `build` short-circuits downstream nodes within a single invocation when a test fails, and carries no memory of a prior run's failures. Sources: `/reference/node-selection/graph-operators`, `/reference/node-selection/methods`.

**27. B.** Without `--full-refresh`, clone leaves an existing target relation alone; with the flag, it recreates it. Independent clone statements can run concurrently, so a higher `--threads` may reduce execution time, subject to adapter and warehouse limits. A incorrectly imposes DAG ordering. C invents a drop-and-skip behavior; D treats an existing relation as a collision. See Ch 12 §12.8 and `/reference/commands/clone`.

**28. C. Rerun from failure** is `dbt retry` wearing a button, and it inherits the command's limits exactly — so it is available only when the failed job's command is one retry supports. **Rerun from start** is the full-rebuild alternative and always works, because it needs nothing from the previous invocation. The reasoning that matters here is recognising the button as a CLI command rather than a separate platform feature, which is what tells you where to look for the constraint.

**29. C.** `DBT_ENGINE_STATE`, `DBT_ENGINE_DEFER` and `DBT_ENGINE_DEFER_STATE` are environment-variable equivalents of the corresponding flags. Where both appear, **the flag wins**: a runner-level default can be overridden by one job. A reverses precedence; B incorrectly replaces a still-valid flag; D invents a conflict. See Ch 12 §12.3.

**30. B.** `--state` is the comparison manifest that `state:modified` reads, and `--defer-state` points deferral at a **different** manifest. Omit `--defer-state` and deferral falls back to `--state`, which is the common single-artifact case. Splitting them lets a CI job compare against the pull request's merge base to decide what changed, while resolving unbuilt refs against production — two genuinely different questions that a single artifact answers badly when the base and production have drifted apart.

**31. C.** Enabling the freshness **checkbox** on a job produces the freshness data — it populates the source-freshness view — but does not fail the job on a stale source. Adding `dbt source freshness` as an explicit **run step** does: the step fails and blocks the steps after it. The distinction matters because the checkbox looks like the obvious way to gate a pipeline on freshness and is not, so a team can believe they have a gate for months without one ever firing. If the intent is to block the run, put the command in the steps.

**32. A.** `--no-write-json` — equivalently the `WRITE_JSON` config — stops dbt writing its JSON artifacts to `target/`, and the documented use case is exactly this multi-invocation shape: one step produces a manifest that a later step depends on, and you do not want an intervening invocation to overwrite it. C is the distractor worth separating: relocating the output is `--target-path`, and reaching for it here would leave the second step's artifacts somewhere the pipeline then has to reason about, rather than simply not producing them.

**33. D.** The statuses are not a single vocabulary shared by every resource type, and that is the whole item. Models, seeds and snapshots record `success`; a test never does — it records `pass`, `fail`, `warn`, `error` or `skipped` — so `result:success` has no test row at all. `result:skipped` does apply to models, seeds, snapshots **and** tests — anything a failed parent prevented from running. And `result:error` is the one that spans the whole graph, matching whatever errored wherever it sits, which is why `result:error+` is the idiomatic "re-run what broke and everything below it".

**34. A.** `dbt retry` resumes the previous invocation from its point of failure; it does not diagnose or repair anything. Retrying a deterministic failure — a SQL error, a broken `ref`, a contract violation — reproduces it exactly. That makes retry the right tool for a *transient* failure such as a warehouse timeout or a lock, and the wrong reflex for a code failure. The useful discipline is to read the error before reaching for the button: if the cause is in the repository, retry only spends the warehouse time again.

**35. D.** Retry is supported after `build`, `compile`, `clone`, `docs generate`, `seed`, `snapshot`, `test`, `run` and `run-operation`. `source freshness` is not on the list, which is worth knowing because it is a common first step in a scheduled job — so a pipeline that fails there cannot be resumed and has to be rerun from the start. The list is short enough to memorise, and the shape of it is that anything producing `run_results.json` in the ordinary way is resumable.

**36. B.** State comparison works on **rendered** values by default, so a config driven by `var()` or `env_var()` is caught only when the rendered result differs. Two different variable values that render the same are invisible, and a slim CI run silently skips a model whose configuration really did change. `state_modified_compare_more_unrendered_values` is not the escape hatch here. It compares the unrendered configuration, which catches the opposite case — the EXPRESSION changed while its rendered value did not, as when `env_var('X')` is replaced by the literal it renders to. Turn it on in this scenario and the config is stored as unrendered Jinja, so a `var()`-driven value becomes less visible to `state:modified`, not more (§12.2). It is off at 1.11 and flips on at 1.12 — so answer from the 1.11 default, and remember that the flag is the reason D is wrong.

# Chapter 13

# Model governance: contracts, versions, access, groups, grants

> **Scope.** Governance is the set of primitives dbt adds on top of a working project to make it safe for multiple teams to share. A single-team project survives on conventions ("don't rename output columns without warning"); a ten-team project survives only when those conventions are declared in code and enforced by the compiler. This chapter covers the three governance bullets the current study guide names — **contracts** (pin the shape of a model's output), **versions** (evolve a model without breaking downstream consumers), and **constraints** (hand enforcement to the platform itself) — plus the configs beneath them: **access** (control which models can be `ref()`ed from where), **groups** (a namespace mechanism that access piggybacks on), and **grants** (post-run warehouse privileges). §13.1 frames the cross-team problem the primitives solve. §13.2–§13.3 cover contracts and constraint-level adapter support. §13.4–§13.5 cover versions and deprecation. §13.6–§13.7 cover access and groups together. §13.8 covers grants and its distinction from access. §13.9 is a short "in practice" sidebar using the fictional Credora project to show selective governance — where a mature project actually reaches for these primitives and where it does not.

**Prerequisites.** Ch 2 (for `ref()` semantics — every governance primitive here is a modifier on `ref()` resolution or on the relation `ref()` points at). Ch 4 (materializations, since `ephemeral` cannot be `public` and grants are issued post-DDL). Ch 6 (for the `config()` / YAML / project-level precedence that applies here the same as everywhere else). No other hard prerequisites.

**Cheat-sheet pointer.** Front-of-book cheat sheet §3 (Topic 2 — Governance) is the one-line recall surface for this chapter.

---

## 13.1 Why governance matters now

Single-team dbt works on trust: everyone on the team reads the same PRs, reviews the same column changes, and coordinates the same renames. At that scale, the governance primitives in this chapter are overkill — the coordination cost of declaring a contract on every model exceeds the cost of an occasional broken downstream.

Multi-team dbt is different. When marketing, finance, and data science all consume from a shared `cr_global` catalog, a column rename in a shared fact table can ripple through dashboards nobody on the producing team has seen. A breaking change that took one hour to write takes three weeks to unwind. The governance primitives each solve a specific version of that cross-team failure mode:

- **Contracts** — "producers cannot silently change a model's output shape" — because the contract is code, checked at build time.

- **Versions** — "producers can publish a breaking change without taking down today's consumers" — by running v1 and v2 side by side and giving consumers a cycle to migrate.
- **Deprecation dates** — "versions and legacy models do not live forever" — by emitting a visible countdown that eventually becomes a hard warning.
- **Access** — "internal models stay internal" — so another team's `ref()` cannot quietly couple to an implementation detail.
- **Groups** — the namespace that access hangs on; without groups, `access: private` collapses to "nobody".
- **Grants** — "BI tools and downstream services get the warehouse privileges they need" — issued automatically after every build, so the privileges cannot drift from the code.

Notice the split: contracts, versions, access and groups operate inside dbt at parse/build time and govern the dbt-level API between teams; grants operate at the warehouse through post-DDL `GRANT` statements and govern warehouse RBAC. They complement rather than duplicate one another — see §13.8 for the exact line between them.

dbt Labs' own governance overview lists two further capabilities beside these — model namespaces and project dependencies. Only project dependencies (cross-project `ref`) is Enterprise-gated; model namespaces is available in dbt Core, and it is the mechanism §13.7 teaches — groups, plus the package namespacing that lets two packages carry a model of the same name and `ref()` take the package as a first argument. Neither is a named bullet in the governance topic, so the page will look wider than this chapter does.

---

## 13.2 Contracts — shape-of-model enforcement

A **contract** pins a model's output schema: the full column list with each column's `data_type`, optionally with column-level or model-level `constraints`. When contracts are enforced, dbt validates the model's SELECT against the contract *before* writing DDL — a "preflight" check. A mismatch fails the build.

**Prerequisites — what contracts apply to.** The contract config is supported on `table` and `view` materializations and on `incremental` with `on_schema_change` set to `append_new_columns` or `fail`. Contracts are *not* supported on `materialized_view`, `ephemeral`, Python models, or on `sources`, `seeds`, or `snapshots`. (The config is model-specific — it doesn't apply to other resource types.) **Unsupported is not the same as refused.** Put `contract: {enforced: true}` on an `ephemeral` or a `materialized_view` model and dbt accepts it in silence — no error, no warning, not a single log line — and the model builds green over a SELECT that plainly violates the contract. The governance control exists only in the YAML, which is what makes the omission expensive: the same violation on a `table`, a `view` or an `incremental` fails the build. The incremental rule is checked early and hard: pair `contract: {enforced: true}` with `on_schema_change: sync_all_columns` and `dbt parse` stops with `Invalid value for on_schema_change: sync_all_columns. Models materialized as incremental with contracts enabled must set on_schema_change to 'append_new_columns' or 'fail'`. The full prerequisite table is on the `/reference/resource-configs/contract` page.

### The `contract` config

Enable enforcement by attaching a `contract` config to the model, typically in its `.yml` entry:

```
version: 2
```

```yaml
models:
  - name: fct_customer_orders
    config:
      contract:
        enforced: true
    columns:
      - name: order_id
        data_type: bigint
        constraints:
          - type: primary_key
          - type: not_null
      - name: customer_id
        data_type: bigint
        constraints:
          - type: not_null
      - name: order_total_cents
        data_type: bigint
        constraints:
          - type: not_null
          - type: check
            expression: "order_total_cents >= 0"
      - name: order_status
        data_type: varchar(20)
        constraints:
          - type: not_null
      - name: ordered_at
        data_type: timestamp
        constraints:
          - type: not_null
```

Three things to notice:

1. **Every output column must be listed, and under an enforced contract every one of them must carry a `data_type`.** Contracts cover *all* columns, never a subset: a SELECT emitting five columns against a contract listing four fails the build, and omitting `order_total_cents` from the list above is a violation rather than a partial contract. And `data_type`, optional documentation on an ordinary `columns:` block, becomes mandatory on every column the instant `enforced: true` is set. §13.3 takes that second rule apart, because it is also what makes `constraints:` work at all.
2. **`constraints:` is optional, and it does nothing on its own.** Column-level constraints nest under the column, as above; constraints spanning more than one column — a composite primary key, say — use a sibling `constraints:` key at the model level. Both placements are inert unless the contract is enforced, and both are covered in §13.3.
3. **`contract:` lives under `config:`.** It is a config (runtime behaviour), and like every config in Ch 6 it can also be set in `dbt_project.yml` (`+contract: {enforced: true}`) or in SQL via `{{ config(contract={'enforced': true}) }}`. The reference is `/reference/resource-configs/contract`.

## What happens on build

With `enforced: true`:

1. **Before DDL is issued — inside the materialization, not during `dbt compile`,** dbt wraps the model's SELECT in an empty preflight query, reads back the output column names and types, and compares them against the contract declared in YAML.

That is why the check needs a warehouse and why a compile-only CI step never runs it (Ch 10 §10.10).

2. **If the SELECT's output shape matches** (same column names, same types, same count), dbt proceeds to issue the DDL (CREATE TABLE AS, MERGE, etc.) as normal.
3. **If the SELECT's output shape does not match**, dbt raises a contract error and the build fails — before any DDL touches the warehouse. The contract page calls this the "preflight check."

The failure modes that most often trigger a contract error:

- A typo in a column alias (`SELECT customer_id AS custmer_id`) — contract says `customer_id`, SELECT emits `custmer_id`, build fails.
- A type drift (`SELECT CAST(order_total_cents AS INT)` when the contract says `bigint`) — dbt compares resolved types and fails.
- A dropped column (the SELECT previously emitted `order_notes`, the code removed it, the YAML still lists it) — build fails.
- An added column with no contract entry (the SELECT now emits `order_channel`, the YAML hasn't been updated) — build fails.

That last bullet is the one that matters most for cross-team hygiene: a producer cannot ship a new column to a contracted model without updating the YAML, which makes the YAML diff visible in the PR. Consumers (and reviewers) see the schema change before it lands.

The concept page is `/docs/mesh/govern/model-contracts`. The contract config reference is `/reference/resource-configs/contract`. The constraints reference is `/reference/resource-properties/constraints`.

## What a contract compares, and what it ignores

The `contract` config has two keys, not one. `enforced` is the one you set, and it defaults to `false`. `alias_types` defaults to `true`, and it is what lets you write a contract in generic types at all: with it on, dbt maps a generic alias to the platform's own spelling before comparing — `string` becomes `text` on Postgres and Redshift — and passes any type it does not recognise straight through. Set it to `false` and the mapping stops, so a column declared `data_type: string` reaches Postgres verbatim and the build dies on `type "string" does not exist`. Leave it alone unless you have a reason.

The comparison itself is narrower than it looks. It compares column **names**, **types** and **count**, and nothing else.

- **Order does not matter.** A contract listing `order_id, order_status` is satisfied by a SELECT emitting them the other way round. dbt then writes the DDL in the contract's order, so the warehouse relation follows the YAML rather than the SQL.
- **Size, precision and scale do not matter.** A SELECT producing `varchar(256)` satisfies a `varchar(257)` contract, and `numeric(10, 2)` satisfies `numeric(38, 6)`. Both sides are reduced to a base type before comparing, so the parenthesised part is invisible to the check. It is not invisible to the warehouse *when the model is a table*: `create table ... (nm varchar(257), ...)` carries the contract's size, which is what the bare-`numeric` warning in §13.3 is about. A view has no column spec in its DDL, so the view carries the SELECT's 256, not the contract's 257.
- **Base types are compared strictly.** An `int` does not satisfy a `bigint` contract, even though every `int` value fits one. There is no widening rule.

When the comparison fails, dbt prints a table rather than a sentence, and reading the table is most of the fix:

```
This model has an enforced contract that failed.
Please ensure the name, data_type, and number of columns in your contract match the
    columns in your model's definition.

| column_name | definition_type | contract_type | mismatch_reason      |
| ----------- | --------------- | ------------- | -------------------- |
| line_count  | INTEGER         |               | missing in contract  |
| order_id    | INTEGER         | LONGINTEGER   | data type mismatch   |
| ordered_at  |                 | DATETIME      | missing in definition |
```

`definition_type` is what the model's SELECT produces; `contract_type` is what the YAML declares; an empty cell means that side has no such column. So `missing in contract` names a column the SQL emits and the YAML does not — the fix is in the YAML. `missing in definition` is the reverse: the YAML lists a column the SQL no longer emits. The types print in dbt's own generic vocabulary rather than the platform's, which is the vocabulary `alias_types` translates from.

### Contract vs data-test — the distinction

A **data test** (Ch 7) asserts something about the *values* in a model's rows: "no nulls in `user_id`", "unique `order_id`". A **contract** asserts something about the *shape* of the model's output: "there are exactly these five columns, with these types". A contract does not replace data tests — contracts do not check row content. Data tests do not replace contracts — data tests run *after* the model has materialized, so they cannot prevent a breaking schema change from ever reaching the warehouse.

In practice: contracts protect downstream *consumers* from schema drift; data tests protect *data* from value drift. Both belong on a shared, high-stakes model.

---

## 13.3 Constraints — platform-level integrity declared in YAML

A contract pins the *shape* of a model's output. A **constraint** goes one step further and asks the data platform itself to police the *contents*: a `NOT NULL` on a column, a `PRIMARY KEY`, a `CHECK` expression written into the CREATE TABLE statement dbt issues. Constraints are the only governance mechanism in this chapter that produces warehouse DDL, and how much any of them actually does depends entirely on which adapter you are running. Two rules govern everything else in this section, and both are worth knowing cold before any syntax.

### Two rules before any syntax

**Constraints are inert without an enforced contract.** A `constraints:` block on a model that has no `contract: {enforced: true}` does nothing at all: no constraint in the DDL, no build failure, no warning. The YAML parses, the model runs, and the relation in the warehouse carries no constraint. The `/reference/resource-properties/constraints` page states the dependency as a prerequisite: to use constraints, your model must declare *and enforce* a contract. In practice the gate is structural rather than advisory — the branch of dbt's table materialization that renders column constraints into the CREATE statement sits inside a test on `contract.enforced`, so with no enforced contract there is no code path that could emit them, and nothing to warn about.

That silence is what makes this the expensive mistake. A model whose constraints never fired looks exactly like a model whose constraints all passed: green build, populated table, no log line. When a question shows you a `constraints:` block and asks what ends up in the warehouse, the first thing to look for is `enforced: true` in the model's config. If it is absent, the answer is "nothing".

The same prerequisite list carries a materialization rule that follows from it: constraints are never applied on `ephemeral` models or on models materialized as `view`. A `view` can carry a contract — dbt will check column names and types — but not constraints. Constraints are a **`table` and `incremental`** feature.

That case is not silent, and the asymmetry is worth holding onto. A constraint on a contracted `view` draws `Constraint types are not supported for view materializations and will be ignored`, and the build continues without it. A constraint on an uncontracted `table` draws nothing at all. The wrong materialization warns; the missing contract does not. Both halves of that rule are about *constraints*: a whole contract on a materialization that cannot enforce one draws nothing at all (§13.2).

**`data_type` becomes mandatory once an enforced contract is actually enforced** — on the materializations named in the prerequisite above, and not on `ephemeral` or `materialized_view`, which accept the config and build green without it. On an ordinary `columns:` block, `data_type` is optional documentation. Set `contract: {enforced: true}` and it becomes required on *every* column in the contract, not merely the constrained ones: the `contract` reference describes an enforced contract as one where dbt ensures the returned dataset matches `name` and `data_type` for every column. Combine that with the first rule and the requirement is transitive — **any model that uses `constraints:` at all needs a `data_type` on every column**, because constraints require an enforced contract and an enforced contract requires the types.

Omit one and the build stops with a message naming the offending columns: contracted models require `data_type` to be defined for each column. The important half is the timing. This is not a parse error — `dbt parse` accepts the project and the manifest builds — and it is not a warehouse error either. It fires during `dbt run`, inside the materialization, *before* the CREATE statement is issued, in the same preflight step §13.2 described. The symptom is a run that fails without having touched the warehouse, and the fix is in YAML rather than in SQL.

One related warning shares that step. Declaring a contracted column with a bare `numeric` or `decimal` `data_type` — no precision, no scale — draws a warning about unintended rounding, because the platform's own default scale (38 and 0, on several) stores whole numbers only, so the column silently rounds what the SELECT produced. It does **not** fail contract enforcement: as §13.2 states, both sides are reduced to a base type before comparing, and `numeric(38,6)` declared over a SELECT casting `numeric(10,2)` builds clean. The cost is wrong numbers, not a red build — which is why the warning exists at all. Write `numeric(38, 6)` rather than `numeric`. The `contract` reference overstates that cost when it says the default scale *"might cause it to fail contract enforcement"*: enforcement compares base types, so a `numeric` declared over a `numeric` result matches whatever the scale does to the values. Executed on dbt 1.11.14 with dbt-postgres 1.11.0, a contracted `data_type: numeric` over `cast(1.234 as numeric(10,2))` logs `Detected columns with numeric type and unspecified precision/ scale, this can lead to unintended rounding: ['amt']` — followed by a stray backtick that dbt's own message-building macro appends — and then builds `OK`. In practice the warning names the columns it found, and that warning is the whole of what you get.

## The six constraint types

dbt defines **six** constraint types. The `constraints` reference lists them in one line — `not_null`, `unique`, `primary_key`, `foreign_key`, `check`, `custom` — and it is worth counting them there, because the per-adapter support table three subsections from now has only five rows, and a reader who learns the count from the table learns it wrong.

| Type | Required extra key | What it declares |
|---|---|---|
| `not_null` | — | The column rejects nulls. |
| `unique` | — | No two rows share the value. |
| `primary_key` | — | Unique and not null; the row identifier. |
| `foreign_key` | `to`, `to_columns` (required in effect — see below) | The value exists in a named column of another relation. |
| `check` | `expression` | A free-text SQL predicate every row must satisfy. |
| `custom` | `expression` | Free-text DDL passed through to the platform. |

Every constraint takes `type` (required) and optionally `name`, a human-friendly label that only some platforms support. `expression` is free text qualifying the constraint; it is required for `check` and `custom` and optional elsewhere. Three details separate the types from one another, and each is the kind of thing a distractor is built from:

1. **`foreign_key` alone carries `to` and `to_columns`.** `to` takes a relation — write it as `ref('dim_customer')` or `source('stripe', 'customers')` — and `to_columns` takes the list of columns on the far side. Because `to` takes a `ref()`, the constraint registers a real dependency in the DAG and resolves correctly across environments. A raw table-name string is not an alternative to it: `to: analytics.fct_customer_orders` stops the parse with `Invalid 'ref' or 'source' syntax on foreign key constraint 'to' on model fct_order_lines: analytics.fct_customer_orders`, at the column level and at the model level alike. `to_columns` is the trap: omit it and dbt does not error. With nothing but `to:` on the constraint the model builds green and the DDL carries no `references` clause at all — the same silent no-op an uncontracted `constraints:` block gives you. dbt writes that clause from `to` **and** `to_columns` together, or from a raw `expression` you supply yourself, and from nothing else.
2. **`check` takes a required `expression`**, written as the predicate alone: `expression: "order_total_cents >= 0"`, not a full `CHECK (...)` clause.
3. **`custom` plus `expression` is the escape hatch** for DDL that has no dbt-level type. A Snowflake masking policy attaches this way — `type: custom` with `expression: "masking policy my_policy"` — and so does anything else your platform accepts inside a column definition. dbt does not interpret the text; it renders it.

## Where a constraint may be declared

Constraints go either on a single column, nested under that column in `columns:`, or at the model level in a sibling `constraints:` key. Prefer the column when the constraint concerns one column — that is the reference page's own recommendation, and it keeps the declaration next to the `data_type` it depends on.

One thing forces the model level: a constraint spanning several columns — a composite primary key, or a `check` comparing two columns — has nowhere else to go. The model level is also the only place the `columns` key appears: `columns: [order_id, line_number]` names the columns the constraint spans, and it is meaningless on a column-level constraint, which already knows which column it sits on.

```yaml
models:
  - name: fct_order_lines
    config:
      materialized: table
      contract:
        enforced: true
    constraints:
      - type: primary_key
        columns: [order_id, line_number]
      - type: foreign_key
        columns: [order_id]
        to: ref('fct_customer_orders')
        to_columns: [order_id]
    columns:
      - name: order_id
        data_type: bigint
      - name: line_number
        data_type: integer
      - name: line_total_cents
        data_type: bigint
        constraints:
          - type: check
            expression: "line_total_cents >= 0"
```

That model builds all three constraints on Postgres, which is what the companion project runs. On Snowflake the two keys become catalog metadata and the `check` is dropped with a warning; the build still succeeds, and nothing about the resulting table stops a duplicate `order_id` or a negative total. The next two subsections are about that gap.

### Three levels of platform support

Six types are *declarable*. What any of them does to your data is a separate question, answered per adapter, and the docs classify the answer into three levels:

1. **Definable and enforced.** The model does not build if the constraint is violated. The platform rejects the write and dbt surfaces the failure.
2. **Definable and not enforced.** The platform accepts the syntax — the constraint appears in the CREATE TABLE DDL and in the catalog — but never checks it. Violating rows land. The declaration is documentation, useful to a reader and to whatever a query planner chooses to make of it, and nothing more.
3. **Not definable and not enforced.** The platform rejects the syntax. dbt drops the constraint from the DDL, warns, and builds the model anyway.

The support matrix covers **five** types, not six. `custom` has no row and cannot have one: dbt does not know what your expression means, so it skips the support check entirely and renders the text into the DDL on every adapter. Whether it then works is a question about the expression and the platform, not about dbt. Six types to declare, five types to reason about enforcement for.

### The adapter matrix, and what to carry out of it

The canonical table is the **Platform constraint support** section of `/docs/mesh/govern/model-contracts#platform-constraint-support`, rendered as one tab per adapter. Note the location, because it is testable in its own right — but note it precisely. `/reference/resource-`

`properties/constraints` carries its **own `Platform constraint support`** section with the same seven-adapter table, Databricks `foreign_key` row included, so the table has two homes in the docs rather than one. What genuinely carries nothing is the **adapter config** pages: `/reference/resource-configs/databricks-configs` has no constraints section at all. That is the trap worth remembering — the instinct to look under the adapter finds nothing, and the absence reads like the feature not existing rather than like the documentation living elsewhere.

| Adapter | `not_null` | `check` | `primary_key` | `foreign_key` | `unique` |
|---|---|---|---|---|---|
| **Postgres** | Enforced | Enforced | Enforced | Enforced | Enforced |
| **Databricks** | Enforced | Enforced | Metadata-only | Metadata-only | Not supported |
| **Redshift** | Enforced | Not supported | Metadata-only | Metadata-only | Metadata-only |
| **Snowflake** | Enforced | Not supported | Metadata-only | Metadata-only | Metadata-only |
| **BigQuery** | Enforced | Not supported | Metadata-only | Metadata-only | Not supported |
| **Athena** | Not supported | Not supported | Not supported | Not supported | Not supported |
| **Spark** | Metadata-only | Metadata-only | Metadata-only | Metadata-only | Metadata-only |

Four statements make the whole table predictable. Learn these and you can reconstruct most of it under pressure:

- **Postgres is the only adapter that enforces every constraint type.** When a question asks which platform genuinely blocks bad data through constraints, that is the answer. It is also the trap this book has to flag against itself: the companion project runs on Postgres, so every constraint you exercise while studying will behave, and none of that behaviour transfers to the Snowflake or BigQuery account you go back to on Monday.
- **Snowflake, Redshift and BigQuery enforce `not_null` and nothing else.** They accept a `primary_key`, put it in the DDL, show it in the catalog, and never check a row against it. *Definable* is not *enforced*, and the gap between those two words is where most of this domain's wrong answers live.
- **Databricks is the one cloud platform that enforces `check`** — and it is also the exception that complicates level 1 above, for the reason in the callout below. Among the adapters that support constraints at all, Databricks and BigQuery are the two that cannot define `unique`.
- **Athena defines no constraint type whatsoever, and Spark enforces none.** Athena rejects all five; Spark accepts all five into the DDL and checks none of them. Neither belongs in a sentence that begins "every warehouse enforces...".

That last point is the correction to a claim you will meet in older study material: `not_null` is *not* universally enforced. It is enforced on Postgres, Snowflake, Redshift, BigQuery and Databricks. It is metadata-only on Spark and not definable on Athena. `not_null` is still the safest single answer to "which constraint is most broadly reliable", but the honest form of the sentence names the two exceptions.

> **Watch out.** The Databricks tab of the platform-support table carries the same note as the Spark tab — that `not_null` and `check` are enforced only *after* a model is built, and that dbt therefore treats such constraints as definable but not enforced — while the table directly beneath that note marks both **Enforced**. The two halves of the tab disagree, so it is worth knowing which one you are answering from. This book teaches the table, because the table is what every published support matrix is derived from. The note is the engineering caveat: on Databricks a `check` violation surfaces after the relation already exists, so the table can be left holding rows the constraint forbids. On Postgres the constraint is live on the CREATE and no violating row ever lands.

## Silencing the unenforced and unsupported warnings

When dbt renders a constraint whose support level is anything short of enforced, it says so. Two optional fields, settable on any constraint, control which of those warnings you hear:

- `warn_unenforced` fires for a constraint the platform *will* accept but *will not* check — `primary_key` on Snowflake. The constraint still goes into the DDL.
- `warn_unsupported` fires for a constraint the platform will not accept at all — `check` on Redshift. The constraint is dropped from the DDL and the build succeeds without it.

Both default to `True`, and setting one to `False` silences that class only. A model on Snowflake declaring both a `primary_key` and a `check` needs `warn_unenforced: false` on the `primary_key` and `warn_unsupported: false` on the `check` for a clean log. Neither flag changes what the warehouse ends up doing: silencing a warning is a decision to stop being reminded, not a decision about enforcement.

Neither warning ever fires for a `custom` constraint, for the reason given above: dbt does not evaluate its support level and so has nothing to warn about.

## The practical guidance

For a team that wants warehouse-enforced data-quality guarantees on a contracted model in a cloud warehouse:

1. **Use `not_null` — on Snowflake, Redshift, BigQuery and Databricks it actually prevents bad rows.** It is the one constraint on those four platforms that does what its name says.
2. **Pair `primary_key` with a dbt `unique` data test.** On those same four platforms the `primary_key` declaration is metadata; the `unique` test runs as a separate query against the materialized table and actually validates. Together you get the declarative intent plus the runtime check.
3. **Use `check` for value-range invariants on Postgres and Databricks, and simulate it elsewhere.** On Snowflake, Redshift, BigQuery and Athena the syntax is not accepted at all, so write a singular data test asserting the condition (`SELECT ... WHERE NOT (order_total_cents >= 0)`). On Databricks the `check` is real but late, so keep the data test if it matters that bad rows can land at all.
4. **Treat `foreign_key` as documentation everywhere except Postgres.** It is metadata-only on Snowflake, Redshift, BigQuery, Databricks and Spark, and not definable on Athena. Where referential integrity actually matters, add a `relationships` data test (Ch 7 §7.2). The `to: ref(...)` form still earns its place on those platforms, because it puts the relationship in the DAG and in the docs even when the warehouse ignores it.

Check the live `/docs/mesh/govern/model-contracts#platform-constraint-support` table whenever a question hinges on one adapter's row. The matrix is maintained as adapters add support, and the Databricks and Spark tabs say in as many words that it will change as the features evolve.

---

## 13.4 Versions — evolving a model without breaking consumers

A **version** is an explicit, named snapshot of a model's shape. The purpose: when a model needs a breaking change (a column rename, a type change, a splitting-into-two), the producer publishes a new version alongside the old one. Consumers who want the new shape pin to it; consumers who need a cycle to migrate continue reading the old version. Nothing downstream breaks on the day of the change.

### Declaring versions

A `versions:` block lives under a model's YAML entry:

```
version: 2

models:
  - name: dim_customer
    latest_version: 2
    config:
      contract:
        enforced: true
    columns:
      - name: customer_id
        data_type: bigint
      - name: customer_display_name
        data_type: varchar(256)
      - name: signup_timestamp
        data_type: timestamp
    versions:
      - v: 2
        columns:
          - name: customer_id
          - name: customer_display_name
          - name: signup_timestamp
      - v: 1
        defined_in: dim_customer_v1
        columns:
          - name: customer_id
          - name: name          # renamed in v2 to customer_display_name
          - name: signup_time   # renamed in v2 to signup_timestamp
```

The keys:

- **`v:`** — the version identifier. Numeric identifiers (`1`, `2`, `3`) are the dominant form; strings are accepted too. The identifier carries no literal `v`: write `v: 2`, not `v: v2`. Always set `latest_version:` explicitly rather than relying on ordering inference.
- **`defined_in:`** — the filename (minus the `.sql` / `.py` extension) that holds this version's SQL. Optional. If omitted, dbt looks for a file named `<model_name>_v<v>.sql` by convention. In the example above, v2's SQL lives in `dim_customer_v2.sql` by default, and v1's SQL lives in `dim_customer_v1.sql` because that's what `defined_in:` points at.
- **`columns:`** — per-version column list, which can differ from the model-level list. A version that declares no `columns:` inherits every top-level column, and a version-level

entry overrides the top-level entry of the same name. The inheritance keys and their legality rules are below.

- latest_version: (sibling of versions:) — names the default version. A consumer calling {{ ref('dim_customer') }} with no version arg gets latest_version. If unset, dbt defaults to the largest version identifier.

One exception to the filename convention rides on latest_version:. A bare <model_name>.sql — dim_customer.sql — is accepted as the file for whichever version is the latest, and for that version only. Move latest_version: elsewhere while that file is still on disk and dbt stops at parse with dbt found versioned and unversioned models with the name "dim_customer".

The reference pages: /reference/resource-properties/versions, /reference/resource-properties/latest_version, and the concept overview at /docs/mesh/govern/model-versions.

## Inheriting columns across versions

A version's columns: list is not only a list of columns. It may also carry a single element built from include: and exclude:, and the rules around that element are exactly what a spot-the-invalid-YAML question is made of.

- include: takes all, '*', or an explicit list of column names. all and '*' mean the same thing.
- exclude: takes a list of names to drop from the inherited set, and it is legal only where include: is all or '*'. Pairing it with an explicit include list is not a warning and not an ignored key — dbt stops at parse, exit 2.
- **At most one** include/exclude element may appear per version. Ordinary column entries sit alongside it and override the top-level definition of the same name.

```
versions:
  - v: 2
  - v: 1
    defined_in: dim_customer_v1
    columns:
      - include: '*'
        exclude: [signup_timestamp]
      - name: name
        description: Renamed to customer_display_name in v2.
```

Two things about where a version lands. In the warehouse, each version materializes to <model_name>_v<v> — dim_customer_v1, dim_customer_v2 — and there is no relation at the bare model name, whichever version is latest. An unpinned ref() resolves to the latest version's own suffixed relation; nothing sits in front of it. Set alias: on a version to override that name, which is how a team keeps the latest version at the database location consumers already query.

The selection vocabulary Ch 11 §11.6 names falls straight out of latest_version:: the version equal to it is latest, anything above it is prerelease, and anything below it is old. With latest_version: 2 over versions 1, 2 and 3, dbt ls --select version:prerelease --output name returns dim_customer.v3 — and that dotted form, <model>.v<v>, is how a versioned node is addressed on the command line.

One config to recognise and not reach for: latest_version_pointer does not exist at 1.11, and its absence is the dangerous kind. dbt accepts config: {latest_version_pointer: {enabled: true}} on a versioned model, builds every version normally, and creates no pointer relation. On Postgres it does that without an error and without a warning — nothing in the run output tells you the config did nothing. Only four adapters run dbt's JSON-schema validation of `config:` blocks — Snowflake, BigQuery, Redshift and Databricks — and on those the unrecognised key draws a deprecation warning; the build still succeeds and the pointer relation still does not appear. The feature and its `latest_version_pointer_enabled_by_default` behaviour flag arrive after 1.11; at the target version, an answer that offers a pointer relation at the bare model name is wrong, however reasonable it sounds.

### How consumers `ref()` a specific version

The `ref()` Jinja function accepts a `v=` keyword argument that pins to a version (Ch 2 §2.2). Three cases:

```
-- Pick the latest_version (v2 in the example above)
SELECT * FROM {{ ref('dim_customer') }}

-- Pin explicitly to v2 (same result as above, but the code declares the intent)
SELECT * FROM {{ ref('dim_customer', v=2) }}

-- Stay on v1 until the consumer has migrated to the new column names
SELECT * FROM {{ ref('dim_customer', v=1) }}
```

The standard reference for the `ref()` signature is `/reference/dbt-jinja-functions/ref`. The `v=` argument is accepted on any versioned model; dbt errors at parse time if the requested version doesn't exist in the `versions:` block. (The same docs page documents `version=` as an accepted alias of `v=` — both forms work — but `v=` is the canonical short form used throughout the model-versions guide and in real-world projects.)

### The migration flow

A breaking change to a shared model typically proceeds as:

1. **Day 0.** Producer adds `v: 2` to the `versions:` block, creates `dim_customer_v2.sql` with the new shape, moves the old SQL into `dim_customer_v1.sql`, and sets `latest_version: 1`. Consumers calling `ref('dim_customer')` still get v1 (unchanged).
2. **Day 0 → Day N.** Consumers who want the new shape update their refs to `ref('dim_customer', v=2)`. Both versions materialize on every build.
3. **Day N (cutover).** Once every consumer has migrated, producer sets `latest_version: 2`. Consumers calling `ref('dim_customer')` (unpinned) now resolve to v2.
4. **Day N + buffer.** Producer adds `deprecation_date:` to v1 (§13.5) — the warning cycle begins.
5. **Day N + buffer + warning cycle.** Producer removes v1 from the `versions:` block and deletes `dim_customer_v1.sql`.

The versioning mechanism runs both versions concurrently during steps 2–4. This is the feature's whole point: a breaking change does not require a coordinated cutover, and consumers migrate at their own pace.

### Contracts and versions work well together

A contracted model combined with versions gives the strongest cross-team safety: the contract declares the shape (so consumers can rely on it), and versions let the shape evolve without taking down unpinned consumers. In practice, contracts and versions almost always appear on the same models — the high-stakes shared facts and dims that multiple teams read from.

---

## 13.5 Deprecating an old version

Once a version has a successor and the migration cycle is winding down, the old version needs a graceful retirement path. `deprecation_date:` is that path.

### The property

`deprecation_date:` takes an RFC-3339 value in one of three shapes: a date (`2026-07-01`), a datetime with an explicit UTC offset (`2026-07-01T12:00:00-06:00`), or a datetime without one (`2026-07-01T12:00:00`). The third shape is the one to watch — with no offset, dbt reads the value in the system timezone of the machine running dbt, so the same YAML crosses the date at a different instant on a developer's laptop and on a CI runner, and either side of that instant a different warning class fires. It can be attached to an individual version entry or to the whole model, and which one you pick decides whether it does anything:

```
models:
  - name: dim_customer
    latest_version: 2
    versions:
      - v: 2
        columns: [...]
      - v: 1
        defined_in: dim_customer_v1
        deprecation_date: "2026-07-01"
        columns: [...]
```

**On a versioned model, put the date on the version — a model-level one is dropped.** A top-level `deprecation_date` alongside a `versions:` block does not fall through to the versions: every version node parses with `deprecation_date: null` and dbt emits nothing at all — no `DeprecatedModel`, no `DeprecatedReference`, past date or future. Executed on 1.11.14 with a control, the identical past date on an *unversioned* model in the same project raised both. dbt builds each version's patch from the version's own key with no fall-back to the model's, unlike the neighbouring `description`, `access` and `constraints`. Nothing tells you the key did nothing, so whole-model deprecation is only for models with no `versions:` block.

The reference page is `/reference/resource-properties/deprecation_date`.

### What happens before and after the date

- **Before the date.** Builds of consumers that `ref()` the deprecated version complete successfully, but dbt emits a warning: the model (or version) is deprecated and will be removed on such-and-such date. If a newer version is available, the warning names it so the consumer can redirect.
- **After the date.** The deprecated model is considered live but unsupported, and the warning stops being advance notice and becomes a statement that the removal date has passed. `--warn-error` is not a post-date mechanism: it promotes *any* dbt warning to an error, so a run with that flag set fails on the deprecation warning either side of the date.

Three distinct warning events carry that, and they differ by who sees them and when. Each has a name, and each can be promoted to an error on its own through `warn_error_options` (Ch 10 §10.9.3) rather than by making every warning fatal:

| Event | Who sees it | When |
|---|---|---|
| `UpcomingReference Deprecation` | the **consumer** — a model that `ref()`s a resource carrying a future `deprecation_date` | before the date |
| `DeprecatedReference` | the **consumer** — the same `ref()`, once the date has passed | after the date |
| `DeprecatedModel` | the **producer** — the deprecated resource itself | after the date |

So the consumer's warning changes class at the date, and the producer's warning only begins there.

The deprecation date's most important job is **visibility**. A consumer whose CI emits "`dim_customer` v1 will be removed on 2026-07-01" on every PR has three months of nudges. Without the date, the migration cycle has no forcing function and v1 outlives its usefulness indefinitely.

### Deleting a contracted model, and why the check needs `--state`

A separate rail sits on deletion rather than on reference: removing, renaming or disabling a contracted model before its `deprecation_date` is a breaking change, and dbt treats it as one. Two preconditions govern whether you ever see it, and both are easy to miss.

**It is a state comparison, so it needs `--state`.** The check lives inside the `state:` selection methods, which compare the current project against a previous run's manifest and walk the nodes that have *disappeared* as well as the ones that changed. A plain `dbt build` has no earlier manifest to miss the model from; it builds what is in front of it and says nothing. A CI job that wants the rail is running something shaped like `dbt build --select state:modified --state ./prior-artifacts` (Ch 12 §12.2). Supplying `--state` without a `state:` selector achieves nothing either — the flag makes the comparison possible, the selector is what performs it.

**Versioned errors; unversioned warns.** With the deleted model carrying a `v:`, dbt raises a contract-breaking-change error and the run stops: `Breaking change to contract Error in model dim_customer ... Contracted model 'model.credora.dim_customer.v1' was deleted or renamed`. With no `versions:` block at all, the same deletion produces `[WARNING]: Breaking change to contracted, unversioned model dim_customer ... was deleted or renamed` and the run exits successfully. The asymmetry is deliberate. A versioned contract is a published interface that consumers pin to a specific `v`, and dropping one out from under them is the failure the rail exists to stop; an unversioned contracted model has no pinned consumers, so the producer gets the warning and keeps the decision.

Past the `deprecation_date` the check stops applying to that model at all. The deletion is exactly what the date announced, so neither the error nor the warning fires.

### The retirement flow

1. **Add `deprecation_date:`** to the old version when the new version has been running in parallel long enough for consumers to migrate (typically one full release cycle — a month or a quarter, depending on the team).
2. **Monitor the warnings.** The CI pipeline's `dbt build` output names every consumer that still `ref()`s the deprecated version. Use that output to drive migration tickets.

3. **Past the date, wait one more cycle.** The deprecation warning continues — the post-date period is the last chance for a laggard consumer to migrate before the version is removed.
4. **Remove the version from `versions:`** and delete its SQL file. If the model was contracted and versioned, a CI job running a `state:` comparison rejects that deletion until the `deprecation_date` has passed.

---

## 13.6 Access — who can `ref()` what

`access:` is a per-model modifier that controls which other models are allowed to call `ref()` against it. Three values:

| Access value | Who can `ref()` this model |
|---|---|
| `private` | Only nodes in the **same group** as this model — any consumer, not only models |
| `protected` | Any model in the **same project**, regardless of group — **or** a model in a project that installs this one as a package. **Default.** |
| `public` | Any model in any project — including external projects that install this project as a package or consume it via `dbt Mesh` cross-project `ref` |

Configure access on the model, either in YAML or via `{{ config(access='private') }}` in the SQL file:

```
models:
  - name: int_customer_ltv_features
    config:
      access: private
      group: ml_feature_engineering
```

The reference pages: concept at `/docs/mesh/govern/model-access`, config reference at `/reference/resource-configs/access`.

### The semantics by example

Consider a project with two groups — `finance` and `marketing` — and several models:

- `fct_finance_revenue_by_region` — `access: private`, `group: finance`. Only finance-group models can `ref()` it.
- `int_finance_revenue_raw` — `access: protected` (default), `group: finance`. Any model in the project can `ref()` it, but the group tag is available for any future `private` tightening.
- `dim_region` — `access: public`, no group. Any project that installs this project as a package can `ref()` it.
- `stg_marketing_events` — no access declared, so `protected` by default. Any model in the project can `ref()` it.

In this layout, a marketing-group model trying to `ref('fct_finance_revenue_by_region')` fails at parse time with a `Parsing Error` reading `... which is not allowed because the referenced node is private to the 'finance' group`: the target is `private` and the caller is not in `finance`. The exception class behind that banner is `DbtReferenceError`, which is what a log parser or a stack trace will name. The error is loud, immediate, and fails the build before any DDL runs — marketing finds out the first time it tries, not after the coupling has shipped.

## Material caveats

- **Ephemeral models cannot be `public`.** The concept page is explicit: a `public` model has to be addressable across project boundaries, and an ephemeral materialization has no warehouse relation for a downstream project to point at.
- **Pair `access: private` with a `group:` — always.** `private` means "same group", and an ungrouped model is in no group: it rejects *every* caller, the producing team's own downstream models included, with `... is private to the '' group`. Ungrouped `private` fails closed, not open.
- **The check is about the consumer's group, not the consumer's kind.** Every node that can call `ref()` is subject to it, and the branch that decides is one condition: the caller has no `group` attribute at all, or an empty one, or one that differs from the target's. A model in another group, a singular test in `tests/` that declares no `group:`, and an exposure's `depends_on:` entry therefore fail identically — and since exposures cannot carry a `group:` at all (§13.7), an exposure can never `ref()` a private model. Being outside the group is what fails, not being inside a named rival one.
- **`access` applies at parse time.** Invalid references are caught before any SQL is compiled to a warehouse. This is the same failure mode as a `ref()` to a misspelled model name (Ch 10 §10.3) and surfaces in the same way.
- **`access` is inherited via config precedence.** A `+access: private` under a directory in `dbt_project.yml` applies to every model under that path, just like any other config. Use the directory-level default for "this whole subtree is internal-only" and override at the model level for the models that are deliberately public.
- **`dbt run-operation` goes around it.** Access and group enforcement is a property of `ref()` resolution during parsing. A macro invoked through `dbt run-operation` can build the relation name itself and query a private model directly, and nothing stops it. Treat `access:` as a discipline over the model graph rather than as a security boundary; the boundary is `grants:` and the warehouse's own RBAC.
- **`restrict-access` is the package-consumer half.** It is a top-level key in `dbt_project.yml`, not a resource config, and it defaults to `False` — which is why the `protected` row above reaches package installers at all. Set it `True` and a project that installs yours can `ref()` only your `public` models; the second half of that row stops applying.

## When to reach for `private`

A common governance trap is declaring everything `private` by default and making other teams request access on demand. That works for twenty models and fails at two hundred: every cross-team consumer becomes a coordination ticket. The more sustainable pattern is:

- **Leave the default (`protected`).** Any model in the project can `ref()` any other — same as pre-access projects. This keeps friction low and matches how most projects actually work internally.

- **Explicitly mark `private` only the models that are implementation details** — intermediate models in a feature-engineering pipeline, staging models a team uses internally, anything that would be dangerous for another team to depend on. These are the models whose shape is most likely to churn, and `private` prevents a downstream team from quietly coupling to a churning target.
- **Explicitly mark `public` only the models that are deliberate cross-project APIs** — the fact and dim models another dbt project installs this project to consume. `public` is the mechanism that lets a dbt Mesh consumer `ref()` across project boundaries. (Cross-project `ref` is a dbt Mesh capability on the Enterprise plans, outside this exam's scope, and `access` is not itself a named study-guide bullet.)

---

## 13.7 Groups — the other half of access

A **group** is a named collection of resources plus an owner. The `owner:` block needs `name:` or `email:` — either one alone is valid, both together is the usual choice, and arbitrary extra keys are allowed beside them. Groups are declared in a `.yml` under `groups:`, with the same top-level syntax as `sources:` or `exposures:`:

```
version: 2

groups:
  - name: finance
    owner:
      name: Finance Analytics
      email: finance-analytics@example.com
  - name: marketing
    owner:
      name: Marketing Analytics
      email: marketing-analytics@example.com
  - name: ml_feature_engineering
    owner:
      name: ML Platform
      email: ml-platform@example.com
```

Attach a model to a group with the `group:` config, in any of the standard config locations:

```
models:
  - name: fct_finance_revenue_by_region
    config:
      access: private
      group: finance
```

Or in `dbt_project.yml`:

```
models:
  my_project:
    finance:
      +group: finance
```

Or in the model SQL:

```
{{ config(group='finance') }}
```

The docs pages: concept at `/docs/build/groups`, config reference at `/reference/resource-configs/group`.

### What groups do

Groups by themselves do three things:

1. **They declare ownership** (the `owner:` block), recorded on the group's own node in `manifest.json`. Each member carries the group's name in its `group` field, so a tool that reads the manifest joins the two — docs site, catalog integrations, lineage viewers. The owner is not copied into any model's `meta`, which stays whatever the model itself sets.
2. **They gate `access: private`.** As discussed in §13.6, `private` means "same-group only". In practice, the private model and any legitimate caller both need group assignments so dbt has a same-group boundary to evaluate.
3. **They give you a selection token.** `dbt build --select group:finance` matches every resource tagged with `group: finance`. This is practically useful for team-specific CI — the finance team's PR gate can build just their group's models.

Groups are not, by themselves, enforcement. A model in `group: finance` is not automatically private; access enforcement requires the combination `access: private` + `group: finance`. Groups are the namespace; access is the policy that uses the namespace.

A model can belong to **at most one** group — there's no multi-group membership. If two teams have a legitimate shared interest in a model, that's a sign the model belongs in a separate, jointly-owned group rather than overlapping memberships.

Membership is not open to every resource type either. Models, tests, seeds, snapshots, analyses and metrics can carry a `group:`; **sources and exposures cannot**. That matters when a team tries to draw a group boundary around a whole domain and finds the source declarations sitting outside it.

### Groups and project structure

A common pattern: one group per top-level directory under `models/`, matching the team that owns that directory. If the project layout is `models/finance/`, `models/marketing/`, and `models/ml/`, the three groups (`finance`, `marketing`, `ml_feature_engineering`) each own their directory via `+group:` in `dbt_project.yml`:

```
models:
  my_project:
    finance:
      +group: finance
    marketing:
      +group: marketing
    ml:
      +group: ml_feature_engineering
```

Now every model in `models/finance/` is tagged `group: finance` by default. Cross-directory references still resolve (the default `access` is `protected`, which is cross-group). When a finance model needs to become implementation-detail-only, the producer adds `access: private` and the gating is already wired.

---

## 13.8 Grants — post-run warehouse privileges

`grants:` is a config that instructs dbt, after materializing a model (or seed or snapshot — the config applies to all three resource types), to issue warehouse `GRANT` statements. It is the mechanism by which BI tools, downstream service accounts, or other warehouse consumers receive `SELECT` (or other) privileges on dbt-built relations.

## The config

```
models:
  - name: fct_finance_revenue_by_region
    config:
      grants:
        select: ['bi_reader_role', 'finance_analysts_role']
```

Or in `dbt_project.yml`:

```
models:
  my_project:
    finance:
      +grants:
        select: ['bi_reader_role', 'finance_analysts_role']
```

After the model's DDL runs, dbt issues something functionally equivalent to:

```
GRANT SELECT ON <schema>.<table> TO bi_reader_role, finance_analysts_role;
```

The reference page is `/reference/resource-configs/grants`.

## Timing: after the DDL, every build

Two semantic points the cert likes to surface:

1. **Grants run after the model's DDL, not before.** A `dbt run` or `dbt build` creates the table, then issues the GRANT. If the table does not materialize (error, `--defer`-resolved), no grants are issued.
2. **Where a `grants:` config is attached, it is applied on every build.** dbt reconciles the relation's warehouse grants to match that config exactly: it adds any listed grantee that is missing and revokes any grantee that is not in the config, so warehouse state tracks code state. The weight is on the opening clause — dbt touches a relation's grants only when a `grants:` config reaches it, and the next subsection is about what that rules out.

## When dbt manages grants, and when it does not

There are three states, and the difference between the second and the third is the one that costs a team access it meant to keep.

| What the config says | What dbt does to the relation |
|---|---|
| `select: ['bi_reader_role']` | Reconciles: grants `bi_reader_role` if it is missing, revokes every other `select` grantee |
| `select: []` | Revokes every `select` grantee, leaving nobody |
| no `grants:` config at all | Nothing. dbt stops managing grants on that relation and leaves whatever privileges are already on it |

An empty list is an instruction; a deleted block is a withdrawal. Delete the block expecting the empty-list behaviour and the old grantees keep their access indefinitely, with nothing in the log to say so.

Reconciliation is a delta, not a blanket reapply. On the first build dbt issues a plain `grant`. On every build after that it queries the privileges already on the relation with adapter-specific SQL and issues only the statements needed to close the gap — so dropping one name from a two-name list produces a single `revoke` and no `grant` at all. Run with `--debug` and the statements are there:

```
revoke SELECT on "credora"."gold"."fct_orders" from "finance_analysts_role"
```

`grants:` also has a boundary, and the reference names four cases where a hook is the right tool instead: privileges on database objects that are not views or tables; row- and column-level access, masking policies and future grants; platform permission features dbt does not wrap; and any custom grant logic of your own. Those belong in a `post-hook` (Ch 6 §6.5).

## Other privileges, and what varies by adapter

`select` is the privilege most teams configure, and on most platforms the value is simply whatever privilege name the warehouse recognises. Three things vary by adapter: which privileges `grants:` carries, the prefix on the *grantee* — which is not the prefix on the privilege — and whether `grants:` is supported at all.

| Adapter | What differs |
|---|---|
| **Databricks** | `read_metadata` and `usage` are not grantable through the config; the reference sends you to a `post-hook` for those two. Reaching for `grants: {read_metadata: [...]}` because the privilege exists on the platform is the mistake to avoid. Grants need no setup on SQL endpoints; an interactive cluster needs table access control enabled first. |
| **BigQuery** | The privilege side takes the `roles/` form (`roles/bigquery.dataViewer`); each grantee carries a type prefix of its own — `user:`, `group:`, `domain:`, or a service account. |
| **Redshift** | A grantee may be a user, a group (`group:`) or a role (`role:`); a bare name is read as a user. |
| **Snowflake** | `grant` and `revoke` are supported for account roles rather than database roles. dbt accounts for `copy_grants` when working out the delta; it defaults to `false`, so a `CREATE OR REPLACE` drops the existing privileges before dbt reapplies its own. |
| **OSS Apache Spark / Delta Lake** | `grants:` does not work at all. |

A privilege's value can also be a Jinja expression, which is how grantees differ per environment without a second config surface:

```
models:
  - name: fct_finance_revenue_by_region
    config:
      grants:
        select: "{{ ['bi_reader_role', 'finance_analysts_role'] if target.name == 'prod'
      else ['analyst_dev_role'] }}"
```

Check the per-adapter section of the grants reference before configuring anything other than select.

## Project-level vs model-level: merge, don't replace

By default, dbt's config precedence (Ch 6 §6.4) says "more specific wins — model-level replaces project-level." For `grants:`, replacement is often the wrong semantics: if `dbt_project.yml` grants `select` to `bi_reader_role` project-wide and a specific model needs to *add* `finance_analysts_role` as well, a model-level `grants: {select: ['finance_analysts_role']}` replaces (not merges) the project-level list — and the BI reader loses access.

The fix is the `+` prefix on the privilege name at the model level:

```
models:
  - name: fct_finance_revenue_by_region
    config:
      grants:
        '+select': ['finance_analysts_role']    # adds to the project-level list, not
   replaces
```

The prefix works per privilege, not per block: in the same `grants:` dict, a privilege written with `+` merges while one written without it still clobbers. `grants` is the only dbt config that takes a merge prefix at all — a different `+` from the `dbt_project.yml` disambiguating prefix in Ch 2 §2.4, in a different position and with a different meaning.

## Grants vs access — the crisp distinction

Both `grants:` and `access:` look like "who can use this model", but they operate at different layers and solve different problems:

| | `access:` (§13.6) | `grants:` (this section) |
|---|---|---|
| Layer | dbt (parse/build-time `ref()` resolution) | Warehouse (post-DDL GRANT statement) |
| Who is being restricted | Other **dbt models** | Any **warehouse principal** — BI tool, service account, human user |
| Failure mode | Parse-time error; the `ref()` is rejected | No failure; the principal simply lacks privilege when they query |
| Typical use | Stop another team's dbt model from coupling to yours | Give BI tools `SELECT`; give downstream services read privileges |

A model can (and often should) have both: `access: public` + `group: finance` + `grants: {select: ['bi_reader_role']}`. The `access: public` advertises the model as a cross-project API; the `group: finance` flags ownership; the `grants:` ensures BI can actually query it. Conversely, an `access: private` model that is never read by any BI tool may not need `grants:` at all.

A third config is confusable with both, and only on BigQuery. `grant_access_to:` makes a view an *authorized view*: readers may query the view even though they have no access to the dataset it selects from. It is a property of the view rather than of a principal, it applies to views only, and it composes with `grants:` rather than replacing it. See `/reference/resource-configs/bigquery-configs`.

**Convention:** use `grants:` for BI-tool roles and warehouse consumers; use `access:` for other dbt projects and internal discipline. They are complements, not substitutes.

---

## 13.9 In practice: Credora's selective governance

> *This section is an "in practice" sidebar. It draws a composite pattern from (a) the main governance pages at `/docs/mesh/govern/model-contracts`, `/docs/mesh/govern/model-versions`, and `/docs/mesh/govern/model-access`, and (b) the dbt Labs blog's recommendations on when to introduce contracts. Credora is fictional (`credora`); Ch 14's opening note has the composite-project disclaimer. Mature projects commonly converge on the selective-governance pattern described below; the choices below are not unique to any single company.*

Credora is a mature multi-market fintech project. Even at its scale — over a thousand models, around a dozen Databricks catalogs, several analytics teams contributing — the project applies governance *selectively*. Which primitives show up where, and which are deliberately absent, is its own teaching lesson.

### Where contracts show up

`fct_lending_offer_clicks_uk` is a gold-layer fact model that powers the primary UK lending dashboard and is consumed by multiple downstream teams (marketing attribution, finance reporting, risk analytics). A breaking schema change here would quietly ripple through three teams' BI. It is **contracted** — the YAML pins every output column's `data_type`, declares `not_null` constraints on the click-level identifiers, and declares a `primary_key` constraint on the event-id column (metadata-only on Databricks, but paired with a `unique` data test to actually validate).

Most other models in `credora` — staging, intermediate, market-specific marts that only one team reads — do not have contracts. The reason is the cost/benefit calculus from §13.1: contracts add YAML overhead and PR review friction on every column change. For internal models that one team reads, that overhead exceeds the breakage risk. For the shared gold layer where three teams read, contracts pay for themselves the first time a breaking change is prevented.

**The rule of thumb:** contract the cross-team gold models; skip the per-team staging and intermediate models.

### Where versions show up

`dim_user_lifecycle_segments_uk_v1` and `dim_user_lifecycle_segments_uk_v2` are the project's one versioned model pair. The story: v1 had a column called `segment_name` with values like `'new_user'`, `'active'`, `'churned'`. Product reorganised the segmentation taxonomy, which needed both a value-set change and a rename to `lifecycle_stage`. A single in-place column change would have broken the three dashboards and one ML feature pipeline that consumed `segment_name`.

Instead:

1. Producer published v2 with `lifecycle_stage` in place of `segment_name`. `latest_version:` stayed on v1.
2. Consumers migrated to `ref('dim_user_lifecycle_segments_uk', v=2)` one by one, over a couple of sprints.
3. Producer moved `latest_version:` to v2. Unpinned consumers (there were none left) would have silently received the new column.

4. Producer added `deprecation_date:` to v1 — three months out.
5. At the deprecation date, producer removed v1 from the `versions:` block and deleted `dim_user_lifecycle_segments_uk_v1.sql`.

This is the standard migration flow from §13.4. It is also the only place Credora uses `versions:` — every other breaking change in the project is coordinated the old-fashioned way (a PR that renames the column, reviewed by every team that consumes the model). Versions are expensive: two SQL files to maintain, two materializations to pay for, and the whole coordination dance above. Projects reach for versions when the blast radius of a coordinated rename is genuinely large — and skip them otherwise.

## Where grants show up

`grants:` is configured **globally via folder-level config** in `dbt_project.yml`:

```
models:
  credora:
    cr_uk:
      gold:
        +grants:
          select: ['credora_bi_reader', 'credora_analytics_reader']
      marts:
        +grants:
          select: ['credora_bi_reader']
```

The rationale: Credora's BI tool and its downstream Databricks dashboards consume from gold and marts layers uniformly. Rather than attach `grants:` to each individual model (tedious, easy to forget), the project uses the directory-level `+grants:` and lets every model in the directory inherit. Individual models that need additional grantees use the `+select:` merge-prefix to add without replacing the directory-level defaults.

## Where `access:` and `groups:` are not

Here is where Credora's selective governance is most instructive: the project **does not use `access:` or `groups:`**. Every model is effectively `access: protected` (the default) and no `groups:` block exists.

The reason is straightforward: Credora is a single-project, single-repo monolith. All its models live in `credora`; cross-project `ref` (via dbt Mesh) does not apply. Within one project, `access: protected` (the default) allows any model to `ref()` any other — which is exactly the permission structure the teams want day-to-day. They coordinate via code review, ownership tags in `meta:`, and the cost/benefit instinct above: tight restrictions pay off when they prevent a specific kind of cross-team breakage, and Credora has not hit that pain point.

What they **could** do — the teaching contrast: if Credora were to split into multiple dbt projects (a data-platform project plus per-market consumer projects, say), the shared `cr_global` project would need `access: public` on its cross-project facts and dims. Similarly, if one market's internal modelling became complex enough that other markets were tempted to `ref()` into it, the producing market could add `access: private` + `group: analytics-<market>` to those internal models and re-establish the boundary. The primitives exist; Credora has not yet needed them.

## The takeaway

Selective governance is the pattern: contracts on the cross-team gold layer, versions on the one model with the coordinated-rename problem, grants globally because every gold-layer model has the same BI consumer, and `access:`/`groups:` deferred until the project actually has the cross-project-coupling problem they solve. At Credora's scale, the overhead of declaring every primitive on every model would swamp the benefit. At ten times the scale, or on a multi-project dbt Mesh, the calculus shifts and `access:`/`groups:` become load-bearing.

Governance primitives are features that stay dormant until their corresponding failure mode becomes real. Adopt them the day the failure mode surfaces; don't carry the cost before then.

---

## Summary

- Governance is the set of primitives that let multiple teams share a dbt project without stepping on each other.
- **Contracts** pin a model's output shape: declare every column's `data_type` in YAML under a `contract: {enforced: true}` config, and dbt validates the model's SELECT against the contract before issuing DDL. A mismatch fails the build, printing a table whose `definition_type` column is the SQL's side and whose `contract_type` column is the YAML's.
- **The comparison covers names, types and count — nothing else.** Column order is ignored and the DDL is written in the contract's order; size, precision and scale are stripped before comparing, so `varchar(256)` satisfies a `varchar(257)` contract while a *table* is still created at 257 (a view keeps the SELECT's 256 — a view's DDL carries no column spec). `alias_types` (default `true`) is what translates a generic `string` into the platform's own spelling.
- **Constraints are inert without an enforced contract** — no DDL, no error, no warning — and they apply only to `table` and `incremental` models, never to `ephemeral` or `view`. The same dependency makes `data_type` transitive: it is optional on an uncontracted model's `columns:` block, mandatory on every column once `enforced: true` is set, and therefore mandatory on any model that declares constraints at all. That failure lands during `dbt run`, before any DDL is issued.
- **Six constraint types are declarable** — `not_null`, `unique`, `primary_key`, `foreign_key`, `check`, `custom`. Only `foreign_key` carries `to` / `to_columns`; `check` and `custom` require an `expression`; `custom` is a pass-through escape hatch for platform-specific DDL, and its absence from the support matrix is why that matrix has five rows rather than six.
- **Enforcement is per adapter, and Postgres is the only one that enforces all five matrix types.** Snowflake, Redshift and BigQuery enforce `not_null` and nothing else; Databricks also enforces `check` but only after the model is built; Spark defines all five and enforces none; Athena defines none. `warn_unenforced` and `warn_unsupported` both default to `True` and each silences one class of warning without changing what the warehouse does.
- **Versions** let a model evolve without breaking consumers: publish v1 and v2 side by side via a `versions:` YAML block, set `latest_version:` to control the default, and let consumers call `ref('my_model', v=2)` to pin. Each version materializes to <model_name>_v<v>; nothing sits at the bare model name, and `latest_version_pointer` — which would put something there — arrives after 1.11 and until then is accepted while creating nothing: silently on Postgres, with a deprecation warning on the four adapters that validate `config:` blocks (Snowflake, BigQuery, Redshift, Databricks).
- **A version's `columns:` may carry one `{include, exclude}` element**, with `exclude` legal only where `include` is `all` or `'*'`; the illegal pairing is a parse failure, not a warning. A version declaring no `columns:` inherits every top-level column.

- `deprecation_date:` retires old versions with a visible warning cycle before removal, carried by three named events — `UpcomingReferenceDeprecation` and `DeprecatedReference` for the consumer, `DeprecatedModel` for the producer. Deleting a contracted model before that date is a breaking change, but only a `state:` comparison against `--state` ever notices, and only a **versioned** model errors; unversioned warns and the run succeeds.
- `access:` controls `ref()` resolution at parse time: `private` (same group only), `protected` (same project, default), `public` (any project). Ephemeral models cannot be `public`; `private` without a group rejects every caller rather than none; and `dbt run-operation` goes around the whole mechanism, which is why `access:` is discipline rather than security.
- **Groups** declare a named collection of resources with an `owner:` block needing `name:` or `email:` (either alone), and are the namespace `access: private` depends on. Models, tests, seeds, snapshots, analyses and metrics can join one; sources and exposures cannot.
- `grants:` issues warehouse `GRANT` statements after DDL, as a delta against the privileges already on the relation; `+`-prefixed privilege names merge with project-level grants instead of replacing them, and `grants` is the only dbt config that takes a merge prefix. A populated list reconciles, `select: []` revokes everyone, and **no `grants:` config at all leaves the relation's grants alone**. `grants:` operates at the warehouse; `access:` operates inside dbt — both are "who can read this model" but at different layers.
- The primitives are selectively adopted: mature projects contract the shared gold layer, version the one model with a coordinated-rename problem, grant broadly via folder-level config, and leave `access:` / `groups:` unused until a cross-project coupling problem emerges.

## Learning-goal checklist (self-assess)

- ☐ **Add a `contract: {enforced: true}`** with typed `columns:` and optional `constraints:` (§13.2).
- ☐ **State the two constraint prerequisites without looking**: constraints do nothing unless `contract: {enforced: true}` is set, and an enforced contract requires a `data_type` on every column (§13.2, §13.3).
- ☐ **Name all six constraint types** — `not_null`, `unique`, `primary_key`, `foreign_key`, `check`, `custom` — and say which one takes `to` / `to_columns`, which two require an `expression`, and which has no row in the adapter matrix (§13.3).
- ☐ **Rebuild the adapter matrix from the rule of thumb** — Postgres enforces all five, Snowflake / Redshift / BigQuery enforce `not_null` only, Databricks adds `check`, Spark enforces none, Athena defines none — and know which of `warn_unenforced` / `warn_unsupported` silences which warning (§13.3).
- ☐ **Say what a contract compares and what it ignores** — names, types and count; not order, not size, precision or scale — and read a mismatch table to find the offending column (§13.2).
- ☐ **Define a model `version:`** plus `latest_version:` plus `deprecation_date:` (§13.4, §13.5).
- ☐ **Write a version's `columns:` inheritance correctly** — one `{include, exclude}` element, `exclude` only under `include: all` / `'*'` — and name the three deprecation warning events (§13.4, §13.5).
- ☐ **State what a contracted model's deletion does** before its `deprecation_date`, and both preconditions: a `state:` comparison, and a versioned model (§13.5).
- ☐ **Set model `access:` to `private | protected | public`** and attach to `groups:` (§13.6, §13.7).
- ☐ **Use `grants:`** for post-run warehouse grants, including `+`-prefix merge (§13.8).

☐ **Distinguish the three `grants:` states** — a populated list, `select: []`, and no config at all — and name a privilege that needs a hook instead (§13.8).

---

## Practice questions

Thirty-six questions covering every §13.1–§13.8 sub-topic, graded recall / apply / analyze.

**1.** A model has `contract: {enforced: true}` in its YAML. When does dbt validate the model's output shape against the contract?
A. After the DDL is submitted to the warehouse
B. Before the DDL is submitted — dbt performs a preflight check on the compiled SELECT
C. When `dbt test` runs, after the model has materialized
D. When `dbt docs generate` runs

**2.** A model has `contract: {enforced: true}` and its YAML lists four columns with `data_type`. The model's SELECT emits five columns. What happens on `dbt build`?
A. The build fails — contracts apply to all columns in a model, and every output column must be declared
B. The build succeeds; the contract is partial and only validates the four listed columns
C. The build succeeds; the fifth column is silently dropped
D. The build fails, but only after the DDL runs — the warehouse rejects the extra column

**3.** Which statement about the `not_null` constraint in a dbt contract is TRUE on Snowflake?
A. `not_null` is metadata-only on Snowflake — violating rows will land
B. `not_null` is enforced — Snowflake rejects every row that violates the constraint
C. `not_null` is not supported on Snowflake at all
D. `not_null` requires a separate `unique_key` config to be enforced

**4.** On which of the following adapters is the `check` constraint definable AND enforced?
A. Snowflake B. BigQuery
C. Redshift D. Databricks

**5.** A team declares `primary_key` as a constraint in a contract on Snowflake. At build time, the contract succeeds and the model materializes. Two weeks later, they discover duplicate rows in the primary-key column. What happened?
A. The `primary_key` constraint failed silently — a dbt bug, since a constraint that builds without error is expected to reject duplicate-key writes
B. On Snowflake, `primary_key` is metadata-only. The DDL was emitted, but Snowflake does not reject duplicate-key writes, so the declaration documents intent while a dbt `unique` test is what enforces it
C. A `primary_key` constraint on a contract automatically prevents duplicates on any warehouse, so the duplicates must have been written outside dbt
D. The team needed `enforced: strict` rather than `enforced: true`, which enables constraint checking instead of only constraint declaration

**6.** Which statement best describes the purpose of a `versions:` block on a dbt model?
A. To roll back a model to a prior state
B. To materialize one model into several schemas at once
C. To tag a model with a semver release number
D. To publish several shapes of the model side by side, so consumers migrate at their own pace

**7.** A model declares three versions (`v: 1`, `v: 2`, `v: 3`) but does not set `latest_version:`. A consumer calls `{{ ref('my_model') }}` with no `v=` argument. Which version does it resolve to?
A. v3 — if `latest_version:` is unset, dbt defaults to the largest version identifier
B. v1 — with `latest_version:` unset, dbt falls back to the first version declared in the YAML
C. An error at parse time — `latest_version:` is required as soon as a model declares more than one version
D. Whichever version dbt resolves first during the parse, so the result can differ between runs

**8.** A model has `latest_version: 1` and `versions:` declared as follows:

```
latest_version: 1
versions:
  - v: 2
  - v: 1
    defined_in: dim_customer_legacy
```

What filenames does dbt expect for the v2 and v1 SQL?
A. v2 → `dim_customer_v2.sql`; v1 → `dim_customer_v1.sql`
B. v2 → `dim_customer.sql`; v1 → `dim_customer_v1.sql`
C. v2 → `dim_customer.sql`; v1 → `dim_customer_legacy.sql`
D. v2 → `dim_customer_v2.sql`; v1 → `dim_customer_legacy.sql`

**9.** A version has `deprecation_date: "2026-07-01"`. The current date is 2026-04-15. A consumer builds with `ref()` targeting the deprecated version. What happens?
A. The build completes and dbt emits a warning that the version is deprecated and names the removal date
B. The build fails with an error
C. The build completes silently — warnings begin only after the date
D. The build completes but dbt refuses to write any rows

**10.** A CI job runs `dbt build --select state:modified --state ./prior-artifacts`. The PR under test deletes `dim_customer_v1.sql` and removes the `v: 1` entry from the `versions:` block of a model configured with `contract: {enforced: true}`, where that version carries `deprecation_date: "2027-01-01"`. The current date is 2026-06-15. What does the job do?
A. It fails — deleting a versioned contracted model before its `deprecation_date` is a contract-breaking change
B. Nothing — a state comparison looks at model SQL, not at contracts
C. It warns and continues — deletion of a contracted model is reported as a warning, not an error
D. It succeeds silently — the restriction takes effect from the `deprecation_date` onward, not before

**11.** A model declares no `access:` config. Which access level does it have?
A. `private` B. `protected`
C. `public` D. None — `access:` is required

**12.** A team declares `access: private` on a finance model. A marketing-group model tries to `ref()` it. What happens?
A. The `ref()` resolves; `access: private` is only a warning
B. The model materializes, but the warehouse denies read access
C. dbt raises `DbtReferenceError` at parse time; the build fails before any SQL is compiled
D. The `ref()` resolves but returns an empty table

**13.** Which combination is NOT allowed in dbt?
A. `access: public` + `materialized: table` B. `access: public` + `group: finance`
C. `access: public` + `materialized: ephemeral` D. `access: private` + `materialized: ephemeral`

**14.** Which statement about dbt `groups:` is TRUE?
A. A `group:` config on a model automatically makes the model `access: private`, so grouping a model is what stops other groups referencing it
B. A model can belong to multiple groups, in the same way it can carry several tags, and each group's owner is recorded against it
C. `groups:` replaces `meta:` for ownership tagging, and the group's owner is copied into each member model's `meta` at parse time
D. `groups:` declares a named collection of resources with an owner; by itself it does not restrict anything — `access: private` is the policy that uses the group as a namespace

**15.** When does dbt issue the GRANT statements declared in a model's `grants:` config?
A. After the model's DDL runs, on every build — if the model materialized successfully
B. Before the model's DDL runs, so the grantee has access during the build
C. Only on the first build, not on subsequent rebuilds
D. Only when `dbt grant` is invoked as a separate command

**16.** `dbt_project.yml` declares `+grants: {select: ['bi_reader']}` at the project level. A specific model needs to additionally grant `select` to `finance_analysts` — without losing the `bi_reader` grant. Which model-level config achieves this without restating the project-level grantee?
A. `grants: {select: ['finance_analysts']}`
B. `grants: {select: ['bi_reader', 'finance_analysts']}`
C. `grants: {'+select': ['finance_analysts']}`
D. `grants: {select: ['finance_analysts'], merge: true}`

**17.** A team wants to prevent a BI tool's service account from reading a specific dbt model. Which config is correct?
A. `access: private` on the model
B. `grants:` with the service account removed from the `select` list
C. `group:` on the model
D. `contract: {enforced: true}` on the model

**18.** A team is considering setting `access: private` on 40 models that are internal implementation details of their data pipeline. What is the best reasoning and approach?
A. Set `access: private` on all 40 without grouping — the declaration by itself prevents cross-team references
B. Leave all 40 on the default `protected` — group assignment is bookkeeping, and a code-review convention already gives you what `private` would
C. Assign the 40 models and their legitimate callers to a group, then set `access: private` now, so a cross-team `ref()` is refused before the coupling forms — an ungrouped `private` model rejects every caller, your own included
D. Set `access: public` on all 40 so other teams at least know the models exist

**19.** A consumer team's `{{ ref('my_model') }}` has started returning a different column set since a recent PR on the producing team's side. The producer renamed `name` to `customer_display_name`. The consumer's dashboards break. What should the producing team have done, and how does the fix look going forward?
A. The producer was correct to rename in place; consumers should always build defensively against any schema change. Going forward: announce breaking changes ahead of the PR and let each consumer team absorb the new column set on its own schedule once it lands
B. The producer should have used `versions:` — publish `my_model_v2` with the renamed column and keep `my_model_v1` materializing the old shape until consumers migrate. Going forward: leave `latest_version:` on v1 while consumers move to `ref('my_model', v=2)`, then promote it and set a `deprecation_date:` on v1 once every consumer has moved
C. The producer should have set `contract: {enforced: true}` — the contract would have prevented the rename. Going forward: enforce a contract on every published model, so any column change fails the producer's own build before it can reach a consumer
D. The producer should have set `access: private` to prevent cross-team reads. Going forward: keep published models private and hand each consumer a copy of the SQL to build inside its own project, where its shape is nobody else's concern

**20.** A contracted model materialized as a table declares `nm` as `varchar(257)` and `amt` as `numeric(38, 6)`. Its SELECT emits `nm` cast to `varchar(256)` and `amt` cast to `numeric(10, 2)`. What happens on `dbt run`?
A. The build fails on both columns — an enforced contract compares the declared type exactly, parentheses included
B. The build succeeds, and the warehouse relation carries the contract's sizes — `varchar(257)` and `numeric(38, 6)`
C. The build succeeds, but the relation carries whatever the SELECT cast to — `varchar(256)` and `numeric(10, 2)`
D. The build succeeds for `nm` and fails for `amt` — length is ignored but scale is compared

**21.** A model sets `materialized: incremental`, `on_schema_change: sync_all_columns` and `contract: {enforced: true}`. What happens, and when?
A. `dbt run` fails at the contract preflight the first time the SELECT's column set changes
B. Both `dbt parse` and `dbt run` succeed; `sync_all_columns` wins and dbt re-derives the contract from the new column set
C. `dbt parse` warns, and `dbt run` falls back to `append_new_columns`
D. `dbt parse` fails with a validation error — a contracted incremental must set `on_schema_change` to `append_new_columns` or `fail`

**22.** A contracted model fails to build, and dbt prints:

```
| column_name | definition_type | contract_type | mismatch_reason       |
| ----------- | --------------- | ------------- | --------------------- |
| line_count  | INTEGER         |               | missing in contract   |
| ordered_at  |                 | DATETIME      | missing in definition |
```

Which pair of edits resolves both rows?
A. Add `line_count` to the YAML `columns:` list, and either emit `ordered_at` from the SELECT or drop it from the YAML
B. Add `ordered_at` to the YAML `columns:` list, and stop emitting `line_count` from the SELECT
C. Give `line_count` a `data_type` of `DATETIME` and `ordered_at` a `data_type` of `INTEGER`
D. Set `alias_types: false`, so the generic type names resolve to the platform's own spelling

**23.** A `foreign_key` constraint on `fct_order_lines.order_id` points at `fct_customer_orders.order_id`, written as `to: ref('fct_customer_orders')`. A reviewer asks why it is not written as the relation name, `analytics.fct_customer_orders`. Which answer is correct?
A. Either spelling parses, but the `ref()` form is preferred because a literal relation name contributes nothing to the DAG
B. The `ref()` form makes `to_columns` unnecessary, since dbt reads the target's `primary_key` declaration
C. The `ref()` form replaces the `relationships` data test, because dbt then validates the reference on every build
D. The literal spelling does not parse — `to:` takes only `ref()` or `source()`, and that expression is what registers the DAG dependency and resolves the target per environment

**24.** A versioned model's `v: 2` entry uses the `columns:` inheritance keys. Which of these `columns:` blocks does dbt reject at parse time?
A. `- {include: '*', exclude: [legacy_flag]}`
B. `- {include: '*'}` and, as a second element, `- {name: order_status, description: "Reworded for v2."}`
C. `- {include: [order_id, order_status], exclude: [legacy_flag]}`
D. `- {name: order_status, description: "Reworded for v2."}` with no include element at all

**25.** A model has three versions and `latest_version: 2`. A developer adds `config: {latest_version_pointer: {enabled: true}}` to it, expecting a `dim_customer` relation that resolves to whichever version is latest. The project runs on Postgres. On dbt Core 1.11, what happens?
A. dbt fails at parse — `latest_version_pointer` is not a recognised config key
B. dbt warns that the config is unavailable at this version, then builds the three versioned relations
C. dbt accepts the config without error or warning, builds the three versioned relations, and creates no pointer relation
D. dbt creates the pointer relation, since the config is enabled explicitly on the model

**26.** A contracted model with no `versions:` block carries `deprecation_date: "2027-01-01"`. A PR deletes it. The current date is 2026-06-15. Which run surfaces the deletion, and how?
A. `dbt build` with no `--state` — it errors, because the contract is in the current manifest
B. `dbt build --select state:modified --state ./prior-artifacts` — it warns and exits successfully, because the deleted model is unversioned
C. `dbt build --select state:modified --state ./prior-artifacts` — it errors and stops, because a contracted model was deleted before its `deprecation_date`
D. `dbt build --state ./prior-artifacts` with no `state:` selector — it warns, because `--state` is what enables the comparison

**27.** A model's YAML has carried `grants: {select: ['bi_reader_role']}` for months. A PR deletes the whole `grants:` block from its config. The model materializes incrementally, so the relation itself is not replaced. What does the next `dbt build` do to `bi_reader_role`'s privilege?
A. It revokes the privilege — an absent config is read as an empty grantee list
B. It revokes the privilege and logs a warning naming the grantee it removed
C. It fails the build — a relation dbt has previously granted on cannot be left unmanaged
D. Nothing — with no `grants:` config attached, dbt stops managing grants on the relation and leaves the privilege in place

**28.** On Databricks, a service principal needs `read_metadata` and `usage` on a dbt-built table, alongside the `select` it already receives through the model's `grants:` config. How are those two privileges configured?
A. As further keys in the same `grants:` config — `grants: {select: [...], read_metadata: [...], usage: [...]}`
B. From a `post-hook` on the model — the `grants:` config does not carry those two privileges on Databricks
C. Under `grants:` with the `+` prefix, which is required for any privilege other than `select`
D. In `dbt_project.yml` rather than on the model, since non-`select` privileges are set at project level

**29.** A project has four models, each carrying `contract: {enforced: true}` and each declaring `id` as `data_type: text` while its SELECT returns an integer: a `table`, a `view`, an `incremental` with `on_schema_change: fail`, and an `ephemeral` that a fifth model selects from. What does `dbt run --full-refresh` report?
A. Four failures — an enforced contract is checked on every materialization that carries one
B. Three failures, and a warning that the ephemeral model's contract cannot be enforced
C. Three failures, and nothing at all said about the ephemeral model — its consumer builds on the violating SQL
D. One failure — only a `table` writes column DDL, so only a table can be checked against a declared type

**30.** A contract declares `not_null` and `check` constraints. On which platform is neither even definable — rejected rather than accepted-and-unenforced?
A. Snowflake
B. Spark
C. Databricks
D. Athena

**31.** How is a `check` constraint declared, compared with `not_null` or `primary_key`?
A. With a `columns:` list naming every column the condition spans
B. With a free-text `expression`, whose SQL dbt passes through to the DDL
C. With an `operator` and a `value`, which dbt renders into a predicate
D. Identically — `check` takes no extra keys and infers the condition from the column's `data_type`

**32.** You need to confirm whether Databricks enforces a `foreign_key`. Where in the dbt docs is that documented?
A. On the Databricks configs page, under its constraints section
B. On the model-contracts page and on the constraints reference page — each carries a `Platform constraint support` table
C. Only on the model-contracts page; the constraints reference points back to it rather than duplicating the table
D. Nowhere in the dbt docs — only in Databricks' own documentation

**33.** A model sets `deprecation_date: 2026-07-01T12:00:00`, with no UTC offset. Which timezone does dbt apply?
A. UTC always — deprecation dates are normalised on parse
B. The warehouse's session timezone
C. The offset of the machine that last wrote `manifest.json`
D. The system timezone of the environment executing the run

**34.** The v1.11 study guide's governance topic names three bullets. Which of these is **not** one of them?
A. Contracts
B. Model versions
C. `access`
D. Constraints

**35.** A contracted column declares `data_type: numeric` with no precision or scale. What does dbt do?
A. Errors — a contract requires a fully specified type
B. Warns about unintended rounding, and builds the model
C. Builds silently; precision and scale are stripped before comparison anyway
D. Warns, and refuses to build until `warn_unenforced: false` is set

**36.** A Snowflake model declares both a `primary_key` (accepted but never checked) and a `check` (not definable there). Which setting silences only the first?
A. `warn_unenforced: false`
B. `warn_unsupported: false`
C. Either — both cover any constraint the platform does not fully honour
D. Neither; both warnings are on unconditionally and cannot be silenced

## Answer key

**1. B.** The contract is enforced at "preflight" — dbt compiles the model's SELECT, introspects the output column names and types, and compares against the YAML contract *before* issuing any DDL. A mismatch fails the build before the warehouse is touched. Option A would be too late — the DDL would have already written the wrong shape. Option C describes data tests, which run after materialization and check row content, not schema. Option D is unrelated — `dbt docs generate` does not enforce contracts. Source: `/docs/mesh/govern/model-contracts`.

**2. A.** dbt's contract documentation is explicit that contracts apply to *all* columns in a model. An undeclared output column is a contract violation, not a partial contract. The build fails with a preflight error. Option C misrepresents dbt's behaviour (dbt does not silently drop columns). Option B describes a different semantic that dbt does not offer. Option D has the phase wrong: the preflight check runs against the compiled SELECT before any DDL is submitted, so the warehouse never sees the extra column. Source: `/docs/mesh/govern/model-contracts`.

**3. B.** On Snowflake, `not_null` is definable and enforced — the warehouse rejects rows that violate it — and it is the only constraint type Snowflake enforces. Option A states the Snowflake behaviour of `primary_key`, `foreign_key` and `unique`, which are metadata-only, and points it at the one row where enforcement does hold. (Per the §13.3 adapter table: Snowflake enforces `not_null`; `primary_key`, `foreign_key`, and `unique` are metadata-only; `check` is **not supported**.) Option C is wrong on Snowflake specifically — `not_null` is the row Snowflake does support; the adapter that supports no constraint at all is Athena, and Spark defines `not_null` without enforcing it. Option D is unrelated — `unique_key` is an incremental-materialization config, not a constraint mechanic. Source: `/reference/resource-properties/constraints`.

**4. D.** `check` constraints are definable-and-enforced on Postgres and Databricks. Snowflake, BigQuery, Redshift, and Athena do not support `check` syntax at all. Spark accepts `check` syntax as metadata-only (definable but not enforced — the DDL carries the constraint, but Spark does not reject violating rows). Databricks is the discriminating case and worth stating precisely. Once a `CHECK` is attached to a Delta table the *platform* enforces it, on that write and every later one — that is real enforcement, not metadata. What is not build-time is the moment dbt attaches it: dbt issues the `CREATE`, loads the rows, and only then `ALTER TABLE ... ADD CONSTRAINT`. If the data already violates the predicate that `ALTER` fails, and what you are left holding is a relation that exists, is populated with the violating rows, and carries no constraint at all. Contrast Postgres, where the constraint is live on the `CREATE` and no violating row ever lands. That ordering is why dbt's own platform note calls a Databricks constraint definable-but-not-enforced *at build time*, while the support matrix marks `check` Enforced (§13.3) — the two are describing different moments, not disagreeing about the platform. Source: `/reference/resource-properties/constraints`.

**5. B.** On Snowflake, BigQuery, Redshift, and Databricks, `primary_key` and `foreign_key` are definable but not enforced — the DDL carries the constraint as metadata, but the warehouse will not reject violating writes. For runtime enforcement of uniqueness on a cloud warehouse, pair the `primary_key` declaration with a dbt `unique` data test that actually queries the materialized table. Option A mischaracterises — this is documented behaviour, not a bug. Option C is incorrect — enforcement varies by adapter and by constraint type. Option D invents a config that does not exist. Source: `/reference/resource-properties/constraints`.

**6. D.** `versions:` allows a model to exist in multiple numbered shapes simultaneously — typically v1 and v2 materialized side by side. Consumers who are ready for the new shape pin to v2 via `ref('my_model', v=2)`; consumers who need a cycle to migrate continue reading v1 via `ref('my_model', v=1)`. Option A is not a dbt feature (rollback is handled via source control, not `versions:`). Option B describes custom schemas, which are a naming config and produce one model per target, not several shapes of one model. Option C is superficial — the semver parallel exists but misses the mechanic (both versions materialize concurrently). Source: `/docs/mesh/govern/model-versions`.

**7. A.** The `latest_version:` property reference is explicit: if unspecified, dbt defaults to the largest numeric version identifier. With versions 1, 2, 3 declared, the default `latest_version` is 3, and an unpinned `ref()` resolves there. Option B would be the case only if `latest_version: 1` were set. Option C invents a requirement (the property is optional). Option D is wrong — version resolution is deterministic. Source: `/reference/resource-properties/latest_version`.

**8. D.** When `defined_in:` is unset on a version entry, dbt looks for a file named `<model_name>_v<v>.sql` — so v2's file is `dim_customer_v2.sql`. When `defined_in:` is set, it overrides the default convention — so v1's file is `dim_customer_legacy.sql` (the `defined_in` value, plus `.sql`). Option A ignores `defined_in:`. Option B assumes the latest version can drop the `_v2` suffix by default, which it cannot in this config. Option C is wrong on v2 for the same reason as B. Source: `/reference/resource-properties/versions`.

**9. A.** Before the deprecation date, dbt emits a deprecation warning on every build that references the deprecated model or version. The warning names the upcoming removal date and, if a newer version is available, names that too. The build itself completes successfully. Option B is what `--warn-error` does — and it does it here, before the date, not only after it (§13.5). Option C is wrong — the warning is the whole point of setting the date in advance. Option D is invented behaviour. Source: `/reference/resource-properties/deprecation_date`.

**10. A.** The restriction is a state-comparison check rather than something a plain `dbt build` notices: dbt compares the current manifest against `--state`, walks the nodes that have been removed as well as those that changed, and treats a contracted model deleted before its `deprecation_date` as a breaking change. On a **versioned** model that breaking change is fatal — `Breaking change to contract Error in model dim_customer ... Contracted model 'model.credora.dim_customer.v1' was deleted or renamed.` — which is the rail that stops a producer dropping a version consumers still pin to. Option B is the trap: `state:modified` does compare contracts, and it inspects removed nodes. Option C is the **unversioned** behaviour — with no `versions:` block the same deletion is a warning and the run exits successfully; that asymmetry is the fact worth carrying into the exam. Option D inverts the rule: once the date has passed, the deletion stops being a breaking change at all. Source: `/reference/resource-properties/deprecation_date`.

**11. B.** `protected` is the default. It allows any model in the same project to `ref()` the model, regardless of group. This matches how projects worked before `access:` existed, so existing projects that have not explicitly declared access continue to work unchanged. Option A would require an explicit declaration plus a group assignment. Option C requires explicit opt-in as a cross-project API. Option D is wrong — `access:` is optional. Source: `/docs/mesh/govern/model-access`.

**12. C.** `access: private` enforces at parse time. A cross-group `ref()` into a private model triggers `DbtReferenceError` immediately — before any SQL compiles and before any DDL runs. This is the same failure class as referencing a non-existent model: loud, immediate, and visible in the PR that introduced the invalid reference. Option A understates the enforcement. Option B confuses `access:` (dbt-level) with `grants:` (warehouse-level). Option D is invented behaviour. Source: `/docs/mesh/govern/model-access`.

**13. C.** Ephemeral models are pure CTEs inlined into consumers — they have no warehouse relation for a cross-project consumer to address. The `model-access` page is explicit: `public` cannot be combined with `ephemeral`. Option A is allowed — a table has a relation to address. Option B is allowed too, and tests a different rule: `access:` and `group:` are orthogonal configs that compose, so a public model can carry a group tag for ownership (§13.8 shows exactly that combination). Option D is allowed — private restrictions apply to `ref()` resolution, which works fine for ephemerals within the same project. Source: `/docs/mesh/govern/model-access`.

**14. D.** Groups are a namespace mechanism. A model with `group: finance` but `access: protected` (the default) is not restricted — any model in the project can still `ref()` it. The group becomes behaviourally meaningful only when combined with `access: private`, which says "same-group only." Option A overstates — groups and access are separate configs that compose. Option C is wrong — `groups:` does not replace `meta:`; ownership flows through both. Option B is wrong — per the docs, a model belongs to **exactly one** group. Sources: `/docs/build/groups`, `/reference/resource-configs/group`.

**15. A.** Grants are applied post-DDL, as part of every materialization. The `grants` reference page shows the sequence: dbt creates the table, then issues `GRANT SELECT ON ... TO ...`.

On every subsequent build dbt reconciles them against the config, issuing only the statements needed to close the gap. If the model does not materialize (error, deferred resolution), no grant is issued. Option B has the timing wrong. Option C would leave grants to drift over time. Option D invents a command — `dbt grant` is not a real invocation. Source: `/reference/resource-configs/grants`.

**16. C.** By default, model-level `grants:` replaces project-level `grants:` — option A would remove `bi_reader`. The `+`-prefix on the privilege name (`+select`) switches to additive semantics: the model-level list is *added* to the project-level list. Option B restates the project-level grantee, which the stem rules out, and drifts the moment that list changes. Option D invents a config key that does not exist. Source: `/reference/resource-configs/grants`.

**17. B.** `grants:` is the warehouse-privilege config. If the service account is not in the `select` list (and no external grant has been applied outside dbt), the account will not have read permission on the materialized relation. `access: private` (A) restricts which dbt models can `ref()` the model — it does not affect warehouse-level reads by BI tools, which query the materialized table directly. Option C is unrelated to warehouse privileges. Option D is about schema enforcement, not access control. Source: `/reference/resource-configs/grants`.

**18. C.** The mechanic comes first: `private` means "same-group only", so the private models *and* every legitimate caller need `group:` assignments before the declaration restricts the right things. That is what defeats option A: an ungrouped model is in no group, so dbt rejects the producing team's own downstream `ref()`s as well — `... is private to the '' group`, exit 2. A does block cross-team references, by breaking the whole pipeline. Order the two steps that way and there is no reason to wait: `access:` is a preventive control, and its value is refusing the first cross-team `ref()` rather than documenting one that already exists. A coupling you discover after the fact is a migration to negotiate; one `private` refused at compile time is a two-line conversation. The cost people fear — every new legitimate consumer becoming a group-membership ticket — is the control working, and it is cheaper than the alternative precisely while the number of couplings is still zero. Option B dismisses the group tags as bookkeeping, which leaves nothing to switch on later; a code-review convention is not something `ref()` resolution can enforce. Option D inverts the intent — `public` advertises cross-project availability, not internal-only. Sources: `/docs/mesh/govern/model-access`, `/docs/build/groups`.

**19. B.** This is the standard versioning use case: a breaking column rename on a cross-team-consumed model. The producer's mistake was renaming in place (which takes down every downstream dashboard that consumed the old column). The right pattern is versions, published and retired following the migration flow in §13.4. Option A is an anti-answer (defensive downstream building doesn't scale — producers owe consumers stable interfaces). Option C describes what a contract would do: contracts *prevent* the rename from being shipped silently (the YAML would change and the build would fail before drift), but they don't *solve* the rename — you still need versions to actually ship the rename without taking down consumers. (A team with serious governance uses contracts AND versions together.) Option D addresses a different problem (cross-team coupling, not schema evolution). Sources: `/docs/mesh/govern/model-versions`, `/reference/resource-properties/versions`, `/reference/resource-properties/latest_version`, `/reference/resource-properties/deprecation_date`.

**20. B.** Contract comparison reduces both sides to a base type before comparing, so a `varchar` matches a `varchar` and a `numeric` matches a `numeric` however either is parameterised. The DDL is then written from the contract, which is why `nm` lands at `varchar(257)` and `amt` at `numeric(38, 6)`. Option C applies the same rule but lets the SELECT win the DDL — a natural reading if you take the contract to be a check and nothing more, and the right answer for a *view*, whose DDL carries no column spec at all. The stem names a table. Option A is the strict reading the docs rule out. Option D invents a split between length and scale; neither is compared. The distinction is what makes §13.3's bare-`numeric` warning coherent:

the risk there is what the platform stores, not what the contract matched. Source: `/reference/resource-configs/contract`.

**21. D.** The pairing is rejected during parsing, not during the run: `Invalid value for on_schema_change: sync_all_columns. Models materialized as incremental with contracts enabled must set on_schema_change to 'append_new_columns' or 'fail'`. The reason is that `sync_all_columns` lets the relation's shape drift to match the SELECT, which is the one thing an enforced contract exists to prevent — so dbt refuses the configuration rather than the run. Option A puts a real failure at the wrong phase, and the phase is the discrimination. Option B inverts the precedence. Option C invents a silent fallback dbt does not perform. Source: `/reference/resource-configs/contract`.

**22. A.** `definition_type` is the model's side and `contract_type` is the YAML's side, so an empty `contract_type` means the SELECT emits a column the YAML has never heard of, and an empty `definition_type` means the YAML lists one the SELECT no longer emits. Row 1 is fixed in the YAML and row 2 in either place. Option B reads the two columns the wrong way round — `ordered_at` is already in the contract, which is why it has a `contract_type` at all. Option C treats both rows as type mismatches, which is a third `mismatch_reason` neither row carries. Option D reaches for `alias_types`, which translates a generic type name into the platform's spelling and has nothing to say about a column that is present on one side only. Source: `/reference/resource-configs/contract`.

**23. D.** `to:` takes a `ref()` or a `source()` expression and nothing else; a literal relation name stops the parse with `Invalid 'ref' or 'source' syntax on foreign key constraint 'to' ...`, at the column level and at the model level alike (§13.3). The expression is also what puts the relationship into the graph: the referenced model becomes a real dependency, and the constraint resolves to whatever schema the target lands in for that target profile. Option A is the belief that parse error refutes — a literal name really would contribute nothing to the DAG, but it is not a spelling dbt accepts. Option B invents an inference; dbt performs no such reading of the target's `primary_key` — omit `to_columns` and it silently emits no constraint rather than inferring one. Option C confuses a declared constraint with a `relationships` test, which is what actually validates on every platform that does not enforce `foreign_key` — that is, everywhere except Postgres (§13.3). Source: `/reference/resource-properties/constraints`.

**24. C.** `exclude:` is legal only where `include:` is `all` or `'*'` (the two spellings are synonyms) — pairing it with an explicit include list is a hard parse failure, not a warning and not an ignored key. Option A is that rule satisfied. Option B is legal because the at-most-one limit applies to include/exclude elements: an ordinary column entry may sit beside one and override the top-level definition of that column. Option D is the plain form — a column list with no inheritance element, which overrides the columns it names and inherits the rest, and which is what most versioned models actually carry. Source: `/reference/resource-properties/versions`.

**25. C.** `latest_version_pointer` arrives after 1.11. At the target version dbt neither rejects the key nor warns about it — the model parses, all three versions build, and no relation appears at the bare model name. That silence is what makes the config worth recognising: nothing in the run output would tell the developer their expectation was not met. Option A assumes unknown config keys are rejected, which dbt does not do. Option B assumes a forward-compatibility warning; none is emitted here, because dbt runs its JSON-schema config validation on Snowflake, Databricks, BigQuery and Redshift only — on any of those four the same YAML raises `CustomKeyInConfigDeprecation`, still without failing. Option D is the expectation the developer brought, and the one the run will appear to confirm. Sources: `/docs/mesh/govern/model-versions`, `/reference/resource-properties/latest_version`.

**26. B.** Two preconditions gate this check, and the stem satisfies one of them. The `state:` selector plus `--state` is what makes dbt compare manifests and notice a node that has disappeared, so B and C are the only invocations that see the deletion at all. Between them, the model's lack of a `versions:` block decides the outcome: an unversioned contracted model deleted before its date produces `[WARNING]: Breaking change to contracted, unversioned model ... was deleted or renamed` and the run exits successfully, while option C's error is what a **versioned** model would raise (Q10). Option A has no earlier manifest to compare against, so nothing fires. Option D supplies `--state` without a `state:` selector, which performs no comparison — the flag makes the comparison possible, the selector is what runs it. Source: `/reference/resource-properties/deprecation_date`.

**27. D.** dbt modifies a relation's grants only where a `grants:` config is attached to the node. Remove the config and dbt stops managing grants there; the privileges already on the relation stay exactly as they are, and no log line reports it. Option A is the trap, and it is the reading a candidate arrives at from the reconciliation rule alone — but revoking-everyone is what `select: []` means, and an empty list is an instruction where a deleted block is a withdrawal. Option B adds observability the deletion case does not have. Option C invents a guard rail; dbt keeps no record that it once granted on the relation. Source: `/reference/resource-configs/grants`.

**28. B.** `read_metadata` and `usage` are the two Databricks privileges the `grants:` config does not carry; the reference sends you to a hook for them, which means a `post-hook` issuing the `GRANT` statements itself (Ch 6 §6.5). The general shape of option A is right on most platforms — a privilege name is a key under `grants:` — which is what makes it the answer to reject knowingly rather than on sight. Option C misreads the `+` prefix, which switches a privilege from replace to merge and has nothing to do with which privileges are supported. Option D invents a project-level restriction; `grants:` is configurable at either level for any privilege it supports. Source: `/reference/resource-configs/grants`.

**29. C.** `Done. PASS=1 WARN=0 ERROR=3 SKIP=0 NO-OP=0 TOTAL=4`, and the summary line above it reads *Completed with 3 errors, 0 partial successes, and **0 warnings***. The `table`, the `view` and the `incremental` each fail with the contract-violation table — `| id | INTEGER | TEXT | data type mismatch |` — which disposes of D: a `view` writes no column DDL and is checked anyway. A is the belief the test point exists to correct. The ephemeral model is *found* (`Found 5 models`) and is genuinely compiled — it arrives in its consumer as `with __dbt__cte__c_eph as (...)` — but it is never a run node, so its contract is never compared to anything, and the consumer is the `PASS=1`. B is the designed near-miss, because the neighbouring case does warn: a *constraint* on a contracted view prints `Constraint types are not supported for view materializations and will be ignored` (§13.3). dbt warns about the part of a contract it cannot honour on a view and says nothing about a whole contract it cannot honour on an ephemeral model — the log carries zero `[WARNING]` lines. Source: `/reference/resource-configs/contract`. Observed on dbt Core 1.11.14.

**30. D.** Athena is the one platform that defines **no** constraint type: all five are rejected outright. Spark is the instructive contrast and the strongest distractor, because it fails the other way — it accepts all five into the DDL and checks none of them, so a contract there looks satisfied and enforces nothing. The difference matters for what you get told: a not-definable constraint raises `warn_unsupported`, while a definable-but-unenforced one raises `warn_unenforced`. Neither Athena nor Spark belongs in a design that leans on constraints for correctness, but only one of them will say so. Source: `/docs/mesh/govern/model-contracts`, whose platform-support table marks every constraint type not definable and not enforced on Athena, and definable but not enforced on Spark.

**31. B.** `check` is the one constraint that carries a condition, and it carries it as a free-text `expression` — ordinary SQL that dbt passes into the DDL without interpreting. That is what makes it the most portable-looking and least portable constraint in practice: the expression is written in the platform's dialect, so a contract that reads fine on Postgres can fail on another warehouse for reasons the YAML does not reveal. A is worth separating because `columns:` is real, just elsewhere: a model-level `primary_key` or `foreign_key` spanning several columns uses it. Source: `/reference/resource-properties/constraints` — "`expression`: Free text input to qualify the constraint."

**32. B.** The per-adapter table has **two** homes. `/docs/mesh/govern/model-contracts#platform-constraint-support` carries it as one tab per adapter, and `/reference/resource-properties/constraints` carries its own `Platform constraint support` section with the same seven adapters — Redshift, Snowflake, BigQuery, Postgres, Spark, Databricks, Athena — and the same five constraint types, Databricks `foreign_key` row included (definable, not enforced). What carries **nothing** is the adapter config page: `/reference/resource-configs/databricks-configs` has no constraints section at all, which is what makes A the instinctive wrong answer and the reason the location is worth memorising. D is defeated by both of the above. Revisit **Ch 13 §13.3**. Cognitive level: recall.

**33. D.** `deprecation_date` accepts three shapes — RFC 3339 with an offset, RFC 3339 without one, and date-only — and a value with no offset falls back to the **system timezone of the environment running dbt**. That is the whole risk: the same manifest deprecates at different instants on a developer's laptop, on a CI runner set to UTC, and on a scheduler in another region, and the difference only shows up as a warning appearing a few hours early or late. Write the offset explicitly for anything a team coordinates around. Source: `/reference/resource-properties/deprecation_date` — "When `deprecation_date` does not include an offset from UTC, then it is interpreted as being in the system time zone of the dbt execution environment."

**34. C.** The three bullets are **contracts**, **versions** and **constraints**. `access` was dropped as a bullet at v1.11 and now sits as a config beneath them, alongside groups and grants. Dropped from the outline is not the same as out of scope — `access` is still real dbt behaviour that a stem can rest on, and it interacts with the three directly, since an `ephemeral` model cannot be `public`. What the change tells you is where the assessment weight sits: the three named bullets are what the guide expects you to be able to design with, and `access` is expected as supporting knowledge. Source: the v1.11 study guide's governance topic for the bullet list itself; `/docs/mesh/govern/model-access` for `access`, including the rule that a model materialized `ephemeral` cannot be `public`.

**35. B.** Declaring a contracted column as a bare `numeric` or `decimal` — no precision, no scale — draws a warning about unintended rounding, and the model still builds. C is the distractor that is half true and worth untangling: size, precision and scale genuinely **are** stripped before the contract comparison, so `numeric(10, 2)` does satisfy a `numeric(38, 6)` contract. The warning is not about the comparison; it is about the DDL, where the platform's own default precision applies and can round values in ways nobody chose. Write the precision you mean. Source: `/reference/resource-configs/contract` — dbt "provides a warning if you don't specify precision and scale when providing a numeric data type", and separately "will not compare granular details such as size, precision, or scale". The same page also says the default scale "might cause it to fail contract enforcement", which overstates it and is what makes A tempting: because the comparison strips precision and scale, there is nothing left for enforcement to fail on. Executed on dbt 1.11.14 with dbt-postgres 1.11.0, the bare `numeric` column warns and the model builds `OK`.

**36. A.** The two warnings split on a precise boundary. `warn_unenforced` fires for a constraint the platform **will accept but will not check** — `primary_key` on Snowflake, which still goes into the DDL. `warn_unsupported` fires for one that is **not definable at all**. Both default to `True`, and setting either to `False` silences that class only. So the model here needs `warn_unenforced: false` on the `primary_key` to quieten it while still being told about the `check`. C is the answer that comes from treating both as a single "this constraint is not real" warning, which is exactly the distinction the pair exists to preserve. Source: `/reference/resource-properties/constraints`, which defines `warn_unenforced` for constraints "supported by your platform but not enforced" and `warn_unsupported` for those the platform "doesn't support at all".

# Chapter 14

# In practice: a Databricks dbt project walkthrough

> **Scope.** This chapter is the book's one integrated walkthrough. It picks up the fictional `credora` project that has appeared in "In practice" sidebars from Ch 2 onward and walks it end-to-end in seven sections — the project file (Ch 2), sources at scale (Ch 3), one Delta-merge incremental (Ch 4), three hook-driven macros (Ch 6), testing (Ch 7), governance (Ch 13), slim CI (Ch 12) — then the disclaimer in §14.8 and the summary in §14.9. Every section exercises a concept from an earlier chapter at production scale; no new concepts are taught. The point is to see how the pieces compose — and where a mature project deliberately *does not* reach for a primitive the blueprint lists.

**Prerequisites.** This chapter assumes you have read Chapters 2, 3, 4, 6, 7, 12, and 13. It cross-references those chapters by section number rather than re-teaching them. If any of those chapters is fuzzy, go back before reading on — this chapter will not repeat the underlying explanations.

**Cheat-sheet pointer.** No cheat-sheet section maps to this chapter on its own. Each section below is a worked example of a cheat-sheet bullet from an earlier chapter; the exam-morning recall surface is still the front-of-book sheet.

**No new blueprint material.** Ch 14 teaches nothing new. Every pattern you see here was introduced in an earlier chapter; this chapter just shows what they look like when stitched together at scale. A reader skimming for exam coverage can skip to §14.9's checklist. A reader who wants an integrated mental model of "what does a real dbt project feel like" should read the whole chapter.

**Credora at a glance.** First introduced in Ch 2 §2.6 and referenced in every "In practice" sidebar since: a multi-market consumer fintech running `credora` on Databricks with Delta Lake and Unity Catalog. Scale signals: **over 1,000 models**, **several hundred macros**, **around a dozen Databricks catalogs**, and a handful of installed open-source packages.

**The runnable counterpart — companion repo.** Credora is illustrative, not cloneable. To *run* a dbt project on your own laptop as you read this chapter, use this book's companion, the open-source repo at `https://github.com/snowleafbooks/dbt-analytics-engineer-certification` — a Postgres project that opens in VS Code Dev Containers and green-builds end to end, pinned by its own `requirements.txt` (§1.6). It exercises every exam concept that works on a local warehouse (four incremental strategies including native Postgres `MERGE`, snapshots, unit tests, custom generic tests, dispatch, contracts, groups and `access:`, grants, state/defer, slim CI) and ships a dedicated `exercises/` folder of deliberately-broken cases for triage practice.

The split is deliberate. Ch 14 shows the shape of a *mature* project at Databricks scale — sharding by market, Unity Catalog tags, Delta-merge incrementals, masking policies, tens-of-thousands of test invocations — and covers what the companion cannot run on Postgres at all: Delta properties, column masks and Unity Catalog governance. Everything you can genuinely run and break is in the companion, and this chapter does not re-demonstrate it at length.

---

## 14.1 Project-file anatomy (cross-ref Ch 2)

Chapter 2 introduced `dbt_project.yml` as a five-line starter. At Credora's scale, the same file is a structured document that nests every market under `models:` and wires every global behaviour into hooks, vars, and dispatch order. The shape below is a condensed fictional excerpt — around eighty lines — that shows every structural move a mature project makes. It is illustrative, not reproduced from any single proprietary source.

```
# dbt_project.yml - condensed ~80-line fictional excerpt
name: 'credora'
version: '1.0.0'
profile: 'credora'
config-version: 2
require-dbt-version: ">=1.11.0,<1.12.0"

model-paths: ["models"]
seed-paths: ["seeds"]
test-paths: ["tests"]
macro-paths: ["macros"]
snapshot-paths: ["snapshots"]
analysis-paths: ["analyses"]
clean-targets: ["target", "dbt_packages"]

vars:
  raw_catalog: "{{ env_var('RAW_CATALOG', 'cr_partner_ingest_dev') }}"
  run_date:    "{{ run_started_at.strftime('%Y-%m-%d') }}"
  enable_masking:       false          # feature-flag: Unity Catalog column masks
  enable_cdf_on_gold:   true           # feature-flag: Delta CDF on gold marts
  limit_in_dev:         true           # dev/CI-only LIMIT injection
  include_experimental_markets: false

dispatch:
  - macro_namespace: dbt_utils
    search_order: ['credora', 'dbt_utils']

on-run-start:
  - "{{ require_select_arg() }}"
  - "{{ generate_masking_functions() if var('enable_masking') else '' }}"
```

```
on-run-end:
  - "{% if target.name == 'prd' %}{{ dbt_artifacts.upload_results(results) }}{% endif
    %}"

query-comment:
  comment: "{{ query_comment(node) }}"
  append: true

models:
  +file_format: delta
  +persist_docs:
    relation: true
    columns:  true

  credora:
    +materialized: view            # project-wide default

    cr_global:
      +database: cr_global
      staging:      { +schema: staging,      +materialized: view }
      intermediate: { +schema: intermediate, +materialized: ephemeral }
      marts:        { +schema: analytics,    +materialized: table }

    cr_uk:
      +database: cr_uk
      +databricks_tags: { market: "uk", owner: "@analytics-uk" }
      staging: { +schema: staging, +materialized: view }
      gold:    { +schema: gold,    +materialized: incremental,
                 +grants: { select: ['credora_bi_reader', 'credora_analytics_reader'] } }

      marts:   { +schema: analytics, +materialized: table,
                 +grants: { select: ['credora_bi_reader'] } }

    cr_us:     { +database: cr_us,     +databricks_tags: { market: "us" } }
    cr_apac_1: { +database: cr_apac_1, +databricks_tags: { market: "apac_1" } }
    cr_apac_2: { +database: cr_apac_2, +databricks_tags: { market: "apac_2" } }
    cr_emea_1: { +database: cr_emea_1, +databricks_tags: { market: "emea_1" } }

seeds:
  credora:
    +schema: reference
    +quote_columns: true

snapshots:
  credora:
    +schema: snapshots
    +file_format: delta
```

Six structural moves are doing the heavy lifting. Each one maps to a specific piece of Ch 2's foundation, scaled up.

**1. Multi-catalog nesting under `models:`.** Each of the six catalogs (`cr_global`, `cr_uk`, `cr_us`, `cr_apac_1`, `cr_apac_2`, `cr_emea_1`) has its own `+database` at the catalog level. Deeper keys (`staging:`, `intermediate:`, `marts:`) set `+schema` and `+materialized` per layer. The `+databricks_tags` block attaches Unity Catalog tags to every table built under that branch. Ch 2 §2.4 introduced the `config-by-path` mechanism; this is what it looks like when a project has to route models across catalogs at Credora's scale without touching each model's YAML.

**2. Global `on-run-start` hooks.** Two hook macros fire before any model builds: `require_select_arg()` (Macro 2, §14.4) raises a compiler error without `--select`/`--exclude`/`--selector`, which abandons the invocation before anything is built, so a bare `dbt build` cannot accidentally rebuild the whole project; and `generate_masking_functions()` (Macro 3, §14.4) issues Unity Catalog mask-function DDL at run start, gated behind the `enable_masking` feature flag. Ch 6 §6.5 covered project-level hooks; this is the idiomatic place for guardrails and run-start infrastructure. The dbt Labs hooks-and-operations reference at `/docs/build/hooks-operations` documents the hook surface both macros build on.

**3. `on-run-end` artifact upload.** `results` is the run-context variable dbt exposes to `on-run-end` and to nothing else; Ch 6 §6.5 covers what it carries. The `dbt_artifacts` package's `upload_results(results)` operation writes a normalised representation of `run_results.json` into warehouse tables, so the platform team can query run history — which models are slowing down, which tests fail most. The `{% if target.name == 'prd' %}` guard is what keeps CI artifacts out of those tables. The package is public at brooklyn-data/dbt_artifacts, and its README documents this exact `on-run-end` pattern.

**4. `vars` as feature-flag toggles.** A handful of project-level vars control run-time behaviour without code changes: `raw_catalog` routes sources between dev/CI/prd catalogs; `enable_masking` and `enable_cdf_on_gold` are boolean toggles that macros and model configs read; `limit_in_dev` controls a row-limit injection that keeps sandbox runs fast; `include_experimental_markets` gates catalogs that are not yet promoted. This is the Ch 6 §6.2 `var()` pattern applied to project-scope feature flags. See also the dbt Labs "Environment variables" guidance at `/reference/dbt-jinja-functions/env_var`.

**5. `dispatch`: search order for adapter-specific macro overrides.** Every `search_order` entry is a package name — the value of that project's `name:` key — so `credora` names the project's own macros, and the block puts them ahead of `dbt_utils`. When a model calls `{{ dbt_utils.generate_surrogate_key(...) }}`, dbt searches the `credora` namespace first for `databricks__generate_surrogate_key`, then `default__generate_surrogate_key`, and falls through to `dbt_utils` only if neither exists. The team ships a Databricks-specific implementation without touching any model's SQL; Ch 8 §8.8 has the full override story. Ch 6 §6.7 and the dbt Labs dispatch reference at `/reference/dbt-jinja-functions/dispatch` are the standard surface.

**6. `+persist_docs` as a global default.** Every model inherits `persist_docs: {relation: true, columns: true}` — every table and column description written into dbt YAML flows into Databricks' Unity Catalog as `COMMENT` metadata. Ch 9 §9.4 introduced the config; setting it once at the top of `models:` avoids repeating it on every layer. `+file_format: delta` sits beside it for the same reason, and §14.3 explains what depends on it. The reference page is `/reference/resource-configs/persist_docs`.

**Dual source.** The structural shape — multi-catalog nesting, global hooks, feature-flag vars, dispatch ordering, project-wide `persist_docs` — is documented as best practice across dbt Labs' How we structure our dbt projects guide (for the `models:` layering convention) and the `/reference/dbt_project.yml` standard reference (for every top-level key shown above).

### What scales and what does not

Not everything in a small project grows with model count. What does:

- `models:` nesting — linear in the number of catalog/layer/schema combinations.
- Feature-flag vars — grows with the number of cross-cutting behaviours the team wants to toggle.
- Hook macros — grows with the number of global guardrails and instrumentation hooks.

What does not:

- Top-level keys (`name`, `version`, `profile`, `*-paths`, `clean-targets`) — the same five to ten lines at any scale.
- `dispatch:` — one block per package namespace being overridden; rarely more than two or three entries even in large projects.
- `require-dbt-version` — a single pin.

The pedagogical point: a `dbt_project.yml` that runs to several hundred lines is not several hundred lines of creative writing. It is the five-line starter plus `models:` nesting driven by the catalog/layer matrix. Read one such file and you can read them all.

---

## 14.2 Sources at scale (cross-ref Ch 3)

Chapter 3 introduced `sources.yml` with a single source and a two-table list. At Credora's scale, each market catalog has its own `sources.yml`, each source uses `env_var()` to route between dev/CI/prd raw catalogs, and freshness is configured selectively — on the handful of critical-path tables that feed real-time pipelines, not on the hundreds of long-tail reference tables that would just generate noisy alerts.

The shape below is a condensed fictional excerpt from one market's sources file.

```
# models/cr_uk/_sources.yml - ~25-line fictional excerpt
version: 2

sources:
  - name: uk_raw_events
    description: >
      Partner ingestion for UK market events - credit checks, offer views,
      application submits. Loaded by the partner ingestion pipeline.
    database: "{{ env_var('RAW_CATALOG', 'cr_partner_ingest_dev') }}"
    schema: uk_events
    loaded_at_field: _ingested_at
    freshness:
      warn_after:  {count: 1, period: hour}
      error_after: {count: 6, period: hour}
    tables:
      - name: credit_check
      - name: offer_view
      - name: application_submit
        freshness:
          warn_after:  {count: 30, period: minute}
          error_after: {count: 2,  period: hour}

  - name: uk_partner_feed
    description: "Third-party credit-bureau extract; weekly cadence."
    database: "{{ env_var('RAW_CATALOG', 'cr_partner_ingest_dev') }}"
    schema: uk_bureau
    tables:
      - name: bureau_score_weekly
      - name: bureau_tradeline_weekly

  - name: uk_internal_telemetry
    description: "Internal product telemetry stream (app events, server logs)."
    database: "{{ env_var('RAW_CATALOG', 'cr_partner_ingest_dev') }}"
    schema: uk_telemetry
    tables:
```

```
      - name: app_event_stream
      - name: session_stream
```

Three patterns worth naming.

**1. Three source systems, not thirty.** Even at Credora's scale, a market's raw-ingestion surface is typically a small number of source systems: an ingest pipeline (`uk_raw_events`), a partner feed (`uk_partner_feed`), and an internal telemetry stream (`uk_internal_telemetry`). The count of source *tables* can be large; the count of source *systems* rarely is. Ch 3 §3.2 introduced the source-system-vs-table distinction; at scale, this distinction is the scaffolding that keeps the sources file legible.

**2. `env_var('RAW_CATALOG', ...)` for dev/CI/prd routing.** Every source's `database:` reads from the same env var, falling back to a dev catalog if unset. The prd CI job exports `RAW_CATALOG=cr_partner_ingest`; the local sandbox uses the default `cr_partner_ingest_dev`; the slim-CI job exports a third catalog that holds the CI fixture data. One project, three environments, zero SQL branching. Ch 3 §3.6 covered this exact pattern; the reference page is `/reference/dbt-jinja-functions/env_var`, which explicitly lists `sources.yml` as a supported call site.

**3. Freshness on the critical path only.** The `uk_raw_events` source has a source-level freshness default (1-hour warn, 6-hour error) that every table inherits. `application_submit` overrides with a tighter 30-minute warn / 2-hour error because it feeds the real-time lending-offer matcher. `uk_partner_feed` has no freshness at all. Note what the argument for that actually is: a weekly feed is not too infrequent to monitor, it is monitored on a weekly scale — thresholds of, say, 8-day warn and 10-day error would be perfectly coherent, and a source-level default of 1 hour / 6 hours would alarm every six days for no operational reason. Credora skips it because a late bureau extract pages nobody: the downstream models tolerate a stale week. Set the numbers from the cadence, and the decision to monitor at all from the consequence. `uk_internal_telemetry` also skips freshness; the team runs its own schema-level monitors on that stream.

The broader rule: **freshness is useful when staleness has an operational consequence**. If a stale source doesn't trigger a page, it doesn't belong under `freshness:` — the alert costs a message per stale table per refresh cycle and buys nothing. Ch 3 §3.5 has the cost/benefit calculus.

**Dual source.** `env_var()` routing inside `sources.yml` is documented per `/reference/dbt-jinja-functions/env_var`; the freshness YAML shape is documented at `/docs/build/sources#source-data-freshness`. The dbt Labs How we structure our dbt projects — staging guide is the reference for layering `stg_*` models on top of these sources.

---

## 14.3 Incremental Delta merge (cross-ref Ch 4)

Chapter 4 introduced the built-in materializations and the five concerns of an incremental model (`materialized`, `is_incremental()`, `unique_key`, `on_schema_change`, `incremental_strategy`). Chapter 4 §4.8 walked the same `fct_lending_offer_clicks_uk` example in depth; this section is a shorter re-statement of the same model with one tightening — `on_schema_change` moves from `sync_all_columns` to `append_new_columns`. The reason is §14.6: once the model is placed under a contract, `sync_all_columns` is no longer legal. The contract reference page requires contracted incremental models to use `append_new_columns` or `fail`, because silently removing a column would break the contract without bumping a version.

```
-- models/cr_uk/gold/fct_lending_offer_clicks_uk.sql
{{ config(
    materialized='incremental',
```

```
    incremental_strategy='merge',
    unique_key='click_event_id',
    on_schema_change='append_new_columns',
    tblproperties={
        'delta.enableChangeDataFeed': 'true',
        'delta.autoOptimize.optimizeWrite': 'true'
    },
    meta={'owner': '@analytics-engineering'}
) }}

with source_events as (
    select * from {{ ref('stg_offer_click_events_uk') }}
    {% if is_incremental() %}
      where event_received_at > (
        select coalesce(max(event_received_at), '1900-01-01'::timestamp) from {{ this }}
      )
    {% endif %}
)

select
    click_event_id,
    user_id,
    offer_id,
    event_received_at,
    clicked_at,
    source_campaign,
    _loaded_at
from source_events
```

Five choices to read carefully, now in the context of the whole project.

1. **`incremental_strategy='merge'`** — Databricks' native `MERGE INTO`. Credora defaults incremental strategy to `merge` at the project level in `dbt_project.yml`; individual models that need a different strategy (`append` for append-only logs) override in their own `config()`. `merge` also carries a table-format prerequisite the `config()` block does not show: on Spark the strategy requires a `file_format` of `delta`, `iceberg` or `hudi`, and on Databricks `delta` or `hudi`. That is why §14.1 sets `+file_format: delta` once at the top of `models:` rather than on each incremental. The reference page is `/docs/build/incremental-strategy` and the Databricks-specific incremental config page at `/reference/resource-configs/databricks-configs`.
2. **`unique_key='click_event_id'`** — single-column identifier guaranteed unique by the ingestion layer. `merge` needs this to match target rows.
3. **`on_schema_change='append_new_columns'`** — new event fields added upstream are picked up automatically (no `--full-refresh` required), but column *removals* are deliberately *not* mirrored to the gold table: an upstream column rename or drop should be a reviewed, contract-versioning event, not an invisible schema change. See `/docs/build/incremental-models` for the four `on_schema_change` values, and `/reference/resource-configs/contract` for why `sync_all_columns` is not legal once a contract is enforced.
4. **`tblproperties` with `delta.enableChangeDataFeed: 'true'`** — Databricks Change Data Feed (CDF) makes row-level change history readable as a stream. Downstream consumers (a feature store, a Kafka bridge) can subscribe to CDF rather than polling the table. The `delta.autoOptimize.optimizeWrite` toggle is Databricks-specific performance tuning, and it is worth naming precisely because its sibling does something else: **optimized writes** right-size the files a write produces, shuffling before the write so it

lands fewer, larger files. **Auto compaction** (`delta.autoOptimize.autoCompact`) is the separate post-write pass that coalesces small files after the fact. Credora sets the first and leaves the second to scheduled maintenance.
5. **The `is_incremental()` guard inside the `source_events` CTE** — keeps the final `select` clean. Functionally equivalent to putting the guard in the outer `select`; readable-at-scale matters.

**Three assumptions the watermark rests on**, because each one has bitten a real pipeline:

- **An empty target.** `max(event_received_at)` over a table with no rows is `NULL`, and `event_received_at > NULL` is `UNKNOWN`, so the filter admits nothing and the run appends zero rows — succeeding, silently, forever. The `coalesce` to a floor date above is what stops that. The case is not hypothetical: it is what you get after a `--full-refresh` that failed partway, or after someone truncates the table to force a reload.
- **Strictly-increasing timestamps.** `>` rather than `>=` assumes no two rows share the boundary value. Where the source can emit ties, `>` drops the ones that arrive after the watermark was read and `>=` reprocesses the boundary — which is safe here only because `merge` on `click_event_id` makes the reprocessing idempotent. On an `append` strategy the same choice duplicates rows.
- **No late arrivals.** A row whose `event_received_at` predates the current watermark is never picked up, because the filter has already moved past it. If the upstream can backfill, the watermark has to be a lookback window (`> max(...) - interval 3 days`) with an idempotent strategy behind it, or the model needs `microbatch` (Ch 4 §4.4) which handles the replay explicitly.

And a fourth that is about the contract rather than the data: **a new upstream column does not arrive on its own.** The `select` here names its columns, and §14.6 puts the model under an enforced contract. So adding a field is a three-part change — the projection, the YAML `columns:` list, and the target schema — coordinated in one PR. `append_new_columns` automates the last of those only for columns the SQL actually selects.

**Dual source.** The Delta-merge incremental pattern with `append_new_columns` + CDF on a contracted gold model is documented at `/reference/resource-configs/databricks-configs` (dbt-databricks adapter configs, including the `file_format` prerequisite, which `/reference/resource-configs/spark-configs` states for Spark), `/docs/build/incremental-strategy` (the incremental-strategy reference), and Databricks' own Change Data Feed documentation. The dbt-databricks GitHub repository ships public examples of the same `merge` + `unique_key` + `tblproperties` shape.

### Scale note

Credora runs `fct_lending_offer_clicks_uk` on a daily schedule against millions of new rows. A full refresh — when the team runs one, which is rarely — takes hours and is reserved for schema migrations or upstream corruption recovery. Ch 4 §4.5 covered when `--full-refresh` is and is not the right answer; in practice, at this scale, it almost never is.

---

## 14.4 Macros in anger (cross-ref Ch 6)

Chapter 6 introduced macros, hooks, and the config-precedence rules. This section describes three macros Credora wires into its project — the same three that appeared in Ch 6 §6.8, now explained by shape and call site rather than by body. Note the call sites differ, and the difference is the point: `query_comment` is named by the project-level `query-comment:` config and runs **per query**, while the other two are `on-run-start` hooks that fire **once per invocation**. Three project integrations, two of which are hooks. The pattern (describe signature + call site, skip the body) matters here: at scale, macros are recognised by the shape of their contract with the project, not by any given implementation.

### Macro 1 — query_comment

**Signature.** `query_comment(node)` — a macro that returns a string. dbt's built-in `query-comment` project config calls it with the current node (or `none` for project-level queries) and attaches the returned string as a SQL comment on every query dbt issues.

**Purpose.** Emit structured JSON telemetry — target name, run start time, node ID, invocation ID, dbt version — so a warehouse query log can be filtered on a comment substring and every statement traced back to the dbt invocation that produced it. Ch 6 §6.8 names the surfaces.

**Call site.** `dbt_project.yml` under the `query-comment:` block, with `append: true` so the comment lands at the end of the statement rather than the beginning (important for some warehouse-side tooling that expects a specific leading pattern):

```
# dbt_project.yml
query-comment:
  comment: "{{ query_comment(node) }}"
  append: true
```

**Reference.** dbt's `/reference/project-configs/query-comment` documents the config and walks through a JSON-payload macro very close to this pattern. Community references include multiple dbt Discourse threads on warehouse cost-attribution via query comments.

### Macro 2 — require_select_arg

**Signature.** `require_select_arg()` — no arguments; returns nothing. Raises a compiler error when a `run`, `build` or `test` invocation passed none of `--select`, `--exclude`, `--selector`. Ch 6 §6.8 has the body, including which context variable actually carries the selectors — `flags` is not it.

**Purpose.** Safety gate against accidental full-project builds. A mature project's full build is expensive; a typo in a scheduled-job config that drops `--select` can cost hours of compute. A three-line macro at `on-run-start` makes that class of mistake impossible.

**Call site.** First entry in the project-level `on-run-start:` list shown in §14.1, so it fires before any model builds. With the macro wired, a bare `dbt build` stops at run start with nothing built and exits 2; `dbt build --select tag:daily` proceeds. The gate holds at the 1.11 defaults because the macro raises a *compiler* error, which abandons the invocation rather than failing one hook — the distinction Ch 6 §6.8 draws, and the reason a guardrail written as a warehouse statement instead would need `skip_nodes_if_on_run_start_fails: true` to stop anything (Ch 10 §10.9.2).

**Reference.** The `on-run-start` guardrail pattern is described in the dbt Labs hooks and operations documentation and in several dbt Discourse threads on CI safety. It is not exotic; it is what any mature project eventually builds.

### Macro 3 — generate_masking_functions

**Signature.** `generate_masking_functions()` — reads a YAML-configured `column_masks` var, iterates it, and emits `CREATE OR REPLACE FUNCTION` DDL for each named mask into a dedicated schema. Each emitted function accepts the column value as its first argument and returns the masked value unless the caller is a member of a whitelisted account group.

**Purpose.** Unity Catalog column-level masking applied through dbt. A mask function is created once per run start; individual models reference it via a `post_hook` that issues `ALTER TABLE ... ALTER COLUMN ... SET MASK`. Readers outside the whitelist see the masked value; readers inside see the raw value. The whole pipeline is gated behind the `enable_masking` project var so the infrastructure can be developed and unit-tested before it is turned on.

**Call site.** Second entry in `on-run-start:`, conditional on the var:

```
# dbt_project.yml
on-run-start:
  - "{{ require_select_arg() }}"
  - "{{ generate_masking_functions() if var('enable_masking') else '' }}"
```

This is "pattern beyond the exam" territory — the cert blueprint does not test Unity Catalog masking directly. It appears here because it exemplifies how a production project wires warehouse-side security through dbt primitives (hooks + macros), not through out-of-band admin consoles.

**Dual source.** Databricks' Column mask SQL reference documents the `ALTER TABLE ... SET MASK` syntax this macro generates. The dbt-databricks GitHub repository ships examples of Unity Catalog integration via hook macros. The pattern — `on-run-start` hook calls a macro that emits DDL — is exactly what `/docs/build/hooks-operations` describes.

### Why three is enough

These three macros exemplify three distinct classes of project integration:

| Macro | Class | When it fires | What it touches |
|---|---|---|---|
| `query_comment` | Per-query instrumentation | Every query dbt issues | SQL string prepended/appended |
| `require_select_arg` | Run-level guardrail | Once at run start | Aborts the run if a precondition fails |
| `generate_masking_functions` | Run-level DDL emission | Once at run start | Issues DDL outside any model |

Most macros wired into a project at scale fit one of these three shapes. One that fits none of them is usually logic that belongs in a model — a per-query integration that mutates state is the standard example.

---

## 14.5 Testing at scale (cross-ref Ch 7)

Chapter 7 introduced the four test taxa and the six test configs. At Credora's scale, the testing surface has three shapes, each solving a different class of problem. Ch 7 §7.9 walked through shapes 1 and 3 in detail; this section summarises all three as one integrated picture.

### Shape A — a graph-iterating singular test as a convention enforcer

Every model in `credora` has to end with a market suffix: `_uk`, `_us`, `_apac_1`, `_apac_2`, `_emea_1`, or `_global`. A model named `fct_offers` in the `cr_uk` catalog is ambiguous when cross-catalog queries reference it; the convention eliminates the ambiguity. Credora enforces it with a **singular test that iterates `graph.nodes`** — the Pattern B shape from Ch 7 §7.9

— emitting one `select` per model that fails if the name does not match the suffix regex. The full test lives in one file:

```
-- tests/valid_market_suffix.sql
-- Fails if any model name does not end in a documented market suffix.
{% set own = graph.nodes.values()
     | selectattr('resource_type', 'equalto', 'model')
     | selectattr('package_name', 'equalto', project_name)
     | list %}
{% for node in own %}
  select '{{ node.name }}' as offending_model
  where not regexp_like('{{ node.name }}', '_(uk|us|apac_[12]|emea_1|global)$')
  {% if not loop.last %}union all{% endif %}
{% endfor %}
```

Ch 7 §7.9 teaches this shape and why the `package_name` filter is load-bearing. What is specific to Credora is the convention itself: the six suffixes in the regex are the six catalogs §14.2 declares, so adding a market means editing both places — which is why the test names the offending model in its output rather than just failing.

**Reference.** Singular tests are documented at `/docs/build/data-tests`; custom generics (the alternative pattern, attached per-resource in `schema.yml`) at `/best-practices/writing-custom-generic-tests`. The `data_tests:` tree in `dbt_project.yml` configures tests that already exist (severity, store_failures, etc.), keyed by each test's own path — for a singular test, its file under `test-paths:` rather than any model folder. It does not attach generics project-wide; see `/reference/data-test-configs`.

## Shape B — a singular test for a cross-market invariant

Some invariants are specific enough that a generic would be overkill. Example: "every `offer_id` that appears in `fct_lending_offer_clicks_uk` should also appear in the cross-market `dim_offers_global` for the same snapshot date." A singular test under `tests/` covers it in one file:

```
-- tests/custom/uk_offers_present_in_global.sql
-- Fails if any UK click references an offer missing from the global dim.
with uk_offer_ids as (
    select distinct offer_id, event_received_at::date as snap_date
    from {{ ref('fct_lending_offer_clicks_uk') }}
),
global_offer_ids as (
    select distinct offer_id, snap_date
    from {{ ref('dim_offers_global') }}
)
select uk.offer_id, uk.snap_date
from uk_offer_ids uk
left join global_offer_ids g
  on uk.offer_id = g.offer_id
 and uk.snap_date = g.snap_date
where g.offer_id is null
```

Singular tests return failing rows — a `select` that returns zero rows is a pass. Ch 7 §7.3 covered the convention. The test is configured with `severity: warn` while the upstream ingestion pipeline is stabilising, and promoted to `severity: error` once clean. The count of singular tests in a project like Credora is small — a handful — but each one encodes a cross-model guarantee that generics cannot express.

**Reference.** Singular tests are documented at `/docs/build/data-tests`. The "small number of singular tests for cross-model invariants" pattern is a direct consequence of the singular-test contract: use a SQL query when the invariant cuts across columns, models, or business rules that a generic test cannot express cleanly.

## Shape C — a home-grown unit-test harness that pre-dates native `unit_tests:`

`credora` existed and was mature before dbt landed native `unit_tests:` YAML. When the team needed to assert on SQL logic — *does the case-when handle the null-market edge case?* — they built a macro harness under `macros/unit_tests/`: a set of run-operation macros that materialise mock-row fixtures as temporary views, execute the target model's SQL against the views, and compare the output to an expected-row fixture. The shape is:

- **Fixtures.** Mock input rows live in seed-like CSVs or inline YAML under `tests/fixtures/`.
- **Harness macros.** `macros/unit_tests/run_unit_tests.sql` is the entry point; `dbt run-operation run_unit_tests` walks the fixtures, invokes each model's compiled SQL against the mocks, and asserts equality to the expected output.
- **Invocation.** Wired into CI as a separate stage, before the main `dbt build`.

It worked, but it was bespoke — the YAML syntax was home-grown, the fixture layout was project-specific, and every new engineer had to learn the harness before writing a unit test.

dbt ships `unit_tests:` YAML as a first-class feature, with a `given:` / `expect:` syntax that covers exactly this use case. Credora's home-grown harness is the kind of project that the feature was built for; migration is on the team's roadmap, not yet in-tree.

**Planned migration tactic — parallel run.** One model at a time, smallest first, never a big-bang cutover: pick a model whose harness fixtures translate cleanly into a `given:` / `expect:` block, write the native `unit_tests:` YAML, and **run both the native test and the legacy harness in parallel** in CI. If the two disagree, **stop and read both against the business specification** — that is the only oracle in the room. The harness has run in production for years, which makes it strong evidence and the first place to look for what the new YAML got wrong; it does not make it correct. A long-lived harness can encode the same misreading of the spec that shipped with it, and a migration is exactly the moment that surfaces, because the disagreement is the first time anyone has computed the answer twice. Treat a mismatch as a defect of unknown location: usually a translation bug in the `given:/expect:` block, sometimes a bug the harness has been hiding. Once the two agree across twenty consecutive PR builds, the legacy entry for that model is retired and the next model migrates. Coverage never dips.

**The scheduled run drops them.** Once a model's native block is in the tree, `dbt build` runs it as part of that model's sequence — which is what the PR gate wants and what the nightly prd job does not. A unit test's inputs are fixtures, so re-running it on production compute asserts nothing CI has not already asserted. Credora's prd job therefore carries `--exclude-resource-type unit_test` and the PR gate does not. Ch 7 §7.8 has the flag, its environment-variable form, and why a graph selector is not the same mechanism.

> **Exam note.** Unit tests as a cert sub-topic mean "recognise the shape and the selector `test_type:unit`"; they are not expected to appear in depth on the exam. Ch 7's unit-test sidebar covers the recall surface.

**Dual source.** Ch 7 §7.9 cites the same dual sources for the home-grown harness story. Community discussion of hand-rolled unit-test approaches lives across multiple dbt Discourse threads; the native feature is at `/docs/build/unit-tests`.

---

## 14.6 Governance, partially applied (cross-ref Ch 13)

Chapter 13 covered five governance primitives: contracts, versions, access, groups, grants. Credora uses three of them (contracts selectively, versions on one model pair, grants project-wide) and deliberately skips two (no `groups:`, no `access:`). The shape of "what a mature project actually reaches for" is its own lesson.

Ch 13 §13.9 walked through each decision in depth. This section is the condensed picture.

### Contracts applied selectively

One model — `fct_lending_offer_clicks_uk` — carries a contract:

```
# models/cr_uk/gold/_schema.yml  (excerpt)
version: 2
models:
  - name: fct_lending_offer_clicks_uk
    config:
      contract: {enforced: true}
    columns:
      - name: click_event_id
        data_type: string
        constraints:
          - type: not_null
          - type: primary_key          # metadata-only on Databricks
      - name: user_id
        data_type: string
        constraints: [{type: not_null}]
      - name: offer_id
        data_type: string
      - name: event_received_at
        data_type: timestamp
      - name: clicked_at
        data_type: timestamp
      - name: source_campaign
        data_type: string
      - name: _loaded_at
        data_type: timestamp
```

Every column has a `data_type`; the event id has a `not_null` and a metadata-only `primary_key`. dbt validates the model's compiled SELECT against the contract *before* issuing DDL — a "preflight" check. A PR that quietly renames `event_received_at` to `received_at_ts` fails the build at compile time, not after three downstream dashboards break.

**Why only this model?** The cost/benefit calculus from Ch 13 §13.1: contracts add YAML overhead on every column change. For internal staging models that one team reads, that overhead exceeds the breakage risk. For shared gold-layer facts that three teams consume, the contract pays for itself the first time a breaking change is prevented. Credora contracts the cross-team gold models — a handful in total — and skips everything else.

**Reference.** `/docs/mesh/govern/model-contracts`, `/reference/resource-configs/contract`, `/reference/resource-properties/constraints`. The "contract only the shared gold layer" pattern is discussed at length in dbt Labs' own guidance on introducing contracts.

## Versions on one model pair

Exactly one versioned model pair exists in the project: `dim_user_lifecycle_segments_uk_v1` and `_v2`. The story (Ch 13 §13.9 has it in full): product reorganised the lifecycle-segment taxonomy, which required both a value-set change and a column rename. Rather than break every consumer simultaneously, the producer published v2 alongside v1, consumers migrated to `{{ ref('dim_user_lifecycle_segments_uk', v=2) }}` on their own schedules, and after a three-month deprecation window v1 was removed. The YAML, caught mid-window:

```
# models/cr_uk/marts/_schema.yml  (excerpt)
version: 2
models:
  - name: dim_user_lifecycle_segments_uk
    latest_version: 2
    versions:
      - v: 1
        defined_in: dim_user_lifecycle_segments_uk_v1
        deprecation_date: '2026-06-30T00:00:00Z'
      - v: 2
        defined_in: dim_user_lifecycle_segments_uk_v2
```

No other model in the project is versioned. Versions are expensive to maintain: two SQL files, two materializations, the coordination dance. Projects reach for versions when the blast radius of a rename is large enough to justify the overhead.

**Reference.** `/docs/mesh/govern/model-versions`, `/reference/resource-properties/versions`, `/reference/resource-properties/latest_version`, `/reference/resource-properties/deprecation_date`.

## Grants globally via folder config

The project runs a central BI tool that reads from every gold-layer model. Rather than attach `grants:` per model, the team sets grants at folder level in `dbt_project.yml`:

```
# dbt_project.yml  (excerpt)
models:
  credora:
    cr_uk:
      gold:
        +grants:
          select: ['credora_bi_reader', 'credora_analytics_reader']
      marts:
        +grants:
          select: ['credora_bi_reader']
```

Every model under `cr_uk/gold/` inherits both grantees; every model under `cr_uk/marts/` inherits only the BI reader. Individual models that need additional grantees use the +-prefix merge syntax (Ch 13 §13.8) to add without replacing the directory defaults.

Two Databricks-specific conditions sit under this, and they are easy to conflate. **Under Unity Catalog**, which is what Credora runs, access is governed by UC privileges — the `GRANT`s dbt issues land on the catalog's own permission model, and they take effect on compute whose *access mode* supports UC governance. A cluster in an access mode that does not enforce UC will not apply them. **The legacy workspace-and-cluster table-access-control toggles are a Hive metastore story**, not a universal Databricks rule: they are what you have to turn on for a legacy interactive cluster against the Hive metastore, and carrying that instruction over to a UC workspace sends people looking for a setting that is not the thing gating them. Check which metastore and which access mode you are on before diagnosing a grant that appears to do nothing. The bare grantee names are also a Databricks spelling rather than a portable one; Ch 13 §13.8 has the prefix form each adapter expects. See Databricks' Unity Catalog and compute configuration references.

**Reference.** `/reference/resource-configs/grants`.

### What's deliberately absent: `groups:` and `access:`

*The reasoning below is Ch 13 §13.9's, applied to this project. Read that section for the general argument; what follows is only what Credora actually decided and why its platform made the decision come out this way.*

Credora uses **neither** `groups:` nor `access:`. Every model defaults to `access: protected`, which inside a single dbt project means "any other model in this project can `ref()` me" — exactly the permission structure the team wants day-to-day. They rely on code review, ownership tags in `meta:`, and the cost/benefit instinct that tight restrictions pay off only when they prevent a specific cross-team coupling problem.

If those boundaries change, Ch 13 §13.9 gives the `access:` and `group:` choices. Credora has not needed them.

The general pattern: **governance primitives stay dormant until their specific failure mode becomes real.** Adopt them the day the failure mode surfaces, not before.

**Reference.** `/docs/mesh/govern/model-access`, `/docs/build/groups`, `/reference/resource-configs/access`, `/reference/resource-configs/group`. dbt Labs' own guidance on when to introduce governance primitives is explicit that cross-project boundaries are the trigger for `access:` / `groups:`.

---

## 14.7 Slim CI (cross-ref Ch 12)

Chapter 12 §12.9 walked through the standard slim-CI recipe in full. This section recasts the same pipeline as a five-step pseudocode sketch of the PR-gate job, with each step annotated. It does not reproduce any single real CI config — the shape below is a composite drawn from dbt's canonical `--defer --state` recipe and public CI examples.

```
# Credora PR-gate pseudocode - 5 numbered steps

1. fetch prior-artifacts from <artifact-store>
      # downloads manifest.json from the last green main-branch build
      # into ./prior-artifacts/

2. dbt parse
      # emits current ./target/manifest.json for the PR's code
      # no warehouse round-trip; single-digit seconds at Credora's scale

3. dbt build                                  \
      --select state:modified+                 \
      --defer --state ./prior-artifacts        \
      --target ci                              \
```

```
      --fail-fast

4. if build succeeded: upload ./target/manifest.json to <artifact-store>
      # tagged with PR commit SHA, for debugging THIS run only.
      # NOT promoted to 'latest-main' -- see step 4 below. That baseline
      # is published by the production job, from a full --target prd build.

5. if build reported a contract violation:
      # emit a contract-drift alert
      # (separate from step 3's --fail-fast: contract preflight
      # failures are a specific subtype the CI job detects by scanning
      # the run log for the contract-enforcement error message)
```

Each step maps directly to a primitive taught earlier.

**Step 1 — Download prior artifacts.** The runner pulls a tarball containing `manifest.json` (and typically `run_results.json` + `sources.json`) from the artifact store — Credora uses S3, but Databricks Volumes, Jenkins-native artifacts, and GitHub Actions cache are all common. Ch 12 §12.1 covered the artifacts; they are the state against which `state:modified+` compares.

**Step 2 — `dbt parse`.** The cheapest way to produce the current `manifest.json`: no compiled SQL, no warehouse. Ch 11 §11.3 covers `parse` vs `compile`; the gate needs only `parse`, because the state diff compares manifests rather than compiled SQL.

**Step 3 — The slim-CI build.** The load-bearing invocation. `state:modified+` diffs the two manifests (current + prior) and selects every modified node plus its descendants. `--defer --state ./prior-artifacts` tells dbt: for any `ref()` target not in the selection **and not already present in the CI target**, resolve against the prior-state relations (production) rather than building it in CI. Credora's gate creates a fresh schema per PR, which is what makes that simplification safe; against a warm schema an unselected ref resolves to whatever is sitting there unless `--favor-state` is passed (Ch 12 §12.3). `--target ci` writes to the CI schema. `--fail-fast` stops on the first failure — engineers prefer a red build at minute 2 over minute 12. Ch 12 §12.2–§12.4 cover every flag.

**Step 4 — Upload on success.** Keep the PR manifest under its commit SHA for debugging; do not promote it to `latest-main`. The **production** job publishes that baseline after a full, successful `--target prd` build. Ch 12 §12.9 explains why a deferred CI run's manifest still names CI-target relations and cannot serve as the production inventory.

**Step 5 — Contract-drift alert.** The CI job scans the build log for the dbt contract-enforcement error pattern. When a contract violation fires, the PR gate fails (via `--fail-fast`), but the platform team also wants a specific alert — contract drifts indicate a producer is about to break consumers, and the alert goes to the producer team's channel. This is the one place the CI job reaches past the raw dbt exit code into log-scanning; every other failure mode is handled by `--fail-fast` alone.

### What this pipeline is not

Worth naming the absences.

- **No `dbt source freshness` in the PR gate.** Freshness is a separate scheduled cadence; PRs change code, not source-load timing. Ch 12 §12.6 covers `source_status:fresher+` for the freshness-triggered rebuild scenario, which is a different pipeline.
- **No `dbt clone`.** Defer is lighter and sufficient for PR-gate CI; clone is for blue/green deploys, which Credora does not run. Ch 12 §12.8 covers clone.
- **No `dbt retry` in CI.** Retry is for operational recovery from partial failures in scheduled jobs, not for PR gates. Ch 12 §12.7 covers retry.

- **`--fail-fast` is a policy choice, not a requirement.** Teams that prefer "finish and report every failure" drop the flag; Credora chose fast-fail to keep engineer feedback tight.

**Reference.** The four-step flow (download artifacts, parse, build-with-defer-and-state, upload) is dbt Labs' canonical slim-CI recipe, documented at `/reference/node-selection/defer` and `/reference/node-selection/state-selection`. The pattern is discussed across multiple dbt Discourse threads on slim CI.

---

## 14.8 What this chapter shows — and what it does not

The seven sections above are what the book calls "pattern teaching": for each concept from Chapters 2–13, show what it looks like in a mature project, and cite the public references that teams converge on. Four explicit disclaimers are load-bearing.

1. **All names, markets, catalogs, and specific model names in this chapter are fictional.** Credora does not exist. The catalog codes (`cr_uk`, `cr_us`, `cr_apac_1`, `cr_apac_2`, `cr_emea_1`, `cr_global`) are an invented multi-market footprint that does not map to any real company's operational geography. The model names (`fct_lending_offer_clicks_uk`, `dim_user_lifecycle_segments_uk_v1`/`_v2`, `stg_offer_click_events_uk`) are invented within the standard dbt taxonomy. The team tags (`@analytics-engineering`, `@analytics-uk`, `@infra-data`) follow dbt's `meta:` conventions but do not name any real team.
2. **Every pattern is drawn from public references.** Cited inline throughout: dbt Labs' official docs and reference pages, dbt Labs' best-practices guides, the dbt Discourse community forum, published dbt Labs blog posts and Coalesce conference talks archived on the dbt Labs events page on slim CI and multi-market patterns, the public open-source projects JaffleShop Classic and JaffleShop, the `dbt-databricks` adapter repository, and Databricks' official platform docs. Every pattern shown has at least one such citation.
3. **No code, config, or log snippet from any proprietary project is reproduced in this chapter.** Every YAML block, every SQL block, and every pseudocode sketch was authored from scratch against the official docs and cross-referenced to the public patterns above. Where this chapter's examples resemble patterns seen in production projects, the resemblance reflects convergent design — mature dbt projects at scale tend to reach the same structural answers because the dbt primitives admit a small number of idiomatic shapes.
4. **The walkthrough is a composite of widely-adopted patterns.** Readers should not infer that Credora corresponds to any specific real company. It is the book's teaching vehicle — a coherent integrated example constructed so that each primitive from Chapters 2–13 has a place to land in a scale context.

---

## 14.9 Summary and learning-goal checklist

- This chapter walks the fictional `credora` project end-to-end in seven sections, each exercising a concept from an earlier chapter at production scale.

- **§14.1** — a condensed `dbt_project.yml`: multi-catalog nesting, global hooks, feature-flag vars, dispatch ordering, project-wide `persist_docs`.
- **§14.2** — a market `sources.yml` with `env_var()` routing for dev/CI/prd and freshness confined to the critical path.
- **§14.3** — one Delta-merge incremental model with CDF enabled, and the `file_format` prerequisite that makes `merge` available at all.
- **§14.4** — three project integrations by signature and call site, only two of them hooks: `query_comment` for telemetry, named by the project-level `query-comment:` config and run **per query**; `require_select_arg` as a safety gate and `generate_masking_functions` for Unity Catalog mask emission, both `on-run-start` hooks firing **once per invocation**.
- **§14.5** — three testing shapes: a graph-iterating singular test as a convention enforcer, a handful of singular tests for cross-model invariants, and a home-grown unit-test harness that pre-dates native `unit_tests:` YAML; the scheduled production run drops unit tests with `--exclude-resource-type`.
- **§14.6** — governance applied selectively: contracts on cross-team gold models, versions on one model pair, grants globally via folder config, with `access:` and `groups:` deliberately absent.
- **§14.7** — the slim-CI PR gate in five steps: download prior artifacts, `dbt parse`, `dbt build --select state:modified+ --defer --state --fail-fast`, upload on success, contract-drift alert on violation.
- The walkthrough is a composite drawn from public references; the four-part disclaimer in §14.8 specifies exactly what the chapter does not show.
- The chapter's learning goals are meta: the reader should be able to *map an existing dbt project onto the book's chapters*, recognise idiomatic patterns at scale, and spot the difference between a primitive that is genuinely useful and one that has been adopted out of a sense of completeness.

## Learning-goal checklist (self-assess)

- ☐ **Read a multi-hundred-line `dbt_project.yml` without flinching** — recognise multi-catalog nesting, global hooks, feature-flag vars, dispatch ordering, `persist_docs`. §14.1.
- ☐ **Recognise source-file patterns at scale** — `env_var()` for dev/CI/prd routing, source-level freshness defaults with per-table overrides, freshness confined to the critical path. §14.2.
- ☐ **Read an incremental model's config block as a five-concern contract** — materialization, strategy, unique key, schema change, `is_incremental()` guard — and name the `file_format` the `merge` strategy presupposes. §14.3.
- ☐ **Classify a project macro integration** — per-query instrumentation through `query-comment:`, or run-level guardrails and DDL emission through hooks. §14.4.
- ☐ **See testing at scale in three complementary shapes** — convention-enforcing singulars over `graph.nodes`, cross-model singular invariants, and home-grown unit-test harnesses as the legacy of projects older than native `unit_tests:` — and keep unit tests out of a production build with the resource-type flag rather than a selector. §14.5.
- ☐ **See governance applied selectively and know which primitives a mature project leaves on the shelf** — contracts on cross-team gold, versions on coordinated-rename problems, grants globally, `access:` / `groups:` only when cross-project coupling becomes real. §14.6.
- ☐ **Describe a slim-CI PR-gate pipeline in terms of the dbt primitives that compose it** — prior artifacts, parse, `state:modified+ --defer --state`, fail-fast, artifact promotion. §14.7.
- ☐ **Spot what the chapter does not show** — no proprietary code, no exact scale numbers, no single-company inference. §14.8.

---

## Practice questions

Twenty questions covering §14.1–§14.7 and the Databricks surfaces this project runs on, each cross-referencing a primitive taught in Chapters 2–13. Every explanation cites the relevant doc and names the chapter to revisit if the question was hard.

**1.** In §14.1's `dbt_project.yml`, the top of the `models:` block sets `+persist_docs: {relation: true, columns: true}`, and the `cr_uk.gold` branch does not mention `persist_docs`. A model in `models/cr_uk/gold/` adds `{{ config(persist_docs={'relation': false, 'columns': false}) }}` at the top of its SQL file. What are the effective `persist_docs` values for that model?
A. `{relation: true, columns: true}` — the project-level config wins.
B. `{relation: true, columns: false}` — a dict config merges key by key across layers, and `columns` is the sole key a model may override.
C. The build errors because `persist_docs` cannot be overridden per-model.
D. `{relation: false, columns: false}` — the SQL `config()` call wins over the project-level `+config`.

**2.** §14.7's PR gate carries one flag copied from an older internal runbook: `--warn-error-options '{"include": ["NoNodesForSelectionCriteria"]}'`. A PR arrives whose `state:modified+` selection matches nothing. What does dbt 1.11 do?
A. Exits 2 before selection runs — `include` was removed, and an unknown key inside `warn_error_options` is a usage error.
B. Exits 2 on the empty selection and prints nothing else; `include` and `error` are interchangeable spellings at 1.11.
C. Exits 0 — an unrecognised key inside `warn_error_options` is dropped, so nothing is promoted and the empty selection stays a warning.
D. Exits 2 on the empty selection, having first printed `[WARNING][WEOIncludeExcludeDeprecation]` and named `error` as the spelling to use instead.

**3.** §14.3's `fct_lending_offer_clicks_uk` has `on_schema_change='append_new_columns'` and is also under a contract (§14.6). A PR adds two new columns (`utm_medium`, `utm_source`) to the model's SELECT and adds them to the YAML contract; the same PR also drops `source_campaign` from the SELECT without bumping the contract version or removing the column from the contract YAML. What happens on the next CI build?
A. Both new columns are added to the target; `source_campaign` is preserved in the target with NULLs going forward.
B. The target's schema is fully synced: `source_campaign` is dropped and the two new columns are added.
C. The build silently continues with the old schema; schema changes always need `--full-refresh`.
D. The build fails at preflight — the compiled SELECT no longer contains `source_campaign`, which the YAML contract still declares.

**4.** §14.3's model is incremental and its `is_incremental()` guard sits inside the `source_events` CTE. The table already exists in the dev target. An engineer runs `dbt run --select fct_lending_offer_clicks_uk --full-refresh`. What does `is_incremental()` return inside that CTE?
A. True — the target exists, and `--full-refresh` governs only whether dbt drops and recreates the relation.
B. False — the flag defeats one of the three conditions the macro tests, so the watermark predicate is skipped and the CTE reads the whole source.
C. True on the first render and false on the second, because dbt renders the model twice under `--full-refresh`.
D. The build errors — `--full-refresh` and an `is_incremental()` guard conflict on one model.

**5.** Credora's nightly prd `dbt build` ends with one failed test on `fct_lending_offer_clicks_uk`. The on-call engineer copies that run's artifacts to `./prior-run`, reruns with `--state ./prior-run`, and wants the model rebuilt and its tests re-run — not the whole DAG. Which selector does that?
A. `result:fail` B. `result:fail+`
C. `result:error+` D. `1+result:fail`

**6.** §14.7's PR gate runs `dbt build --select state:modified+ --state ./prior-artifacts`. A PR edits one properties file and nothing else: it adds `tags: ['pii']` to `fct_lending_offer_clicks_uk`'s `config:` block and `meta: {owner: '@analytics-uk'}` to `dim_offers_global`'s. No SQL moves. What does the gate select?
A. `dim_offers_global` and its descendants only — a model-level `meta` change is a modification, a model-level `tags` change is not.
B. Both models and their descendants — `state:modified` compares every config key, and both edits are config edits.
C. Neither model — `state:modified` diffs compiled SQL, and no SQL changed.
D. `fct_lending_offer_clicks_uk` and its descendants only — `tags` drive selection, so a tag change must invalidate the node; `meta` is documentation and is excluded.

**7.** §14.5 Shape A enforces the market-suffix convention with a singular test that iterates `graph.nodes`. A team wants to **exempt** the folder `models/cr_global/experimental/` — models there are allowed to skip the suffix. What is the idiomatic way?
A. Filter the `graph.nodes` loop in the test itself, skipping models for which `node.fqn[1:3] == ['cr_global', 'experimental']`.
B. Add `valid_market_suffix: false` to the experimental folder's `data_tests:` block in `dbt_project.yml`, which disables the test for that branch.
C. Delete `tests/valid_market_suffix.sql` — one exempt folder is not worth the convention.
D. Move `models/cr_global/experimental/` outside `model-paths:` so dbt never parses those models at all.

**8.** §14.5 Shape C's harness runs as its own CI stage, but a model's native `unit_tests:` block runs inside `dbt build` instead, at that model's position in the sequence. Its inputs are fixtures, so the nightly prd job should not pay for them while the PR gate still does. Which invocation leaves the rest of that build intact and skips only the unit tests?
A. `dbt build --exclude-resource-type unit_test`
B. `dbt build --exclude unit_test`
C. `dbt build --select test_type:data`
D. `dbt build --exclude-resource-type unit_test test`

**9.** In §14.6's contract YAML, `offer_id`, `clicked_at` and `_loaded_at` each declare a `data_type` and no `constraints:` at all. A PR deletes the `data_type:` line under `clicked_at` and changes nothing else. What happens on the next build?
A. Nothing changes — `data_type` is required only on columns that carry a constraint, so the remaining entries are documentation.
B. The model builds; dbt infers `clicked_at`'s type from the compiled SELECT and warns that the contract is now partial.
C. Parsing fails for the whole project — `data_type` is mandatory on every `columns:` entry in any properties file, contract or not.
D. The model errors while dbt assembles its CREATE statement: an enforced contract needs a `data_type` on every column, so no DDL reaches the warehouse.

**10.** §14.6's `cr_uk.marts` entry, `+grants: {select: ['credora_bi_reader']}`, names its grantee bare, which is what Databricks expects. A sister market runs the same gold layer on Redshift, where `credora_bi_reader` is a Redshift group. What does the block need there?
A. `select: ['group:credora_bi_reader']` — Redshift reads an unprefixed grantee name as a user.
B. `select: ['credora_bi_reader']` — Redshift resolves an unprefixed name against users, groups and roles in turn.
C. `select: ['role:credora_bi_reader']` — `role:` is the Redshift prefix for a grantee that is not a user.
D. `select: ['roles/credora_bi_reader']` — Redshift takes the same `roles/` grantee form that BigQuery does.

**11.** §14.6 sets `+grants: {select: ['credora_bi_reader', 'credora_analytics_reader']}` at the `cr_uk.gold` folder level. A specific model in that folder adds `{{ config(grants={'select': ['credora_risk_reader']}) }}` in SQL. After `dbt run`, which roles does dbt itself grant SELECT to on that model's table?
A. All three roles — `grants:` always merges across config layers.
B. Only `credora_bi_reader` and `credora_analytics_reader` — the folder config wins.
C. Only `credora_risk_reader` — without a `+`-prefix, the SQL-level grant replaces rather than merges.
D. The build fails — declaring `grants:` at both layers is a configuration conflict.

**12.** §14.6 notes that Credora uses neither `access:` nor `groups:`. A reader asks: "Couldn't they still use `access: private` + `groups:` to enforce module boundaries inside one repo, as a form of self-discipline?" Which is the best answer?
A. Yes in principle — `private` restricts `ref()` to the same group, and that works inside one project — but for Credora as described in §14.6 the group bookkeeping buys little that its single platform team and PR review do not already give; the payoff grows with the number of independently-owned teams.
B. No — `access:` only works across projects (dbt Mesh), not within a single project.
C. No — `groups:` require a paid dbt platform tier.
D. Yes, and it would be enforced at run time: the warehouse rejects a query issued from outside the group, which is stronger than anything code review can catch.

**13.** §14.7's five-step PR gate orders: (1) fetch prior artifacts, (2) `dbt parse`, (3) `dbt build --select state:modified+ --defer --state`, (4) upload on success, (5) contract-drift alert. A team proposes dropping step 1 entirely and running only steps 2–5. What goes wrong?
A. `dbt parse` requires the warehouse connection, and step 1 is what sets it up.
B. `dbt parse` succeeds, but step 3 then has no prior manifest to diff against — `state:modified+` with an empty `--state` directory fails.
C. Nothing — step 1 is redundant because `dbt parse` produces all the state dbt needs.
D. `dbt parse` automatically downloads prior artifacts, so step 1 is redundant.

**14.** §14.7's step 3 uses `--defer --state ./prior-artifacts`. A team removes `--state ./prior-artifacts` but keeps `--defer`. What happens?
A. `--defer` alone is sufficient; dbt auto-detects the prior state.
B. The build runs without deferral, silently — `--defer` without `--state` is a no-op.
C. The build errors — deferral requires `--state` or `--defer-state`, and neither was passed.
D. The build rebuilds every upstream node in CI, since without `--state` there is nothing to defer to.

**15.** §14.7 step 3 uses `state:modified+`. A PR modifies exactly one model, `stg_offer_click_events_uk`. `fct_lending_offer_clicks_uk` refs `stg_offer_click_events_uk`. Three downstream marts ref `fct_lending_offer_clicks_uk`. What does `state:modified+` select?
A. Just `stg_offer_click_events_uk`.
B. `stg_offer_click_events_uk` and `fct_lending_offer_clicks_uk` — direct children only.
C. `stg_offer_click_events_uk` plus every descendant: `fct_lending_offer_clicks_uk` and the three downstream marts.
D. Every model in the project.

**16.** §14.7 step 5 describes a contract-drift alert that fires on contract violations. A PR author receives this alert after step 3 fails. What is the most likely root cause?
A. A `not_null` data test on the model failed after the model itself built cleanly.
B. A `dbt source freshness` check reported a source past its `error_after` threshold and stopped the run.
C. The PR changed a contracted model's output and the preflight check rejected it before DDL.
D. The CI warehouse credentials expired and step 3 could not open a connection.

**17.** §14.4 Macro 3 wires `generate_masking_functions()` conditional on `var('enable_masking')`. The team wants to enable masking in prd only. Which is the best wiring?
A. Hard-code `var('enable_masking')` to true inside the macro, so the masking DDL is part of the macro rather than a project setting.
B. Set `enable_masking: true` globally in `dbt_project.yml` vars, so every target inherits it and no invocation has to pass anything.
C. Leave `enable_masking: false` as the default in `dbt_project.yml` vars; override to true at invocation time via `--vars '{enable_masking: true}'` only in the prd scheduled job.
D. Delete the conditional so the macro always runs, and rely on prd being the only target where the masking functions are actually referenced.

**18.** §14.5 Shape C describes Credora's home-grown unit-test harness. It pre-dates the team's adoption of native `unit_tests:` YAML, it is still in the tree, and the migration off it is planned but unfinished. Which migration step is the smallest and most useful first move?
A. Rewrite the harness macros so they emit `unit_tests:` YAML automatically, then run the generator across the project.
B. Pick one model with clear mock-input/expected-output fixtures in the existing harness and author its `unit_tests:` YAML block; run both in parallel until the native test reproduces the harness's result.
C. Reproduce the harness's assertions as singular tests under `tests/` first, and treat the move to `unit_tests:` as a later step.
D. Delete the harness in the migration PR and reinstate coverage once the native blocks are written.

**19.** §14.1's `dispatch:` block puts `credora` before `dbt_utils`. A model calls `{{ dbt_utils.generate_surrogate_key(['col_a', 'col_b']) }}`. Which implementation runs, and why?
A. `dbt_utils.default__generate_surrogate_key` — the namespace prefix on the call names the package whose implementation dispatch will use.
B. `credora.databricks__generate_surrogate_key` if defined, else that namespace's `default__` — `search_order` resolves the project's own namespace first.
C. Neither — dbt raises an ambiguous-macro error, because `credora` and `dbt_utils` both define a macro of that name.
D. `dbt_utils.databricks__generate_surrogate_key` — `search_order` is evaluated back to front, so the package listed last is the one dispatch settles on whatever the project defines.

**20.** A Databricks Python model runs once nightly in a scheduled dbt job. Start-up latency is acceptable, there is no all-purpose cluster the team keeps warm for other work, and the platform team wants the run's compute cost attributed to it rather than shared. Which `submission_method` fits, and why not the default?
A. `all_purpose_cluster` — the default, and the cheapest because the cluster is shared
B. `job_cluster` — it spins up per run, so a nightly job never pays to keep a cluster warm
C. `workflow_job` — the only method that supports scheduled execution
D. `serverless_cluster` — the only method that avoids cluster management

## Answer key

**1. D.** Model config precedence runs in-SQL `{{ config() }}` > properties-file `config:` > `dbt_project.yml` `+config`, so the SQL call wins and both keys resolve false. Executed on dbt 1.11.14 against the same project shape: a model carrying that `config()` call resolves to `{relation: false, columns: false}` in the manifest, while a sibling that says nothing inherits `{relation: true, columns: true}` — the override is real, not a failure to apply. The same run also settles option B: a model naming one key resolves to that key alone, so a dict config replaces the inherited dict rather than merging into it, and there is no key that a model is barred from overriding. Option A inverts the order; note that the test-side chain runs the other way, which is the trap. Option C invents a conflict dbt does not raise. Source: `/reference/define-configs`, `/reference/resource-configs/persist_docs`. **Revisit Ch 2 §2.4 and Ch 6 §6.4 if this was hard.**

**2. D.** `include` and `exclude` are the legacy spellings of `warn_error_options`' `error` and `warn` keys. dbt still reads them and tells you so. Executed on dbt 1.11.14: a selection under `'{"include": [...]}'` emits `[WARNING][WEOIncludeExcludeDeprecation]` telling you to use `error` instead — **and still honours the key**, promoting the warning it names to an error and exiting 2. The same selection written `'{"error": [...]}'` exits 2 with no deprecation line, which is the half B denies. A is wrong twice: the key is read, and the run reaches selection. C describes a real behaviour attached to the wrong key — a *misspelled* key such as `"errors"` is dropped in silence, promoting nothing and exiting 0, so "unrecognised keys are ignored" is true of `errors` and false of `include`, which dbt recognises and warns about. Source: `/reference/global-configs/warnings`. **Revisit Ch 10 §10.9.3 if this was hard.**

**3. D.** Two rules intersect. (1) `append_new_columns` adds new columns to the target but does not remove dropped ones; on its own, dropping `source_campaign` from the SELECT would simply stop new rows from populating that column. (2) The contract on the model declares the full column list; dbt compiles the SELECT and compares it to the contract YAML *before* any DDL — a missing column is a preflight failure. Because the PR did not bump the model version or remove `source_campaign` from the YAML contract, preflight rejects the build. Sources: `/docs/build/incremental-models` on `append_new_columns` semantics; `/reference/resource-configs/contract` on the contracted-model column constraint; `/docs/mesh/govern/model-versions` on versioning breaking changes. **Revisit Ch 4 §4.3.3 and Ch 13 §13.2 if this was hard.**

**4. B.** `is_incremental()` is true only when all three hold: the model is materialized `incremental`, the target relation already exists, **and** the run is not in full-refresh mode. The flag defeats the third condition on its own, so the watermark predicate never renders and the CTE reads the source in full — which is exactly what a full refresh needs it to do. Executed on dbt 1.11.14 with a model that logs the macro's value: first run, no target, False; second run, target present, no flag, True; third run, target present with `--full-refresh`, False. Option A treats the flag as purely a relation-level instruction. Option C misreads the double render: dbt does render the model more than once per invocation, and the same run shows the value identical each time. Option D invents a conflict — every run above completed. Source: `/docs/build/incremental-models`. **Revisit Ch 4 §4.3.1 if this was hard.**

**5. D.** `result:` selectors read the prior run's `run_results.json`, so the rerun needs `--state`; the item then turns on which side of the failed node the graph operator sits. A test is a leaf, so a trailing `+` reaches nothing. Executed on dbt 1.11.14 against a run carrying one failed test: `result:fail` and `result:fail+` each returned the same single test node and zero models — a test is a leaf, so the trailing `+` reaches nothing — while `1+result:fail` returned the model the failed test is attached to, plus that model's other tests, which eager indirect selection brings along. So A and B rerun the failing test against the same relation that produced the failure, and it fails again for the same reason. C fails differently and is worth its own beat: `result:error` selects nodes whose status was *error*, and this run had a failing test rather than an errored node, so the selection is empty and dbt exits having built nothing. `result:error+` keeps its trailing `+` because an errored *model* has descendants; the asymmetry is where tests sit in the graph, not the selector. Source: `/reference/node-selection/methods`, `/reference/node-selection/graph-operators`. **Revisit Ch 12 §12.5 and Ch 11 §11.7 if this was hard.**

**6. A.** `state:modified` excludes a model-level `tags` change and a `group` reassignment; a model-level `meta` change it treats as a modification. Executed on dbt 1.11.14 against a baseline manifest of the same project: adding `config: tags: ['probe_tag_xyz']` to one model left `dbt ls --select state:modified --state <dir>` reporting `The selection criterion 'state:`

`modified' does not match any enabled nodes`, while `dbt ls --select tag:probe_tag_xyz` returned that model — the tag was applied and simply not compared. `state:modified.configs` said the same. Replacing the tag with `config: meta: {owner: "probe-team"}` selected the model under both `state:modified` and `state:modified.configs`. Reassigning another model between two declared groups selected nothing under either. B is wrong on one half, `tags`; D is wrong on both, being the exact inverse of the key. C is the intuition that `state:modified` is a SQL diff; `state:modified.body` is the sub-selector that would be, and the bare form compares configs too, which is why the `meta` edit lands at all. The reference page has both halves the wrong way round, calling a group change a modification and a `meta` change metadata-only; where the page and the runtime disagree, answer from the runtime. Source: `/reference/node-selection/state-comparison-caveats`, `/reference/node-selection/methods`. **Revisit Ch 12 §12.2 if this was hard.**

**7. A.** Singular tests are SQL files with Jinja — there is no per-folder "disable this test" config because the test is not attached to specific resources. The test is one file, so the exemption is one extra condition in the `{% for %}` clause, filtering on `node.fqn` (or `node.path` / `node.tags`). Option C removes the test everywhere, not just one folder. Option B keys the `data_tests:` tree on a model folder, but a singular test's config path is its own file under `test-paths:`, so the entry never reaches it — executed on 1.11.14, the test still reports `PASS` with that block in place. Nor does anything warn you: the stray keypath resolves to the folder, and a folder holding any data test counts as used. Only a folder with none draws `Configuration paths exist in your dbt_project.yml file which do not apply to any resources`, and even that names the folder, not the test. `valid_market_suffix: false` is not the disable syntax either, and the form that works, `+enabled: false` on the test's own path, is option C by another route. Option D drops every model in the folder from the project to exempt them from one naming rule. Source: `/docs/build/data-tests` on singular-test mechanics; `graph.nodes` shape at `/reference/dbt-jinja-functions/graph`. **Revisit Ch 7 §7.9 if this was hard.**

**8. A.** `--exclude-resource-type` is a CLI flag that takes resource types, and `unit_test` is one of them; models, seeds, snapshots and data tests are untouched. Executed on dbt 1.11.14 against a project carrying two unit tests: selecting a model with the flag returns the model and its data tests and neither unit test, while the same selection without it returns both. B reaches for the wrong mechanism — `--exclude` takes graph selectors, and a bare `unit_test` handed to it matches no node, exits clean, and leaves both unit tests in the run. C narrows the run to data tests, so no model, seed or snapshot builds at all. D is the right flag with one token too many: `test` and `unit_test` are separate resource types, and excluding both strips every data test as well. The environment-variable form is `DBT_ENGINE_EXCLUDE_RESOURCE_TYPES`. Source: `/reference/global-configs/resource-type`. **Revisit Ch 7 §7.8 if this was hard.**

**9. D.** `data_type` is optional on an uncontracted model's `columns:` entries. On a materialization that ENFORCES contracts — `table`, `view`, and `incremental` with `on_schema_change` set to `append_new_columns` or `fail`, which is the case here — it becomes mandatory on **every** column, and constraints have nothing to do with it. (An `ephemeral` or `materialized_view` model accepts the same config and builds green with the column missing, no error and no warning.) Executed on dbt 1.11.14: the run raises `Contracted models require data_type to be defined for each column`, names the offending column, exits 1, and leaves no relation behind, because the check runs inside `create_table_as` while the CREATE statement is being assembled. Restoring the `data_type` makes the same model build; flipping `enforced` to false makes the incomplete YAML legal again. Option A reads the requirement as constraint-gated. Option B credits dbt with inferring the missing type, which is the opposite of what a contract is for — the YAML is the assertion, not a hint. Option C has the right requirement and the wrong scope and stage: `dbt parse` accepts this project, and an uncontracted model may omit `data_type` entirely — both confirmed by execution. Source: `/reference/resource-`

configs/contract, /reference/resource-properties/columns. **Revisit Ch 13 §13.2 if this was hard.**

**10. A.** Redshift grants to users, groups and roles, and it tells them apart by prefix: `group:` for a group, `role:` for a role, and an unprefixed name for a user. `credora_bi_reader` is a group, so it needs `group:`. B is the Databricks spelling carried over unchanged; there is no fallback resolution, so dbt would issue the grant against a user of that name. C picks the wrong non-user kind — Redshift groups and Redshift roles are separate objects with separate prefixes. D borrows BigQuery's vocabulary and misplaces it: there, `roles/` prefixes the *privilege* (`roles/bigquery.dataViewer` in place of `select`), while grantees carry `user:`, `group:`, `serviceAccount:` or `domain:`. Source: /reference/resource-configs/grants. **Revisit Ch 13 §13.8 if this was hard.**

**11. C.** Without the +-prefix merge syntax (e.g., `grants={'+select': ['credora_risk_reader']}`), the more-specific config replaces the broader one rather than merging. The folder-level roles are overridden entirely. If the team wanted additive behaviour, they would write `+select:` to merge. Read the stem's scope carefully: it asks what **dbt grants**, which is what `grants:` controls and what dbt reconciles on each run. Who can actually *read* the table is a larger question the warehouse answers — under Unity Catalog a principal can hold SELECT through a privilege inherited from the catalog or schema, through ownership of the relation, or through membership of a group that holds one, and dbt neither sets nor revokes any of those. Source: /reference/resource-configs/grants. **Revisit Ch 13 §13.8 if this was hard.**

**12. A.** Two halves, and only the first is a fact about dbt. The mechanic: `access:` does work within a single project — `access: private` restricts `ref()` to models in the same group, resolved at parse time — so anyone answering "it only works across projects" has the boundary wrong. The judgement: whether the bookkeeping is worth it is scenario-specific, and A is keyed on Credora as §14.6 describes it — one repo, one platform team, PR review already catching cross-module `ref()`s. Change the scenario and the answer changes with it: several independently-owned teams in one monorepo, or a consumer the producers cannot see in review, and declaring the boundary starts paying for itself (Ch 13 §13.6 argues that case). Option B is wrong — `access:` applies within single projects as well as across. Option C is wrong — there is no paid-tier gate. Option D puts the enforcement in the wrong place: `access:` is resolved while dbt builds the graph and rejects the offending `ref()` there, and nothing about it reaches the warehouse. Warehouse-side enforcement is what `grants:` does (Ch 13 §13.8); the two are separate surfaces. Source: /docs/mesh/govern/model-access. **Revisit Ch 13 §13.6–§13.7 if this was hard.**

**13. B.** `dbt parse` emits only the *current* `manifest.json`. `state:modified+` requires a *prior* `manifest.json` at the `--state` directory path, and without step 1 to download it there is none. Executed on dbt 1.11.14 three ways — `--state` pointing at an empty directory, at a missing one, and omitted entirely — all three fail identically before selection, with `Runtime Error / Got a state selector method, but no comparison manifest`, exit code 2. Source: /reference/node-selection/state-selection. **Revisit Ch 12 §12.2 if this was hard.**

**14. C.** Defer resolves unselected `ref()` calls against the prior state's relations, so the prior `manifest.json` has to be locatable. Executed on dbt 1.11.14, `dbt run --defer` and `dbt test --defer` with no state flag both stop before any node runs, with `Runtime Error / --state or --defer-state are required for deferral, but neither was provided`. So A is wrong on auto-detection — the message names the two flags that work and neither is inferred — and B is wrong that the flag quietly no-ops. D describes running CI with no deferral at all, which is a different invocation from a malformed one. Source: /reference/node-selection/defer. **Revisit Ch 12 §12.3 if this was hard.**

**15. C.** `state:modified` matches modified nodes; the trailing `+` is the graph operator meaning "this node plus every descendant". One modified source propagates through the

DAG to every downstream reachable from it. Option B would be `state:modified+1` (descendants to depth 1). Source: `/reference/node-selection/graph-operators`, `/reference/node-selection/state-selection`. **Revisit Ch 11 §11.7 and Ch 12 §12.2 if this was hard.**

**16. C.** A contract violation means the model's compiled SELECT no longer matches the YAML contract — a column renamed on `fct_lending_offer_clicks_uk` and not renamed in `_schema.yml` is the shape it usually takes, and it is what §14.7's step 5 alert exists to route. Option A would be a `dbt test` failure, a different error class and one raised after the model itself built cleanly. Option B would be a `dbt source freshness` result, which is not in the PR gate at all (§14.7 notes this). Option D would surface as a connection error at step 2 or 3, not as a contract violation. Source: `/docs/mesh/govern/model-contracts`. **Revisit Ch 13 §13.2 and Ch 12 §12.9 if this was hard.**

**17. C.** Project-level `vars:` sets the default; invocation-level `--vars` overrides at the CLI. Keeping the safe default (`false`) and opting in at the specific invocation site is the idiomatic multi-environment pattern — dev and CI do not accidentally trigger DDL that belongs in prd. Option B would run in dev, which is often undesirable for masking (dev runs under different permissions). Source: `/reference/dbt-jinja-functions/var`, `/docs/build/hooks-operations`. **Revisit Ch 6 §6.2 if this was hard.**

**18. B.** The migration tactic is a parallel run on one model: author the native `unit_tests:` block for a model whose fixtures already exist, keep the harness case running beside it, and retire the harness case only once the native test agrees. Coverage never dips, and a disagreement is scoped to a single model instead of a release. Note what the parallel run buys and what it does not: the harness is strong *evidence*, not an oracle — a disagreement means one of the two is wrong, usually the freshly-written YAML, occasionally the harness itself, and the tiebreaker is the business specification rather than seniority. Option A automates the wrong artefact — a generator built from the harness inherits whatever the harness gets wrong, at project scale, with nothing left to check it against. Option C swaps the test type: a singular test queries the built relation, while the harness and `unit_tests:` both assert model logic against mocked input, so the assertions do not survive the translation and the mocks have nowhere to go. Option D gives up coverage for the length of the migration to buy nothing. Source: `/docs/build/unit-tests`, `/reference/resource-properties/unit-tests`, `/docs/build/data-tests`. **Revisit Ch 7 §7.8 if this was hard.**

**19. B.** Dispatch's `search_order` is first-match-wins in the order written, and every entry is a package name — the value of `name:` in that project's `dbt_project.yml`, which is why `credora` resolves to the project's own macros. So the call resolves in the `credora` namespace first (the adapter-specific `databricks__`, then the `default__` fallback), falling through to `dbt_utils` only if neither exists — §14.1's structural move 5. One failure mode is worth carrying out of this: an entry naming a package that does not exist is skipped in silence — no warning, no error, exit 0 — so the override never fires and there is nothing in the log to find the typo by. A has the namespace prefix on the call deciding the implementation, which is the thing `dispatch` exists to override. C expects an error, but two definitions of one macro name across two packages is the ordinary case dispatch resolves. D reverses the order, and a `search_order` read back to front would make the block a no-op — `dbt_utils` is already where the call lands without it. Source: `/reference/dbt-jinja-functions/dispatch`, `/reference/project-configs/dispatch-config`. **Revisit Ch 6 §6.7 and Ch 8 §8.6 if this was hard.**

**20. B.** On Databricks, `submission_method` takes `all_purpose_cluster` (the default), `job_cluster`, `serverless_cluster` and `workflow_job`, and the choice is a cost and latency trade rather than a capability one. All-purpose is fastest to start because the cluster is already warm, and the most expensive to leave running — which makes it right for development and wrong for a nightly job. A job cluster spins up per run: slower to start, cheaper for scheduled work. Serverless removes cluster management at the platform's own pricing, and `workflow_job` submits the model as a Databricks workflow, which is what you want when the run must appear in that platform's orchestration rather than only in dbt's. Development on all-purpose and scheduled runs on job or serverless is the usual split. B is keyed on the three conditions the stem states, and each one is load-bearing: if start-up latency mattered, a warm all-purpose cluster would win; if the team already kept one running for other work, the marginal cost of reusing it could beat paying for a fresh cluster; and if attribution did not matter, serverless would be at least as good an answer. Without those conditions "job cluster is best" is a defensible default rather than a determinate answer, which is why the stem supplies them. Source: `/reference/resource-configs/databricks-configs`, `/docs/build/python-models`. **Revisit Ch 4 §4.7 if this was hard.**

# Chapter 15

# Exam day: strategy and format drills

> **Scope.** By the time you open this chapter, the fourteen preceding chapters have given you the dbt knowledge. This chapter is the last-mile layer: how to convert that knowledge into marks on exam day.

Knowing the content is not the same as scoring it. The exam is 65 questions against a 120-minute clock, with no room for an avoidable mistake on any of them, and that execution gap — not missing knowledge — is where prepared candidates lose marks.

---

## 15.1 The six official buckets, seven tactics

The current study guide lists six official format buckets (see Chapter 1, §1.3 for first-principles coverage). This book splits multiple-choice into single-answer and multi-answer tactics, because they behave differently under time pressure.

### 1. Multiple-choice — single answer

The dominant format. Four to five options, one correct.

**Tactic.** Read the stem first, in full. Before your eyes scan the options, **articulate your own answer in your head**. Only then read the options and match yours to one of them. If your pre-guess maps cleanly onto option C, pick C and move on. If your pre-guess matches none of the options, re-read the stem — you may have misunderstood the question.

Why this works: dbt single-answer MCQs almost always carry one "plausible-but-wrong" distractor that sounds right if you read the options first — "incremental models must be dropped and rebuilt after a schema change", say, which is true-sounding (incrementals *are* fiddly under schema change) and false (that is what `on_schema_change` policies and `--full-refresh` are for). Pre-answering is what makes it visible.

### 2. Multiple-choice — multi-answer ("select N")

Same visual layout as single-answer, but the stem says "select two" or "select all that apply." No partial credit: an exactly-correct set is the only correct answer.

Before reading the options, **count the N in the prompt**, and count your selections against N before you submit. The failure mode is the "and this one is also true" impulse on a "select two": three individually-true selections still mark the whole item wrong. Where the stem gives no N and says only "select all that apply", it is asking for **every** true option — judge each one on its own merits and select all that pass. Do not fall back on the smallest set you can defend: an unknown count is not a reason to under-select, and a true option left unchecked is as wrong as a false one checked.

### 3. Fill-in-the-blank (FITB)

A sentence, command, or YAML snippet with one or more blanks. You type the exact token, case- and spacing-sensitive, with no decoration — no trailing space, no quotes unless the surrounding syntax requires them, no extra flags. `is_incremental()` not `is_incremental ()` and not `{{ is_incremental() }}` unless the blank is already inside a Jinja expression. The decoration trap bites specifically where the blank's surrounding syntax already provides the wrapper: `materialized: "______"` wants `incremental`, not `"incremental"`, because the quotes are already rendered.

The tokens worth drilling letter-perfect are listed in Chapter 1 §1.3; run them from the cheat sheet before you sit down.

### 4. Matching

Two columns. Drag items from the right column onto items in the left column. Typical use: command-to-effect, selector-to-semantics, or config-to-resource-type.

Eliminate as you go. Lock in the pairings you are certain of first — matching is the format where a confident first pass pays off most, and a single wrong pair marks the whole item incorrect. Do not assume the two columns pair off one-to-one, though: nothing published says the right-hand pool is exactly the size of the left, and a pool with a spare item breaks the "the last one is forced" shortcut. Read the stem for what it actually asks, and check the leftover against the item it would land on rather than assigning it by elimination.

### 5. Hotspot

A screenshot — usually a YAML file, a SQL model, or a DAG — with clickable regions. You click the single region that answers the stem.

Read the stem first, twice. Hotspot screenshots are crowded on purpose; the stem narrows what you are actually being asked. Common stems: "click the line that is misconfigured," "click the key that controls where compiled SQL is written," "click the resource that would be built first." The skimmer's failure mode is clicking the first thing that looks wrong without checking the others — a hotspot YAML with a clear typo on line 3 and a subtle semantic error on line 7, plus a stem asking "click the line that would cause a compile error," will punish you for stopping at the typo.

> **Note for this book.** In the chapter drills and mocks, hotspot items are framed as MCQs labelled "Which line is incorrect: A. Line 3, B. Line 5, ..." because markdown does not render click regions. On the real exam you click the region directly. The reasoning skill is identical; only the input mechanic differs.

### 6. Build-list

An unordered pool of items. Click items in order to build an ordered list. Typical use: "order these commands for a slim-CI run" or "order these build steps for a first-time project setup."

Do not assume every pool item belongs in the answer — a build list can carry a distractor that appears in no correct ordering, so the question can be "which items belong, and in what sequence?" rather than only the second half of that. Settle the whole ordering, and confirm the stem's direction (beginning-to-end vs. end-to-beginning) before your first click. Reordering costs more than choosing, so the mistake to avoid is committing early.

### 7. Discrete Option Multiple Choice (DOMC)

The format most candidates have never seen outside this exam. One option is shown at a time, and you click Yes (this statement is correct) or No (this statement is not correct). Another option appears. You cannot see multiple options simultaneously, cannot go back, and the engine draws from a larger pool — the options you see are not necessarily the options another candidate sees.

Treat every option as an **independent true/false question**. Do NOT ask yourself "is this the best answer?" — DOMC does not give you that frame, and the reflex to pick-the-best from MCQ-land will cause you to click No on statements that are individually correct but feel "less correct" than a remembered alternative. A DOMC item might show you two or three statements that are all independently true; each gets a Yes. The same reflex in its other form is just as costly: because you cannot see the pool, a statement that is not on your mental list of correct answers is not thereby false. Judge what is on the screen, on its own merits.

Two disciplines carry DOMC items:

1. **Read only the statement on screen.** Do not rely on comparison with an option you saw earlier — you may have misremembered it, and anyway each statement is judged on its own merit.
2. **Pre-compute the answer from the stem before clicking.** If the stem is "which statement about `dbt deps` is true," mentally list 3–4 true statements about `dbt deps` before the first option appears. When an option appears, check whether it matches any of your pre-computed truths. If yes, click Yes. If no, click No.

### Time budget per format

Target first-pass times — flag and move on if you blow past them:

| Format | Target | Hard ceiling |
|---|---|---|
| MCQ single | 45–60s | 90s |
| MCQ multi | 60–90s | 120s |
| FITB | 30–45s | 60s (these are the fastest) |
| Matching | 60–90s | 120s |
| Hotspot | 90–120s | 150s (reading tax) |
| Build-list | 60–90s | 120s |
| DOMC | ~15s per statement | n/a — pool size varies |

---

## 15.2 Time budget — 1.8 minutes per question

The math: **65 questions × 1.8 minutes = 117 minutes**, inside a 120-minute window. Do not treat the leftover 3 minutes as a buffer — the three-pass structure below fills all 120. Your only real cushion is what you bank by moving fast on easy items in the first pass, and that tightness is where the exam bites.

### What 1.8 minutes actually buys you

In practice, the 65 questions do not consume 1.8 minutes each. Based on the format tactics above:

- ~15 questions will feel instant (≤30 seconds each — format-recall MCQs, short FITB).

- ~40 questions will feel normal (60–90 seconds each — most MCQs and matching).
- ~10 questions will take real thought (2–3+ minutes each, spread across the first and second passes — hotspot with a 20-line YAML, build-list with 7 items, DOMC with a long tail).

A first pass at those rates, with the hard ten flagged at 90 seconds, runs to about 80 minutes — inside the 93-minute first-pass window. The 27 minutes that remain split 22 for the flagged ten and 5 for a final sanity check.

### The three-pass structure

**First pass (minute 0–93): answer everything you are confident about in ≤90 seconds.**

- If a question takes over 90 seconds without converging, best-guess it, flag it, and move on. Never flag a blank — §15.4 has the arithmetic.
- Aim to reach question 65 with the flagged questions marked and the rest answered.

**Second pass (minute 93–115): revisit the flagged questions.**

- Re-read the stem from scratch. Often the mis-read from the first pass becomes obvious on a fresh read.
- Use elimination. Even if you cannot identify the correct answer, you can usually eliminate two options, which takes a 1-in-5 guess to a 1-in-3.
- Lock in "best guess" on anything that still resists. Do not spend more than 3 minutes on any single flagged question — at that point you are speculating, and speculation on one question costs you the chance to revisit another.

**Third pass (minute 115–120): sanity check the easy ones you rushed.**

- Spot-check five or six of the questions you answered in under 30 seconds. The most common error here is mis-counting on a multi-answer question (you selected two when the prompt said "select three"), followed by misreading a FITB (you typed `is_incremental` without noticing).
- Do not second-guess on confidence. If you answered it fast and the answer still looks right, move on.

### When to break the budget

Break the first-pass budget when a question is a **gift** — a fast FITB or a single-answer MCQ where you know the answer in 15 seconds. Banking 30 seconds of buffer here is worth more than rigidly holding 90 seconds per question.

Break the second-pass budget when you are within sight of finishing — if 3 minutes on a genuinely hard flagged question converts "guess" to "certain," it is worth it. Do not break the second-pass budget on question 1 of 10 flagged ones; break it on question 9 or 10 when no others remain.

---

## 15.3 Five recurring trap patterns

These five shapes trip up candidates who know the dbt content, because the trap is in how the question is built rather than in the material. Each ends with a pointer to the chapter that teaches the underlying skill.

## Pattern 1: Source counting by (database + schema)

**Shape.** A question shows SQL that references several warehouse tables and asks how many sources and how many tables need to be declared in sources.yml.

**The trap.** A source in dbt is a logical grouping — typically one per <database>.<schema> — that contains many tables. The naive reader counts every distinct warehouse table as its own source and over-declares. Four tables in one <db>.<schema> are **one source and four tables**.

**How to solve on the fly.** List every table reference from the SQL as <db>.<schema>.<table>. Deduplicate on the first two fields to count sources. Deduplicate on the full triple to count tables. The two counts are usually different.

**See Chapter 3 §3.4** for source() and sources.yml structure.

## Pattern 2: Every dbt-managed table must be behind ref()

A question presents a small set of model files where one or more models hard-code a schema-qualified table name; the models build in the wrong order or fail. dbt builds its DAG from ref() and source() calls, so a hard-coded <schema>.<table> is invisible to the scheduler. The fix lives in the **downstream** model, not the upstream one: replace the literal with ref('upstream_model_name') and the edge re-registers. The on-the-fly check runs per warehouse-table reference: produced by another model in this project, ref(); a raw table, source(); never hard-coded. See Chapter 2 §2.2 for ref() and DAG ordering.

## Pattern 3: Incremental models need an is_incremental() guard

A question asks you to identify a true (or false) statement about incremental materializations, with one or more options claiming an incremental model can do without the is_incremental() macro, without a unique_key, or without an on_schema_change policy. Think of these as three knobs a standard incremental tunes — and only one of them is hard-required:

| Knob | What it buys | Required? |
|---|---|---|
| is_incremental() | filtered-delta behaviour | not required *syntax* — a standard incremental parses and runs without it, and simply reprocesses its whole source every run. It is the usual way to get the delta behaviour that makes the materialization worth using, and a microbatch body carries no guard at all (§4.4.2) |
| unique_key | the merge and delete+insert strategies | no on a standard incremental — but microbatch is adapter-dependent (§4.4.5) |
| on_schema_change | schema evolution — only under append_new_columns or sync_all_columns. fail aborts on divergence; the default ignore adapts nothing and still errors when the SQL drops a column | no — documented as optional |

So on a "which is FALSE?" item over a standard incremental, "`unique_key` is required" is itself the false option — and read an `is_incremental()` option with the same care: "required to avoid reprocessing the whole source" is true, "required for the model to build" is not. Do not carry either row across to `microbatch`: the body takes no guard, and the key requirement follows the adapter's replacement mechanism, where "never needs one" is as wrong as "always needs one". See Chapter 4 §4.3 for the must-haves list, §4.4.2 and §4.4.5 for the microbatch exceptions.

### Pattern 4: Test-scope reduction on incrementals

A question describes an incremental model with a large volume of data and asks how to avoid re-testing the whole table on every run. The multi-select stem offers several test-config parameters and most of them are red herrings:

| Test config | What it does | Shrinks test scope? |
|---|---|---|
| `where:` | applies a predicate to the test's scan — `where: "loaded_at > dateadd(day, -7, current_date)"` tests only the recent window | **yes — this is the one** |
| `limit:` | caps the rows the failing-rows query returns, and so what gets counted | no — the classic distractor; it shrinks the result, not what the test asserts over |
| `severity`, `store_failures`, `error_if` / `warn_if` | shape what happens to results | no — failure handling, not scope |

On a "select N" stem, eliminate the valid-but-orthogonal options first, then confirm the remaining selections number exactly N. See Chapter 7 §7.5 for test configs.

### Pattern 5: Git is tested but is not in the outline

Git is not named in any domain of the topic outline, so candidates write it off as ungraded prerequisite knowledge — and then meet it, because one of the official sample questions is a git-branching item. Treat it as in scope, at intermediate depth. The discriminator is `git fetch` vs `git pull`. Appendix A §A.2 is the refresher, and it is worth one re-read the week before.

---

## 15.4 The skip-and-return plan

The ten or so questions that will eat your time are not distributed by topic — they are distributed by "did you happen to memorise this specific config key." The skip-and-return plan is what keeps one of them from tanking the other 64.

### What triggers a flag

Everything in this section assumes the exam interface lets you mark a question and come back to it. Check that in the tutorial screen before the timer starts; where it does not, answer each question when you first see it and use the time you save at the end for a straight re-read. Flag a question when **either** of these is true:

1. **You have been on it for 90 seconds without converging on an answer.** The 90-second trigger is a ceiling, not a target — if at 60 seconds you already know this will take 3 minutes, flag at 60.
2. **You are unsure of definitional scope.** You know the general area but cannot remember whether the specific config key is `store_failures` or `store_failures_as`. Flag and move on — the second pass sometimes jogs memory from context elsewhere in the exam.

### The no-blank rule

Never leave a flagged question unanswered. **Best-guess first, then flag.** The reasoning is arithmetic: a flag-and-blank you never get back to is a guaranteed zero, while a flag-and-guess is a 1-in-4 or 1-in-5 shot on a single-answer MCQ and roughly 1-in-2 on a DOMC statement (Yes/No being roughly equiprobable). Across ten flagged questions that is 2–5 expected points — the width of the gap between a fail and a pass.

### Return-pass discipline

On the second pass:

1. **Re-read the stem from scratch.** Do not read your own flagged notes first; read the stem fresh. First-pass misreads are the single biggest source of flag-pass wins.
2. **Eliminate more aggressively.** On a single-answer MCQ you guessed A on, can you eliminate B and C? That shifts the expected value of your guess from 0.25 to 0.5 even if you still do not know whether A or D is right.
3. **Lock in and move on.** Revising a third time without a new insight means you are selecting on the pattern of your own indecision, which is no better than random.

### When to stop returning

Stop when **a second revision has not improved your confidence**. Lock in whatever it gave you and move to another flagged question.

If you reach the end of your flagged list and have time left, use it on the third pass (sanity-check the easy ones you rushed).

---

## 15.5 The final 24 hours

The final day is a maintenance day, not a learning day. Anything you have not studied by the morning of the exam will not be studied productively now.

### Recommended checklist

- **Take Mock Test 2** if you have not yet — or re-scan the one you took. It is this book's stretch-difficulty diagnostic, written a notch harder than Mock 1, so clearing its 65% bar (43 of 65) is a good sign. It is not a prediction of your exam result — use it to find the concepts you missed or guessed at, and re-drill those.
- **Review the questions you got wrong on Mock 2.** Name the error mode for each — recall gap, mis-read, MCQ frame applied to a DOMC item, or mis-count on a multi-answer question. Each mode has its own corrective tactic, so recognising the class beats memorising the specific question.

- **Re-read the cheat sheet front-to-back.** You have seen it enough times now that a single pass should take 15 minutes. Pay extra attention to the commands grid and the node-selection grid — those are the sections where subtle discrimination questions live.
- **No new content.** If you have not studied Python models, governance contracts, or `--defer --state` by now, skip them. The expected-value gain from a half-day of new-topic cramming is negative once exam fatigue is accounted for.
- **Sleep. Hydrate.** Not optional. Do not take the exam on 4 hours of sleep to squeeze in one more mock. The 1.8-minute budget is unforgiving when your working memory is impaired.
- **Know your exam-day tech setup.** Re-read the proctoring bullet in Chapter 1 §1.4 and check the browser, webcam, desk and ID requirements the day before — not 20 minutes before your window opens.

### What not to do

- Do not take Mock Test 1 for the first time 24 hours before the exam. Mock 1 is set at real-exam difficulty; it should be taken 2–3 weeks out, with time for the weak-domain re-drill in the middle of the 6-week study track.
- Do not memorise chapters you have skimmed. If Chapter 12 (state/defer) has been light reading, the 24-hour window is too late to internalize `state:modified.body` vs. `state:modified.configs`. The cheat sheet covers the recall layer; trust it.
- Do not arrive in the exam expecting to look things up. The exam is closed-book. The cheat sheet lives in your head by now — trust that.

---

## 15.6 Common post-exam feedback patterns

Three reactions are worth anticipating, because each one points at a preparation gap this chapter's tactics address. They are the patterns this book expects, not a survey of what candidates report.

### "Harder than I expected"

Usually means the candidate under-accounted for multi-answer questions. The study guide groups single-answer and multi-answer MCQs under one "multiple-choice" heading, so candidates sometimes walk in assuming every MCQ is single-answer. Multi-answer MCQs punish the "add one more for good measure" reflex; §15.1 has the exact-set rule.

**Corrective tactic.** Count the N in every multi-answer stem, every time. Treat N as the question's load-bearing word.

### "Easier than I expected"

Often means the candidate under-recognised DOMC items and over-committed to single-answer MCQ framing. On a DOMC, if two independent statements are both true, the correct action is to click Yes on both — but an MCQ-trained candidate will click Yes on one and No on the other because "only one can be correct." This candidate's score will be worse than their perceived experience.

**Corrective tactic.** When a question shows one option at a time with Yes/No buttons, it is DOMC. Drop the MCQ frame. Judge each statement on its own merit.

### "Ran out of time"

The 1.8-minute figure is what 65 questions in 120 minutes averages out to; no rule stops you spending five minutes on one item, which is exactly the problem. Candidates who discover this too late usually burned 4–5 minutes on the first 3–4 hard questions, then had to rush the last 30 questions in under an hour. First-pass discipline — best-guess and move on at 90 seconds — is the protection against that failure mode.

**Corrective tactic.** Practice the 90-second discipline on Mock 1 and Mock 2. Time yourself per-question (or at checkpoints: on pace for 1.8 min/Q means roughly question 17 by minute 30 and question 33 by minute 60). These are pacing targets of this book's own choosing, not exam rules.

---

## Summary

- The exam is **65 questions in 120 minutes**, 65% to pass, and six official format buckets: multiple-choice, FITB, matching, hotspot, build-list, and DOMC. This book treats single-answer and multi-answer MCQ as separate tactics.
- Each format has an **optimal attack tactic**: pre-guess for single MCQ, count-the-N for multi MCQ, letter-perfect typing for FITB, eliminate-as-you-go for matching, read-the-stem-twice for hotspot, sequence-first-then-click for build-list, independent-true-false for DOMC.
- **1.8 minutes per question is an average, not a per-item ceiling**: the recommended structure is three passes (first pass ≤90 seconds per question, setting aside the hard ones; second pass return to them; third pass sanity-check the easy ones) — available in full only if the exam interface lets you revisit, so check that in the tutorial first.
- Five recurring trap patterns absorb most of the avoidable lost marks: source = db + schema, ref everything, `is_incremental()` is the conditional filter a standard incremental needs to avoid reprocessing, test scope (where), and git is in scope.
- **Skip-and-return plan**, where the interface supports one: set aside at 90 seconds or on definitional uncertainty; never leave a blank; stop revisiting after two revisions without improved confidence.
- **Final 24 hours**: Mock 2, review wrong questions, re-read cheat sheet, no new content, sleep, verify exam-day tech setup.

# Chapter 16

# Mock Test 1 (Baseline Difficulty)

Calibrated to the median tranche of the real exam. Mock Test 2 is the stretch paper. Ch 1 §1.8 places both papers in each study track — sit this one first.

---

## Instructions

- **This mock paper is 65 questions in 2 hours, and 65% or higher passes** — at least **43 correct**.
- **Single attempt.** Do all 65 before checking any answers. The point is to build stamina across the full 120-minute window, not to iterate.
- **No notes, no cheat sheet, no docs site.** If you can't answer a question, flag it and move on — exactly as you would in the live exam.
- **Time-budget target:** ~1.8 minutes per question. If a question crosses 3 minutes, flag and skip.
- Write your answers on a separate sheet (A/B/C/D, or free-form for fill-in-the-blank / matching / build-list). The answer key follows the questions — don't skim ahead.
- Scoring: each question is 1 point. Multi-answer questions score 1 point only if **all** correct options are selected and no incorrect ones — no partial credit, matching the exam's published basis: one point for a correct answer, zero for an incorrect one, all questions weighted equally.
- After scoring, read every explanation — including the ones you got right — to catch questions where you guessed well. Revisit the flagged chapters in priority order.

Format shapes used in this mock — each stem is self-describing; recognise the shape from its phrasing:

- **Single-answer MCQ** — one correct option. Four options A–D, except Q42, which has five.
- **Multi-answer** — the stem says so: "Which two..." or "(Select all that apply.)". Option count is not the tell. All correct options must be selected.
- **Fill in the blank** — the stem carries "Fill in the blank:" and an `______` placeholder; answer is the missing token.
- **Matching** — a two-column table; answer with pairs like `1→b, 2→c`.
- **Hotspot** — a numbered YAML or SQL snippet, with each option naming a line; answer with the letter.
- **Build-list** — stem says "Order..." or "reorder..."; answer with the sequence of item numbers.

## Questions

**1.** Which statement about the `{{ ref() }}` function is true?
A. `ref()` executes at run time inside the warehouse and returns a row set.
B. `ref()` is a shortcut for hard-coding `<database>.<schema>.<table>` and has no effect on the DAG.
C. `ref()` resolves at compile time to a target-aware, schema-qualified relation identifier and registers a dependency edge in the project's graph.
D. `ref()` works inside models whose materialization is `table`, and compiles to a literal elsewhere.

**2.** You are writing a staging model `stg_payments.sql` that reads from a raw table named `payments` in a database `raw_prd` and schema `finance`. A `sources.yml` file declares a source named `finance` under that database/schema with a table called `payments`. Which line in the staging model is correct?
A. `select * from raw_prd.finance.payments`
B. `select * from {{ ref('finance', 'payments') }}`
C. `select * from {{ source('finance', 'payments') }}`
D. `select * from {{ source('raw_prd', 'finance.payments') }}`

**3.** Given this `sources.yml` fragment, how many sources and tables are declared?

```
sources:
  - name: salesforce
    database: raw
    schema: salesforce
    tables:
      - name: accounts
      - name: opportunities
      - name: contacts
  - name: stripe
    database: raw
    schema: stripe
    tables:
      - name: charges
      - name: customers
```

A. 1 source with 5 tables B. 5 sources with 2 tables
C. 2 sources with 2 tables D. 2 sources with 5 tables

**4.** In the following model SQL, which line introduces a bug that will cause the DAG to build in the wrong order?

```
1: {{ config(materialized='table') }}
2:
3: with accounts as (
4:   select * from {{ ref('stg_accounts') }}
5: ),
6: opportunities as (
7:   select * from raw_prd.salesforce.opportunities
8: )
9: select a.*, o.total_amount
10: from accounts a
11: left join opportunities o on o.account_id = a.id
```

A. Line 1 — materialization should be `view`
B. Line 4 — the `ref()` should be wrapped in `source()` instead.
C. Line 7 — hard-coded identifier bypasses the DAG; should be `{{ source(...) }}` or `{{ ref(...) }}`
D. Line 11 — the join should use `inner join` instead of `left join`

**5.** Which is the default materialization for a model with no `materialized` config set anywhere in the project?
A. `table` B. `incremental`
C. `ephemeral` D. `view`

**6.** You are building a reporting mart that is queried by ~30 dashboards every few minutes. The source data changes once per day. The mart takes 45 seconds to compute. Which materialization is the most appropriate default?
A. `view` — logical, so it stays in step with upstream on each query.
B. `ephemeral` — let dbt inline the SQL into each downstream model that refs it.
C. `table` — rebuild once per day, read cheaply from the materialized object many times.
D. `incremental` with an `append` strategy and a daily filter.

**7.** A model uses a conventional incremental strategy — `merge` or `delete+insert`. Which of the following does it need in order to load only new or changed rows correctly, rather than reprocessing its whole source every run? (Select all that apply.)
A. `materialized='incremental'`
B. `strategy='scd2'`, naming the SCD2 history strategy
C. An `{% if is_incremental() %}` guard around the filter
D. `unique_key`, for the `merge` and `delete+insert` strategies
E. `persist_docs: {relation: true}` to publish the description
F. `snapshot: true` to register the model for history tracking

**8.** An incremental model has been running nightly for months. A contributor adds a `promo_code` column to its SELECT and, in the same PR, sets `on_schema_change: append_new_columns`. After the next `dbt run`, what does `promo_code` hold in the target table?
A. Values for every row — dbt reprocesses the table when the schema changes.
B. Values on the rows this run and later runs insert; `NULL` on every row already in the table.
C. Nothing yet — `append_new_columns` takes effect only on the following `--full-refresh`.
D. Nothing: dbt errors, because widening a model that has already been built requires `sync_all_columns`.

**9.** Fill in the blank: the built-in Jinja macro that returns `True` when an incremental model's target table already exists and the run is not in full-refresh mode is `{{ ______ }}`.

**10.** A fact model on dbt-postgres receives late-arriving corrections: rows already loaded are restated, matched on `order_id`. The team wants the corrections applied rather than duplicated. Which incremental configuration does that, on this adapter?
A. `incremental_strategy='append'` — the corrected rows are added, and consumers take the latest by `loaded_at`.
B. `incremental_strategy='delete+insert'` with `unique_key='order_id'` — dbt deletes the matching rows, then inserts the new versions.
C. `incremental_strategy='insert_overwrite'` with no `unique_key` — the affected partitions are replaced wholesale.
D. `incremental_strategy='merge'` with no `unique_key` — Postgres matches on the table's primary key automatically.

**11.** A model sets `materialized='incremental'` and `incremental_strategy='microbatch'`. Which set of configs must it also declare for the project to parse?
A. `event_time`, `begin`, `batch_size`
B. `event_time`, `lookback`, `unique_key`
C. `partition_by`, `begin`, `batch_size`
D. `event_time`, `begin`, `concurrent_batches`

**12.** A microbatch model on dbt-postgres declares `event_time`, `batch_size='month'` and a `begin` several months before today, so the run plans a number of monthly batches. It declares no `unique_key`. You run `dbt run --select that_model --full-refresh`. What happens?
A. The run fails at parse time, before dbt plans a single batch.
B. The first batch builds, then batch 2 fails with a compilation error demanding a `unique_key` config.
C. Every batch builds; `unique_key` matters to the `merge` strategy alone.
D. dbt falls back to `append` and duplicates rows across the overlapping batch windows.

**13.** Fill in the blank: a relative sample window is written as an integer and a grain, as in `dbt run --sample='3 days'`. A sample window narrows only those `ref()` and `source()` relations that declare an ______ config; without it the run succeeds and quietly processes every row.

**14.** A SQL table model `fct_orders` has this complete query and only the built-in `unique` and `not_null` tests on `order_id`, at their default configuration:

```
select order_id from {{ ref('stg_orders') }}
```

A CI job runs `dbt build --select fct_orders --empty --full-refresh` with `stg_orders` already materialized in the target schema. The model and both tests pass. What has that result established?
A. The table was created empty and its two tests passed vacuously; production data quality remains untested.
B. The production orders have unique, non-null IDs; the run validated those warehouse rows.
C. The SQL compiled without executing; `--empty` bypassed table creation and the test phase.
D. The table contains all production orders; `--empty` changed only the displayed row counts.

**15.** Which statement about dbt **snapshots** is correct?
A. Snapshots are defined in `models/` and selected with `materialized='snapshot'`.
B. Snapshots are an optimization of incremental models — faster on large tables.
C. Snapshots track SCD2 history with `dbt_valid_from` and `dbt_valid_to` columns, and run via `dbt snapshot`.
D. Snapshots require a `unique_key` but take no strategy configuration.

**16.** A snapshot uses the `check` strategy. Which configuration determines which columns dbt compares between runs?
A. `unique_key` B. `updated_at`
C. `loaded_at_field` D. `check_cols`

**17.** The `country_codes` seed is already loaded. A developer changes CSV values only; its column names and types do not change. The downstream `dim_locations` table model and `rpt_sales_by_country` reporting model, plus their direct tests, must use the new lookup values. No upstream node needs work. Which one command meets all requirements?
A. `dbt seed --select country_codes`
B. `dbt run --select country_codes+`
C. `dbt build --select country_codes+`
D. `dbt build --select country_codes`

**18.** A team wants to rewrite a heavy SQL model as a **Python model** and keep it materialized as a `view` so downstream queries always see current data. What happens?
A. It works — Python models support the same five materializations as SQL models.
B. Python models take no `materialized` config at all; the adapter chooses one per run.
C. It works, but dbt silently downgrades the view to `ephemeral` and inlines it downstream.
D. Python models support `table` and `incremental` only, so `view` is rejected; the model has to be a table.

**19.** Which of the following warehouse/runtime combinations support dbt Python models? (Select all that apply.)
A. Snowflake, via Snowpark
B. Databricks, via PySpark on a cluster or serverless compute
C. BigQuery, via PySpark on Dataproc (Serverless or cluster)
D. Postgres, via the `plpython3u` procedural language
E. Redshift, via a Python user-defined function

**20.** You have this `dbt_project.yml` fragment:

```
1: models:
2:   acme:
3:     staging:
4:       +materialized: view
5:     marts:
6:       +materialized: table
7:       finance:
8:         +materialized: incremental
9:         +unique_key: order_id
```

A model at `models/marts/finance/fct_orders.sql` has no `{{ config() }}` block and no YAML `config:` entry. Which line defines the materialization this model will have?

A. Line 4 B. Line 6
C. Line 8 D. Line 9

**21.** A `dbt_project.yml` declares `config-version: 2`, `model-paths: ["models"]` and `seed-paths: ["seeds"]`, and nothing else. `dbt parse` fails. Which keys is the file missing?

A. `version` and `target-path`
B. `name` and `profile`
C. `profile` and `packages-install-path`
D. `name` and `require-dbt-version`

**22.** Order these four locations from **highest** to **lowest** in dbt's config-precedence chain:

1. `dbt_project.yml` `+config` block under `models:`
2. `{{ config(...) }}` inside the model's `.sql` file
3. YAML `config:` block in a properties (schema) file
4. dbt's built-in defaults

**23.** The `vars:` block in `dbt_project.yml` and the `--vars` CLI flag both feed which Jinja function?

Fill in the blank: `{{ ______('my_var') }}`.

**24.** Match the Jinja context function on the left to its purpose on the right.

| Function | Purpose |
|---|---|
| 1. `ref('model_name')` | a. Return the current target's name / schema / database / type |
| 2. `source('src', 'tbl')` | b. Register a dependency on a dbt-managed model and resolve to its relation |
| 3. `doc('block_name')` | c. Register a dependency on a raw table declared in `sources.yml` |
| 4. `env_var('MY_VAR')` | d. Read a value from the host process's environment |
| 5. `target` | e. Insert a reusable description defined in a `.md` doc block |
| 6. `this` | f. Return the relation identifier of the model being compiled |

**25.** In the following `dbt_project.yml` snippet, which block sets warehouse grants for every model under `models/marts/`?

```
models:
  acme:
    marts:
      +grants:
        select: ['reporter', 'analyst']
```

A. `grants:` is only valid inside a model's `{{ config() }}` block, so this snippet has no effect.
B. The grants apply at dbt parse time, before any model is built.
C. `grants:` can only be set at the project root, not under `models:`.
D. `+grants: {select: [...]}` applies the listed `SELECT` grants to every materialization produced under `models/marts/`.

**26.** Which statement about pinning a package in `packages.yml` is correct?
A. Pinning is discouraged; leaving a package unpinned lets `dbt deps` pick up upstream fixes as they ship.
B. Pinning applies to git packages alone; hub packages are resolved from the registry at install time.
C. `packages.yml` ignores version numbers; `dbt deps` resolves to the newest release each time it runs.
D. `version: "x.y.z"` for a hub package or `revision:` for a git package pins the install, and `dbt deps` records the resolved set in `package-lock.yml`.

**27.** Which command installs the packages declared in `packages.yml` into the project's `dbt_packages/` directory?
A. `dbt install` B. `dbt build --deps`
C. `dbt packages install` D. `dbt deps`

**28.** Which statement about `dbt build` vs `dbt run` is correct?
A. `dbt build` is an alias for `dbt run` that also prints a resource summary.
B. `dbt build` runs models, then tests, then seeds, then snapshots in that order as separate phases without short-circuiting.
C. `dbt build` executes models, tests, seeds, and snapshots in DAG order, and short-circuits rather than pressing on past a failure.
D. `dbt build` runs only the models whose code has changed since the last invocation.

**29.** Which command generates the two JSON artifacts that the dbt docs site renders from?
A. `dbt parse` B. `dbt compile`
C. `dbt docs generate` D. `dbt build --docs`

**30.** Which artifact contains warehouse-introspected column types and table statistics for each node, and is written by `dbt docs generate`?
A. `manifest.json` B. `run_results.json`
C. `sources.json` D. `catalog.json`

**31.** Which statement about **model contracts** is correct?
A. On a `table`, `view` or `incremental` model, an enforced contract requires every column of the SELECT to be declared in `columns:` with a `data_type`.
B. Contracts are supported only on Snowflake; other adapters ignore the config.
C. Enforcing a contract forces dbt to re-materialize the model as a `view` regardless of its original materialization.
D. Contracts replace data tests — once enforced, tests configured under `data_tests:` are skipped.

**32.** Which of these can be declared under a model's `constraints:` block at dbt Core 1.11? (Select all that apply.)
A. `check`
B. `custom`, with an `expression` dbt emits verbatim into the DDL
C. `exclusion`, mapping to the Postgres `EXCLUDE` clause
D. `foreign_key`
E. `masking_policy`, for Snowflake column masking
F. `default`, to supply a column default value

**33.** A model's YAML declares a `primary_key` constraint on one column and a `not_null` constraint on another. The model has no `contract:` block. What does dbt do on the next `dbt run`?
A. It emits both constraints in the `CREATE TABLE` DDL and the warehouse enforces them.
B. It raises a parsing error, because constraints require an enforced contract to be declared.
C. It ignores both constraints — they are inert without `contract: {enforced: true}`.
D. It enforces them itself after the build, failing the model when a row violates one.

**34.** Your team declares `primary_key`, `foreign_key` and `not_null` constraints under an enforced contract, and deploys the same project to Postgres and to Snowflake. Which outcome should you expect?
A. Both platforms reject rows that violate any of the three; the contract makes enforcement uniform.
B. Snowflake enforces all three, and Postgres accepts `not_null` while ignoring the rest.
C. Neither platform enforces anything: constraints are dbt-side documentation that never reaches the DDL.
D. Postgres enforces all three at build time; on Snowflake `not_null` is enforced and the key constraints are recorded as metadata.

**35.** You have declared versions 1 and 2 of the model `dim_users` under `versions:`, with `latest_version: 2`. A downstream model calls `{{ ref('dim_users') }}` with no `v=` argument. Which version does dbt resolve to?
A. Version 1 — an unpinned `ref()` resolves to the lowest declared version identifier.
B. dbt raises an error, because `v=` is required once `versions:` is declared.
C. Version 2 — `latest_version` is what an unpinned `ref()` resolves to.
D. dbt resolves to whichever version was defined last in the YAML file.

**36.** Fill in the blank: to pin a downstream reference to version 2 of `dim_users` instead of following `latest_version`, write `{{ ref('dim_users', ______) }}`.

**37.** Which statement about `access:` on a model is true?
A. `access: private` means only resources in the same group as the model may `ref()` it — and a model with no group is in no group, so it rejects every caller.
B. `access: public` is the default for all models.
C. `access` is a warehouse-level grant — it controls which warehouse roles can `SELECT` from the table.
D. `access: private` is refused at parse time unless the model also declares a `group:`.

**38.** A CI step runs `dbt build`. Three models fail their tests, dbt prints a complete run summary, and the shell captures exit code `1`. What does that exit code tell you?
A. dbt itself crashed partway through, so the summary it printed cannot be trusted.
B. The warehouse refused a connection; a refused connection is the only source of exit code `1`.
C. Exit code `1` is dbt's success code; `0` is reserved for an invocation that selected no nodes.
D. The run completed and reported a handled failure — nodes failed, but dbt finished and wrote `run_results.json`.

**39.** Two models `a.sql` and `b.sql` contain `{{ ref('b') }}` and `{{ ref('a') }}` respectively. What does `dbt compile` do?
A. Picks a compile order arbitrarily and renders both models into `target/compiled/`.
B. Drops one of the two refs, compiles both, and reports nothing about the loss.
C. Fails with `Found a cycle:` naming both models — the graph cannot be linked.
D. Compiles both and defers the cycle to a warning on the next `dbt run`.

**40.** When a `dbt run` fails with a wrapped "Database Error" message quoting warehouse vocabulary like "invalid identifier 'ORDER_I'", what is the most useful first diagnostic step?
A. Re-run with `--full-refresh` so the target relation is rebuilt from scratch.
B. Run `dbt debug` to confirm the warehouse connection is still healthy.
C. Open `target/compiled/<path>.sql`, read the resolved SELECT, and run it in the warehouse query editor.
D. Run `dbt clean` to clear `target/` and `dbt_packages/`, then retry the model.

**41.** Which is the standard fix path for a YAML indentation error in a properties file? Order these steps as the fastest working-to-merged sequence:

1. Open the file in an editor and locate the reported line:column.
2. Run `dbt parse` (or `dbt compile`) to reproduce the error on the same branch.
3. Correct the indentation, replacing any tabs with spaces.
4. Re-run `dbt parse` to confirm the error is gone.
5. Open a pull request and add the fix as a commit.

**42.** A project calls `{{ generate_surrogate_key(['a', 'b']) }}` and `dbt compile` fails with `'generate_surrogate_key' is undefined`. The project's `packages.yml` declares `dbt-labs/dbt_utils`, and `dbt_packages/` holds it. Which action resolves the failure?
A. Run `dbt deps` again to reinstall the package so its macros become available.
B. Call the macro namespaced as `{{ dbt_utils.generate_surrogate_key([...]) }}`.
C. Move the macro call into `on-run-start`.
D. Rename the macro file under `macros/`.
E. Run `dbt clean` and try again.

**43.** An engineer's `dbt run` on dbt Core 1.11 fails immediately with `relation "analytics_qa.fct_orders" does not exist`, before any model builds. The project's `dbt_project.yml` has an `on-run-start` hook that issues `select * from {{ target.schema }}.fct_orders limit 0`. Which is the most likely cause?
A. The hook's SELECT probes a relation that does not exist yet in this engineer's target schema, so it fails before any model builds.
B. `on-run-start` does not fire on `dbt run`; that hook is reserved for `dbt build` invocations.
C. `dbt run` reads `on-run-end` hooks and ignores `on-run-start`, so the SQL belongs there instead.
D. dbt rejects `select` statements in project hooks; hooks accept DDL and DML statements.

**44.** The standard "slim CI" command recipe is:
A. `dbt build --select state:modified+ --defer --state ./prior-artifacts`
B. `dbt build --full-refresh`
C. `dbt run --select @state:modified`
D. `dbt build --select result:error+ --target ci`

**45.** An engineer opens a PR that touches one model, `fct_orders`. The CI job runs `dbt build --select state:modified+ --defer --state ./prior-artifacts`. The unchanged upstreams are never built into the CI schema, and `fct_orders`'s refs to them still resolve. What makes the refs resolve?

A. `--defer --state` tells dbt that a `ref()` to an unmodified upstream resolves against the prior run's relation rather than rebuilding it in the CI target.

B. `state:modified+` selects downstream of modified nodes and deliberately excludes unchanged upstreams.

C. The CI target sets `full_refresh: false`, which suppresses upstream rebuilds.

D. `dbt build` walks the graph downstream by default, so ancestors fall outside the selection.

**46.** In a DAG with a parent model `stg_events` that has three direct descendants `int_events_daily`, `int_events_weekly`, and `int_events_monthly`, a `dbt build` run fails on `stg_events`. What happens to its three descendants?

A. They all run; dbt only short-circuits when the failure is in a test.

B. They are marked as `skipped` because their upstream dependency failed.

C. They run sequentially; the second and third are cancelled when the first fails.

D. dbt restarts from `stg_events` with `--full-refresh`.

**47.** A CI job orchestrated by an external tool (e.g., Airflow, Jenkins) runs `dbt build` and fails. Which selector re-runs only the failed node and everything downstream on the next invocation?

A. `--select result:error+` B. `--select state:modified+`

C. `--select result:success+` D. `--select source_status:error+`

**48.** A CI job needs a full, queryable copy of the production schema for a smoke test, without paying to rebuild any incremental model. Which command gets it, and how?

A. `dbt clone --state ./prod-artifacts` — zero-copy clones where the adapter supports them, and a pointer view where it does not.

B. `dbt build --full-refresh --target ci` — rebuilds every relation from source in the CI schema.

C. `dbt run --defer --state ./prod-artifacts` — defers reads to production without creating relations.

D. `dbt clone --full-refresh` — a physical `CREATE TABLE AS SELECT` of each production relation.

**49.** A `dbt build` running with `--threads 8` and `--fail-fast` hits an error on one model while seven other nodes are mid-query. What does dbt do?

A. It lets the seven in-flight nodes finish, then stops before scheduling anything new.

B. It cancels the in-flight queries, then marks every node that had not run as skipped.

C. It retries the failed model once, and stops the run only if the retry fails too.

D. It stops the run and reports the seven in-flight nodes as errors alongside the first.

**50.** You are authoring a **custom generic test**. Which two statements about writing the test are true?
A. The test is defined inside a `{% test my_test(model, column_name) %}` / `{% endtest %}` block, where `my_test` is the generic name callers will invoke.
B. The test body is a SQL `SELECT` statement; dbt fails the test when that SELECT returns zero rows.
C. Custom generic tests must be defined in the `tests/` directory — files placed under `macros/` are ignored.
D. The test body must explicitly `return` a boolean; dbt fails the test when the return value is `false`.
E. A custom generic test can be invoked from YAML under a column's `tests:` key the same way a built-in (`unique`, `not_null`) is invoked.

**51.** A **singular test** is:
A. A generic test with exactly one argument.
B. A `.sql` file in the `tests/` directory whose SELECT returns zero rows when the assertion passes.
C. A test that runs against a single column only.
D. A macro in `macros/` wrapped in `{% test %}` tags.

**52.** Which statement about **unit tests** at dbt Core 1.11 is correct?
A. A unit test is a `.sql` file under `tests/` that passes when its SELECT returns zero rows.
B. A unit test declares mock inputs under `given:` and expected rows under `expect:` in a `unit_tests:` block in a `models/` properties file, and dbt runs it before the model materializes.
C. A unit test queries the model's materialized relation, so the model must be built before its unit tests can run.
D. A unit test is a data test with `severity: error`, so a failure short-circuits the downstream graph.

**53.** Which pair is correct about `severity` in test configs?
A. `severity: warn` stops the build on failure; `severity: error` records the failure in the log and continues.
B. `severity: error` (default) → test failure fails the build; `severity: warn` → test failure is reported as a warning but does not fail the build.
C. `severity:` takes `high` or `low`, and `error_if` converts one into the other.
D. `severity: warn` sets `store_failures: true` for you, so failing rows are kept for inspection.

**54.** You add `store_failures: true` to a test config. Where do failing rows land?
A. Appended to `target/compiled/<test_name>.sql` alongside the compiled test SQL.
B. Written to a warehouse table in the test's audit schema, `<schema>_dbt_test__audit` by default.
C. Printed to stdout in the run log and discarded when the invocation ends.
D. Written to a `failures.yml` file in the project root for review before the next run.

**55.** Match each test config on the left to its effect on the right.

| Config | Effect |
|---|---|
| 1. `config: {fail_calc: "sum(amount_over_limit)"}` | a. Narrow the rows the test operates on (e.g., tested only where `created_at >= ...`) |
| 2. `config: {where: "created_at >= current_date - 7"}` | b. Persist the retained failures as a view rather than a table |
| 3. `config: {store_failures_as: view}` | c. Report the aggregate the expression computes instead of a row count |
| 4. `config: {limit: 10}` | d. Cap the number of rows returned per failing test |

**56.** You want to run every test in the project that is tagged `nightly`. Which command does that?

A. `dbt test --select tag:nightly` B. `dbt run --select tag:nightly`
C. `dbt test --tag nightly` D. `dbt build --select test_type:nightly`

**57.** You are running `dbt build` with the default indirect selection mode. You pass `--select tag:nightly`. How does dbt decide which tests run?

A. It runs the tests that carry the `nightly` tag themselves, and nothing attached to the selected models.
B. In the default `eager` mode dbt runs any test whose referenced resources intersect the selected set.
C. It runs the project's whole test suite, because tag selection applies to models rather than to tests.
D. Tags select models; tests are reached through a separate `--select test_type:` clause.

**58.** Which statement about **exposures** is correct?

A. Exposures are a materialization that renders a dashboard from a model's result set.
B. Exposures are YAML-declared downstream consumers with a required `name`, `type` and `owner`, plus a `depends_on:` list; they appear on the lineage graph and execute no SQL.
C. Exposures replace `ref()` for BI-facing marts, wiring the dashboard straight to the warehouse.
D. Exposures are a dbt platform feature; dbt Core parses them but ignores them entirely.

**59.** An exposure has `type: dashboard`, `depends_on: [ref('fct_revenue')]`, and `owner: {email: 'data@acme.io'}`. Which command lists every upstream node that feeds this exposure?

A. `dbt ls --select +exposure:my_dashboard` B. `dbt run --exposure my_dashboard`
C. `dbt exposures list` D. `dbt docs generate --exposure my_dashboard`

**60.** A source's YAML nests `freshness: {warn_after: {count: 12, period: hour}, error_after: {count: 2, period: day}}` and `loaded_at_field: inserted_at` under a `config:` key. The project runs on Snowflake. Which statement about that declaration at dbt Core 1.11 is correct?
A. The `config:` nesting is now required; the older top-level form was removed and raises a parsing error.
B. Both forms are valid — `config:` nesting is the recommended shape, and the top-level form parses, binds, and raises a deprecation warning on this adapter.
C. `period: day` is invalid; `warn_after` and `error_after` accept `minute`, `hour` and `week` alone.
D. Both forms are valid and the top-level form raises no deprecation warning on any adapter — "recommended" is not "deprecated".

**61.** Your nightly job runs `dbt source freshness`, then `dbt build --select source_status:fresher+ --state ./prior-artifacts`. On the very first night the build fails before it selects anything. Why?
A. The selector compares two freshness results — the prior run's `sources.json` inside `--state` and the one just written to `target/` — and night one has only the current file.
B. The selector reads `run_results.json`, which the freshness command does not write.
C. Night one has no prior to compare against, so the selector matches nothing and the build completes green over an empty selection.
D. `--state` must point at `target/`, not at a prior-artifacts directory.

**62.** Which artifacts does dbt read out of the directory passed to `--state ./prior-artifacts`? (Select all that apply.)
A. `manifest.json`
B. `run_results.json`
C. `catalog.json`
D. `sources.json`
E. `partial_parse.msgpack`

**63.** Which state-selector variant would you use if you want to re-run a model whenever the **body** of its SQL changed, but not when only its `{{ config() }}` values changed?
A. `state:modified` B. `state:modified+`
C. `state:modified.configs` D. `state:modified.body`

**64.** A `dbt build` on dbt Core 1.11 fails partway through. You want to resume, but only across the `marts` subtree. Which statement is correct?
A. `dbt retry --select marts` narrows the replay to the marts subtree.
B. `dbt retry` rejects `--select` outright; narrowing needs a fresh `dbt build` with a `result:` selector.
C. `dbt retry` replays the failed nodes and silently ignores any `--select` you pass it.
D. `dbt retry --full-refresh` is the documented way to scope a resume to one subtree.

**65.** You are in a CI job that has a fresh `./prior-artifacts/` directory containing the previous production run's artifacts. You want to: (1) build only the nodes whose definitions changed and everything downstream, (2) have tests run as part of the invocation, and (3) re-run any unresolved model execution errors from a prior partial run too. Which single command does all three?

A. `dbt build --select state:modified+ --exclude result:error --defer --state ./prior-artifacts`

B. `dbt build --select state:modified+ result:error+ --defer --state ./prior-artifacts`

C. `dbt run --select state:modified+ result:error+ --defer --state ./prior-artifacts`

D. `dbt retry --select state:modified+ --defer --state ./prior-artifacts`

---

## Answer key

Score yourself first. Each entry cites the doc ref that grounds the claim, plus a book-chapter pointer if you want to re-drill the topic.

---

**1. C.** `ref()` resolves at compile time to a schema-qualified relation reference (e.g., `"analytics"."staging"."stg_orders"`) using the active target's schema and database, and registers a dependency edge in the manifest so dbt can order the DAG. It is not a run-time function (A), and it is emphatically more than a shortcut — it is what makes dbt a DAG engine rather than a SQL templating tool (B). Source: `/reference/dbt-jinja-functions/ref`. Revisit **Ch 2 §2.2** if this was hard. Cognitive level: recall.

**2. C.** A table declared in `sources.yml` is read via `{{ source('source_name', 'table_name') }}` — the source name is the top-level `name:` in the YAML, and the table name is the `- name:` under `tables:`. Hard-coding the identifier (A) bypasses dbt's source registration; `ref()` (B) is for dbt-managed models, not raw tables; the `source()` call in D has its arguments malformed. Source: `/reference/dbt-jinja-functions/source`, `/docs/build/sources`. Revisit **Ch 3 §3.2**. Cognitive level: recall.

**3. D.** Two distinct `name:` entries under `sources:` = 2 sources. Across both sources, the `tables:` lists sum to 3 + 2 = 5. By the §3.4 modeling convention, each source declaration corresponds to a distinct `(database, schema)` pair; counting distinct `name:` values under `sources:` is the quickest way to count sources. Source: `/reference/source-properties`. Revisit **Ch 3 §3.4**. Cognitive level: apply.

**4. C (Line 7).** `raw_prd.salesforce.opportunities` is a hard-coded identifier that bypasses the DAG — dbt cannot infer this as a dependency, so it may run this model against an environment where that raw object doesn't exist, or in the wrong order. The fix is to declare the raw table in `sources.yml` and reference it with `{{ source('salesforce', 'opportunities') }}` (or, if it is in fact a dbt-managed staging model, with `{{ ref('stg_opportunities') }}`). Hard-coded relation spotting is one of the exam's favourite traps. Source: `/reference/dbt-jinja-functions/source`. Revisit **Ch 3 §3.2**. Cognitive level: apply.

**5. D.** The default materialization for any model without a `materialized` config is `view` — the cheapest to build and the one most tolerant of upstream schema drift. Source: `/docs/build/materializations`. Revisit **Ch 4 §4.1**. Cognitive level: recall.

**6. C.** A mart read many times per day but refreshed once should be a `table`: rebuild cost is paid once, read cost is minimal on the materialized object. A `view` would re-compute the 45-second SELECT on every dashboard query — the exact anti-pattern. `ephemeral` would inline the SQL into each dashboard-facing model, which is worse again. `incremental` is defensible for very large marts but adds configuration (`unique_key`, `is_incremental()`, a strategy) not justified here. Source: `/docs/build/materializations`. Revisit **Ch 4 §4.1**. Cognitive level: apply.

**7. A, C, D.** Read the stem's test: *load only new or changed rows correctly.* `materialized='incremental'` (A) is what selects the materialization at all. The `is_incremental()` guard (C) is what confines the filter to subsequent runs — note the precise claim, since this is where the item is won or lost: a model without the guard still parses and still builds, it just re-reads its entire source every run, which is the behaviour the stem rules out. And `unique_key` (D) is what `merge` and `delete+insert` match target rows on; without it `merge` silently degrades to an append and `delete+insert` has nothing to delete by, so both stop being correct on a re-processed row. `strategy='scd2'` (B) is not a config; snapshots do SCD2, not incrementals. `persist_docs` (E) is a documentation feature, orthogonal to incrementality. `snapshot: true` (F) is not a real config. The stem names the two conventional strategies deliberately: a `microbatch` model needs no `is_incremental()` guard at all, because dbt filters the upstream `ref()` per batch. Sources: `/docs/build/incremental-models`, `/reference/resource-configs/unique_key`, `/docs/build/incremental-microbatch`. Revisit **Ch 4 §4.3**. Cognitive level: recall.

**8. B.** `on_schema_change` reconciles the target's SHAPE, not its history. `append_new_columns` issues the `ALTER TABLE ... ADD COLUMN`, so the column exists from this run on and every row the run inserts carries a value — but dbt does not revisit rows that are already there, and no value is computed for them. They hold `NULL`, and they will hold `NULL` until something reprocesses them. That something is `--full-refresh`, which is the only way to populate history for a newly added column, and the reason a widening change to a large incremental is a scheduling decision rather than a one-line edit. **None of the four `on_schema_change` values backfill.** A is the assumption the config's name invites and the one to break. C inverts the mechanism: the config works on the incremental path and is what a full refresh makes unnecessary, not the other way round. D invents an error; `sync_all_columns` differs from `append_new_columns` in that it also *drops* columns the SQL no longer selects, which is a wider blast radius, not a prerequisite. Source: `/docs/build/incremental-models`. Revisit **Ch 4 §4.3.3**. Cognitive level: analyze.

**9. `is_incremental()`.** The `is_incremental()` built-in returns `True` only when (a) the model is configured as `incremental`, (b) the target table already exists in the warehouse, and (c) the run is not in full-refresh mode. On the first run (when the target does not yet exist) it returns `False` and the guard compiles away. Read (c) carefully: `--full-refresh` on the CLI is the usual way in, but a model configured `full_refresh: false` overrides that flag and keeps the model on the incremental branch — so "`--full-refresh` was not passed" and "not in full-refresh mode" are not the same condition. Source: `/docs/build/incremental-models`. Revisit **Ch 4 §4.3.1**. Cognitive level: recall.

**10. B.** `delete+insert` is the strategy that restates a row: for the keys in the incoming batch it deletes the matching target rows and inserts the new versions, which is why it needs a `unique_key` to mean anything. Note what it does **not** do: without one dbt does not refuse — `default__get_delete_insert_merge_sql` wraps the whole `delete` block in `{% if unique_key %}` and emits the `insert` regardless, so the model runs green and accumulates duplicates (§4.3). And it is the **unnamed** default strategy that dbt-postgres resolves to `delete+insert`; ask for `merge` by name and Postgres issues a real `MERGE`. Naming `delete+insert` explicitly is therefore a real choice, not a synonym. A is the shape of the bug the stem describes: `append` writes the correction beside the original and leaves every consumer to deduplicate, which is the work the incremental was supposed to do. C names a strategy dbt-postgres does not implement, and pairs it with a partition concept Postgres has no equivalent config for here. D is the trap worth carrying: `merge` with **no** `unique_key` does not fall back to a primary key or raise — it silently degrades to append-only, so it looks configured and behaves like A. Sources: `/docs/build/incremental-strategy`, `/reference/resource-configs/unique_key`. Revisit **Ch 4 §4.3**. Cognitive level: apply.

**11. A.** Microbatch has exactly three required configs: `event_time` (the timestamp column dbt filters on), `begin` (the earliest timestamp to build from), and `batch_size`. Omit any one and the project fails to parse with a message naming the missing config. `lookback` and `concurrent_batches` (D) are optional; `unique_key` (B) is required by some adapters but is not part of the universal trio; `partition_by` (C) belongs to warehouse-side partitioning, not to microbatch. `batch_size` accepts `hour`, `day`, `month` or `year` — there is no `week`. Source: `/docs/build/incremental-microbatch`. Revisit **Ch 4 §4.4.1**. Cognitive level: recall.

**12. B.** This is the microbatch trap that only shows up at run time. On dbt-postgres the microbatch strategy replaces a batch with a `MERGE` keyed on `unique_key`, so the adapter requires one — but batch 1 of a full refresh writes into an empty target and succeeds, and the failure surfaces only at batch 2, the first one dbt treats as incremental — under `--full-refresh` batch 1 is submitted non-incrementally whether or not the target already exists. The error is `dbt-postgres 'microbatch' requires a unique_key config`, raised from `postgres__get_incremental_microbatch_sql`. Adapters with native partition replacement do not need it, which is why the requirement reads as adapter trivia until it bites. Source: `/docs/build/incremental-microbatch`. Revisit **Ch 4 §4.4.5**. Cognitive level: analyze.

**13.** **`event_time`.** A sample window filters a `ref()` or `source()` only when the referenced relation declares an `event_time` config — and note that a *source* needs its own `event_time`, not just the model reading it. Without it, `--sample` fails **open**: no error, no warning, a green run, and every row processed. That silent-success mode is what makes it worth a question. The window itself takes two shapes: relative (`--sample='3 days'`, grain `hour`/`day`/`month`/`year`) or static (`--sample='{"start": "...", "end": "..."}'`). Source: `/docs/build/sample-flag`. Revisit **Ch 11 §11.12**. Cognitive level: recall.

**14. A.** `--empty` limits the `ref()` input to zero rows. This query only projects that input, so the table is empty and both default tests count zero failures. That validates SQL execution and table creation, not production IDs (B). The tests still execute (C), and the table contains no production rows (D). The explicit query matters: zero input does not guarantee zero output for every SQL model, such as one selecting a literal or an aggregate. See `/docs/build/empty-flag` and **Ch 11 §11.11**. Cognitive level: analyze.

**15. C.** Snapshots are the dbt SCD2 construct: they track source-row history and write `dbt_valid_from` / `dbt_valid_to` (plus `dbt_scd_id` and `dbt_updated_at`) columns, and they run via `dbt snapshot` — also included in `dbt build`. A `{% snapshot %}` **block** lives under `snapshot-paths`, never `models/`; the YAML form is looser, and convention keeps it there too. A snapshot is its own resource type, and setting `materialized='snapshot'` on a model does not produce one: dbt does ship a `snapshot` materialization, and a model carrying it alongside `unique_key` and `strategy` builds — but what it builds is a model (A). They carry a `strategy:` config, `timestamp` or `check`, which makes D wrong. The primary definition syntax is a top-level `snapshots:` YAML block with `relation:` plus `config:`; the older `{% snapshot %}` Jinja block is legacy but still valid. Source: `/docs/build/snapshots`. Revisit **Ch 5 §5.1–§5.2**. Cognitive level: recall.

**16. D.** The `check` strategy compares the columns listed in `check_cols` between the previous snapshot row and the current source row. `updated_at` is used by the `timestamp` strategy. `unique_key` is required for either strategy to identify the same logical row. `loaded_at_field` belongs to source freshness, not snapshots. Sources: `/reference/resource-configs/strategy`, `/reference/resource-configs/check_cols`. Revisit **Ch 5 §5.2**. Cognitive level: recall.

**17. C.** The suffix `+` selects `country_codes` and its downstream nodes. `dbt build` loads the selected seed, materializes the selected models, and runs tests that directly depend on those models in DAG order. Because only CSV values changed, an ordinary reload is sufficient; `--full-refresh` is for a structural change. `dbt seed` reloads only the CSV, `dbt run --select country_codes+` leaves the seed's existing rows in place and runs no tests, and bare `dbt build --select country_codes` does not select downstream models. Sources: `dbt build`, `dbt seed`, `Graph operators`. Revisit **Ch 5 §5.4 and Ch 11 §11.2, §11.7**. Cognitive level: apply.

**18. D.** Python models support two materializations, `table` and `incremental`. `view` and `ephemeral` are SQL-only, because both are compile-time constructs — a view is a stored SELECT and an ephemeral model is inlined as a CTE, and neither has any meaning for a

DataFrame-returning Python function. A team that needs always-current data from a Python model materializes it as a table and schedules it, or moves the logic back to SQL. Source: `/docs/build/python-models`. Revisit **Ch 4 §4.7**. Cognitive level: apply.

**19. A, B, C.** Python models are supported on Snowflake (Snowpark), Databricks (PySpark), and BigQuery (PySpark on Dataproc — Serverless or cluster) — the three platforms dbt Labs documents. `plpython3u` and a Redshift Python UDF are real warehouse features, but neither is a dbt Python-model runtime: the materialization macro has to declare `supported_languages=['sql', 'python']` and the adapter has to implement `submit_python_job`, and dbt-postgres and dbt-redshift ship neither half. Asking dbt-postgres for one fails with `Materialization "materialization_table_default" only supports languages ['sql']; got "python"`. Source: `/docs/build/python-models`. Revisit **Ch 4 §4.7**. Cognitive level: recall.

**20. C (Line 8).** Config precedence in `dbt_project.yml` cascades from general to specific — the deeper path `models: acme: marts: finance:` sets `+materialized: incremental` on line 8, which wins over the `marts` parent's `+materialized: table` on line 6. Line 9 sets `+unique_key`, not the materialization. Source: `/reference/define-configs`, `/reference/resource-configs/materialized`. Revisit **Ch 2 §2.4 and Ch 4 §4.2**. Cognitive level: apply.

**21. B.** `dbt_project.yml` has exactly two required keys: `name` (the project's name, used as the top-level key under `models:`) and `profile` (which profile in `profiles.yml` supplies the connection). Everything else has a default — `version`, `target-path`, `packages-install-path`, `require-dbt-version` are all optional, and `config-version: 2` is the only supported value at 1.11 and is already present here. Sources: `/reference/project-configs/name`, `/reference/project-configs/profile`. Revisit **Ch 2 §2.1**. Cognitive level: recall.

**22. Correct order: 2, 3, 1, 4.** SQL-level `{{ config(...) }}` wins; then YAML `config:` blocks in properties files; then `dbt_project.yml +config`; then dbt's built-in defaults. "More specific wins" is the mnemonic — and note that a *generic* test inverts it, its instance `config:` in YAML beating the `{{ config() }}` in its own definition, which is a separate trap (Ch 7 §7.5). Source: `/reference/define-configs`. Revisit **Ch 6 §6.4 and Ch 2 §2.4**. Cognitive level: recall.

**23. `var`.** Both `dbt_project.yml`'s `vars:` block and the CLI `--vars '{key: value}'` flag are read by the Jinja `var()` function at compile time. `env_var()` is a different mechanism (it reads the host environment), and `config()` / `target` / `this` are unrelated. Source: `/reference/dbt-jinja-functions/var`. Revisit **Ch 6 §6.2**. Cognitive level: recall.

**24. 1→b, 2→c, 3→e, 4→d, 5→a, 6→f.** Each function maps to one canonical purpose: `ref()` registers a dbt-model dependency; `source()` registers a raw-table dependency; `doc()` splices in a description defined once in a `.md` doc block; `env_var()` reads the host-process environment; `target` exposes target attributes (`target.name`, `target.schema`, etc.); `this` resolves to the relation identifier of the current model. Source: `/reference/dbt-jinja-functions/ref` and the sibling pages in that index. Revisit **Ch 6 §6.1–§6.3**. Cognitive level: recall.

**25. D.** `+grants: {select: ['...']}` under a `models:` path applies those grants to every materialization produced under that path. Grants are applied at materialization time, as DDL issued after the warehouse object is created — not at parse time (B). They are valid both in `dbt_project.yml` and in an individual model's `{{ config() }}`, which rules out A and C. Source: `/reference/resource-configs/grants`. Revisit **Ch 13 §13.8**. Cognitive level: recall.

**26. D.** Pin with `version: "x.y.z"` for a Hub package or `revision: <branch|tag|hash>` for a Git package. `dbt deps` resolves the whole dependency tree and writes `package-lock.yml`, which records the fully resolved versions so a teammate's install matches yours; `dbt deps --upgrade` is what re-resolves it deliberately. Pinning is strongly recommended and works for every package source, which rules out A and B; version numbers are honoured, which rules out C. Source: `/docs/build/packages`. Revisit **Ch 8 §8.3**. Cognitive level: recall.

**27. D.** `dbt deps` installs packages declared in `packages.yml` into `dbt_packages/` (the path is configurable via `packages-install-path`). There is no `dbt install` or `dbt packages install` command; `dbt build` does not install packages. Source: `/reference/commands/deps`. Revisit **Ch 8 §8.4**. Cognitive level: recall.

**28. C.** `dbt build` executes models, tests, seeds, snapshots and user-defined functions in one DAG-ordered pass, and it short-circuits: if an upstream node fails (or a test on it fails with `severity: error`), downstream execution is gated as described in Ch 11 §11.2. C names four supported types without claiming an exhaustive list; the discriminators are DAG order and short-circuiting. B incorrectly runs separate resource-type phases end to end. Source: `/reference/commands/build`. Revisit **Ch 11 §11.2**. Cognitive level: recall.

**29. C.** `dbt docs generate` writes `target/catalog.json` (warehouse-introspected column types and table stats) and updates `target/manifest.json` (the project graph). `dbt docs serve` renders those artifacts as the local docs site. `parse` and `compile` do not produce `catalog.json`; `--docs` is not a real `build` flag. Source: `/reference/commands/cmd-docs` (note: this command retains the `cmd-` prefix in its URL). Revisit **Ch 9 §9.1**. Cognitive level: recall.

**30. D.** `catalog.json` is the warehouse-introspection artifact — produced by `dbt docs generate`, it captures column types, table statistics, and per-node metadata read back from the live warehouse. `manifest.json` is the project graph; `run_results.json` is the last invocation's per-node status; `sources.json` is produced by `dbt source freshness`. Source: `/reference/artifacts/catalog-json`. Revisit **Ch 9 §9.1 and Ch 12 §12.1**. Cognitive level: recall.

**31. A.** On a materialization that supports contracts — `table`, `view`, and `incremental` with `on_schema_change` set to `append_new_columns` or `fail` (§13.2) — `contract: {enforced: true}` requires every column in the model's compiled SELECT to be declared in the YAML `columns:` block with a `data_type`; any mismatch in name or type fails at build time. `data_type` is optional on an uncontracted model and becomes mandatory once the contract is enforced — that promotion is the mechanism the exam tests. The scope matters: an `ephemeral` or `materialized_view` model accepts the same config and builds green with columns missing, no error and no warning, which is §13.2's "unsupported is not the same as refused". Contracts are adapter-agnostic at the dbt level (B is wrong), they do not change materialization (C), and they coexist with data tests (D). Source: `/reference/resource-configs/contract`, `/reference/resource-properties/columns`. Revisit **Ch 13 §13.2–§13.3**. Cognitive level: recall.

**32. A, B, D.** Six constraint types are declarable: `not_null`, `unique`, `primary_key`, `foreign_key`, `check`, and `custom`. Of the options offered, `check`, `custom` and `foreign_key` are on that list. `custom` is the escape hatch — it pairs with an `expression` that dbt emits verbatim into the DDL, which is how you reach a platform-specific clause such as a Snowflake masking policy. `exclusion` (C) and `default` (F) are real SQL concepts but are not dbt constraint types, and `masking_policy` (E) is precisely the case `custom` exists to cover rather than a type of its own. Source: `/reference/resource-properties/constraints`. Revisit **Ch 13 §13.3**. Cognitive level: recall.

**33. C.** Constraints do nothing on their own: they are emitted into the DDL only under `contract: {enforced: true}`. Declared without a contract they are parsed, stored on the node, and ignored — no DDL, no error, no warning. That silence is what makes it a good exam item and a real production trap, because the YAML *looks* like it is doing something. dbt does not enforce constraints itself (D); enforcement, where it happens at all, is the warehouse's job. Source: `/reference/resource-configs/contract`, `/docs/mesh/govern/model-contracts`. Revisit **Ch 13 §13.3**. Cognitive level: apply.

**34. D.** "Declarable" and "enforced" are two different questions, and the contracts page carries a per-adapter matrix for exactly that reason. Postgres is the only adapter that enforces every constraint type at build time. On most cloud warehouses, `not_null` is the broadly-enforced one and `primary_key` / `foreign_key` are accepted and recorded as metadata the optimizer may use, without blocking a violating row. A contract guarantees the *shape* of the model — column names and types — not the *values* in it. Source: `/docs/mesh/govern/model-contracts`. Revisit **Ch 13 §13.3**. Cognitive level: analyze.

**35. C.** With latest_version: 2 declared, a bare {{ ref('dim_users') }} (no v=) resolves to version 2. latest_version exists precisely so downstream callers can opt into "whatever is current" without hard-coding a version number. If latest_version is not set, dbt resolves to the largest declared version identifier — not the lowest (A) and not the last one written in the file (D). Source: /reference/resource-properties/latest_version, /reference/dbt-jinja-functions/ref. Revisit **Ch 13 §13.4**. Cognitive level: recall.

**36.** v=2 (version=2 is the accepted long form). ref() takes the version as a keyword argument and reads version first, falling back to v — so the two spellings are interchangeable and ref('dim_users', v=2) and ref('dim_users', version=2) compile identically. Pinning is how a consumer opts out of following latest_version while a producer migrates. Source: /reference/dbt-jinja-functions/ref. Revisit **Ch 13 §13.4**. Cognitive level: recall.

**37. A.** private means same-group-only: only resources in the model's own group may ref() it, and a ref from outside raises DbtReferenceError at parse time. What dbt does *not* do is require the pairing, which is what defeats D — nothing checks that a private model has a group:, and an ungrouped one parses and then rejects every caller, the producing team's own downstream models included, with ... is private to the '' group. Pairing private with a group: is the book's standing advice (§13.6), not a rule dbt enforces. The default access is protected, not public (B). Access is dbt-metadata-side — it restricts who can ref() the model inside the project — and is distinct from grants:, which is the warehouse-role side (C). Sources: /docs/mesh/govern/model-access, /reference/resource-configs/access. Revisit **Ch 13 §13.6** and **§13.8**. Cognitive level: recall.

**38. D.** dbt has three process exit codes and they mean different things to a CI step. 0 is success. 1 is a **handled** error: dbt ran to completion, some nodes failed, the summary is accurate and run_results.json was written — which is exactly what a failing test produces. 2 is an **unhandled** error, meaning dbt itself did not complete and the artifacts may be absent or partial. Reading 1 as a crash (A) sends you looking for the wrong bug; it is the ordinary "the build is red" code. Keep these separate from a node's status, which is a string in run_results.json — success, error, fail, warn, skipped. Sources: /reference/exit-codes, /reference/commands/run. Revisit **Ch 10 §10.1**. Cognitive level: analyze.

**39. C.** The cycle bites at graph-link time, not at parse: dbt parse exits 0 and writes a manifest, because parsing reads files and never links the graph. The first command that does link it — compile, run, build, even ls — fails with Found a cycle: model.<project>.a --> model.<project>.b, and with no error-category banner in front of it. The guide files this under *Dependency errors*, its name for the category rather than a label you will see on screen. No silent recovery: dbt picks no order (A), drops no ref() (B), and cannot defer the error to run time (D), because nothing can be scheduled from a graph that will not build. The fix is to extract the shared logic into a third model both nodes can ref. Source: /guides/debug-errors. Revisit **Ch 10 §10.3**. Cognitive level: recall.

**40. C.** Wrapped "Database Error" messages originate from the warehouse; the most productive first move is to read the compiled SQL in target/compiled/, find the exact SELECT dbt sent, and run it in the warehouse query editor to reproduce it in isolation. --full-refresh (A) is expensive and diagnoses nothing. dbt debug (B) tests connectivity, which a Database Error has already demonstrated works. dbt clean (D) removes compile artifacts, which is the opposite of what you want when the compiled SQL is the evidence. Source: /guides/debug-errors, /reference/commands/compile. Revisit **Ch 10 §10.1, §10.2**. Cognitive level: apply.

**41. Correct order: 2, 1, 3, 4, 5.** First reproduce (2), then open the file at the reported location (1), fix the indentation (3), re-run to confirm (4), and then commit and open the PR (5). The "reproduce before editing" step is the one people skip; without it, you don't actually know whether you've fixed anything. Source: /guides/debug-errors, /docs/platform/git/version-control-basics. Revisit **Ch 10 §10.4 + §10.8**. Cognitive level: apply.

**42. B.** A package macro is only in scope under its package namespace. Installing the package puts generate_surrogate_key in dbt_utils's namespace, not in the root project's, so a bare call stays undefined however many times you install it — which is what rules A out. Note the detail the stem pins deliberately: `dbt_packages/` already holds the package. Had it been **absent**, you would never have seen this error at all; dbt stops at project load with `dbt found N package(s) specified in packages.yml, but only 0 package(s) installed in dbt_packages`, exit 2, naming no model and no macro. So a per-model undefined-macro error is itself evidence that `dbt deps` has already run (Ch 8 §8.4). C changes when the call happens, not what is in scope. D renames a file dbt does not resolve macros by. E removes build artefacts and touches neither. Source: `/reference/dbt-jinja-functions/dispatch`. Revisit **Ch 8 §8.4** and **Ch 10 §10.5**. Cognitive level: apply.

**43. A.** `on-run-start` does fire on `dbt run` — the project-hook trigger list runs to six commands at 1.11: `build`, `run`, `seed`, `snapshot`, `test`, and `source freshness`, the last added when its behaviour flag matured. That rules out B and C. The reference page lists `compile` and `docs generate` too, and at 1.11 neither fires a project hook. dbt accepts arbitrary SQL in hooks, SELECTs included, which rules out D. So the hook ran and the warehouse rejected its SELECT: `fct_orders` does not exist yet in this engineer's `analytics_qa` schema. Version boundary: at its 1.11 default of `false`, `skip_nodes_if_on_run_start_fails` leaves the models to build after the failed hook — the run still exits 1 — and it is scheduled to mature at 1.12, after which dbt skips them instead. Sources: `/reference/project-configs/on-run-start-on-run-end`, `/reference/global-configs/behavior-changes`. Revisit **Ch 10 §10.2 + Ch 6 §6.5**. Cognitive level: analyze.

**44. A.** The canonical slim-CI recipe is `dbt build --select state:modified+ --defer --state ./prior-artifacts` — build what changed and its downstream (`state:modified+`), and resolve refs to unchanged upstreams against the prior run's relations instead of rebuilding them (`--defer --state`). Source: `/reference/node-selection/defer`, `/reference/node-selection/state-selection`. Revisit **Ch 12 §12.4**. Cognitive level: apply.

**45. A.** `--defer --state` is the mechanism that lets the CI job skip rebuilding unchanged upstreams: when a selected node refs an unmodified upstream, dbt resolves that ref to the prior-state relation — the production table — instead of creating a duplicate in the CI schema. B answers a different question: `state:modified+` explains why the upstreams are not *selected*, and says nothing about resolution — on its own it leaves every such ref pointing at a relation the CI schema does not hold. C invents a config — `full_refresh` governs incremental rebuild, not selection. D is false as written: with no selector `dbt build` builds the whole project, ancestors included; it is the trailing `+` that adds descendants. Source: `/reference/node-selection/defer`. Revisit **Ch 12 §12.3**. Cognitive level: analyze.

**46. B.** `dbt build` propagates failures downstream by marking descendants as `skipped`. They are not run (A is wrong); there is no per-descendant cancellation logic (C mischaracterises); `--full-refresh` is a separate flag with no auto-trigger here (D). One caveat the build doc spells out: when a test has several parents that are independent of each other, dbt skips a downstream node only if that node depends on all of them. The stem here is the simple single-parent case where the distinction does not arise. Source: `/reference/commands/build`. Revisit **Ch 11 §11.2 and Ch 10 §10.1**. Cognitive level: apply.

**47. A.** `result:error+` selects nodes that errored in the last run plus everything downstream of them, reading `run_results.json` from the state directory. It is the standard resumption selector when an external orchestrator, rather than `dbt retry`, owns the retry. `state:modified+` (B) is for code-change-driven CI. `result:success+` (C) is valid syntax but selects the wrong set — everything that worked. `source_status:` (D) selects on source-freshness results, not on build results. Source: `/reference/node-selection/methods`. Revisit **Ch 12 §12.5**. Cognitive level: apply.

**48. A.** `dbt clone --state <dir>` reads a prior manifest and clones the recorded relations. The gate is two-axis, not one: dbt takes the zero-copy branch only where the adapter supports it — Snowflake, Databricks, BigQuery — **and** the source relation's catalog type is exactly `table`. Everywhere else, Postgres included, and for a `view` or materialized view even on a zero-copy adapter, it creates a pointer view (create view ... as select * from <source>). Either way nothing is recomputed, which is the whole point for a smoke-test environment. B pays the full rebuild the stem is trying to avoid. C is the subtlest distractor: --defer resolves refs against production but creates no relations of its own, so there is nothing for the smoke test to query. D describes the behaviour clone specifically avoids. Source: /reference/commands/clone. Revisit **Ch 12 §12.8**. Cognitive level: apply.

**49. B.** --fail-fast (-x) stops the run at the first error rather than letting the rest of the graph play out. Two things then happen, and the exam likes the pair: dbt terminates the thread pool and cancels the adapter connections still executing, so the in-flight queries are cancelled rather than allowed to finish; and every node dbt has not already recorded — the cancelled in-flight ones included — is appended to the results as skipped, with Skipping due to fail_fast. Nothing is retried (C), and the cancelled nodes are not reported as errors of their own (D) — CANCEL is a log line, never a node status. Source: /reference/global-configs/failing-fast. Revisit **Ch 10 §10.1 and Ch 11 §11.10**. Cognitive level: apply.

**50. A, E.** A custom generic test is defined as a Jinja {% test <name>(...) %} / {% endtest %} block, where <name> is the public name callers invoke (A). Once defined, it is invoked in YAML exactly like a built-in (E) — and note that tests: remains a valid backward-compatible alias for data_tests: at 1.11, so option E's spelling still holds. B inverts the pass/fail convention: the body is a SELECT that returns *failing* rows, so zero rows means pass. C is false — a custom generic can live under macros/ or tests/generic/. D is false: the body is SQL, not a Jinja return. Source: /best-practices/writing-custom-generic-tests, /docs/build/data-tests. Revisit **Ch 7 §7.4**. Cognitive level: recall.

**51. B.** A singular test is a .sql file under tests/ whose SELECT returns zero rows when the assertion passes and one-or-more rows when it fails. The test's name is its filename. It is not a generic with one argument (A), is not per-column (C), and is not a {% test %} macro (D — that is a custom generic). Source: /docs/build/data-tests. Revisit **Ch 7 §7.3**. Cognitive level: recall.

**52. B.** The given: mocks are substituted for each ref() and source() before the model materializes and the result is compared against expect: — which is what lets a unit test catch a logic regression at PR time without the table existing. A describes a singular test: a .sql file under tests/, not a unit_tests: block in a properties file. C inverts the ordering — under dbt build a model's unit tests run first, so a failing one skips the model rather than validating it after the fact. D confuses the two axes: a unit test validates SQL *logic* against mocked input, while a data test validates warehouse *rows*. Source: /docs/build/unit-tests, /reference/resource-properties/unit-tests. Revisit **Ch 7 §7.8**. Cognitive level: recall.

**53. B.** The default severity is error; a test failure then fails the build and, under dbt build, short-circuits everything downstream. Setting severity: warn demotes the failure to a warning — reported in the logs, build continues. A inverts the pair. C invents a scale that does not exist. D confuses severity with store_failures, which is an independent config. The warn_if / error_if thresholds layer on top and are worth knowing separately. Source: /reference/resource-configs/severity. Revisit **Ch 7 §7.5**. Cognitive level: recall.

**54. B.** store_failures: true writes the failing rows to a warehouse table in an audit schema, named <schema>_dbt_test__audit — the suffix is appended to the active schema — unless you override it, so engineers can query the rows that triggered the failure instead of re-deriving them. It does not append to compiled files (A), print and discard (C), or write a YAML sink (D). The neighbouring fact worth carrying: with store_failures: true and store_failures_as unset, the failures land as a **table**. Source: /reference/resource-configs/store_failures. Revisit **Ch 7 §7.5**. Cognitive level: recall.

**55. 1→c, 2→a, 3→b, 4→d.** fail_calc replaces the default count(*) so the number dbt compares against the thresholds is whatever the expression computes (c); where: narrows the tested rows (a) — the standard way to avoid full-table rescans on incremental tests; store_failures_as: view persists the retained failures as a view rather than the default table, and overrides `store_failures` in both directions (b); `limit:` caps the rows returned per failing test (d). Note the shape of the left column: at 1.11 the nested `config:` key is the current shape for all four. A bare sibling key still parses: dbt folds it into the test's config and warns that the property has moved, so the signal to watch for is a deprecation line rather than an error. Source: `/reference/data-test-configs`. Revisit **Ch 7 §7.5**. Cognitive level: apply.

**56. A.** `dbt test --select tag:foo` runs tests tagged `foo` — either through the test's own `tags:` config or, under default eager indirect selection, tests attached to models tagged `foo`. There is no `--tag` flag (C). `dbt run` does not run tests (B). `test_type:nightly` is not a valid value (D): `test_type:` takes `data`, `unit`, `generic` or `singular`. Tag selection also composes: `dbt test --select "test_type:generic,tag:nightly"` intersects, narrowing the same run to the generic tests among the tagged nodes, while replacing that comma with a space unions the two instead. Sources: `/reference/commands/test`, `/reference/node-selection/methods`. Revisit **Ch 7 §7.6, Ch 11 §11.5, Ch 11 §11.8**. Cognitive level: recall.

**57. B.** The default indirect-selection mode is `eager`: dbt runs any test whose referenced resources intersect the selected set. A test on `stg_orders` therefore runs whenever `stg_orders` is selected, even though the test itself carries no `nightly` tag. The other three modes narrow this — `cautious` requires every parent to be selected, `buildable` sits between the two, and `empty` selects no tests at all. Source: `/reference/global-configs/indirect-selection`. Revisit **Ch 7 §7.6**. Cognitive level: apply.

**58. B.** Exposures are YAML-declared downstream consumers — dashboards, notebooks, analyses, ML pipelines, applications. `name`, `type` and `owner` are required (the `owner:` block must itself supply a `name`, an `email`, or both), and `depends_on:` accepts `ref()`, `source()` and `metric()` calls. They render as first-class nodes on the lineage graph and execute no SQL; their value is metadata — ownership, discoverability, and answering "which dashboards break if I change this model". Source: `/docs/build/exposures`, `/reference/exposure-properties`. Revisit **Ch 9 §9.5**. Cognitive level: recall.

**59. A.** `dbt ls --select +exposure:my_dashboard` lists every node upstream of the exposure — the models, sources, snapshots and seeds it depends on transitively. The `+` prefix is the all-ancestors graph operator, and the `exposure:` method matches by exposure name. Drop the `+` and you select the exposure alone, which is the mistake the question is looking for. Sources: `/reference/node-selection/methods`, `/reference/commands/list`. Revisit **Ch 9 §9.5 + Ch 11 §11.5**. Cognitive level: apply.

**60. B.** Nesting `freshness` and `loaded_at_field` under `config:` is the recommended shape at 1.11, and the top-level form still parses and binds on every adapter. On Snowflake it also raises `PropertyMovedToConfigDeprecation`, once per key, because dbt runs its JSON-schema property validation on Snowflake, Databricks, BigQuery and Redshift only; the identical YAML is silent on Postgres. A overstates the change — a `[WARNING]` is not a parsing error and the parse exits 0. C is wrong on the enum: `period` accepts `minute`, `hour` and `day`, with no default and no `week`, so `{count: 2, period: day}` is a perfectly valid 48-hour threshold. D is the belief the adapter gate refutes, and it is the one to lose: silence on Postgres means the check did not run, not that the form is approved. Source: `/reference/source-configs`, `/reference/resource-properties/freshness`. Revisit **Ch 3 §3.1** (the adapter gate) and **§3.3**. Cognitive level: apply.

**61. A.** `source_status:fresher+` is a *comparison*, and a comparison needs two sides: the `sources.json` in the `--state` directory from the previous freshness check, and the `sources.json` the current `dbt source freshness` just wrote to `target/`. Night one has only the second — and dbt does not treat a missing side as an empty result. It stops:

```
Encountered an error:
Internal Error
  No previous state comparison freshness results in sources.json
```

Exit 2, nothing built, and the output is byte-identical whether the --state directory is empty or absent. From night two on, with the prior artifact promoted into prior-artifacts/ , it works. C is the belief this item exists to correct, and it is the comfortable one: a first night that is quietly a no-op would let the pipeline self-heal, so a CI author who assumes it writes no guard and meets a hard failure instead. Seed the prior directory, or gate the step on the artifact existing. B names the wrong artifact: sources.json is written only by dbt source freshness, and run_results.json has no freshness data in it. Source: /reference/node-selection/methods, /reference/artifacts/sources-json. Revisit **Ch 12 §12.6**. Cognitive level: analyze.

**62. A, B, D.** dbt reads exactly three artifacts out of a state directory. manifest.json is the baseline that state: selectors diff against. run_results.json backs the result: selectors. sources.json backs source_status:. catalog.json (C) is docs metadata and is never consulted by state comparison — a clean negative fact and a reliable distractor. partial_parse.msgpack (E) is dbt's own parse cache in target/, not a state artifact. Sources: /reference/node-selection/state-selection, /reference/artifacts/manifest-json, /reference/artifacts/sources-json, /reference/artifacts/catalog-json. Revisit **Ch 12 §12.1**. Cognitive level: recall.

**63. D.** state:modified.body matches nodes whose SQL body changed, ignoring config-only diffs. state:modified.configs is the complementary selector. state:modified is the union of every sub-selector — body, configs, relation, persisted descriptions, macros, contract — and state:modified+ adds downstream propagation on top of that union. Source: /reference/node-selection/methods, /reference/node-selection/state-selection. Revisit **Ch 12 §12.2**. Cognitive level: recall.

**64. B.** dbt retry reads run_results.json and re-runs the nodes recorded as error, fail, skipped, runtime error or partial success, inside the same selection the failed command used. It does not accept --select: passing it is a usage error, not a silently ignored argument as C claims. To choose a different selection, use a fresh invocation: dbt build --select "result:error+,marts" --state <dir> intersects the errored nodes and their descendants with the subtree you want. result: reads the prior run_results.json from --state and has no target/ fallback, so the flag is not optional. Source: /reference/commands/retry. Revisit **Ch 12 §12.7**. Cognitive level: apply.

**65. B.** A single dbt build with the union selector state:modified+ result:error+ plus --defer --state does all three: state:modified+ picks up the code-change-driven nodes, result:error+ picks up the unresolved model execution errors, build runs tests alongside models and short-circuits on failure, and --defer --state points refs-to-unchanged-upstreams at the prior-state relations. A does the opposite of requirement 3 — --exclude result:error drops exactly the unresolved model execution errors you wanted back. C fails requirement 2, because dbt run executes models only. D fails on two counts: retry rejects --select at 1.11 and replays the prior invocation rather than computing a state diff. Space-separated selectors form a **union**. Sources: /reference/node-selection/set-operators, /reference/node-selection/state-selection, /reference/commands/build. Revisit **Ch 11 §11.5 and Ch 12 §12.3–§12.5**. Cognitive level: analyze.

---

## After the mock

- **Scored 43 or higher ($\geq$65%)?** You pass the mock. Identify your weakest two domains by counting wrong answers per domain (see the table below). Re-drill those chapters' practice Qs before Mock Test 2.

- **Scored 35–42?** Near-miss. Go back to the two or three weakest domains and re-read each chapter's core sections, redo its practice Qs, then retake Mock Test 1 after 48–72 hours before attempting Mock Test 2.
- **Scored below 35?** Foundation gap. The most productive move is to re-read Ch 2, Ch 4, Ch 7, and Ch 10 — the four load-bearing chapters — and retake Mock Test 1 a week later.

### Domain tally sheet

Mark your correct/incorrect tally per domain to see where you are weakest. Domain numbering and titles follow the dbt Core 1.11 study guide's seven topics.

| Domain | Questions | Correct | Incorrect | Revisit chapter |
|---|---|---|---|---|
| 1. Developing and optimizing dbt models | Q1–Q30 (30 Qs) | | | Ch 2, 3, 4, 5, 6, 8, 11 (+ Ch 9 for `dbt docs`, Ch 13 for `grants`) |
| 2. Managing dbt models governance | Q31–Q37 (7 Qs) | | | Ch 13 |
| 3. Debugging data modeling errors | Q38–Q45 (8 Qs) | | | Ch 10 (§10.9 owns the `flags:` block), Ch 12 |
| 4. Troubleshooting and optimizing dbt pipelines | Q46–Q49 (4 Qs) | | | Ch 10, Ch 11, Ch 12 |
| 5. Implementing dbt tests | Q50–Q57 (8 Qs) | | | Ch 7 |
| 6. Implementing and maintaining external dependencies | Q58–Q61 (4 Qs) | | | Ch 3, Ch 9, Ch 12 |
| 7. Leveraging the dbt state | Q62–Q65 (4 Qs) | | | Ch 12, Ch 11 |

Mock 1 and Mock 2 cover the same seven-domain blueprint, in the same per-domain shape as the table above. dbt Labs does not publish domain weights; that distribution is this book's inference from bullet counts and the ten official sample questions, and Ch 1 §1.2 says so explicitly. The two papers do not differ by domain: both tally sheets allocate the same 30 / 7 / 8 / 4 / 8 / 4 / 4. They differ in how those questions are laid out — this paper groups each domain into one contiguous run, while Mock 2 interleaves them, which is closer to how a real sitting feels and is why its tally rows read as scattered lists. Where Mock 2 is harder is cognitive level, and that one is measured rather than allocated — every question carries its own tag. This paper leans recall, with a little over half its items tagged that way; Mock 2 leans apply, with barely a third recall and appreciably more analyze. Same map, harder questions. If your weak domains differ between the two papers, prioritise re-drilling the chapters that show up in both.

# Chapter 17

# Mock Test 2 (Stretch Difficulty)

Tuned one notch harder than the real exam. If you score 65%+ on this paper, you are almost certainly over-prepared — the real sitting should feel easier. Take this 1–3 days before your exam, after Chapter 15 and a final pass of the cheat sheet. Not before Mock 1.

---

## Instructions

- **65 questions. 2 hours. Passing: 65%.** That's **43 correct** minimum. Multi-answer questions score 1 point only if every correct option is selected and no incorrect ones — no partial credit, same as the real exam.
- **Single attempt, no lookups.** Do all 65, then check the key. Flag and skip anything that crosses 3 minutes. Target ~1.8 min per question.
- **Stretch mix:** weighted toward *apply* and *analyze* where Mock 1 is weighted toward *recall* — each answer key tags its own level. Expect multi-step reasoning and negative framing more often. After scoring, read every explanation — including for questions you got right.

Format shapes used in this mock: **MCQ** single-answer, **Select N** multi-answer, **FITB** fill-in-the-blank, **Matching**, **Hotspot** answer with a line number, **Build-list** reorder steps.

---

## Questions

**1.** A colleague's model reads `from {{ ref('stg_orders', v=2) }}` but `dbt parse` fails with `Model 'model.project.consumer' (models/consumer.sql) depends on a node named 'stg_orders' with version '2' which was not found`, after a warning that no matching node was found for the patch named `stg_orders_v2`. The `stg_orders.yml` declares `versions: [{v: 1}, {v: 2}]` and `latest_version: 2`. What is the most likely cause?

A. The `stg_orders_v2.sql` file does not exist alongside the versions YAML — declaring a version does not create the file.
B. `v=` cannot be passed as a keyword argument to `ref()`; use positional form.
C. `latest_version` must equal `1` for version 2 to be resolvable.
D. Versioned models must be materialized as `table` for `v=` to work.

**2.** Which is **NOT** true about `source()` and `sources.yml`?
A. A source's `database:` and `schema:` together define the warehouse location; two YAML sources with the same pair are still two distinct dbt sources.
B. Omitting `database:` forces dbt to raise a runtime error during `dbt source freshness`.
C. Source freshness thresholds are declared on the source or the table, not on columns.
D. `{{ source('raw', 'orders') }}` resolves at compile time using the declared `database`/`schema` (or a package source's `overrides:` block).

**3.** Review this `dbt_project.yml` fragment. A model at `models/marts/finance/fct_ar.sql` has `{{ config(materialized='table', tags=['q_close']) }}` at the top of the file. Which tag list is attached to the model?

```
models:
  acme:
    +tags: ['acme']
    marts:
      +tags: ['mart']
      finance:
        +tags: ['finance']
```

A. `['q_close']` only — SQL-level `config` replaces project-level `+tags`.
B. `['acme', 'mart', 'finance', 'q_close']` — dbt unions all matching path tags with the SQL-level list.
C. `['finance', 'q_close']` — most-specific path wins, then adds the SQL level.
D. `['acme']` only — the top-level path always wins.

**4.** An incremental model has `on_schema_change='fail'`. The SELECT drops a column that the target table already has. On the next `dbt run` (no `--full-refresh`), what happens?
A. dbt silently drops the column from the target and runs the MERGE with the narrower schema.
B. dbt runs the MERGE against the existing target schema; the dropped column retains its last value.
C. dbt auto-promotes the run to `--full-refresh` and rebuilds.
D. dbt raises a run-time error naming the schema-drift and refuses to write; the fix is a manual `--full-refresh` or a change to `sync_all_columns`.

**5.** `dbt show --select stg_customers stg_orders --limit 5` exits 0. What does it print?
A. One preview table — `stg_orders`, up to five rows; the last node named is the one previewed.
B. Two preview tables, `stg_customers` then `stg_orders`, up to five rows each.
C. One preview table — `stg_customers`, up to five rows; `stg_orders` is compiled and queried, but never printed.
D. No preview at all — `dbt show` raises a usage error when `--select` resolves to more than one node.

**6.** Fill in the blank: the incremental config that controls what dbt does when the model's SELECT adds new columns is ______; its default is `ignore`.

**7.** Select the **two** statements about **Python models** at dbt 1.11 that are true.
A. The function signature must be `def model(dbt, session):` and return a DataFrame.
B. Inside the function, upstream models are referenced with `{{ ref('model') }}`.
C. Python models may be materialized as `table` or `incremental`, but not as `view` or `ephemeral`.
D. Python models are supported on Postgres, Snowflake, and BigQuery.
E. Configs are set with `{{ config(...) }}` in a Jinja header comment.

**8.** A project's `dbt_project.yml` sets `+materialized: view` on the whole package and `+materialized: table` on the `dims/` folder inside it. Match each model to what it materializes as.

| Model, and what else is set for it | Materialization |
|---|---|
| 1. `stg_orders.sql` — nothing else, anywhere | a. `table` |
| 2. `int_orders.sql` — `config: {materialized: ephemeral}` in its properties YAML | b. `view` |
| 3. `fct_orders.sql` — `config: {materialized: incremental}` in its properties YAML, and `{{ config(materialized='table') }}` in the SQL | c. `ephemeral` |
| 4. `dims/dim_users.sql` — `{{ config(materialized='incremental') }}` in the SQL | d. `incremental` |

**9.** A project's `dbt_project.yml` declares `require-dbt-version: [">=1.9.0", "<1.11.0"]`. An engineer runs `dbt run` on a machine with dbt 1.11.14 installed. What happens?
A. dbt proceeds but logs a version warning.
B. dbt refuses to run the project and exits non-zero with a version-mismatch error before parsing any model.
C. dbt auto-downgrades itself to the newest in-range version for the run.
D. The directive only applies to `dbt build`; `dbt run` ignores it.

**10.** You want a seed CSV loaded with `country_code` explicitly typed as `varchar(2)` on a Postgres warehouse (the equivalent on other adapters is whatever string-with-length type they expose). Which configuration achieves that?
A. Add a `constraints:` block under the seed.
B. `quote_columns: true` on the seed.
C. `column_types: {country_code: 'varchar(2)'}` under the seed's config.
D. Rename the CSV column to `country_code:VARCHAR(2)`.

**11.** Which statement about **model groups** and `access: private` is correct?
A. Groups are defined under `dbt_project.yml`'s `vars:` block.
B. `access: private` and `access: protected` are synonyms — both block cross-project refs.
C. An `access: private` model is visible only inside its own group; a `ref()` from outside that group raises `DbtReferenceError` at parse time.
D. A model can belong to multiple groups simultaneously via a list.

**12.** Review this YAML. What is the effective behavior for downstream refs to `dim_customer`?

```
models:
  - name: dim_customer
    access: public
    latest_version: 2
    deprecation_date: 2031-06-30
    versions:
      - v: 1
        deprecation_date: 2030-12-31
      - v: 2
```

A. Refs using `v=1` stay silent until 2030-12-31 and only begin warning once that date has passed.
B. `{{ ref('dim_customer') }}` errors because a `deprecation_date` is declared at the model level.
C. Both versions are unusable — `deprecation_date` at the model level blocks all refs.
D. `{{ ref('dim_customer') }}` resolves to v2; refs using `v=1` warn on every run once the `deprecation_date` is declared, and the warning can be promoted to an error via dbt's warn/error settings.

**13.** Which constraint type is **NOT** declarable under a model's `constraints:` block?
A. `primary_key` B. `foreign_key`
C. `check` D. `default`

**14.** A `dbt build` run fails. The log shows: `Database Error in model fct_orders (models/marts/fct_orders.sql): Invalid identifier 'ORDR_DATE'`. Identify the irrelevant step in the pool below and order the remaining three into the most efficient triage:

1. Open `target/compiled/<project-name>/models/marts/fct_orders.sql` and read the compiled SELECT dbt actually sent.
2. Run `dbt debug --connection` to verify the warehouse is reachable before triaging further.
3. Paste the compiled SELECT into the warehouse query editor to reproduce the error in isolation.
4. Fix the typo in the source model and re-run `dbt build --select fct_orders+`.

**15.** You edit `models/staging/stg_orders.yml` and `dbt parse` fails with `yaml.scanner.ScannerError: while scanning for the next token ... found character '\t'`. Which error family is this?
A. Database error — the warehouse rejected a character.
B. Compilation error — a `ref()` failed to resolve.
C. Parse error on a YAML file — tabs are forbidden; use spaces.
D. Connection error — the warehouse session timed out.

**16.** `dbt run` passes on your branch but fails in CI with `Compilation Error: Model 'int_customer_orders' depends on a node named 'stg_orders' which is disabled.` The file `models/staging/stg_orders.sql` exists on the branch. Which is the **most likely** cause?
A. The CI job pulled a stale `dbt_packages/` directory.
B. `stg_orders.sql` has `{{ config(enabled=false) }}` (or YAML `enabled: false`) in a path that only applies in the CI target.
C. The warehouse's schema `analytics_ci` needs to be created first.
D. `dbt_project.yml` is missing a `profile:` key.

**17.** A nightly `dbt build --threads 8` is twenty models in when one model errors; seven other models are mid-execution on the remaining threads. The on-call engineer re-runs the job with `-x` (`--fail-fast`) added. What does that flag change?
A. dbt re-executes the failed model up to three times and only aborts the invocation if all three attempts fail.
B. dbt lets the seven in-flight models finish and then, because the run is ending early, builds the failed model's descendants anyway so the schema is left consistent.
C. dbt aborts at the first failure, cancelling the statements still in flight on the other threads; nothing further is built.
D. dbt aborts the invocation and drops the relations the run had already created, so the target is left as it was before the run.

**18.** A nightly `dbt build --select tag:nightly --target prod` must fail on any warning it raises, with one exception: the team has accepted an `UpcomingReferenceDeprecation` on a versioned model and does not want that one warning to break the job. Which flags do exactly that?
A. `--warn-error --warn-error-options '{"silence": ["UpcomingReferenceDeprecation"]}'`
B. `--warn-error-options '{"error": "all", "silence": ["UpcomingReferenceDeprecation"]}'`
C. `--warn-error UpcomingReferenceDeprecation`
D. `--warn-error-options '{"include": "all", "exclude": ["UpcomingReferenceDeprecation"]}'`

**19.** In the following log excerpt, which stage of the triage path (YAML parse → compile → warehouse) is the failure?

```
1: 14:02:11 Running with dbt=1.11.14
2: 14:02:12 Registered adapter: snowflake=1.11.0
3: 14:02:13 Found 84 models, 3 snapshots, 210 data tests, 4 seeds, 12 sources, 6
     exposures, 512 macros, 3 groups, 9 unit tests
4: 14:02:14 Concurrency: 8 threads (target='ci')
5: 14:02:15 Encountered an error:
6: Compilation Error in model int_revenue_rollup (models/intermediate/int_revenue_rollup.
     sql)
7:   'dbt_utils' is undefined.
```

A. Line 3 — parse stage; sources.yml malformed.
B. Line 6 — compile stage; a macro namespace is unresolved.
C. Line 7 — warehouse stage; database reported an undefined schema.
D. Line 1 — dbt version mismatch.

**20.** `dbt build` vs `dbt run --select ... --defer --state`: which statement is correct about **what `build` adds** on top of `run`?
A. `build` enables `--defer` by default.
B. `build` runs only snapshots; tests and seeds are never bundled.
C. `build` is `run` plus `dbt docs generate` at the end.
D. `build` additionally invokes tests, seeds, and snapshots, in one DAG-ordered pass rather than four separate invocations.

**21.** A CI job seeds a scratch schema with `dbt clone --select state:modified+ --state ./prod-artifacts --target ci`. The warehouse is Postgres. What does dbt create?
A. Nothing — `dbt clone` needs `--defer` alongside `--state` everywhere except the dbt platform's own CLI, and the job passed only `--state`.
B. One physical `create table ... as select` copy per selected node, since Postgres cannot produce a zero-copy clone.
C. One pointer view per selected node — `create view ... as select * from` the production relation — because true zero-copy cloning is available only on Snowflake, Databricks and BigQuery.
D. Nothing — `dbt clone` only re-points the target schema's search path at production; it creates no relations of its own.

**22.** Which pair is the correct test config → effect mapping?
A. `severity: warn` → fails the build; `error_if` → raises the severity when row count exceeds a threshold.
B. `severity: warn` → logs a warning without failing the build; `error_if: ">100"` (under the default `severity: error`) → the test errors only when failing rows exceed 100.
C. `severity: high` and `severity: low` are the two valid levels.
D. `store_failures: true` implies `severity: warn` automatically.

**23.** The standard arguments for the built-in `relationships` test are:
A. `model:` and `column:`
B. `to:` (accepts `ref('...')` or `source('...','...')`) and `field:`
C. `parent_table:` and `parent_column:`
D. `ref:` and `fk:`

**24.** A column in `fct_orders.yml` has both `tests: [unique, not_null]` and, under the model, `constraints: [{type: primary_key, columns: [order_id]}]` plus `contract: {enforced: true}`. Which statement is correct?
A. Declaring the same column as `primary_key` under constraints and `unique` under tests raises a duplicate-declaration error.
B. Declaring a `primary_key` constraint makes the `unique` data test redundant and dbt skips it.
C. Contracts override data tests — once `enforced: true`, all data tests are skipped.
D. The data tests and the contract constraint are complementary: the tests run at `dbt test` time; the `primary_key` constraint is declared at build time and (on supporting adapters) enforced by the warehouse.

**25.** You have a custom generic test defined in `macros/tests/non_negative.sql`. Which invocation in `schema.yml` correctly attaches it to a column?

```
columns:
  - name: amount_cents
    tests:
      - ????
```

A. `- ref('non_negative')` B. `- macros.non_negative`
C. `- non_negative` D. `- test: non_negative`

**26.** Fill in the blank: the flag that builds a model against **zero input rows** — so the DDL and the contract are exercised without scanning any data — is `dbt run --______`.

**27.** A model is configured `persist_docs: {relation: true, columns: true}` and its YAML supplies a `description:` for the model and for every column. Which statement is correct?
A. `persist_docs` reads the comment already on the warehouse object and overwrites the YAML `description:` with it.
B. `persist_docs` is what puts descriptions on the docs site; with it unset the site shows the model with an empty description.
C. The comment statements are issued by `dbt docs generate`, which reads the descriptions while it introspects the warehouse for the catalog.
D. The descriptions reach the warehouse as object comments the next time the model is materialized; the docs site renders those same descriptions from `manifest.json` whether or not `persist_docs` is set.

**28.** Which of the following is **NOT** true about dbt exposures?
A. An exposure is declared in `.yml` under `exposures:` with a `type:` from `dashboard | notebook | analysis | ml | application`.
B. An exposure's `depends_on:` field accepts `ref()`, `source()`, and `metric()` expressions.
C. An exposure appears on the lineage graph in the docs site with edges to every node in its `depends_on:` list.
D. Running `dbt run --exposure my_dashboard` executes the exposure as if it were a model.

**29.** A package in `packages.yml` is declared as `- package: dbt-labs/dbt_utils` with `version: [">=1.1.0", "<2.0.0"]`. The project has no `package-lock.yml` yet. What happens on `dbt deps`?
A. dbt installs every version in the range, one alongside the other.
B. dbt errors — range pins are not supported; only exact `version: x.y.z` or a Git `revision:`.
C. dbt resolves the newest release inside the range and writes it into `package-lock.yml`.
D. `dbt deps` ignores the range and installs `latest`.

**30.** Review this `sources.yml`. Which tables does `dbt source freshness` check?

```
sources:
  - name: raw
    config:
      loaded_at_field: ingested_at
      freshness:
        warn_after: {count: 6, period: hour}
        error_after: {count: 24, period: hour}
    tables:
      - name: orders
      - name: payments
      - name: legacy_regions
        config:
          freshness: null
```

A. None — a `freshness: null` on one table invalidates the source-level block for its siblings too.
B. All three, at 6h/24h — a table-level `freshness:` block is advisory, so the source-level thresholds win.
C. `orders` and `payments` at 6h/24h and `legacy_regions` with no thresholds, so it is reported but can only ever pass.
D. `orders` and `payments`; `legacy_regions` is not checked at all, because a table-level `freshness: null` cancels the inherited thresholds.

**31.** Which statement about `run_results.json` is correct?
A. It holds the parsed node graph, which is the artifact `state:modified` compares the current parse against.
B. It is written by `dbt run` and `dbt build` only; `dbt test` records its outcomes in `manifest.json` instead.
C. It records a per-node `status` — the field that both `result:` selectors and `dbt retry` read — and every command that executes resources writes it, `docs generate` and `run-operation` included.
D. It is written only when an invocation fails; a clean run leaves the previous file in place untouched.

**32.** A legacy SQL script joins four hard-coded references: `warehouse_raw.crm.accounts`, `warehouse_raw.crm.contacts`, `warehouse_raw.billing.invoices`, and `warehouse_raw.billing.line_items`. You are migrating this into dbt. How many distinct sources and tables should the `sources.yml` declare, if each source is keyed on `(database, schema)`?
A. 4 sources, 4 tables. B. 2 sources, 4 tables.
C. 1 source, 4 tables. D. 1 source, 2 tables.

**33.** Select the **three** statements that are true about `is_incremental()` on an incremental model.
A. It returns `True` only when the model is configured `materialized='incremental'`, the target relation already exists, and the run is not in full-refresh mode.
B. On the very first run of an incremental (target missing), `is_incremental()` returns `False` and the guarded `WHERE` clause compiles away.
C. Omitting the `is_incremental()` guard on an incremental model means every run reprocesses the full source through the configured incremental strategy — e.g., `merge` re-merges every row, `append` duplicates rows on every run.
D. `is_incremental()` is only available on the Snowflake and BigQuery adapters; on other warehouses the macro is undefined and the model fails to compile.
E. It returns `True` whenever a `unique_key` is declared, regardless of whether the target relation exists, so the guarded `WHERE` clause is active on the very first run.

**34.** Review this incremental model. Which line introduces a bug that causes the **first run** to fail with `relation "fct_events" does not exist`?

```
1: {{ config(
2:    materialized='incremental',
3:    unique_key='event_id',
4:    incremental_strategy='merge'
5: ) }}
6:
7: select *
8: from {{ ref('stg_events') }}
9: where event_ts > (select max(event_ts) from {{ this }})
```

A. Line 2 — `materialized='incremental'` is invalid on the first run; use `table`.
B. Line 4 — `merge` strategy is not supported without a schema contract.
C. Line 9 — the `(select max from {{ this }})` subquery is not guarded by `is_incremental()`, so on first-run dbt references a table that does not yet exist.
D. Line 8 — `ref('stg_events')` should be `source('stg','events')`.

**35.** An incremental reporter model has `unique_key=['order_id','line_no']`, `incremental_strategy='merge'`, and `on_schema_change='append_new_columns'`. A contributor renames an existing column `gross_amt` to `gross_amount_usd` in the SELECT. What happens on the next `dbt run` (no `--full-refresh`)?
A. dbt auto-drops `gross_amt` and backfills `gross_amount_usd` with the old column's values, so no history is lost.
B. `append_new_columns` detects the rename and issues an ALTER RENAME on the target, carrying the existing values across.
C. dbt raises a hard error and stops, because a rename requires `sync_all_columns` and the configured value cannot handle it.
D. `append_new_columns` treats the rename as an add: a new column `gross_amount_usd` is added; the old `gross_amt` stays with NULLs for new rows; existing rows keep their `gross_amt` values.

**36.** Fill in the blank: to make a specific incremental model rebuild from scratch on the next invocation without passing `--full-refresh` at the CLI, set the config `______` to `True` in the model's `{{ config() }}` block.

**37.** A snapshot sets `snapshot_meta_column_names={'dbt_valid_from': 'valid_from', 'dbt_valid_to': 'valid_to'}` and is built for the first time. Which metadata columns does the target table carry?
A. `valid_from`, `valid_to` — the two metadata columns the mapping does not name are dropped.
B. `dbt_scd_id`, `dbt_updated_at`, `valid_from`, `valid_to` — a partial mapping renames the keys it names and leaves the rest.
C. `dbt_scd_id`, `dbt_updated_at`, `dbt_valid_from`, `dbt_valid_to` — the config is rejected unless it maps the full set of four.
D. `scd_id`, `updated_at`, `valid_from`, `valid_to` — setting the config drops the `dbt_` prefix across the metadata set.

**38.** Which statement about the **ephemeral** materialization is correct?
A. Ephemeral models support `unique_key` and `is_incremental()` just like incrementals, so they can process only new rows on each run.
B. An ephemeral model is built as a temporary table at the start of the run and dropped at the end of the `dbt run` invocation.
C. An ephemeral model is compiled into a CTE inlined at each downstream model that refs it; it is never materialized in the warehouse and is not selectable in the docs catalog.
D. `dbt run --select my_ephemeral` materializes it as a view for that invocation, so downstream models can select from the relation directly.

**39.** Two microbatch models run on an adapter that supports parallel batch execution. Both target relations already exist, and neither model sets `concurrent_batches`. `fct_a` self-joins `{{ this }}`; `fct_b` does not. Whose batches run in parallel?
A. `fct_a`'s only — a self-join is the case parallelism is designed for, since each batch reads the relation as it stood when the run began.
B. Both — an unset `concurrent_batches` means dbt parallelises wherever the adapter can.
C. Neither — parallel batch execution requires `concurrent_batches: true` written out.
D. `fct_b`'s only — with the config unset, dbt reads each model's raw SQL, and a `this` reference is what makes it hold that model's batches in order.

**40.** Review this YAML fragment for `stg_payments.sql`. Which statement about the compiled model is correct?

```
models:
  - name: stg_payments
    config:
      materialized: table
      tags: ['finance']
    description: "One row per payment."
```

```
-- stg_payments.sql top
{{ config(materialized='view', tags=['staging']) }}

select * from {{ source('raw','payments') }}
```

A. The model materializes as a `table` — YAML `config:` wins over SQL `{{ config() }}`.
B. The model materializes as a `view` with tags `['finance','staging']` — SQL-level materialization wins; tags union.
C. The model fails to parse — conflicting `config` blocks must be resolved manually.
D. The model materializes as a `view` with only the tag `['staging']` — SQL-level config replaces the YAML list entirely.

**41.** Match each adapter to the mechanism dbt uses to replace a batch under `incremental_strategy='microbatch'`.

| Adapter | Batch replacement |
|---|---|
| 1. Postgres | a. `insert_overwrite` — the batch's partition is swapped in whole. |
| 2. Snowflake | b. `replace_where` — the rows matching the batch predicate are rewritten in place. |
| 3. BigQuery | c. `merge` — matched on the model's `unique_key`, which this adapter therefore requires. |
| 4. Databricks | d. `delete+insert` — the batch window is deleted from the target, then the batch is inserted. |

**42.** Which statement about **dispatch** is correct?
A. Dispatch only works inside packages, never inside the root project; a root-project `dispatch:` block in `dbt_project.yml` is ignored at parse time.
B. `dispatch` is a post-hook that runs arbitrary SQL after a model materializes; the macro search order is fixed and cannot be configured.
C. `{{ adapter.dispatch('my_macro', 'dbt_utils') }}` searches your root project before `dbt_utils`, and inside each namespace in turn it tries `<adapter>__my_macro` and then `default__my_macro`; a project-level `dispatch:` config in `dbt_project.yml` lets you declare or reorder that search path per macro namespace.
D. `dispatch-config` accepts only one override per project, applied globally to every macro namespace rather than per namespace.

**43.** A Postgres model runs with `materialized: table` and `contract: {enforced: true}`. Its YAML declares every selected column with a matching `data_type`, and declares `amount` as `numeric` with `constraints: [{type: check, expression: "amount >= 0"}]`. The SELECT returns one row with `amount = -5`. During `dbt build --select fct_payments`, what happens?
A. dbt fails its preflight before DDL, because a value that violates `check` does not match the contract's output shape.
B. dbt creates the table and treats `check` as metadata only; a separately configured data test is the first chance to reject the negative value.
C. The shape preflight passes, then Postgres rejects the violating row through the `check` constraint while dbt materializes the table.
D. dbt builds the model because contracts can compare column names and data types but cannot carry a value predicate into platform DDL.

**44.** Your group config in `schema.yml` declares `groups: [{name: finance, owner: {email: 'fin@acme.io'}}]`. A model `fct_ar` has `config: {group: finance, access: private}`. Which downstream ref works without error?
A. `{{ ref('fct_ar') }}` from a downstream exposure's `depends_on:` list.
B. `{{ ref('fct_ar') }}` from a model with `{group: marketing}`.
C. `{{ ref('fct_ar') }}` from a singular test in `tests/`, which carries no `group:` of its own.
D. `{{ ref('fct_ar') }}` from a model whose own config is `{group: finance}`.

**45.** A teammate's `fct_revenue.sql` contains the hard-coded join `LEFT JOIN warehouse.analytics.dim_customers d`. Their branch builds locally. In a new environment target with `analytics_prod` as the schema, `dbt run` fails with `Database Error: relation "analytics.dim_customers" does not exist`. What is the cleanest fix?
A. Add an `on-run-start` hook that creates an `analytics` schema in every environment, so the hard-coded path resolves everywhere.
B. Replace `warehouse.analytics.dim_customers` with `{{ ref('dim_customers') }}` so dbt resolves the relation against the active target, and registers the edge in the DAG.
C. Hard-code `warehouse.{{ target.schema }}.dim_customers` so the schema follows the active target while the rest of the path stays explicit.
D. Add `dim_customers` as a source in `sources.yml` and select from it with `source()`, so the relation is declared rather than hard-coded.

**46.** A CI job runs `dbt parse` as a cheap pre-merge gate. It passes, exit 0. The deploy then runs `dbt compile` and fails with `Compilation Error in model int_flights (models/int_flights.sql)` followed by `'generate_surrogate_key' is undefined. This can happen when calling a macro that does not exist. Check for typos and/or install package dependencies with "dbt deps".` `dbt_utils` is declared in `packages.yml` and installed in `dbt_packages/`; the model calls the macro without its namespace. Why did the gate not catch it?
A. `dbt parse` skips any model whose SQL contains Jinja it cannot resolve
B. `dbt parse` renders the Jinja, but an unknown macro *name* becomes a permissive `Undefined` that raises nothing until compile renders the model's SQL
C. `dbt parse` reads `packages.yml` but not `dbt_packages/`, so it saw the package as absent
D. `dbt parse` reused the previous run's manifest and reported that instead

**47.** A scheduled production `dbt build` failed last night. This morning you read the logs: 3 models `error`, 12 models `skipped`, 40 models `success`. You want to re-build only the failed tree without recomputing the 40 successes. Which selector, on a fresh `dbt build --state ./prior` invocation, does this?
A. `--select result:all+` — every node from the prior run, successes included, plus their downstream.
B. `--select state:modified+` — but only after editing each failed model, since the selector keys on code changes rather than on last night's results.
C. `--select +result:error` — the error nodes and everything upstream of them, rebuilding the inputs before the models that failed.
D. `--select result:error+` — re-runs error nodes and everything downstream; `result:skipped` is not needed because every downstream-of-error node is already captured by `+`.

**48.** A model's `dbt run` succeeds, but `dbt test` fails with a `unique` violation on `order_id`. Which is the **most efficient** analyze path to find the offending duplicates?
A. Set `store_failures: true` on the `unique` test, re-run `dbt test --select order_id_unique`, and read the persisted failure table in the warehouse.
B. Run `dbt test --select order_id_unique --fail-fast` so dbt halts at the first duplicate and prints the offending rows in the log.
C. Switch the model to `materialized='view'` so the duplicates are no longer persisted and the `unique` test stops failing.
D. Run `dbt retry`, which replays the failed test node and reports the duplicate `order_id` values it found on the second pass.

**49.** A `dbt build` runs a DAG of `stg_a` → `test_a` → `int_a` → `test_b` → `fct_a`. `test_a` fails at `severity: error`. What happens?
A. `int_a`, `test_b`, and `fct_a` are all skipped — a test `error` short-circuits every downstream resource.
B. `int_a` and `fct_a` still build; tests don't affect model DAG ordering.
C. `int_a` is skipped but `fct_a` still builds off `stg_a` directly.
D. Only `test_b` is skipped; downstream models continue.

**50.** A model calls `{{ ref('stg_orders').render() }}`. Which of dbt's reference rewrites does that one call opt the reference out of?
A. All three — `--empty`'s zero-row subquery, `--sample`'s event-time window, and a microbatch model's per-batch auto-filter.
B. `--empty`'s zero-row subquery only — `--sample` and the microbatch filter key off `event_time`, which `.render()` does not reach.
C. `--sample`'s window and the microbatch auto-filter only — `--empty` rewrites the model's own `select`, not its references.
D. None of them — `.render()` returns the bare identifier, and dbt applies each rewrite after the reference has rendered.

**51.** You have an incremental model `fct_events`. You add a `unique` test on `event_id`. On every run, the test scans the full target table (100M rows) and takes 12 minutes. You want the test to evaluate only the newly-inserted rows. Which approach is documented per the dbt docs?
A. Add a `where:` config on the test — e.g., `where: "event_ts > dateadd(day, -1, current_date)"` — so the SELECT only scans recent rows.
B. Add a `post-hook` to `fct_events` that `DELETE`s rows older than a day, so the table the test scans stays small.
C. Set `severity: warn` on the test, which narrows the assertion to the rows written by the current invocation.
D. Add `limit: 1000` on the test so only 1k rows are scanned.

**52.** Select the **two** statements that are true about the `accepted_values` built-in generic test.
A. The test passes when every value in the column appears in the `values:` list; it fails when any row's value is outside the list.
B. It supports a `quote: false` argument, useful when the column is a numeric type so values aren't wrapped in quotes.
C. It accepts a `regex:` argument to express the value set as a pattern.
D. It requires the column to be `not_null`.
E. It produces `warn` severity by default.

**53.** A custom generic test `positive` lives in `tests/generic/positive.sql` and is attached to a column of a **source**. Which `{% test %}` signature is standard?
A. `{% test positive(model, column_name) %} select * from {{ model }} where {{ column_name }} < 0 {% endtest %}`
B. `{% macro positive(model, column_name) %} ... {% endmacro %}`
C. `{% test positive(source, column_name) %} select * from {{ source }} where {{ column_name }} < 0 {% endtest %}`
D. `{% generic test positive(model, column_name) %} ... {% end %}`

**54.** A singular test `tests/no_orphan_lines.sql` reads:

```
select ol.order_line_id
from {{ ref('fct_order_lines') }} ol
left join {{ ref('dim_orders') }} o on ol.order_id = o.order_id
where o.order_id is null
```

Which statement is correct?
A. The test passes when zero rows are returned; any orphan line fails the test.
B. The test passes when one or more rows are returned (proof of orphans found).
C. Singular tests require a `{% test %}` wrapper; this file would not execute.
D. Singular tests cannot `ref()` intermediate models, only marts.

**55.** Which statement about `--sample` is **NOT** true?
A. It narrows an upstream relation to a time window, and only if *that relation* declares `event_time`.
B. If the sampled relation declares no `event_time`, dbt reports OK and quietly processes the whole table — no error, no warning.
C. It is accepted by `dbt run` and `dbt build`.
D. It is accepted by `dbt compile` and `dbt snapshot`, which is how you preview a window without writing anything.

**56.** `dbt docs generate` produces which artifacts? Select **two**.
A. `catalog.json` — warehouse-introspected column types, table stats, and relation metadata per node.
B. `manifest.json` — the full resource graph (refreshed by generate; parse-only commands also emit this).
C. `state.json` — the diff of modified nodes since the last build.
D. `docs.html` — the rendered static documentation site.
E. `sources.json` — the per-source freshness results, refreshed whenever the catalog is rebuilt.

**57.** A dashboard exposure named `revenue_tracker` declares `depends_on: ["ref('dim_customer', v=1)"]`. In the same project `dim_customer` declares versions 1, 2 and 3, with `latest_version: 2`. What does `dbt ls --select +exposure:revenue_tracker --resource-type model` return?
A. `dim_customer.v1` and its upstream models — the exposure's edge is pinned to the version it names
B. `dim_customer.v2` and its upstream models, because a selector resolves a versioned model to `latest_version`
C. All three versions and their shared upstream, because the exposure names the model rather than one version
D. `dim_customer.v3` and its upstream models, because `v: 3` is the highest version defined

**58.** A package in `packages.yml` is declared as:

```
packages:
  - git: "https://github.com/acme/internal-dbt-macros.git"
    revision: main
```

Which statement about this declaration is correct?
A. `revision:` accepts all three of a branch, tag, or commit SHA; pinning to `main` lets the resolved commit drift on the next `dbt deps --upgrade` and is discouraged for production reproducibility — pin to a commit SHA or tag instead.
B. An internal repository must be declared with the `private:` key instead of `git:`; the `git:` key only accepts public HTTPS URLs.
C. Git packages install into `dbt_packages/<revision>/`, so two revisions of the same repository can sit side by side.
D. `revision:` accepts only tags; a branch needs a separate `branch:` key and a commit SHA a `commit:` key.

**59.** Match each state selector to the artifact it reads from. An artifact may be used more than once, or not at all.

Selectors:

1. state:modified+
2. result:error+
3. source_status:fresher+
4. state:new

Artifacts:

A. run_results.json
B. sources.json
C. manifest.json (current vs --state <dir>/manifest.json)
D. manifest.json (current only)

**60.** state:modified.body selects nodes where:
A. The raw SQL body changed between the prior manifest and the current parse — a config change made in YAML rather than in the model file does not select the node.
B. Any YAML property changed, including tests and descriptions — an edit to the model's schema file selects the node even when its SQL is untouched.
C. The compiled SQL output changed, accounting for macro resolution — so a macro edit selects every model that calls it, even with no change to the model file.
D. The upstream sources were reported fresher since the prior run, so the node is selected whenever new rows landed beneath it.

**61.** A Slim CI job is structured as:

```
1: dbt deps
2: dbt compile --target ci --defer --state ./prod-artifacts
3: dbt build --select state:modified+ --defer --state ./prod-artifacts --target ci
4: dbt docs generate --target ci
```

The team reports that step 3 sometimes rebuilds the whole DAG, not just the modified subtree. What is the most likely cause?
A. ./prod-artifacts/manifest.json was produced by an older dbt version, or under a different state_modified_compare_more_unrendered_values setting, so the comparison is still made but nearly every node comes back "modified".
B. --defer and state:modified+ cannot be combined; when both are passed dbt drops the selector and builds the full DAG.
C. dbt build ignores --select whenever --state is supplied, so state selection only ever narrows dbt run and dbt test.
D. --state reads artifacts only from a directory named target/; a directory named prod-artifacts is ignored, so no comparison is possible and every node is selected.

**62.** A previous dbt build left 3 models in error and 8 in skipped. dbt retry is invoked. Which nodes does retry re-execute?
A. The 3 error and 8 skipped nodes, using all the same selectors and flags recorded in the prior run_results.json.
B. Only the 3 error nodes.
C. Every node in the project, in DAG order — retry discards the prior selection and starts a clean build.
D. Only the 8 skipped nodes.

**63.** `dbt source freshness` ran at 09:00; three sources were `fresher`, two `stale`. You then run `dbt build --select source_status:fresher+ --state ./prior` immediately afterwards. Order these stages, in the order dbt executes them:

1. Load `sources.json` from `./prior/` and compare its per-source `max_loaded_at` to the current `sources.json`.
2. Resolve the `source_status:fresher+` selector to the list of sources whose `max_loaded_at` advanced.
3. Compute the `+` closure: every downstream model of the `fresher` sources.
4. Build the resolved node set in DAG order.
5. Write a fresh `run_results.json` and updated `manifest.json` to `target/`.

**64.** A `dbt build` invocation prints two error lines in the log:

```
Compilation Error in model fct_orders (models/marts/fct_orders.sql)
  'date_trunc' takes one argument, two were given
Database Error in model dim_customers (models/marts/dim_customers.sql)
  syntax error at or near "ORDER"
```

Which classification of the two errors is correct, and where should the developer look first for each?
A. Both are warehouse errors; both fixes live in the model SQL. Look in `target/run/` for both.
B. The first is a Jinja/macro error raised before any warehouse round-trip — read the source `.sql` and the macros it calls. The second is a warehouse-side SQL error — read the compiled file under `target/compiled/`.
C. The first is an adapter incompatibility; the fix is to switch warehouses. The second is a typo; fix in the source.
D. Both are transient failures recoverable by `dbt retry` without code changes; read `logs/dbt.log` for each.

**65.** `dbt parse` fails on `stg_orders.sql`; `dbt debug` against the same profile reports all checks passed. The model's SQL has `from {{ source('raw', 'orders') }}`. Which is the **most likely** root cause and the most targeted fix?
A. The `source()` call's first argument doesn't match a top-level `name:` in any `sources.yml`, so dbt cannot resolve the relation at compile time. Fix: add (or correct) a matching `sources.yml` entry, or fix the typo in the `source()` arguments.
B. The warehouse is unreachable, so the source relation cannot be looked up while the project is parsed. Fix: run `dbt debug --connection` and correct the credentials in `profiles.yml`.
C. The model needs to be marked `materialized='ephemeral'` before `source()` will resolve, because parsing skips relation lookup for ephemeral nodes. Fix: set the materialization in the model's config block.
D. `dbt parse` does not support `source()` — only `ref()` is resolved at parse time. Fix: replace the `source()` call with a `ref()` to a staging model that reads the raw table directly.

## Answer key

Score yourself first. Each entry cites the doc that grounds the answer plus a chapter cross-ref.

**1. A.** Declaring `versions: [{v: 1}, {v: 2}]` in YAML does not materialize the version files; a `stg_orders_v2.sql` (or `stg_orders.sql` if v2 is `defined_in` pointing at the base) must exist on disk. `v=` is a valid kwarg (B wrong). Source: `/reference/dbt-jinja-functions/ref`, `/reference/resource-properties/versions`. Revisit **Ch 13 §13.4**. Cognitive level: apply.

**2. B.** Omitting `database:` does NOT raise a runtime error — dbt silently falls back to the target's database (per `profiles.yml`) via the source-config resolution chain. No error is emitted during `dbt source freshness` for this reason alone. A, C, D are true. Source: `/reference/source-properties`. Revisit **Ch 3 §3.1**. Cognitive level: analyze.

**3. B.** `tags` is a list-merge config: `dbt_project.yml` path-level `+tags` accumulate down the path, and SQL-level `config(tags=[...])` unions on top. Result: `['acme','mart','finance', 'q_close']`. Source: `/reference/resource-configs/tags`, `/reference/define-configs`. Revisit **Ch 2 §2.4**. Cognitive level: apply.

**4. D.** With `on_schema_change='fail'`, any detected schema mismatch (new column, dropped column, type change) raises an error at run time — that is the point of `fail` relative to the other three values: `ignore` is silent on *added* columns (a removed column still fails); `append_new_columns` adds new columns but never removes them; `sync_all_columns` is destructive reconciliation (it adds new columns and drops removed ones). The fix is usually `--full-refresh` once the team agrees the drop is intentional, or change to `sync_all_columns` for automatic reconciliation going forward. Source: `/docs/build/incremental-models`. Revisit **Ch 4 §4.3**. Cognitive level: apply.

**5. C.** `dbt show` previews one node; the selection is an ordinary selection. Both models are compiled and executed, and only the node named by the first `--select` argument is printed — executed on dbt Core 1.11.14, the invocation exits 0 and emits a single `Previewing node 'stg_customers':` table. The fixture returned five rows; `--limit 5` is a cap, not a promise — it is applied as a SQL `limit` inside the rewritten query, so a relation holding fewer prints fewer. Reverse the two names and `stg_orders` prints instead, which is what A inverts. B is the expectation the command invites and does not meet; D reads the one-node limit as a guard, but nothing is rejected and nothing warns. Source: `/reference/commands/show`. Revisit **Ch 11 §11.1**. Cognitive level: apply.

**6.** `on_schema_change`. The four valid values are `ignore` (default), `fail`, `append_new_columns`, `sync_all_columns`. The default is the one that bites: under `ignore` a column added to the SELECT is dropped from the INSERT/MERGE, so the target table never receives it. Source: `/docs/build/incremental-models`. Revisit **Ch 4 §4.3.3**. Cognitive level: recall.

**7. A, C.** The signature is `def model(dbt, session):` returning a DataFrame (A), and the materialization set is `table` or `incremental` only — `view` and `ephemeral` are SQL-only (C). B is wrong: inside the function you call `dbt.ref("...")`, not Jinja `{{ ref() }}`. D is wrong on Postgres: Python models run on Snowflake, BigQuery and Databricks, and dbt-postgres refuses one outright with `Materialization "materialization_table_default" only supports languages ['sql']; got "python"`. E is wrong: configs are set with `dbt.config(...)` inside the function. Source: `/docs/build/python-models`. Revisit **Ch 4 §4.7**. Cognitive level: recall.

**8. 1→b, 2→c, 3→a, 4→d.** Precedence, highest to lowest: SQL `{{ config() }}` → YAML properties `config:` → `dbt_project.yml +config` → dbt's built-in defaults. Model 1 has only the package-level default to fall back on, so it is a view. Model 2's properties YAML outranks the project file. Model 3 sets both, and the SQL wins — the YAML `incremental` never applies. Model 4 is the trap: a *deeper* `dbt_project.yml` path beats a shallower one, so `dims/` would make it a table, but folder depth only breaks ties *within* layer 3 and never lifts it above the SQL header. Executed: the four resolve to view / ephemeral / table / incremental, and the run builds three relations, not four — the ephemeral model is inlined as a CTE and writes nothing. Source: `/reference/define-configs`. Revisit **Ch 6 §6.4, Ch 2 §2.4**. Cognitive level: apply.

**9. B.** `require-dbt-version` is checked when dbt loads the project, before any model is parsed: an out-of-range installed version aborts the invocation with a Runtime Error naming both the installed and the required version, and dbt exits non-zero. There is no auto-downgrade (C) and no warning-only mode (A); the directive is a property of the project, so it gates every command, `dbt run` included (D). The one documented escape hatch is `--no-`

`version-check`, which the error message itself names. Source: `/reference/project-configs/require-dbt-version`. Revisit **Ch 2 §2.4**. Cognitive level: recall.

**10. C.** `column_types` under seed config is the standard knob. `quote_columns` is about identifier quoting. Constraints do not apply to seeds. Source: `/reference/resource-configs/column_types`. Revisit **Ch 5 §5.4**. Cognitive level: recall.

**11. C.** `access: private` narrows visibility to the model's own group; a ref from outside it hits `DbtReferenceError` at parse. dbt does not *require* the `group:` binding — an ungrouped `private` model loads and then rejects every caller, including the producing team's own, so pairing the two is advice rather than a validation rule (Ch 13 §13.6). `protected` is the default and allows same-project refs. Source: `/docs/mesh/govern/model-access`, `/docs/build/groups`. Revisit **Ch 13 §13.6 + §13.7**. Cognitive level: recall.

**12. D.** A `deprecation_date` starts warning the moment it is declared, not when it arrives. Before the date every downstream `ref()` draws `UpcomingReferenceDeprecation` — *slated for deprecation on* — and once it passes the same ref draws `DeprecatedReference` — *was deprecated on* — plus a `DeprecatedModel` warning on the model itself (Ch 13 §13.5). Executed on 1.11.14: a `deprecation_date` of 2099-12-31 already warns today. A bare `{{ ref('dim_customer') }}` resolves to `latest_version: 2`, which declares no date of its own, and `{{ ref('dim_customer', v=1) }}` still resolves normally — a deprecation warns, it never blocks, which is what B and C get wrong. `--warn-error` promotes either warning to a compilation error and exit 2. A is the discriminator: it is the intuitive reading of `deprecation_date` and the runtime refutes it. Source: `/reference/resource-properties/deprecation_date`. Revisit **Ch 13 §13.5**. Cognitive level: apply.

**13. D.** Six constraint types are declarable: `not_null`, `unique`, `check`, `primary_key`, `foreign_key`, and `custom` — the last a free-form `expression` you use when a platform needs DDL dbt has no keyword for. All six are in scope. `default` is not among them and never has been: a column default is a warehouse-side DDL concern, not something a contract declares. Source: `/reference/resource-properties/constraints`. Revisit **Ch 13 §13.3**. Cognitive level: recall.

**14. Exclude step 2; correct order: 1, 3, 4.** The standard triage for a "Database Error ... Invalid identifier" is to read the compiled SQL (1), reproduce it in the warehouse editor in isolation (3), then fix the typo and re-run the failed subtree (4). Step 2 (`dbt debug --connection`) is a deliberate distractor: a "Database Error" message means the warehouse already accepted the connection and rejected the SQL; verifying connectivity is wasted motion. Source: `/guides/debug-errors`, `/reference/commands/compile`, `/reference/commands/debug`. Revisit **Ch 10 §10.2 + §10.6**. Cognitive level: apply.

**15. C.** A YAML scanner error with a line:column pointer is a parse error, pre-graph. Tabs are invalid YAML indentation — replace with spaces. Source: `/reference/configs-and-properties`, `/guides/debug-errors`. Revisit **Ch 10 §10.4**. Cognitive level: recall.

**16. B.** Read the error string precisely: dbt distinguishes **"which is disabled"** from **"which was not found"**, and only a node it located and found disabled produces the first (Ch 10 §10.3.2). That rules out every cause in which the node is absent or unreadable, and points at a `config(enabled=...)` whose value differs by target. Compilation-error-on-ref despite the file existing on-branch is most often caused by `enabled: false` in a target-specific config (e.g., `models: +enabled: "{{ target.name == 'dev' }}"`). Stale `dbt_packages/` (A) produces a different "macro undefined" shape, not a node lookup. Source: `/reference/resource-configs/enabled`, `/reference/dbt-jinja-functions/ref`. Revisit **Ch 10 §10.3**. Cognitive level: analyze.

**17. C.** `--fail-fast` (short flag `-x`) stops the invocation at the first failing node and terminates the open warehouse connections, so the statements still running on the other threads are cancelled rather than allowed to finish — the log prints a `CANCEL query` line for each. Everything not already built is left unbuilt. B inverts the flag: `--fail-fast` only ever ends a run *earlier*, so it can never cause a node that would have been skipped to build instead.

A invents a retry loop — replaying failures is `dbt retry`'s job, on a separate invocation, and it does not retry automatically. D invents a transaction boundary around the whole run: relations already created stay created, which is exactly why `dbt retry` and `result:error+` exist. Source: `/reference/global-configs/failing-fast`, `/reference/commands/retry`. Revisit **Ch 11 §11.10 + Ch 12 §12.7**. Cognitive level: apply.

**18. B.** Only `--warn-error-options` is granular. Its `error` key takes either the string `"all"` / `"*"` or an array of warning names, while `warn` and `silence` take an array only, so `error: "all"` with `silence: ["UpcomingReferenceDeprecation"]` escalates everything except the one accepted event. Executed on dbt-core 1.11.14 against a project carrying that deprecation: B exits 0 and the warning is gone, while `--warn-error-options '{"error": "all"}'` alone exits 2 on it. A is the trap for anyone who reaches for both surfaces at once — dbt refuses the combination outright with `warn_error_options: not allowed with argument warn_error`, exit 2. C is the belief the flag is granular: `--warn-error` is all-or-nothing and takes no warning-name argument, so the name is parsed as a stray positional and the invocation dies with `Error: Got unexpected extra argument (UpcomingReferenceDeprecation)`, exit 2. D uses the pre-rename `include` / `exclude` keys; they still map onto `error` / `warn`, but doing so raises `WEOIncludeExcludeDeprecation`, which `include: "all"` then escalates into a Compilation Error — exit 2, and the job fails on the very warning the team wanted kept. Source: `/reference/global-configs/warnings`. Revisit **Ch 11 §11.10 + Ch 10 §10.9.3**. Cognitive level: apply.

**19. B (Line 6).** `Compilation Error … 'dbt_utils' is undefined` is a compile-stage failure, and the signature tells you which of two faults it is. The **namespace** is named and not in scope — so the package is not installed under that name, and the fix is to declare it in `packages.yml` and run `dbt deps`, or to correct the namespace if it is misspelled. Contrast the other signature, `'generate_surrogate_key' is undefined`, which names a bare MACRO: there the package IS installed and the call simply lacks its namespace (Ch 8 §8.4). Telling the two apart is the skill; the fixes are not interchangeable. Line 3 is the resource census, which is a healthy parse, not a malformed `sources.yml` (A). Line 7 is the *body* of the same compile error, not a warehouse message — no SQL was sent (C). Line 1 is the version banner every invocation prints, and is the classic red herring in a log-reading item (D). Source: `/reference/dbt-jinja-functions/dispatch`, `/guides/debug-errors`. Revisit **Ch 10 §10.5 + Ch 8 §8.2**. Cognitive level: apply.

**20. D.** `build` = `run` + `test` + `seed` + `snapshot`, interleaved in one DAG-ordered invocation rather than run as four separate commands. That single-pass ordering is the whole point of the command. B is wrong on scope; C attaches a docs step that `build` has never had; A confuses `build` with `clone`, where deferral is intrinsic to the command rather than a flag it implies — clone needs only `--state`. Source: `/reference/commands/build`. Revisit **Ch 11 §11.2**. Cognitive level: recall.

**21. C.** Zero-copy cloning is an adapter capability, available on Snowflake, Databricks and BigQuery. Everywhere else — Postgres included — dbt falls back to a **pointer view**: `create view … as select * from` the source relation, which costs nothing to create and reads through to production data. B is the tempting near-miss: the fallback is a view, not a `create table … as select` copy, so it moves no data. A is false in the direction that matters — deferral is intrinsic to `clone` rather than a flag the command implies, so the `--state` path the job passed is all it needs. D invents a search-path mechanism dbt has no equivalent of. Use `--full-refresh` when the target relations already exist and you want them recreated. Source: `/reference/commands/clone`. Revisit **Ch 12 §12.8**. Cognitive level: apply.

**22. B.** Two facts. (1) `severity: warn` makes the test log a warning but not fail the build (the default is `error`, which fails). (2) `warn_if` / `error_if` are row-count thresholds that gate *which* condition triggers — but the caveat is strict: under `severity: warn`, dbt **never consults** `error_if` — the compiled query still computes a `should_error` column and nothing reads it, so only `warn_if` reaches the verdict (per `/reference/resource-configs/severity`). So `error_if: '>100'` only promotes to error under the default `severity: error`. Option

A inverts severity. C invents level names (`error` and `warn` are the only two). D conflates two unrelated configs. Source: `/reference/resource-configs/severity`. Revisit **Ch 7 §7.5**. Cognitive level: apply.

**23. B.** `relationships` takes `to:` — a `ref()` or `source()` call, which is also what registers the DAG edge — and `field:`, the column in the referenced relation. The other key names are inventions. One thing has moved that the argument *names* do not show: under the `require_generic_test_arguments_property` behaviour flag, a generic test's inputs nest under an `arguments:` block rather than sitting flat beside `severity:` and the other configs, so the shape you write these two keys in has changed even though the keys have not. Source: `/reference/resource-properties/data-tests`, `/reference/data-test-configs`. Revisit **Ch 7 §7.2**. Cognitive level: recall.

**24. D.** Data tests and contract constraints are orthogonal: tests run at `dbt test` time as SELECTs; constraints are declared in DDL and enforced by the warehouse where supported. Source: `/reference/resource-properties/constraints`, `/docs/mesh/govern/model-contracts`. Revisit **Ch 13 §13.2, Ch 7 §7.2**. Cognitive level: analyze.

**25. C.** A custom generic test is invoked by its bare name under `tests:` — same shape as a built-in (`unique`, `not_null`). Namespacing (`macros.x`, `ref(...)`, `test: x`) is invented syntax. Source: `/best-practices/writing-custom-generic-tests`. Revisit **Ch 7 §7.4**. Cognitive level: recall.

**26. `empty`.** `--empty` rewrites every upstream `ref()` and `source()` into a `limit 0` subquery, so the model's SQL runs and its relation is created against no rows at all. Executed on 1.11.14, the compiled SQL for a staging model carries `_dbt_limit_subq_orders`, `limit 0` and `where false`; without the flag none of the three appears. That is what makes it a schema-and-contract check rather than a data build. It is accepted by `run`, `build`, `snapshot` and `compile`, and rejected by `test` and `seed` — `dbt seed --empty` exits 2 with `No such option: --empty`. Do not confuse it with `--sample`, which narrows a window rather than emptying it and is accepted by `run` and `build` only. Source: `/docs/build/empty-flag`. Revisit **Ch 11 §11.11**. Cognitive level: recall.

**27. D.** `persist_docs` is a materialization-time concern: dbt appends `comment on table` … and `comment on column` … statements to the DDL it runs when the model is next built, so a description edit alone changes nothing in the warehouse until the model runs again. It has no bearing on the docs site, which renders `description:` out of `manifest.json` — which is why B is backwards and why C names the wrong command: `dbt docs generate` introspects the warehouse to build `catalog.json` and issues no comment DDL. A inverts the direction of travel: the YAML is the source of truth and the warehouse comment is the copy, never the other way round. Source: `/reference/resource-configs/persist_docs`, `/reference/artifacts/manifest-json`. Revisit **Ch 9 §9.4**. Cognitive level: analyze.

**28. D.** There is no `dbt run --exposure` command: an exposure holds no SQL, so there is nothing for dbt to execute. It is a first-class node on the lineage graph and nothing more, which is why you reach it with a selector rather than a command of its own. A, B and C are all accurate — and while you are here, note what is *required*: `name` and `type`, plus an `owner:` block carrying a name, an email, or both. `owner` being required is the detail most readers get wrong, because it looks like documentation garnish. Source: `/reference/exposure-properties`, `/docs/build/exposures`. Revisit **Ch 9 §9.5**. Cognitive level: recall.

**29. C.** Range pins are valid. With no lockfile to consult, `dbt deps` resolves the range to the newest release that satisfies every constraint and records that resolved version in `package-lock.yml` — which is what makes the next install reproducible: once the lockfile is present and its `packages.yml` hash still matches, the recorded version wins and the range is not re-resolved. Exact versions and Git revisions also work. Source: `/docs/build/packages`. Revisit **Ch 8 §8.3**. Cognitive level: apply.

**30. D.** Table-level freshness config overrides the source-level block, and the specific value `null` is an **opt-out**: it cancels the inherited thresholds for that table, and `dbt source` `freshness` then skips the table entirely rather than checking it against nothing. The trap is that *omitting* the key is what inherits — B has that exactly backwards. C is the near-miss: a table with no thresholds is not checked at all, so there is no pass to report. A over-generalises one table's opt-out to the whole source. Source: `/reference/resource-properties/freshness`, `/reference/source-configs`. Revisit **Ch 3 §3.3**. Cognitive level: analyze.

**31. C.** `run_results.json` is the invocation log in artifact form: one entry per executed node, each carrying a `status`, and that status field is the single thing `result:error`, `result:fail` and `dbt retry` all read. The producer list is broader than most readers expect — `build`, `clone`, `compile`, `docs generate`, `retry`, `run`, `run-operation`, `seed`, `show`, `snapshot` and `test` all write it, which is why B is wrong twice over. A describes `manifest.json`, the artifact `state:` selectors diff against. D is wrong in the direction that costs a CI job: the file is rewritten on every invocation, so a green run overwrites the failure record the previous one left behind — capture it before you re-run. Source: `/reference/artifacts/run-results-json`, `/reference/node-selection/methods`. Revisit **Ch 12 §12.1 + §12.5**. Cognitive level: apply.

**32. B.** By the §3.4 modeling convention, tables sharing a `(database, schema)` pair are grouped under one source declaration with its own `name:` (dbt does not enforce this — it's how teams model). Here `(warehouse_raw, crm)` and `(warehouse_raw, billing)` are two distinct pairs, so two sources, with four distinct tables across them. Source-counting is one of the most reliably-tested traps. Source: `/reference/source-properties`, `/docs/build/sources`. Revisit **Ch 3 §3.4**. Cognitive level: apply.

**33. A, B, C.** A, B are the standard semantics. C is a subtle but true implication — without the guard, every run reprocesses the full source through the configured strategy (merge re-merges everything, append duplicates rows). Note C is *not* equivalent to `table` materialization: `table` replaces contents wholesale, while an unguarded incremental still runs its strategy. D is false (all adapters that support incrementals support `is_incremental()`). E is false — existence of the target is the key condition, not `unique_key`. Source: `/docs/build/incremental-models`. Revisit **Ch 4 §4.3.1**. Cognitive level: analyze.

**34. C (Line 9).** The `(select max(event_ts) from {{ this }})` reads from the target on the first run, when the target does not yet exist. Wrap the WHERE in `{% if is_incremental() %} ... {% endif %}`. Source: `/docs/build/incremental-models`. Revisit **Ch 4 §4.3.1, Ch 10 §10.3**. Cognitive level: analyze.

**35. D.** `append_new_columns` only adds columns; renames look like "new column appears + old column disappears from SELECT." The target keeps the old column (back-populated as NULL for new rows since the SELECT no longer emits it). `sync_all_columns` would drop the old one but also requires a rebuild for full consistency. Source: `/docs/build/incremental-models`. Revisit **Ch 4 §4.3.3**. Cognitive level: analyze.

**36.** `full_refresh`**.** Per-model `{{ config(full_refresh=true) }}` forces rebuild-from-scratch on **every** invocation while the config remains set — the docs note the resource "always performs a full refresh, regardless of whether you pass the `--full-refresh` flag." Toggle the config back to `false` (or remove it) after a one-time backfill to avoid unintended every-run rebuilds. Source: `/reference/resource-configs/full_refresh`. Revisit **Ch 4 §4.5**. Cognitive level: recall.

**37. B.** `snapshot_meta_column_names` maps dbt's name to yours, and it is honoured key by key: name two and two are renamed, while the metadata columns the mapping leaves out keep their defaults. Executed on dbt Core 1.11.14 / dbt-postgres 1.11.0, the mapping in the stem produced a target carrying `dbt_scd_id`, `dbt_updated_at`, `valid_from` and `valid_to`, exit 0. A treats an unnamed column as a deleted one; C invents an all-or-nothing rule the config does not have; D generalises two renames into a blanket prefix strip. The semantics travel with the name — the current version is still the row whose `valid_to` is `NULL`. Applying the config to a snapshot that already holds rows is the separate trap: that errors and writes nothing. Source: `/reference/resource-configs/snapshot_meta_column_names`. Revisit **Ch 5 §5.1**. Cognitive level: apply.

**38. C.** Ephemerals compile into CTEs inlined at every downstream ref. They are not materialized as warehouse objects, do not appear in the catalog, and cannot be selected for standalone build. Source: /docs/build/materializations. Revisit **Ch 4 §4.6**. Cognitive level: recall.

**39. D.** concurrent_batches is unset by default, and unset does not mean off — it means dbt decides. The decision is a static scan of the model's raw SQL: a model that references this writes to the relation it is reading, so its batches are held in order; a model that does not is free to run them in parallel. The two models therefore diverge under one identical config, which is what the stem isolates. B and C each collapse the fallback into a fixed answer — parallel regardless, sequential regardless — and both lose the per-model discrimination. A inverts the rule outright. Two gates sit in front of the scan and the stem satisfies both: the adapter must support concurrency, and the relation must already exist — which is why a first run is sequential whatever the SQL says. Source: /reference/resource-properties/concurrent_batches, /docs/build/parallel-batch-execution. Revisit **Ch 4 §4.4**. Cognitive level: analyze.

**40. B.** SQL-level {{ config() }} wins precedence over YAML config:. tags is list-merge (both entries union to ['finance','staging']); materialized is scalar-replace (SQL's view wins). Source: /reference/define-configs. Revisit **Ch 6 §6.4**. Cognitive level: analyze.

**41. 1→c, 2→d, 3→a, 4→b.** Microbatch is one strategy with one config surface and no core implementation: default__get_incremental_microbatch_sql raises not-implemented, so each adapter supplies its own statement. dbt-postgres dispatches to the merge macro, which is why unique_key is mandatory there and optional where a partition is replaced wholesale. Snowflake and Redshift delete the batch window and insert it back; BigQuery and Spark overwrite the partition the batch covers; Databricks rewrites the rows the batch predicate matches. Source: /docs/build/incremental-microbatch. Revisit **Ch 4 §4.4**. Cognitive level: recall.

**42. C.** adapter.dispatch is dbt's mechanism for adapter-specific macro resolution. Naming dbt_utils as the macro namespace does not send dbt there first: whenever that namespace is an installed dependency, the default search path is your root project and then the package, and each namespace is exhausted (<adapter>__, then default__) before the next is tried. The dispatch: config in dbt_project.yml declares or reorders that path per namespace. The default__ fallback is what makes a package portable — omit it, ship only snowflake__ and bigquery__, and the macro is undefined the moment someone runs the project on Postgres. Source: /reference/dbt-jinja-functions/dispatch. Revisit **Ch 6 §6.7 + Ch 8 §8.6**. Cognitive level: apply.

**43. C.** dbt's preflight compares the SELECT's column names and data types with the contract, not row values, so it passes here. For an enforced table contract, dbt includes the declared constraint in the DDL. Postgres enforces check, so it rejects the negative row while dbt materializes the table. This is a warehouse constraint failure, not a shape mismatch or a data-test result. Source: /docs/mesh/govern/model-contracts, /reference/resource-configs/contract. Revisit **Ch 13 §13.2–§13.3**. Cognitive level: analyze.

**44. D.** access: private restricts ref() to consumers inside the same group, and D is the only option that satisfies that. The rule is enforced at parse time and it is about the *consumer node*, not about what kind of node it is: a model in another group (B), a singular test that declares no group (C) and an exposure's depends_on: entry (A) each fail the same check, with a parse-time error naming the node, the private model and the group it belongs to. Source: /docs/mesh/govern/model-access, /docs/build/groups. Revisit **Ch 13 §13.6 + §13.7**. Cognitive level: apply.

**45. B.** {{ ref('dim_customers') }} is the standard fix: dbt resolves the relation per target, and the dependency appears in the DAG so build order is guaranteed. Every hard-coded reference to a dbt-managed table must be replaced with ref() — it is the trap the exam returns to most often. Source: /reference/dbt-jinja-functions/ref, /docs/build/

`models`. Revisit **Ch 2 §2.2 (the `ref()` and DAG section), Ch 10 §10.3**. Cognitive level: apply.

**46. B.** `dbt parse` *does* render each model's Jinja — what it does not produce is **compiled SQL**. It renders with macro capture on, and that path installs a permissive `Undefined`, so a macro name it cannot resolve evaluates to nothing instead of raising. The error waits for `dbt compile`, the first command that renders model bodies into SQL. Measured on 1.11.14: a model calling a macro name that is not in scope — here a package macro written without its namespace — parses at exit 0 and then fails compile with `'...' is undefined`. The decisive contrast is a **known** macro called wrongly — `{{ probe_one_arg(1, 2) }}` against a one-argument macro raises `takes not more than 1 argument(s)` **at parse**, and a model containing both faults raises the arity one at parse, which proves parse rendered the very file holding the undefined name (Ch 10 §10.5). So the lesson is about what the gate buys: `parse` gives you a syntax-and-DAG gate and catches a mis-*called* macro; only `compile` tells you the SQL renders (Ch 11 §11.3). A is wrong on mechanism: nothing is skipped, the name is resolved permissively. C inverts what parse reads — an uninstalled package is precisely what parse WOULD catch, with the package-count error at project load (Ch 8 §8.4), and the stem pins the package as installed. D describes partial parsing, which reuses an unchanged manifest rather than manufacturing a pass. Source: `/reference/commands/parse`, `/reference/commands/compile`. Revisit **Ch 10 §10.5** and **Ch 11 §11.3**. Cognitive level: analyze.

**47. D.** `result:error+` selects error nodes and their downstream closure, reading `run_results.json` from the directory `--state` names — there is no `target/` fallback. Upstream of an error is already complete (they ran successfully to reach the error), so `+result:error` is not what you want here. Source: `/reference/node-selection/methods`. Revisit **Ch 12 §12.5**. Cognitive level: apply.

**48. A.** `store_failures: true` persists the failing rows into the test-audit schema, so you can query the duplicates directly instead of reverse-engineering them from a row count. With `store_failures_as` left unset, the storage shape is a **table** — `store_failures_as` accepts `table`, `view` or `ephemeral` and overrides `store_failures` wherever both are set, and its `ephemeral` value means do-not-store rather than naming a third storage format. B misreads `--fail-fast`, which stops the invocation at the first failing node and still reports a count rather than the rows. C swaps the materialization without touching the rows the SELECT returns, so the test fails identically against the view. D misreads `retry`, which replays the same node against the same data and surfaces no rows. Source: `/reference/resource-configs/store_failures`, `/reference/resource-configs/store_failures_as`. Revisit **Ch 7 §7.5**. Cognitive level: apply.

**49. A.** A test `error` short-circuits every downstream resource in `dbt build` — including models that are only downstream of the tested upstream, not downstream of the test itself. This is the key differentiator vs. `dbt run`. Source: `/reference/commands/build`. Revisit **Ch 11 §11.2**. Cognitive level: apply.

**50. A.** `.render()` asks a reference for its relation and nothing else. All three rewrites land on the *reference* rather than on the model, which is why one method exempts a reference from any of them — it is a family of rewrites, not a per-flag trick. Executed on dbt Core 1.11.14 / dbt-postgres 1.11.0: a plain `{{ ref('stg_orders') }}` compiled to `(select * from "credora"."dev"."stg_orders" where false limit 0) _dbt_limit_subq_stg_orders` under `--empty`, to a `_dbt_et_filter_subq_stg_orders` subquery under `--sample`, and to the same event-time subquery inside a microbatch model's batch; `{{ ref('stg_orders').render() }}` compiled to `"credora"."dev"."stg_orders"` in all three. B reads the hatch as an `--empty` trick. C repeats the misreading that `--empty` limits the model's own `select` — it wraps the references and leaves the `create` alone. D confuses `.render()` with `.identifier`, which in the same run yielded the bare `stg_orders`; `.render()` returns the fully-qualified relation, and returns it *instead of* the rewrite. Source: `/reference/dbt-jinja-functions/ref`, `/docs/build/incremental-microbatch`. Revisit **Ch 11 §11.11** and **Ch 4 §4.4.6**. Cognitive level: apply.

**51. A.** `where:` on a test narrows the test SELECT — the standard way to scope a generic test to new rows on an incremental model. B narrows the scan by deleting history, which trades the assertion's cost against the data the model exists to hold; scope the test, not the table. C misreads `severity`, which governs what a failure *does* — warn instead of error — and never what the SELECT scans, so the 12 minutes are unchanged. `limit:` (D) is also a narrower but doesn't guarantee coverage of new rows. Source: `/reference/resource-properties/data-tests`, `/reference/resource-configs/where`. Revisit **Ch 7 §7.5**. Cognitive level: apply.

**52. A, B.** A is the core semantic — set membership, failing on any value outside `values:`. B is the `quote` argument, which you set to `false` so a numeric column's values are not wrapped in quotes in the generated `not in (…)` list. C is invented; pattern matching is what a custom generic is for. D is wrong, and the mechanism is worth getting exactly right: `accepted_values` does not require `not_null`, and a `NULL` row does not fail it — but nothing in the macro filters nulls out. The compiled test is a bare `where value_field not in (…)`, and `NULL not in (…)` evaluates to NULL rather than TRUE, so SQL's three-valued logic drops the row before dbt sees it. `unique` reaches the same outcome differently, through an explicit `where <column> is not null` the macro writes itself. Either way, attach a separate `not_null` test if you want nulls to fail. E is wrong — `error` is the default severity. Source: `/reference/resource-properties/data-tests`; mechanism verified against the installed macro source and a live Postgres execution on dbt 1.11.14. Revisit **Ch 7 §7.2**. Cognitive level: recall.

**53. A.** `{% test <name>(model, column_name) %} ... {% endtest %}` is the documented signature, and the first parameter is spelled `model` whatever the test is attached to — a source, a seed or a snapshot arrives as `model` too, and the compiled query selects from that relation. C renames it to match the resource, which binds nothing: dbt still passes the relation under the keyword `model`, so the run stops before any SQL is sent, with *macro 'dbt_macro___test_positive' takes no keyword argument 'model'*. `{% macro %}` is for helpers, not tests; `{% generic test %}` is invented. Source: `/best-practices/writing-custom-generic-tests`. Revisit **Ch 7 §7.4**. Cognitive level: recall.

**54. A.** A singular test is a `.sql` file under `tests/` whose SELECT returns the failing rows: zero rows is a pass, one row is a failure. `{% test %}` wrapping belongs to custom generics (C), and singular tests resolve `ref()` like any other model (D). The comparison worth holding on to is with the built-in `relationships` test, which excludes rows whose child column is `NULL` — the one null-exclusion the docs state outright. This hand-written query is **stricter**: `relationships` would pass an orphan line whose `order_id` is `NULL`, and the left join above will not. Reach for a singular when you need that strictness, when you want extra columns in the failure output, or when the assertion reads better in domain language. Source: `/docs/build/data-tests`, `/reference/resource-properties/data-tests`. Revisit **Ch 7 §7.3**. Cognitive level: apply.

**55. D.** Executed on 1.11.14: `dbt compile --sample=...` and `dbt snapshot --sample=...` both exit 2 with `No such option: --sample`. The flag is accepted by `run` and `build` **only** — which is the line that separates it from `--empty`, accepted by `run`, `build`, `snapshot` and `compile`. A and C are true. **B is the one worth carrying out of this item**: `--sample` fails *open*. Point it at a relation that declares no `event_time` and dbt neither errors nor warns — it runs, reports OK, and processes the whole table, so the only signal that your window was ignored is the row count you were not watching. Source: `/docs/build/sample-flag`. Revisit **Ch 11 §11.12**. Cognitive level: recall.

**56. A, B.** `dbt docs generate` introspects the warehouse to write `catalog.json` and re-parses the project to refresh `manifest.json`. **C** names a file dbt has never written — there is no `state.json`; "state" is a *directory* of prior artifacts you point `--state` at, not an artifact of its own. **D** is wrong only on the filename: `generate` does write a rendered static site, but it is `target/index.html`, and `dbt docs serve` then serves that file rather than rendering one on demand. **E** is wrong on the producer: `sources.json` comes from `dbt source freshness` and from nothing else, so rebuilding the catalog never refreshes it. Worth knowing separately: `target/`

`graph.gpickle` is real, and `docs generate` does write it — along with `graph_summary.json` and `run_results.json` — but as a byproduct of building the DAG, which every graph-building command does. Source: `/reference/commands/cmd-docs`, `/reference/artifacts/manifest-json`, `/reference/artifacts/catalog-json`, `/reference/artifacts/sources-json`. Revisit **Ch 9 §9.1 + Ch 12 §12.1**. Cognitive level: recall.

**57. A.** An exposure's `depends_on:` edge is version-precise. `ref('dim_customer', v=1)` pins the edge to the `.v1` node, so the `+` prefix walks v1's ancestry and nothing else — verified on 1.11.14 against a bare-ref control in the same project, where `ref('dim_customer')` in the same position landed on `.v2` instead. B states the rule that governs the BARE form and applies it to the pinned one; it is what you get if you assume a selector always resolves to `latest_version`, and it is the likeliest wrong answer here. C treats the exposure as naming a logical model rather than a node — versions are separate DAG nodes, and `dbt ls` returns one of them. D confuses the highest version DEFINED with the LATEST version: with `latest_version: 2`, `v: 3` is a **prerelease** that no unversioned reference reaches, and `version:prerelease` is the selector that names it. Source: `/reference/exposure-properties`; the versioned form carries no worked example in the docs, so this item rests on execution. Revisit **Ch 9 §9.5**. Cognitive level: apply.

**58. A.** `revision:` accepts branch/tag/SHA. A branch pin is not a stable pin: `dbt deps` resolves `main` to whatever commit it points at today and records it in `package-lock.yml`, so the drift arrives on the next `dbt deps --upgrade` — or on every `deps` run where the lock file is gitignored rather than committed. Pin to a SHA or tag for reproducibility. B inverts the private-package rule: `private:` is the recommended shape for an internal repository, but it is not the required one — `git:` reaches a private repository too, with a full SSH URL, which is the alternative the docs name. C names the wrong directory: a package installs under the name it declares in its own `dbt_project.yml`, not under the revision, so one repository resolves to one directory. D invents two keys — `revision:` carries the branch, the tag and the SHA between them. Source: `/docs/build/packages`. Revisit **Ch 8 §8.2** and **§8.3**. Cognitive level: apply.

**59. 1→C, 2→A, 3→B, 4→C.** `state:*` selectors — including `state:new` — read the current manifest against a prior manifest supplied via `--state`. `result:*` selectors read `run_results.json` from the previous invocation. `source_status:fresher+` reads `sources.json` from the previous `dbt source freshness` run. All four selector families are documented at `/reference/node-selection/methods` and `/reference/node-selection/state-selection`. Revisit **Ch 12 §12.2–§12.5**. Cognitive level: apply.

**60. A.** `state:modified.body` compares the model file's raw text — a `{{ config() }}` edit inside the `.sql` selects; a config change made only in YAML does not. Companion sub-selectors: `.configs`, `.relation`, `.persisted_descriptions`, `.macros`, `.contract`. Source: `/reference/node-selection/methods`, `/reference/node-selection/state-selection`. Revisit **Ch 12 §12.2**. Cognitive level: recall.

**61. A.** The failure mode the stem describes — the job *runs* and selects far too much — needs a baseline dbt can still read. That is the stale-but-comparable case: a manifest written by an older dbt version, or under a different `state_modified_compare_more_unrendered_values` setting, still compares, but compares against differently-computed values, so node after node comes back "modified". Distinguish it from outright artifact incompatibility: a manifest whose *schema version* dbt cannot handle does not quietly over-select, it fails the invocation. Overbuilding and erroring are different symptoms with different causes, and the stem gives you the first. The fix either way: regenerate the baseline from the production run on the same dbt version and flag settings, and upload that as the CI prior. B contradicts the documented Slim CI recipe, where `--defer` and `state:modified+` are the standard pairing rather than a conflict. C is wrong about `dbt build`, which honours `--select` like every other command — `--state` supplies the artifacts the selector compares against, it does not switch selection off. D invents a naming rule: `--state` takes any directory holding prior artifacts, which is why step

3 can name `./prod-artifacts` at all. Source: `/reference/node-selection/state-comparison-caveats`. Revisit **Ch 12 §12.4**. Cognitive level: analyze.

**62. A.** `retry` reads the prior `run_results.json` and re-runs every node that did not complete successfully — `error`, `fail` and `skipped` — with the same selectors/flags. Here that is the 3 errored and the 8 skipped. `--select` is not accepted: passing it fails before anything runs, with `Error: No such option: --select`. Nor does retry ever replay the whole project (C) — the node list is frozen to the prior invocation's unsuccessful set. Source: `/reference/commands/retry`. Revisit **Ch 12 §12.7**. Cognitive level: recall.

**63. Correct order: 1, 2, 3, 4, 5.** Load prior `sources.json` → compute `fresher` set → compute downstream closure (`+`) → run the resolved nodes → write the new artifacts. Source: `/reference/artifacts/sources-json`, `/reference/node-selection/methods`. Revisit **Ch 12 §12.6 + Ch 3 §3.3**. Cognitive level: apply.

**64. B.** The error-classification taxonomy from Ch 10 §10.1 ("YAML vs dbt vs SQL vs Connection"): a **Compilation Error** is raised by dbt before that model's statement is submitted — usually a macro call with the wrong arity, an undefined Jinja symbol, or a `ref()` to a model that doesn't exist. Read the source `.sql` and the macros it calls; the compiled file may not even exist for that model. (Compilation itself is not warehouse-free — dbt still opens a connection for the relation cache and for `run_query` — but the failing model's SQL never leaves dbt. See Ch 10 §10.2.) A **Database Error** is the warehouse rejecting SQL dbt did send — read target/compiled/<path>/<model>.sql for the rendered model query, which is where a syntax error in your own SQL will be, and target/run/<path>/<model>.sql for the same query inside the materialization wrapper dbt actually submitted. The run file and the query history are what to check when the compiled SQL looks correct on its own. Source: `/guides/debug-errors`, `/reference/commands/compile`. Revisit **Ch 10 §10.1 (error taxonomy) and §10.2 (compiled-file inspection workflow)**. Cognitive level: apply.

**65. A.** `source()` resolves against the project's `sources.yml` declarations — the first argument is the source `name:`, the second the `tables: - name:`. If neither matches, dbt cannot construct a `database.schema.table`; that resolution happens as the graph is linked, so the failure lands during `dbt parse` as a Compilation Error, before the warehouse is touched. Option B is wrong because parse opens no connection: an unreachable warehouse leaves `dbt parse` at exit 0 and surfaces at `dbt compile`, and `dbt debug` has already cleared the profile. C and D are inventions (`materialized:` doesn't affect Jinja resolution; `source()` resolves the same way `ref()` does). Source: `/reference/dbt-jinja-functions/source`, `/docs/build/sources`. Revisit **Ch 3 §3.1–§3.2 (source declaration and resolution) + Ch 10 §10.1 (error taxonomy)**. Cognitive level: analyze.

---

## After the mock

- **Scored 43 or higher (≥65%)?** Passing the stretch paper puts the real sitting comfortably in reach. Count wrong answers per domain in the table below to find your weakest two, then do a final spaced re-read of their cheat-sheet sections in the 24 hours before the exam.
- **Scored 34–42?** On-track for a real-exam pass. Re-drill the two weakest domains' chapter Qs and re-read those chapters' Summary + Learning-goal checklist. Do **not** retake Mock 2 within 48 hours — the recall would be from memory, not understanding.
- **Scored below 34?** Postpone the exam by at least a week. Re-read Ch 4, Ch 7, Ch 10, Ch 12 and Ch 13 — Mock 2's stretch concentrates in those five chapters — then retake Mock 1 to confirm the foundation before returning to Mock 2.

### Domain tally sheet

Mark your correct/incorrect tally per domain to see where you are weakest:

| Domain | Questions | Correct | Incorrect | Revisit chapter |
|---|---|---|---|---|
| 1. Developing and optimizing dbt models | Q2–Q10, Q20, Q26–Q27, Q29, Q32–Q42, Q45, Q49–Q50, Q55–Q56, Q58 (30 Qs) | | | Ch 2, 3, 4, 6, 8, 9, 11 |
| 2. Managing dbt models governance | Q1, Q11–Q13, Q24, Q43–Q44 (7 Qs) | | | Ch 13 |
| 3. Debugging data modeling errors | Q14–Q16, Q18–Q19, Q46, Q64–Q65 (8 Qs) | | | Ch 10 |
| 4. Troubleshooting and optimizing dbt pipelines | Q17, Q21, Q31, Q47 (4 Qs) | | | Ch 11, Ch 12 |
| 5. Implementing dbt tests | Q22–Q23, Q25, Q48, Q51–Q54 (8 Qs) | | | Ch 7 |
| 6. Implementing and maintaining external dependencies | Q28, Q30, Q57, Q63 (4 Qs) | | | Ch 3, Ch 9 |
| 7. Leveraging the dbt state | Q59–Q62 (4 Qs) | | | Ch 12 |

Both papers carry the same per-domain shape. Mock 2 changes the difficulty, not the spread.

# Appendix A

# SQL and Git prerequisites

## Preface

The current study guide lists two Checkpoint 0 prerequisites, and this appendix adds one sub-topic to each.

| Prerequisite | The guide lists | This appendix adds | What the exam does with it |
|---|---|---|---|
| **SQL** | joins, aggregations, CTEs, window functions | NULL handling | Assumed, not separately quizzed — no "what does this `SELECT` return" question is in the blueprint — but every dbt-fragment question rewards clean CTE reading. |
| **Git** | branching strategies, basic commands, pull requests | `git fetch` vs `git pull` | Appears in one of the 10 official sample questions, despite git having left the scored domain bullets — see Ch 1 §1.5. |

Treat the SQL recap as confidence-building; treat the Git recap as exam material.

This appendix is a **checkpoint, not a tutorial**. Each sub-section is a short recap of a required skill. If a recap reads as review, you're in good shape. If it reads as new information, pause the book and work through one of the resources in §A.3 before continuing.

---

## A.1 SQL checkpoint

The exam's SQL fragments are idiomatic analytics SQL — no warehouse-specific dialect. The Jinja wrapped around them is not this checkpoint's subject either: `ref` belongs to Chapter 2, `source` to Chapter 3, and `config` and macros to Chapter 6. Five topics you need cold.

### Joins

Five kinds, distinguished by which rows survive:

| Join | Keeps | Fills `NULL` for |
|---|---|---|
| `INNER JOIN` | rows where the key matches on both sides | nothing |
| `LEFT JOIN` | every row from the left input | unmatched right-side columns |
| `RIGHT JOIN` | every row from the right input | unmatched left-side columns |
| `FULL OUTER JOIN` | every row from both inputs | whichever side is absent |
| `CROSS JOIN` | every left row paired with every right row — the Cartesian product | n/a |

`RIGHT JOIN` is the mirror of `LEFT JOIN` and is rare in analytics SQL — most teams rewrite it as a `LEFT JOIN` with the inputs swapped. `CROSS JOIN` is intentional only for number/date spines or deliberate fan-outs. dbt models almost always join via `LEFT JOIN` or `INNER JOIN`; a `FULL OUTER` in a fragment is usually testing whether you notice unmatched rows on both sides.

**Anti-join** — the "rows in A with no match in B" pattern. Databricks SQL *does* have the keyword — `LEFT ANTI JOIN` — and so does Spark SQL; ANSI SQL does not, and neither do Snowflake, BigQuery or Redshift. Because a fragment has to read the same way on every adapter, the pattern is normally written one of two portable ways, which return the same rows:

| Form | Expression |
|---|---|
| Outer join + NULL filter | `LEFT JOIN B ON ... WHERE B.key IS NULL` |
| Correlated subquery | `WHERE NOT EXISTS (SELECT 1 FROM B WHERE B.key = A.key)` |

The `IS NULL` filter on the right-side key is what keeps only the unmatched left rows. A third form, `NOT IN (SELECT key FROM B)`, looks equivalent and is not: one NULL anywhere in the subquery stops `NOT IN` from ever evaluating TRUE — it is FALSE for a value that *does* match and UNKNOWN for one that does not — and `WHERE` keeps only TRUE, so the query returns zero rows. dbt's own `relationships` generic test is exactly this shape: it selects the child key, `LEFT JOIN`s the parent, and keeps the rows `where parent.to_field is null`. Recognise `LEFT JOIN ... WHERE ... IS NULL` on sight when reading a SQL fragment.

Refresher: ThoughtSpot (ex-Mode) SQL Tutorial, "Joining tables" section — `https://www.thoughtspot.com/sql-tutorial/sql-joins/`.

### Aggregations

`GROUP BY` collapses rows into one per distinct combination of the grouping columns. The counting variants are what a fragment usually turns on:

| Expression | Counts |
|---|---|
| `COUNT(*)` | rows, NULLs included |
| `COUNT(col)` | non-NULL values of `col` |

| Expression | Counts |
|---|---|
| `COUNT(DISTINCT col)` | distinct non-NULL values of `col` |

`SUM`, `AVG`, `MIN`, and `MAX` ignore NULL values silently. `WHERE` filters rows before grouping; `HAVING` filters aggregated rows after it — the exam occasionally tests this sequencing. In dbt models, `GROUP BY` appears mostly in the intermediate layer where metrics are first calculated.

Refresher: ThoughtSpot (ex-Mode) SQL Tutorial, "SQL aggregate functions" section — `https://www.thoughtspot.com/sql-tutorial/sql-aggregate-functions/`.

## CTEs

A Common Table Expression is `WITH name AS (query) SELECT ... FROM name`. CTEs beat subqueries for dbt modularity because they read top-to-bottom and can be chained (`WITH a AS (...), b AS (SELECT * FROM a ...), c AS (...) SELECT * FROM c`). Every dbt model in the "how we structure" guide is a chain of CTEs: one per logical transformation, ending in a `final` or `renamed` CTE whose `SELECT` is the model's output. The exam rewards readers who can trace column lineage through a 3–5-CTE fragment at sight. A CTE can reference an earlier CTE in the same `WITH` clause but never a later one; recursive CTEs are out of scope for the exam.

Refresher: dbt Labs' "How we structure our dbt projects" guide, `/best-practices/how-we-structure/1-guide-overview` — shows standard staging → intermediate → marts CTE chains.

## Window functions

A window function uses an `OVER` clause. When specified, `PARTITION BY` turns a global window into a per-group window, and `ORDER BY` defines the ordering inside it. Supply ranking criteria explicitly; for deterministic `ROW_NUMBER()`, include a tie-breaker that uniquely orders each partition.

| Function | Returns |
|---|---|
| `ROW_NUMBER()` | a 1-based sequence per partition — tied rows still get distinct numbers |
| `RANK()` | the same rank for tied rows, then a gap |
| `DENSE_RANK()` | the same rank for tied rows, no gap |
| `LAG(col, 1)` / `LEAD(col, 1)` | the previous / next row's `col` within the partition |

Omitting `PARTITION BY` is a common fragment bug. Window functions appear on the exam mainly in debugging-style questions — "why does this column have the wrong value?" — where the answer is usually a missing `PARTITION BY` or a wrong `ORDER BY`.

References: PostgreSQL window function syntax and Databricks `ROW_NUMBER()`.

## NULL handling

`NULL` is not equal to anything, including itself — use `IS NULL` / `IS NOT NULL`, never `= NULL`. Most operators propagate NULLs: `NULL + 1` is NULL, and `NULL = NULL` is NULL, not TRUE. `COALESCE(a, b, c)` returns the first non-NULL argument; `NULLIF(a, b)` returns NULL when `a = b` and `a` otherwise, which is how you protect a division: `NULLIF(denominator, 0)`. How aggregates treat NULLs is in "Aggregations" above. The dbt `not_null` generic test catches NULL-handling bugs at test time.

Refresher: W3Schools, "SQL NULL Values" — `https://www.w3schools.com/sql/sql_null_values.asp`. Databricks' own `https://docs.databricks.com/aws/en/sql/language-manual/sql-ref-null-semantics` is the reference to use where the exact three-valued result matters.

---

## A.2 Git checkpoint

The exam's Git questions are at intermediate depth — it does not test rebasing, cherry-picking, or interactive workflows. Five topics you need cold.

### Branching

`git switch -c feature/my-change` creates a new branch from the current `HEAD` and moves your working copy to it (`git checkout -b feature/my-change` is the older form). `git switch main` moves between existing branches. `git branch -d branch-name` deletes a merged branch; `-D` force-deletes an unmerged one. The workflow these commands serve is in "Feature-branch discipline" below.

Refresher: dbt Labs' "Version control basics" guide, `/docs/platform/git/version-control-basics`.

### Merging and conflict resolution

`git merge other-branch` brings `other-branch`'s commits into your current branch, producing a merge commit if the histories have diverged. A conflict happens where the two sides touch the same or adjacent lines, or where one side deleted what the other modified; Git marks the conflict with `<<<<<<<`, `=======`, `>>>>>>>` blocks in the affected files, and you edit the file to pick the correct resolution before `git add` + `git commit`. The exam does not drill conflict-marker syntax, but it does test that you know conflicts arise from divergent edits and are resolved by a human, not by a dbt command — in a `.sql` model, a `.yml` file and `dbt_project.yml` alike.

Refresher: dbt Labs' "Version control basics" guide.

### `git fetch` vs `git pull`

`git fetch` downloads remote commits into your local copy's `remotes/origin/*` tracking refs without touching your working branch — it updates your view of the remote, nothing else. `git pull` runs `git fetch` **plus an integration step** against your current branch, which changes your working tree. In the merge-based workflow every exam scenario assumes, that step is `git merge`; configuration and flags can make it a rebase or restrict it to a fast-forward instead. The exam tests this exact distinction: the correct tool for "reconcile with the head branch" is `git pull` (because reconciling means integrating the remote work); `git fetch` alone does not reconcile.

Refresher: Atlassian's "Syncing" tutorial at `https://www.atlassian.com/git/tutorials/syncing` (covers fetch vs pull).

### Pull requests and code review

A pull request is a request to merge your feature branch into `main` (or another integration branch), opened against the hosting platform (GitHub, GitLab, Bitbucket). The reviewer reads the diff, leaves comments, and approves or requests changes; once approved and passing CI, the PR is merged. The exam expects you to know that (a) merging is a reviewed event, not a solo action, (b) CI usually runs `dbt compile` + `dbt test` (or `dbt build --select state:modified+ --defer --state ./prior-artifacts`) against the PR, (c) the PR author is responsible for addressing comments and re-running CI. Chapter 10 walks through a branch → fix → PR example.

Refresher: Atlassian's "Making a pull request" tutorial at `https://www.atlassian.com/git/tutorials/making-a-pull-request`. (dbt Labs' `/docs/platform/git/pr-template` page sets the PR URL dbt Studio opens; it does not teach the review workflow.)

### Feature-branch discipline

The baseline workflow every exam scenario assumes: `main` is protected, every change lives on its own short-lived feature branch, feature branches merge via reviewed PR, CI gates the merge. A feature branch should not accumulate weeks of work — rebase or re-branch if it does. `git fetch origin main` + `git merge origin/main` (or `git pull origin main`) keeps a long-running feature branch aligned with new `main` commits. Never force-push to `main`; force-push to your own feature branch is acceptable to clean up local history before review.

Refresher: Atlassian's "Feature branch workflow" tutorial at `https://www.atlassian.com/git/tutorials/comparing-workflows/feature-branch-workflow`, or Pro Git §3.4 (Branching Workflows).

---

## A.3 If you're rusty on either

### SQL — where to go

- **The Databricks SQL language manual** — `https://docs.databricks.com/aws/en/sql/language-manual/`. Somewhere precise to settle join, NULL and window-function semantics rather than infer them. It is the dialect Chapter 14's real-project examples use; its three-valued-logic pages are a clear reference for the semantics every warehouse shares.
- **ThoughtSpot (ex-Mode) SQL Tutorial** — `https://www.thoughtspot.com/sql-tutorial/`. Browser-based sandbox with progressive chapters.
- **SQLZoo** — `https://sqlzoo.net/`. Problem-set-driven; if you prefer learning by solving exercises rather than reading, use this.
- **The dbt Fundamentals course** — `https://learn.getdbt.com/courses/dbt-fundamentals`. Free with a dbt Learn login. It is a dbt course, not a pure SQL course, but the modelling-layer exercises force SQL fluency.

Plan: two evenings on joins + aggregations + CTEs, one evening on window functions, one evening on NULL handling. After four sessions, return to Chapter 2 and the SQL-heavy questions should read cleanly.

### Git — where to go

- **dbt Labs' "Version control basics"** — `/docs/platform/git/version-control-basics`. dbt Labs' own primer, pitched at the depth the exam expects. Checkpoint 0 names no resources of its own, so this is the nearest dbt-side page.
- **Atlassian's Git tutorials** — `https://www.atlassian.com/git/tutorials`. Strong on the branch / merge / PR workflow. "Syncing" and "Making a pull request" are the two exam-relevant articles.

- **The official Git book, Pro Git** — `https://git-scm.com/book/en/v2`. Chapters 1–3 cover the branching and command work; pull requests, which Checkpoint 0 also names, are a forge feature rather than a git one — see ch 6 or your provider's own docs.

Plan: one evening on branching + merging + PRs (Atlassian's "Making a pull request"), one evening specifically on `git fetch` vs `git pull` (dbt Labs' page plus a hands-on try with a practice repo). After two sessions, the Git questions on the exam read cleanly.

---

## Learning-goal checklist (self-assess)

- ☐ I can read a 5-CTE dbt model end-to-end and name the output of each CTE.
- ☐ I know which join kind keeps unmatched rows on the left, right, both, or neither.
- ☐ I recognise `LEFT JOIN ... WHERE ... IS NULL` as an anti-join on sight, and I know `NOT IN` is not a safe substitute for it.
- ☐ I can state the difference between `WHERE` and `HAVING` without looking it up.
- ☐ I can read a `ROW_NUMBER() OVER (PARTITION BY x ORDER BY y)` expression and predict the output for a small input.
- ☐ I know that `NULL = NULL` is NULL and that `COUNT(col)` skips NULLs.
- ☐ I can create a feature branch, commit, push, and open a pull request without reading instructions.
- ☐ I can explain `git fetch` vs `git pull` to a colleague in one sentence.
- ☐ I can resolve a three-line merge conflict by hand, and I know no dbt command does it for me.
- ☐ I have merged a reviewed PR into `main` at least once in the past month (or completed the Atlassian PR tutorial end-to-end).

Six or more boxes unchecked: spend a week on the resources above before starting Chapter 2. Three to five unchecked: the recaps here plus targeted reading on the weak sub-topics is enough. Two or fewer: you're ready.

# Appendix B

# The official dbt Learn path, mapped to this book

## Preface

The current study guide (dbt Core 1.11) publishes a **4-checkpoint learning path** (0–3): one recommended route for someone new to dbt, which the guide says explicitly you can reorder. Each checkpoint lists some mix of dbt Learn courses, docs pages to read, hands-on experience to gain, and commands to practice.

This book is **not a substitute** for the official path — **use both**. dbt Labs' guidance is "complete the official path"; this book's position is "the official path plus this book", because the exam rewards conceptual clarity and operational familiarity alike. The courses assume a working warehouse and weeks to experiment; this book walks every blueprint item, with decision trees for the trap-heavy topics, drills after every technical chapter, and two full-length mocks before you sit. That is the whole of the argument, and it is not repeated below.

The four checkpoints line up with the blueprint domains (Ch 1 §1.2) like this:

- **Checkpoint 1 is essentially all of Topic 1**, which carries nearly half the outline's sub-bullets. That is why it takes seven of the path's eleven courses and a documentation list long enough to be a study plan on its own. Budget accordingly.
- **Checkpoint 2 is Topics 2 and 3** — governance and debugging, paired.
- **Checkpoint 3 is Topics 5, 6 and 7**, plus Topic 4's `dbt clone`.

Each checkpoint below repeats what the guide lists for it and adds one entry: the chapters of this book that cover the same material. Topics that are **in scope but absent from the reading lists** get their own section at the end — they are the easiest thing here to misread.

---

## Checkpoint 0 — Prerequisites

**Official resource:** No specific course; dbt Labs lists SQL and Git as pre-reading.

**Docs pages the checkpoint lists:** None from dbt docs — SQL and Git are outside the dbt surface.

**Book chapters that pair with this checkpoint:** Appendix A — SQL and Git checkpoint.

**Optional reading / experience:**

- SQL: joins, aggregations, CTEs, window functions — see Appendix A §A.1, which adds NULL handling.

- Git: branching strategies, basic commands, pull requests — see Appendix A §A.2.

**Read this checkpoint more carefully than its length suggests.** Git moved out of the developing-models domain and into the prerequisites, framed as assumed knowledge. That is not a de-scoping — the official sample set still ships a git-branching item (Ch 1 §1.5), so Appendix A §A.2 is doing more work under the current blueprint, not less.

---

## Checkpoint 1 — Build a Foundation

This is the largest checkpoint by a wide margin — seven of the path's eleven courses sit in it.

**Official resources (seven courses, all free with a dbt Learn login):**

- **dbt Fundamentals (dbt Studio)** — the parenthetical is the dbt Cloud IDE → dbt Studio rename surfacing, and this is the only place the guide uses the new naming.
- **Materialization Fundamentals** — `https://learn.getdbt.com/courses/materializations`.
- **Refactoring SQL for Modularity** — `https://learn.getdbt.com/courses/refactoring-sql-for-modularity`.
- **Analyses and Seeds** — `https://learn.getdbt.com/courses/analyses-and-seeds`.
- **Snapshots** — `https://learn.getdbt.com/courses/snapshots`.
- **Incremental Models** — `https://learn.getdbt.com/courses/incremental-models`.
- **Jinja, Macros, and Packages** — `https://learn.getdbt.com/courses/jinja-macros-and-packages`.

Course titles and their URLs move. Every course named in this appendix is findable from the catalogue at `https://learn.getdbt.com/`; look them up by title there rather than by a link printed here.

**Readings the checkpoint lists:**

- "The dbt viewpoint" — `https://docs.getdbt.com/community/resources/viewpoint`.
- "How we structure our dbt projects" — `/best-practices/how-we-structure/1-guide-overview` and its sub-pages `/2-staging`, `/3-intermediate`, `/4-marts`, `/5-the-rest-of-the-project`.
- "Refactoring legacy SQL to dbt" — `/guides/refactoring-legacy-sql`.

**Docs pages the checkpoint lists, and where the book teaches each:**

| Docs page | Book section |
|---|---|
| Add sources to your DAG — `/docs/build/sources` | Ch 3 §3.1, §3.2 |
| Source configurations — `/reference/source-configs` | Ch 3 §3.1 |
| Materializations — `/docs/build/materializations` | Ch 4 §4.1, §4.2 |
| Materialization best practices — `/best-practices/materializations/1-guide-overview` | Ch 4 §4.1, §4.6 |
| Best practice workflows — `/best-practices/best-practice-workflows` | Ch 2 §2.3, Ch 14 |

| Docs page | Book section |
|---|---|
| About the `build` / `run` / `test` / `docs` / `show` / `snapshot` / `seed` commands | Ch 11 §11.1–§11.3, plus Ch 9 §9.1 for `docs` |
| `dbt_project.yml` — `/reference/dbt_project.yml` | Ch 2 §2.4, Ch 6 §6.4 |
| dbt Packages — `/docs/build/packages` | Ch 8 §8.1–§8.5 |
| Python models — `/docs/build/python-models` | Ch 4 §4.7 |
| `grants` — `/reference/resource-configs/grants` | Ch 13 §13.8 |
| Add snapshots to your DAG — `/docs/build/snapshots` | Ch 5 §5.1–§5.3 |
| About incremental models — `/docs/build/incremental-models` | Ch 4 §4.3 |
| About incremental strategy — `/docs/build/incremental-strategy` | Ch 4 §4.3 |
| About microbatch incremental models — `/docs/build/incremental-microbatch` | Ch 4 §4.4 |
| About the `--empty` flag — `/docs/build/empty-flag` | Ch 11 §11.11 |
| About the `--sample` flag — `/docs/build/sample-flag` | Ch 11 §11.12 |

**Commands the checkpoint expects you to practice:** `dbt build`, `dbt run`, `dbt test`, `dbt show`, `dbt snapshot`, `dbt seed`, `dbt docs generate`. Ch 11 §11.1 is the command grid, and gives `dbt show` its own treatment: it previews one node, but its `--select` resolves nodes — attached tests included — exactly as on every other command.

**Book chapters that pair with this checkpoint:** Ch 1 (logistics and setup), Ch 2 (project structure, `ref()`, `dbt_project.yml`, the model life cycle), Ch 3 (sources), Ch 4 (materializations, incremental, microbatch, `event_time`, Python models), Ch 5 (snapshots in YAML, `hard_deletes`, seeds), Ch 6 (Jinja, macros, config precedence), Ch 8 (packages), Ch 11 (the CLI, `--empty`, `--sample`).

**Optional reading / experience the checkpoint recommends:** build a dbt pipeline from scratch; refactor SQL for performance; implement all core materializations; use packages and macros. Ch 1 §1.6 points at the companion repo, which is the fastest way to get all four reps on a laptop.

**Worth extra attention.** Five of the entries above — incremental strategy, microbatch, `--empty`, `--sample`, and `dbt show` inside the commands row — are named in the topic outline and are the densest material in this checkpoint.

---

## Checkpoint 2 — Govern and Debug Your Models

**Official resource:** the **dbt Mesh — Model Governance** module. Governance is a named course rather than a docs footnote — read that as contracts, versions and constraints being expected knowledge here, not advanced reading.

**Reading the checkpoint lists:**

- "Data product management: best practices" (dbt Labs post).

**Docs pages the checkpoint lists, and where the book teaches each:**

| Docs page | Book section |
| --- | --- |
| Model contracts — `/docs/mesh/govern/model-contracts` | Ch 13 §13.2 |
| Model versions — `/docs/mesh/govern/model-versions` | Ch 13 §13.4, §13.5 |
| Constraints — `/reference/resource-properties/constraints` | Ch 13 §13.3 |
| Debugging errors — `/guides/debug-errors` | Ch 10 §10.1–§10.7 |
| `dbt compile` command — `/reference/commands/compile` | Ch 11 §11.3, Ch 10 §10.2 |
| About behavior changes — `/reference/global-configs/behavior-changes` | Ch 10 §10.9 |
| About flags (global configs) — `/reference/global-configs/about-global-configs` | Ch 10 §10.9, Ch 2 §2.4 for where the `flags:` block sits |

**Book chapters that pair with this checkpoint:** Ch 13 (contracts, constraints, versions, access, groups), Ch 10 (triage, compiled SQL, behaviour flags), Ch 11 §11.3 (`compile` versus `parse`), Ch 2 §2.4 (where a `flags:` block sits in `dbt_project.yml`; Ch 10 §10.9 owns what goes in it).

**Optional reading / experience the checkpoint recommends:** familiarity with model access, contracts and versions; data-product producer and consumer management practices; identifying, understanding and debugging errors in dbt logs. Ch 14 §14.6 shows governance applied selectively in a large project, which is what "producer and consumer practices" looks like in the wild.

**Why governance and debugging share a checkpoint.** A governed model is one whose failures you can diagnose. A contract that fires turns a silent downstream break into a mismatch table naming the offending column (Ch 13 §13.2), and reading that table is the skill, not merely declaring the contract. Read Ch 13, then Ch 10.

Note also that **model access survives in this checkpoint's experience list** even though it is no longer a printed bullet in the topic outline. Ch 13 §13.6 and §13.7 keep it. Nothing published says how deeply access is examined, so treat the split as this book's recommendation: read those two sections, and drill them if the topic feels unfamiliar.

---

## Checkpoint 3 — Build Resilient Pipelines at Scale

**Official resources (three courses, all free with a dbt Learn login):**

- **Advanced Testing** — `https://learn.getdbt.com/courses/advanced-testing`.
- **Unit Testing**.
- **Exposures**.

Unit Testing and Exposures are standalone courses rather than sub-topics of a larger one. That is a promotion, and it is why Ch 7 §7.8 and Ch 9 §9.5 are full sections in this book rather than sidebars.

**Readings the checkpoint lists:**

- "How we structure our dbt projects" — `/best-practices/how-we-structure/1-guide-overview`. Its second appearance on the path; the checkpoint wants you re-reading it with tests in mind.
- "Test smarter not harder" (dbt Labs post).

- "Test smarter not harder: Where should tests go in your pipeline?" (dbt Labs post).
- "Your Essential dbt Project Checklist" (dbt Labs post).
- "To defer or to clone, that is the question" (dbt Labs post).

**Docs pages the checkpoint lists, and where the book teaches each:**

| Docs page | Book section |
|---|---|
| About the `dbt clone` command — `/reference/commands/clone` | Ch 12 §12.8 |
| Clone incremental models — `/best-practices/clone-incremental-models` | Ch 12 §12.8, read alongside §12.9 |
| Add data tests to your DAG — `/docs/build/data-tests` | Ch 7 §7.1–§7.3 |
| Testing and documenting sources — `/docs/build/sources` | Ch 3 §3.1, Ch 7 §7.2 |
| Writing custom generic data tests — `/best-practices/writing-custom-generic-tests` | Ch 7 §7.4 |
| Data test configurations — `/reference/data-test-configs` | Ch 7 §7.5 |
| Unit tests — `/docs/build/unit-tests` | Ch 7 §7.8 |
| About the `dbt test` command — `/reference/commands/test` | Ch 7 §7.6, Ch 11 §11.1 |
| Add Exposures to your DAG — `/docs/build/exposures` | Ch 9 §9.5 |
| Exposure properties — `/reference/exposure-properties` | Ch 9 §9.5 |
| dbt source freshness — `/reference/commands/source` | Ch 3 §3.3 |
| About state in dbt, and the `state` method — `/reference/node-selection/state-selection` | Ch 12 §12.1, §12.2 |
| `dbt retry` — `/reference/commands/retry` | Ch 12 §12.7 |

**Commands the checkpoint expects you to practice:** `dbt test`, `dbt source freshness`, `dbt clone`, `dbt retry`, and the `state` selector method. The guide lists `state` alongside four real commands; it is not one — `state:modified+` is something you type after a command, not instead of one.

**Book chapters that pair with this checkpoint:** Ch 7 (all four test types, custom generic tests, test configs, unit tests), Ch 9 §9.5 (exposures and exposure properties), Ch 3 §3.3 (source freshness), Ch 11 §11.1 (`dbt test` in the command grid), Ch 12 (state artifacts, `state:` sub-methods, `--defer --state`, `dbt retry`, `dbt clone`), Ch 14 §14.5 and §14.7 (testing and slim CI at scale).

**What the checkpoint's readings push you toward** (Checkpoint 3 is the one checkpoint with no Experience block — it lists Courses, Readings, Documentation and Commands only): design a test strategy that catches regressions without drowning the pipeline in redundant assertions; document downstream consumers so a breaking change has a blast radius you can name; use state to rebuild only what changed. Ch 12 §12.9 assembles the last of those into a working CI pipeline.

## What left the reading list is not what left the exam

Eleven documentation pages are absent from the path's reading lists. **That is not a de-scoping**, and reading it as one is the expensive mistake here.

Two published counter-examples settle it. Node-selection syntax appears in no docs list, yet one official sample question is a pure graph-operator item turning on where you place `+` relative to a model name. The `schema` property appears in none either, yet another turns on `schema` inside `sources.yml`. The path's docs list is a *reading suggestion*; the topic outline in Ch 1 §1.2 is the assessment scope.

Here is every such page and the chapter that teaches it:

| Dropped from the path | Still taught in |
| --- | --- |
| Node selection syntax | Ch 11 §11.5–§11.9 — the full selector, graph-operator and set-operator treatment |
| General resource properties | Ch 2 §2.4 (config precedence), Ch 6 §6.4 |
| `env_var` | Ch 6 §6.2, Ch 3 §3.6 (multi-environment sources) |
| `target` | Ch 6 §6.2 |
| `schema` | Ch 2 §2.3 (introduced), Ch 2 §2.4 (`+schema:` appends; `generate_schema_name`), Ch 3 §3.1 |
| `database` | Ch 2 §2.4 (`+database:` replaces rather than appends), Ch 3 §3.1 |
| Tags | Ch 11 §11.6 (`tag:` selector method), Ch 11 §11.9 (which levels tests inherit a tag from), Ch 7 §7.6 |
| Hooks and operations | Ch 6 §6.5 |
| Custom schemas | Ch 2 §2.3 (introduced), Ch 2 §2.4 (the append behaviour and the macro override) |
| Threads | Ch 2 §2.1, §2.5 |
| `dbt run-operation` | Ch 6 §6.5, Ch 11 §11.1 |

Read that table as a set of chapters to keep drilling, not to skip. Ch 11 keeps its full node-selection treatment, and Ch 15 §15.5's last-day advice to re-read the node-selection grid still holds.

---

## Summary table

| Checkpoint | Official courses | Book chapter pairing | Primary blueprint domains covered |
| --- | --- | --- | --- |
| 0 — Prerequisites | none (SQL + git self-study) | Appendix A | (prerequisite; none) |

| Checkpoint | Official courses | Book chapter pairing | Primary blueprint domains covered |
|---|---|---|---|
| 1 — Build a Foundation | dbt Fundamentals (dbt Studio); Materialization Fundamentals; Refactoring SQL for Modularity; Analyses and Seeds; Snapshots; Incremental Models; Jinja, Macros, and Packages | Ch 1, Ch 2, Ch 3, Ch 4, Ch 5, Ch 6, Ch 8, Ch 11 | 1 (developing and optimizing models) |
| 2 — Govern and Debug Your Models | dbt Mesh — Model Governance | Ch 13, Ch 10, Ch 11 §11.3, Ch 2 §2.4 | 2 (governance), 3 (debugging) |
| 3 — Build Resilient Pipelines at Scale | Advanced Testing; Unit Testing; Exposures | Ch 3, Ch 7, Ch 9, Ch 11, Ch 12, Ch 14 | 5 (tests), 6 (external dependencies), 7 (state), and 4 (pipelines, via `dbt clone`) |

**Note on the mocks and Chapter 15:** none of the three is part of the official learning path. They add what the courses do not — format drill, time-budget practice, and two full-length timed rehearsals; Ch 1 §1.8 places the mocks in the study plan. Ch 14 has no counterpart either: no checkpoint asks you to read a project at Credora's scale, and that is the gap it fills.

---

## Using this appendix with the official path

**If you've completed the official courses** but haven't sat the exam: read the book in chapter order, spending more time on any chapter whose official course you found thin. Then check the five entries under Checkpoint 1's **Worth extra attention** — a course you took before those joined the path did not cover them. The cheat sheet and the mocks are the pieces hardest to reproduce from the courses alone.

**If you haven't completed the official courses:** work through the book first — it is more compact than the courses combined — then take the official courses for any domain still weak after Mock 1. They are strongest on Checkpoint 1, where hands-on practice with materializations and Jinja sticks better than reading; Ch 1 §1.6's companion repo gives you the same reps locally.

# Appendix C

# Dimensional modeling primer

Read this when the modeling vocabulary in Ch 2, Ch 4 or Ch 14 feels rusty: facts, dimensions, grain, star schemas, SCD types, surrogate keys, and what each one means inside a dbt project. Sources are listed at the end — note that `/terms/dimensional-modeling` is not a docs page; it redirects to a dbt Labs blog post.

---

## C.1 The four building blocks

### Fact table

A fact table records the **measurements of a business event** — orders, payments, page views, support tickets. Each row is one event at the table's grain. Most columns are either:

- **Foreign keys** to dimension tables (`customer_id`, `product_id`, `date_id`) — the "who / what / when" of the event,
- **Numeric measures** (`order_total_cents`, `quantity`, `duration_seconds`) — the "how much" of the event.

In a dbt project the convention is the `fct_` prefix: `fct_orders`, `fct_page_views`, `fct_support_tickets`. The dbt "How we structure" guide (`/best-practices/how-we-structure/4-marts`) uses bare entity names (`orders`) instead — §C.7 has the exam-relevant reading of the two conventions.

### Dimension table

A dimension table holds the **descriptive attributes** of an entity that a fact references — `dim_customers` (name, email, signup date, region), `dim_products` (SKU, category, brand). Dimension tables are typically smaller than fact tables, change less frequently, and are joined to facts at query time to answer "by what" / "describe me" questions.

The convention is the `dim_` prefix. Dimensions are usually materialized as `table` (Ch 4) so dashboard joins read cheaply.

### Grain

The **grain** of a fact table is the level of detail one row represents. "One row per order" and "one row per order line item" are different grains; mixing them in one table is the classic modeling bug. Always state the grain in the model's `description:` so downstream consumers cannot mis-aggregate.

### Star schema

A **star schema** is one central fact table joined to several dimension tables via foreign keys. Drawn as a diagram, the fact sits in the middle and the dimensions radiate outward — hence "star." Most BI tools assume star-shaped data and produce predictable joins from it.

---

## C.2 Variations

### Snowflake schema

A **snowflake schema** extends a star by *normalizing* dimension tables — instead of `dim_products` carrying a `category_name` column, the products dimension links to a separate `dim_product_categories` table. The diagram now has dimensions linking to other dimensions, fanning out like a snowflake.

Snowflake schemas save storage on highly repeated attribute strings but cost more joins at query time. Modern cloud warehouses make storage cheap and joins (relatively) expensive, so most dbt projects denormalize back to a star — which is why the dbt marts guide explicitly favors **wide tables**.

Note the unfortunate name collision: "Snowflake schema" (a modeling pattern) is unrelated to **Snowflake** (the warehouse vendor).

### Bridge table

A **bridge table** resolves a many-to-many relationship between a fact and a dimension. Example: an orders fact and a promotions dimension where one order can have multiple promotions applied. The bridge table `bridge_order_promotions` carries `(order_id, promotion_id)` pairs — one row per applied promotion. The bridge *represents* the association; it does not by itself stop double-counting. Joining a fact through it fans the fact out to one row per promotion, so an order-grain measure summed over that join is counted once per promotion. You still have to aggregate back to the intended grain, or allocate the measure across the promotions with a weighting factor, before summing. Build one only when the cardinality forces it.

In a dbt project a bridge is just another model under `marts/`, often prefixed `bridge_`.

### Wide / one-big-table (OBT)

A **wide table** pre-joins fact + dimensions into a single denormalized output, so consumers don't join at all. The trade-off is storage and refresh cost (every dimension update propagates) against query simplicity. OBT is the modern dbt-flavored alternative to a strict star — see the marts guide.

---

## C.3 Why dimensional modeling pays off — performance and maintenance

Dimensional modeling buys two things: **query performance** and **project maintainability**.

### Performance benefits

| Benefit | Why it holds |
| --- | --- |
| **Fewer joins at query time** | A star asks a dashboard to join one fact to a handful of dimensions on their key columns — a join shape every modern query planner handles well. Do not carry an index assumption over from a row-store: Databricks Delta has no traditional relational indexes and its `FOREIGN KEY` constraints are informational and unenforced, so the gain comes from the join *shape* and from file pruning, not from an index seek. A wide table pre-joins everything, so the query is a single scan with no joins at all. Both normally beat joining ten normalized tables on every dashboard refresh. |
| **Predictable, cacheable join paths** | BI tools (Looker, Tableau, Power BI) generate SQL by traversing a known join graph, and a star is the shape they assume. Query plans cache cleanly across users and time windows. |
| **Pre-computed aggregations** | A fact table can be pre-aggregated to a higher grain (`fct_orders_daily` rolled from `fct_orders`) and exposed as a materialized table. The expensive `GROUP BY` runs once per build, not once per dashboard load. |
| **Materialization choice maps cleanly** | Dimensions are small and read-heavy → `table` (cheap reads, infrequent rebuild). Facts are large and append-heavy → `incremental` (cheap appends, no full rebuild). `ephemeral` and `view` are the usual staging and intermediate choices. Read all of this as a workload default rather than a layering rule: materialization follows cost and read pattern, not the layer a model sits in, and a small mart may legitimately stay a `view` until querying it gets expensive. |
| **Surrogate keys give a single-column join** | One equality on a fixed-width hash replaces a multi-column join predicate. Whether that is measurably faster depends on the engine and the data; the reliable gain is that the join key is one column and the same shape everywhere. `dbt_utils.generate_surrogate_key` makes this a one-liner. |
| **Selective refresh** | Dimension changes are decoupled from fact rows, so `dim_customers` rebuilds without touching `fct_orders`. dbt's DAG selectors (`+dim_customers`, `dim_customers+`) make this surgical. |

## Maintenance benefits

| Benefit | Why it holds |
|---|---|
| **Conformed dimensions = single source of truth** | "Customer" is defined once in `dim_customers` and referenced by every fact — orders, payments, support tickets, page views. One column-rename in one place, not five. |
| **Schema changes localized** | A new customer attribute adds one column to `dim_customers`: no fact-table change, no consumer SQL change. In a denormalized warehouse that attribute lives in five fact tables and every consumer query has to be rewritten. |
| **Convention-driven onboarding** | A new engineer who reads `fct_orders` and `dim_customers` knows the grain, the join keys, and the layer from the name alone (Ch 2 §2.3). |
| **SCD2 decouples history from query logic** | History lives in the snapshot, not in consumer SQL, so queries don't change shape when history requirements evolve. Which current-row predicate is correct depends on whether the snapshot sets `dbt_valid_to_current`; Ch 5 §5.1 has both forms and the trap in each. |
| **Modular layers contain refactors** | Staging → intermediate → marts gives each layer one responsibility. Refactoring a join in `int_orders_enriched` touches neither `stg_orders` nor `fct_orders` — the blast radius of any change is bounded by the layer it lives in. |
| **Tests target stable identities** | A `unique` test on `fct_orders.order_id` and a `relationships` test from `fct_orders.customer_id` to `dim_customers.customer_id` survive every schema evolution. Tests that target a denormalized blob break every time the blob's column set shifts. |
| **The DAG mirrors the business** | Marts named after business processes (orders, payments, support) make the dbt DAG read like a business-process map. Debugging starts at the right model because the model name describes the domain. |

## Trade-offs to remember

Dimensional modeling is not free:

- **Storage overhead.** Wide tables and SCD2 history grow data volume. Cheap on cloud warehouses, expensive on legacy systems.
- **ETL/ELT complexity.** Maintaining surrogate keys, conformed dimensions, and SCD logic adds pipeline steps. dbt absorbs most of this complexity through snapshots, `dbt_utils`, and tests, but the discipline is still there.

- **Refresh latency.** A pre-aggregated fact is one build behind real time. For sub-hour reporting needs, dimensional marts may need to be supplemented with views over the staging layer.

The trade is a bounded up-front design cost against ongoing query-performance and maintenance wins; dbt's layered project structure assumes it is worth making.

---

## C.4 Slowly Changing Dimensions (SCD)

Dimension attributes change over time — a customer moves to a new region, a product gets re-categorized. The **SCD type** is your policy for handling that change.

| Type | Behaviour | When to use |
|---|---|---|
| **SCD Type 1** | Overwrite the old value in place. No history. | Attribute never needs to be reported on historically (typo fixes, irrelevant updates). |
| **SCD Type 2** | Insert a new row with `valid_from` / `valid_to` columns; the old row is closed out. Full history. | Reporting needs to answer "what was true on date X?" — most analytics use cases. |
| **SCD Type 3** | Add a "previous" column on the same row. Limited history (one prior value). | Rare; specific transitions you want to compare against current. |
| **SCD Type 4–7** | Hybrids and audit-tables variants. Industry-niche. | Out of scope for the exam. |

dbt's **snapshot** primitive (Ch 5) implements SCD Type 2 mechanically. A snapshot with `unique_key` plus a `timestamp` (or `check`) strategy is the supported way to capture SCD2 history without writing the merge SQL by hand.

---

## C.5 Surrogate keys

A **surrogate key** is a key generated by your warehouse — typically an md5 / sha256 hash of the natural key columns — that joins facts to dimensions in place of the source-system key. Two reasons to use one:

1. The natural key may be a tuple (e.g., `(account_id, region)`); a single hashed surrogate is easier to join on.
2. It gives every dimension the same key shape, so joins and tests look alike across the mart.

**A hash is stable only while its inputs are.** `md5`/`sha2` are deterministic functions of the columns you feed them, so re-running on unchanged input reproduces the key exactly — but a renamed SKU or a re-allocated customer ID changes the input and therefore changes the hash, which is precisely the case where you wanted the key to hold still. A hashed surrogate is not persistent assigned identity. Where the business key can genuinely mutate and history must survive it, hash a column that does not change, assign an identity of your own and carry it forward, or keep a mapping table from old key to new — and let the snapshot (Ch 5) hold the versions.

In dbt, `dbt_utils.generate_surrogate_key(['col_a', 'col_b'])` is the standard helper — covered in Ch 8 §8.5.

---

## C.6 Kimball's four-step design (for context)

Ralph Kimball's *The Data Warehouse Toolkit* prescribes four steps for designing a star schema. When a question uses Kimball-flavored language, this is the framework behind it:

1. **Pick the business process.** "Orders," "Payments," "Page views" — one process per fact table.
2. **Declare the grain.** "One row per order line item." The grain pins everything else.
3. **Identify the dimensions.** "Each line item involves a customer, a product, a date, a store." → `dim_customers`, `dim_products`, `dim_dates`, `dim_stores`.
4. **Identify the facts.** "Quantity, unit price, line total, discount applied." → numeric columns on the fact table.

dbt's modern position (per the marts guide) is that this process is still a useful *thought exercise* even when the output is a wide entity table rather than a strict star. The four-step ordering — process, grain, dimensions, facts — is the load-bearing part.

---

## C.7 Where dbt diverges from the textbook

Kimball-flavored options do not always map to modern dbt practice. The divergences:

| Divergence | dbt's position | The dbt-flavored answer |
|---|---|---|
| **Naming** | The "How we structure" guide names marts after **business entities** (`orders`, `customers`), not `fct_orders` / `dim_customers`. Both are seen in the wild and either is acceptable in practice. | whichever the stem's own project or excerpt already uses; where the stem asks what the dbt Labs guide recommends, the entity-name form |
| **Denormalization** | Wide marts over strict snowflakes: storage is cheap, compute is expensive. | the star, or the wide table, over a snowflake at equal grain |

| Divergence | dbt's position | The dbt-flavored answer |
| --- | --- | --- |
| **SCD2** | Strict Kimball SCD2 is a hand-authored merge pattern; in dbt it is a one-config-block snapshot (Ch 5). A snapshot can only reconstruct changes it observed, so it answers "what did this row look like on a given date" only for versions captured since it started running — though under the `timestamp` strategy the oldest captured version is dated from the source's own `updated_at`, which may predate the first run (Ch 5). | the `dbt snapshot` option over any option that writes the merge logic by hand, and a temporal join on `dbt_valid_from` / `dbt_valid_to` when the question is what a fact saw at the time |
| **Bridges** | Still built when a genuine many-to-many forces one, but uncommon — most marts denormalize the relationship into the fact's columns instead. | denormalizing into the fact where the cardinality allows it; a bridge where it does not, with the re-aggregation stated |
| **Junk dimensions** | A separate device: it collapses several low-cardinality flags into one small dimension holding their distinct COMBINATIONS. Many fact rows share one junk row — ordinary many-to-one, like any dimension. What matters is that it does not fan the fact out, so it is not a bridge. | for a 3-attribute, 5-value set of flags, inlining those three columns into the fact is usually simpler than either a junk dimension or a bridge |

---

## C.8 What to memorize for the exam

This material is pure recall, and the recognition surface is small:

- Fact = events + measures; Dimension = descriptive attributes.
- Star = one fact + many dimensions; Snowflake = dimensions linked to other dimensions.
- Grain = one row's level of detail; mis-stated grain is the classic modeling bug.
- Bridge = represents a many-to-many association between a fact and a dimension; it fans the fact out, so re-aggregate or allocate at the intended grain.
- Junk dimension = several low-cardinality flags collapsed into one small dimension of their distinct combinations. Joins many-to-one like any dimension and does NOT fan the fact out, which is what separates it from a bridge.

- SCD2 = "track history of dimension changes" → in dbt, that is `dbt snapshot` with `strategy: 'timestamp'` or `'check'`.
- Surrogate key = warehouse-generated single-column key (often `md5`/`sha2` of natural-key columns); deterministic, so it is stable exactly as long as its inputs are. `dbt_utils.generate_surrogate_key` is the standard helper.

Recall these on sight and the vocabulary costs you no time in the exam.

---

## References


- Daniel Poppy, *Guide to dimensional modeling*, dbt Labs blog (published 2024-07-01). The fullest dbt-side treatment of the material in this appendix.
- dbt Labs, *How we structure our dbt projects — Marts*, `/best-practices/how-we-structure/4-marts`. The docs-page take on marts; §C.7 reads it against the Kimball textbook.
- Ralph Kimball & Margy Ross, *The Data Warehouse Toolkit*, 3rd ed. (Wiley, 2013). The textbook reference. Out of scope for the exam, but the source of every term in this appendix.

Made in the USA
Coppell, TX
04 November 2026

11273937R00324